fundamentals of
Human Resource Management

Third Edition

Raymond A. Noe
The Ohio State University

John R. Hollenbeck
Michigan State University

Barry Gerhart
University of Wisconsin–Madison

Patrick M. Wright
Cornell University

**McGraw-Hill
Irwin**

Boston   Burr Ridge, IL   Dubuque, IA   New York   San Francisco   St. Louis
Bangkok   Bogotá   Caracas   Kuala Lumpur   Lisbon   London   Madrid   Mexico City
Milan   Montreal   New Delhi   Santiago   Seoul   Singapore   Sydney   Taipei   Toronto

The McGraw-Hill Companies

McGraw-Hill
Irwin

FUNDAMENTALS OF HUMAN RESOURCE MANAGEMENT

Published by McGraw-Hill/Irwin, a business unit of The McGraw-Hill Companies, Inc., 1221 Avenue of the Americas, New York, NY, 10020. Copyright © 2009, 2007, 2004 by The McGraw-Hill Companies, Inc. All rights reserved. No part of this publication may be reproduced or distributed in any form or by any means, or stored in a database or retrieval system, without the prior written consent of The McGraw-Hill Companies, Inc., including, but not limited to, in any network or other electronic storage or transmission, or broadcast for distance learning.

Some ancillaries, including electronic and print components, may not be available to customers outside the United States.

This book is printed on acid-free paper.

4 5 6 7 8 9 0 DOW/ DOW 0

ISBN   978-0-07-338147-3
MHID   0-07-338147-0

Vice president and editor-in-chief: *Brent Gordon*
Publisher: *Paul Ducham*
Executive editor: *John Weimeister*
Developmental editor: *Donielle Xu*
Editorial assistant: *Heather Darr*
Marketing manager: *Natalie Zook*
Marketing coordinator: *Michael Gedatus*
Project manager: *Kathryn D. Mikulic*
Senior production supervisor: *Debra R. Sylvester*
Interior designer: *Pam Verros*
Senior photo research coordinator: *Jeremy Cheshareck*
Photo researcher: *Ira C. Roberts*
Lead media project manager: *Brian Nacik*
Cover design: *Pam Verros*
Cover image: *www.veer.com*
Typeface: *10.5/12 Goudy*
Compositor: *Aptara®, Inc.*
Printer: *RR Donnelley, Willard*

Library of Congress Cataloging-in-Publication Data

Fundamentals of human resource management / Raymond A. Noe ... [et al.]. —3rd ed.
   p. cm.
   Includes index.
   ISBN-13: 978-0-07-338147-3 (alk. paper)
   ISBN-10: 0-07-338147-0 (alk. paper)
   1. Personnel management. I. Noe, Raymond A.
HF5549.F86 2009
658.3—dc22

                                                                                    2008029819

www.mhhe.com

In tribute to the lives of Raymond and Mildred Noe
—R.A.N.

To my parents, Harold and Elizabeth, my wife, Patty, and
my children, Jennifer, Marie, Timothy, and Jeffrey
—J.R.H.

To my parents, Robert and Shirley, my wife, Heather,
and my children, Chris and Annie
—B.G.

To my parents, Patricia and Paul, my wife, Mary, and my
sons, Michael and Matthew
—P.M.W.

About the Authors

Raymond A. Noe is the Robert and Anne Hoyt Professor of Management at The Ohio State University. He was previously a professor in the Department of Management at Michigan State University and the Industrial Relations Center of the Carlson School of Management, University of Minnesota. He received his BS in psychology from The Ohio State University and his MA and PhD in psychology from Michigan State University. Professor Noe conducts research and teaches undergraduate as well as MBA and PhD students in human resource management, managerial skills, quantitative methods, human resource information systems, training, employee development, and organizational behavior. He has published articles in the *Academy of Management Journal, Academy of Management Review, Journal of Applied Psychology, Journal of Vocational Behavior,* and *Personnel Psychology*. Professor Noe is currently on the editorial boards of several journals including *Personnel Psychology, Journal of Applied Psychology,* and *Journal of Organizational Behavior*. Professor Noe has received awards for his teaching and research excellence, including the Herbert G. Heneman Distinguished Teaching Award in 1991 and the Ernest J. McCormick Award for Distinguished Early Career Contribution from the Society for Industrial and Organizational Psychology in 1993. He is also a fellow of the Society for Industrial and Organizational Psychology.

John R. Hollenbeck received his PhD in Management from New York University in 1984, and is currently the Eli Broad Professor of Management at the Eli Broad Graduate School of Business Administration at Michigan State University. Dr. Hollenbeck was the first recipient of the Ernest J. McCormick Award for Early Contributions to the field of Industrial and Organizational Psychology in 1992, and is currently a Fellow of the Academy of Management, the American Psychological Association, and the Society of Industrial and Organizational Psychology. He has published over 70 articles and book chapters on the topics of work motivation and group behavior with more than 40 of these appearing in the most highly cited refereed outlets. According to the Institute for Scientific Research, this body of work has been cited over 1,300 times by other researchers. Dr. Hollenbeck was the acting editor at *Organizational Behavior and Human Decision Processes* in 1995, the associate editor at *Decision Sciences* between 1998 and 2004, and the editor of *Personnel Psychology* from 1996 to 2002. He currently serves on the editorial board of the *Academy of Management Journal,* the *Journal of Applied Psychology, Personnel Psychology,* and *Organizational Behavior and Human Decision Processes*. Dr. Hollenbeck's teaching has been recognized with several awards, including the Michigan State University Teacher-Scholar Award in 1987 and the Michigan State University Distinguished Faculty Award in 2006. Within the Broad School of Business, he was awarded the Dorothy Withrow Teaching Award in 2002, the Lewis Quality of Excellence Award in both 2001 and 2004, and Most Outstanding MBA Faculty Award in 2007.

Barry Gerhart is the Bruce R. Ellig Distinguished Chair in Pay and Organizational Effectiveness and Director of the Strategic Human Resources Program at the University of Wisconsin–Madison. He was previously the Frances Hampton Currey Chair in Organizational Studies at the Owen School of Management at Vanderbilt University and Associate Professor and Chairman of the Department of Human Resource Studies, School of Industrial and Labor Relations at Cornell University. He received his BS in psychology from Bowling Green State University in 1979 and his PhD in industrial relations from the University of Wisconsin–Madison in 1985. His research is in the areas of compensation/rewards, staffing, and employee attitudes. Professor Gerhart has worked with a variety of organizations, including TRW, Corning, and Bausch & Lomb. His work has appeared in the *Academy of Management Journal, Industrial Relations, Industrial and Labor Relations Review, Journal of Applied Psychology, Personnel Psychology,* and *Handbook of Industrial and Organizational Psychology,* and he has served on the editorial boards of the *Academy of Management Journal, Industrial and Labor Relations Review,* and the *Journal of Applied Psychology.* He was a corecipient of the 1991 Scholarly Achievement Award, Human Resources Division, Academy of Management.

Patrick M. Wright is Professor of Human Resource Studies and Director of the Center for Advanced Human Resource Studies in the School of Industrial and Labor Relations at Cornell University. He was formerly Associate Professor of Management and Coordinator of the Master of Science in Human Resource Management program in the College of Business Administration and Graduate School of Business at Texas A&M University. He holds a BA in psychology from Wheaton College and an MBA and a PhD in organizational behavior/human resource management from Michigan State University. He teaches, conducts research, and consults in the areas of personnel selection, employee motivation, and strategic human resource management. His research articles have appeared in journals such as the *Academy of Management Journal, Journal of Applied Psychology, Organizational Behavior and Human Decision Process, Journal of Management,* and *Human Resource Management Review.* He has served on the editorial boards of *Journal of Applied Psychology* and *Journal of Management* and also serves as an ad hoc reviewer for *Organizational Behavior* and *Human Decision Processes, Academy of Management Journal,* and *Academy of Management Review.* In addition, he has consulted for a number of organizations, including Whirlpool Corporation, Amoco Oil Company, and the North Carolina State government.

He has co-authored two textbooks, has co-edited a number of special issues of journals dealing with the future of Strategic HRM as well as Corporate Social Responsibility. He has taught in Executive Development programs and has conducted programs and/or consulted for a number of large public and private sector organizations. Dr. Wright served as the Chair of the HR Division of the Academy of Management and on the Board of Directors for SHRM Foundation, World at Work, and Human Resource Planning Society.

Preface

The management of human resources is critical for companies to provide "value" to customers, shareholders, employees, and the community where they are located. Value includes not only profits but also employee growth and satisfaction, creation of new jobs, protection of the environment, and contributions to community programs. All aspects of human resource management including acquiring, preparing, developing, and compensating employees can help companies meet their competitive challenges and create value. Also, effective human resource management requires an awareness of broader contextual issues affecting business such as changes in the labor force, legal issues, and globalization. Both the popular press and academic research show that effective human resource management practices do result in greater value for shareholders and employees. For example the human resource management practices at companies such as Google, Wegman Food Markets, Starbucks, and JM Smucker help them earn recognition on *Fortune* magazine's list of "The 100 Best Companies to Work For." This publicity creates a positive vibe for these companies, helping them attract talented new employees, motivate and retain current employees, and make their services and products more desirable to consumers.

Engaging, Focused, and Applied: Our Approach in *Fundamentals of Human Resource Management*

Following graduation most students will find themselves working in businesses or not-for-profit organizations. Regardless of their position or career aspirations, their role in either directly managing other employees or understanding human resource management practices is critical for ensuring both company and personal success. As a result, *Fundamentals of Human Resource Management* focuses on human resource issues and how HR is used at work. *Fundamentals of Human Resource Management* is applicable to both HR majors and students from other majors or colleges who are taking a human resource course as an elective or a requirement. Our approach to teaching human resource management involves *engaging* the student in learning through the use of examples and best practices, *focusing* them on the important HR issues and concepts, and providing them the opportunity to *apply* what they have learned through end-of-chapter cases and in-chapter features. Students not only learn about best practices but they are actively engaged through the use of cases and decision making. As a result, students will be able to take what they have learned in the course and apply it to solving human resource management problems they will encounter on their jobs.

For example, as described in detail in the guided tour of the book, each chapter includes "Thinking Ethically" which confronts students with ethical issues that occur in managing human resources, "HR Oops!" (a new feature in the third edition of *Fundamentals* that highlights human resource management issues that were handled poorly), and several different cases (*BusinessWeek* cases and additional end-of-chapter cases). All of these features encourage students to critically evaluate human resource–related situations and problems that have occurred in companies and apply the chapter concepts.

"Did You Know" boxes are included in each chapter. The information provided in these boxes shows how the issues discussed in the chapter play out in companies. Some examples include how much time employees waste at work, the kinds of Internet searches that companies conduct to find out about prospective employees, and the top 10 causes of workplace injuries.

Adopters of *Fundamentals* have access to Manager's Hot Seat exercises which include video segments showing scenarios that are critical for HR success including ethics, diversity, working in teams, and the virtual workplace. Students assume the role of manager as they watch the video and answer questions that appear during the segment—forcing them to make on-the-spot decisions. *Fundamentals of Human Resource Management* also provides students with "how to" perform HR activities such as interviewing that they are likely to have to perform in their jobs. Finally, *Fundamentals of Human Resource Management* shows how the Internet can be useful for managing human resources.

The author team believes that the focused, engaging, and applied approach distinguishes this book from others that have similar coverage of HR topics. The book has timely coverage of important HR issues, is easy to read, has many features that grab the students' attention, and gets the students actively involved in learning. We would like to thank those of you who have adopted previous editions of *Fundamentals,* and we hope that you will continue to use upcoming editions! For those of you considering *Fundamentals* for adoption, we believe that our approach makes *Fundamentals* your text of choice for human resource management.

Organization

Fundamentals of Human Resource Management includes an introductory chapter (Chapter 1) and five parts.

Chapter 1 discusses why human resource management is an essential element for an organization's success. The chapter introduces human resource management practices and human resource professionals and managers' roles and responsibilities in managing human resources. Also, ethics in human resource management is emphasized.

Part 1 discusses the environmental forces that companies face in trying to effectively utilize their human resources. These forces include economic, technological, and social trends, employment laws, and work design. Employers typically have more control over work design than development of equal employment law or economic, technological, or social trends, but all affect how employers attract, retain, and motivate human resources. Some of the major trends discussed in Chapter 2 include greater availability of new and inexpensive technology for human resource management, the growth of the use of human resources on a global scale, changes in the labor force and the types of skills needed in today's jobs, and a focus on aligning human resource management with the company's strategy. Chapter 3, "Providing Equal Employment Opportunity and a Safe Workplace," presents an overview of the major laws affecting employers in these areas and ways that organizations can develop human resource practices that are in compliance with the laws. Chapter 4, "Analyzing Work and Designing Jobs," shows how jobs and work systems determine the knowledge, skills, and abilities that employees need to provide services or produce products and influence employees' motivation, satisfaction, and safety at work. The process of analyzing and designing jobs is discussed.

Part 2 deals with identifying the types of employees needed, recruiting and choosing them, and training them to perform their jobs. Chapter 5, "Planning for and Recruiting Human Resources," discusses how to develop a human resource plan. The strengths and weaknesses of different employment options for dealing with shortages or excesses of human resources including outsourcing, use of contract workers, and downsizing are emphasized. Strategies for recruiting talented employees including use of electronic recruiting sources such as job boards and blogs are emphasized. Chapter 6, "Selecting Employees and Placing Them in Jobs," emphasizes that selection is a process starting with screening applications and résumés and concluding with a job offer. The chapter takes a look at the most widely used methods for minimizing errors in choosing employees including applications and résumés, employment tests, and interviews. Selection method standards such as reliability and validity are discussed in understandable terms. Chapter 7, "Training Employees," covers the features of effective training systems. Effective training includes not only creating a good learning environment, but managers who encourage employees to use training content in their jobs and employees who are motivated to learn. The advantages and disadvantages of different training methods, including e-learning, are discussed.

Part 3 discusses how to assess employee performance and capitalize on their talents through retention and development. In "Managing Employees' Performance" (Chapter 8), we examine the strengths and weaknesses of different performance management systems including controversial forced distribution or ranking systems. "Developing Employees for Future Success" (Chapter 9) shows the student how assessment, job experiences, formal courses, and mentoring relationships can be used to develop employees for future success. Chapter 10, "Separating and Retaining Employees," discusses how to maximize employee satisfaction and productivity and retain valuable employees as well as how to fairly and humanely separate employees if the need arises because of poor performance or economic conditions.

Part 4 covers rewarding and compensating human resources, including how to design pay structures, recognize good performers, and provide benefits. In Chapter 11, "Establishing a Pay Structure," we discuss how managers weigh the importance and costs of pay to develop a compensation structure and levels of pay for each job given the worth of the jobs, legal requirements, and employee's judgments about the fairness of pay levels. The advantages and disadvantages of different types of incentive pay including merit pay, gainsharing, and stock ownership are discussed in Chapter 12, "Recognizing Employee Contributions with Pay." Chapter 13, "Providing Employee Benefits," highlights the contents of employee benefit packages, the ways that organizations administer benefits, and what companies can do to help employees understand the value of benefits and control benefits costs.

Part 5 covers other HR goals including collective bargaining and labor relations, managing human resource globally, and creating and maintaining high-performance organizations. "Collective Bargaining and Labor Relations" (Chapter 14) explores human resource activities where employees belong to unions or are seeking to join unions. Traditional issues in labor-management relations such as union structure and membership, the labor organizing process, and contract negotiations are discussed, as well as new ways unions and management are working together in less adversarial and more cooperative relationships. In "Managing Human Resources Globally" (Chapter 15), HR planning, selection, training, and compensating in international settings are discussed. We show how global differences among countries affect decisions about human resources. The role of human resources in creating an organization that achieves a high level of performance for employees, customers, community, shareholders, and managers is the focus of Chapter 16, "Creating and Maintaining High-Performance Organizations." The chapter describes high-performance work systems and the conditions that contribute to high performance and introduces students to the ways to measure the effectiveness of human resource management.

Acknowledgments

The third edition of *Fundamentals of Human Resource Management* would not have been possible without the staff of McGraw-Hill/Irwin and Elm Street Publishing Services. John Weimeister, our editor, helped us in developing the vision for the book and gave us the resources we needed to develop a top-of-the-line HRM teaching package. Donielle Xu's valuable insights and organizational skills kept the author team on deadline and made the book more visually appealing than the authors could have ever done on their own. Karen Hill of Elm Street worked diligently to make sure that the book was interesting, practical, and readable, and remained true to findings of human resource management research. We also thank Natalie Zook for her marketing efforts for this new book.

Our supplement authors deserve thanks for helping us create a first-rate teaching package. Julie Gedro of Empire State College wrote the newly custom-designed *Instructor's Manual* and Les Wiletzky of Pierce College authored the new PowerPoint presentation.

We would like to extend our sincere appreciation to all of the professors who gave of their time to offer their suggestions and insightful comments that helped us to develop and shape this new edition:

Angela D. Boston
The University of Texas–Arlington

Diane Galbraith
Slippery Rock University

Jerry Anthony Carbo II
Fairmont State University

Jane Whitney Gibson
Nova Southeastern University

William P. Ferris
Western New England College

Nancy Elizabeth Waldeck
University of Toledo

We would also like to thank the professors who gave of their time to review the previous editions through various stages of development.

Cheryl Adkins
Longwood University

Barry Armandi
SUNY–Old Westbury

Michelle Alarcon
Hawaii Pacific University

Kristin Backhaus
State University of New York at New Paltz

Lydia Anderson
Fresno City College

Charlene Barker
Spokane Falls Community College

Brenda Anthony
Tallahassee Community College

Melissa Woodard Barringer
University of Massachusetts at Amherst

Wendy Becker
University of Albany

Jerry Bennett
Western Kentucky University

Tom Bilyeu
Southwestern Illinois College

Genie Black
Arkansas Tech University

Larry Borgen
Normandale Community College

Kay Braguglia
Hampton University

John Brau
Alvin Community College

Jon Bryan
Bridgewater State College

Susan Burroughs
Roosevelt University

Tony Cafarelli
Ursuline College

Jerry Carbo
Fairmont State College

Kevin Carlson
Virginia Tech

Xiao-Ping Chen
University of Washington

Sharon Clark
Lebanon Valley College

Gary Corona
Florida Community College

Craig Cowles
Bridgewater State College

Suzanne Crampton
Grand Valley State University

Denise Daniels
Seattle Pacific University

K. Shannon Davis
North Carolina State University

Cedric Dawkins
Ashland University

Tom Diamante
Adelphi University

Anita Dickson
Northampton Community College

Robert Ericksen
Craven Community College

Dave Erwin
Athens State University

Philip Ettman
Westfield State College

Angela Farrar
University of Nevada at Las Vegas

Ronald Faust
University of Evansville

David Foote
Middle Tennessee State University

Lucy Ford
Rutgers University

Wanda Foster
Calumet College of St. Joseph

Marty Franklin
Wilkes Community College

Rusty Freed
Tarleton State University

Walter Freytag
University of Washington

Donald Gardner
University of Colorado–Colorado Springs

Michael Gavlik
Vanderbilt University

Treena Gillespie
California State University–Fullerton

Kris Gossett
Ivy Tech State College

Samuel Hazen
Tarleton State University

James Hess
Ivy Tech State College

Kim Hester
Arkansas State University

Chad Higgins
University of Washington

Nancy Higgins
Montgomery College

Charles Hill
UC Berkeley

Mary Hogue
Kent State University

MaryAnne Hyland
Adelphi University

Linda Isenhour
University of Central Florida

Henry Jackson
Delaware County Community College

Pamela Johnson
California State University–Chico

Coy Jones
The University of Memphis

Gwendolyn Jones
University of Akron

Kathleen Jones
University of North Dakota

Jordan Kaplan
Long Island University

Jim Kennedy
Angelina College

Shawn Komorn
University of Texas Health Sciences Center

Lee W. Lee
Central Connecticut State University

Leo Lennon
Webster University

Dan Lybrook
Purdue University

Patricia Martinez
University of Texas at San Antonio

Jalane Meloun
Kent State University

Angela Miles
Old Dominion University

James Morgan
California State University–Chico

Vicki Mullenex
Davis & Elkins College

Cliff Olson
Southern Adventist University

Laura Paglis
University of Evansville

Teresa Palmer
Illinois State University

Jack Partlow
Northern Virginia Community College

Dana Partridge
University of Southern Indiana

Brooke Quizz
Peirce College

Barbara Rau
University of Wisconsin–Oshkosh

Mike Roberson
Eastern Kentucky University

Foreman Rogers, Jr.
Northwood University

Mary Ellen Rosetti
Hudson Valley Community College

Joseph Salamone
State University of New York at Buffalo

Lucian Spataro
Ohio University

James Tan
University of Wisconsin—Stout

Steven Thomas
Southwest Missouri State University

Alan Tilquist
West Virginia State College

Tom Tudor
University of Arkansas

Fraya Wagner-Marsh
Eastern Michigan University

Richard Wagner
University of Wisconsin–Whitewater

Melissa Waite
SUNY Brockport

Barbara Warschawski
Schenectady County Community College

Gary Waters
Hawaii Pacific University

Bill Waxman
Edison Community College

Steven Wolff
Marist College

John Zietlow
Lee University

John Zummo
York College

Raymond A. Noe
John R. Hollenbeck
Barry Gerhart
Patrick M. Wright

fundamentals of **human**
resource
management

Noe   Hollenbeck   Gerhart   Wright

fundamentals of
Human Resource Management
third edition

engaging.
focused.
applied.

The third edition of
*Fundamentals of Human
Resource Management*
continues to offer students
a brief introduction to
HRM that is rich with
examples and engaging in
its application.

**Please take a moment to
page through some of the
highlights of this new
edition.**

FEATURES

WHAT DO I NEED TO KNOW?

Assurance of learning:

- Learning objectives open each chapter.
- Learning objectives are referenced in the page margins where the relevant discussion begins.
- The chapter summary is written around the same learning objectives.
- The student quiz on the textbook OLC and instructor testing questions are tagged to the appropriate objective they cover.

Training Employees

What Do I Need to Know?
After reading this chapter, you should be able to:

LO1 Discuss how to link training programs to organizational needs.

LO2 Explain how to assess the need for training.

LO3 Explain how to assess employees' readiness for training.

LO4 Describe how to plan an effective training program.

LO5 Compare widely used training methods.

LO6 Summarize how to implement a successful training program.

LO7 Evaluate the success of a training program.

LO8 Describe training methods for employee orientation and diversity management.

Introduction

With 78,000 employees working in 294 offices in 48 countries, computer-chip maker Intel has to foster collaboration across many cultures and languages. Although English is widely used as a common language for international businesses, misunderstandings can arise, especially among people who usually speak a different language. Intel's solution is to offer a voluntary training program. Employees can take classes in Mandarin, Japanese, and Spanish at various offices throughout the United States. The classes help employees work with colleagues or clients from other countries. As the demand for language training increased, the company began planning similar programs for employees outside the United States. Intel also offers one-day classes that deliver basic information about other cultures' history and business practices so that employees can learn how to work effectively with people from those cultures. Company spokeswoman Tracy Koon explains, "You're not going to be an effective team if you are constantly offending the other members without knowing it." At Intel, the solution is training.[1]

Training consists of an organization's planned efforts to help employees acquire job-related knowledge, skills, abilities, and behaviors, with the goal of applying these on the job. A training program may range from formal classes to one-on-one mentoring, and it may take place on the job or at remote locations. No matter what its form, training can benefit the organization when it is linked to organizational needs and when it motivates employees.

This chapter describes how to plan and carry out an effective training program. We begin by discussing how to develop effective training in the context of the organization's strategy. Next, we discuss how organizations assess employees' training needs. We then review training methods and the process of evaluating a training program. The chapter concludes by discussing some special applications of training: orientation of new employees and the management of diversity.

chapter seven

HR Oops!

Training without Results

If diversity training works, companies using it should have more managers from groups that experience discrimination. But in a study by three sociologists, most companies that introduced diversity training saw no significant change in the number of women and minority managers.

At the companies studied, talking about differences did not make people value diversity, at least not enough to promote women and minorities. However, assigning mentors to female and minority employees helped. Making managers responsible for achieving diversity targets made a bigger difference. And doing all three had the most impact.

An example shows the problem with focusing on training alone. A law firm trying to attract and retain more female attorneys provided training to foster respect for female colleagues. The trainers did their assignment, but no one was assigned to look for the real problem: the firm routinely assigned big clients to its male attorneys. For a successful career, the female attorneys needed polite colleagues less than they did experience with key clients.

Source: Alana Conner Snibbe, "Diversity Training Doesn't Work," *Stanford Social Innovation Review,* Winter 2007, www.ssireview.com; Lisa Takeuchi, "The Diversity Delusion," *Time,* May 7,

2007, downloaded from General Reference Center Gold, http://find.galegroup.com; and A. Kalev, F. Dobbin, and E. Kelly, "Best Practices or Best Guesses? Assessing the Efficacy of Corporate Affirmative Action and Diversity Policies," *American Sociological Review* 71 (2006), pp. 589–617.

Questions

1. In the example of the law firm, what step(s) in the training process did the firm skip before it set up training?

2. What business goals can a diversity training program reasonably be expected to achieve? How can it be made more goal-oriented?

HR Oops!

Engage students through examples of companies where the HR department has fallen short. Discussion questions at the end of each example encourage student analysis of the situation. Examples include: "When Employees Steal," "Discriminating against Pregnant Workers," and "Sneaky Recruiters."

NEW!

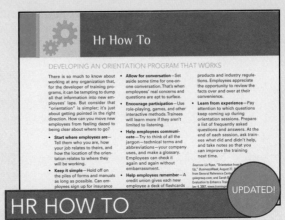

BEST PRACTICES

Engage students through examples of companies where the HR department is working well. Examples include: "Healthwise Knows the Value of a Valued Employee," "Gallup Helps Wesley Medical Center Find Practical Selection Methods," and "Valuing Diversity at JPMorgan Chase."

HR HOW TO

Engage students through specific steps to creating HRM programs and tackling common challenges. Examples include: "Employee Surveys," "Supervising Your Parents' Generation," and "Interviewing Effectively."

eHRM

Engage students through examples of how HR departments are utilizing technology today. Examples include: "High-Tech Flexibility at Bank of the West" and "Video Résumés—Perilous Policy?"

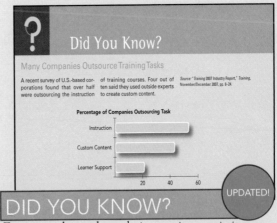

DID YOU KNOW?

Engage students through interesting statistics related to chapter topics. Examples include: "Even Office Work Can Tire You," "One in Three Positions Are Filled with Insiders," and "Employers Are Googling and Social Networking, Too."

FEATURES

that spill over into their personal lives. E-mail, pagers, and cell phones bombard employees with information and work demands. In the car, on vacation, on planes, and even in the bathroom, employees can be interrupted by work demands. More demanding work results in greater employee stress, less satisfied employees, loss of productivity, and higher turnover—all of which are costly for companies.

Many organizations are taking steps to provide more flexible work schedules, to protect employees' free time, and to more productively use employees' work time. Workers consider flexible schedules a valuable way to ease the pressures and conflicts of trying to balance work and nonwork activities. Employers are using flexible schedules to recruit and retain employees and to increase satisfaction and productivity. For example, Best Buy created its Results-Only Work Environment (ROWE) to give employees control over how, when, and where they get the job done, as long as they achieve the desired results.[52] The idea of this experiment is to let employees focus on productivity, rather than whether they are physically present in a meeting or seated behind their desk at a particular time of day. In divisions that have tried ROWE, employees say they are more engaged at work, are more committed to the company, and have improved their family relationships at the same time.

THINKING ETHICALLY

THE ETHICS OF OFFSHORING

When companies use offshoring, they are eliminating higher-paid U.S. jobs and replacing them with lower-paid jobs elsewhere. The debate has raged over whether this practice is ethical.

Businesses certainly need to make a profit, and offshoring can help lower costs. One manager who endorses offshoring is George Hefferan, vice president and general counsel for Mindcrest, a legal services firm based in Chicago. According to Hefferan, the company would not even exist if it couldn't hire lawyers in Mumbai and Pune, India. At far lower rates than U.S. attorneys charge, the Indian lawyers review lease agreements and do other routine tasks. This assistance frees employees in Chicago to tackle more complicated assignments.

But viewed from U.S. workers' standpoint, offshoring has its downside. Business owner Valarie King-Bailey

once lost her own engineering job to offshoring. King-Bailey then started her own company, OnShore Technology, an information technology (IT) engineering firm. The company now has eight employees and a mission of "keeping technology jobs on America's shores."

SOURCE: Ann Meyer, "U.S. Exit Strategy Splits Employers," *Chicago Tribune*, October 29, 2007, sec. 3, p. 2.

Questions

1. When a company moves jobs to another [country], who benefits? Who loses? Given the [win]ners and losers, do you think offshoring is [ethical]? Why or why not?
2. Imagine you are an HR manager at a comp[any that] is planning to begin offshoring its produ[ction or] customer service operations. How could [you help] the company proceed as ethically as poss[ible]?

Focused on ethics. Reviewers indicated that the Thinking Ethically feature, which confronts students in each chapter with an ethical issue regarding managing human resources, was a highlight. This feature has been updated throughout the text.

---

given the way the brain processes information. Generally, this means reducing the information-processing requirements of a job. In these simpler jobs, workers may be less likely to make mistakes or have accidents. Of course, the simpler jobs also may be less motivating. Research has found that challenging jobs tend to fatigue and dissatisfy workers when they feel little control over their situation, lack social support, and feel motivated mainly to avoid errors. In contrast, they may enjoy the challenges of a difficult job where they have some control and social support, especially if they enjoy learning and are unafraid of making mistakes.[34] Because of this drawback to simplifying jobs, it can be most beneficial to simplify jobs where employees will most appreciate having the mental demands reduced (as in a job that is extremely challenging) or where the costs of errors are severe (as in the job of a surgeon or air-traffic controller).

There are several ways to simplify a job's mental demands. One is to limit the amount of information and memorization that the job requires. Organizations can also provide adequate lighting, easy-to-understand gauges and displays, simple-to-operate equipment, and clear instructions. Often, employees try to simplify some of the mental demands of their own jobs by creating checklists, charts, or other aids. Finally, every job requires some degree of thinking, remembering, and paying attention, so for every job, organizations need to evaluate whether their employees can handle the job's mental demands.

Changes in technology sometimes reduce job demands and errors, but in some cases, technology has made the problem worse. Some employees try to juggle information from several sources at once—say, talking on a cell phone while typing, surfing the Web for information during a team member's business presentation, or repeatedly stopping work on a project to check e-mail or instant messages. In these cases, the cell phone, handheld computer, and e-mail or instant messages are distracting the employees from their primary task. They may convey important information, but they also break the employee's train of thought, reducing performance and increasing the likelihood of errors.[35] The problem may be aggravated by employees downplaying the significance of these interruptions. For example, in a recent survey of workers, only half said they check their e-mail at work more than once an hour, and more than a third said they check every 15 minutes. However, monitoring software on their computers determined that they were actually changing applications to check e-mail up to 30 or 40 times an hour.[36] The sheer volume of e-mail, as illustrated by Figure 4.8, can be a drain on employee time. Even if an employee spends just a minute or two on each message, e-mail will consume a significant part of the day.

Information-processing errors also are greater in situations in which one person hands off information to another. Such transmission problems have become a major concern in the field of medicine, because critical information is routinely shared among nurses, doctors, and medical technicians, as well as between hospital employees changing shifts. Problems during shift changes are especially likely as a result of fatigue and burnout among employees with stressful jobs.[37] Some hospitals have coped by introducing a method called SBAR (situation, background, assessment, and recommendation), which standardizes the information delivered at handoff points. In a

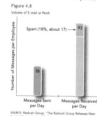

Figure 4.8
Volume of E-mail at Work

Spam (18%, about 17)

Number of Messages per Employee

Messages Sent per Day — 38
Messages Received per Day — 93

SOURCE: Radicati Group, "The Radicati Group Releases New Study, 'Messaging and Collaboration—Business User Survey, 2007,'" news release, December 17, 2007, www.radicati.com.

Focused on current evidence. Figures and tables have been updated throughout the text with the most recent statistics and information available.

---

to Toulouse, where they could learn the new software and work with French engineers in redesigning the parts. The cross-border teamwork, unprecedented for Airbus, began to see results. Finally, the first A380s were ready for takeoff. Unfortunately, because the delays reduced sales, profits are still years away.

SOURCES: Daniel Michaels, "Airbus, Amid Turmoil, Revives Troubled Plane," *Wall Street Journal*, October 15, 2007, http://online.wsj.com; "The Giant on the Runway: The Airbus A380," *Economist*, October 13, 2007.

inside jets and others teamed up with colleagues in France, how did these changes affect the knowledge, skills, and abilities and other characteristics required for performing these engineers' jobs?

3. Suppose you had been an HR manager working at Airbus headquarters or in Hamburg when the production of the A380 was first delayed. Could you have helped the company meet its business goals? If so, how? If not, why not?

 IT'S A WRAP!

www.mhhe.com/noefund3e is your source for Reviewing, Applying, and Practicing the concepts you learned about in Chapter 4.

Review	Application	Practice
• Chapter learning objectives	• Manager's Hot Seat segment: "Virtual Workplace: Out of Office Reply"	• Chapter quiz
• Narrated lecture and iPod content	• Video case and quiz: "Working Smart"	• Pre-test and Post-test
	• Self-assessments Find Your Match: O*NET	
	• Web-exercise: Comparative Job Analysis	

Focused on student resources. The end-of-chapter 'It's a WRAP!' box clearly indicates options students have for Reviewing, Applying, and Practicing the concepts learned in each chapter at www.mhhe.com/noe3e.

Apply the concepts in each chapter through comprehensive review and discussion questions.

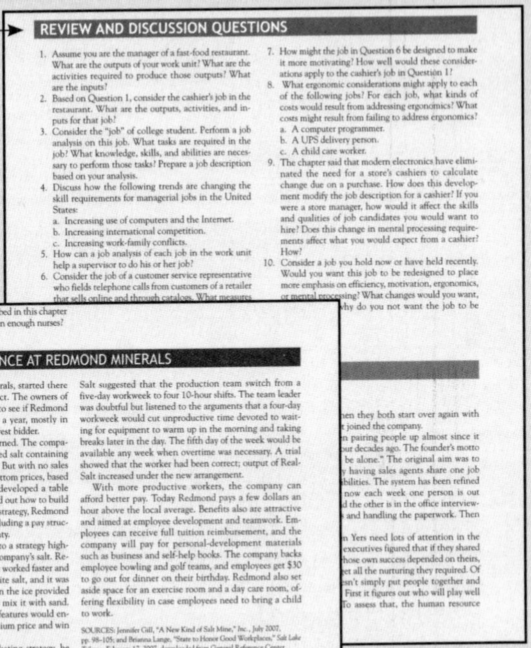

REVIEW AND DISCUSSION QUESTIONS

1. Assume you are the manager of a fast-food restaurant. What are the outputs of your work unit? What are the activities required to produce those outputs? What are the inputs?
2. Based on Question 1, consider the cashier's job in the restaurant. What are the outputs, activities, and inputs for that job?
3. Consider the "job" of college student. Perform a job analysis on this job. What tasks are required in the job? What knowledge, skills, and abilities are necessary to perform those tasks? Prepare a job description based on your analysis.
4. Discuss how the following trends are changing the skill requirements for managerial jobs in the United States:
   a. Increasing use of computers and the Internet.
   b. Increasing international competition.
   c. Increasing work-family conflicts.
5. How can a job analysis of each job in the work unit help a supervisor to do his or her job?
6. Consider the job of a customer service representative who fields telephone calls from customers of a retailer that sells online and through catalogs. What measures ...
7. How might the job in Question 6 be designed to make it more motivating? How well would these considerations apply to the cashier's job in Question 1?
8. What ergonomic considerations might apply to each of the following jobs? For each job, what kinds of costs would result from addressing ergonomics? What costs might result from failing to address ergonomics?
   a. A computer programmer.
   b. A UPS delivery person.
   c. A child care worker.
9. The chapter said that modern electronics have eliminated the need for a store's cashiers to calculate change due on a purchase. How does this development modify the job description for a cashier? If you were a store manager, how would it affect the skills and qualities of job candidates you would want to hire? Does this change in mental processing requirements affect what you would expect from a cashier? How?
10. Consider a job you hold now or have held recently. Would you want this job to be redesigned to place more emphasis on efficiency, motivation, ergonomics, or mental processing? What changes would you want, ... why do you not want the job to be ...

Apply the concepts in each chapter through two cases looking at companies and how their practices illustrate chapter content. These cases can be used in class lecture, and the questions provided at the end of each case are suitable for assignments or discussion.

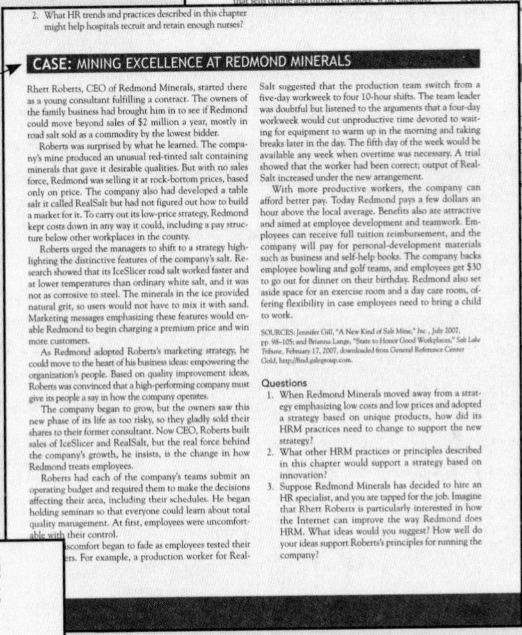

2. What HR trends and practices described in this chapter might help hospitals recruit and retain enough nurses?

CASE: MINING EXCELLENCE AT REDMOND MINERALS

Rhett Roberts, CEO of Redmond Minerals, started there as a young consultant fulfilling a contract. The owners of the family business had brought him in to see if Redmond could move beyond sales of $2 million a year, mostly in road salt sold as a commodity by the lowest bidder.

Roberts was surprised by what he learned. The company's mine produced an unusual red-tinted salt containing minerals that gave it desirable qualities. But with no sales force, Redmond was selling it at rock-bottom prices, based only on price. The company also had developed a table salt it called RealSalt but had not figured out how to build a market for it. To carry out its low-price strategy, Redmond kept costs down in any way it could, including a pay structure below other workplaces in the county.

Roberts urged the managers to shift to a strategy highlighting the distinctive features of the company's salt. Research showed that its IceSlicer road salt worked faster and at lower temperatures than ordinary white salt, and it was not as corrosive to steel. The minerals in the ice provided natural grit, so users would not have to mix it with sand. Marketing messages emphasizing these features would enable Redmond to begin charging a premium price and win more customers.

As Redmond adopted Roberts's marketing strategy, he could move to the heart of his business ideas: empowering the organization's people. Based on quality improvement ideas, Roberts was convinced that a high-performing company must give its people a say in how the company operates.

The company began to grow, but the owners saw this new phase of its life as too risky, so they gladly sold their shares to their former consultant. Now CEO, Roberts built sales of IceSlicer and RealSalt, but the real force behind the company's growth, he insists, is the change in how Redmond treats employees.

Roberts had each of the company's teams submit an operating budget and required them to make the decisions affecting their area, including their schedules. He began holding seminars so that everyone could learn about total quality management. At first, employees were uncomfortable with their control.

... discomfort began to fade as employees tested their ... ers. For example, a production worker for RealSalt suggested that the production team switch from a five-day workweek to four 10-hour shifts. The team leader was doubtful but listened to the arguments that a four-day workweek would cut unproductive time devoted to waiting for equipment to warm up in the morning and taking breaks later in the day. The fifth day of the week would be available any week when overtime was necessary. A trial showed that the worker had been correct; output of RealSalt increased under the new arrangement.

With more productive workers, the company can afford better pay. Today Redmond pays a few dollars an hour above the local average. Benefits also are attractive and aimed at employee development and teamwork. Employees can receive full tuition reimbursement, and the company will pay for personal-development materials such as business and self-help books. The company backs employee bowling and golf teams, and employees get $30 to go out for dinner on their birthday. Redmond also set aside space for an exercise room and a day care room, offering flexibility in case employees need to bring a child to work.

SOURCES: Jennifer Gill, "A New Kind of Salt Mine," *Inc.*, July 2007, pp. 98–105; and Brianna Lange, "State to Honor Good Workplaces," *Salt Lake Tribune*, February 17, 2007, downloaded from General Reference Center Gold, http://find.galegroup.com.

Questions

1. When Redmond Minerals moved away from a strategy emphasizing low costs and low prices and adopted a strategy based on unique products, how did its HRM practices need to change to support the new strategy?
2. What other HRM practices or principles described in this chapter would support a strategy based on innovation?
3. Suppose Redmond Minerals has decided to hire an HR specialist, and you are tapped for the job. Imagine that Rhett Roberts is particularly interested in how the Internet can improve the way Redmond does HRM. What ideas would you suggest? How well do your ideas support Roberts's principles for running the company?

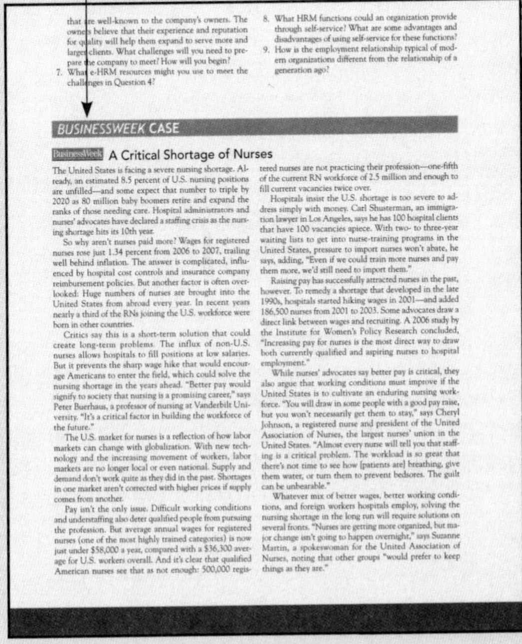

that are well-known to the company's owners. The owners believe that their experience and reputation for quality will help them expand to serve more and larger clients. What challenges will you need to prepare the company to meet? How will you begin?

7. What e-HRM resources might you use to meet the challenges in Question 4?
8. What HRM functions could an organization provide through self-service? What are some advantages and disadvantages of using self-service for these functions?
9. How is the employment relationship typical of modern organizations different from the relationship of a generation ago?

BUSINESSWEEK CASE

BusinessWeek A Critical Shortage of Nurses

The United States is facing a severe nursing shortage. Already, an estimated 8.5 percent of U.S. nursing positions are unfilled—and some expect that number to triple by 2020 as 80 million baby boomers retire and expand the ranks of those needing care. Hospital administrators and nurses' advocates have declared a staffing crisis as the nursing shortage hits its 10th year.

So why aren't nurses paid more? Wages for registered nurses rose just 1.34 percent from 2006 to 2007, trailing well behind inflation. The answer is complicated, influenced by hospital cost controls and insurance company reimbursement policies. But another factor is often overlooked: Huge numbers of nurses are brought into the United States from abroad every year. In recent years nearly a third of the RNs joining the U.S. workforce were born in other countries.

Critics say this is a short-term solution that could create long-term problems. The influx of non-U.S. nurses allows hospitals to fill positions at low salaries. But it prevents the sharp wage hike that would encourage Americans to enter the field, which could solve the nursing shortage in the years ahead. "Better pay would signify to society that nursing is a promising career," says Peter Buerhaus, a professor of nursing at Vanderbilt University. "It's a critical factor in building the workforce of the future."

The U.S. market for nurses is a reflection of how labor markets can change with globalization. With new technology and the increasing movement of workers, labor markets are no longer local or even national. Supply and demand don't work quite as they did in the past. Shortages in one market aren't corrected with higher prices if supply comes from another.

Pay isn't the only issue. Difficult working conditions and understaffing also deter qualified people from pursuing the profession. But average annual wages for registered nurses (one of the most highly trained categories) is now just under $58,000 a year, compared with a $36,300 average for U.S. workers overall. And it's clear that qualified American nurses see that as not enough: 500,000 registered nurses are not practicing their profession—one-fifth of the current RN workforce of 2.5 million and enough to fill current vacancies twice over.

Hospitals insist the U.S. shortage is too severe to address simply with money. Carl Shusterman, an immigration lawyer in Los Angeles, says he has 100 hospital clients that have 100 vacancies apiece. With two- to three-year waiting lists to get into nurse-training programs in the United States, pressure to import nurses won't abate, he says, adding, "Even if we could train more nurses and pay them more, we'd still need to import them."

Raising pay has successfully attracted nurses in the past, however. To remedy a shortage that developed in the late 1990s, hospitals started hiking wages in 2001—and added 186,500 nurses from 2001 to 2003. Some advocates draw a direct link between wages and recruiting. A 2006 study by the Institute for Women's Policy Research concluded, "Increasing pay for nurses is the most direct way to draw both currently qualified and aspiring nurses to hospital employment."

While nurses' advocates say better pay is critical, they also argue that working conditions must improve if the United States is to cultivate an enduring nursing workforce. "You will draw in some people with a good pay raise, but you won't necessarily get them to stay," says Cheryl Johnson, a registered nurse and president of the United Association of Nurses, the largest nurses' union in the United States. "Almost every nurse will tell you that staffing is a critical problem. The workload is so great that there's not time to see how [patients are] breathing, give them water, or turn them to prevent bedsores. The guilt can be unbearable."

Whatever mix of better wages, better working conditions, and foreign workers hospitals employ, solving the nursing shortage in the long run will require solutions on several fronts. "Nurses are getting more organized, but major change isn't going to happen overnight," says Suzanne Martin, a spokeswoman for the United Association of Nurses, noting that other groups "would prefer to keep things as they are."

Here's what our reviewers have said:

"I definitely would say this is the best introduction to HRM text on the market. I find it easy to read and understand, yet it contains the necessary level of knowledge needed to be successful in an entry level HR generalist role." *Jerry Carbo, Fairmont State University*

"The features are outstanding . . . very easy to read and understand and allow for application of the information." *Angela Boston, The University of Texas-Arlington*

"The features are outstanding and add a lot to the book. They keep the book current and give insight to real-life applications." *Jane Gibson, Nova Southeastern University*

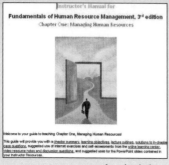

Instructor's Manual

The newly custom-designed Instructor's Manual includes chapter summaries, learning objectives, an extended chapter outline, key terms, description of text boxes, discussion questions, summary of end-of-chapter cases, video notes, and additional activities.

Test Bank

The test bank includes multiple choice, true/false, and essay questions for each chapter. Rationales and page references are also provided for the answers. Available on the IRCD or the Instructor OLC.

IRCD (Instructor Presentation CD-ROM)

This multimedia CD-ROM allows instructors to create dynamic classroom presentations by incorporating PowerPoint, videos, and the Instructor's Manual and Test Bank. (ISBN: 007336441X)

Videos

Videos for each chapter, along with accompanying video cases and quizzes, are located on the OLC and highlight companies and current HRM issues. (Instructor DVD ISBN: 0073283088)

PowerPoint

The slides include lecture material, key terms, additional content to expand concepts in the text, hotlinks, and discussion questions that can be used in CPS (see below). The PowerPoint is found on the Instructor CD-ROM and on the Instructor and Student Center of the Online Learning Center. The PPT also now includes detailed teaching notes.

CPS (Wireless Classroom Performance System) by eInstruction

If you've ever asked yourself, "How can I measure class participation, or "How do I encourage class participation?" then CPS might be the product for you. CPS enables you to record responses from students to questions posed in a PowerPoint slide, even record attendance, and offers a variety of reporting features, including easy export to WebCT or Blackboard grade books. For your students, it's as easy as using buttons on a remote control. Questions can be designed by you, or questions are already included in the Fundamentals of Human Resource Management PowerPoint. Ask your local sales representative how to get CPS for your classroom.

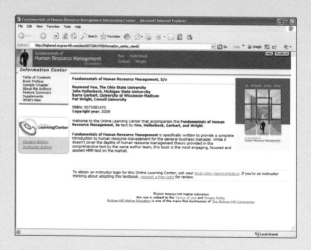

Online Learning Center

(www.mhhe.com/noefund3e)

This text-specific Web site follows the text chapter by chapter. Students can go online to take self-grading quizzes, watch video clips and answer discussion questions, read relevant and current HR news, and work through interactive exercises. There is a guide linking the PHR/SPHR certification exam with the text. Instructors can also access downloadable supplements such as the Instructor's Manual and Manager's Hot Seat notes. Professors and students can access this content directly through the textbook Web site, through PageOut, or within a course management system (i.e., WebCT or Blackboard).

Self-Assessments, Test Your Knowledge Quizzes, and iPod Content

These interactive features provide students with tools to study chapter concepts in a variety of environments, and provide instructors with additional assignments or in-class discussion opportunities. These are premium content features and require a purchased access code.

Manager's Hot Seat

The Manager's Hot Seat is an interactive online feature that allows students to watch as 15 real managers apply their years of experience to confront issues, Students assume the role of the manager as they watch the video and answer multiple choice questions that pop up during the segment—forcing them to make decisions on the spot. Students learn from the manager's mistakes and successes, and then do a report critiquing the manager's approach by defending their reasoning. Reports can be e-mailed or printed out for credit. If you choose to package the Hot Seat with this text, there are individual and group exercises related to most of the segments on the online learning center, as well as accompanying teaching notes in the Instructor's Manual. This is a premium content feature and requires a purchased access code.

Brief Contents

Contents

PART 5

Meeting Other HR Goals 399

xxx   Contents

Managing Human Resources

What Do I Need to Know?

After reading this chapter, you should be able to:

LO1 Define human resource management, and explain how HRM contributes to an organization's performance.

LO2 Identify the responsibilities of human resource departments.

LO3 Summarize the types of skills needed for human resource management.

LO4 Explain the role of supervisors in human resource management.

LO5 Discuss ethical issues in human resource management.

LO6 Describe typical careers in human resource management.

Introduction

Imagine trying to run a business where you have to replace every employee two or three times a year. If that sounds chaotic, you can sympathize with the challenge facing Rob Cecere when he took the job of regional manager for a group of eight Domino's Pizza stores in New Jersey. In Cecere's region, store managers were quitting after a few months on the job. The lack of consistent leadership at the store level contributed to employee turnover rates of up to 300 percent a year (one position being filled three times in a year). In other words, new managers constantly had to find, hire, and train new workers—and rely on inexperienced people to keep customers happy. Not surprisingly, the stores in Cecere's new territory were failing to meet sales goals.

Cecere made it his top goal to build a stable team of store managers who in turn could retain employees at their stores. He held a meeting with the managers and talked about improving sales, explaining, "It's got to start with people": hiring good people and keeping them on board. He continues to coach his managers, helping them build sales and motivate their workers through training and patience. In doing so, he has the backing of Domino's headquarters. When the company's current chief executive, David Brandon, took charge, he was shocked by the high employee turnover (then 158 percent nationwide), and he made that problem his priority. Brandon doubts the pay rates are what keeps employees with any fast-food company; instead, he emphasizes careful hiring, extensive coaching, and opportunities to earn promotions. In the years since Brandon became CEO, employee turnover at Domino's has fallen. And in New Jersey, Cecere is beginning to see results from his store managers as well.[1]

The challenges faced by Domino's are important dimensions of **human resource management (HRM),** the policies, practices, and systems that influence employees' behavior, attitudes, and performance. Many companies refer to HRM as involving "people practices." Figure 1.1 emphasizes

chapter one

Figure 1.1

Human Resource Management Practices

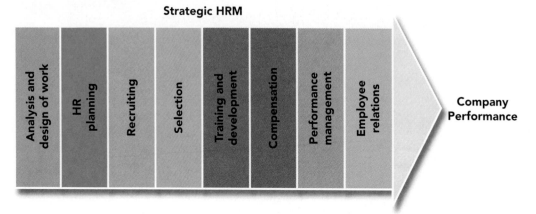

LO1 Define human resource management, and explain how HRM contributes to an organization's performance.

human resource management (HRM)
The policies, practices, and systems that influence employees' behavior, attitudes, and performance.

that there are several important HRM practices: analyzing work and designing jobs, attracting potential employees (recruiting), choosing employees (selection), teaching employees how to perform their jobs and preparing them for the future (training and development), evaluating their performance (performance management), rewarding employees (compensation), creating a positive work environment (employee relations), and supporting the organization's strategy (HR planning and change management). An organization performs best when all of these practices are managed well. At companies with effective HRM, employees and customers tend to be more satisfied, and the companies tend to be more innovative, have greater productivity, and develop a more favorable reputation in the community.[2]

In this chapter, we introduce the scope of human resource management. We begin by discussing why human resource management is an essential element of an organization's succcess. We then turn to the elements of managing human resources: the roles and skills needed for effective human resource management. Next, the chapter describes how all managers, not just human resource professionals, participate in the activities related to human resource management. The following section of the chapter addresses some of the ethical issues that arise with regard to human resource management. We then provide an overview of careers in human resource management. The chapter concludes by highlighting the HRM practices covered in the remainder of this book.

Human Resources and Company Performance

Managers and economists traditionally have seen human resource management as a necessary expense, rather than as a source of value to their organizations. Economic value is usually associated with *capital*—cash, equipment, technology, and facilities. However, research has demonstrated that HRM practices can be valuable.[3] Decisions such as whom to hire, what to pay, what training to offer, and how to evaluate employee performance directly affect employees' motivation and ability to provide goods and services that customers value. Companies that attempt to increase their competitiveness by investing in new technology and promoting quality throughout the organization also invest in state-of-the-art staffing, training, and compensation practices.[4]

Figure 1.2

Impact of Human
Resource Management

The concept of "human resource management" implies that employees are *resources* of the employer. As a type of resource, **human capital** means the organization's employees, described in terms of their training, experience, judgment, intelligence, relationships, and insight—the employee characteristics that can add economic value to the organization. In other words, whether it manufactures automobiles or forecasts the weather, for an organization to succeed at what it does, it needs employees with certain qualities, such as particular kinds of training and experience. This view means employees in today's organizations are not interchangeable, easily replaced parts of a system but the source of the company's success or failure. By influencing *who* works for the organization and *how* those people work, human resource management therefore contributes to such basic measures of an organization's success as quality, profitability, and customer satisfaction. Figure 1.2 shows this relationship.

Athleta Corporation, a catalog and Internet retailer of sports apparel, based in Petaluma, California, demonstrates the importance of human capital to the company's bottom line. Athleta's workforce is so committed to the company that turnover is less than 1 percent (1 out of 100 employees leave the company in an average year), productivity (output per worker) is increasing, and the company's growth is skyrocketing—it grew by five times in one year alone. One way the company has built a committed workforce is by cultivating a positive work environment. Most of Athleta's 60 employees set their own work schedules and are permitted to take personal time during the day. Employees take the initiative to learn one another's jobs, so they can fill in for one another during the day. Those who take time off for personal reasons willingly work odd hours. The company encourages employees to take breaks for physical activity, and employees can even bring along their dogs, which join employees outside for a run or to play catch. Employees use the open space preserve behind Athleta's facility to run, or they work out with the gym equipment set up in the company's storage area.[5] The "Best Practices" box tells about another company that appreciates the importance of human capital.

Human resource management is critical to the success of organizations because human capital has certain qualities that make it valuable. In terms of business strategy, an organization can succeed if it has a *sustainable competitive advantage* (is better than competitors at something and can hold that advantage over a sustained period of

human capital
An organization's employees, described in terms of their training, experience, judgment, intelligence, relationships, and insight.

Healthwise Knows the Value of a Valued Employee

Healthwise, a nonprofit organization based in Boise, Idaho, seeks to maintain a culture based on respect, teamwork, and "doing the right thing." In its treatment of employees, doing the right thing means creating a workplace that is "healthy, flexible, and employee-centered." As the leaders of Healthwise know, the company relies on intelligent and dedicated staff members to fulfill its mission of developing information resources that people can use to make smart health-care decisions. Executives meet with a counselor every six weeks to build stronger working relationships.

Consistent with the company's mission of empowering its clients' customers to make good decisions, Healthwise offers benefits that help its own employees stay healthy. Employees can take on-site classes in aerobics, yoga, and weight loss; borrow company-owned bicycles; walk on a treadmill while working at their computer; and visit an on-site gym. Many employees hold meetings while hiking on trails behind the office building. To reinforce healthy choices, the company pays employees up to $200 a year in bonuses for such activities as getting a physical or walking to work.

The workplace design also helps promote employees' health. Flowing water and natural lighting provide a relaxing atmosphere. Most employees have private offices with views of the nearby foothills.

Jim Balkins, the chief strategic officer for Healthwise, says these benefits are more than luxuries; they make business sense. According to Balkins, employee-friendly policies make it easier to recruit and keep talented people. In fact, Healthwise receives roughly 100 applications for each vacant position, and its employee turnover is about one-third the industry average. "If you have happier employees," says Balkins, "you have happier customers, and you can retain them." CEO Donald Kemper agrees: "When you want to come to work, you do better, work harder and smarter, and have better ideas." Another part of the proof? Revenues at Healthwise are climbing fast.

Sources: "About Us" and "Careers," Healthwise Web site, http://www.healthwise.org, accessed January 2, 2008; Kelly K. Spors, "Top 15 Small Workplaces: Outshining the Big Names," *Career Journal,* October 17, 2007, http://www.careerjournal.com; and Sandra Forester, "Boise's Healthwise Has Been Recognized for Its Design, Perks, and Atmosphere," *(Boise) Idaho Statesman,* November 28, 2007, downloaded from General Reference Center Gold, http://find.galegroup.com.

---

time). Therefore, we can conclude that organizations need the kind of resources that will give them such an advantage. Human resources have these necessary qualities:

- Human resources are *valuable*. High-quality employees provide a needed service as they perform many critical functions.
- Human resources are *rare* in the sense that a person with high levels of the needed skills and knowledge is not common. An organization may spend months looking for a talented and experienced manager or technician.
- Human resources *cannot be imitated*. To imitate human resources at a high-performing competitor, you would have to figure out which employees are providing the advantage and how. Then you would have to recruit people who can do precisely the same thing and set up the systems that enable those people to imitate your competitor.
- Human resources have *no good substitutes*. When people are well trained and highly motivated, they learn, develop their abilities, and care about customers. It is difficult to imagine another resource that can match committed and talented employees.

These qualities imply that human resources have enormous potential. An organization realizes this potential through the ways it practices human resource management.

At Southwest Airlines, the company's focus is on keeping employees loyal, motivated, trained, and compensated. In turn, there is a low turnover rate and a high rate of customer satisfaction.

Effective management of human resources can form the foundation of a **high-performance work system**—an organization in which technology, organizational structure, people, and processes all work together to give an organization an advantage in the competitive environment. As technology changes the ways organizations manufacture, transport, communicate, and keep track of information, human resource management must ensure that the organization has the right kinds of people to meet the new challenges. Maintaining a high-performance work system may include development of training programs, recruitment of people with new skill sets, and establishment of rewards for such behaviors as teamwork, flexibility, and learning. In the next chapter, we will see some of the changes that human resource managers are planning for, and Chapter 16 examines high-performance work systems in greater detail.

high-performance work system
An organization in which technology, organizational structure, people, and processes all work together to give an organization an advantage in the competitive environment.

Responsibilities of Human Resource Departments

LO2 Identify the responsibilities of human resource departments.

In all but the smallest organizations, a human resource department is responsible for the functions of human resource management. On average, an organization has one HR staff person for every 93 employees served by the department.[6] Table 1.1 details the responsibilities of human resource departments. These responsibilities include the practices introduced in Figure 1.1 plus two areas of responsibility that support those practices: (1) establishing and administering personnel policies and (2) ensuring compliance with labor laws. As the "Did You Know?" box suggests, these activities shape many aspects of work that give employees their greatest satisfaction.

FUNCTION	RESPONSIBILITIES
Analysis and design of work	Work analysis; job design; job descriptions
Recruitment and selection	Recruiting; job postings; interviewing; testing; coordinating use of temporary labor
Training and development	Orientation; skills training; career development programs
Performance management	Performance measures; preparation and administration of performance appraisals; discipline
Compensation and benefits	Wage and salary administration; incentive pay; insurance; vacation leave administration; retirement plans; profit sharing; stock plans
Employee relations	Attitude surveys; labor relations; employee handbooks; company publications; labor law compliance; relocation and outplacement services
Personnel policies	Policy creation; policy communication; record keeping; HR information systems
Compliance with laws	Policies to ensure lawful behavior; reporting; posting information; safety inspections; accessibility accommodations
Support for strategy	Human resource planning and forecasting; change management

TABLE 1.1

Responsibilities of HR Departments

Source: Based on SHRM-BNA Survey No. 66, "Policy and Practice Forum: Human Resource Activities, Budgets, and Staffs, 2000–2001," Bulletin to Management, Bureau of National Affairs Policy and Practice Series (Washington, DC: Bureau of National Affairs, June 28, 2001).

Did You Know?

Most Workers Are Satisfied with Their Jobs

In a Gallup survey of employed adults, most said they are somewhat or completely satisfied with each aspect of their jobs.

Source: Joseph Carroll, "U.S. Workers Remain Largely Satisfied with Their Jobs," Gallup news release, November 27, 2007, www.gallup.com.

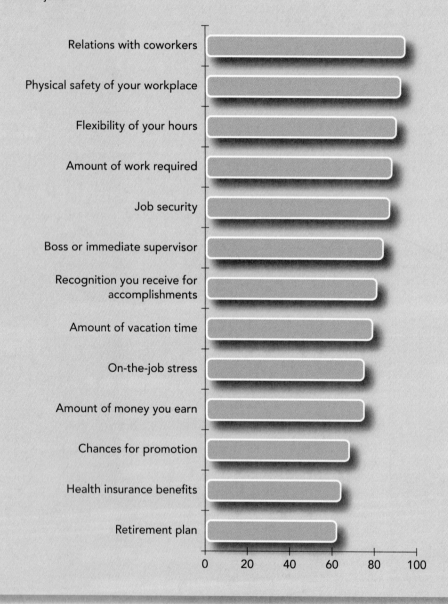

Although the human resource department has responsibility for these areas, many of the tasks may be performed by supervisors or others inside or outside the organization. No two human resource departments have precisely the same roles because of differences in organization sizes and characteristics of the workforce, the industry, and management's values. In some companies, the HR department handles all the activities listed in Table 1.1. In others, it may share the roles and duties with managers of other departments such as finance, operations, or information technology. In some companies, the HR department actively advises top management. In others, the department responds to top-level management decisions and implements staffing, training, and compensation activities in light of company strategy and policies.

Let's take an overview of the HR functions and some of the options available for carrying them out. Human resource management involves both the selection of which options to use and the activities involved with using those options. Later chapters of the book will explore each function in greater detail.

Analyzing and Designing Jobs

To produce their given product or service (or set of products or services), companies require that a number of tasks be performed. The tasks are grouped together in various combinations to form jobs. Ideally, the tasks should be grouped in ways that help the organization to operate efficiently and to obtain people with the right qualifications to do the jobs well. This function involves the activities of job analysis and job design. **Job analysis** is the process of getting detailed information about jobs. **Job design** is the process of defining the way work will be performed and the tasks that a given job requires.

In general, jobs can vary from having a narrow range of simple tasks to having a broad array of complex tasks requiring multiple skills. At one extreme is a worker on an assembly line at a poultry-processing facility; at the other extreme is a doctor in an emergency room. In the past, many companies have emphasized the use of narrowly defined jobs to increase efficiency. With many simple jobs, a company can easily find workers who can quickly be trained to perform the jobs at relatively low pay. However, greater concern for innovation and quality has shifted the trend to more use of broadly defined jobs. Also, as we will see in Chapters 2 and 4, some organizations assign work even more broadly, to teams instead of individuals.

Recruiting and Hiring Employees

Based on job analysis and design, an organization can determine the kinds of employees it needs. With this knowledge, it carries out the function of recruiting and hiring employees. **Recruitment** is the process through which the organization seeks applicants for potential employment. **Selection** refers to the process by which the organization attempts to identify applicants with the necessary knowledge, skills, abilities, and other characteristics that will help the organization achieve its goals. An organization makes selection decisions in order to add employees to its workforce, as well as to transfer existing employees to new positions.

Approaches to recruiting and selection involve a variety of alternatives. Some organizations may actively recruit from many external sources, such as Internet job postings, newspaper want-ads, and college recruiting events. Other organizations may rely heavily on promotions from within, applicants referred by current employees, and the availability of in-house people with the necessary skills.

job analysis
The process of getting detailed information about jobs.

job design
The process of defining the way work will be performed and the tasks that a given job requires.

recruitment
The process through which the organization seeks applicants for potential employment.

selection
The process by which the organization attempts to identify applicants with the necessary knowledge, skills, abilities, and other characteristics that will help the organization achieve its goals.

Home Depot and other retail stores use in-store kiosks similar to the Career Center shown here to recruit applicants for employment.

At some organizations the selection process may focus on specific skills, such as experience with a particular programming language or type of equipment. At other organizations, selection may focus on general abilities, such as the ability to work as part of a team or find creative solutions. The focus an organization favors will affect many choices, from the way the organization measures ability, to the questions it asks in interviews, to the places it recruits. Table 1.2 lists the top five qualities that employers say they are looking for in job candidates, based on a survey by the National Association of Colleges and Employers.

Training and Developing Employees

training
A planned effort to enable employees to learn job-related knowledge, skills, and behavior.

development
The acquisition of knowledge, skills, and behaviors that improve an employee's ability to meet changes in job requirements and in customer demands.

Although organizations base hiring decisions on candidates' existing qualifications, most organizations provide ways for their employees to broaden or deepen their knowledge, skills, and abilities. To do this, organizations provide for employee training and development. **Training** is a planned effort to enable employees to learn job-related knowledge, skills, and behavior. For example, many organizations offer safety training to teach employees safe work habits. **Development** involves acquiring knowledge, skills, and behavior that improve employees' ability to meet the challenges of a variety of new or existing jobs, including the client and customer demands of those jobs. Development programs often focus on preparing employees for management responsibility. Likewise, if a company plans to set up teams to manufacture products, it might offer a development program to help employees learn the ins and outs of effective teamwork.

Decisions related to training and development include whether the organization will emphasize enabling employees to perform their current jobs, preparing them for future jobs, or both. An organization may offer programs to a few employees in whom the organization wants to invest, or it may have a philosophy of investing in the training of all its workers. Some organizations, especially large ones, may have extensive formal training programs, including classroom sessions and training programs online. Other organizations may prefer a simpler, more flexible approach of encouraging employees to participate in outside training and development programs as needs are identified.

Managing Performance

performance management
The process of ensuring that employees' activities and outputs match the organization's goals.

Managing human resources includes keeping track of how well employees are performing relative to objectives such as job descriptions and goals for a particular position. The process of ensuring that employees' activities and outputs match the organization's goals is called **performance management.** The activities of performance management

Table 1.2

Top Five Qualities Employers Seek in Job Candidates

1.	Communication skills (written and verbal)
2.	Honesty/integrity
3.	Interpersonal skills
4.	Motivation/initiative
5.	Strong work ethic

Source: Reprinted from Job Outlook 2007, with permission of the National Association of Colleges and Employers, copyright holder.

include specifying the tasks and outcomes of a job that contribute to the organization's success. Then various measures are used to compare the employee's performance over some time period with the desired performance. Often, rewards—the topic of the next section—are developed to encourage good performance.

The human resource department may be responsible for developing or obtaining questionnaires and other devices for measuring performance. The performance measures may emphasize observable behaviors (for example, answering the phone by the second ring), outcomes (number of customer complaints and compliments), or both. When the person evaluating performance is not familiar with the details of the job, outcomes tend to be easier to evaluate than specific behaviors.[7] The evaluation may focus on the short term or long term and on individual employees or groups. Typically, the person who completes the evaluation is the employee's supervisor. Often employees also evaluate their own performance, and in some organizations, peers and subordinates participate, too.

Planning and Administering Pay and Benefits

The pay and benefits that employees earn play an important role in motivating them. This is especially true when rewards such as bonuses are linked to the individual's or group's achievements. Decisions about pay and benefits can also support other aspects of an organization's strategy. For example, a company that wants to provide an exceptional level of service or be exceptionally innovative might pay significantly more than competitors in order to attract and keep the best employees. At other companies, a low-cost strategy requires knowledge of industry norms, so that the company does not spend more than it must.

Planning pay and benefits involves many decisions, often complex and based on knowledge of a multitude of legal requirements. An important decision is how much to offer in salary or wages, as opposed to bonuses, commissions, and other performance-related pay. Other decisions involve which benefits to offer, from retirement plans to various kinds of insurance to time off with pay. All such decisions have implications for the organization's bottom line, as well as for employee motivation.

Pay and benefits have the greatest impact when they are based on what employees really want and need. At Cronin and Company, a small advertising agency in Glastonbury, Connecticut, midway between Boston and New York, the challenge is to keep talent from leaving for the many attractions of those major cities. Cronin makes it a priority that the workplace be comfortable and attractive, with an environment that makes people want to linger. The company has a posh employee lounge with leather chairs, piped-in jazz, and a cappuccino machine. The lounge is meant not only to keep employees happy but to stimulate creative interaction.[8]

Administering pay and benefits is another big responsibility. Organizations need systems for keeping track of each employee's earnings and benefits. Employees need information about their health plan, retirement plan, and other benefits. Keeping track of this involves extensive record keeping and reporting to management, employees, the government, and others.

Maintaining Positive Employee Relations

Organizations often depend on human resource professionals to help them maintain positive relations with employees. This function includes preparing and distributing employee handbooks that detail company policies and, in large organizations, company publications such as a monthly newsletter or a Web site on the organization's intranet. Preparing these communications may be a regular task for the human resource department.

The human resource department can also expect to handle certain kinds of communications from individual employees. Employees turn to the HR department for answers to questions about benefits and company policy. If employees feel they have been discriminated against, see safety hazards, or have other problems and are dissatisfied with their supervisor's response, they may turn to the HR department for help. Members of the department should be prepared to address such problems.

In organizations where employees belong to a union, employee relations entail additional responsibilities. The organization periodically conducts collective bargaining to negotiate an employment contract with union members. The HR department maintains communication with union representatives to ensure that problems are resolved as they arise.

Establishing and Administering Personnel Policies

All the human resource activities described so far require fair and consistent decisions, and most require substantial record keeping. Organizations depend on their HR department to help establish policies related to hiring, discipline, promotions, and benefits. For example, with a policy in place that an intoxicated worker will be immediately terminated, the company can handle such a situation more fairly and objectively than if it addressed such incidents on a case-by-case basis. The company depends on its HR professionals to help develop and then communicate the policy to every employee, so that everyone knows its importance. If anyone violates the rule, a supervisor can quickly intervene—confident that the employee knew the consequences and that any other employee would be treated the same way. Not only do such policies promote fair decision making, but they also promote other objectives, such as workplace safety and customer service.

All aspects of human resource management require careful and discreet record keeping, from processing job applications, to performance appraisals, benefits enrollment, and government-mandated reports. Handling records about employees requires accuracy as well as sensitivity to employee privacy. Whether the organization keeps records in file cabinets or on a sophisticated computer information system, it must have methods for ensuring accuracy and for balancing privacy concerns with easy access for those who need information and are authorized to see it.

Ensuring Compliance with Labor Laws

As we will discuss in later chapters, especially Chapter 3, the government has many laws and regulations concerning the treatment of employees. These laws govern such matters as equal employment opportunity, employee safety and health, employee pay and benefits, employee privacy, and job security. Government requirements include filing reports and displaying posters, as well as avoiding unlawful behavior. Most managers depend on human resource professionals to help them keep track of these requirements.

Ensuring compliance with laws requires that human resource personnel keep watch over a rapidly changing legal landscape. For example, the increased use of and access to electronic databases by employees and employers suggest that in the near future legislation will be needed to protect employee privacy rights. Currently, no federal laws outline how to use employee databases in such a way as to protect employees' privacy while also meeting employers' and society's concern for security.

Lawsuits that will continue to influence HRM practices concern job security. As companies are forced to close facilities and lay off employees because of economic or competitive conditions, cases dealing with the illegal discharge of employees have increased. The issue of "employment at will"—that is, the principle that an employer may terminate employment at any time without notice—will be debated. As the age of the overall workforce increases, as described in the next chapter, the number of cases dealing with age discrimination in layoffs, promotions, and benefits will likely rise. Employers will need to review work rules, recruitment practices, and performance evaluation systems, revising them if necessary to ensure that they do not falsely communicate employment agreements the company does not intend to honor (such as lifetime employment) or discriminate on the basis of age.

One reason W. L. Gore & Associates is repeatedly named one of the 100 Best Companies to Work for in America is their unusual corporate culture where all employees are known as associates and bosses are not to be found. How do you think this boosts morale in the workplace?

Supporting the Organization's Strategy

At one time, human resource management was primarily an administrative function. The HR department focused on filling out forms and processing paperwork. As more organizations have come to appreciate the significance of highly skilled human resources, however, many HR departments have taken on a more active role in supporting the organization's strategy. As a result, today's HR professionals need to understand the organization's business operations, project how business trends might affect the business, reinforce positive aspects of the organization's culture, develop talent for present and future needs, craft effective HR strategies, and make a case for them to top management.[9]

An important element of this responsibility is **human resource planning,** identifying the numbers and types of employees the organization will require in order to meet its objectives. Using these estimates, the human resource department helps the organization forecast its needs for hiring, training, and reassigning employees. Planning also may show that the organization will need fewer employees to meet anticipated needs. In that situation, human resource planning includes how to handle or avoid layoffs.

As part of its strategic role, one of the key contributions HR can make is to engage in evidence-based HR. **Evidence-based HR** refers to demonstrating that human resource practices have a positive influence on the company's profits or key stakeholders (employees, customers, community, shareholders). This practice helps show that the money invested in HR programs is justified and that HRM is contributing to the company's goals and objectives. For example, data collected on the relationship between HR practices and productivity, turnover, accidents, employee attitudes, and medical costs may show that HR functions are as important to the business as finance, accounting, and marketing. As the "HR How To" box describes, HR decisions should be made on the basis of hard data, not just intuition.

Often, an organization's strategy requires some type of change—for example, adding, moving, or closing facilities; applying new technology; or entering markets in other regions or countries. Common reactions to change include fear, anger, and confusion. The organization may turn to its human resource department for help in managing the change process. Skilled human resource professionals can apply knowledge of human behavior, along with performance management tools, to help the organization manage change constructively.

human resource planning
Identifying the numbers and types of employees the organization will require to meet its objectives.

evidence-based HR
Collecting and using data to show that human resource practices have a positive influence on the company's bottom line or key stakeholders.

HR How To

EMPLOYEE SURVEYS

To measure employee attitudes, Healthwise, a nonprofit provider of health information, has been using regular employee surveys since 1990. As the company has grown from a dozen employees to more than 200, it has used the survey results to maintain a positive culture.

Healthwise's founder and chief executive Don Kemper taps his experience to offer advice on effective employee surveys:

- *Keep the survey simple*—At Healthwise, this means nine straightforward questions in which employees rate their satisfaction with seven aspects of the company's culture.
- *Invite constructive feedback*—Surveys also ask employees what the company can do to improve and what the employees value about the company.

E-mails from Kemper to the employees explain that the purpose of the questions is to generate ideas, not to invite complaining, but Kemper is prepared for criticism.

- *Let employees be anonymous*—Online surveys are a convenient way to gather anonymous data. The computer can group responses so that specific ratings can't be associated with individual employees.
- *Encourage responses*—To be an accurate reflection of what employees are thinking, the survey has to generate responses from all the employees. At Healthwise, e-mails and encouragement by team leaders during meetings get out the word that participation is important.

- *Act on what you learn*—If survey results show employees are dissatisfied with some practice or have an idea for doing things differently, respond by either making changes or explaining the rationale for not taking action. Respond with respect and honesty.
- *Follow a systematic schedule*—Healthwise asks the same basic questions twice a year. That way it can see whether satisfaction is improving, whether changes in the business are associated with changes in satisfaction, and what areas might require more attention in the future.

Source: Kate Milani, "Taking the Pulse of Workplace Culture," *CareerJournal.com,* October 2, 2007, www.careerjournal.com.

LO3 Summarize the types of skills needed for human resource management.

Skills of HRM Professionals

With such varied responsibilities, the human resource department needs to bring together a large pool of skills. These skills fall into the four basic categories shown in Figure 1.3:

- *Human relations skills*—The ability to understand and work well with other people is important to virtually any career, but human relations skills are especially significant for human resource management today. Given the significance of human resources, many managers are calling for HRM to become the "source of people expertise" in the organization.[10] HR managers therefore need to know how people play a role in giving the organization an advantage against the competition as well as the policies, programs, and practices that can help the organization's people do so. Today's HR professionals must be skilled at communicating, negotiating, and team development.
- *Decision-making skills*—Human resource managers must make a wide variety of decisions that affect whether employees are qualified and motivated and whether

the organization is operating efficiently and complying with the law. Especially at organizations that give HRM departments a role in supporting strategy, HR decision makers also must be able to apply decision-making skills to strategic issues. This requires knowledge of the organization's line of business and the ability to present options in terms of costs and benefits to the organization, stated in terms of dollars.[11] Decisions must also take into account social and ethical implications of the alternatives.

Figure 1.3

Skills of HRM Professionals

- *Leadership skills*—HR managers need to play a leadership role with regard to the organization's human resources. In today's environment, leadership often requires helping the organization manage change. Fulfilling this leadership role includes diagnosing problems, implementing organizational changes, and evaluating results, especially in terms of employees' skills and attitudes. Changes typically produce conflict, resistance, and confusion. HR professionals must oversee the change to ensure success. HRM provides tools for overcoming resistance to change, teaching employees to operate under new conditions and encouraging innovation. A survey of large corporations found that in 87 percent of the companies, organization development and change were managed by the HR department.[12]

- *Technical skills*—In any field, including management, "technical skills" are the specialized skills of that field. In human resource management, professionals need knowledge of state-of-the-art practices in such areas as staffing, development, rewards, organizational design, and communication. New selection techniques, performance appraisal methods, training programs, and incentive plans are constantly being developed and often include the use of new software and computer systems. New laws are passed every year, and technical skills require knowledge of how to comply. Professionals must be able to evaluate the worth of new techniques and critically evaluate them in light of HRM principles and business value to determine which are beneficial.

HR Responsibilities of Supervisors

LO4 Explain the role of supervisors in human resource management.

Although many organizations have human resource departments, HR activities are by no means limited to the specialists who staff those departments. In large organizations, HR departments advise and support the activities of the other departments. In small organizations, there may be an HR specialist, but many HR activities are carried out by line supervisors. Either way, non-HR managers need to be familiar with the basics of HRM and their role with regard to managing human resources.

At a start-up company, the first supervisors are the company's founders. Not all founders recognize their HR responsibilities, but those who do have a powerful

Figure 1.4

Supervisors' Involvement in HRM: Common Areas of Involvement

advantage. When Rene Larrave and two partners founded the consulting firm they called Tactica, Larrave felt certain that the only way the firm could grow profitably was with a clear vision of the numbers and kinds of employees who could enable that growth. Larrave and his partners drew up career paths for all the employees they planned to hire, including the requirements for the jobs to which they would be promoted during the company's first few years. To help their future employees find their way along those career paths, they published the details in their company's Employee Atlas. The partners also set up a plan for reviewing performance by collecting feedback from peers as well as supervisors. Using this plan, implemented by its HR department, Tactica in several years grew to a $40 million firm, staffed by almost 200 highly committed, hardworking employees—most of them holding the positions that Larrave and his partners had planned for them.[13]

As we will see in later chapters, supervisors typically have responsibilities related to all the HR functions. Figure 1.4 shows some HR responsibilities that supervisors are likely to be involved in. Organizations depend on supervisors to help them determine what kinds of work need to be done (job analysis and design) and in what quantities (HR planning). Supervisors typically interview job candidates and participate in the decisions about which candidates to hire. Many organizations expect supervisors to train employees in some or all aspects of the employees' jobs. Supervisors conduct performance appraisals and may recommend pay increases. And, of course, supervisors play a key role in employee relations, because they are most often the voice of management for their employees, representing the company on a day-to-day basis. In all these activities, supervisors can participate in HRM by taking into consideration the ways that decisions and policies will affect their employees. Understanding the principles of communication, motivation, and other elements of human behavior can help supervisors inspire the best from the organization's human resources.

LO5 Discuss ethical issues in human resource management.

ethics
The fundamental principles of right and wrong.

Ethics in Human Resource Management

Whenever people's actions affect one another, ethical issues arise, and business decisions are no exception. **Ethics** refers to fundamental principles of right and wrong; ethical behavior is behavior that is consistent with those principles. Business decisions, including HRM decisions, should be ethical, but the evidence suggests that is not always what happens. Recent surveys indicate that the general public and managers do not have positive perceptions of the ethical conduct of U.S. businesses. For example, in a survey conducted by the *Wall Street Journal*, 4 out of 10 executives reported they had been asked to behave unethically.[14]

Many ethical issues in the workplace involve human resource management. Nationwide Insurance has a three-person ethics office that offers a confidential "help line" for employees. About two-thirds of the calls to the help line involve issues related to human resource management—for example, conflicts with coworkers or supervisors or complaints of sexual harassment. When employees raise these concerns, the human resource team investigates them and takes action when necessary. Other departments handle other issues, such as those involving security or legal matters. The goal of these efforts is to keep employees focused on living up to the company's values, rather than just staying out of legal trouble.[15]

Employee Rights

In the context of ethical human resource management, HR managers must view employees as having basic rights. Such a view reflects ethical principles embodied in the U.S. Constitution and Bill of Rights. A widely adopted understanding of human rights, based on the work of the philosopher Immanuel Kant, as well as the tradition of the Enlightenment, assumes that in a moral universe, every person has certain basic rights:

- *Right of free consent*—People have the right to be treated only as they knowingly and willingly consent to be treated. An example that applies to employees would be that employees should know the nature of the job they are being hired to do; the employer should not deceive them.
- *Right of privacy*—People have the right to do as they wish in their private lives, and they have the right to control what they reveal about private activities. One way an employer respects this right is by keeping employees' medical records confidential.
- *Right of freedom of conscience*—People have the right to refuse to do what violates their moral beliefs, as long as these beliefs reflect commonly accepted norms. A supervisor who demands that an employee do something that is unsafe or environmentally damaging may be violating this right if it conflicts with the employee's values. (Such behavior could be illegal as well as unethical.)
- *Right of freedom of speech*—People have the right to criticize an organization's ethics, if they do so in good conscience and their criticism does not violate the rights of individuals in the organization. Many organizations address this right by offering hot lines or policies and procedures designed to handle complaints from employees.
- *Right to due process*—If people believe their rights are being violated, they have the right to a fair and impartial hearing. As we will see in Chapter 3, Congress has addressed this right in some circumstances by establishing agencies to hear complaints when employees believe their employer has not provided a fair hearing. For example, the Equal Employment Opportunity Commission may prosecute complaints of discrimination if it believes the employer did not fairly handle the problem.

One way to think about ethics in business is that the morally correct action is the one that minimizes encroachments on and avoids violations of these rights.

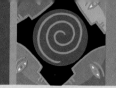

HR Oops!

When Employees Steal

Every year retailers lose billions of dollars to theft. A lot of attention focuses on shoplifters; but while a shoplifter steals $114 worth of merchandise on average, employees who steal take over $900 worth of merchandise.

Strangely, retailers seem almost reluctant to tackle this problem. Measures that help are easy to identify: surveillance cameras near cash registers, active supervision in stores and back rooms, routine background screening of job applicants *before* they are hired, and database programs that mine sales data for suspicious patterns. With the tools available, "supermarket shrink" is down only slightly, however. And Kelly Evely Ansboury, director of IntelliCorp Records, says retailers that use her company to screen job applicants tend to avoid doing the checks until after the applicants have been hired.

Sources: Len Lewis, "To Catch a Thief," *Grocery Headquarters,* September 2007; Liz Parks, "Keeping a Watchful Eye," *Supermarket News,* October 22, 2007; and Katherine Field, "Shrinking Shrink," *Chain Store Age,* July 2007, all downloaded from General Reference Center Gold, http://find.galegroup.com.

Questions

1. What ethical considerations do retailers need to consider in implementing the anti-theft measures described here?

2. Which of the HR responsibilities described in this chapter could play a role in reducing employee theft?

As the examples above suggest, organizations often face situations in which the rights of employees are affected. In particular, the right of privacy has received much attention in recent years. Computerized record keeping and computer networks have greatly increased the ways people can gain (authorized or unauthorized) access to records about individuals. Human resource records can be particularly sensitive. HRM responsibilities therefore include the ever-growing challenge of maintaining confidentiality. The HR Oops! box highlights the financial costs that occur from employee theft and asks you to consider the role of ethics in stopping it.

Standards for Ethical Behavior

Ethical, successful companies act according to four principles.[16] First, in their relationships with customers, vendors, and clients, ethical and successful companies emphasize mutual benefits. Second, employees assume responsibility for the actions of the company. Third, such companies have a sense of purpose or vision that employees value and use in their day-to-day work. Finally, they emphasize fairness; that is, another person's interests count as much as their own.

United Parcel Service (UPS) has made a commitment to ensure that every employee takes responsibility for ethical behavior. At the top of the organization, UPS's chief executive officer emphasizes that employees who get results by violating laws or ethical principles harm the company by undermining its customer relationships and ability to grow. The company has developed a set of ethics-related processes and procedures, embodied in a Code of Business Conduct. All employees must read and agree to follow that code, which describes the kinds of behavior required in a variety of business situations. UPS has also hired a company to provide a hotline employees can call if they have concerns that ethical standards have been violated. All information received by the hotline is forwarded to UPS's compliance department, whose employees investigate and ensure that appropriate action is taken. Managers of business units are evaluated based on ethical as well as financial standards. Each year, managers evaluate their unit's employee and business relationships in terms of ethical issues.[17]

Figure 1.5

Standards for Identifying Ethical Practices

For human resource practices to be considered ethical, they must satisfy the three basic standards summarized in Figure 1.5.[18] First, HRM practices must result in the greatest good for the largest number of people. Second, employment practices must respect basic human rights of privacy, due process, consent, and free speech. Third, managers must treat employees and customers equitably and fairly. These standards are most vexing when none of the alternatives in a situation meets all three of them. For instance, most employers hesitate to get involved in the personal affairs of employees, and this attitude is in keeping with employees' right to privacy. But when personal matters include domestic violence, employees' safety may be in jeopardy, both at home and in the workplace. For Barbara Marlowe of the Boston law firm Mintz Levin Cohn Ferris Glovsky and Popeo, the choice is clear: Helping employees protect themselves does good for employees and also helps employees do better on the job, she says. Mintz Levin set up a group called Employers Against Domestic Violence. Companies that join the group take measures such as posting the phone number of a victim help line, allowing employees to keep flexible hours (to shake off stalkers), and removing victims' names from dial-by-name directories (so harassers can't easily call and disturb them at work).[19]

Careers in Human Resource Management

LO6 Describe typical careers in human resource management.

There are many different types of jobs in the HRM profession. Figure 1.6 shows selected HRM positions and their salaries. The salaries vary depending on education and experience, as well as the type of industry in which the person works. As you can see from Figure 1.6, some positions involve work in specialized areas of HRM such as recruiting, training, or labor and industrial relations. Usually, HR generalists make between $60,000 and $80,000, depending on their experience and education level. Generalists usually perform the full range of HRM activities, including recruiting, training, compensation, and employee relations.

The vast majority of HRM professionals have a college degree, and many also have completed postgraduate work. The typical field of study is business (especially human resources or industrial relations), but some HRM professionals have degrees in the social sciences (economics or psychology), the humanities, and law programs. Those

Figure 1.6

Median Salaries for
HRM Positions

SOURCE: John Dooney and Evren Esen, "Incentive Pay Fuels HR Salaries," *HRMagazine*, November 2007, downloaded from General Reference Center Gold, http://find.galegroup.com, citing the Society for Human Resource Management 2007/2008 Survey Report on Human Resources Personnel Compensation.

who have completed graduate work have master's degrees in HR management, business management, or a similar field. A well-rounded educational background will serve a person well in an HRM position.

HR professionals can increase their career opportunities by taking advantage of training and development programs. General Motors offers its human resource employees a curriculum designed to improve their ability to contribute to the company's business success. The training program details the goals of HRM at General Motors, explains how these relate to business changes at the company, and teaches business topics such as finance and the management of change.[20]

Some HRM professionals have a professional certification in HRM, but many more are members of professional associations. The primary professional organization for HRM is the Society for Human Resource Management (SHRM). SHRM is the world's largest human resource management association, with more than 210,000 professional and student members throughout the world. SHRM provides education and information services, conferences and seminars, government and media representation, and online services and publications (such as *HR Magazine*). You can visit SHRM's Web site to see their services at www.shrm.org.

Organization of This Book

This chapter has provided an overview of human resource management to give you a sense of its scope. In this book, the topics are organized according to the broad areas of human resource management shown in Table 1.3. The numbers in the table refer to the part and chapter numbers.

Part 1 discusses aspects of the human resource environment: trends shaping the field (Chapter 2), legal requirements (Chapter 3), and the work to be done by the organization, which is the basis for designing jobs (Chapter 4). Part 2 explores the responsibilities involved in acquiring and preparing human resources: HR planning and recruiting (Chapter 5), selection and placement of employees (Chapter 6), and training (Chapter 7). Part 3 turns to the assessment and development of human resources through performance management (Chapter 8) and employee development (Chapter 9), as well as appropriate ways to handle employee separation when the organization determines it no longer wants or needs certain employees (Chapter 10). Part 4 addresses topics related to compensation: pay structure (Chapter 11), pay to recognize performance (Chapter 12), and benefits (Chapter 13). Part 5 explores special topics faced by HR managers today: human resource management in organizations where employees have or are seeking union representation (Chapter 14), international human resource management (Chapter 15), and high-performance organizations (Chapter 16).

Along with examples highlighting how HRM helps a company maintain high performance, the chapters offer various other features to help you connect the principles to real-world situations. "Best Practices" boxes tell success stories related to the chapter's topic. "HR Oops!" boxes identify situations gone wrong and invite you to find better alternatives. "HR How To" boxes provide details about how to carry out a practice in each HR area. "Did You Know . . . ?" boxes are snapshots of interesting statistics related to chapter topics. Many chapters also include an "e-HRM" box identifying ways that human resource professionals are applying information technology and the Internet to help their organizations excel in the fast-changing modern world.

SHRM provides education, information services (such as this conference), seminars, government and media representation, and online services and publications.

THINKING ETHICALLY

WHO'S RESPONSIBLE FOR YOUR COMPANY'S REPUTATION?

In a recent poll, almost 7 out of 10 Americans rated the reputation of American companies as either "not good" or "terrible." But they did identify some firms they thought had good reputations. Ranked among the best were Microsoft, Johnson & Johnson, and 3M Corporation. Respondents admired companies that focused on quality, were environmentally responsible, and were engaged in activities that helped the needy. Philanthropy by Microsoft's founder, Bill Gates, helped put his company in first place.

In general, companies that believe they have an obligation to go beyond legal requirements and act on a concern for the environment, labor issues, and human rights are said to practice "social responsibility." For example, a socially responsible company might try to ensure that all workers earn enough to meet their basic needs and that the company uses renewable resources whenever possible. Companies have found that they improve their reputation when they let customers and the

public know about their efforts to become socially responsible. However, these efforts do have financial costs.

SOURCES: Ronald Alsop, "How Boss's Deeds Buff a Firm's Reputation," *Wall Street Journal*, January 31, 2007, http://online.wsj.com; and Beckey Bright, "Managing Corporate Social Responsibility," *Wall Street Journal*, March 3, 2007, http://online.wsj.com.

Questions

1. Should social responsibility be a matter of business strategy (deciding whether the practices will boost profits in the long term), ethics (deciding whether the practices are morally right), or both? Why?
2. Review the functions and responsibilities of human resource management and identify areas where HRM might contribute to social responsibility. In deciding whether to take a socially responsible approach in each of these areas, consider what ethical principles you could apply.

SUMMARY

LO1 Define human resource management, and explain how HRM contributes to an organization's performance.

Human resource management consists of an organization's "people practices"—the policies, practices, and systems that influence employees' behavior, attitudes, and performance. HRM influences who works for the organization and how those people work. These human resources, if well managed, have the potential to be a source of sustainable competitive advantage, contributing to basic objectives such as quality, profits, and customer satisfaction.

LO2 Identify the responsibilities of human resource departments.

By carrying out HR activities or supporting line management, HR departments have responsibility for a variety of functions related to acquiring and managing employees. The HRM process begins with analyzing and designing jobs, then recruiting and selecting employees to fill those jobs. Training and development equip employees to carry out their present jobs and follow a career path in the organization. Performance management ensures that employees' activities and outputs match the organization's goals. Human resource departments also plan and administer the organization's pay and benefits. They carry out activities

in support of employee relations, such as communications programs and collective bargaining. Conducting all these activities involves the establishment and administration of personnel policies. Management also depends on human resource professionals for help in ensuring compliance with labor laws, as well as for support for the organization's strategy—for example, human resource planning and change management.

LO3 Summarize the types of skills needed for human resource management.

Human resource management requires substantial human relations skills, including skill in communicating, negotiating, and team development. Human resource professionals also need decision-making skills based on knowledge of the HR field as well as the organization's line of business. Leadership skills are necessary, especially for managing conflict and change. Technical skills of human resource professionals include knowledge of current techniques, applicable laws, and computer systems.

LO4 Explain the role of supervisors in human resource management.

Although many organizations have human resource departments, non-HR managers must be familiar with the basics of HRM and their own role with regard to managing human resources. Supervisors typically have responsibilities related to all the HR functions. Supervisors help analyze work, interview job candidates, participate in selection decisions, provide training, conduct performance appraisals, and recommend pay increases. On a day-to-day basis, supervisors represent the company to their employees, so they also play an important role in employee relations.

LO5 Discuss ethical issues in human resource management.
Like all managers and employees, HR professionals should make decisions consistent with sound ethical principles. Their decisions should result in the greatest good for the largest number of people; respect basic rights of privacy, due process, consent, and free speech; and treat employees and customers equitably and fairly. Some areas in which ethical

issues arise include concerns about employee privacy, protection of employee safety, and fairness in employment practices (for example, avoiding discrimination).

LO6 Describe typical careers in human resource management.
Careers in human resource management may involve specialized work in fields such as recruiting, training, or labor relations. HR professionals may also be generalists, performing the full range of HR activities described in this chapter. People in these positions usually have a college degree in business or the social sciences. Human resource management means enhancing communication with employees and concern for their well-being, but it also involves a great deal of paperwork and a variety of non–people skills, as well as knowledge of business and laws.

KEY TERMS

development, p. 8
ethics, p. 14
evidence-based HR, p. 11
high-performance work system, p. 5
human capital, p. 3

human resource management (HRM), p. 2
human resource planning, p. 11
job analysis, p. 7
job design, p. 7

performance management, p. 8
recruitment, p. 7
selection, p. 7
training, p. 8

REVIEW AND DISCUSSION QUESTIONS

1. How can human resource management contribute to a company's success?
2. Imagine that a small manufacturing company decides to invest in a materials resource planning (MRP) system. This is a computerized information system that improves efficiency by automating such work as planning needs for resources, ordering materials, and scheduling work on the shop floor. The company hopes that with the new MRP system, it can grow by quickly and efficiently processing small orders for a variety of products. Which of the human resource functions are likely to be affected by this change? How can human resource management help the organization carry out this change successfully?
3. What skills are important for success in human resource management? Which of these skills are already strengths of yours? Which would you like to develop?
4. Traditionally, human resource management practices were developed and administered by the company's human resource department. Line managers are now playing a major role in developing and implementing HRM practices. Why do you think non-HR managers are becoming more involved?

5. If you were to start a business, which aspects of human resource management would you want to entrust to specialists? Why?
6. Why do all managers and supervisors need knowledge and skills related to human resource management?
7. Federal law requires that employers not discriminate on the basis of a person's race, sex, national origin, or age over 40. Is this also an ethical requirement? A competitive requirement? Explain.
8. When a restaurant employee slipped on spilled soup and fell, requiring the evening off to recover, the owner realized that workplace safety was an issue to which she had not devoted much time. A friend warned the owner that if she started creating a lot of safety rules and procedures, she would lose her focus on customers and might jeopardize the future of the restaurant. The safety problem is beginning to feel like an ethical dilemma. Suggest some ways the restaurant owner might address this dilemma. What aspects of human resource management are involved?
9. Does a career in human resource management, based on this chapter's description, appeal to you? Why or why not?

BUSINESSWEEK CASE

BusinessWeek   How to Make a Microserf Smile

Steven A. Ballmer, Microsoft Corporation's CEO, had an epic morale problem on his hands. Microsoft's stock had been drifting sideways for years, and Google envy was rampant. The chronically delayed Windows Vista was irking the Microserfs and blackening their outlook. So was the perception that their company was flabby, middle-aged, and unhip.

Management knew morale was bad. After all, many employees' options were under water. And Google Inc. was getting all the press as a paradise with free food and cushy perks. But Microsoft offered its own gold-plated bennies—free health care, for one. Why was this not registering with employees? Why had turnover crept up?

Ballmer decided he needed a new human resources chief, someone to help improve the mood. Rather than promoting an HR professional or looking outside, he turned to perhaps the most unlikely candidate on his staff, a veteran product manager named Lisa Brummel.

When Ballmer floated the HR job in April 2005, Brummel was deeply conflicted. She had built a solid career developing software, getting customer feedback, launching it, and then making revisions. HR was foreign territory. Yet she loved Microsoft and recognized the internal challenges the company was facing. By the next morning, she had relented. Ballmer named Brummel HR chief and telegraphed to employees that she would be his consigliere of happiness.

In her first weeks as HR chief, Brummel felt as though she were flying at night without instruments. At first she was receiving about two e-mails a day from employees. "There was no communication with employees—none," she says. Internal surveys presented a picture of a happy, contented workforce. Brummel didn't buy the rosy findings. "People weren't connected to the company or our mission anymore," she says.

So she launched a listening tour, holding town hall meetings from Redmond to Bangalore to London. She started an internal blog to get people talking and created a portal on the intranet where people could suggest solutions to HR shortcomings. She held focus groups and mined her network for on-the-ground intelligence agents: the people, from managers to coders, she had come to know since joining the company in 1989.

Time and again, Brummel heard the same refrain: HR was a black box; it had to open up and get employee input. People loathed the forced curve in performance reviews. They wanted clarity in compensation, more direction on how to get promoted, and better managers. They were fed up with the nickel-and-diming on creature comforts. "The

coffee was just really, really bad," says corporate vice president Chris Capossela.

In May 2006, Brummel went live with a reimagined HR, dubbed myMicrosoft 1.0. Nothing got people buzzing more than Brummel's overhaul of the performance review. Employees dreaded Microsoft's ranking system. It pitted coworkers against one another; it made frank evaluations less likely. Microsoft has always had two rankings: one measuring annual performance and one that captures long-term potential. Brummel created a new system that preserved grades and the chance for stars to win bigger paychecks. But no longer would employees' yearly performance be subject to the curve. Bosses would have freedom to pass out whatever grade they wanted, and raises and bonuses would be tied to that grade.

In May 2007, Brummel released myMicrosoft 2.0. Based on feedback from employees, she discontinued desk-side delivery of groceries, since barely any employees were using it, and introduced new ways to hold managers accountable for how they lead. She hopes to begin tailoring HR to individual work styles and life stages, using customized benefits and compensation as a way of differentiating between the needs of Gen Y-ers and their aging boomer colleagues. She's considering satellite offices so commuters don't have to waste time driving when they could be working.

So how's she doing so far? Attrition is down from 10 percent in 2005 to 8.3 percent in 2007. The new performance rating system has not yet led to grade inflation. And employees, who give Brummel rock-star positive reviews, describe a more buoyant mood. Of course, Brummel can't do anything about the stock price. Still, in what may be the most personally satisfying response to her efforts, a memo has been popping up on Microsoft message boards, listing all the ways Microsoft is superior to Google.

SOURCE: Excerpted from Michelle Conlin and Jay Greene, "How to Make a Microserf Smile," *BusinessWeek*, September 10, 2007, pp. 57–59.

Questions

1. According to the information given, how has human resource management hindered or enhanced Microsoft's performance? What other aspects of performance do you think effective HRM *could* improve at Microsoft?

2. Which HRM responsibilities has Brummel addressed? What other HRM responsibilities might be important, given the situation described here?

CASE: CAN THE TSA SECURE TOP-FLIGHT PERFORMANCE?

If you've flown in the United States recently, you've passed through security checkpoints staffed by the Transportation Security Administration, a federal agency created in November 2001 to protect all modes of transportation. TSA agents are best known for scanning baggage and screening persons headed for gates in the nation's airports. Most travelers appreciate the concern for safety following the 2001 terrorist attacks, but many also grumble about times they have encountered a TSA employee who was unpleasant or seemed capricious in enforcing rules.

For its part, TSA management has been challenged to maintain a workforce that is knowledgeable, well qualified, ethical, and vigilant about identifying risky persons and behavior. Occasional news reports have identified lapses such as items stolen from luggage (perhaps when TSA agents are inspecting checked bags) and claims that security screeners have cheated on tests of their ability to spot smuggled weapons.

In a recent year, TSA received an average of 1,443 claims for lost, stolen, or damaged items, affecting a small share of the 65 million passengers who travel each month. Geoff Rabinowitz, a business traveler whose laptop computer disappeared from one of his bags, worries that theft by TSA or airline employees could signal a huge security risk: "If they can get away with taking something out of bags, what can they put in bags without getting caught?" Lauren Suhre lost jewelry and sees theft as a sign of poor management: "I can't imagine working for them." TSA responds to such complaints by noting that it has a zero-tolerance policy for employees caught stealing and investigates charges aggressively.

Cheating on security tests is another problem that raises ethics questions. One report said agents at airports in San Francisco and Jackson, Mississippi, allegedly were tipped off about undercover tests to be conducted. According to the allegations, TSA employees described to screeners the undercover agents, the type of weapons they would attempt to smuggle through checkpoints, and the way the weapons would be hidden.

What is the TSA doing to improve the professionalism of its employees? Many of the efforts involve human resource management. One practice involves the design of jobs. TSA wants employees to see themselves not just as "screeners" who sit in airports but as part of a larger law enforcement effort. So that job title was eliminated and replaced with the term *security officers*, and career paths were developed. The agency also improved its training in job tasks such as interpreting X rays and searching property. It added performance-based pay to its compensation plan, so high-performing employees are rewarded in a practical way. Such changes have helped reduce employee turnover substantially. A survey also found greater job satisfaction among TSA workers.

These improvements are no small achievement, considering that government agencies have tended to lag behind many businesses in creating a focus on high performance. In a government agency, which is not ruled by sales and profits, it can be difficult to develop measurable performance outcomes—measuring what individuals and groups actually achieve, rather than merely tracking their day-to-day activities. As a result, employees may not always see how their individual efforts can help the agency achieve broader goals. Without this vision, they have less incentive to excel.

TSA, part of the Department of Homeland Security (DHS), has tried to become an exception, a performance-oriented government agency. Marta Perez, chief human capital officer of DHS, says TSA defined its overall objective as "to deploy layers of security to protect the traveling public and the nation's transportation system." To achieve that objective, the agency set specific goals for individual airports, including goals to improve the efficiency and effectiveness of airport screening, as well as safety targets. For example, one goal is that the wait time for 80 percent of the passengers going through airport security should be 10 minutes or less. Individuals at each airport have specific goals aimed at achieving the airport's overall goals. According to Perez, the goals help employees and managers talk about what is expected and how they will be evaluated.

SOURCES: Mark Schoeff Jr., "TSA Sees Results from Revamped People Practices," *Workforce Management*, December 11, 2006, p. 20; Bill Trahant, "Realizing a Performance Culture in Federal Agencies," *Public Manager*, Fall 2007, pp. 45–50; Tom Belden, "Reports of Thefts from Luggage at PHL," *Philadelphia Inquirer*, August 27, 2007, downloaded from General Reference Center Gold, http://find.galegroup.com; and Thomas Frank, "Investigation Looks at Airport-Screener Testing," *USA Today*, October 5, 2007, http://find.galegroup.com.

Questions

1. Which, if any, of the HR practices described in this case do you think can contribute to greater efficiency and effectiveness of TSA employees? What other practices would you recommend?
2. Which, if any, of the HR practices described in this case do you think can contribute to ethical behavior by TSA employees? What other practices would you recommend?

IT'S A WRAP!

www.mhhe.com/noefund3e is your source for **R**eviewing, **A**pplying, and **P**racticing the concepts you learned about in Chapter 1.

Review	**Application**	**Practice**
• Chapter learning objectives	• Manager's Hot Seat segment: "Ethics, Let's Make a Fourth Quarter Deal"	• Chapter quiz
• Narrated lecture and iPod content		
• Test Your Knowledge: What Do You Know about HRM?	• Video case and quiz: "Creative Corporation"	
	• Self-Assessments: Do You Have What It Takes for a Career in HR? and Assessing Your Ethical Decision-Making Skills	
	• Web exercise: Society for Human Resource Management	

NOTES

1. Erin White, "To Keep Employees, Domino's Decides It's Not All about Pay," *Wall Street Journal*, February 17, 2005, http://online.wsj.com.

2. A. S. Tsui and L. R. Gomez-Mejia, "Evaluating Human Resource Effectiveness," in *Human Resource Management: Evolving Rules and Responsibilities*, ed. L. Dyer (Washington, DC: BNA Books, 1988), pp. 1187–227; M. A. Hitt, B. W. Keats, and S. M. DeMarie, "Navigating in the New Competitive Landscape: Building Strategic Flexibility and Competitive Advantage in the 21st Century," *Academy of Management Executive* 12, no. 4 (1998), pp. 22–42; J. T. Delaney and M. A. Huselid, "The Impact of Human Resource Management Practices on Perceptions of Organizational Performance," *Academy of Management Journal* 39 (1996), pp. 949–69.

3. W. F. Cascio, *Costing Human Resources: The Financial Impact of Behavior in Organizations*, 3rd ed. (Boston: PWS-Kent, 1991).

4. S. A. Snell and J. W. Dean, "Integrated Manufacturing and Human Resource Management: A Human Capital Perspective," *Academy of Management Journal* 35 (1992), pp. 467–504; M. A. Youndt, S. Snell, J. W. Dean Jr., and D. P. Lepak, "Human Resource Management, Manufacturing Strategy, and Firm Performance," *Academy of Management Journal* 39 (1996), pp. 836–66.

5. Athleta Corporation Web site, www.athleta.com, September 22, 2001; K. Dobbs, "Knowing How to Keep Your Best and Brightest," *Workforce*, April 2001, pp. 56–60.

6. F. Hansen, "2006 Data Bank Annual," *Workforce Management*, December 11, 2006, p. 48.

7. S. Snell, "Control Theory in Strategic Human Resource Management: The Mediating Effect of Administrative Information," *Academy of Management Journal* 35 (1992), pp. 292–327.

8. Jill Hecht Maxwell, "New to the HR Brew," *Inc.*, April 2001, p. 100.

9. R. Grossman, "New Competencies for HR," *HRMagazine*, June 2007, pp. 58–62; HR Competency Assessment Tools, www.shrm.org/competencies/benefits.asp.

10. G. McMahan and R. Woodman, "The Current Practice of Organization Development within the Firm: A Survey of Large Industrial Corporations," *Group and Organization Studies* 17 (1992), pp. 117–34.

11. G. Jones and P. Wright, "An Economic Approach to Conceptualizing the Utility of Human Resource Management Practices," *Research in Personnel/Human Resources* 10 (1992), pp. 271–99.

12. R. Schuler and J. Walker, "Human Resources Strategy: Focusing on Issues and Actions," *Organizational Dynamics*, Summer 1990, pp. 5–19.

13. Kate O'Sullivan, "Why You're Hiring All Wrong," *Inc.*, February 2002, p. 86.

14. R. Ricklees, "Ethics in America," *Wall Street Journal*, October 31–November 3, 1983, p. 33.

15. D. Buss, "Working It Out," *HR Magazine*, June 2004, www.shrm.org.

16. M. Pastin, *The Hard Problems of Management: Gaining the Ethics Edge* (San Francisco: Jossey-Bass, 1986); and T. Thomas, J. Schermerhorn Jr., and J. Dienhart, "Strategic Leadership of Ethical Behavior in Business," *Academy of Management Executive* 18 (2004), pp. 56–66.

17. R. Stolz, "What HR Will Stand For," *Human Resource Executive*, January 2003, pp. 20–28.

18. G. F. Cavanaugh, D. Moberg, and M. Velasquez, "The Ethics of Organizational Politics," *Academy of Management Review* 6 (1981), pp. 363–74.

19. Mike Hofman, "The Shadow of Domestic Violence," *Inc.*, March 2001, p. 85.

20. S. Caudron, "HR Is Dead, Long Live HR," *Workforce*, January 2003, pp. 26–29; and S. Bates, "Business Partners," *HR Magazine*, March 2003, pp. 50–57.

The Human Resource Environment

PART ONE

Trends in Human Resource Management

Introduction

The early years of the 21st century shook the complacency of U.S. workers and forced them to take a fresh look at the ways they are working. The previous decade of turbulent growth gave way to caution as hiring slowed and many companies created jobs overseas. Terrorist attacks on U.S. soil followed by wars in two countries forced a new sense of life's uncertainties. And a revolution in information technology redefined such fundamental notions as what it means to be "in touch" or "at work." More and more voices in the workplace, in the community, and in the media tell of people who are mulling over why they work the way they do, what the future holds, and how they want to change to meet new demands and opportunities.

More than ever, organizations today must be able to respond creatively to uncertainty and change. For some companies, the challenge involves juggling the workload when some employees who are military reservists or National Guard members are called into active duty. When these service members return home, their employers must return them to their jobs at the pay level they would have received had they not been away, and they must try to make accommodations for them if they have become disabled.

Another source of change is the sizable number of U.S. workers who are retiring, taking decades of experience with them. Employers must not only fill the positions but also make sure that important knowledge is not lost. Solutions to transfer knowledge may involve combinations of face-to-face and online mentoring programs. Also, more companies are handling fluctuating personnel needs by hiring temporary employees to fill professional and management positions. For example, Stephen McElfresh takes temporary jobs as an HR manager, leading projects such as product launches and facility openings. He says, "There is more opportunity to make a real difference in an interim role, because I am touching people and organizations at the moment of change."[1]

These creative responses to change and uncertainty illustrate the kinds of people and situations that shape the nature of human resource management today. This chapter describes major trends that are affecting human resource management. It begins with an examination of the modern labor force, including trends that are determining who will participate in the workforce of the future. Next is an exploration of the ways HRM can support a number of trends in organizational strategy, from efforts to maintain high-performance work systems to changes in the organization's size and structure. Often, growth includes the use of human resources on a global scale, as more and more organizations hire immigrants or open operations overseas. The chapter then turns to major changes in technology, especially the role of the Internet. As we will explain, the Internet is changing organizations themselves, as well as providing new ways to carry out human resource management. Finally, we explore the changing nature of the employment relationship, in which careers and jobs are becoming more flexible.

LO1 Describe trends in the labor force composition and how they affect human resource management.

internal labor force
An organization's workers (its employees and the people who have contracts to work at the organization).

external labor market
Individuals who are actively seeking employment.

Change in the Labor Force

The term *labor force* is a general way to refer to all the people willing and able to work. For an organization, the **internal labor force** consists of the organization's workers—its employees and the people who have contracts to work at the organization. This internal labor force has been drawn from the organization's **external labor market,** that is, individuals who are actively seeking employment. The number and kinds of people in the external labor market determine the kinds of human resources available to an organization (and their cost). Human resource professionals need to be aware of trends in the composition of the external labor market, because these trends affect the organization's options for creating a well-skilled, motivated internal labor force.

An Aging Workforce

In the United States, the Bureau of Labor Statistics (BLS), an agency of the Department of Labor, tracks changes in the composition of the U.S. labor force and forecasts employment trends. The BLS has projected that from 2006 to 2016, the total U.S. civilian labor force will grow from 151 million to 164 million workers.[2] This 8.5 percent increase is noticeably lower than the 13.1 increase experienced during the previous decade.

Some of the expected change involves the distribution of workers by age. From 2006 to 2016, the fastest-growing age group is expected to be workers 55 and older. The 25- to 44-year-old group will increase its numbers only slightly, so its share of the total workforce will fall. And young workers between the ages of 16 and 24 will actually be fewer in number. This combination of trends will cause the overall workforce to age. Figure 2.1 shows the change in age distribution, as forecast by the Bureau of Labor Statistics, between 2006 and 2016. By 2010, more than half of U.S. workers will be older than 40, and a significant share will be nearing retirement.[3] Human resource professionals will therefore spend much of their time on concerns related to retirement

As more and more of the workforce reaches retirement age, some companies have set up mentoring programs between older and younger workers so that knowledge is not lost but passed on. How does the company benefit from these mentoring programs?

HR How To

SUPERVISING YOUR PARENTS' GENERATION

With more of tomorrow's workers hitting the 55-plus age group and a sizable share of people past retirement age looking for part-time work, many of tomorrow's managers will be supervising workers older than themselves. Organizations and their HR staffs will have to develop managers who can navigate this potentially tricky situation. Here are some ideas for making this arrangement succeed:

- *Keep an open mind*—Young managers may have in-depth training and fresh ideas about new methods, but older workers have experience that might translate into important wisdom. Managers shouldn't just assume that their way is best.

When an older worker critiques an idea, offer to listen.

- *Focus on results*—When older and younger employees have different ideas about how to handle an assignment, the manager should not take sides. Instead, everyone should be on the "side" of getting the best results. The solution may be to test each approach and see which one delivers.

- *Be discreet about your age*—Achieving a management post before age 30 is impressive, but pointing it out to older employees probably won't inspire them. They are likely to appreciate a more modest type of leadership.

- *Offer consulting positions*—Professional workers, such as accountants and engineers, may be more comfortable serving as a consultant to a young manager than as the manager's employee. A consulting assignment may feel less risky to the older worker, and it may open the door to opportunities for the older professional to mentor the less-experienced manager.

Source: Based on Sarah E. Needleman, "Overseeing Workers Who Are Closer in Age to Your Parents," *CareerJournal.com,* June 21, 2007, www.careerjournal.com.

planning, retraining older workers, and motivating workers whose careers have plateaued. Organizations will struggle with ways to control the rising costs of health care and other benefits, and many of tomorrow's managers will supervise employees much older than themselves (see the "HR How To" feature). At the same time, organizations will have to find ways to attract, retain, and prepare the youth labor force.

Older people want to work, and many say they plan a working retirement. Despite myths to the contrary, worker performance and learning do not suffer as a result of aging.[4] Older employees are willing and able to learn new technology. More older

Figure 2.1

Age Distribution of U.S. Labor Force, 2006 and 2016

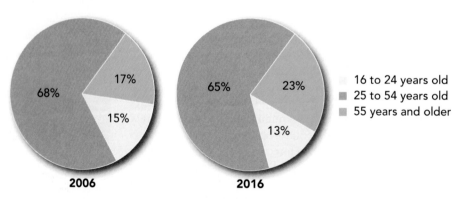

SOURCE: Bureau of Labor Statistics, "Employment Projections: 2006–16," news release, December 4, 2007, www.bls.gov.

workers are asking to work part-time or for only a few months at a time as a way to transition to full retirement. Employees and companies are redefining the meaning of retirement to include second careers as well as part-time and temporary work assignments. Although recruiting and retaining older workers may present some challenges related to costs of health care and other benefits, companies also are benefiting from these employees' talents and experience.

Borders Group, for example, has adapted hiring and retention practices to capitalize on older workers.[5] Half of book purchases in the United States are made by customers over the age of 45, so the company believes older workers can relate well to these customers. To attract and retain older workers, Borders added medical and dental benefits for part-time workers and began developing a "passport" program in which workers can work half the year at a Borders store in one part of the country and half the year at another location, which accommodates those who want to spend winters in warm climates. Since Borders launched the program, employee turnover has plunged, and the turnover rate among workers over age 50 is one-tenth the turnover of employees under 30.

A Diverse Workforce

Another kind of change affecting the U.S. labor force is that it is growing more diverse in racial, ethnic, and gender terms. As Figure 2.2 shows, the 2016 workforce is expected to be 80 percent white, 12 percent black, and 8 percent Asian and other minorities. The fastest-growing of these categories are Asian and "other groups," because these groups are experiencing immigration and birthrates above the national average. In addition to these racial categories, the ethnic category of Hispanics is growing equally fast, and the Hispanic share of the U.S. labor force is expected to reach 16 percent of the total in 2016.[6] Along with greater racial and ethnic diversity, there is also greater gender diversity. More women are in the paid labor force than in the past, and the labor force participation rate for men has been slowly declining. By 2016, the share of women in the labor force is expected to reach about 59 percent.[7]

One important source of racial and ethnic diversity is immigration. The U.S. government establishes procedures for foreign nationals to follow if they wish to live and work permanently in the United States, and it sets limits on the number of immigrants who are admitted through these channels. Of the more than 1 million immigrants who come to the United States legally each year, more than six out of ten are relatives of U.S. citizens. Another one-fourth come on work-related visas, some of which are set aside for workers with exceptional qualifications in science, business, or the arts. (About half of the work-related visas go to the immediate relatives of those coming to the United States to work, allowing workers to bring their spouse and children.) The U.S. government also grants temporary work visas to a limited number of highly educated workers, permitting them to work in the United States for a set period of time but not to remain as immigrants. U.S. law requires employers to verify that any job candidate who is not a U.S. citizen has received permission to work in the United States

Figure 2.2

Projected Racial/Ethnic Makeup of the U.S. Workforce, 2016

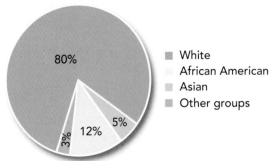

SOURCE: "Labor Force," *Occupational Outlook Quarterly,* Fall 2007, pp. 40–47.

as an immigrant or with a temporary work permit. (This requirement is discussed in Chapter 6.)

Other foreign-born workers in the United States arrived to this country without meeting the legal requirements for immigration or asylum. These individuals, known as undocumented or illegal immigrants, likely number in the millions. While government policy toward immigrants is a matter of heated public debate, the human resource implications have two practical parts. The first involves the supply of and demand for labor. Many U.S. industries, including meatpacking, construction, farming, and services, rely on immigrants to perform demanding work that may be low paid. In other industries, such as computer software development, employers say they have difficulty finding enough qualified U.S. workers to fill technical jobs. These employers are pressing for immigration laws to allow a greater supply of foreign-born workers.

The other HR concern is the need to comply with laws. Recently, Immigration and Customs Enforcement agents have been cracking down on employers who allegedly knew they were employing undocumented immigrants. Businesses that have justified hiring these people on the grounds that they work hard and are needed for the business to continue operating now are facing greater legal risks.[8] Even as some companies are lobbying for changes to immigration laws, the constraints on the labor supply force companies to consider a variety of ways to meet their demand for labor, including job redesign (see Chapter 4), higher pay (Chapter 11), and foreign operations (Chapter 15).

The greater diversity of the U.S. labor force challenges employers to create HRM practices that ensure they fully utilize the talents, skills, and values of all employees. As a result, organizations cannot afford to ignore or discount the potential contributions of women and minorities. Employers will have to ensure that employees and HRM systems are free of bias and value the perspectives and experience that women and minorities can contribute to organizational goals such as product quality and customer service. As we will discuss further in the next chapter, managing cultural diversity involves many different activities. These include creating an organizational culture that values diversity, ensuring that HRM systems are bias-free, encouraging career development for women and minorities, promoting knowledge and acceptance of cultural differences, ensuring involvement in education both within and outside the organization, and dealing with employees' resistance to diversity.[9] Figure 2.3 summarizes ways in which HRM can support the management of diversity for organizational success.

Many U.S. companies have already committed themselves to ensuring that they recognize the diversity of their internal labor force and use it to gain a competitive advantage. According to a recent survey of HR professionals, the most common approaches include recruiting efforts with the goal of increasing diversity and training programs related to diversity.[10] The majority of respondents believed that these efforts were beneficial; 91 percent said they helped the company maintain a competitive advantage.

Valuing diversity is part of Safeway's approach to competing with specialty grocers and big-box stores such as Wal-Mart and Target.[11] Safeway invested in programs to attract, develop, and retain its best talent and to position the company as an employer of choice. Although 70 percent of Safeway's customers are women, male leaders had been the norm in the retail grocery industry. Safeway took initiatives to help women, including women of color, advance into management. The CEO speaks regularly with employees about diversity issues, and employees have access to DVDs featuring interviews with successful employees who are women and people of color. The company

Figure 2.3

HRM Practices That Support Diversity Management

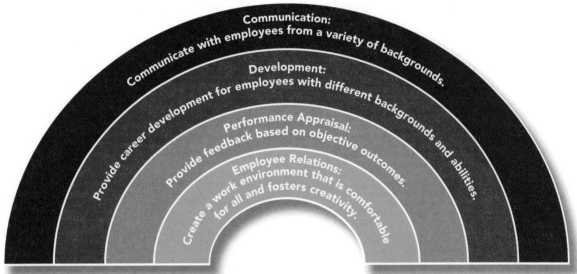

SOURCE: Based on M. Loden and J. B. Rosener, *Workforce America!* (Homewood, IL: Business One Irwin, 1991).

ensures that all employees who qualify for its Retail Leadership Program, including those who work part-time and have flexible schedules to juggle work and family responsibilities, have the same opportunities for coaching, development, and advancement. A women's leadership network sponsors development meetings between promising women and executives who suggest new job opportunities that can help them advance to the next level. With these and other efforts, the number of female store managers has risen a dramatic 42 percent, and financial analysts have concluded that the advancement of women and minorities has increased Safeway's sales and earnings.

Throughout this book, we will show how diversity affects HRM practices. For example, from a staffing perspective, it is important to ensure that tests used to select employees are not unfairly biased against minority groups. From the perspective of work design, employees need flexible schedules that allow them to meet nonwork needs. In terms of training, it is clear that employees must be made aware of the damage that stereotypes can do. With regard to compensation, organizations are providing benefits such as elder care and day care as a way to accommodate the needs of a diverse workforce. As we will see later in the chapter, successfully managing diversity is also critical for companies that compete in international markets.

Skill Deficiencies of the Workforce

The increasing use of computers to do routine tasks has shifted the kinds of skills needed for employees in the U.S. economy. Such qualities as physical strength and mastery of a particular piece of machinery are no longer important for many jobs. More employers are looking for mathematical, verbal, and interpersonal skills, such as the ability to solve math or other problems or reach decisions as part of a team. Often, when organizations are looking for technical skills, they are looking for skills related to computers and using the Internet. Today's employees must be able to handle a variety of responsibilities, interact with customers, and think creatively.

To find such employees, most organizations are looking for educational achievements. A college degree is a basic requirement for many jobs today. Competition for qualified college graduates in many fields is intense. At the other extreme, workers with less education often have to settle for low-paying jobs. Some companies are unable to find qualified employees and instead rely on training to correct skill deficiencies.[12] Other companies team up with universities, community colleges, and high schools to design and teach courses ranging from basic reading to design blueprint reading.

Not all the skills employers want require a college education. Employers surveyed by the National Association of Manufacturers report a deficiency in qualified production workers—not just engineers and computer experts. At Whirlpool, for example, production workers need algebra skills to ensure that steel sizes conform to specifications; the company has had to develop training programs to provide those skills.[13] Today's U.S. production jobs rely on intelligence and skills as much as on strength. Workers often must operate sophisticated computer-controlled machinery and monitor quality levels. In some areas, companies and communities have set up apprenticeship and training programs to fix the worker shortage. The gap between skills needed and skills available has decreased U.S. companies' ability to compete because as a consequence of the deficiency they sometimes lack the capacity to upgrade technology, reorganize work, and empower employees.

High-Performance Work Systems

LO2 Summarize areas in which human resource management can support the goal of creating a high-performance work system.

Human resource management is playing an important role in helping organizations gain and keep an advantage over competitors by becoming **high-performance work systems.** These are organizations that have the best possible fit between their social system (people and how they interact) and technical system (equipment and processes).[14] As the nature of the workforce and the technology available to organizations have changed, so have the requirements for creating a high-performance work system. Customers are demanding high quality and customized products, employees are seeking flexible work arrangements, and employers are looking for ways to tap people's creativity and interpersonal skills. Such demands require that organizations make full use of their people's knowledge and skill, and skilled human resource management can help organizations do this.

high-performance work systems
Organizations that have the best possible fit between their social system (people and how they interact) and technical system (equipment and processes).

Among the trends that are occurring in today's high-performance work systems are reliance on knowledge workers; the empowerment of employees to make decisions; and the use of teamwork. The following sections describe those three trends, and Chapter 16 will explore the ways HRM can support the creation and maintenance of a high-performance work system. HR professionals who keep up with change are well positioned to help create high-performance work systems.

Knowledge Workers

The growth in e-commerce, plus the shift from a manufacturing to a service and information economy, has changed the nature of employees that are most in demand. The Bureau of Labor Statistics forecasts that between 2006 and 2016, most new jobs will be in service occupations, especially education and health services.

The number of service jobs has important implications for human resource management. Research shows that if employees have a favorable view of HRM practices—say, their career opportunities, training, pay, and feedback on performance—they are

Did You Know?

Top 10 Occupations for Job Growth

The following graph shows the occupations that are expected to add the most new jobs between 2006 and 2016. These jobs require widely different levels of training and responsibility, and pay levels vary considerably.

Source: Bureau of Labor Statistics, "Occupational Employment," *Occupational Outlook Quarterly*, Fall 2007, pp. 6–29.

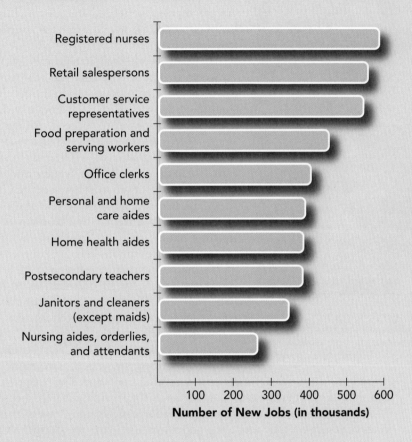

more likely to provide good service to customers. Therefore, quality HRM for service employees can translate into customer satisfaction.

Besides differences among industries, job growth varies according to the type of job. The "Did You Know?" box lists the 10 occupations expected to gain the most jobs between 2006 and 2016. Of the jobs expected to have the greatest percentage increases, most are related to health care and computers. The fastest-growing occupations are network systems and data communications analysts, personal and home care aides, home health aides, computer software engineers, and veterinary technologists and technicians.[15] Many of these occupations require a college degree. In contrast, the occupations expected to have the largest numerical increases more often require only on-the-job training. (Exceptions are registered nurses and postsecondary teachers.) This means that many companies' HRM departments will need to provide excellent training as well as hiring.

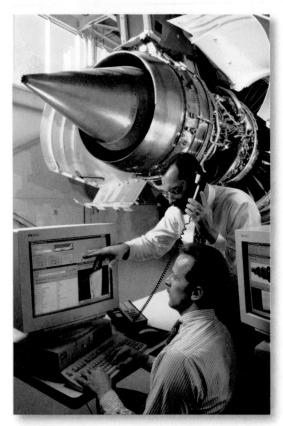

Knowledge workers are employees whose value to their employers stems primarily from what they know. Engineers such as the ones pictured here have in-depth knowledge of their field and are hard to replace because of their special knowledge.

knowledge workers
Employees whose main contribution to the organization is specialized knowledge, such as knowledge of customers, a process, or a profession.

What most of these high-growth jobs have in common is specialized knowledge. To meet their human capital needs, companies are increasingly trying to attract, develop, and retain knowledge workers. **Knowledge workers** are employees whose main contribution to the organization is specialized knowledge, such as knowledge of customers, a process, or a profession. Knowledge workers are especially needed for jobs in health services, business services, social services, engineering, and management.

Knowledge workers are in a position of power, because they own the knowledge that the company needs in order to produce its products and services, and they must share their knowledge and collaborate with others in order for their employer to succeed. An employer cannot simply order these employees to perform tasks. Managers depend on the employees' willingness to share information. Furthermore, skilled knowledge workers have many job opportunities, even in a slow economy. If they choose, they can leave a company and take their knowledge to another employer. Replacing them may be difficult and time-consuming.

As more organizations become knowledge-based, they must promote and capture learning at the level of employees, teams, and the overall organization. At Nissan Motor's U.S. operations, 16 teams each bring together 8 to 16 high-performing salaried employees from different departments.[16] They meet weekly to discuss issues such as quality and diversity, proposing new ideas that can benefit the company. One team looking for ways to save money developed a proposal for working at home. The team conducted a study that showed working at home could improve morale while cutting expenses.

The reliance on knowledge workers also affects organizations' decisions about the kinds of people they are recruiting and selecting.[17] They are shifting away from focusing on specific skills, such as how to operate a particular kind of machinery, and toward a greater emphasis on general cognitive skills (thinking and problem solving) and interpersonal skills. Employers are more interested in evidence that job candidates will excel at working in teams or interacting with customers. These skills also support an employee's ability to gather and share knowledge, helping the organization to innovate and meet customer needs. To the extent that technical skills are important, employers often are most interested in the ability to use information technology, including the Internet and statistical software.

LO3 Define employee empowerment, and explain its role in the modern organization.

Employee Empowerment

To completely benefit from employees' knowledge, organizations need a management style that focuses on developing and empowering employees. **Employee empowerment** means giving employees responsibility and authority to make decisions regarding all aspects of product development or customer service.[18] Employees are then held accountable for products and services. In return, they share the resulting losses and rewards.

HRM practices such as performance management, training, work design, and compensation are important for ensuring the success of employee empowerment. Jobs must be designed to give employees the necessary latitude for making a variety of decisions. Employees must be properly trained to exert their wider authority and use information resources such as the Internet, as well as tools for communicating information. Employees also need feedback to help them evaluate their success. Pay and other rewards should reflect employees' authority and be related to successful handling of their responsibility. In addition, for empowerment to succeed, managers must be trained to link employees to resources within and outside the organization, such as customers, coworkers in other departments, and Web sites with needed information. Managers must also encourage employees to interact with staff throughout the organization, must ensure that employees receive the information they need, and must reward cooperation. Finally, empowered employees deliver the best results if they are fully engaged in their work. *Employee engagement*—full involvement in one's work and commitment to one's job and company—is associated with higher productivity, better customer service, and lower turnover.[19]

As with the need for knowledge workers, use of employee empowerment shifts the recruiting focus away from technical skills and toward general cognitive and interpersonal skills. Employees who have responsibility for a final product or service must be able to listen to customers, adapt to changing needs, and creatively solve a variety of problems.

Teamwork

Modern technology places the information that employees need for improving quality and providing customer service right at the point of sale or production. As a result, the employees engaging in selling and producing must also be able to make decisions about how to do their work. Organizations need to set up work in a way that gives employees the authority and ability to make those decisions. One of the most popular ways to increase employee responsibility and control is to assign work to teams. **Teamwork** is the assignment of work to groups of employees with various skills who interact to assemble a product or provide a service. Work teams often assume many activities traditionally reserved for managers, such as selecting new team members, scheduling work, and coordinating work with customers and other units of the organization. Work teams also contribute to total quality by performing inspection and quality-control activities while the product or service is being completed.

In some organizations, technology is enabling teamwork even when workers are at different locations or work at different times. These organizations use *virtual teams*—teams that rely on communications technology such as videoconferences, e-mail, and cell phones to keep in touch and coordinate activities.

Teamwork can motivate employees by making work more interesting and significant. At organizations that rely on teamwork, labor costs may be lower as well. Spurred by such advantages, a number of companies are reorganizing assembly operations—abandoning the assembly line in favor of operations that combine mass production with jobs in which employees perform multiple tasks, use many skills, control the pace of work, and assemble the entire final product. One example of this type of teamwork is the Marion, North Carolina, factory of Rockwell Automation's Power Systems Division, where almost every employee works on a team. The facility is organized into 20 manufacturing cells; 16 make routine products accounting for 80 percent of the division's revenue, and the other 4 make special-order products in lots as small as one unit. These

employee empowerment
Giving employees responsibility and authority to make decisions regarding all aspects of product development or customer service.

teamwork
The assignment of work to groups of employees with various skills who interact to assemble a product or provide a service.

machining and assembly employees are cross-trained to perform at least three jobs, so they can step in wherever they are needed. Management also is carried out by teams, each of which brings together a supervisor, an engineer, and a planner. These management teams are responsible for buying materials, hiring employees, providing customer service, and scheduling overtime. Employees and management are all involved in monitoring product data and introducing improvements to products and processes. This setup has enabled Power Systems to produce excellent quality with fast turnaround times, exceptionally low costs, high customer satisfaction, and no accidents.[20]

Focus on Strategy

LO4 Identify ways HR professionals can support organizational strategies for quality, growth, and efficiency.

As we saw in Chapter 1, traditional management thinking treated human resource management primarily as an administrative function, but managers today are beginning to see a more central role for HRM. They are beginning to look at HRM as a means to support a company's *strategy*—its plan for meeting broad goals such as profitability, quality, and market share.[21] For an example of this role, see the "Best Practices" box. This strategic role for HRM has evolved gradually. At many organizations, managers still treat HR professionals primarily as experts in designing and delivering HR systems. But at a growing number of organizations, HR professionals are strategic partners with other managers.

This means they use their knowledge of the business and of human resources to help the organization develop strategies and to align HRM policies and practices with those strategies. To do this, human resource managers must focus on the future as well as the present, and on company goals as well as human resource activities. They may, for example, become experts at analyzing the business impact of HR decisions or at developing and keeping the best talent to support business strategy. An example of an HRM professional who understands this new role is Kiyoski Shinozaki, a manager with Nikkei, a Japanese business publishing company. Shinozaki's education includes a master's degree in human resource management, and he is adding to his business credentials by taking further courses in finance and accounting. He predicts that deeper business knowledge will help him plan and suggest initiatives, rather than merely reacting to strategies devised by other managers.[22]

The specific ways in which human resource professionals support the organization's strategy vary according to their level of involvement and the nature of the strategy. Strategic issues include emphasis on quality and decisions about growth and efficiency. Human resource management can support these strategies, including efforts such as quality improvement programs, mergers and acquisitions, and restructuring. Decisions to use reengineering and outsourcing can make an organization more efficient and also give rise to many human resource challenges. International expansion presents a wide variety of HRM challenges and opportunities. Figure 2.4 summarizes these strategic issues facing human resource management.

High Quality Standards

total quality management (TQM)
A companywide effort to continuously improve the ways people, machines, and systems accomplish work.

To compete in today's economy, companies need to provide high-quality products and services. If companies do not adhere to quality standards, they will have difficulty selling their product or service to vendors, suppliers, or customers. Therefore, many organizations have adopted some form of **total quality management (TQM)**—a companywide effort to continuously improve the ways people, machines, and systems accomplish work.[23] TQM has several core values:[24]

Best Practices

HR Refreshes Strategy at Coca-Cola Company

When Neville Isdell took over as chief executive of Coca-Cola a few years ago, profit growth was stalling, morale was poor, and employee turnover was a major problem. Efforts to reorganize the company had failed to generate the desired improvements. Isdell decided that the solution had to focus on people.

Isdell made his commitment to people issues real in his second day on the job, when he appointed Cynthia McCague, an experienced HRM professional, as Coke's director of human resources, reporting directly to the CEO. McCague had a winning track record for supporting strategy, having brought success to a struggling facility in the Philippines and led the company's move into Eastern Europe and Russia. Her reporting relationship with Isdell positioned her to become directly involved in strategy.

The effort started with careful analysis of the company's problems. HR staff surveyed Coke's top 400 managers, asking about leadership, performance, and obstacles to success. The surveys were followed by in-depth interviews of 70 of the managers.

Analysis showed that the company lacked a clear direction and shared purpose, and it confirmed that morale was low and working relationships had been strained by the past efforts to reorganize. In addition, Coke's people focused on short-term performance at the expense of long-term results.

The company assembled its 150 top leaders to form teams addressing each of the problems uncovered. One team developed statements of the company's mission, vision, and values. Another improved the ways Coke recognizes and rewards employees.

Within a year, the company was ready to begin rolling out changes. HR staff worked with employees in public affairs and communications to teach the new mission, vision, and values. Face-to-face meetings were held worldwide, video messages were posted online, and a company blog was launched so that associates could post comments about the values and their successes. In addition, the company's intranet was reworked into a portal offering up-to-the-minute news.

Such efforts have helped managers at all levels get their people focused on shared goals. That change, in turn, has boosted performance. According to follow-up surveys, employees are more engaged and more aware of goals, and have a higher opinion of their leadership. Those sentiments appear to be well grounded, as Coke's employee turnover has fallen, while sales and stock value have begun to climb again.

Isdell continued his focus on people issues when he announced that his chief operating officer, Muhtar Kent, would replace him as CEO in July 2008, while he retained his position of chairman of the board. Isdell planned to make the succession as smooth as possible, saying, "Management succession is the key final measure of any CEO's success, and I will do all I can to ensure our progress is secure for many years ahead."

Sources: Associated Press, "Coca-Cola CEO Neville Isdell to Step Down," *CBS News,* December 6, 2007, www.cbsnews.com; Adrienne Fox, "Refreshing a Beverage Company's Culture," *HRMagazine,* November 2007, downloaded from General Reference Center Gold, http://find.galegroup.com; and Laila Karamally, "Coke's New CEO Focuses on Workers," *Workforce Management,* July 1, 2004, http://find.galegroup.com.

- Methods and processes are designed to meet the needs of internal and external customers (that is, whomever the process is intended to serve).
- Every employee in the organization receives training in quality.
- Quality is designed into a product or service so that errors are prevented from occurring, rather than being detected and corrected in an error-prone product or service.
- The organization promotes cooperation with vendors, suppliers, and customers to improve quality and hold down costs.
- Managers measure progress with feedback based on data.

Based on these values, the TQM approach provides guidelines for all the organization's activities, including human resource management. To promote quality, organizations need an environment that supports innovation, creativity, and risk taking to meet

Figure 2.4

Business Strategy: Issues
Affecting HRM

customer demands. Problem solving should bring together managers, employees, and customers. Employees should communicate with managers about customer needs.

Human resource management supports the strong commitment to quality at TRW Automotive Holdings Corporation's factory in Fowlerville, Michigan. The facility produces automotive slip-control units, a category that encompasses automobile components such as antilock brakes and vehicle stability systems. Auto companies are always looking for product and price improvements, but in spite of constant changes, the Fowlerville plant continues to operate efficiently and with an amazing defect rate of just three customer rejections out of every million items. In addition, all deliveries have been made on time. The company credits its efficient plant layout and its workforce for the exceptional practices. With low turnover, the facility benefits from employees' experience, and training ensures that its people are knowledgeable. Plant manager Bob Holman comments, "People here know what to do without being told," and manufacturing employee Andrew Bogdan explains, "This is probably the most multitasked plant floor you'll ever see. Seventy percent of our people can do 90 percent of the jobs here." In addition, the organization fosters employee involvement and teamwork. For example, production workers serve on Policy and Procedure Panels, which have a voice in administrative decisions.[25]

Mergers and Acquisitions

Often, organizations join forces through mergers (two companies becoming one) and acquisitions (one company buying another). Some mergers and acquisitions result in consolidation within an industry, meaning that two firms in one industry join to hold a greater share of the industry. For example, British Petroleum's acquisition of Amoco Oil represented a consolidation, or reduction of the number of companies in the oil industry. Other mergers and acquisitions cross industry lines. In a merger to form Citigroup,

Citicorp combined its banking business with Traveller's Group's insurance business. Furthermore, these deals more frequently take the form of global megamergers, or mergers of big companies based in different countries (as in the case of BP-Amoco).

HRM should have a significant role in carrying out a merger or acquisition. Differences between the businesses involved in the deal make conflict inevitable. Training efforts should therefore include development of skills in conflict resolution. Also, HR professionals have to sort out differences in the two companies' practices with regard to compensation, performance appraisal, and other HR systems. Settling on a consistent structure to meet the combined organization's goals may help to bring employees together.

Downsizing

It would have been hard to ignore the massive "war for talent" that went on during the late 1990s, particularly with the dot-com craze, as Internet-based companies seemingly became rich overnight. During this time, organizations sought to become "employers of choice," to establish "employment brands," and to develop "employee value propositions." All these slogans were meant as ways to ensure that the organizations would be able to attract and retain talented employees. However, what was less noticeable was that in spite of the hiring craze, massive layoffs also were occurring. In fact, as shown in Figure 2.5, 1998, the height of the war for talent, also saw the largest number of layoffs in the decade.[26]

This pattern seems to represent a "churning" of employees. In other words, organizations apparently were laying off employees with outdated skills or cutting whole businesses that were in declining markets while simultaneously building businesses and employee bases in newer, higher-growth markets. For example, IBM cut 69,256 people yet increased its workforce by 16,000 in 1996. Although downsizing always poses problems for human resource management, the impact can be especially confusing in an organization that "churns" employees. How can such an organization develop a reputation as an employer of choice and motivate employees to care about the organization? The way organizations answer such questions will play a significant part in determining the quality of employees on the payroll.

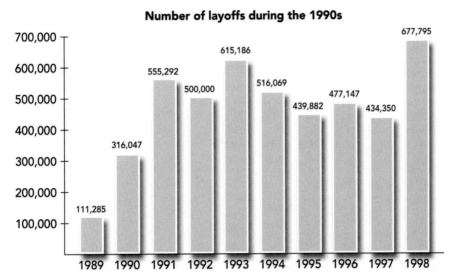

Number of layoffs during the 1990s

SOURCE: Challenger, Gray, and Christmas, Outplacement Firm, Workforce Reports 1998.

Figure 2.5

Number of Employees Laid Off during the 1990s

Whether or not the organization is churning employees, downsizing presents a number of challenges and opportunities for HRM. In terms of challenges, the HRM function must "surgically" reduce the workforce by cutting only the workers who are less valuable in their performance. Achieving this is difficult because the best workers are most able (and often willing) to find alternative employment and may leave voluntarily before the organization lays off anyone. Early-retirement programs are humane, but they essentially reduce the workforce with a "grenade" approach—not distinguishing good from poor performers but rather eliminating an entire group of employees. In fact, research indicates that when companies downsize by offering early-retirement programs, they usually end up rehiring to replace essential talent within a year. Often the company does not achieve its cost-cutting goals because it spends 50 to 150 percent of the departing employee's salary in hiring and retraining new workers.[27]

Another HRM challenge is to boost the morale of employees who remain after the reduction; this is discussed in greater detail in Chapter 5. HR professionals should maintain open communication with remaining employees to build their trust and commitment, rather than withholding information.[28] All employees should be informed why the downsizing is necessary, what costs are to be cut, how long the downsizing will last, and what strategies the organization intends to pursue. Finally, HRM can provide downsized employees with outplacement services to help them find new jobs. Such services are ways an organization can show that it cares about its employees, even though it cannot afford to keep all of them on the payroll.

Reengineering

Rapidly changing customer needs and technology have caused many organizations to rethink the way they get work done. For example, when an organization adopts new technology, its existing processes may no longer result in acceptable quality levels, meet customer expectations for speed, or keep costs to profitable levels. Therefore, many organizations have undertaken **reengineering**—a complete review of the organization's critical work processes to make them more efficient and able to deliver higher quality.

reengineering
A complete review of the organization's critical work processes to make them more efficient and able to deliver higher quality.

Ideally, reengineering involves reviewing all the processes performed by all the organization's major functions, including production, sales, accounting, and human resources. Therefore, reengineering affects human resource management in two ways. First, the way the HR department itself accomplishes its goals may change dramatically. Second, the fundamental change throughout the organization requires the HR department to help design and implement change so that all employees will be committed to the success of the reengineered organization. Employees may need training for their reengineered jobs. The organization may need to redesign the structure of its pay and benefits to make them more appropriate for its new way of operating. It also may need to recruit employees with a new set of skills. Often, reengineering results in employees being laid off or reassigned to new jobs, as the organization's needs change. HR professionals should also help with this transition, as they do for downsizing.

outsourcing
The practice of having another company (a vendor, third-party provider, or consultant) provide services.

Outsourcing

Many organizations are increasingly outsourcing business activities. **Outsourcing** refers to the practice of having another company (a vendor, third-party provider, or consultant) provide services. For instance, a manufacturing company might outsource its accounting and transportation functions to businesses that specialize in these activities. Outsourcing gives the company access to in-depth expertise and is often more economical as well.

Not only do HR departments help with a transition to outsourcing, but many HR functions are being outsourced. One study suggests that 8 out of 10 companies outsource at least one human resource activity, and a more recent study found that 91 percent of U.S. companies have taken steps to standardize their HR processes to prepare for outsourcing.[29] Cardinal Health, a provider of health care products, services, and technology, signed a contract with ExcellerateHRO to provide administrative functions.[30] HR professionals remaining at Cardinal work in strategic areas such as talent management, organizational effectiveness, and total rewards, while ExcellerateHRO provides routine services.

Expanding into Global Markets

LO5 Summarize ways in which human resource management can support organizations expanding internationally.

Companies are finding that to survive they must compete in international markets as well as fend off foreign competitors' attempts to gain ground in the United States. To meet these challenges, U.S. businesses must develop global markets, keep up with competition from overseas, hire from an international labor pool, and prepare employees for global assignments.

Study of companies that are successful and widely admired suggests that these companies not only operate on a multinational scale, but also have workforces and corporate cultures that reflect their global markets.[31] These companies, which include General Electric, Coca-Cola, Microsoft, Walt Disney, and Intel, focus on customer satisfaction and innovation. In addition, they operate on the belief that people are the company's most important asset. Placing this value on employees requires the companies to emphasize human resource practices, including rewards for superior performance, measures of employee satisfaction, careful selection of employees, promotion from within, and investment in employee development.

The Global Workforce

For today's and tomorrow's employers, talent comes from a global workforce. Organizations with international operations hire at least some of their employees in the foreign countries where they operate. In fact, regardless of where their customers are located, more and more organizations are looking overseas to hire talented people willing to work for less pay than the U.S. labor market requires. Intel, for example, has projected that most of its future employees will be hired outside U.S. borders. The efforts to hire workers in other countries are common enough that they have spurred the creation of a popular name for the practice: **offshoring.** Just a few years ago, most offshoring involved big manufacturers building factories in countries with lower labor costs. But today it is so easy to send information and software around the world that even start-ups are hiring overseas. In one study, almost 4 out of 10 new companies employed foreign analysts, marketers, engineers, and other employees. In contrast to computer and printer manufacturer Hewlett-Packard, which hired its first foreign workers 20 years after its founding in 1939, search engine Google employed people outside the United States just three years after its 1998 start.[32]

offshoring
Moving operations from the country where a company is headquartered to a country where pay rates are lower but the necessary skills are available.

Technology is lowering barriers to overseas operations. OfficeTiger, which provides business services to banks, insurance companies, and other clients, has 200 employees in the United States and 2,000 in southern India. Whether its clients need typesetting or marketing research, the Indian employees can readily submit their work over the Internet. Because Indian workers are generally paid only about one-fifth of U.S.

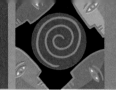

HR Oops!

No Great Bargain

With Chinese wage rates far below those in the United States, China would seem to be the logical place for a manufacturer to keep costs down. But one U.S. manufacturer recently discovered that low wage rates don't always translate into a bargain.

The manufacturer was preparing to produce a component for automobiles, and it intended to set up production in China. Fortunately, before moving ahead, the company hired a consultant to verify the savings. According to the consultant, going to China would reduce costs by just 5 percent.

How could that be? One reason was that the piece required little handling; it was simply stamped. As a result, labor costs were a small fraction of manufacturing costs. Also, the piece weighed so much that a standard 20-foot shipping container would reach its weight limit before it was full. The company would have to ship partially filled containers all the way from China to its customers.

Source: "But I Thought Everyone Saved Money in China," *Industry Week,* October 1, 2007, www.industryweek.com.

Questions

1. What are some risks or drawbacks of an HR strategy based only on paying the lowest wages?

2. Imagine you work for a company that has a low-cost strategy and is considering operations in China. As an HR manager, how would you support the strategy?

---

earnings for comparable jobs, OfficeTiger offers attractive prices. The company is growing, and it expects that two-thirds of its future hires will be in India, Sri Lanka, and countries other than the United States.[33]

Hiring in developing nations such as India, Mexico, and Brazil gives employers access to people with potential who are eager to work yet who will accept lower wages than elsewhere in the world. Challenges, however, may include employees' lack of familiarity with technology and corporate practices, as well as political and economic instability in the areas. Important issues that HR experts can help companies weigh include whether workers in the offshore locations can provide the same or better skills, how offshoring will affect motivation and recruitment of employees needed in the United States, and whether managers are well prepared to manage and lead offshore employees (see the HR Oops! box).

Even hiring at home may involve selection of employees from other countries. The 1990s and the beginning of the 21st century, like the beginning of the last century, have been years of significant immigration, with over 1.2 million people obtaining permanent resident status in 2006 alone.[34] Figure 2.6 shows the distribution of immigration by continent of origin. The impact of immigration will be especially large in some regions of the United States. In the states on the Pacific Coast, 7 out of 10 entrants to the labor force are immigrants.[35] About 70 percent of immigrant workers will be Hispanics and Asians. Employers in tight labor markets—such as those seeking experts in computer science, engineering, and information systems—are especially likely to recruit international students.[36]

International Assignments

expatriates
Employees who take assignments in other countries.

Besides hiring an international workforce, organizations must be prepared to send employees to other countries. This requires HR expertise in selecting employees for international assignments and preparing them for those assignments. Employees who take assignments in other countries are called **expatriates.**

Figure 2.6

Where Immigrants to the United States Came from in 2006

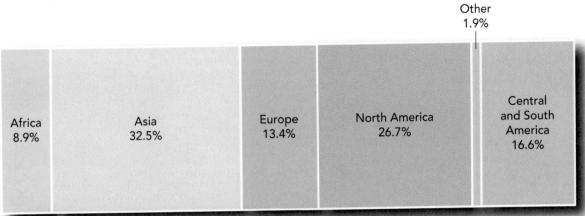

SOURCE: Department of Homeland Security, Office of Immigration Statistics, *2006 Yearbook of Immigration Statistics*, Table 2, downloaded at http://uscis.gov (December 5, 2007).

U.S. companies must better prepare employees to work in other countries. The failure rate for U.S. expatriates is greater than that for European and Japanese expatriates.[37] To improve in this area, U.S. companies must carefully select employees to work abroad based on their ability to understand and respect the cultural and business norms of the host country. Qualified candidates also need language skills and technical ability. In Chapter 15, we discuss practices for training employees to understand other cultures.

Technological Change in HRM

Advances in computer-related technology have had a major impact on the use of information for managing human resources. Large quantities of employee data (including training records, skills, compensation rates, and benefits usage and cost) can easily be stored on personal computers and manipulated with user-friendly spreadsheets or statistical software. Often these features are combined in a **human resource information system (HRIS),** a computer system used to acquire, store, manipulate, analyze, retrieve, and distribute information related to an organization's human resources.[38] An HRIS can support strategic decision making, help the organization avoid lawsuits, provide data for evaluating programs or policies, and support day-to-day HR decisions. Table 2.1 describes some of the technologies that may be included in an organization's HRIS.

The support of an HRIS can help HR professionals navigate the challenges of today's complex business environment. For example, rapidly changing technology can cause employees' skills to become obsolete. Organizations must therefore carefully monitor their employees' skills and the organization's needed skills. Often the employees and needs are distributed among several locations, perhaps among several countries. Florida Power & Light Company, based in Juno Beach, Florida, uses HRIS applications to provide information to employees and to support decision making by managers. More than 10,000 employees in 20 states can use the information system to learn about their benefits. Managers use the system to track employees' vacation and sick days and to make changes in staffing and pay. If managers want a personnel report, they no longer have to call the human resource department to request one; the HRIS will prepare it automatically.[39]

LO6 Discuss how technological developments are affecting human resource management.

human resource information system (HRIS)
A computer system used to acquire, store, manipulate, analyze, retrieve, and distribute information related to an organization's human resources.

TABLE 2.1

New Technologies Influencing HRM

TECHNOLOGY	WHAT IT DOES	EXAMPLE
Internet portal	Combines data from several sources into a single site; lets user customize data without programming skills.	A company's manager can track labor costs by work group.
Shared service centers	Consolidate different HR functions into a single location; eliminate redundancy and reduce administrative costs; process all HR transactions at one time.	AlliedSignal combined more than 75 functions, including finance and HR, into a shared service center.
Application service provider (ASP)	Lets companies rent space on a remote computer system and use the system's software to manage its HR activities, including security and upgrades.	KPMG Consulting uses an ASP to host the company's computerized learning program.
Business intelligence	Provides insight into business trends and patterns and helps businesses improve decisions.	Managers use the system to analyze labor costs and productivity among different employee groups.

The Internet and e-HRM are helpful for employees who work outside the office because they can receive and share information online easily. The benefits of products such as PDAs and Blackberrys are enormous but is it possible to be too accessible?

The Internet Economy

The way business is conducted has changed rapidly during the past decade and will continue to do so. Much of the change is related to the widespread adoption of the Internet by businesses and individuals.

The Internet economy creates many HRM challenges.[40] The fast pace of change in information technology requires companies to continually update their skill requirements and then recruit and train people to meet those requirements. The competition for such employees may be stiff and, as described earlier, often involves recruiting on an international scale.

Motivation can also be a challenge. A decade ago, many Internet-based organizations were small start-up companies founded by young, forward-looking people who saw the potential of a then-new technology. These companies sometimes made up for inexperienced management with a culture based on creativity, enthusiasm, and intense commitment. Policies and procedures sometimes took a backseat to team spirit and workplace fun. But as competition from established companies heated up and as investors withdrew funding, the start-up companies were acquired, went out of business, or had to radically cut back hiring and spending. In this environment, HRM needs to help companies comply with labor laws, motivate employees, and craft human resource policies that seem fair to workers and meet employers' competitive demands.

electronic human resource management (e-HRM)
The processing and transmission of digitized HR information, especially using computer networking and the Internet.

Electronic Human Resource Management (e-HRM)

Many HRM activities have moved onto the Internet. Electronic HRM applications let employees enroll in and participate in training programs online. Employees can go online to select from items in a benefits package and enroll in the benefits they choose. They can look up answers to HR-related questions and read company news, perhaps downloading it as a podcast. This processing and transmission of digitized HR information is called **electronic human resource management (e-HRM).**

TABLE 2.2

Implications of e-HRM
for HRM Practices

HRM PRACTICES	IMPLICATIONS OF E-HRM
Analysis and design of work	Employees in geographically dispersed locations can work together in virtual teams using video, e-mail, and the Internet.
Recruiting	Post job openings online; candidates can apply for jobs online.
Training	Online learning can bring training to employees anywhere, anytime.
Selection	Online simulations, including tests, videos, and e-mail, can measure job candidates' ability to deal with real-life business challenges.
Compensation and benefits	Employees can review salary and bonus information and seek information about and enroll in benefit plans.

E-HRM has the potential to change all traditional HRM functions. Table 2.2 shows some major implications of e-HRM. For example, employees in different geographic areas can work together. Use of the Internet lets companies search for talent without geographic limitations. Recruiting can include online job postings, applications, and candidate screening from the company's Web site or the Web sites of companies that specialize in online recruiting, such as Monster.com or Yahoo! HotJobs. Employees from different geographic locations can all receive the same training over the company's computer network.

Privacy is an important issue in e-HRM. A great deal of HR information is confidential and not suitable for posting on a Web site for everyone to see. One solution is to set up e-HRM on an *intranet,* which is a network that uses Internet tools but limits access to authorized users in the organization. However, to better draw on the Internet's potential, organizations are increasingly replacing intranets with Web portals (Web sites designed to serve as a gateway to the Internet, highlighting links to relevant information).[41] Whether a company uses an intranet or a Web portal, it must ensure that it has sufficient security measures in place to protect employees' privacy.

Sharing of Human Resource Information

Information technology is changing the way HR departments handle record keeping and information sharing. Today, HR employees use technology to automate much of their work in managing employee records and giving employees access to information and enrollment forms for training, benefits, and other programs. As a result, HR employees play a smaller role in maintaining records, and employees now get information through **self-service.** This means employees have online access to information about HR issues such as training, benefits, compensation, and contracts; go online to enroll themselves in programs and services; and provide feedback through online surveys. Today, employees routinely look up workplace policies and information about their benefits online, and they may receive electronic notification when deposits are made directly to their bank accounts.

Mapics, a software developer based in Atlanta, provides self-service software geared to managers as well as nonmanagement employees. Self-service at Mapics includes enrollment in benefits plans, and managers use the system for such tasks as performance appraisals and payroll planning. Mapics lacked reliable information on vacation time used by its employees, many of whom work from home or at client sites. The company used HR self-service to solve this information problem. Not only was the existing information tracked on paper inaccurate, but many employees were too engrossed in their work to take their vacations, and the days rolled over year

self-service
System in which employees have online access to information about HR issues and go online to enroll themselves in programs and provide feedback through surveys.

after year, until the company was recording a liability of a million dollars' worth of accrued, unused vacation time. Mapics set up a vacation management system in which managers can look up the amount of vacation time their employees have used and the amount of remaining vacation. Employees keep track of their vacation time too. This helps with scheduling and also enables managers to encourage employees to use their remaining time. Mapics changed its vacation policy to require that employees take their vacation or lose the time at the end of the year. At Mapics, self-service has improved management and employee satisfaction with HR services at the same time it has cut costs.[42]

Like Mapics, a growing number of companies are combining employee self-service with management self-service, such as the ability to go online to authorize pay increases, approve expenses, and transfer employees to new positions. More sophisticated systems extend management applications to decision making in areas such as compensation and performance management. For example, managers can schedule job interviews or performance appraisals, guided by the system to provide the necessary information and follow every step called for by the company's procedures.[43] To further support management decisions, the company may create an *HR dashboard,* or a display of how the company is performing on specific HR metrics, such as productivity and absenteeism. For example, Cisco Systems helps with talent management by displaying on its HR dashboard how many of its people move and why.[44] The data can help management identify divisions where the managers are successfully developing new talent.

LO7 Explain how the nature of the employment relationship is changing.

Change in the Employment Relationship

Technology and the other trends we have described in this chapter require managers at all levels to make rapid changes in response to new opportunities, competitive challenges, and customer demands. These changes are most likely to succeed in flexible, forward-thinking organizations, and the employees who will thrive in such organizations need to be flexible and open to change as well. In this environment, employers and employees have begun to reshape the employment relationship.[45]

A New Psychological Contract

psychological contract
A description of what an employee expects to contribute in an employment relationship and what the employer will provide the employee in exchange for those contributions.

We can think of that relationship in terms of a **psychological contract,** a description of what an employee expects to contribute in an employment relationship and what the employer will provide the employee in exchange for those contributions.[46] Unlike a written sales contract, the psychological contract is not formally put into words. Instead, it describes unspoken expectations that are widely held by employers and employees. In the traditional version of this psychological contract, organizations expected their employees to contribute time, effort, skills, abilities, and loyalty. In return, the organizations would provide job security and opportunities for promotion.

However, this arrangement is being replaced with a new type of psychological contract.[47] To stay competitive, modern organizations must frequently change the quality, innovation, creativeness, and timeliness of employee contributions and the skills needed to make those contributions. This need has led to organizational restructuring, mergers and acquisitions, layoffs, and longer hours for many employees. Companies demand excellent customer service and high productivity levels. They expect employees to take more responsibility for their own careers, from seeking training to balancing work and family. These expectations result in less job security for employees, who can count on working for several companies over the course of a career. The average length of time a person holds a job has declined during this decade from nine years to just seven.[48]

In exchange for top performance and working longer hours without job security, employees want companies to provide flexible work schedules, comfortable working conditions, more control over how they accomplish work, training and development opportunities, and financial incentives based on how the organization performs. (Figure 2.7 provides a humorous look at an employee who seems to have benefited from this modern psychological contract by obtaining a family-friendly work arrangement.) Employees realize that companies cannot provide employment security, so they want *employability*. This means they want their company to provide training and job experiences to help ensure that they can find other employment opportunities.

MTW, a successful information technology company, is exceptional in that it puts its psychological contracts into writing. Whenever a new employee joins the company, that person writes an "expectations agreement" stating his or her most important goals. Every six months or so, the employee and the team leader of the employee's project team review the expectations agreement and modify it if the employee's expectations have changed.[49]

Figure 2.7

A Family-Friendly Work Arrangement

SPEED BUMP   **Dave Coverly**

BY permission of Dave Coverly and Creators Syndicate, Inc.

Flexibility

The new psychological contract largely results from the HRM challenge of building a committed, productive workforce in turbulent economic conditions that offer opportunity for financial success but can also quickly turn sour, making every employee expendable. From the organization's perspective, the key to survival in a fast-changing environment is flexibility. Organizations want to be able to change as fast as customer needs and economic conditions change. Flexibility in human resource management includes flexible staffing levels and flexible work schedules.

LO8 Discuss how the need for flexibility affects human resource management.

Flexible Staffing Levels

A flexible workforce is one the organization can quickly reshape and resize to meet its changing needs. To be able to do this without massive hiring and firing campaigns, organizations are using more alternative work arrangements. **Alternative work arrangements** are methods of staffing other than the traditional hiring of full-time employees. There are a variety of methods, with the following being most common:

- *Independent contractors* are self-employed individuals with multiple clients.
- *On-call workers* are persons who work for an organization only when they are needed.

alternative work arrangements
Methods of staffing other than the traditional hiring of full-time employees (for example, use of independent contractors, on-call workers, temporary workers, and contract company workers).

HIGH-TECH FLEXIBILITY AT BANK OF THE WEST

Bank of the West, which specializes in commercial lending and small-business accounts, competes with banking giants by using technology to help it offer top-quality service efficiently. A software program called Planet, provided by GMT Corporation, analyzes the needs of the company's 700 branches to create staffing schedules based on seasonal and local usage.

With Planet, banks can analyze personnel needs and staff branches with a basic level of employees. A pool of floating employees is prepared to move from branch to branch as needed. The balanced level of staffing gives customers a good banking experience at any time of year, while the software ensures that schedules are drawn up fairly, automatically taking into account employee preferences and requests for time off.

Employees like the system, because they can easily request time off or make changes to the schedule. Managers like it because it simplifies a difficult task and helps them plan ahead.

Sources: "Case in Point: Bank of the West Bullish on Workforce Optimization Software," *ABA Banking Journal*, July 2007, downloaded from General Reference Center Gold, http://find.galegroup.com; and Global Management Technologies, "Products: Workforce Management," GMT Web site, www.gmt.com, accessed December 7, 2007.

- *Temporary workers* are employed by a temporary agency; client organizations pay the agency for the services of these workers.
- *Contract company workers* are employed directly by a company for a specific time specified in a written contract.

The Bureau of Labor Statistics estimates that about one-tenth of employed individuals work in alternative employment arrangements.[50] The majority, about 10.3 million, are independent contractors. Another 2.5 million are on-call workers, 1.2 million work for temporary-help agencies, and over 800,000 are workers provided by contract firms. In addition, about 11 percent of noninstitutionalized civilians who are old enough to work have part-time jobs; most of them work part-time by choice. Nike uses 3,700 temporary employees each year. These employees help Nike meet labor needs during upturns in the business cycle, as well as ongoing needs for specialized talent related to particular initiatives such as new-product development or retail store concepts.[51]

Multitasking has become a way of life for many employees who need to make the most of every minute. This is a new, but prevalent, trend that is affecting human resource management and the employees it supports.

More workers in alternative employment relationships are choosing these arrangements, but preferences vary. Most independent contractors and contract workers have this type of arrangement by choice. In contrast, temporary agency workers and on-call workers are likely to prefer traditional full-time employment. There is some debate about whether nontraditional employment relationships are good or bad. Some labor analysts argue that alternative work arrangements are substandard jobs featuring low pay, fear of unemployment, poor health insurance and retirement benefits, and dissatisfying work. Others claim that these jobs provide flexibility for companies and employees alike. With alternative work arrangements, organizations can more easily modify the number of their employees. Continually adjusting staffing levels is especially cost-effective for an organization that has fluctuating demand for its products and services. And when an organization downsizes by laying off temporary and part-time employees, the damage to morale among permanent full-time workers is likely to be less severe.

Flexible Work Schedules

The globalization of the world economy and the development of e-commerce have made the notion of a 40-hour workweek obsolete. As a result, companies need to be staffed 24 hours a day, seven days a week. Employees in manufacturing environments and service call centers are being asked to work 12-hour days or to work afternoon or midnight shifts. Similarly, professional employees face long hours and work demands that spill over into their personal lives. E-mail, pagers, and cell phones bombard employees with information and work demands. In the car, on vacation, on planes, and even in the bathroom, employees can be interrupted by work demands. More demanding work results in greater employee stress, less satisfied employees, loss of productivity, and higher turnover—all of which are costly for companies.

Many organizations are taking steps to provide more flexible work schedules, to protect employees' free time, and to more productively use employees' work time. Workers consider flexible schedules a valuable way to ease the pressures and conflicts of trying to balance work and nonwork activities. Employers are using flexible schedules to recruit and retain employees and to increase satisfaction and productivity. For example, Best Buy created its Results-Only Work Environment (ROWE) to give employees control over how, when, and where they get the job done, as long as they achieve the desired results.[52] The idea of this experiment is to let employees focus on productivity, rather than whether they are physically present in a meeting or seated behind their desk at a particular time of day. In divisions that have tried ROWE, employees say they are more engaged at work, are more committed to the company, and have improved their family relationships at the same time.

THINKING ETHICALLY

THE ETHICS OF OFFSHORING

When companies use offshoring, they are eliminating higher-paid U.S. jobs and replacing them with lower-paid jobs elsewhere. The debate has raged over whether this practice is ethical.

Businesses certainly need to make a profit, and offshoring can help lower costs. One manager who endorses offshoring is George Hefferan, vice president and general counsel for Mindcrest, a legal services firm based in Chicago. According to Hefferan, the company would not even exist if it couldn't hire lawyers in Mumbai and Pune, India. At far lower rates than U.S. attorneys charge, the Indian lawyers review lease agreements and do other routine tasks. This assistance frees employees in Chicago to tackle more complicated assignments.

But viewed from U.S. workers' standpoint, offshoring has its downside. Business owner Valarie King-Bailey once lost her own engineering job to offshoring. King-Bailey then started her own company, OnShore Technology, an information technology (IT) engineering firm. The company now has eight employees and a mission of "keeping technology jobs on America's shores."

SOURCE: Ann Meyer, "U.S. Exit Strategy Splits Employers," *Chicago Tribune*, October 29, 2007, sec. 3, p. 2.

Questions

1. When a company moves jobs to another country, who benefits? Who loses? Given the mix of winners and losers, do you think offshoring is ethical? Why or why not?
2. Imagine you are an HR manager at a company that is planning to begin offshoring its production or customer service operations. How could you help the company proceed as ethically as possible?

SUMMARY

LO1 Describe trends in the labor force composition and how they affect human resource management.

An organization's internal labor force comes from its external labor market—individuals who are actively seeking employment. In the United States, this labor market is aging and becoming more racially and ethnically diverse. The share of women in the U.S. workforce has grown to nearly half of the total. To compete for talent, organizations must be flexible enough to meet the needs of older workers, possibly redesigning jobs. Organizations must recruit from a diverse population, establish bias-free HR systems, and help employees understand and appreciate cultural differences. Organizations also need employees with skills in decision making, customer service, and teamwork, as well as technical skills. The competition for such talent is intense. Organizations facing a skills shortage often hire employees who lack certain skills, then train them for their jobs.

LO2 Summarize areas in which human resource management can support the goal of creating a high-performance work system.

HRM can help organizations find and keep the best possible fit between their social system and technical system. Organizations need employees with broad skills and strong motivation. Recruiting and selection decisions are especially important for organizations that rely on knowledge workers. Job design and appropriate systems for assessment and rewards have a central role in supporting employee empowerment and teamwork.

LO3 Define employee empowerment, and explain its role in the modern organization.

Employee empowerment means giving employees responsibility and authority to make decisions regarding all aspects of product development or customer service. The organization holds employees accountable for products and services, and in exchange, the employees share in the rewards (or losses) that result. Selection decisions should provide the organization people who have the necessary decision-making and interpersonal skills. HRM must design jobs to give employees latitude for decision making and train employees to handle their broad responsibilities. Feedback and rewards must be appropriate for the work of empowered employees. HRM can also play a role in giving employees access to the information they need.

LO4 Identify ways HR professionals can support organizational strategies for quality, growth, and efficiency.

HR professionals should be familiar with the organization's strategy and may even play a role in developing the strategy. Specific HR practices vary according to the type of strategy. Job design is essential for empowering employees to practice total quality management. In organizations planning major changes such as a merger or acquisition, downsizing, or reengineering, HRM must provide leadership for managing the change in a way that includes skillful employee relations and meaningful rewards. HR professionals can bring "people issues" to the attention of the managers leading these changes. They can provide training in conflict resolution skills, as well as knowledge of the other organization involved in a merger or acquisition. HR professionals also must resolve differences between the companies' HR systems, such as benefits packages and performance appraisals. For a downsizing, the HR department can help to develop voluntary programs to reduce the workforce or can help identify the least valuable employees to lay off. Employee relations can help maintain the morale of employees who remain after a downsizing. In reengineering, the HR department can lead in communicating with employees and providing training. It will also have to prepare new approaches for recruiting and appraising employees that are better suited to the reengineered jobs. Outsourcing presents similar issues related to job design and employee selection.

LO5 Summarize ways in which human resource management can support organizations expanding internationally.

Organizations with international operations hire employees in foreign countries where they operate, so they need knowledge of differences in culture and business practices. Even small businesses discover that qualified candidates include immigrants, as they account for a significant and growing share of the U.S. labor market. HRM needs to understand and train employees to deal with differences in cultures. HRM also must be able to help organizations select and prepare employees for overseas assignments. To support efficiency and growth, HR staff can prepare companies for offshoring, in which operations are moved to lower-wage countries. HR experts can help organizations determine whether workers in offshore locations can provide the same or better skills, how offshoring will affect motivation and recruitment of employees needed in the United States, and whether managers are prepared to manage offshore employees.

LO6 Discuss how technological developments are affecting human resource management.

Information systems have become a tool for more HR professionals, and often these systems are provided through the Internet. The widespread use of the Internet includes HRM applications. Organizations search for talent globally using online job postings and screening candidates online. Organizations' Web sites feature information directed toward potential employees. Employees may receive training online. At many companies, online information sharing enables employee self-service for many HR needs, from application forms to training modules to information about the details of company policies and benefits. Organizations can now structure work that involves collaboration among employees at different times and places. In such situations, HR professionals must ensure that communications remain effective enough to detect and correct problems when they arise.

LO7 Explain how the nature of the employment relationship is changing.

The employment relationship takes the form of a "psychological contract" that describes what employees and employers expect from the employment relationship. It includes unspoken expectations that are widely held. In the traditional version, organizations expected their employees to contribute time, effort, skills, abilities, and loyalty in exchange for job security and opportunities for promotion. Today, modern organizations' needs are constantly changing, so organizations are requiring top performance and longer work hours but cannot provide job security. Instead, employees are looking for flexible work schedules, comfortable working conditions, greater autonomy, opportunities for training and development, and performance-related financial incentives. For HRM, the changes require planning for flexible staffing levels.

LO8 Discuss how the need for flexibility affects human resource management.

Organizations seek flexibility in staffing levels through alternatives to the traditional employment relationship. They may use outsourcing as well as temporary and contract workers. The use of such workers can affect job design, as well as the motivation of the organization's permanent employees. Organizations also may seek flexible work schedules, including shortened work weeks. They may offer flexible schedules as a way for employees to adjust work hours to meet personal and family needs. Organizations also may move employees to different jobs to meet changes in demand.

KEY TERMS

alternative work arrangements, p. 47
electronic human resource management (e-HRM), p. 44
employee empowerment, p. 35
expatriates, p. 42
external labor market, p. 27

high-performance work systems, p. 32
human resource information system (HRIS), p. 43
internal labor force, p. 27
knowledge workers, p. 34
offshoring, p. 41

outsourcing, p. 40
psychological contract, p. 46
reengineering, p. 40
self-service, p. 45
teamwork, p. 35
total quality management (TQM), p. 36

REVIEW AND DISCUSSION QUESTIONS

1. How does each of the following labor force trends affect HRM?
   a. Aging of the labor force.
   b. Diversity of the labor force.
   c. Skill deficiencies of the labor force.
2. At many organizations, goals include improving people's performance by relying on knowledge workers, empowering employees, and assigning work to teams. How can HRM support these efforts?
3. Merging, downsizing, and reengineering all can radically change the structure of an organization. Choose one of these changes, and describe HRM's role in making the change succeed. If possible, apply your discussion to an actual merger, downsizing, or reengineering effort that has recently occurred.

4. When an organization decides to operate facilities in other countries, how can HRM practices support this change?
5. Why do organizations outsource HRM functions? How does outsourcing affect the role of human resource professionals? Would you be more attracted to the role of HR professional in an organization that outsources many HR activities or in the outside firm that has the contract to provide the HR services? Why?
6. Suppose you have been hired to manage human resources for a small company that offers business services including customer service calls and business report preparation. The 20-person company has been preparing to expand from serving a few local clients

that are well known to the company's owners. The owners believe that their experience and reputation for quality will help them expand to serve more and larger clients. What challenges will you need to prepare the company to meet? How will you begin?

7. What e-HRM resources might you use to meet the challenges in Question 4?

8. What HRM functions could an organization provide through self-service? What are some advantages and disadvantages of using self-service for these functions?

9. How is the employment relationship typical of modern organizations different from the relationship of a generation ago?

BUSINESSWEEK CASE

BusinessWeek A Critical Shortage of Nurses

The United States is facing a severe nursing shortage. Already, an estimated 8.5 percent of U.S. nursing positions are unfilled—and some expect that number to triple by 2020 as 80 million baby boomers retire and expand the ranks of those needing care. Hospital administrators and nurses' advocates have declared a staffing crisis as the nursing shortage hits its 10th year.

So why aren't nurses paid more? Wages for registered nurses rose just 1.34 percent from 2006 to 2007, trailing well behind inflation. The answer is complicated, influenced by hospital cost controls and insurance company reimbursement policies. But another factor is often overlooked: Huge numbers of nurses are brought into the United States from abroad every year. In recent years nearly a third of the RNs joining the U.S. workforce were born in other countries.

Critics say this is a short-term solution that could create long-term problems. The influx of non-U.S. nurses allows hospitals to fill positions at low salaries. But it prevents the sharp wage hike that would encourage Americans to enter the field, which could solve the nursing shortage in the years ahead. "Better pay would signify to society that nursing is a promising career," says Peter Buerhaus, a professor of nursing at Vanderbilt University. "It's a critical factor in building the workforce of the future."

The U.S. market for nurses is a reflection of how labor markets can change with globalization. With new technology and the increasing movement of workers, labor markets are no longer local or even national. Supply and demand don't work quite as they did in the past. Shortages in one market aren't corrected with higher prices if supply comes from another.

Pay isn't the only issue. Difficult working conditions and understaffing also deter qualified people from pursuing the profession. But average annual wages for registered nurses (one of the most highly trained categories) is now just under $58,000 a year, compared with a $36,300 average for U.S. workers overall. And it's clear that qualified American nurses see that as not enough: 500,000 registered nurses are not practicing their profession—one-fifth of the current RN workforce of 2.5 million and enough to fill current vacancies twice over.

Hospitals insist the U.S. shortage is too severe to address simply with money. Carl Shusterman, an immigration lawyer in Los Angeles, says he has 100 hospital clients that have 100 vacancies apiece. With two- to three-year waiting lists to get into nurse-training programs in the United States, pressure to import nurses won't abate, he says, adding, "Even if we could train more nurses and pay them more, we'd still need to import them."

Raising pay has successfully attracted nurses in the past, however. To remedy a shortage that developed in the late 1990s, hospitals started hiking wages in 2001—and added 186,500 nurses from 2001 to 2003. Some advocates draw a direct link between wages and recruiting. A 2006 study by the Institute for Women's Policy Research concluded, "Increasing pay for nurses is the most direct way to draw both currently qualified and aspiring nurses to hospital employment."

While nurses' advocates say better pay is critical, they also argue that working conditions must improve if the United States is to cultivate an enduring nursing workforce. "You will draw in some people with a good pay raise, but you won't necessarily get them to stay," says Cheryl Johnson, a registered nurse and president of the United Association of Nurses, the largest nurses' union in the United States. "Almost every nurse will tell you that staffing is a critical problem. The workload is so great that there's not time to see how [patients are] breathing, give them water, or turn them to prevent bedsores. The guilt can be unbearable."

Whatever mix of better wages, better working conditions, and foreign workers hospitals employ, solving the nursing shortage in the long run will require solutions on several fronts. "Nurses are getting more organized, but major change isn't going to happen overnight," says Suzanne Martin, a spokeswoman for the United Association of Nurses, noting that other groups "would prefer to keep things as they are."

Questions

1. Which trends described in this chapter are contributing to the nursing shortage?
2. What HR trends and practices described in this chapter might help hospitals recruit and retain enough nurses?
3. Imagine that you are an HR manager working for a hospital. In general terms, suggest how you might support the hospital's ability to attract and retain nursing talent. Which HRM topics will you need to explore further to develop your ideas?

CASE: MINING EXCELLENCE AT REDMOND MINERALS

Rhett Roberts, CEO of Redmond Minerals, started there as a young consultant fulfilling a contract. The owners of the family business had brought him in to see if Redmond could move beyond sales of $2 million a year, mostly in road salt sold as a commodity by the lowest bidder.

Roberts was surprised by what he learned. The company's mine produced an unusual red-tinted salt containing minerals that gave it desirable qualities. But with no sales force, Redmond was selling it at rock-bottom prices, based only on price. The company also had developed a table salt it called RealSalt but had not figured out how to build a market for it. To carry out its low-price strategy, Redmond kept costs down in any way it could, including a pay structure below other workplaces in the county.

Roberts urged the managers to shift to a strategy highlighting the distinctive features of the company's salt. Research showed that its IceSlicer road salt worked faster and at lower temperatures than ordinary white salt, and it was not as corrosive to steel. The minerals in the ice provided natural grit, so users would not have to mix it with sand. Marketing messages emphasizing these features would enable Redmond to begin charging a premium price and win more customers.

As Redmond adopted Roberts's marketing strategy, he could move to the heart of his business ideas: empowering the organization's people. Based on quality improvement ideas, Roberts was convinced that a high-performing company must give its people a say in how the company operates.

The company began to grow, but the owners saw this new phase of its life as too risky, so they gladly sold their shares to their former consultant. Now CEO, Roberts built sales of IceSlicer and RealSalt, but the real force behind the company's growth, he insists, is the change in how Redmond treats employees.

Roberts had each of the company's teams submit an operating budget and required them to make the decisions affecting their area, including their schedules. He began holding seminars so that everyone could learn about total quality management. At first, employees were uncomfortable with their control.

The discomfort began to fade as employees tested their new powers. For example, a production worker for Real-Salt suggested that the production team switch from a five-day workweek to four 10-hour shifts. The team leader was doubtful but listened to the arguments that a four-day workweek would cut unproductive time devoted to waiting for equipment to warm up in the morning and taking breaks later in the day. The fifth day of the week would be available any week when overtime was necessary. A trial showed that the worker had been correct; output of Real-Salt increased under the new arrangement.

With more productive workers, the company can afford better pay. Today Redmond pays a few dollars an hour above the local average. Benefits also are attractive and aimed at employee development and teamwork. Employees can receive full tuition reimbursement, and the company will pay for personal-development materials such as business and self-help books. The company backs employee bowling and golf teams, and employees get $30 to go out for dinner on their birthday. Redmond also set aside space for an exercise room and a day care room, offering flexibility in case employees need to bring a child to work.

Questions

1. When Redmond Minerals moved away from a strategy emphasizing low costs and low prices and adopted a strategy based on unique products, how did its HRM practices need to change to support the new strategy?
2. What other HRM practices or principles described in this chapter would support a strategy based on innovation?
3. Suppose Redmond Minerals has decided to hire an HR specialist, and you are tapped for the job. Imagine that Rhett Roberts is particularly interested in how the Internet can improve the way Redmond does HRM. What ideas would you suggest? How well do your ideas support Roberts's principles for running the company?

IT'S A WRAP!

www.mhhe.com/noefund3e is your source for **R**eviewing, **A**pplying, and **P**racticing the concepts you learned about in Chapter 2.

Review
- Chapter learning objectives
- Narrated lecture and iPod content

Application
- Manager's Hot Seat segment: "Privacy: Burned by the Firewall"
- Video case and quiz: "Hotjobs.com"
- Self-assessment: Trends in Human Resource Management
- Web exercise: HRM and new technologies

Practice
- Chapter quiz

NOTES

1. Martha Frase-Blunt, "Short-Term Executives," *HR Magazine*, June 2004, downloaded from Infotrac at http://web4.infotrac.galegroup.com.
2. Bureau of Labor Statistics, "Employment Projections: 2006–16," news release, December 4, 2007, www.bls.gov.
3. Anne Fisher, "How to Battle the Coming Brain Drain," *Fortune*, March 21, 2005, downloaded from Infotrac at http://web7.infotrac.galegroup.com.
4. N. Lockwood, *The Aging Workforce* (Alexandria, VA: Society for Human Resource Management, 2003).
5. J. Marquez, "Novel Ideas at Borders Lure Older Workers," *Workforce Management*, May 2005, pp. 28, 30.
6. "Labor Force," *Occupational Outlook Quarterly*, Fall 2007, pp. 40–47.
7. Ibid.
8. For background and examples related to immigration, see U.S. Citizenship and Immigration Services, "How Do I Become a Lawful Permanent Resident while in the United States?" *Services and Benefits: Permanent Resident (Green Card)*, CIS website, www.uscis.gov, accessed December 10, 2007; Federation for American Immigration Reform, "Overview of Annual Immigration," last updated July 2007, www.fairus.org; Center for Immigration Studies, "Legal Immigration," *Topics*, www.cis.org, accessed December 10, 2007; U.S. State Department, "Temporary Workers," June 2007, http://travel.state.gov; Barry Newman, "Immigration Crackdown Targets Bosses This Time," *Wall Street Journal*, February 27, 2007, http://online.wsj.com; and Juliana Barbassa, "Legal Immigrant High-Tech Workers Speak," *Yahoo News*, October 29, 2007, http://news.yahoo.com.
9. T. H. Cox and S. Blake, "Managing Cultural Diversity: Implications for Organizational Competitiveness," *The Executive* 5 (1991), pp. 45–56.
10. "Impact of Diversity Initiatives on the Bottom Line Survey," *SHRM/Fortune*, June 2001.
11. A. Pomeroy, "Cultivating Female Leaders," *HRMagazine*, February 2007, pp. 44–50.
12. J. Rossi, "The 'Future' of U.S. Manufacturing," *TD*, March 2006, pp. 12–13; and R. Davenport, "Eliminate the Skills Gap," *TD*, February 2006, pp. 26–34.
13. M. Schoeff, "Amid Calls to Bolster U.S. Innovation, Experts Lament Paucity of Basic Math Skills," *Workforce Management*, March 2006, pp. 46–49.
14. J. A. Neal and C. L. Tromley, "From Incremental Change to Retrofit: Creating High-Performance Work Systems," *Academy of Management Executive* 9 (1995), pp. 42–54.
15. "Occupational Employment," *Occupational Outlook Quarterly*, Fall 2007, pp. 6–29.
16. J. Marquez, "Driving Ideas Forward at Nissan," *Workforce Management*, July 17, 2006, p. 28.
17. A. Carnevale and D. Desrochers, "Training in the Dilbert Economy," *Training & Development*, December 1999, pp. 32–36.
18. T. J. Atchison, "The Employment Relationship: Untied or Re-Tied," *Academy of Management Executive* 5 (1991), pp. 52–62.
19. R. Vance, *Employee Engagement and Commitment* (Alexandria, VA: Society for Human Resource Management, 2006); M. Huselid, "The Impact of Human Resource Management Practices on Turnover, Productivity, and Corporate Financial Performance," *Academy of Management Journal* 38 (1995), pp. 635–72; S. Payne and S. Webber, "Effects of Service Provider Attitudes and Employment Status on Citizenship Behaviors and Customers' Attitudes and Loyalty Behavior," *Journal of Applied Psychology* 91 (2006), pp. 365–68; and J. Hartner, F. Schmidt, and T. Hayes, "Business-Unit Level Relationship between Employee

Satisfaction, Employee Engagement, and Business Outcomes: A Meta-analysis," *Journal of Applied Psychology* 87 (2002), pp. 268–79.

20. John S. McClenahen, "Bearing Necessities," *Industry Week*, October 2004, downloaded from Infotrac at http://web4.infotrac.galegroup.com.
21. Steve Bates, "Facing the Future," *HR Magazine*, July 2002, downloaded from Infotrac at http://web2.infotrac.galegroup.com.
22. Ibid.
23. J. R. Jablonski, *Implementing Total Quality Management: An Overview* (San Diego: Pfeiffer, 1991).
24. R. Hodgetts, F. Luthans, and S. Lee, "New Paradigm Organizations: From Total Quality to Learning to World-Class," *Organizational Dynamics*, Winter 1994, pp. 5–19.
25. William H. Miller, "Instability? Not a Problem," *Industry Week*, October 2004, downloaded from Infotrac at http://web4.infotrac.galegroup.com.
26. J. Laabs, "Has Downsizing Missed Its Mark?" *Workforce*, April 1999, pp. 31–38.
27. J. Lopez, "Managing: Early-Retirement Offers Lead to Renewed Hiring," *Wall Street Journal*, January 26, 1993, p. B1.
28. A. Church, "Organizational Downsizing: What Is the Role of the Practitioner?" *Industrial-Organizational Psychologist* 33, no. 1 (1995), pp. 63–74.
29. S. Caudron, "HR Is Dead, Long Live HR," *Workforce*, January 2003, pp. 26–29; and P. Ketter, "HR Outsourcing Accelerates," *TD*, February 2007, pp. 12–13.
30. M. Schoeff Jr., "Cardinal Health HR to Take More Strategic Role," *Workforce Management*, April 24, 2006, p. 7.
31. J. Kahn, "The World's Most Admired Companies," *Fortune*, October 26, 1998, pp. 206–26; A. Fisher, "The World's Most Admired Companies," *Fortune*, October 27, 1997, p. 232.
32. Jim Hopkins, "To Start Up Here, Companies Hire over There," *USA Today*, February 10, 2005, downloaded at www.usatoday.com.
33. Ibid.
34. Department of Homeland Security, Office of Immigration Statistics, *2006 Yearbook of Immigration Statistics*, Table 2, http://uscis.gov (December 5, 2007).
35. "The People Problem," *Inc.*, State of Small Business 2001 issue, May 29, 2001, pp. 84–85.
36. National Association of Colleges and Employers, "Job Outlook 2002," www.jobweb.com.
37. R. L. Tung, "Expatriate Assignments: Enhancing Success and Minimizing Failure," *Academy of Management Executive* 12, no. 4 (1988), pp. 93–106.

38. M. J. Kavanaugh, H. G. Guetal, and S. I. Tannenbaum, *Human Resource Information Systems: Development and Application* (Boston: PWS-Kent, 1990).
39. Bill Roberts, "Empowerment or Imposition?" *HR Magazine*, June 2004, downloaded from Infotrac at http://web7.infotrac.galegroup.com.
40. This section is based on L. Grensing-Pophal, "Are You Suited for a Dot-Com?" *HR Magazine*, November 2000, pp. 75–80; Leslie A. Weatherly, "HR Technology: Leveraging the Shift to Self-Service," *HR Magazine*, March 2005, downloaded from Infotrac at http://web7.infotrac.galegroup.com; and Roberts, "Empowerment or Imposition?"
41. See Weatherly, "HR Technology."
42. Roberts, "Empowerment or Imposition?"
43. Weatherly, "HR Technology."
44. N. Lockwood, *Maximizing Human Capital: Demonstrating HR Value with Key Performance Indicators* (Alexandria, VA: SHRM Research Quarterly, 2006).
45. J. O'Toole and E. Lawler III, *The New American Workplace* (New York: Palgrave Macmillan, 2006).
46. D. M. Rousseau, "Psychological and Implied Contracts in Organizations," *Employee Rights and Responsibilities Journal* 2 (1989), pp. 121–29.
47. D. Rousseau, "Changing the Deal while Keeping the People," *Academy of Management Executive* 11 (1996), pp. 50–61; and M. A. Cavanaugh and R. Noe, "Antecedents and Consequences of the New Psychological Contract," *Journal of Organizational Behavior* 20 (1999), pp. 323–40.
48. C. Tejada, "For Many, Taking Work Home Is Often a Job without Reward," *Wall Street Journal*, Interactive Edition, March 5, 2002, http://online.wsj.com.
49. E. O. Welles, "Great Expectations," *Inc.*, March 2001, pp. 68–70, 72–73.
50. Bureau of Labor Statistics (BLS), "Charting the U.S. Labor Market in 2006," *Current Population Survey*, www.bls.gov, last modified September 28, 2007; BLS, "Alternative Employment Arrangements and Worker Preferences," *Monthly Labor Review: The Editor's Desk*, August 4, 2005, www.bls.gov, last updated August 8, 2005; and BLS, "Independent Contractors in 2005," *Monthly Labor Review: The Editor's Desk*, July 29, 2005, www.bls.gov, last updated August 1, 2005.
51. F. Hansen, "A Permanent Strategy for Temporary Hires," *Workforce Management*, February 26, 2007, pp. 25–30.
52. P. Kiger, "Flexibility to the Fullest," *Workforce Management*, September 25, 2006, pp. 1, 16–23.

Providing Equal Employment Opportunity and a Safe Workplace

Introduction

Learning about employees and customers guided Weyerhaeuser Company as it developed a human resource policy suitable for a diverse business environment. From an employee survey, Weyerhaeuser, which produces forest products such as paper, lumber, and cardboard and paper packaging, learned that it needed to improve recruitment and retention of talented men and women from diverse ethnic groups. The company determined that growing populations of Hispanic and other ethnic groups in its markets could be better served by a workforce that represented these groups. For instance, Hispanic employees might be aware of new product ideas that would meet a demand unfamiliar to the company's mostly non-Hispanic managers.

To cultivate a diverse workforce, human resource management at Weyerhaeuser cast a wider net to recruit through organizations like the National Society of Hispanic MBAs, the National Society of Black Engineers, Women in Construction, and similar groups. The company added hiring and retention of minorities to the goals for which bonuses are awarded to managers. These efforts apply lessons Weyerhaeuser learned from a safety program in which it combined training, communication, and rewards to reduce accident rates. The safety program cultivated a broad definition of safety, including a work environment that feels emotionally as well as physically safe for employees. That program paved the way for the diversity program—to create an environment in which no employee should be harassed because of race or gender. Although the company's jobs in forestry and paper mills are outside fields that have traditionally drawn women and members of racial and ethnic minorities, Weyerhaeuser began to see progress early in the program.[1]

As we saw in Chapter 1, human resource management takes place in the context of the company's goals and society's expectations for how a company should operate. In the United States, the federal government has set some limits on how an

chapter three

organization can practice human resource management. Among these limits are requirements intended to prevent discrimination in hiring and employment practices and to protect the health and safety of workers while they are on the job. Questions about a company's compliance with these requirements can result in lawsuits and negative publicity that often cause serious problems for a company's success and survival. Conversely, a company that skillfully navigates the maze of regulations can gain an advantage over its competitors. A further advantage may go to companies that, like Weyerhaeuser, go beyond mere legal compliance to find ways of linking fair employment and worker safety to business goals such as building a workforce that is highly motivated and attuned to customers.

This chapter provides an overview of the ways government bodies regulate equal employment opportunity and workplace safety and health. It introduces you to major laws affecting employers in these areas, as well as the agencies charged with enforcing those laws. The chapter also discusses ways organizations can develop practices that ensure they are in compliance with the laws.

One point to make at the outset is that managers often want a list of dos and don'ts that will keep them out of legal trouble. Some managers rely on strict rules such as "Don't ever ask a female applicant if she is married," rather than learning the reasons behind those rules. Clearly, certain practices are illegal or at least inadvisable, and this chapter will provide guidance on avoiding such practices. However, managers who merely focus on how to avoid breaking the law are not thinking about how to be ethical or how to acquire and use human resources in the best way to carry out the company's mission. This chapter introduces ways to think more creatively and constructively about fair employment and workplace safety.

Regulation of Human Resource Management

LO1 Explain how the three branches of government regulate human resource management.

All three branches of the U.S. government—legislative, executive, and judicial—play an important role in creating a legal environment for human resource management. The legislative branch, which consists of the two houses of Congress, has enacted a number of laws governing human resource activities. Senators and U.S. Representatives generally develop these laws in response to perceived societal needs. For example, during the civil rights movement of the early 1960s, Congress enacted Title VII of the Civil Rights Act to ensure that various minority groups received equal opportunities in many areas of life.

The executive branch, including the many regulatory agencies that the president oversees, is responsible for enforcing the laws passed by Congress. Agencies do this through a variety of actions, from drawing up regulations detailing how to abide by the laws to filing suit against alleged violators. Some federal agencies involved in regulating human resource management include the Equal Employment Opportunity Commission and the Occupational Safety and Health Administration. In addition, the president may issue executive orders, which are

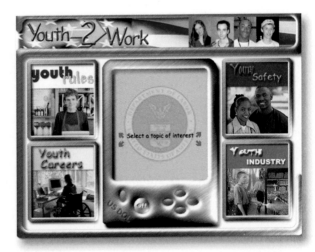

One way the executive branch communicates information about laws is through Web sites like Youth2Work. This site is designed to provide young workers with a safe workplace by making them aware of laws that, for example, restrict the amount of work they can do and the machinery they can operate.

directives issued solely by the president, without requiring congressional approval. Some executive orders regulate the activities of organizations that have contracts with the federal government. For example, President Lyndon Johnson signed Executive Order 11246, which requires all federal contractors and subcontractors to engage in affirmative-action programs designed to hire and promote women and minorities. (We will explore the topic of affirmative action later in this chapter.)

The judicial branch, the federal court system, influences employment law by interpreting the law and holding trials concerning violations of the law. The U.S. Supreme Court, at the head of the judicial branch, is the court of final appeal. Decisions made by the Supreme Court are binding; they can be overturned only through laws passed by Congress. The Civil Rights Act of 1991 was partly designed to overturn Supreme Court decisions.

Equal Employment Opportunity

L02 Summarize the major federal laws requiring equal employment opportunity.

Among the most significant efforts to regulate human resource management are those aimed at achieving **equal employment opportunity (EEO)**—the condition in which all individuals have an equal chance for employment, regardless of their race, color, religion, sex, age, disability, or national origin. The federal government's efforts to create equal employment opportunity include constitutional amendments, legislation, and executive orders, as well as court decisions that interpret the laws. Table 3.1 summarizes major EEO laws discussed in this chapter. These are U.S. laws; equal employment laws in other countries may differ.

equal employment opportunity (EEO)
The condition in which all individuals have an equal chance for employment, regardless of their race, color, religion, sex, age, disability, or national origin.

Constitutional Amendments

Two amendments to the U.S. Constitution—the Thirteenth and Fourteenth—have implications for human resource management. The Thirteenth Amendment abolished slavery in the United States. Though you might be hard-pressed to cite an example of race-based slavery in the United States today, the Thirteenth Amendment has been applied in cases where discrimination involved the "badges" (symbols) and "incidents" of slavery.

The Fourteenth Amendment forbids the states from taking life, liberty, or property without due process of law and prevents the states from denying equal protection of the laws. Recently it has been applied to the protection of whites in charges of reverse discrimination. In a case that marked the early stages of a move away from race-based quotas, Alan Bakke alleged that as a white man he had been discriminated against in the selection of entrants to the University of California at Davis medical school.[2] The university had set aside 16 of the available 100 places for "disadvantaged" applicants who were members of racial minority groups. Under this quota system, Bakke was able to compete for only 84 positions, whereas a minority applicant was able to compete for all 100. The federal court ruled in favor of Bakke, noting that this quota system had violated white individuals' right to equal protection under the law.

An important point regarding the Fourteenth Amendment is that it applies only to the decisions or actions of the government or of private groups whose activities are deemed government actions. Thus, a person could file a claim under the Fourteenth Amendment if he or she had been fired from a state university (a government organization) but not if the person had been fired by a private employer.

Legislation

The periods following the Civil War and during the civil rights movement of the 1960s were times when many voices in society pressed for equal rights for all without

Table 3.1

Summary of Major EEO Laws and Regulations

ACT	REQUIREMENTS	COVERS	ENFORCEMENT AGENCY
Thirteenth Amendment	Abolished slavery	All individuals	Court system
Fourteenth Amendment	Provides equal protection for all citizens and requires due process in state action	State actions (e.g., decisions of government organizations)	Court system
Civil Rights Acts (CRAs) of 1866 and 1871 (as amended)	Grant all citizens the right to make, perform, modify, and terminate contracts and enjoy all benefits, terms, and conditions of the contractual relationship	All individuals	Court system
Equal Pay Act of 1963	Requires that men and women performing equal jobs receive equal pay	Employers engaged in interstate commerce	EEOC
Title VII of CRA	Forbids discrimination based on race, color, religion, sex, or national origin	Employers with 15 or more employees working 20 or more weeks per year; labor unions; and employment agencies	EEOC
Age Discrimination in Employment Act of 1967	Prohibits discrimination in employment against individuals 40 years of age and older	Employers with 15 or more employees working 20 or more weeks per year; labor unions; employment agencies; federal government	EEOC
Rehabilitation Act of 1973	Requires affirmative action in the employment of individuals with disabilities	Government agencies; federal contractors and subcontractors with contracts greater than $2,500	OFCCP
Pregnancy Discrimination Act of 1978	Treats discrimination based on pregnancy-related conditions as illegal sex discrimination	All employees covered by Title VII	EEOC
Americans with Disabilities Act of 1990	Prohibits discrimination against individuals with disabilities	Employers with more than 15 employees	EEOC
Executive Order 11246	Requires affirmative action in hiring women and minorities	Federal contractors and subcontractors with contracts greater than $10,000	OFCCP
Civil Rights Act of 1991	Prohibits discrimination (same as Title VII)	Same as Title VII, plus applies Section 1981 to employment discrimination cases	EEOC
Uniformed Services Employment and Reemployment Rights Act of 1994	Requires rehiring of employees who are absent for military service, with training and accommodations as needed	Veterans and members of reserve components	Veterans' Employment and Training Service

regard to a person's race or sex. In response, Congress passed laws designed to provide for equal opportunity. In later years, Congress has passed additional laws that have extended EEO protection more broadly.

Civil Rights Acts of 1866 and 1871

During Reconstruction, Congress passed two Civil Rights Acts to further the Thirteenth Amendment's goal of abolishing slavery. The Civil Rights Act of 1866 granted all persons the same property rights as white citizens, as well as the right to enter into and enforce contracts. Courts have interpreted the latter right as including employment contracts. The Civil Rights Act of 1871 granted all citizens the right to sue in federal court if they feel they have been deprived of some civil right. Although these laws might seem outdated, they are still used because they allow the plaintiff to recover both compensatory and punitive damages (that is, payment to compensate them for their loss plus additional damages to punish the offender).

Equal Pay Act of 1963

Under the Equal Pay Act of 1963, if men and women in an organization are doing equal work, the employer must pay them equally. The act defines *equal* in terms of skill, effort, responsibility, and working conditions. However, the act allows for reasons why men and women performing the same job might be paid differently. If the pay differences result from differences in seniority, merit, quantity or quality of production, or any factor other than sex (such as participating in a training program or working the night shift), then the differences are legal.

Title VII of the Civil Rights Act of 1964

The major law regulating equal employment opportunity in the United States is Title VII of the Civil Rights Act of 1964. Title VII directly resulted from the civil rights movement of the early 1960s, led by such individuals as Dr. Martin Luther King Jr. To ensure that employment opportunities would be based on character or ability rather than on race, Congress wrote and passed Title VII, and President Lyndon Johnson signed it into law in 1964. The law is enforced by the **Equal Employment Opportunity Commission (EEOC),** an agency of the Department of Justice.

Equal Employment Opportunity Commission (EEOC)
Agency of the Department of Justice charged with enforcing Title VII of the Civil Rights Act of 1964 and other antidiscrimination laws.

Title VII prohibits employers from discriminating against individuals because of their race, color, religion, sex, or national origin. An employer may not use these characteristics as the basis for not hiring someone, for firing someone, or for discriminating against them in the terms of their pay, conditions of employment, or privileges of employment. In addition, an employer may not use these characteristics to limit, segregate, or classify employees or job applicants in any way that would deprive any individual of employment opportunities or otherwise adversely affect his or her status as an employee. The act applies to organizations that employ 15 or more persons working 20 or more weeks a year and that are involved in interstate commerce, as well as state and local governments, employment agencies, and labor organizations.

Title VII also states that employers may not retaliate against employees for either "opposing" a perceived illegal employment practice or "participating in a proceeding" related to an alleged illegal employment practice. *Opposition* refers to expressing to someone through proper channels that you believe an illegal employment act has taken place or is taking place. *Participation in a proceeding* refers to testifying in an investigation, hearing, or court proceeding regarding an illegal employment act. The purpose of this provision is to protect employees from employers' threats and other forms of intimidation aimed at discouraging employees from bringing to light acts they believe to be illegal. Companies that violate this prohibition may be liable for punitive damages.

Age Discrimination in Employment Act (ADEA)

One category of employees not covered by Title VII is older workers. Older workers sometimes are concerned that they will be the targets of discrimination, especially when a company is downsizing. Older workers tend to be paid more, so a company that wants to cut labor costs may save by laying off its oldest workers. To counter such discrimination, Congress in 1967 passed the Age Discrimination in Employment Act (ADEA), which prohibits discrimination against workers who are over the age of 40. Similar to Title VII, the ADEA outlaws hiring, firing, setting compensation rates, or other employment decisions based on a person's age being over 40.

Many firms have offered early-retirement incentives as an alternative or supplement to involuntary layoffs. Because this approach to workforce reduction focuses on older employees, who would be eligible for early retirement, it may be in violation of the ADEA. Early-retirement incentives require that participating employees sign an agreement waiving their rights to sue under the ADEA. Courts have tended to uphold the use of early-retirement incentives and waivers as long as the individuals were not coerced into signing the agreements, the agreements were presented in a way the employees could understand, and the employees had enough time to make a decision.[3] However, the Equal Employment Opportunity Commission recently expanded the interpretation of discriminatory retirement policies when it charged a law firm with having an illegal "age-based retirement policy." According to the charges, Sidley Austin Brown & Wood, based in Chicago, gave more than 30 lawyers older than age 40 notice that their status was being lowered from partner to special counsel or counsel and that they would be expected to leave the firm in a few years. The firm described the action as a way to provide more opportunities for young lawyers, but lawyers who were pressured to retire contended they were forced out as a way to boost profits by replacing highly paid partners with less-experienced, lower-paid lawyers. Sidley Austin settled the suit at a cost of $27.5 million, to be paid to the former partners. The consent decree bars the firm from "maintaining any formal or informal policy or practice requiring retirement as a partner or requiring permission to continue as a partner once the partner has reached a certain age."[4]

Age discrimination complaints make up a large percentage of the complaints filed with the Equal Employment Opportunity Commission, and whenever the economy is slow, the number of complaints grows. For example, as shown in Figure 3.1, the number

Figure 3.1

Age Discrimination Complaints, 1991–2006

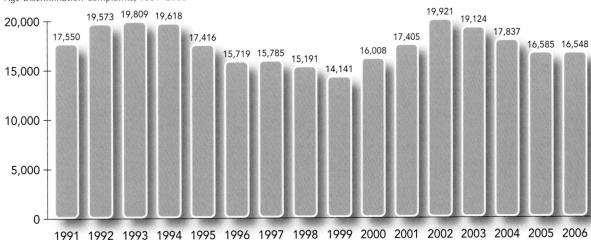

SOURCE: Equal Employment Opportunity Commission, http://eeoc.gov/stats/adea.html.

of age discrimination cases increased during the early 1990s, when many firms were downsizing. Another increase in age discrimination claims accompanied the economic slowdown at the beginning of this decade.

In today's environment, in which firms are seeking talented individuals to achieve the company's goals, older employees can be a tremendous pool of potential resources. Baptist Health South Florida addresses the worker shortage in health care by making it easier for employees to stick around when they reach the usual retirement age. At Baptist, under a policy it calls Bridgement of Service, employees who have retired but want to return within five years are able to come back with the same level of seniority and benefits they had earned before leaving. Some of these employees work part-time and use their retirement savings to make up the difference in pay. Another policy that makes it easier to stay with Baptist allows workers to accumulate up to 1,000 hours of paid time off. As workers near retirement age, they can save up time and take an extended vacation to see if they really want to be away from work. Two of Baptist's recruiters specialize in transferring employees within the company, and they spend a large share of their time helping older workers change to jobs that are less physically demanding. The company also modifies jobs; for example, spring lifts in laundry containers permit housekeepers to move loads without bending over. Efforts such as these have helped to keep employee turnover, especially among older employees, far below the industry average.[5]

Vocational Rehabilitation Act of 1973

affirmative action
An organization's active effort to find opportunities to hire or promote people in a particular group.

In 1973, Congress passed the Vocational Rehabilitation Act to enhance employment opportunity for individuals with disabilities. This act covers executive agencies and contractors and subcontractors that receive more than $2,500 annually from the federal government. These organizations must engage in affirmative action for individuals with disabilities. **Affirmative action** is an organization's active effort to find opportunities to hire or promote people in a particular group. Thus, Congress intended this act to encourage employers to recruit qualified individuals with disabilities and to make reasonable accommodations to all those people to become active members of the labor market. The Department of Labor's Employment Standards Administration enforces this act.

Vietnam Era Veteran's Readjustment Act of 1974

Similar to the Rehabilitation Act, the Vietnam Era Veteran's Readjustment Act of 1974 requires federal contractors and subcontractors to take affirmative action toward employing veterans of the Vietnam War (those serving between August 5, 1964, and May 7, 1975). The Office of Federal Contract Compliance Procedures, discussed later in this chapter, has authority to enforce this act.

Pregnancy Discrimination Act of 1978

An amendment to Title VII of the Civil Rights Act of 1964, the Pregnancy Discrimination Act of 1978 defines discrimination on the basis of pregnancy, childbirth, or related medical conditions to be a form of illegal sex discrimination. According to the EEOC, this means that employers must treat "women who are pregnant or affected by related conditions . . . in the same manner as other applicants or employees with similar abilities or limitations."[6] For example, an employer may not refuse to hire a woman because she is pregnant. Decisions about work absences or accommodations must be based on the same policies as the organization uses for other disabilities (see the HR Oops! box). Benefits, including health insurance, should cover pregnancy and related medical conditions in the same way that it covers other medical conditions.

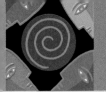

HR Oops!

Discriminating against Pregnant Workers

A record number of pregnancy discrimination charges were filed with the EEOC in 2006, and the uptick continued the following year. At a California software company, for example, a public relations employee said that when she was six months pregnant, the company's chief executive insisted that she decide whether she wanted a promotion. She replied that the timing wasn't right, and the CEO told her that the lack of dedication meant she should leave the company. In Spokane, Washington, a pregnant employee of an advertising agency was laid off. Her supervisor told her that

the decision of which employee would go was based on the facts that she would soon be taking maternity leave and was not her family's sole breadwinner. And in Maryland, a newly hired receptionist was asked what size uniform she would need. When the receptionist revealed that she was unsure which size to request because she was pregnant, the hiring manager rescinded the job offer and suggested she reapply after the baby was born.

Sources: "2006 Saw Increase in Number of Discrimination Charges Filed," *HRMagazine,* April 2007, General Reference Center Gold, http://find.galegroup.com; Kristen Gerencher, "Six Tips

for Fighting Bias against Pregnant Workers," *Career Journal.com,* October 22, 2007, www.careerjournal.com; Tom Sowa, "EEOC Sues Spokane Company over Layoff," September 28, 2007, http://find.galegroup.com; and Hanah Cho, "Pregnancy Complaints Called 'Career Killers,'" *Baltimore Sun,* March 28, 2007, http://find.galegroup.com.

Questions

1. In each of the examples given, how did the employer allegedly discriminate? What actions, as described, were wrong?

2. What would have been a legal way to handle the situations described here?

Americans with Disabilities Act (ADA) of 1990

One of the farthest-reaching acts concerning the management of human resources is the Americans with Disabilities Act. This 1990 law protects individuals with disabilities from being discriminated against in the workplace. It prohibits discrimination based on disability in all employment practices such as job application procedures, hiring, firing, promotions, compensation, and training. Other employment activities covered by the ADA are employment advertising, recruitment, tenure, layoff, leave, and fringe benefits.

The ADA defines **disability** as a physical or mental impairment that substantially limits one or more major life activities, a record of having such an impairment, or being regarded as having such an impairment. The first part of the definition refers to individuals who have serious disabilities—such as epilepsy, blindness, deafness, or paralysis—that affect their ability to perform major life activities such as walking, seeing, performing manual tasks, learning, caring for oneself, and working. The second part refers to individuals who have a history of disability, such as someone who has had cancer but is currently in remission, someone with a history of mental illness, and someone with a history of heart disease. The third part of the definition, "being regarded as having a disability," refers to people's subjective reactions, as in the case of someone who is severely disfigured; an employer might hesitate to hire such a person on the grounds that people will react negatively to such an employee.[7]

The ADA covers specific physiological disabilities such as cosmetic disfigurement and anatomical loss affecting the body's systems. In addition, it covers mental and psychological disorders such as mental retardation, organic brain syndrome, emotional or mental illness, and learning disabilities. Conditions not covered include obesity, substance abuse, eye and hair color, and lefthandedness.[8] Also, if a person uses mitigating measures (for example, medicine or equipment) that enable him or her to perform each major life activity with little or no difficulty, the person is not considered

disability
Under the Americans with Disabilities Act, a physical or mental impairment that substantially limits one or more major life activities, a record of having such an impairment, or being regarded as having such an impairment.

63

Figure 3.2

Disabilities Associated
with Complaints Filed
under ADA

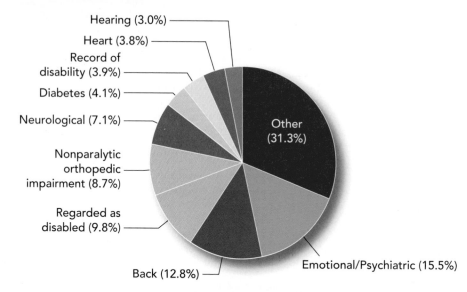

Hearing (3.0%)
Heart (3.8%)
Record of
disability (3.9%)
Diabetes (4.1%)
Neurological (7.1%)
Nonparalytic
orthopedic
impairment (8.7%)
Regarded as
disabled (9.8%)
Other
(31.3%)
Back (12.8%)
Emotional/Psychiatric (15.5%)

Total complaints: 235,515

SOURCE: Equal Employment Opportunity Commission, "ADA Charge Data by Impairments/Bases: Receipts,"
www.eeoc.gov, cumulative data for July 26, 1992–September 30, 2006.

disabled under the ADA. Figure 3.2 shows the types of disabilities associated with complaints filed under the ADA.

In contrast to other EEO laws, the ADA goes beyond prohibiting discrimination to require that employers take steps to accommodate individuals covered under the act. If a disabled person is selected to perform a job, the employer (perhaps in consultation with the disabled employee) determines what accommodations are necessary for the employee to perform the job. Examples include using ramps and lifts to make facilities accessible, redesigning job procedures, and providing technology such as TDD lines for hearing-impaired employees. Some employers have feared that accommodations under the ADA would be expensive. However, in the years since the ADA went into effect, the Equal Employment Opportunity Commission has determined that the median cost of an accommodation is only $240, and one-fifth of accommodations cost nothing.[9] As technology advances, the cost of many technologies has been falling.

Civil Rights Act of 1991

In 1991 Congress broadened the relief available to victims of discrimination by passing a Civil Rights Act (CRA 1991). CRA 1991 amends Title VII of the Civil Rights Act of 1964, as well as the Civil Rights Act of 1866, the Americans with Disabilities Act, and the Age Discrimination in Employment Act of 1967. One major change in EEO law under CRA 1991 has been the addition of compensatory and punitive damages in cases of discrimination under Title VII and the Americans with Disabilities Act. Before CRA 1991, Title VII limited damage claims to *equitable relief*, which courts have defined to include back pay, lost benefits, front pay in some cases, and attorney's fees and costs. CRA 1991 allows judges to award compensatory and punitive damages when the plaintiff proves the discrimination was intentional or reckless. Compensatory damages include such things as future monetary loss, emotional pain, suffering, and loss of enjoyment of life. Punitive damages are a punishment; by requiring violators to pay the plaintiff an amount beyond the actual losses suffered, the courts try to discourage employers from discriminating.

EMPLOYER SIZE	DAMAGE LIMIT
14 to 100 employees	$ 50,000
101 to 200 employees	100,000
201 to 500 employees	200,000
More than 500 employees	300,000

Recognizing that one or a few discrimination cases could put an organization out of business, and so harm many innocent employees, Congress has limited the amount of punitive damages. As shown in Table 3.2, the amount of damages depends on the size of the organization charged with discrimination. The limits range from $50,000 per violation at a small company (14 to 100 employees) to $300,000 at a company with more than 500 employees. A company has to pay punitive damages only if it discriminated intentionally or with malice or reckless indifference to the employee's federally protected rights.

Uniformed Services Employment and Reemployment Rights Act of 1994

When members of the armed services were called up following the terrorist attacks of September 2001, a 1994 employment law—the Uniformed Services Employment and Reemployment Rights Act (USERRA)—assumed new significance. Under this law, employers must reemploy workers who left jobs to fulfill military duties for up to five years. When service members return from active duty, the employer must reemploy them in the job they would have held if they had not left to serve in the military, including the same seniority, status, and pay. Disabled veterans also have up to two years to recover from injuries received during their service or training, and employers must make reasonable accommodations for a remaining disability.

Service members also have duties under USERRA. Before leaving for duty, they are to give their employers notice, if possible. After their service, the law sets time limits for applying to be reemployed. Depending on the length of service, these limits range from approximately 2 to 90 days. Veterans with complaints under USERRA can obtain assistance from the Veterans' Employment and Training Service of the Department of Labor.

Executive Orders

Two executive orders that directly affect human resource management are Executive Order 11246, issued by Lyndon Johnson, and Executive Order 11478, issued by Richard Nixon. Executive Order 11246 prohibits federal contractors and subcontractors from discriminating based on race, color, religion, sex, or national origin. In addition, employers whose contracts meet minimum size requirements must engage in affirmative action to

Aric Miller, an Army reservist sergeant, was deployed for service with the 363rd military police unit in Iraq for over a year. When he returned to the states, he was able to resume his job as an elementary school teacher thanks to the 1994 Uniformed Services Employment and Reemployment Rights Act. The act requires employers to reemploy service members in the job they would have held if they had not left to serve in the military. Why is this act important?

ensure against discrimination. Those receiving more than $10,000 from the federal government must take affirmative action, and those with contracts exceeding $50,000 must develop a written affirmative-action plan for each of their establishments. This plan must be in place within 120 days of the beginning of the contract. This executive order is enforced by the Office of Federal Contract Compliance Procedures.

Executive Order 11478 requires the federal government to base all its employment policies on merit and fitness. It specifies that race, color, sex, religion, and national origin may not be considered. Along with the government, the act covers all contractors and subcontractors doing at least $10,000 worth of business with the federal government. The U.S. Office of Personnel Management is in charge of ensuring that the government is in compliance, and the relevant government agencies are responsible for ensuring the compliance of contractors and subcontractors.

LO3 Identify the federal agencies that enforce equal employment opportunity, and describe the role of each.

The Government's Role in Providing for Equal Employment Opportunity

At a minimum, equal employment opportunity requires that employers comply with EEO laws. To enforce those laws, the executive branch of the federal government uses the Equal Employment Opportunity Commission and the Office of Federal Contract Compliance Procedures.

Equal Employment Opportunity Commission (EEOC)

The Equal Employment Opportunity Commission (EEOC) is responsible for enforcing most of the EEO laws, including Title VII, the Equal Pay Act, and the Americans with Disabilities Act. To do this, the EEOC investigates and resolves complaints about discrimination, gathers information, and issues guidelines.

When individuals believe they have been discriminated against, they may file a complaint with the EEOC or a similar state agency. They must file the complaint within 180 days of the incident. Figure 3.3 illustrates the number of charges filed with

Figure 3.3

Types of Charges Filed with the EEOC

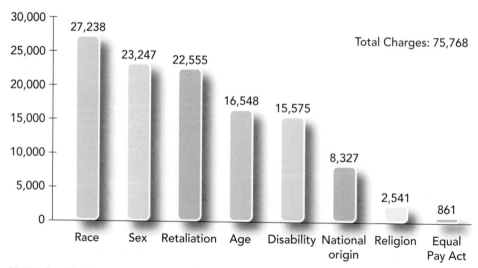

SOURCE: Equal Employment Opportunity Commission, "Charge Statistics FY 1997 through FY 2006," www.eeoc.gov, modified February 26, 2007.

the EEOC for different types of discrimination in 2006. Many individuals file more than one type of charge (for instance, both race discrimination and retaliation), so the total number of complaints filed with the EEOC is less than the total of the amounts in each category.

After the EEOC receives a charge of discrimination, it has 60 days to investigate the complaint. If the EEOC either does not believe the complaint to be valid or fails to complete the investigation within 60 days, the individual has the right to sue in federal court. If the EEOC determines that discrimination has taken place, its representatives will attempt to work with the individual and the employer to try to achieve a reconciliation without a lawsuit. Sometimes the EEOC enters into a consent decree with the discriminating organization. This decree is an agreement between the agency and the organization that the organization will cease certain discriminatory practices and possibly institute additional affirmative-action practices to rectify its history of discrimination. A settlement with the EEOC can be costly, including such remedies as back pay, reinstatement of the employee, and promotions.

If the attempt at a settlement fails, the EEOC has two options. It may issue a "right to sue" letter to the alleged victim. This letter certifies that the agency has investigated the victim's allegations and found them to be valid. The EEOC's other option, which it uses less often, is to aid the alleged victim in bringing suit in federal court.

The EEOC also monitors organizations' hiring practices. Each year organizations that are government contractors or subcontractors or have 100 or more employees must file an Employer Information Report (EEO-1) with the EEOC. The **EEO-1 report** is an on-line questionnaire requesting the number of employees in each job category (such as managers, professionals, and laborers), broken down by their status as male or female, Hispanic or non-Hispanic, and members of various racial groups. The EEOC analyzes those reports to identify patterns of discrimination, which the agency can then attack through class-action lawsuits. Employers must display EEOC posters detailing employment rights. These posters must be in prominent and accessible locations—for example, in a company's cafeteria or near its time clock. Also, employers should retain copies of documents related to employment decisions—recruitment letters, announcements of jobs, completed job applications, selections for training, and so on. Employers must keep these records for at least six months or until a complaint is resolved, whichever is later.

Besides resolving complaints and suing alleged violators, the EEOC issues guidelines designed to help employers determine when their decisions violate the laws enforced by the EEOC. These guidelines are not laws themselves. However, the courts give great consideration to them when hearing employment discrimination cases. For example, the *Uniform Guidelines on Employee Selection Procedures* is a set of guidelines issued by the EEOC and other government agencies. The guidelines identify ways an organization should develop and administer its system for selecting employees so as not to violate Title VII. The courts often refer to the *Uniform Guidelines* to determine whether a company has engaged in discriminatory conduct. Similarly, in the *Federal Register*, the EEOC has published guidelines providing details about what the agency will consider illegal and legal in the treatment of disabled individuals under the Americans with Disabilities Act.

Office of Federal Contract Compliance Programs (OFCCP)

The **Office of Federal Contract Compliance Programs (OFCCP)** is the agency responsible for enforcing the executive orders that cover companies doing business with the federal government. As we stated earlier in the chapter, businesses with contracts

EEO-1 report
The EEOC's Employer Information Report, which counts employees sorted by job category, sex, ethnicity, and race.

Uniform Guidelines on Employee Selection Procedures
Guidelines issued by the EEOC and other agencies to identify how an organization should develop and administer its system for selecting employees so as not to violate antidiscrimination laws.

Office of Federal Contract Compliance Programs (OFCCP)
The agency responsible for enforcing the executive orders that cover companies doing business with the federal government.

for more than $50,000 may not discriminate in employment based on race, color, religion, national origin, or sex, and they must have a written affirmative-action plan on file. This plan must include three basic components:

1. *Utilization analysis*—A comparison of the race, sex, and ethnic composition of the employer's workforce with that of the available labor supply. The percentages in the employer's workforce should not be greatly lower than the percentages in the labor supply.
2. *Goals and timetables*—The percentages of women and minorities the organization seeks to employ in each job group, and the dates by which the percentages are to be attained. These are meant to be more flexible than quotas, requiring only that the employer have goals and be seeking to achieve the goals.
3. *Action steps*—A plan for how the organization will meet its goals. Besides working toward its goals for hiring women and minorities, the company must take affirmative steps toward hiring Vietnam veterans and individuals with disabilities.

Each year, the OFCCP audits government contractors to ensure they are actively pursuing the goals in their plans. The OFCCP examines the plan and conducts on-site visits to examine how individual employees perceive the company's affirmative-action policies. If the agency finds that a contractor or subcontractor is not complying with the requirements, it has several options. It may notify the EEOC (if there is evidence of a violation of Title VII), advise the Department of Justice to begin criminal proceedings, request that the Secretary of Labor cancel or suspend any current contracts with the company, and forbid the firm from bidding on future contracts. For a company that depends on the federal government for a sizable share of its business, that last penalty is severe.

Businesses' Role in Providing for Equal Employment Opportunity

LO4 Describe ways employers can avoid illegal discrimination and provide reasonable accommodation.

Rare is the business owner or manager who wants to wait for the government to identify that the business has failed to provide for equal employment opportunity. Instead, out of motives ranging from concern for fairness to the desire to avoid costly lawsuits and settlements, most companies recognize the importance of complying with these laws. Often, management depends on the expertise of human resource professionals to help in identifying how to comply. These professionals can help organizations take steps to avoid discrimination and provide reasonable accommodation.

Avoiding Discrimination

How would you know if you had been discriminated against? Decisions about human resources are so complex that discrimination is often difficult to identify and prove. However, legal scholars and court rulings have arrived at some ways to show evidence of discrimination.

Disparate Treatment

disparate treatment
Differing treatment of individuals, where the differences are based on the individuals' race, color, religion, sex, national origin, age, or disability status.

One sign of discrimination is **disparate treatment**—differing treatment of individuals, where the differences are based on the individuals' race, color, religion, sex, national origin, age, or disability status. For example, disparate treatment would include hiring or promoting one person over an equally qualified person because of the individual's race.

VIDEO RÉSUMÉS—PERILOUS POLICY?

Internet technology makes it easy for almost anyone to shoot a video and post it online. Some people are applying their technical talents to their own careers by creating video résumés. These résumés let people tell their story creatively and just might set a job applicant apart from the crowd.

The risk is that the technique might also set a candidate apart from the crowd in a harmful way. Employers know they must avoid discrimination based on race, color, national origin, disability, and so on. But if the video shows an applicant from a group the employer is biased against, it might be all too easy for that employer to think of a reason not to interview the candidate.

On the up side, some experts think a well-executed video résumé can help a person shine and may even overcome bias in some cases. Deborah Dagit, who heads diversity programs at Merck and Company, says, "If you are someone with a disability . . . [that] has a high degree of stigma, a video résumé could work to your advantage" by dispelling preconceived notions of what a person with that disability can do.

In a recent survey by Vault.com, 89 percent of employers said they would look at a video résumé. Yet, companies crafting a policy for this use of technology should consider not only the benefits but also the possible drawbacks.

Source: Aysha Hussain, "Do Video Résumés Help or Lead to Discrimination?" *DiversityInc,* June 26, 2007, www.diversityinc.com.

Or suppose a company fails to hire women with school-age children (claiming the women will be frequently absent) but hires men with school-age children. In that situation, the women are victims of disparate treatment, because they are being treated differently based on their sex. To sustain a claim of discrimination based on disparate treatment, the women would have to prove that the employer intended to discriminate.

To avoid disparate treatment, companies can evaluate the questions and investigations they use in making employment decisions. These should be applied equally. For example, if the company investigates conviction records of job applicants, it should investigate them for all applicants, not just for applicants from certain racial groups. Companies may want to avoid some types of questions altogether. For example, questions about marital status can cause problems, because interviewers may unfairly make different assumptions about men and women. (Common stereotypes about women have been that a married woman is less flexible or more likely to get pregnant than a single woman, in contrast to the assumption that a married man is more stable and committed to his work.)

Sometimes a company can develop a more appropriate approach by focusing on the job requirement behind or implied by a question it would rather not ask. At the Teachers' College of Columbia University in New York, interviewers avoid questions about candidates' child care arrangements. Instead, says Diane Dobry, director of communications for the college, the interviewers discuss the work schedule. Dobry explains, "We say there are evening hours and weekend hours, but we don't ask [candidates] how they'll manage it. It's up to them."[10]

Is disparate treatment ever legal? The courts have held that in some situations, a factor such as sex or race may be a **bona fide occupational qualification (BFOQ)**, that is, a necessary (not merely preferred) qualification for performing a job. A typical example is a job that includes handing out towels in a locker room. Requiring that employees who perform this job in the women's locker room be female is a BFOQ. However, it is very difficult to think of many jobs where criteria such as sex and race

bona fide occupational qualification (BFOQ)
A necessary (not merely preferred) qualification for performing a job.

are BFOQs. In a widely publicized case from the 1990s, Johnson Controls, a manufacturer of car batteries, instituted a "fetal protection" policy that excluded women of childbearing age from jobs that would expose them to lead, which can cause birth defects. Johnson Controls argued that the policy was intended to provide a safe workplace and that sex was a BFOQ for jobs that involved exposure to lead. However, the Supreme Court disagreed, ruling that BFOQs are limited to policies directly related to a worker's ability to do the job.[11]

disparate impact
A condition in which employment practices are seemingly neutral yet disproportionately exclude a protected group from employment opportunities.

four-fifths rule
Rule of thumb that finds evidence of discrimination if an organization's hiring rate for a minority group is less than four-fifths the hiring rate for the majority group.

Disparate Impact

Another way to measure discrimination is by identifying **disparate impact**—a condition in which employment practices are seemingly neutral yet disproportionately exclude a protected group from employment opportunities. In other words, the company's employment practices lack obvious discriminatory content, but they affect one group differently than others. An example is a complaint by police officers and dispatchers in Jackson, Mississippi, that younger workers were receiving higher-percentage pay increases than the department was granting to older workers. Rather than intending to discriminate on the basis of age, the department was trying to bring starting pay into line with that of other police departments, but the policy had a disparate impact on different age groups.[12] A commonly used test of disparate impact is the **four-fifths rule,** which finds evidence of discrimination if the hiring rate for a minority group is less than four-fifths the hiring rate for the majority group. Keep in mind that this rule of thumb compares *rates* of hiring, not numbers of employees hired. Figure 3.4 illustrates how to apply the four-fifths rule.

Figure 3.4

Applying the Four-Fifths Rule

Example: A new hotel has to hire employees to fill 100 positions. Out of 300 total applicants, 200 are black, and the remaining 100 are white. The hotel hires 40 of the black applicants and 60 of the white applicants.

Step 1: Find the Rates

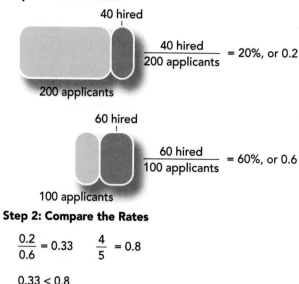

40 hired

$$\frac{40 \text{ hired}}{200 \text{ applicants}} = 20\%, \text{ or } 0.2$$

200 applicants

60 hired

$$\frac{60 \text{ hired}}{100 \text{ applicants}} = 60\%, \text{ or } 0.6$$

100 applicants

Step 2: Compare the Rates

$$\frac{0.2}{0.6} = 0.33 \qquad \frac{4}{5} = 0.8$$

$$0.33 < 0.8$$

The four-fifths requirement is not satisfied, and thus discrimination is proved.

An important distinction between disparate treatment and disparate impact is the role of the employer's intent. Proving disparate treatment in court requires showing that the employer intended the disparate treatment, but a plaintiff need not show intent in the case of disparate impact. It is enough to show that the result of the treatment was unequal. For example, the requirements for some jobs, such as firefighters or pilots, have sometimes included a minimum height. Although the intent may be to identify people who can perform the jobs, an unintended result may be disparate impact on groups that are shorter than average. Women tend to be shorter than men, and people of Asian ancestry tend to be shorter than people of European ancestry.

One way employers can avoid disparate impact is to be sure that employment decisions are really based on relevant, valid measurements. If a job requires a certain amount of strength and stamina, the employer would want measures of strength and stamina, not simply individuals' height and weight. The latter numbers are easier to obtain but more likely to result in charges of discrimination. Assessing validity of a measure can be a highly technical exercise requiring the use of statistics. The essence of such an assessment is to show that test scores or other measurements are significantly related to job performance. In the case of age discrimination, the Supreme Court's recent ruling allows a somewhat easier standard: To justify disparate impact on older employees, the employer must be able to show that the impact results from "reasonable factors other than age."[13] The Jackson police department set up a pay policy to help it recruit new officers, and the Supreme Court considered this plan reasonable.

EEO Policy

Employers can also avoid discrimination and defend against claims of discrimination by establishing and enforcing an EEO policy. The policy should define and prohibit unlawful behaviors, as well as provide procedures for making and investigating complaints. The policy also should require that employees at all levels engage in fair conduct and respectful language. Derogatory language can support a court claim of discrimination.

Affirmative Action and Reverse Discrimination

In the search for ways to avoid discrimination, some organizations have used affirmative-action programs, usually to increase the representation of minorities. In its original form, affirmative action was meant as taking extra effort to attract and retain minority employees. These efforts have included extensively recruiting minority candidates on college campuses, advertising in minority-oriented publications, and providing educational and training opportunities to minorities. However, over the years, many organizations have resorted to quotas, or numerical goals for the proportion of certain minority groups, to ensure that their workforce mirrors the proportions of the labor market. Sometimes these organizations act voluntarily; in other cases, the quotas are imposed by the courts or the EEOC.

Regina Genwright talks to a voice-activated copier at the American Foundation for the Blind. The copier has a Braille keyboard and wheelchair-accessible height. Equipment like this can help employers make reasonable accommodation for their disabled employees.

Whatever the reasons for these hiring programs, by increasing the proportion of minority or female candidates hired or promoted, they necessarily reduce the proportion of white or male candidates hired or promoted. In many cases, white and/or male individuals have fought against affirmative action and quotas, alleging what is called *reverse discrimination.* In other words, the organizations are allegedly discriminating against white males by preferring women and minorities. Affirmative action remains controversial in the United States. Surveys have found that Americans are least likely to favor affirmative action when programs use quotas.[14]

Providing Reasonable Accommodation

reasonable accommodation
An employer's obligation to do something to enable an otherwise qualified person to perform a job.

Especially in situations involving religion and individuals with disabilities, equal employment opportunity may require that an employer make **reasonable accommodation.** In employment law, this term refers to an employer's obligation to do something to enable an otherwise qualified person to perform a job. Electrolux Group recently settled a case in which Muslim workers from Somalia complained they were disciplined for using an unscheduled break as prayer time. Observant Muslims pray five times a day, with two of the prayers offered within restricted time periods (early morning and at sunset). The Electrolux employees observed the sunset prayer by taking an unscheduled break traditionally offered to line employees on an as-needed basis. In the settlement, Electrolux arranged to allow the sunset prayer so that it could accommodate the religious practices of its Muslim workers without creating a business hardship.[15]

In the context of religion, this principle recognizes that for some individuals, religious observations and practices may present a conflict with work duties, dress codes, or company practices. For example, some religions require head coverings, or individuals might need time off to observe the sabbath or other holy days, when the company might have them scheduled to work. When the employee has a legitimate religious belief requiring accommodation, the employee should demonstrate this need to the employer. Assuming that it would not present an undue hardship, employers are required to accommodate such religious practices. They may have to adjust schedules so that employees do not have to work on days when their religion forbids it, or they may have to alter dress or grooming requirements.

For employees with disabilities, reasonable accommodations also vary according to the individuals' needs. As shown in Figure 3.5, employers may restructure jobs, make facilities in the workplace more accessible, modify equipment, or reassign an employee to a job that the person can perform. In some situations, a disabled individual may provide his or her own accommodation, which the employer allows, as in the case of a blind worker who brings a guide dog to work.

If accommodating a disability would require significant expense or difficulty, however, the employer may be exempt from the reasonable accommodation requirement (although the employer may have to defend this position in court). An accommodation is considered "reasonable" if it does not impose an undue hardship on the employer, such as an expense that is large in relation to a company's resources.

sexual harassment
Unwelcome sexual advances as defined by the EEOC.

Preventing Sexual Harassment

LO5 Define sexual harassment, and tell how employers can eliminate or minimize it.

Based on Title VII's prohibition of sex discrimination, the EEOC defines sexual harassment of employees as unlawful employment discrimination. **Sexual harassment** refers to unwelcome sexual advances. The EEOC has defined the types of behavior and the situations under which this behavior constitutes sexual harassment:

Figure 3.5

Examples of Reasonable Accommodations under the ADA

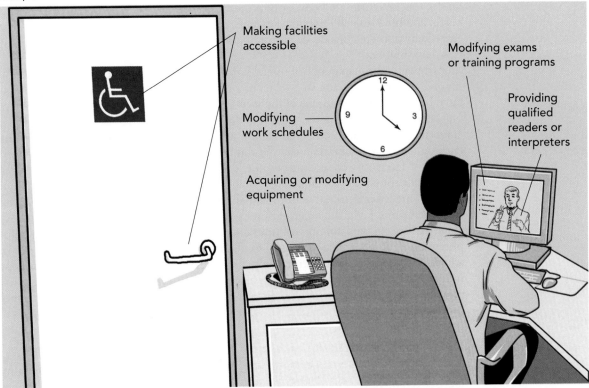

Note: Reasonable accommodations do *not* include hiring an unqualified person, lowering quality standards, or compromising co-workers' safety.

SOURCE: Based on Equal Employment Opportunity Commission, "The ADA: Your Responsibilities as an Employer," www.eeoc.gov, modified March 21, 2005.

Unwelcome sexual advances, requests for sexual favors, and other verbal or physical contact of a sexual nature constitute sexual harassment when

1. Submission to such conduct is made either explicitly or implicitly a term or condition of an individual's employment,
2. Submission to or rejection of such conduct by an individual is used as the basis for employment decisions affecting such individual, or
3. Such conduct has the purpose or effect of unreasonably interfering with an individual's work performance or creating an intimidating, hostile, or offensive working environment.[16]

Under these guidelines, preventing sexual discrimination includes managing the workplace in a way that does not permit anybody to threaten or intimidate employees through sexual behavior.

In general, the most obvious examples of sexual harassment involve *quid pro quo harassment,* meaning that a person makes a benefit (or punishment) contingent on an employee's submitting to (or rejecting) sexual advances. For example, a manager who promises a raise to an employee who will participate in sexual activities is engaging in quid pro quo harassment. Likewise, it would be sexual harassment to threaten to reassign someone to a less desirable job if that person refuses sexual favors.

A more subtle, and possibly more pervasive, form of sexual harassment is to create or permit a "hostile working environment." This occurs when someone's behavior in the workplace creates an environment in which it is difficult for someone of a particular sex to work. Common complaints in sexual harassment lawsuits include claims that harassers ran their fingers through the plaintiffs' hair, made suggestive remarks, touched intimate body parts, posted pictures with sexual content in the workplace, and used sexually explicit language or told sex-related jokes. The reason that these behaviors are considered discrimination is that they treat individuals differently based on their sex.

Although a large majority of sexual harassment complaints received by the EEOC involve women being harassed by men, a growing share of sexual harassment claims have been filed by men. Some of the men claimed that they were harassed by women, but same-sex harassment also occurs and is illegal. Babies "R" Us recently settled a claim in which a male employee said he was subjected to a sexually hostile working environment. He maintained that he was the target of mocking behavior and unwelcome and derogatory comments because he did not conform to society's stereotypes of how a male should appear or behave.[17]

To ensure a workplace free from sexual harassment, organizations can follow some important steps. First, the organization can develop a policy statement making it very clear that sexual harassment will not be tolerated in the workplace. Second, all employees, new and old, can be trained to identify inappropriate workplace behavior. In addition, the organization can develop a mechanism for reporting sexual harassment in a way that encourages people to speak out. Finally, management can prepare to act promptly to discipline those who engage in sexual harassment, as well as to protect the victims of sexual harassment.

Valuing Diversity

As we mentioned in Chapter 2, the United States is a diverse nation, and becoming more so. In addition, many U.S. companies have customers and operations in more than one country. Managers differ in how they approach the challenges related to this diversity. Some define a diverse workforce as a competitive advantage that brings them a wider pool of talent and greater insight into the needs and behaviors of their diverse customers. These organizations say they have a policy of *valuing diversity*.

The practice of valuing diversity has no single form; it is not written into law or business theory. Organizations that value diversity may practice some form of affirmative action, discussed earlier. They may have policies stating their value of understanding and respecting differences. Organizations may try to hire, reward, and promote employees who demonstrate respect for others. They may sponsor training programs designed to teach employees about differences among groups. Whatever their form, these efforts are intended to make each individual feel respected. The "Best Practices" box provides an example. Also, these actions can support equal employment opportunity by cultivating an environment in which individuals feel welcome and able to do their best.

Occupational Safety and Health Act (OSH Act)
U.S. law authorizing the federal government to establish and enforce occupational safety and health standards for all places of employment engaging in interstate commerce.

LO6 Explain employers' duties under the Occupational Safety and Health Act.

Occupational Safety and Health Act (OSH Act)

Like equal employment opportunity, the protection of employee safety and health is regulated by the government. Through the 1960s, workplace safety was primarily an issue between workers and employers. By 1970, however, roughly 15,000 work-related fatalities occurred every year. That year, Congress enacted the **Occupational Safety and Health Act (OSH Act),** the most comprehensive U.S. law regarding worker safety. The OSH Act authorized the federal government to establish and enforce occupational safety and health standards for all places of employment engaging in interstate commerce.

Best Practices

Valuing Diversity at JPMorgan Chase

JPMorgan Chase, a global financial-services firm, has 170,000 employees in more than 50 countries. The company has won awards for its commitment to diversity, but CEO Jamie Dimon says diversity is valued simply because it benefits the company: "Our collective diversity is our strength."

Diversity at JPMorgan is defined as all the qualities that individuals possess, including primary characteristics such as age, gender, and ethnic heritage, as well as secondary characteristics such as work experience, work style, religion, and economic status. To create an inclusive environment, the company sponsors employee networking groups serving employees with disabilities, administrative staff, employees concerned about balancing family and career demands, employees from various ethnic groups, and lesbian, gay, bisexual, and transgender employees. The company also holds diversity events around the world to increase understanding and foster professional development. And recruiting events, internships, and partnerships with professional associations aim to reach a diverse pool of candidates.

One employee who has been able to thrive at JPMorgan is Amita Mehta, the firm's diversity manager and the HR department's liaison to the company's Asian employees. Mehta helps her company understand how qualities of Asian cultures may affect how Asian employees interact with management and coworkers. For example, she points out that many Asian cultures value group more than individual achievements, so an Asian employee might avoid displaying his or her individual accomplishments. Respecting their boss's position, they may tend to avoid bragging or frank comments, especially during performance appraisals. Learning about such cultural patterns can help managers and employees notice situations where they may need to gather accurate performance information, rather than waiting for employees to speak up.

Another JPMorgan employee who has experienced the value placed on diversity is credit underwriter Lina Sayed. Sayed asked her boss to help her find a space where she could fulfill the Muslim obligation of praying five times a day. They worked with the HR department to identify a suitable location. Sayed also has found that her colleagues respect her fast during the Muslim holy month of Ramadan, scheduling meetings with this requirement in mind. Sayed says, "When you're open about things and people can ask questions, it's less likely they'll be discriminatory."

Sources: Rebecca R. Hastings, "The Forgotten Minority," *HRMagazine,* July 2007, General Reference Center Gold, http://find.galegroup.com; Yoji Cole, "Six Years after September 11, Muslims See More Inclusive Workplaces," *DiversityInc.,* September 11, 2007, http://diversityinc.com; and JPMorgan Chase, "About Us" and "Careers: Diversity," www.jpmorganchase.com, accessed January 3, 2008.

The OSH Act divided enforcement responsibilities between the Department of Labor and the Department of Health. Under the Department of Labor, the **Occupational Safety and Health Administration (OSHA)** is responsible for inspecting employers, applying safety and health standards, and levying fines for violation. The Department of Health is responsible for conducting research to determine the criteria for specific operations or occupations and for training employers to comply with the act. Much of the research is conducted by the National Institute for Occupational Safety and Health (NIOSH).

General and Specific Duties

The main provision of the OSH Act states that each employer has a general duty to furnish each employee a place of employment free from recognized hazards that cause or are likely to cause death or serious physical harm. This is called the act's *general-duty clause*. Employers also must keep records of work-related injuries and illnesses and post an annual summary of these records from February 1 to April 30 in the following year. Figure 3.6 shows a sample of OSHA's Form 300A, the annual summary that must be posted, even if no injuries or illnesses occurred.

Occupational Safety and Health Administration (OSHA) Labor Department agency responsible for inspecting employers, applying safety and health standards, and levying fines for violation.

LO7 Describe the role of the Occupational Safety and Health Administration.

Figure 3.6

OSHA Form 300A: Summary of Work-Related Injuries and Illnesses

OSHA's Form 300A

Summary of Work-Related Injuries and Illnesses

Year 20___

U.S. Department of Labor
Occupational Safety and Health Administration

Form approved OMB no. 1218-0176

All establishments covered by Part 1904 must complete this Summary page, even if no work-related injuries or illnesses occurred during the year. Remember to review the Log to verify that the entries are complete and accurate before completing this summary.

Using the Log, count the individual entries you made for each category. Then write the totals below, making sure you've added the entries from every page of the Log. If you had no cases, write "0."

Employees, former employees, and their representatives have the right to review the OSHA Form 300 in its entirety. They also have limited access to the OSHA Form 301 or its equivalent. See 29 CFR Part 1904.35, in OSHA's recordkeeping rule, for further details on the access provisions for these forms.

Number of Cases

Total number of deaths	Total number of cases with days away from work	Total number of cases with job transfer or restriction	Total number of other recordable cases
_____ (G)	_____ (H)	_____ (I)	_____ (J)

Number of Days

Total number of days of job transfer or restriction	Total number of days away from work
_____ (K)	_____ (L)

Injury and Illness Types

Total number of . . .
(M)

(1) Injuries _____

(2) Skin disorders _____

(3) Respiratory conditions _____

(4) Poisonings _____

(5) All other illnesses _____

Establishment information

Your establishment name _____

Street _____

City _____ State _____ ZIP _____

Industry description (e.g., Manufacture of motor truck trailers) _____

Standard Industrial Classification (SIC), if known (e.g., SIC 3715) _____

Employment information (If you don't have these figures, see the Worksheet on the back of this page to estimate.)

Annual average number of employees _____

Total hours worked by all employees last year _____

Sign here

Knowingly falsifying this document may result in a fine.

I certify that I have examined this document and that to the best of my knowledge the entries are true, accurate, and complete.

Company executive _____ Title _____

Phone (___) _____ Date __ / __ / __

Post this Summary page from February 1 to April 30 of the year following the year covered by the form.

Public reporting burden for this collection of information is estimated to average 50 minutes per response, including time to review the instructions, search and gather the data needed, and complete and review the collection of information. Persons are not required to respond to the collection of information unless it displays a currently valid OMB control number. If you have any comments about these estimates or any other aspects of this data collection, contact: US Department of Labor, OSHA Office of Statistics, Room N-3644, 200 Constitution Avenue, NW, Washington, DC 20210. Do not send the completed forms to this office.

HR How To

OFF TO A SAFE START

Starting a new business usually entails long hours for the owners and managers. It's no wonder, when you think of all the issues involved—raising money, finding a place to work, crafting the details of a business plan, hiring all the employees. And regardless of whether the business will manufacture goods or consist entirely of office workers, the government expects that the owners will address health and safety issues from the very start.

OSHA regulations have a (sometimes justifiable) reputation for being complex and difficult to follow. But the agency has prepared materials designed to help businesses succeed. A good place to begin is to visit the agency's Web site (www.osha.gov), where you can find helpful links, including the *Small Business Handbook* and a step-by-step guide called Compliance Assistance Quick Start. The General Industry Quick Start leads new-business owners step by step through the basics of OSHA

requirements, including links to the necessary forms.

When planning the setup of operations, new-business owners should also be planning how to keep their employees safe. According to OSHA, employers should have an Emergency Action Plan that describes what workers should do in case of a fire or other emergency. The workplace must have exit routes, and workers should know the routes. Employers also must identify any hazardous chemicals used in the workplace to provide information about those chemicals. Planning should identify potential hazards and determine whether any can be eliminated. Avoiding hazards may be as simple as arranging rooms so that electrical cords do not cause accidents.

Employers must display OSHA's Safe and Healthful Workplaces poster in a location where it is conspicuous to employees and job candidates. The poster tells about employees' rights and responsibilities under the OSH Act.

New-business owners must obtain copies of OSHA's Log of Work-Related Injuries and Illnesses. Recording any work-related injuries and illnesses on the log is another duty under the OSH Act. (Some businesses, such as employers in many services industries, are exempt, however.)

Employers may request free and confidential on-site consultations to help them identify and correct hazards. Several OSHA training centers conduct courses related to worker safety and health. At the OSHA Web site, employers can download interactive training materials on general and specific topics related to occupational safety and health.

By getting off to a safe start, employers help to create an environment in which employees recognize safety and health as important values of the organization.

Source: Occupational Safety and Health Administration, "Compliance Assistance Quick Start," www.osha.gov, updated November 6, 2007.

The act also grants specific rights; for example, employees have the right to:

- Request an inspection.
- Have a representative present at an inspection.
- Have dangerous substances identified.
- Be promptly informed about exposure to hazards and be given access to accurate records regarding exposure.
- Have employer violations posted at the work site.

The above "HR How To" box summarizes key points from OSHA's guidance on how new companies can ensure that they follow these requirements.

The Department of Labor recognizes many specific types of hazards, and employers must comply with all the occupational safety and health standards published by NIOSH. NIOSH has, for instance, determined that a noise level of 85 decibels (comparable to the noise of heavy city traffic) is potentially dangerous. A person exposed to this much noise over a long enough period of time could experience hearing loss as

OSHA is responsible for inspecting businesses, applying safety and health standards, and levying fines for violations. OSHA regulations prohibit notifying employers of inspections in advance.

a result. Researchers in San Francisco measured noise levels at five local restaurants and found that the levels reached 85 decibels and often reached 105 decibels. Such levels could be a health risk for waiters working in the restaurant for eight hours at a time. Employers could respond in a number of ways, from permitting ear plugs to educating workers to reconsidering restaurant design (large bars, open kitchens, and high ceilings are a number of features that intensify noise levels).[18]

Although NIOSH publishes numerous standards, it is impossible for regulators to anticipate all possible hazards that could occur in the workplace. Thus, the general-duty clause requires employers to be constantly alert for potential sources of harm in the workplace (as defined by the standard of what a reasonably prudent person would do) and to correct them. Information about hazards can come from employees or from outside researchers. A recent study found that health care workers are unusually likely to develop work-related asthma. The researchers found that the disease occurred because the workers were frequently exposed to latex and disinfectants known to cause asthma. They also worked around asthma-aggravating materials, including cleaning products and materials used in renovating buildings. Hospitals and other health care providers can protect their workers from asthma by substituting nonlatex or powder-free gloves for powdered latex gloves. They also can be more selective in their use of disinfectants.[19]

Enforcement of the OSH Act

To enforce the OSH Act, the Occupational Safety and Health Administration conducts inspections. OSHA compliance officers typically arrive at a workplace unannounced; for obvious reasons, OSHA regulations prohibit notifying employers of inspections in advance. After presenting credentials, the compliance officer tells the employer the reasons for the inspection and describes, in a general way, the procedures necessary to conduct the investigation.

An OSHA inspection has four major components. First, the compliance officer reviews the company's records of deaths, injuries, and illnesses. OSHA requires this kind of record keeping at all firms with 11 or more full- or part-time employees. Next, the officer—typically accompanied by a representative of the employer (and perhaps by a representative of the employees)—conducts a "walkaround" tour of the employer's premises. On this tour, the officer notes any conditions that may violate specific published standards or the less specific general-duty clause. The third component of the inspection, employee interviews, may take place during the tour. At this time, anyone who is aware of a violation can bring it to the officer's attention. Finally, in a closing conference, the compliance officer discusses the findings with the employer, noting any violations.

Following an inspection, OSHA gives the employer a reasonable time frame within which to correct the violations identified. If a violation could cause serious injury or death, the officer may seek a restraining order from a U.S. District Court. The restraining order compels the employer to correct the problem immediately. In addition, if an OSHA violation results in citations, the employer must post each citation in a prominent place near the location of the violation.

Besides correcting violations identified during the inspection, employers may have to pay fines. These fines range from $20,000 for violations that result in death of an employee to $1,000 for less serious violations. Other penalties include criminal charges for falsifying records that are subject to OSHA inspection or for warning an employer of an OSHA inspection without permission from the Department of Labor.

Employee Rights and Responsibilities

Although the OSH Act makes employers responsible for protecting workers from safety and health hazards, employees have responsibilities as well. They have to follow OSHA's safety rules and regulations governing employee behavior. Employees also have a duty to report hazardous conditions.

Along with those responsibilities go certain rights. Employees may file a complaint and request an OSHA inspection of the workplace, and their employers may not retaliate against them for complaining. Employees also have a right to receive information about any hazardous chemicals they handle in the course of their jobs. OSHA's Hazard Communication Standard and many states' **right-to-know laws** require employers to provide employees with information about the health risks associated with exposure to substances considered hazardous. State right-to-know laws may be more stringent than federal standards, so organizations should obtain requirements from their state's health and safety agency, as well as from OSHA.

Under OSHA's Hazard Communication Standard, organizations must have **material safety data sheets (MSDSs)** for chemicals that employees are exposed to. An MSDS is a form that details the hazards associated with a chemical; the chemical's producer or importer is responsible for identifying these hazards and detailing them on the form. Employers must also ensure that all containers of hazardous chemicals are labeled with information about the hazards, and they must train employees in safe handling of the chemicals. Office workers who encounter a chemical infrequently (such as a secretary who occasionally changes the toner in a copier) are not covered by these requirements. In the case of a copy machine, the Hazard Communication Standard would apply to someone whose job involves spending a large part of the day servicing or operating such equipment.

right-to-know laws
State laws that require employers to provide employees with information about the health risks associated with exposure to substances considered hazardous.

material safety data sheets (MSDSs)
Forms on which chemical manufacturers and importers identify the hazards of their chemicals.

Impact of the OSH Act

The OSH Act has unquestionably succeeded in raising the level of awareness of occupational safety. Yet legislation alone cannot solve all the problems of work site safety. Indeed, the rate of occupational illnesses more than doubled between 1985 and 1990, according to the Bureau of Labor Statistics, while the rate of injuries rose by about 8 percent. However, as depicted in Figure 3.7, both rates have shown an overall downward trend since then.[20] The "Did You Know?" box shows the leading causes of injuries at work in 2004.

Many industrial accidents are a product of unsafe behaviors, not unsafe working conditions. Because the act does not directly regulate employee behavior, little behavior change can be expected unless employees are convinced of the standards' importance.[21]

Figure 3.7

Rates of Occupational
Injuries and Illnesses

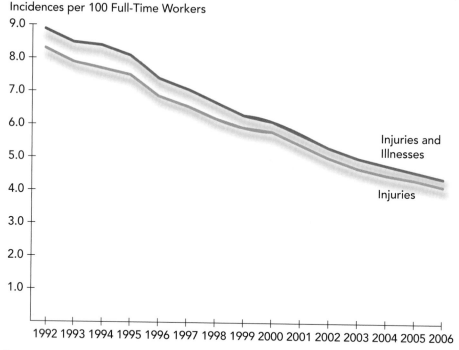

Incidences per 100 Full-Time Workers

Note: Data do not include fatal work-related injuries and illnesses.

SOURCE: Bureau of Labor Statistics, "Industry, Injury, and Illness Data," www.bls.gov, accessed March 31, 2005.

Conforming to the law alone does not necessarily guarantee their employees will be safe, so many employers go beyond the letter of the law. In the next section we examine various kinds of employer-initiated safety awareness programs that comply with OSHA requirements and, in some cases, exceed them.

LO8 Discuss ways employers promote worker safety and health.

Employer-Sponsored Safety and Health Programs

Many employers establish safety awareness programs to go beyond mere compliance with the OSH Act and attempt to instill an emphasis on safety. A safety awareness program has three primary components: identifying and communicating hazards, reinforcing safe practices, and promoting safety internationally.

job hazard analysis technique
Safety promotion technique that involves breaking down a job into basic elements, then rating each element for its potential for harm or injury.

Identifying and Communicating Job Hazards

Employees, supervisors, and other knowledgeable sources need to sit down and discuss potential problems related to safety. One method for doing this is the **job hazard analysis technique.**[22] With this technique, each job is broken down into basic elements, and each of these is rated for its potential for harm or injury. If there is agreement that some job element has high hazard potential, the group isolates the element and considers possible technological or behavior changes to reduce or eliminate the hazard.

Did You Know?

Top 10 Causes of Workplace Injuries

Every year, Liberty Mutual conducts research it calls the Workplace Safety Index. In 2004, serious work-related injuries cost employers $48.6 billion. The leading cause was overexertion (for example, excessive lifting, pushing, carrying, or throwing), followed by falls on the same level (rather than from a height, such as a ladder), and bodily reaction (injury from movements such as bending, climbing, or slipping).

Source: Liberty Mutual, "2006 Liberty Mutual Workplace Safety Index," www.libertymutual.com.

10 leading causes of workplace injuries in 2004

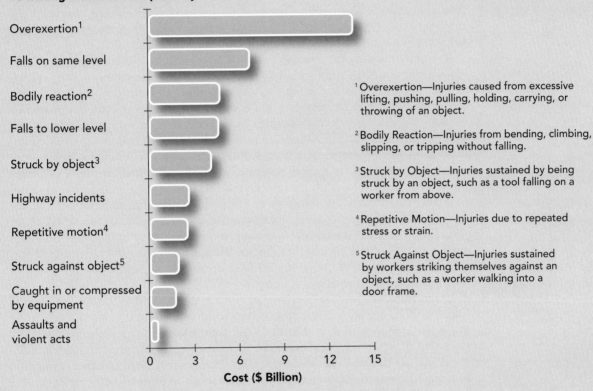

[1] Overexertion—Injuries caused from excessive lifting, pushing, pulling, holding, carrying, or throwing of an object.

[2] Bodily Reaction—Injuries from bending, climbing, slipping, or tripping without falling.

[3] Struck by Object—Injuries sustained by being struck by an object, such as a tool falling on a worker from above.

[4] Repetitive Motion—Injuries due to repeated stress or strain.

[5] Struck Against Object—Injuries sustained by workers striking themselves against an object, such as a worker walking into a door frame.

Another means of isolating unsafe job elements is to study past accidents. The **technic of operations review (TOR)** is an analysis method for determining which specific element of a job led to a past accident.[23] The first step in a TOR analysis is to establish the facts surrounding the incident. To accomplish this, all members of the work group involved in the accident give their initial impressions of what happened. The group must then, through discussion, come to an agreement on the single, systematic failure that most likely contributed to the incident, as well as two or three major secondary factors that contributed to it.

United Parcel Service combined job analysis with employee empowerment to reduce injury rates dramatically. Concerned about the many sprains, strains, and other injuries experienced by its workers, UPS set up Comprehensive Health and Safety

technic of operations review (TOR)
Method of promoting safety by determining which specific element of a job led to a past accident.

Process (CHSP) committees that bring together management and nonmanagement employees. Each committee investigates and reports on accidents, conducts audits of facilities and equipment, and advises employees on how to perform their jobs more safely. For example, the committees make sure delivery people know safe practices for lifting packages and backing up trucks. Whenever committee members see someone behaving unsafely, they are required to intervene. Since the CHSP committees began their work, the injury rate at UPS has fallen from over 27 injuries per 200,000 hours worked to just 10.2 injuries per 200,000, well on the way to the company's target injury rate of 3.2.[24]

To communicate with employees about job hazards, managers should talk directly with their employees about safety. Memos also are important, because the written communication helps establish a "paper trail" that can later document a history of the employer's concern regarding the job hazard. Posters, especially if placed near the hazard, serve as a constant reminder, reinforcing other messages.

In communicating risk, managers should recognize that different groups of individuals may constitute different audiences. Women and immigrants may be vulnerable in some situations, but for different reasons.[25] Certain jobs that are highly repetitive—for example, cashiers and administrative support—are dominated by women, who are therefore vulnerable to repetitive-strain injuries such as carpal tunnel syndrome. In addition, until recently, most of the personal protective equipment available for workers was designed to fit male bodies. When equipment does not fit properly, workers are less motivated to wear it, and they may have difficulty performing their jobs safely and accurately. Immigrants are vulnerable to safety problems when there are language or cultural barriers that make it difficult for them to learn safety procedures, question situations that sound unsafe, or ask about tasks they don't understand fully. On a supplemental form to OSHA Form 300, the agency has begun asking whether language was a barrier to safety. Because of this risk, efforts to improve communication in organizations benefit safety as well as motivation and productivity.

Other workers who may be at higher risk are at each end of the age spectrum.[26] Older workers are more likely than others to submit disability claims, and if they are injured, they tend to be absent longer than their younger colleagues. Conditions that may put older workers at risk include vision and hearing changes and decreases in coordination and balance. Organizations may need to make reasonable accommodations in response to such changes, both to protect their employees and to meet the challenges of an aging workforce, described in Chapter 2. With young workers, the safety challenge is to protect them from risk taking. Young workers may be especially eager to please the adults they work with, and they may be more fearful than their older colleagues when safety requires challenging authority. Employees who are new to the workforce may not be aware of the health and safety laws that are supposed to protect them. Research by the National Safety Council indicates that 40 percent of accidents happen to individuals in the 20-to-29 age group and that 48 percent of accidents happen to workers during their first year on the job.[27]

Reinforcing Safe Practices

To ensure safe behaviors, employers should not only define how to work safely but reinforce the desired behavior. One common technique for reinforcing safe practices is implementing a safety incentive program to reward workers for their support of and commitment to safety goals. Such programs start by focusing on monthly or quarterly goals or by encouraging suggestions for improving safety. Possible goals might include good housekeeping practices, adherence to safety rules, and proper use of protective equipment. Later, the program expands to include more wide-ranging, long-term goals. Typically, the employer distributes prizes in highly public forums, such as company or department meetings. Using merchandise for prizes, instead of cash, provides a lasting symbol of achievement. A good deal of evidence suggests that such incentive programs are effective in reducing the number and cost of injuries.[28]

Besides focusing on specific jobs, organizations can target particular types of injuries or disabilities, especially those for which employees may be at risk. For example, Prevent Blindness America estimates that 2,000 eye injuries occur every day in occupational settings.[29] Organizations can prevent such injuries through a combination of job analysis, written policies, safety training, protective eyewear, rewards and sanctions for safe and unsafe behavior, and management support for the safety effort. Similar practices for preventing other types of injuries are available in trade publications, through the National Safety Council, and on the Web site of the Occupational Safety and Health Administration (www.osha.gov).

Promoting Safety Internationally

Given the increasing focus on international management, organizations also need to consider how to ensure the safety of their employees regardless of the nation in which they operate. Cultural differences may make this more difficult than it seems. For example, a study examined the impact of one standardized corporationwide safety policy on employees in three different countries: the United States, France, and Argentina. The results of this study indicate that employees in the three countries interpreted the policy differently because of cultural differences. The individualistic, control-oriented culture of the United States stressed the role of top management in ensuring safety in a top-down fashion. However, this policy failed to work in Argentina, where the culture is more "collectivist" (emphasizing the group). Argentine employees tend to feel that safety is everyone's joint concern, so the safety programs needed to be defined from the bottom of the organization up.[30]

Another challenge in promoting safety internationally is that laws, enforcement practices, and political climates vary from country to country. With the increasing use of offshoring, described in Chapter 2, more companies have operations in countries where labor standards are far less strict than U.S. standards. Managers and employees in these countries may not think the company is serious about protecting workers' health and safety. In that case, strong communication and oversight will be necessary if the company intends to adhere to the ethical principle of valuing its foreign workers' safety as much as the safety of its U.S. workers. In an extreme example, Unocal Corporation recently settled a lawsuit in which people near a natural-gas pipeline in Myanmar (formerly Burma) said they were forced into slave labor and victimized by other crimes, including rape by soldiers guarding the pipeline. Unocal—which has since been acquired by ChevronTexaco—was one partner in the pipeline venture and agreed it would compensate those who sued and also contribute to aid programs providing health care and education in the region.[31] Although this type of situation might be unthinkable in North America, companies that wish to operate globally have to consider the extent to which they have ethical as well as legal obligations toward their workers and communities.

THINKING ETHICALLY

A HOSTILE ENVIRONMENT AT MADISON SQUARE GARDEN

Anucha Browne Sanders recently won a civil trial in which she claimed she had been sexually and verbally harassed at work by Isiah Thomas, coach of the New York Knicks. (Thomas has since been reassigned to other duties.) Also, the jury agreed, when Browne Sanders complained to her managers at Madison Square Garden (home of the Knicks), they retaliated against her by firing her.

Browne Sanders was awarded $11.6 million, but the Garden also paid with its reputation. During the course of the testimony, the public heard about the quick temper of the Garden's chairman, James Dolan, and the culture of an organization that tried to meet Dolan's every whim. The very decision to go to trial, rather than settle Browne Sanders's case quietly, raised questions about management's judgment. Testimony during the trial described an environment in which crude language was routine.

Since the trial, employees of the New York Rangers and Memphis Grizzlies have also indicated they were sexually harassed at the Garden. More lawsuits are possible.

SOURCE: Selena Roberts, "The Garden Needs a Warning Label," *New York Times*, October 3, 2007, www.nytimes.com; and Jeremy Smerd, "The 'Big' News Stories That Weren't," *Workforce Management*, December 10, 2007, downloaded from General Reference Center Gold, http://find.galegroup.com.

Questions

1. Can a commitment to ethics make illegal behavior less likely? How does this example illustrate the legal risks of failing to create an ethical climate?
2. How can human resource management help create an environment that promotes ethical treatment of diverse coworkers and discourages harassment?

SUMMARY

LO1 Explain how the three branches of government regulate human resource management.

The legislative branch develops laws such as those governing equal employment opportunity and worker safety and health. The executive branch establishes agencies such as the Equal Employment Opportunity Commission and Occupational Safety and Health Administration to enforce the laws by publishing regulations, filing lawsuits, and performing other activities. The president may also issue executive orders, such as requirements for federal contractors. The judicial branch hears cases related to employment law and interprets the law.

LO2 Summarize the major federal laws requiring equal employment opportunity.

The Civil Rights Acts of 1866 and 1871 grants all persons equal property rights, contract rights, and the right to sue in federal court if they have been deprived of civil rights. The Equal Pay Act of 1963 requires equal pay for men and women who are doing work that is equal in terms of skill, effort, responsibility, and working conditions. Title VII of the Civil Rights Act of 1964 prohibits employment discrimination on the basis of race, color, religion, sex, or national origin. The Age Discrimination in Employment Act prohibits employment discrimination against persons older than 40. The Vocational Rehabilitation Act of 1973 requires that federal contractors engage in affirmative action in the employment of persons with disabilities. The Vietnam Era Veteran's Readjustment Act of 1974 requires affirmative action in employment of veterans who served during the Vietnam War. The Pregnancy Discrimination Act of 1978 treats discrimination based on pregnancy-related conditions as illegal sex discrimination. The Americans with Disabilities Act requires reasonable accommodations for qualified workers with disabilities. The Civil Rights Act of 1991 provides for compensatory and punitive damages in cases of discrimination. The Uniformed Services Employment and Reemployment Rights Act of 1994 requires that employers reemploy service members who left jobs to fulfill military duties.

LO3 Identify the federal agencies that enforce equal employment opportunity, and describe the role of each.

The Equal Employment Opportunity Commission is responsible for enforcing most of the EEO laws, including Title VII and the Americans with Disabilities Act. It investigates and resolves complaints, gathers information, and issues guidelines. The Office of Federal Contract Compliance Procedures is responsible for enforcing executive orders that call for affirmative action by companies that do business with the federal government. It monitors affirmative-action plans and takes action against companies that fail to comply.

LO4 Describe ways employers can avoid illegal discrimination and provide reasonable accommodation.

Employers can avoid discrimination by avoiding disparate treatment of job applicants and employees, as well as policies that result in disparate impact. Companies can develop and enforce an EEO policy coupled with policies and practices that demonstrate a high value placed on diversity. Affirmative action may correct past discrimination, but quota-based activities can result in charges of reverse discrimination. To provide reasonable accommodation, companies should recognize needs based on individuals' religion or disabilities. Employees may need to make such accommodations as adjusting schedules or dress codes, making the workplace more accessible, or restructuring jobs.

LO5 Define sexual harassment, and tell how employers can eliminate or minimize it.

Sexual harassment is unwelcome sexual advances and related behavior that makes submitting to the conduct a term of employment or the basis for employment decisions, or that interferes with an individual's work performance or creates a work environment that is intimidating, hostile, or offensive. Organizations can prevent sexual harassment by developing a policy that defines and forbids it, training employees to recognize and avoid this behavior, and providing a means for employees to complain and be protected.

LO6 Explain employers' duties under the Occupational Safety and Health Act.

Under the Occupational Safety and Health Act, employers have a general duty to provide employees a place of employment free from recognized safety and health hazards. They must inform employees about hazardous substances, maintain and post records of accidents and illnesses, and comply with NIOSH standards about specific occupational hazards.

LO7 Describe the role of the Occupational Safety and Health Administration.

The Occupational Safety and Health Administration publishes regulations and conducts inspections. If OSHA finds violations, it discusses them with the employer and monitors the employer's response in correcting the violation.

LO8 Discuss ways employers promote worker safety and health.

Besides complying with OSHA regulations, employers often establish safety awareness programs designed to instill an emphasis on safety. They may identify and communicate hazards through the job hazard analysis technique or the technic of operations review. They may adapt communications and training to the needs of different employees, such as differences in experience levels or cultural differences from one country to another. Employers may also establish incentive programs to reward safe behavior.

KEY TERMS

affirmative action, p. 62
bona fide occupational qualification (BFOQ), p. 69
disability, p. 63
disparate impact, p. 70
disparate treatment, p. 68
EEO-1 report, p. 67
equal employment opportunity (EEO), p. 58

Equal Employment Opportunity Commission (EEOC), p. 60
four-fifths rule, p. 70
job hazard analysis technique, p. 80
material safety data sheets (MSDSs), p. 79
Occupational Safety and Health Act (OSH Act), p. 74
Occupational Safety and Health Administration (OSHA), p. 75

Office of Federal Contract Compliance Procedures (OFCCP), p. 67
reasonable accommodation, p. 72
right-to-know laws, p. 79
sexual harassment, p. 72
technic of operations review (TOR), p. 81
Uniform Guidelines on Employee Selection Procedures, p. 67

REVIEW AND DISCUSSION QUESTIONS

1. What is the role of each branch of the federal government with regard to equal employment opportunity?
2. For each of the following situations, identify one or more constitutional amendments, laws, or executive orders that might apply.
   a. A veteran of the Vietnam conflict experiences lower-back pain after sitting for extended periods

   of time. He has applied for promotion to a supervisory position that has traditionally involved spending most of the workday behind a desk.
   b. One of two female workers on a road construction crew complains to her supervisor that she feels uncomfortable during breaks, because the other employees routinely tell off-color jokes.

c. A manager at an architectural firm receives a call from the local newspaper. The reporter wonders how the firm wishes to respond to calls from two of its employees alleging racial discrimination. About half of the firm's employees (including all of its partners and most of its architects) are white. One of the firm's clients is the federal government.

3. For each situation in the preceding question, what actions, if any, should the organization take?

4. The Americans with Disabilities Act requires that employers make reasonable accommodations for individuals with disabilities. How might this requirement affect law enforcement officers and fire fighters?

5. To identify instances of sexual harassment, the courts may use a "reasonable woman" standard of what constitutes offensive behavior. This standard is based on the idea that women and men have different ideas of what behavior is appropriate. What are the implications of this distinction? Do you think this distinction is helpful or harmful? Why?

6. Given that the "reasonable woman" standard referred to in Question 5 is based on women's ideas of what is appropriate, how might an organization with mostly male employees identify and avoid behavior that could be found to be sexual harassment?

7. What are an organization's basic duties under the Occupational Safety and Health Act?

8. OSHA penalties are aimed at employers, rather than employees. How does this affect employee safety?

9. How can organizations motivate employees to promote safety and health in the workplace?

10. For each of the following occupations, identify at least one possible hazard and at least one action employers could take to minimize the risk of an injury or illness related to that hazard.
   a. Worker in a fast-food restaurant
   b. Computer programmer
   c. Truck driver
   d. House painter

BUSINESSWEEK CASE

BusinessWeek HOW TO HEAL A SICK OFFICE

Ever since cubicles sprouted up in office buildings 40 years ago, inhabitants have been under assault. Chemicals in carpet glue, cleaning supplies, and printer cartridges can cause headaches, dizziness, lethargy, rashes, nausea, and respiratory irritation. This could be solved by pumping in lots of fresh air, but the windows in most modern office buildings are sealed shut. Then there's the space allocation: A typical office worker gets about 40 square feet—less than a third as much as in the 1970s. Dozens of studies have documented the toll all this takes on body and mind. How are we ever going to blossom into globally networked, branded superstars while trapped in shrinking cubicle farms bathed in foul fumes?

The fix may be simpler than you think. Healing sick offices is generally a matter of replacing synthetic materials with natural alternatives, improving the flow of fresh air, and letting some natural light shine in. Healthy options—including clever techniques for pumping sunlight deep into a building's recesses—are proliferating. And while it's hard right now to know which microscopic evils may be lurking in your cubicle, the next decade will bring cheap consumer tests for airborne toxins and pathogens. Scientists are also working on newfangled materials to mix into coatings that can suck toxins out of the air.

But don't wait for these magic developments. Managers who start cleaning and brightening up their employees' workspaces right away can expect to be rewarded with lower costs, fewer incidences of illness and absenteeism, higher productivity, and the recruitment of better-qualified staff. A 2003 study of call centers found that workers with window views processed calls 6 to 12 percent faster, performed up to 25 percent better on mental acuity tests, and reported fewer health problems than their peers in conventionally lit spaces.

Businesses that do right by cubicle dwellers may also find that they're doing good for the environment. That will bring benefits down the road. Letting in more natural light cuts a company's energy consumption, and that matters to earth-conscious job seekers. In a study by office goods supplier Corporate Express, 64 percent of workers—from the mail room to the executive suite—said their decision to work for a company is guided in part by its green practices.

Here are some of the things that sap health and morale in the work space, and ways to make them better:

- Lighting
  Problem: Compared with natural light, fluorescent tubes can drain productivity.
  Fix: Skylights from Ciralight and others use mirrors to track the sun and deliver more rays. Pairing them with sensors that dim overhead fixtures can cut lighting bills by up to 75 percent.
- Cleaning agents
  Problem: A big office building may release tons of toxic chemicals from cleansers into the workplace each year.

Fix: Several companies are rolling out new lines of plant-based cleaners for carpets, glass, and other surfaces.

- Carpets and fabrics
Problem: Rugs harbor molds and fungi, and glues that anchor them to the floor emit fumes.
Fix: To replace glue, Interface devised TacTiles, hand-sized adhesive squares that connect carpet titles to one another, but not directly to the floor. It also makes a natural agent from phosphoric acid and coconut oil to stop molds.

- Furniture
Problem: Formaldehyde is a common ingredient in processed woods used in office furniture.
Fix: Green desks and dividers from Steelcase, Knoll, and others are made from sunflower husks, wheat straw, and nontoxic wood products.

- Electronics
Problem: Some laser printers and copiers emit ozone, volatile organic compounds, and ultrafine toner specks that can damage lung tissue.
Fix: Move office equipment into well-ventilated areas away from desks.

SOURCE: Adam Aston, "How to Heal a Sick Office," *BusinessWeek*, August 20, 2007, downloaded from General Reference Center Gold, http://find. galegroup.com.

Questions

1. Do you agree with the idea that workplace safety and health are an important concern for offices, not just manufacturing and construction sites? Why or why not?
2. Should HR managers raise the issue of healthy offices, or should they wait for employees to complain about specific problems? Why?

CASE: EMC CONFRONTS HARASSMENT CHARGES

Since 2003, at least half a dozen lawsuits have been filed against EMC Corporation, based in Hopkinton, Massachusetts, claiming the company discriminated against female employees. Recently, two former EMC saleswomen asked that their suit be given class-action status. EMC, which provides software for information management, denies that the company tolerates discrimination or sexual harassment.

According to the complaints in the lawsuits, EMC subjected saleswomen to demeaning sexual comments, company-paid trips to strip clubs, and retaliation against women who complained. Three women said managers took away accounts they had built up and gave them to male colleagues. One woman said her boss wouldn't give her a big account because she refused to "smoke, drink, swear, hunt, fish, and tolerate strip clubs." The law firm requesting the class action gathered 30 sworn affidavits from saleswomen supporting allegations that the workplace was hostile and discriminatory.

Pay data show that saleswomen at EMC have earned less than salesmen with the same length of experience. During one year, for salespeople with two to three years of service, the women's median pay was $266,063, compared with $305,417 for men. EMC responds that the pay gap reflects differences in performance. The lawsuits include claims that employment decisions were based in part on consideration of individuals' sex, pregnancy, and marital and parental status.

One problem may be that women are poorly represented at EMC. While 40 percent of the sales force is female at IBM, another big software company, just 13.5 percent of EMC's salespeople are women. Gillian Thomas, a lawyer for a women's legal-rights association called Legal Momentum, says, "Hostile environments for women tend to occur where they're dramatically in the minority." At EMC, salespeople traditionally have been recruited from among former college athletes, and the culture is aggressive. Salespeople call clients daily and are expected to spend evenings taking them out to dinner and weekends playing golf with them.

EMC's Web site says the company values diversity, and the company has a formal policy defining and banning sexual harassment. The company sponsors a Women's Leadership Forum. Frank Hauck, who has been in charge of marketing at EMC for several years, insists that sexual harassment is not tolerated. He recalls a situation that arose shortly after he took the top marketing job: a salesman's expense account included a visit to a strip club with a client, and Hauck told the company's controller that, in accordance with company policy, EMC should not pay the bill.

EMC points out that its saleswomen hold important accounts, including Chrysler and Citigroup. Emily Stampiglia, who has been selling for EMC for seven years, describes the sales force as "the most aggressive," adding, "I'm comfortable in that competitive world."

SOURCES: William M. Bulkeley, "A Data-Storage Titan Confronts Bias Claims," *Wall Street Journal*, September 12, 2007, http://online.wsj.com; EMC Corporation, "Corporate Profile" and "Our Commitment to Diversity," EMC Web site, www.emc.com, accessed January 3, 2008; "More Men Behaving Badly—WSJ Blasts EMC for Sexual-Harassment Lawsuit," *DiversityInc*, September 12, 2007, www.diversityinc.com; and "Bias Suit Depicts EMC as Frat House–esque," *eWeek*, September 13, 2007, General Reference Center Gold, http://find.galegroup.com.

Questions

1. Compare the behavior described in this case with this chapter's description of sex discrimination and sexual harassment. Does EMC seem to have violated any laws? If so, which ones, and how?

2. Can EMC continue to sell as aggressively yet avoid charges of sexual harassment and sexual discrimination? If so, how? If not, why not, and how should it resolve this conflict?

3. Imagine that you are an HR manager at EMC. Recommend two actions the company can take to avoid sex discrimination lawsuits in the future. Explain how your recommendations will help EMC's business performance.

IT'S A WRAP!

www.mhhe.com/noefund3e is your source for Reviewing, Applying, and Practicing the concepts you learned about in Chapter 3.

Review

- Chapter learning objectives
- Narrated lecture and iPod content
- Review HR Forms: EEOC Form 100: Employer Information Report and OSHA Form 300A: Summary of Work-Related Injuries and Illnesses
- Test Your Knowledge: Comparing Affirmative Action, Valuing and Managing Diversity

Application

- Manager's Hot Seat segment: "Office Romance: Groping for Answers"
- Video case and quiz: "Working through a Medical Crisis"
- Self-assessments: What Do You Know about Sexual Harassment? and Appreciating and Valuing Diversity
- Web exercise: Equal Employment Opportunity Commission

Practice

- Chapter quiz

NOTES

1. Frank Jossi, "Cultivating Diversity," *Human Resource Executive*, December 2004, pp. 37–40.

2. *Bakke v. Regents of the University of California*, 17 F.E.P.C. 1000 (1978).

3. "Labor Letter," *Wall Street Journal*, August 25, 1987, p. 1.

4. Henry Weinstein, "U.S. Charges Law Partnership with Age Bias," *Los Angeles Times*, January 20, 2005, downloaded at Yahoo News, http://story.news.yahoo.com; and Equal Employment Opportunity Commission, "$27.5 Million Consent Decree Resolves EEOC Age Bias Suit against Sidley Austin," news release, www.eeoc.gov/press/ October 5, 2007.

5. Joe Mullich, "New Ideas Draw Older Workers," *Workforce Management*, March 2004, www.workforce.com.

6. Equal Employment Opportunity Commission, "Pregnancy Discrimination," *Discrimination by Type: Facts and Guidance*, www.eeoc.gov, modified March 2, 2005.

7. "ADA: The Final Regulations (Title I): A Lawyer's Dream/An Employer's Nightmare," *Employment Law Update* 16, no. 9 (1991), p. 1; and Equal Employment Opportunity Commission, "The Americans with Disabilities Act: A Primer for Small Business," www.eeoc.gov, modified February 4, 2004.

8. "ADA Supervisor Training Program: A Must for Any Supervisor Conducting a Legal Job Interview," *Employment Law Update* 7, no. 6 (1992), pp. 1–6; and Equal Employment Opportunity Commission, "The ADA: Your Responsibilities as an Employer," www.eeoc.gov, modified March 21, 2005.

9. EEOC, "The Americans with Disabilities Act: A Primer for Small Business."

10. Jacqueline Fitzgerald, "Drawing the Line in Interviews," *Chicago Tribune*, February 20, 2002, sec. 8, p. 2.

11. *UAW v. Johnson Controls, Inc.*, 499 U.S. 187 (1991).

12. Jan Crawford Greenburg, "Age-Bias Law Expanded," *Chicago Tribune*, March 31, 2005, sec. 1, pp. 1, 17; and Jess Bravin, "Court Expands Age Bias Claims for

Work Force," *Wall Street Journal*, March 31, 2005, http://online.wsj.com.

13. Greenburg, "Age-Bias Law Expanded"; and Bravin, "Court Expands Age Bias Claims."

14. D. Kravitz and J. Platania, "Attitudes and Beliefs about Affirmative Action: Effects of Target and of Respondent Sex and Ethnicity," *Journal of Applied Psychology* 78 (1993), pp. 928–38.

15. Equl Employment Opportunity Commission, "EEOC and Electrolux Reach Voluntary Resolution in Class Religious Accommodation Case," news release, September 24, 2003, www.eeoc.gov.

16. EEOC guideline based on the Civil Rights Act of 1964, Title VII.

17. Equal Employment Opportunity Commission, "Babies 'R' Us to Pay $205,000, Implement Training Due to Same-Sex Harassment of Male Employee," news release, January 15, 2003, www.eeoc.gov/press/.

18. National Safety Council, "Waiters' Work Is Risky Business," *Safety and Health Magazine*, NSC Web site, www.nsc.org, September 2000.

19. Reuters Limited, "Healthcare Workers Risk Getting Asthma on the Job," *Yahoo News*, March 24, 2005, http://news.yahoo.com.

20. Bureau of Labor Statistics, "Injuries, Illnesses, and Fatalities," www.bls.gov/iif/, accessed April 4, 2005; and Occupational Health and Safety Administration, "Statement of Labor Secretary Elaine L. Chao on Historic Lows in Workplace Injury and Illness," OSHA Web site, www.osha.gov, December 18, 2001.

21. J. Roughton, "Managing a Safety Program through Job Hazard Analysis," *Professional Safety* 37 (1992), pp. 28–31.

22. Roughton, "Managing a Safety Program."

23. R. G. Hallock and D. A. Weaver, "Controlling Losses and Enhancing Management Systems with TOR Analysis," *Professional Safety* 35 (1990), pp. 24–26.

24. Douglas P. Shuit, "A Left Turn for Safety," *Workforce Management*, March 2005, pp. 49–50.

25. Sandy Smith, "Protecting Vulnerable Workers," *Occupational Hazards*, April 2004, downloaded from Infotrac at http://web5.infotrac.galegroup.com.

26. Ibid.

27. J. F. Mangan, "Hazard Communications: Safety in Knowledge," *Best's Review* 92 (1991), pp. 84–88.

28. R. King, "Active Safety Programs, Education Can Help Prevent Back Injuries," *Occupational Health and Safety* 60 (1991), pp. 49–52.

29. Prevent Blindness America, "2,000 Employees Suffer Work-Related Eye Injuries Every Day in the United States," news release, March 1, 2005, downloaded at www.preventblindness.org.

30. M. Janssens, J. M. Brett, and F. J. Smith, "Confirmatory Cross-Cultural Research: Testing the Viability of a Corporation-wide Safety Policy," *Academy of Management Journal* 38 (1995), pp. 364–82.

31. "Unocal Settles Four Lawsuits over Alleged Myanmar Abuses," *Wall Street Journal*, March 21, 2005, http://online.wsj.com; and Marc Lifsher, "Unocal Settles Human Rights Lawsuit over Alleged Abuses at Myanmar Pipeline," *Los Angeles Times*, March 22, 2005, http://news.yahoo.com.

Analyzing Work and Designing Jobs

What Do I Need to Know?

After reading this chapter, you should be able to:

LO1 Summarize the elements of work flow analysis.

LO2 Describe how work flow is related to an organization's structure.

LO3 Define the elements of a job analysis, and discuss their significance for human resource management.

LO4 Tell how to obtain information for a job analysis.

LO5 Summarize recent trends in job analysis.

LO6 Describe methods for designing a job so that it can be done efficiently.

LO7 Identify approaches to designing a job to make it motivating.

LO8 Explain how organizations apply ergonomics to design safe jobs.

LO9 Discuss how organizations can plan for the mental demands of a job.

Introduction

Teach for America, a national organization that encourages college graduates to take teaching jobs in inner-city schools, has seen the number of applicants soar to 18,000 for fewer than 3,000 openings as the program heads toward its goal of doubling in size by 2010. Elissa Clapp, the organization's vice president of recruitment and selection, says that one reason is a teacher's ability to make a difference in the lives of others: "People are seeking to ensure that all parts of their lives—professional as well as personal—are fulfilling and meaningful." Kay McElroy, a high school teacher and mother, sees another attraction: a work schedule that matches her children's school schedule. Along with the academic schedule and the ability to make a difference in children's lives comes a job that combines great responsibility with an administrative trend toward greater oversight of school performance. Teachers must plan lessons that meet wide differences in skill levels and learning styles, and their success is regularly evaluated with a battery of standardized tests administered to their students. Typically, the result is a workload that extends beyond classroom hours and walls.[1]

Heavy responsibility, duties that range from planning to paperwork to inspiring children, and a work schedule that runs from September to June— all these are elements of the teacher's job. These elements give rise to the types of skills and personalities required for success, and they in turn help to narrow the field of people who will succeed at teaching. Consideration of such elements is at the heart of analyzing work, whether in a school district or a multinational corporation.

This chapter discusses the analysis and design of work and, in doing so, lays out some considerations that go into making informed decisions about how to create and link jobs. The chapter begins with a look at the big-picture issues related to analyzing work flow and organizational structure. The discussion then turns to the more specific issues of analyzing and designing jobs. Traditionally, job analysis has emphasized the study of existing jobs in order

chapter four

to make decisions such as employee selection, training, and compensation. In contrast, job design has emphasized making jobs more efficient or more motivating. However, as this chapter shows, the two activities are interrelated.

Work Flow in Organizations

Informed decisions about jobs take place in the context of the organization's overall work flow. Through the process of **work flow design,** managers analyze the tasks needed to produce a product or service. With this information, they assign these tasks to specific jobs and positions. (A **job** is a set of related duties. A **position** is the set of duties performed by one person. A school has many teaching *positions*; the person filling each of those positions is performing the *job* of teacher.) Basing these decisions on work flow design can lead to better results than the more traditional practice of looking at jobs individually.

Work Flow Analysis

Before designing its work flow, the organization's planners need to analyze what work needs to be done. Figure 4.1 shows the elements of a work flow analysis. For each type of work, such as producing a product line or providing a support service (accounting, legal support, and so on), the analysis identifies the output of the process, the activities involved, and three categories of inputs: raw inputs (materials and information), equipment, and human resources.

Outputs are the products of any work unit, whether a department, team, or individual. An output can be as readily identifiable as a completed purchase order, an employment

LO1 Summarize the elements of work flow analysis.

work flow design
The process of analyzing the tasks necessary for the production of a product or service.

job
A set of related duties.

position
The set of duties (job) performed by a particular person.

Figure 4.1

Developing a Work Flow Analysis

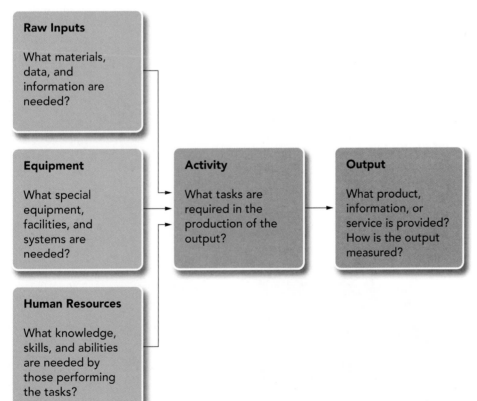

test, or a hot, juicy hamburger. An output can also be a service, such as transportation, cleaning, or answering questions about employee benefits. Even at an organization that produces tangible goods, such as computers, many employees produce other outputs, such as components of the computers, marketing plans, and building security. Work flow analysis identifies the outputs of particular work units. The analysis considers not only the amount of output but also quality standards. This attention to outputs has only recently gained attention among HRM professionals. However, it gives a clearer view of how to increase the effectiveness of each work unit.

For the outputs identified, work flow analysis then examines the work processes used to generate those outputs. Work processes are the activities that members of a work unit engage in to produce a given output. Every process consists of operating procedures that specify how things should be done at each stage of developing the output. These procedures include all the tasks that must be performed in producing the output. Usually, the analysis breaks down the tasks into those performed by each person in the work unit. This analysis helps with design of efficient work systems by clarifying which tasks are necessary. Typically, when a unit's work load increases, the unit adds people, and when the work load decreases, some members of the unit may busy themselves with unrelated tasks in an effort to appear busy. Without knowledge of work processes, it is more difficult to identify whether the work unit is properly staffed. Knowledge of work processes also can guide staffing changes when work is automated, outsourced, or restructured. At Toyota, employees at all levels are constantly on the lookout for ways to ensure reliability and high quality. After many years of study and continuous improvement, the company has developed thousands of pages of documentation that lays out precisely what needs to be done for every step of each job to avoid defects, prevent wasted time and effort, and minimize inventories of finished goods and work in process. Toyota management expects all employees to continue identifying ways to improve these work processes and eliminate unnecessary tasks.[2]

The final stage in work flow analysis is to identify the inputs used in the development of the work unit's product. As shown in Figure 4.1, these inputs can be broken down into the raw inputs (materials and knowledge), equipment, and human skills needed to perform the tasks. Makers of athletic shoes need nylon and leather, shoe-making machinery, and workers to operate the machinery, among other inputs. Nike and Reebok minimize the cost of inputs by subcontracting manufacturing to factories in countries where wages are low. In contrast, New Balance Athletic Shoes operates a factory in Norridgewock, Maine, where modern technology and worker training enable the company to afford U.S. workers. Teams of employees use automated equipment that operates over 20 sewing machines simultaneously. The employees are

Firefighters work as a team. They and their equipment are the "inputs" (they do the work), and the "output" is an extinguished fire and the rescue of people and pets. In any organization or team, workers need to be cross-trained in several skills to create an effective team. If these firefighters are trained to do any part of the job, the chief can deploy them rapidly as needed.

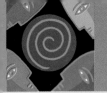

HR Oops!

Software Can't Do It Alone

One high-tech input that has promised to boost sales is a type of software known as a customer relationship management (CRM) system. Companies have invested large sums in these systems, which are supposed to give salespeople ready access to all the data they need about customers, products, and selling methods. Together with talented salespeople, CRM should be delivering greater sales.

The problem is that, even as companies have invested in these inputs, they have failed to provide a necessary ingredient: data for the system to analyze and retrieve.

A recent survey of 1,000 companies found that their salespeople had trouble getting the information they needed from their CRM systems. For example, about one-fifth said it takes significant effort to get information about strategic account plans and best practices used by the sales force; in fact, they said they rarely find this type of information when they try. Over one-fourth said it takes significant effort to get competitive analysis information. With these and other types of data missing, only about one in five companies say they have seen significantly greater

revenues as a result of investing in CRM systems.

Source: Jim Dickie, "Fueling the CRM Engine," *CRM Magazine,* April 2007, Business & Company Resource Center, http://galenet.galegroup.com.

Questions

1. In this example, which categories of inputs shown in Figure 4.1 are companies providing? Which categories are they failing to focus on?

2. How can HR professionals help their sales organizations better analyze the work flow to improve sales results?

---

cross-trained in all tasks. The highly efficient factory produces shoes much faster than a typical Chinese shoe factory.[3]

Work Flow Design and an Organization's Structure

LO2 Describe how work flow is related to an organization's structure.

Besides looking at the work flow of each process, it is important to see how the work fits within the context of the organization's structure. Within an organization, units and individuals must cooperate to create outputs. Ideally, the organization's structure brings together the people who must collaborate to efficiently produce the desired outputs. The structure may do this in a way that is highly centralized (that is, with authority concentrated in a few people at the top of the organizaton) or decentralized (with authority spread among many people). The organization may group jobs according to functions (for example, welding, painting, packaging), or it may set up divisions to focus on products or customer groups.

Although there are an infinite number of ways to combine the elements of an organization's structure, we can make some general observations about structure and work design. If the structure is strongly based on function, workers tend to have low authority and to work alone at highly specialized jobs. Jobs that involve teamwork or broad responsibility tend to require a structure based on divisions other than functions. When the goal is to empower employees, companies therefore need to set up structures and jobs that enable broad responsibility, such as jobs that involve employees in serving a particular group of customers or producing a particular product, rather than performing a narrowly defined function. The organization's structure also affects managers' jobs. Managing a division responsible for a product or customer group tends to require more experience and cognitive (thinking) ability than managing a department that handles a particular function.[4]

Work design often emphasizes the analysis and design of jobs, as described in the remainder of this chapter. Although all of these approaches can succeed, each focuses on one isolated job at a time. These approaches do not necessarily consider how that single job fits into the overall work flow or structure of the organization. To use these techniques effectively, human resource personnel should also understand their organization as a whole. Without this big-picture appreciation, they might redesign a job in a way that makes sense for the particular job but is out of line with the organization's work flow, structure, or strategy.

Job Analysis

LO3 Define the elements of a job analysis, and discuss their significance for human resource management.

job analysis
The process of getting detailed information about jobs.

To achieve high-quality performance, organizations have to understand and match job requirements and people. This understanding requires **job analysis,** the process of getting detailed information about jobs. Analyzing jobs and understanding what is required to carry out a job provide essential knowledge for staffing, training, performance appraisal, and many other HR activities. For instance, a supervisor's evaluation of an employee's work should be based on performance relative to job requirements. In very small organizations, line managers may perform a job analysis, but usually the work is done by a human resource professional. A large company may have a compensation management department that includes job analysts (also called personnel analysts). Organizations may also contract with firms that provide this service.

Job Descriptions

job description
A list of the tasks, duties, and responsibilities (TDRs) that a particular job entails.

An essential part of job analysis is the creation of job descriptions. A **job description** is a list of the tasks, duties, and responsibilities (TDRs) that a job entails. TDRs are observable actions. For example, a news photographer's job requires the jobholder to use a camera to take photographs. If you were to observe someone in that position for a day, you would almost certainly see some pictures being taken. When a manager attempts to evaluate job performance, it is most important to have detailed information about the work performed in the job (that is, the TDRs). This information makes it possible to determine how well an individual is meeting each job requirement.

A job description typically has the format shown in Figure 4.2. It includes the job title, a brief description of the TDRs, and a list of the essential duties with detailed specifications of the tasks involved in carrying out each duty. Although organizations may modify this format according to their particular needs, all job descriptions within an organization should follow the same format. This helps the organization make consistent decisions about such matters as pay and promotions. It also helps the organization show that it makes human resource decisions fairly.

Whenever the organization creates a new job, it needs to prepare a job description, using a process such as the one detailed in the "HR How To" box nearby. Job descriptions should then be reviewed periodically (say, once a year) and updated if necessary. Performance appraisals can provide a good opportunity for updating job descriptions, as the employee and supervisor compare what the employee has been doing against the details of the job description.

Organizations should give each newly hired employee a copy of his or her job description. This helps the employee to understand what is expected, but it shouldn't be presented as limiting the employee's commitment to quality and customer satisfaction.

Figure 4.2

Sample Job Description

TRAIN CREW/SERVICE AT UNION PACIFIC

OVERVIEW

When you work on a Union Pacific train crew, you're working at the very heart of our railroad. Moving trains. Driving trains. Making sure our customers' freight gets delivered safely and on time.

JOB DESCRIPTION

In this entry-level position, you'll start as a Switchperson or Brakeperson, working as on-the-ground traffic control. You don't need any previous railroad experience; we provide all training. These jobs directly lead to becoming a Conductor and a Locomotive Engineer, where you will have a rare opportunity to work on board a moving locomotive. The Conductor is responsible for the train, the freight and the crew. The Locomotive Engineer actually operates the locomotive.

DUTIES

As a Switchperson or Brakeperson, you'll learn to move trains safely in the yards and over the road. You'll be climbing ladders, boarding freight cars, operating track switches, inspecting cars, and using radio communications to control train movement.

MAJOR TASKS AND RESPONSIBILITIES

You won't work a standard 40-hour work week. Train crews are always on-call, even on weekends and holidays. You'll travel with our trains, sometimes spending a day or more away from your home terminal.

SOURCE: Union Pacific Web site, www.unionpacific.jobs/careers/explore/train/train_service.shtml, accessed April 24, 2008.

Ideally, employees will want to go above and beyond the listed duties when the situation and their abilities call for that. Many job descriptions include the phrase *and other duties as requested* as a way to remind employees not to tell their supervisor, "But that's not part of my job."

Job Specifications

Whereas the job description focuses on the activities involved in carrying out a job, a **job specification** looks at the qualities or requirements the person performing the job must possess. It is a list of the knowledge, skills, abilities, and other characteristics (KSAOs) that an individual must have to perform the job. *Knowledge* refers to factual or procedural information that is necessary for successfully performing a task. For example, this course is providing you with knowledge in how to manage human resources. A *skill* is an individual's level of proficiency at performing a particular task—that is, the capability to perform it well. With knowledge and experience, you could acquire skill in the task of preparing job specifications. *Ability*, in contrast to skill, refers to a more general enduring capability that an individual possesses. A person might have the ability to cooperate with others or to write clearly and precisely. Finally, *other characteristics* might be personality traits such as someone's persistence or motivation

job specification
A list of the knowledge, skills, abilities, and other characteristics (KSAOs) that an individual must have to perform a particular job.

HR How To

WRITING A JOB DESCRIPTION

Preparing a job description begins with gathering information from sources who can identify the details of performing a task—for example, persons already performing the job, the supervisor or team leader, or if the job is new, managers who are creating the new position. Other sources of information may include the company's human resource files, such as past job advertisements and job descriptions, as well as general sources of information about similar jobs, such as O*NET (http://online. onetcenter.org).

There are several ways to gather information about the duties of a job:

- Employees can fill out a questionnaire that asks about what they do or complete a diary that details their activities over several days.

- A job analyst can visit the workplace and watch or videotape an employee performing the job. This method is most appropriate for jobs that are repetitive and involve physical activity.

- A job analyst can visit the workplace and ask an employee to show what the job entails. This method is most appropriate for clerical and technical jobs.

- A manager or supervisor can describe what a person holding the job must do to be successful. What would the job holder's outputs be? The analyst can identify the activities necessary to create these outputs.

- A supervisor or job analyst can review company records related to performing the job—for example, work orders or summaries of customer calls. These records can show the kinds of problems a person solves in the course of doing a job.

The next step is to list all the activities and evaluate which are essential duties. Rate all the duties on a scale of 1 to 5, where 1 is most important, or rank the tasks according to how much time the person spends on them. Perhaps the ratings will show that some tasks are desirable but not essential.

When people analyzing a job come to different conclusions about which activities are essential, the person writing the job description should compare the listed activities with the company's goals and work flow to see which are essential.

From these sources, the writer of the job description obtains the important elements of the description:

- *Title of the job*—The title should be descriptive and, if appropriate, indicate the job's level in the organization.

- *Administrative information about the job*—The job description may identify a division, department, supervisor's title, date of the analysis, name of the analyst, and other information for administering the company's human resource activities.

- *Summary of the job, focusing on its purpose and duties*—This summary should be brief and as specific as possible, including types of responsibilities, tools and equipment used, and level of authority.

- *Essential duties of the job*— These should be listed in order of importance to successful performance and should include details such as physical requirements (for example, the amount of weight to be lifted), the persons with whom an employee in this job interacts, and the results to be accomplished. This section should include only duties that the job analysis identified as essential.

- *Additional responsibilities*— The job description may state that the position requires additional responsibilities as requested by the supervisor.

Sources: Small Business Administration, "Writing Effective Job Descriptions," *Small Business Planner,* www.sba.gov/smallbusinessplanner/, accessed January 8, 2008; "How to Write a Job Analysis and Description," *Entrepreneur,* www. entrepreneur.com, accessed January 8, 2008; "Job Descriptions and the ADA," HRNext, www.hrnext. com, downloaded March 7, 2002; "Simple Job Analysis," HRNext, www.hrnext.com, downloaded March 7, 2002; and Lou Adler, "Know What You're Looking For," *Inc.com,* March 2005, www.inc.com.

to achieve. Some jobs also have legal requirements, such as licensing or certification. Figure 4.3 is a set of sample job specifications for the job description in Figure 4.2.

In developing job specifications, it is important to consider all of the elements of KSAOs. As with writing a job description, the information can come from a combination of people performing the job, people supervising or planning for the

Figure 4.3

Sample Job Specifications

TRAIN CREW/SERVICE AT UNION PACIFIC

REQUIREMENTS

You must be at least 18 years old. You must speak and read English because you'll be asked to follow posted bulletins, regulations, rule books, timetables, switch lists, etc. You must pass a reading comprehension test (see sample) to be considered for an interview.

JOB REQUIREMENTS

You must be able to use a computer keyboard, and you must be able to count and compare numbers. (You might, for example, be asked to count the cars on a train during switching.) You must be able to solve problems quickly and react to changing conditions on the job.

You must have strong vision and hearing, including the ability to: see and read hand signals from near and far; distinguish between colors; visually judge the speed and distance of moving objects; see at night; and recognize changes in sounds.

You must also be physically strong: able to push, pull, lift and carry up to 25 pounds frequently; up to 50 pounds occasionally; and up to 83 pounds infrequently. You'll need good balance to regularly step on and off equipment and work from ladders to perform various tasks. And you must be able to walk, sit, stand and stoop comfortably.

You'll be working outdoors in all weather conditions – including snow, ice, rain, cold, and heat – and frequently at elevations more than 12 feet above the ground.

SOURCE: Union Pacific Web site, www.unionpacific.jobs/careers/explore/train/train_service.shtml, accessed April 24, 2008.

job, and trained job analysts. At Acxiom Corporation, job specifications are based on an analysis of employees' roles and competencies (what they must be able to do), stated in terms of behaviors. To reach these definitions, groups studied what the company's good performers were doing and looked for the underlying abilities. For example, according to Jeff Standridge, Acxiom's organizational development leader, they might ask a panel about a high-performing software developer, and panel members might identify the employee's knowledge of the Java and C^{++} programming languages. Then the job analysts would probe for the abilities behind this knowledge. In the case of the software developer, the employee's strength was not just in his specific skills but in his ability to learn.[5]

In contrast to tasks, duties, and responsibilities, KSAOs are characteristics of people and are not directly observable. They are observable only when individuals are carrying out the TDRs of the job—and afterward, if they can show the product of their labor. Thus, if someone applied for a job as a news photographer, you could not simply look at the individual to determine whether he or she can spot and take effective photographs. However, you could draw conclusions later about the person's skills by looking at examples of his or her photographs.

Accurate information about KSAOs is especially important for making decisions about who will fill a job. A manager attempting to fill a position needs information about the characteristics required and about the characteristics of each applicant. Interviews and selection decisions should therefore focus on KSAOs. In the earlier example of computer programming at Acxiom, the company would look for someone who knows the computer languages currently used and has a track record of taking the initiative to learn new computer languages as they are developed.

Sources of Job Information

LO4 Tell how to obtain information for a job analysis.

Information for analyzing an existing job often comes from incumbents, that is, people who currently hold that position in the organization. They are a logical source of information because they are most acquainted with the details of the job. Incumbents should be able to provide very accurate information.

A drawback of relying solely on incumbents' information is that they may have an incentive to exaggerate what they do in order to appear more valuable to the organization. Information from incumbents should therefore be supplemented with information from observers, such as supervisors, who look for a match between what incumbents are doing and what they are supposed to do. Research suggests that supervisors may provide the most accurate estimates of the importance of job duties, while incumbents may be more accurate in reporting information about the actual time spent performing job tasks and safety-related risk factors.[6] For analyzing skill levels, the best source may be external job analysts who have more experience rating a wide range of jobs.[7]

The government also provides background information for analyzing jobs. In the 1930s, the U.S. Department of Labor created the *Dictionary of Occupational Titles (DOT)* as a vehicle for helping the new public employment system link the demand for skills and the supply of skills in the U.S. workforce. The *DOT* described over 12,000 jobs, as well as some of the requirements of successful job holders. This system served the United States well for over 60 years, but it became clear to Labor Department officials that jobs in the new economy were so different that the *DOT* no longer served its purpose. The Labor Department therefore introduced a new system, called the Occupational Information Network (O*NET).

Instead of relying on fixed job titles and narrow task descriptions, O*NET uses a common language that generalizes across jobs to describe the abilities, work styles, work activities, and work context required for 1,000 broadly defined occupations. Users can visit O*NET OnLine (http://online.onetcenter.org) to review jobs' tasks, work styles and context, and requirements including skills, training, and experience. In Oklahoma City, Workforce Oklahoma's Eastside Career Connection Center used O*NET to guide small employers in listing job vacancies. For example, a metal fabrication company was having difficulty finding knowledgeable welders, so it decided to set up its own training program. The Eastside center worked with the company to define the desired skills, prepare job descriptions, and set up training aimed to fill the jobs described.[8]

Manpower, an employment services company, uses O*Net to classify its jobs and track demand nationwide.

Position Analysis Questionnaire (PAQ)
A standardized job analysis questionnaire containing 194 questions about work behaviors, work conditions, and job characteristics that apply to a wide variety of jobs.

Position Analysis Questionnaire

After gathering information, the job analyst uses the information to analyze the job. One of the broadest and best-researched instruments for analyzing jobs is the **Position Analysis Questionnaire (PAQ).** This is a standardized job analysis questionnaire containing 194 items that represent work behaviors, work conditions, and job characteristics that apply to a wide variety of jobs. The questionnaire organizes these items into six sections concerning different aspects of the job:

1. *Information input*—Where and how a worker gets information needed to perform the job.
2. *Mental processes*—The reasoning, decision making, planning, and information-processing activities involved in performing the job.
3. *Work output*—The physical activities, tools, and devices used by the worker to perform the job.
4. *Relationships with other persons*—The relationships with other people required in performing the job.
5. *Job context*—The physical and social contexts where the work is performed.
6. *Other characteristics*—The activities, conditions, and characteristics other than those previously described that are relevant to the job.

The person analyzing a job determines whether each item on the questionnaire applies to the job being analyzed. The analyst rates each item on six scales: extent of use, amount of time, importance to the job, possibility of occurrence, applicability, and special code (special rating scales used with a particular item). The PAQ headquarters uses a computer to score the questionnaire and generate a report that describes the scores on the job dimensions.

Using the PAQ provides an organization with information that helps in comparing jobs, even when they are dissimilar. The PAQ also has the advantage that it considers the whole work process, from inputs through outputs. However, the person who fills out the questionnaire must have college-level reading skills, and the PAQ is meant to be completed only by job analysts trained in this method. In fact, the ratings of job incumbents tend to be less reliable than ratings by supervisors and trained analysts.[9] Also, the descriptions in the PAQ reports are rather abstract, so the reports may not be useful for writing job descriptions or redesigning jobs.

Fleishman Job Analysis System

To gather information about worker requirements, the **Fleishman Job Analysis System** asks subject-matter experts (typically job incumbents) to evaluate a job in terms of the abilities required to perform the job.[10] The survey is based on 52 categories of abilities, ranging from written comprehension to deductive reasoning, manual dexterity, stamina, and originality. As in the example in Figure 4.4, the survey items are arranged into a scale for each ability. Each begins with a description of the ability and a comparison to related abilities. Below this is a seven-point scale with phrases describing extemely high and low levels of the ability. The person completing the survey indicates which point on the scale represents the level of the ability required for performing the job being analyzed.

When the survey has been completed in all 52 categories, the results provide a picture of the ability requirements of a job. Such information is especially useful for employee selection, training, and career development.

Fleishman Job Analysis System
Job analysis technique that asks subject-matter experts to evaluate a job in terms of the abilities required to perform the job.

Importance of Job Analysis

Job analysis is so important to HR managers that it has been called the building block of everything that personnel does.[11] The fact is that almost every human

Figure 4.4

Example of an Ability
from the Fleishman Job
Analysis System

Written Comprehension

This is the ability to understand written sentences and paragraphs.
How written comprehension is different from other abilities:

This Ability	Other Abilities

Understand written English words, sentences, and paragraphs.   vs.   *Oral comprehension (1): Listen and understand spoken* English words and sentences.

vs.   *Oral expression (3)* and *written expression (4): Speak or write* English words and sentences so others will understand.

Requires understanding of complex or detailed information in **writing** containing unusual words and phrases and involving fine distinctions in meaning among words.

- 7
- 6   ← Understand an instruction book on repairing a missile guidance system.
- 5
- 4
- 3   ← Understand an apartment lease.
- 2
- 1   ← Read a road map.

Requires understanding short, simple **written** information containing common words and phrases.

SOURCE: From E. A. Fleishman and M. D. Mumford, "Evaluating Classifications of Job Behavior: A Construct Validation of the Ability Requirements Scales," *Personnel Psychology* 44 (1991), pp. 423–576. Copyright © 1991 by Blackwell Publishing. Reproduced with permission of Blackwell Publishing via Copyright Clearance Center.

resource management program requires some type of information that is gleaned from job analysis:[12]

- *Work redesign*—Often an organization seeks to redesign work to make it more efficient or to improve quality. The redesign requires detailed information about the existing job(s). In addition, preparing the redesign is similar to analyzing a job that does not yet exist.
- *Human resource planning*—As planners analyze human resource needs and how to meet those needs, they must have accurate information about the levels of skill required in various jobs, so that they can tell what kinds of human resources will be needed.
- *Selection*—To identify the most qualified applicants for various positions, decision makers need to know what tasks the individuals must perform, as well as the necessary knowledge, skills, and abilities.
- *Training*—Almost every employee hired by an organization will require training. Any training program requires knowledge of the tasks performed in a job, so that the training is related to the necessary knowledge and skills.
- *Performance appraisal*—An accurate performance appraisal requires information about how well each employee is performing in order to reward employees who

perform well and to improve their performance if it is below standard. Job analysis helps in identifying the behaviors and the results associated with effective performance.

- *Career planning*—Matching an individual's skills and aspirations with career opportunities requires that those in charge of career planning know the skill requirements of the various jobs. This allows them to guide individuals into jobs in which they will succeed and be satisfied.
- *Job evaluation*—The process of job evaluation involves assessing the relative dollar value of each job to the organization in order to set up fair pay structures. If employees do not believe pay structures are fair, they will become dissatisfied and may quit, or they will not see much benefit in striving for promotions. To put dollar values on jobs, it is necessary to get information about different jobs and compare them.

Job analysis is also important from a legal standpoint. As we saw in Chapter 3, the government imposes requirements related to equal employment opportunity. Detailed, accurate, objective job specifications help decision makers comply with these regulations by keeping the focus on tasks and abilities. These documents also provide evidence of efforts made to engage in fair employment practices. For example, to enforce the Americans with Disabilities Act, the Equal Employment Opportunity Commission may look at job descriptions to identify the essential functions of a job and determine whether a disabled person could have performed those functions with reasonable accommodations. Likewise, lists of duties in different jobs could be compared to evaluate claims under the Equal Pay Act. However, job descriptions and job specifications are not a substitute for fair employment practices.

Besides helping human resource professionals, job analysis helps supervisors and other managers carry out their duties. Data from job analysis can help managers identify the types of work in their units, as well as provide information about the work flow process, so that managers can evaluate whether work is done in the most efficient way. Job analysis information also supports managers as they make hiring decisions, review performance, and recommend rewards.

Trends in Job Analysis

LO5 Summarize recent trends in job analysis.

As we noted in the earlier discussion of work flow analysis, organizations are beginning to appreciate the need to analyze jobs in the context of the organization's structure and strategy. In addition, organizations are recognizing that today's workplace must be adaptable and is constantly subject to change. Thus, although we tend to think of "jobs" as something stable, they actually tend to change and evolve over time. Those who occupy or manage jobs often make minor adjustments to match personal preferences or changing conditions.[13] Indeed, although errors in job analysis can have many sources, most inaccuracy is likely to result from job descriptions being outdated. For this reason, job analysis must not only define jobs when they are created, but also detect changes in jobs as time passes.

In today's world of rapidly changing products and markets, some observers have even begun to suggest that the concept of a "job" is obsolete. Some researchers and businesspeople have observed a trend they call *dejobbing*—viewing organizations as a field of work needing to be done, rather than as a set or series of jobs held by individuals. For example, at Amazon.com, HR director Scott Pitasky notes, "Here, a person might be in the same 'job,' but three months later be doing completely different

Amazon.com practices "dejobbing," or designing work by project rather than by jobs. What would appeal to you about working for a company organized like this?

work."[14] This means Amazon.com puts more emphasis on broad worker specifications ("entrepreneurial and customer-focused") than on detailed job descriptions ("HTML programming"), which may not be descriptive one year down the road.

These changes in the nature of work and the expanded use of "project-based" organizational structures require the type of broader understanding that comes from an analysis of work flows. Because the work can change rapidly and it is impossible to rewrite job descriptions every week, job descriptions and specifications need to be flexible. At the same time, legal requirements (as discussed in Chapter 3) may discourage organizations from writing flexible job descriptions. So, organizations must balance the need for flexibility with the need for legal documentation. This presents one of the major challenges to be faced by HRM departments in the next decade. Many professionals are meeting this challenge with a greater emphasis on careful job design.

Job Design

LO6 Describe methods for designing a job so that it can be done efficiently.

Although job analysis, as just described, is important for an understanding of existing jobs, organizations also must plan for new jobs and periodically consider whether they should revise existing jobs. When an organization is expanding, supervisors and human resource professionals must help plan for new or growing work units. When an organization is trying to improve quality or efficiency, a review of work units and processes may require a fresh look at how jobs are designed.

job design
The process of defining how work will be performed and what tasks will be required in a given job.

These situations call for **job design,** the process of defining how work will be performed and what tasks will be required in a given job, or *job redesign*, a similar process that involves changing an existing job design. To design jobs effectively, a person must thoroughly understand the job itself (through job analysis) and its place in the larger work unit's work flow process (through work flow analysis). Having a detailed knowledge of the tasks performed in the work unit and in the job, a manager then has many alternative ways to design a job. As shown in Figure 4.5, the available approaches emphasize different aspects of the job: the mechanics of doing a job efficiently, the job's impact on motivation, the use of safe work practices, and the mental demands of the job.

Figure 4.5

Approaches to Job Design

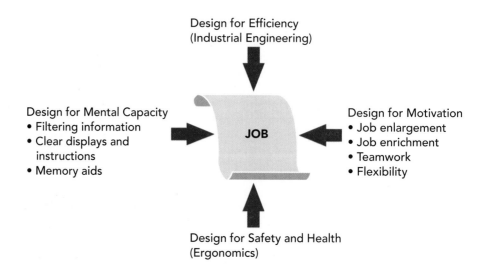

Design for Efficiency
(Industrial Engineering)

Design for Mental Capacity
• Filtering information
• Clear displays and instructions
• Memory aids

JOB

Design for Motivation
• Job enlargement
• Job enrichment
• Teamwork
• Flexibility

Design for Safety and Health
(Ergonomics)

Designing Efficient Jobs

If workers perform tasks as efficiently as possible, not only does the organization benefit from lower costs and greater output per worker, but workers should be less fatigued. This point of view has for years formed the basis of classical **industrial engineering,** which looks for the simplest way to structure work in order to maximize efficiency. Typically, applying industrial engineering to a job reduces the complexity of the work, making it so simple that almost anyone can be trained quickly and easily to perform the job. Such jobs tend to be highly specialized and repetitive.

industrial engineering The study of jobs to find the simplest way to structure work in order to maximize efficiency.

In practice, the scientific method traditionally seeks the "one best way" to perform a job by performing time-and-motion studies to identify the most efficient movements for workers to make. Once the engineers have identified the most efficient sequence of motions, the organization should select workers based on their ability to do the job, then train them in the details of the "one best way" to perform that job. The company also should offer pay structured to motivate workers to do their best. (Chapters 11 and 12 discuss pay and pay structures.)

Industrial engineering provides measurable and practical benefits. However, a focus on efficiency alone can create jobs that are so simple and repetitive that workers get bored. Workers performing these jobs may feel their work is meaningless. Hence, most organizations combine industrial engineering with other approaches to job design.

Designing Jobs That Motivate

Especially when organizations must compete for employees, depend on skilled knowledge workers, or need a workforce that cares about customer satisfaction, a pure focus on efficiency will not achieve human resource objectives. These organizations need jobs that employees find interesting and satisfying, and job design should take into account factors that make jobs motivating to employees.

LO7 Identify approaches to designing a job to make it motivating.

A model that shows how to make jobs more motivating is the Job Characteristics Model, developed by Richard Hackman and Greg Oldham. This model describes jobs in terms of five characteristics:[15]

1. *Skill variety*—The extent to which a job requires a variety of skills to carry out the tasks involved.
2. *Task identity*—The degree to which a job requires completing a "whole" piece of work from beginning to end (for example, building an entire component or resolving a customer's complaint).
3. *Task significance*—The extent to which the job has an important impact on the lives of other people.
4. *Autonomy*—The degree to which the job allows an individual to make decisions about the way the work will be carried out.
5. *Feedback*—The extent to which a person receives clear information about performance effectiveness from the work itself.

As shown in Figure 4.6, the more of each of these characteristics a job has, the more motivating the job will be, according to the Job Characteristics Model. The model predicts that a person with such a job will be more satisfied and will produce more and better work. For example, to increase the meaningfulness of making artery stents (devices that are surgically inserted to promote blood flow), the maker of these products invites its production workers to an annual party, where they meet patients whose lives were saved by the products they helped to manufacture.[16] To read about

Best Practices

Joie de Vivre Hospitality Puts Joy in the Job

The three dozen boutique hotels that operate under the corporate umbrella of Joie de Vivre Hospitality aim not so much merely to provide a good night's sleep as to deliver wonderful experiences to certain travelers defined by their lifestyles and tastes. The company's name—a French phrase for the "joy of living"—defines not only the guest's experience but also the company's HR goal of keeping its employees happy and enthusiastic, because they are the "critical starting point for successful business."

Hotel workers are traditionally paid low wages, but Joie de Vivre counters that down side by giving employees plenty of say in how they do their work. When the company took over the Hotel Carlton in San Francisco, management learned that the cleaning staff were frustrated with their worn-out vacuum cleaners. Joie de Vivre's manager bought a new vacuum for each housekeeper and began replacing them yearly. New vacuum cleaners are cheaper than hiring new employees. The front desk manager also gained more control over his job. Joie de Vivre let him rearrange the phones at the reception desk so that they would be easier to answer, and he shifted work hours to be increasingly available in the evenings, when he could dream up more ways to keep guests delighted with little extras.

To keep the focus on why employees' performance is important, managers construct the agenda for each executive meeting to include 15 minutes for participants to tell anecdotes of staff members who are doing something extraordinary. At the end of each meeting, one of the executives is chosen to call these employees and express appreciation. Management also invites groups of workers to meetings where they discuss how their work makes a difference to guests.

Sources: Phred Dvorak, "Hotelier Finds Happiness, Keeps Staff Checked In," *Wall Street Journal,* December 17, 2007, http://online.wsj.com; Mike Hofman, "The Idea That Saved My Company," *Inc.,* October 2007, downloaded from General Reference Center Gold, http://find.galegroup.com (interview with Chip Conley); and Joie de Vivre Hospitality, "Joie de Vivre Fact Sheet," www.jdvhotels.com, accessed January 8, 2008.

another company that has applied principles of the job characteristics approach, see the "Best Practices" box.

Applications of the job characteristics approach to job design include job enlargement, job enrichment, self-managing work teams, flexible work schedules, and telework.

Figure 4.6

Characteristics of a Motivating Job

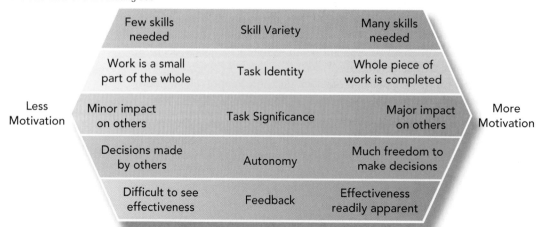

Job Enlargement

In a job design, **job enlargement** refers to broadening the types of tasks performed. The objective of job enlargement is to make jobs less repetitive and more interesting. Methods of job enlargement include job extension and job rotation.

Job extension is enlarging jobs by combining several relatively simple jobs to form a job with a wider range of tasks. An example might be combining the jobs of receptionist, typist, and file clerk into jobs containing all three kinds of work. This approach to job enlargement is relatively simple, but if all the tasks are dull, workers will not necessarily be more motivated by the redesigned job.

Job rotation does not actually redesign the jobs themselves, but moves employees among several different jobs. This approach to job enlargement is common among production teams. During the course of a week, a team member may carry out each of the jobs handled by the team. Team members might assemble components one day and pack products into cases another day. As with job extension, the enlarged jobs may still consist of repetitive activities, but with greater variation among those activities.

Job Enrichment

The idea of **job enrichment,** or empowering workers by adding more decision-making authority to their jobs, comes from the work of Frederick Herzberg. According to Herzberg's two-factor theory, individuals are motivated more by the intrinsic aspects of work (for example, the meaningfulness of a job) than by extrinsic rewards such as pay. Herzberg identified five factors he associated with motivating jobs: achievement, recognition, growth, responsibility, and performance of the entire job. Thus, ways to enrich a manufacturing job might include giving employees authority to stop production when quality standards are not being met and having each employee perform several tasks to complete a particular stage of the process, rather than dividing up the tasks among the employees. For a salesperson in a store, job enrichment might involve the authority to resolve customer problems, including the authority to decide whether to issue refunds or replace merchandise.

Self-Managing Work Teams

Instead of merely enriching individual jobs, some organizations empower employees by designing work to be done by self-managing work teams. As described in Chapter 2, these teams have authority for an entire work process or segment. Team members typically have authority to schedule work, hire team members, resolve problems related to the team's performance, and perform other duties traditionally handled by management. Teamwork can give a job such motivating characteristics as autonomy, skill variety, and task identity.

Because team members' responsibilities are great, their jobs usually are defined broadly and include sharing of work assignments. Team members may, at one time or another, perform every duty of the team. The challenge for the organization is to provide enough training so that the team members can learn the necessary skills. Another approach, when teams are responsible for particular work processes or customers, is to assign the team responsibility for the process or customer, then let the team decide which members will carry out which tasks.

A study of work teams at a large financial services company found that the right job design was associated with effective teamwork.[17] In particular, when teams are self-managed and team members are highly involved in decision making, teams are more productive, employees more satisfied, and managers more pleased with performance.

job enlargement
Broadening the types of tasks performed in a job.

job extension
Enlarging jobs by combining several relatively simple jobs to form a job with a wider range of tasks.

job rotation
Enlarging jobs by moving employees among several different jobs.

job enrichment
Empowering workers by adding more decision-making authority to jobs.

Figure 4.7

Alternatives to the
8-to-5 Job

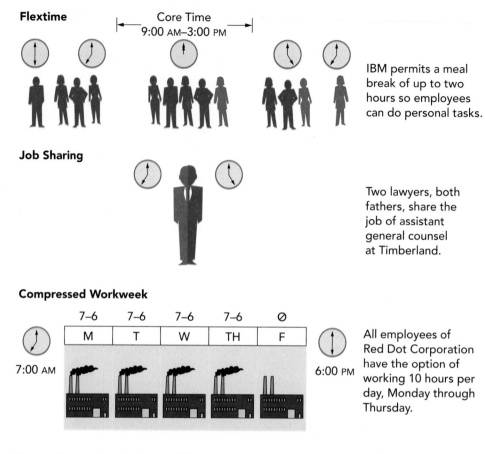

Flextime

Core Time
9:00 AM–3:00 PM

IBM permits a meal
break of up to two
hours so employees
can do personal tasks.

Job Sharing

Two lawyers, both
fathers, share the
job of assistant
general counsel
at Timberland.

Compressed Workweek

7–6	7–6	7–6	7–6	∅
M	T	W	TH	F

7:00 AM

6:00 PM

All employees of
Red Dot Corporation
have the option of
working 10 hours per
day, Monday through
Thursday.

Teams also tend to do better when each team member performs a variety of tasks and when team members view their effort as significant.

Flexible Work Schedules

One way in which an organization can give employees some say in how their work is structured is to offer flexible work schedules. Depending on the requirements of the organization and the individual jobs, organizations may be able to be flexible in terms of when employees work. As introduced in Chapter 2, types of flexibility include flextime and job sharing. Figure 4.7 illustrates alternatives to the traditional 40-hour workweek.

Flextime is a scheduling policy in which full-time employees may choose starting and ending times within guidelines specified by the organization. The flextime policy may require that employees be at work between certain hours, say, 10:00 AM and 3:00 PM. Employees work additional hours before or after this period in order to work the full day. One employee might arrive early in the morning in order to leave at 3:00 PM to pick up children after school. Another employee might be a night owl who prefers to arrive at 10:00 AM and work until 6:00, 7:00, or even later in the evening. A flextime policy also may enable workers to adjust a particular day's hours in order to make time for doctor's appointments, children's activities, hobbies, or volunteer work. A work schedule that allows time for community and family interests can be extremely motivating for some employees.

Job sharing is a work option in which two part-time employees carry out the tasks associated with a single job. Such arrangements can enable an organization to attract

flextime
A scheduling policy in which full-time employees may choose starting and ending times within guidelines specified by the organization.

job sharing
A work option in which two part-time employees carry out the tasks associated with a single job.

TECHNOLOGY GETS ACCENTURE EMPLOYEES OUT OF THE OFFICE

When the consultants of Arthur Andersen broke off to form Accenture, they had offices in 47 countries. Where should the headquarters be located? After much debate, the partners settled on an unusual answer: everywhere. Accenture's consultants work wherever they can best get the job done, whether at a client's site, in their own homes, or at Accenture branches located near the world's major airports.

On any given day, the typical Accenture employee logs in to the company's Web site to record where he or she is that day. If the consultant needs a desk, he or she can be directed to the closest Accenture office, where a fully networked cubicle is waiting. Each consultant has an individual telephone number and can have phone calls routed automatically to the current location.

Collaboration software on each employee's laptop computer lets the consultants share data and documents. When they want to communicate visually, they can use videoconferencing technology and whiteboards in most Accenture offices.

This work arrangement helps Accenture's consultants stay close to its clients. The greater time spent with clients increases trust and understanding, which help retain clients. Consultant Bill Green travels more than 165,000 miles a year but says the effort is well worth it: "We get information we would never get if we were stuck back at some headquarters."

Sources: C. Hymowitz, "Have Advice, Will Travel," *Wall Street Journal,* June 5, 2006, pp. B1, B5; R. King, "Working from Home: It's in the Details," *BusinessWeek,* February 12, 2007, pp. 39–40; A. Hesseldahl, "Tech Support for the Home Office," *BusinessWeek,* February 12, 2007, p. 40; and R. King, "Virtual Workplace Do's and Don'ts," *BusinessWeek,* April 16, 2007, p. 30.

or retain valued employees who want more time to attend school or to care for family members. The job requirements in such an arrangement include the ability to work cooperatively and coordinate the details of one's job with another person.

Although not strictly a form of flexibility on the level of individual employees, another scheduling alternative is the *compressed workweek*. A compressed workweek is a schedule in which full-time workers complete their weekly hours in fewer than five days. For example, instead of working eight hours a day for five days, the employees could complete 40 hours of work in four 10-hour days. This alternative is most common, but some companies use other alternatives, such as scheduling 80 hours over nine days (with a three-day weekend every other week) or reducing the workweek from 40 to 38 or 36 hours. Employees may appreciate the extra days available for leisure, family, or volunteer activities. An organization might even use this schedule to offer a kind of flexibility—for example, letting workers vote whether they want a compressed workweek during the summer months. This type of schedule has a couple of drawbacks, however. One is that employees may become exhausted on the longer workdays. Another is that if the arrangement involves working more than 40 hours during a week, the Fair Labor Standards Act requires the payment of overtime wages to nonsupervisory employees.

Atlanta law firm Alston & Bird combined flexibility with the use of work teams to make paralegals' jobs more motivating. In the high pressure of a law firm, paralegals often put in long hours. At Alston & Bird, paralegals are assigned to teams, and each team develops its own work schedules for members, using flexible work hours and job sharing as needed. Turnover is far below the industry average, and one employee notes, "I can't imagine a more interesting job or a better place to work."[18]

Did You Know?

Even Office Work Can Tire You

Muscle fatigue is usually associated with physically demanding jobs such as those in manufacturing and construction, but even office workers can benefit from ergonomic job design.

Source: Derek Timm, "Ergonomic Workplace Strategies Don't Have to Break the Bank," *Healthcare Purchasing News* 31 (November 2007), downloaded from General Reference Center Gold, http://find.galegroup.com.

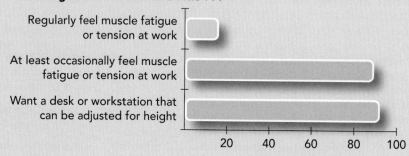

Percentage of Office Workers Who . . .

- Regularly feel muscle fatigue or tension at work
- At least occasionally feel muscle fatigue or tension at work
- Want a desk or workstation that can be adjusted for height

20   40   60   80   100

Telework

Flexibility can extend to work locations as well as work schedules. Before the Industrial Revolution, most people worked either close to or inside their own homes. Mass production technologies changed all this, separating work life from home life, as people began to travel to centrally located factories and offices. Today, however, skyrocketing prices for office space, combined with drastically reduced prices for portable communication and computing devices, seem ready to reverse this trend. The broad term for doing one's work away from a centrally located office is *telework* or telecommuting.

For employers, advantages of telework include less need for office space and the ability to offer greater flexibility to employees who are disabled or need to be available for children or elderly relatives. The employees using telework arrangements may be absent less often than employees with similar demands who must commute to work. Also, a recent study found that the majority of teleworkers say they are at least as productive working from home rather than from a central office.[19] Telework is easiest to implement for people in managerial, professional, or sales jobs, especially those that involve working and communicating on a computer. A telework arrangement is generally difficult to set up for manufacturing workers.

Given the possible benefits, it is not surprising that telework is a growing trend. Estimates indicate that 14 percent of the U.S. workforce operated off-site for at least two days a week in 2007, up from 11 percent in 2004. Projections are that this share will reach 17 percent by 2009.[20]

LO8 Explain how organizations apply ergonomics to design safe jobs.

ergonomics
The study of the interface between individuals' physiology and the characteristics of the physical work environment.

Designing Ergonomic Jobs

The way people use their bodies when they work—whether toting heavy furniture onto a moving van or sitting quietly before a computer screen—affects their physical well-being and may affect how well and how long they can work. The "Did You Know?" box presents data on fatigue. The study of the interface between individuals' physiology and the characteristics of the physical work environment is called **ergonomics.**

The goal of ergonomics is to minimize physical strain on the worker by structuring the physical work environment around the way the human body works. Ergonomics therefore focuses on outcomes such as reducing physical fatigue, aches and pains, and health complaints. Ergonomic research includes the context in which work takes place, such as the lighting, space, and hours worked.[21]

Ergonomic job design has been applied in redesigning equipment used in jobs that are physically demanding. Such redesign is often aimed at reducing the physical demands of certain jobs so that anyone can perform them. In addition, many interventions focus on redesigning machines and technology—for instance, adjusting the height of a computer keyboard to minimize occupational illnesses, such as carpal tunnel syndrome. The design of chairs and desks to fit posture requirements is very important in many office jobs. One study found that having employees participate in an ergonomic redesign effort significantly reduced the number and severity of cumulative trauma disorders (injuries that result from performing the same movement over and over), lost production time, and restricted-duty days.[22]

Although employers in all industries are supposed to protect workers under the "general duty" clause, nursing homes, grocery stores, and poultry-processing plants are the only three industries for which OSHA has published ergonomic standards.

Often, redesigning work to make it more worker-friendly also leads to increased efficiencies. For example, at International Truck and Engine Corporation, one of the most difficult aspects of truck production was pinning the axles to the truck frame. Traditionally, the frame was lowered onto the axle and a crew of six people, armed with oversized hammers and crowbars, forced the frame onto the axle. Because the workers could not see the bolts they had to tighten under the frame, the bolts were often fastened improperly, and many workers injured themselves in the process. After a brainstorming session, the workers and engineers concluded that it would be better to flip the frame upside down and attach the axles from above. The result was a job that could be done twice as fast by half as many workers, who were much less likely to make mistakes or get injured.[23]

The Occupational Safety and Health Administration has a "four-pronged" strategy for encouraging ergonomic job design. The first prong is to issue guidelines (rather than regulations) for specific industries. As of the end of 2007, these guidelines have been issued for the nursing home, grocery store, and poultry-processing industries. Second, OSHA enforces violations of its requirement that employers have a general duty to protect workers from hazards, including ergonomic hazards. Third, OSHA works with industry groups to advise employers in those industries. And finally, OSHA established a National Advisory Committee on Ergonomics to define needs for further research. You can learn more about OSHA's guidelines at the agency's Web site, www.osha.gov.

Designing Jobs That Meet Mental Capabilities and Limitations

LO9 Discuss how organizations can plan for the mental demands of a job.

Just as the human body has capabilities and limitations, addressed by ergonomics, the mind, too, has capabilities and limitations. Besides hiring people with certain mental skills, organizations can design jobs so that they can be accurately and safely performed given the way the brain processes information. Generally, this means reducing the information-processing requirements of a job. In these simpler jobs, workers may be less likely to make mistakes or have accidents. Of course, the simpler jobs also may be less motivating. Research has found that challenging jobs tend to fatigue and dissatisfy workers when they feel little control over their situation, lack social support, and feel motivated mainly to avoid errors. In contrast, they may enjoy the challenges of a difficult job where they have some control and social support, especially if they enjoy learning and are unafraid of making mistakes.[24] Because of this drawback to simplifying jobs, it can be most beneficial to simplify jobs where employees will most appreciate having the mental demands reduced (as in a job that is extremely challenging) or where the costs of errors are severe (as in the job of a surgeon or air-traffic controller).

There are several ways to simplify a job's mental demands. One is to limit the amount of information and memorization that the job requires. Organizations can also provide adequate lighting, easy-to-understand gauges and displays, simple-to-operate equipment, and clear instructions. Often, employees try to simplify some of the mental demands of their own jobs by creating checklists, charts, or other aids. Finally, every job requires some degree of thinking, remembering, and paying attention, so for every job, organizations need to evaluate whether their employees can handle the job's mental demands.

Changes in technology sometimes reduce job demands and errors, but in some cases, technology has made the problem worse. Some employees try to juggle information from several sources at once—say, talking on a cell phone while typing, surfing the Web for information during a team member's business presentation, or repeatedly stopping work on a project to check e-mail or instant messages. In these cases, the cell phone, handheld computer, and e-mail or instant messages are distracting the employees from their primary task. They may convey important information, but they also break the employee's train of thought, reducing performance and increasing the likelihood of errors.[25] The problem may be aggravated by employees downplaying the significance of these interruptions. For example, in a recent survey of workers, only half said they check their e-mail at work more than once an hour, and more than a third said they check every 15 minutes. However, monitoring software on their computers determined that they were actually changing applications to check e-mail up to 30 or 40 times an hour.[26] The sheer volume of e-mail, as illustrated by Figure 4.8, can be a drain on employee time. Even if an employee spends just a minute or two on each message, e-mail will consume a significant part of the day.

Information-processing errors also are greater in situations in which one person hands off information to another. Such transmission problems have become a major concern in the field of medicine, because critical information is routinely shared among nurses, doctors, and medical technicians, as well as between hospital employees changing shifts. Problems during shift changes are especially likely as a result of fatigue and burnout among employees with stressful jobs.[27] Some hospitals have coped by introducing a method called SBAR (situation, background, assessment, and recommendation), which standardizes the information delivered at handoff points. In a

Figure 4.8

Volume of E-mail at Work

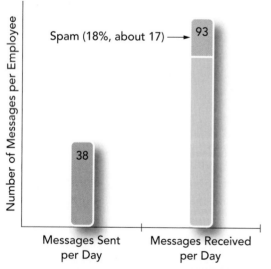

SOURCE: Radicati Group, "The Radicati Group Releases New Study, 'Messaging and Collaboration—Business User Survey, 2007,'" news release, December 17, 2007, www.radicati.com.

few seconds, the person handing off the care of a patient gets control of the situation by engaging the listener's attention (situation), relays enough information to establish the context of the problem (background), gives an overall evaluation of the condition (assessment), and makes a specific suggestion about the best action to take next (recommendation). At one hospital that began using the SBAR method, the rate of adverse events (unexpected medical problems causing harm) was reduced by more than half, from 90 to just 40 of every thousand patients treated.[28]

THINKING ETHICALLY

IS TELECOMMUTING FAIR TO THOSE AT THE OFFICE?

For a growing number of workers who are sick of sitting in rush-hour traffic, the cure is telework, or telecommuting. Researchers have found that people who use computers and other devices to work outside a traditional central-office setting feel more in control of their work and have better morale. Teleworkers also appreciate the cost savings from not having to buy a train ticket or make yet another trip to the gas station.

More recently, however, researchers have taken a closer look at the impact of telecommuting on other employees—those who have to or choose to go to the office every day. When colleagues start telecommuting, those at the workplace enjoy their work less and feel less connected to their coworkers. Traditional commuters may feel that their workload has increased and that their schedule has become less flexible. Overall, they are less satisfied with their work and more likely to consider quitting.

Sources: Timothy Golden, "Co-Workers Who Telework and the Impact on Those in the Office: Understanding the Implications of Virtual Work for Co-Worker Satisfaction and Turnover Intentions," *Human Relations* 60 no. 11 (2007) (abstract), http://hum.sagepub.com; Kristina Cooke, "Telecommuting Not So Great for Those Left in Office," *Yahoo News*, January 11, 2008, http://news.yahoo.com; and Patricia Reaney, "Telecommuting Found to Boost Morale, Cut Stress," *Yahoo News*, November 20, 2007, http://news.yahoo.com.

Questions

1. According to this research, telework benefits some employees at the expense of others. Reviewing the ethical principles from Chapter 1, what can a person ethically do when a course of action benefits some people and hurts others?
2. Imagine that you work in human resource management at a company that has decided to adopt telework as a way to retain valued employees. Suggest ways you can help the company proceed with this plan as ethically as possible.

SUMMARY

LO1 Summarize the elements of work flow analysis.

The analysis identifies the amount and quality of a work unit's outputs, which may be products, parts of products, or services. Next, the analyst determines the work processes required to produce these outputs, breaking down tasks into those performed by each person in the work unit. Finally, the work flow analysis identifies the inputs used to carry out the processes and produce the outputs.

LO2 Describe how work flow is related to an organization's structure.

Within an organization, units and individuals must cooperate to create outputs, and the organization's structure brings people together for this purpose. The structure may be centralized or decentralized, and people may be grouped according to function or into divisions focusing on particular products or customer groups. A functional structure is most appropriate for people who perform highly specialized jobs and hold relatively little authority. Employee empowerment and teamwork succeed best in a divisional structure. Because of these links between structure and types of jobs, considering such issues improves the success of job design.

LO3 Define the elements of a job analysis, and discuss their significance for human resource management.

Job analysis is the process of getting detailed information about jobs. It includes preparation of job descriptions and job specifications. A job description lists the tasks, duties, and responsibilities of a job. Job specifications look at the qualities needed in a person performing the job. They list the knowledge, skills, abilities, and other characteristics that are required for successful performance of a job. Job analysis provides a foundation for carrying out many HRM responsibilities, including work redesign, human resource planning, employee selection and training, performance appraisal, career planning, and job evaluation to determine pay scales.

LO4   Tell how to obtain information for a job analysis.

Information for analyzing an existing job often comes from incumbents and their supervisors. The Labor Department publishes general background information about jobs in the *Dictionary of Occupational Titles* and Occupational Information Network (O*NET). Job analysts, employees, and managers may complete a Position Analysis Questionnaire or fill out a survey for the Fleishman Job Analysis System.

LO5   Summarize recent trends in job analysis.

Some organizations are "dejobbing," or viewing organizations in terms of a field of work needing to be done, rather than as a set or series of jobs. These organizations look for employees who can take on different responsibilities as the field of work changes. Organizations are also adopting project-based structures and teamwork, which also require flexibility and the ability to handle broad responsibilities.

LO6   Describe methods for designing a job so that it can be done efficiently.

The basic technique for designing efficient jobs is industrial engineering, which looks for the simplest way to structure work to maximize efficiency.

Through methods such as time-and-motion studies, the industrial engineer creates jobs that are relatively simple and typically repetitive. These jobs may bore workers because they are so simple.

LO7   Identify approaches to designing a job to make it motivating.

According to the Job Characteristics Model, jobs are more motivating if they have greater skill variety, task identity, task significance, autonomy, and feedback about performance effectiveness. Ways to create such jobs include job enlargement (through job extension or job rotation) and job enrichment. In addition, self-managing work teams offer greater skill variety and task identity. Flexible work schedules and telework offer greater autonomy.

LO8   Explain how organizations apply ergonomics to design safe jobs.

The goal of ergonomics is to minimize physical strain on the worker by structuring the physical work environment around the way the human body works. Ergonomic design may involve modifying equipment to reduce the physical demands of performing certain jobs or redesigning the jobs themselves to reduce strain. Ergonomic design may target work practices associated with injuries.

LO9   Discuss how organizations can plan for the mental demands of a job.

Employers may seek to reduce mental as well as physical strain. The job design may limit the amount of information and memorization involved. Adequate lighting, easy-to-read gauges and displays, simple-to-operate equipment, and clear instructions also can minimize mental strain. Computer software can simplify jobs—for example, by performing calculations or filtering out spam from important e-mail. Finally, organizations can select employees with the necessary abilities to handle a job's mental demands.

KEY TERMS

ergonomics, p. 108
Fleishman Job Analysis System, p. 99
flextime, p. 106
industrial engineering, p. 103
job, p. 91
job analysis, p. 94

job description, p. 94
job design, p. 102
job enlargement, p. 105
job enrichment, p. 105
job extension, p. 105
job rotation, p. 105
job sharing, p. 106

job specification, p. 95
position, p. 91
Position Analysis Questionnaire (PAQ), p. 98
work flow design, p. 91

REVIEW AND DISCUSSION QUESTIONS

1. Assume you are the manager of a fast-food restaurant. What are the outputs of your work unit? What are the activities required to produce those outputs? What are the inputs?

2. Based on Question 1, consider the cashier's job in the restaurant. What are the outputs, activities, and inputs for that job?

3. Consider the "job" of college student. Perform a job analysis on this job. What tasks are required in the job? What knowledge, skills, and abilities are necessary to perform those tasks? Prepare a job description based on your analysis.

4. Discuss how the following trends are changing the skill requirements for managerial jobs in the United States:
   a. Increasing use of computers and the Internet.
   b. Increasing international competition.
   c. Increasing work-family conflicts.

5. How can a job analysis of each job in the work unit help a supervisor to do his or her job?

6. Consider the job of a customer service representative who fields telephone calls from customers of a retailer that sells online and through catalogs. What measures can an employer take to design this job to make it efficient? What might be some drawbacks or challenges of designing this job for efficiency?

7. How might the job in Question 6 be designed to make it more motivating? How well would these considerations apply to the cashier's job in Question 2?

8. What ergonomic considerations might apply to each of the following jobs? For each job, what kinds of costs would result from addressing ergonomics? What costs might result from failing to address ergonomics?
   a. A computer programmer.
   b. A UPS delivery person.
   c. A child care worker.

9. The chapter said that modern electronics have eliminated the need for a store's cashiers to calculate change due on a purchase. How does this development modify the job description for a cashier? If you were a store manager, how would it affect the skills and qualities of job candidates you would want to hire? Does this change in mental processing requirements affect what you would expect from a cashier? How?

10. Consider a job you hold now or have held recently. Would you want this job to be redesigned to place more emphasis on efficiency, motivation, ergonomics, or mental processing? What changes would you want, and why? (Or why do you not want the job to be redesigned?)

BUSINESSWEEK CASE

BusinessWeek Bridging the Generation Gap

For a pair of colleagues born four decades apart, Penelope Burns and Rinath Benjamin spend a lot of time together. Burns, 68, and Benjamin, 29, are sales agents at the Manhattan office of employment agency Randstad USA. They sit inches apart, facing each other. They hear every call the other makes. They read every e-mail the other sends or receives. Sometimes they finish each other's sentences.

This may seem a little strange, but the unconventional pairing is all part of Randstad's effort to ensure that its twentysomething employees—the flighty, praise-seeking Generation Y that we have read so much about—fit in and stick around. The Dutch company, which has been expanding in the United States, is hoping to win the hearts, minds, and loyalty of its young employees by teaming them up with older, more experienced hands. Every new sales agent is assigned a partner to work with until their business has grown to a certain size, which usually

takes a few years. Then they both start over again with someone who has just joined the company.

Randstad has been pairing people up almost since it opened for business four decades ago. The founder's motto was "Nobody should be alone." The original aim was to boost productivity by having sales agents share one job and trade off responsibilities. The system has been refined over the years, and now each week one person is out making sales calls, and the other is in the office interviewing potential workers and handling the paperwork. Then they switch.

Knowing that Gen Yers need lots of attention in the workplace, Randstad executives figured that if they shared a job with someone whose own success depended on theirs, they were certain to get all the nurturing they required. Of course, Randstad doesn't simply put people together and hope it all works out. First it figures out who will play well with other people. To assess that, the human resource department conducts extensive interviews and requires candidates to shadow a sales agent for half a day.

One of the most compelling features of Randstad's partnering program is that neither person is "the boss." And both are expected to teach the other.

Soon after Benjamin started, she suggested they begin to use the electronic payroll system Randstad offers to save time and reduce their paperwork. Burns hesitated: She had been filling out time sheets for the talent (as the temporary employees are called) and wasn't sure how they would take to the new task. But Benjamin persuaded her it would ultimately be simpler for everyone.

These are relationships like any other, full of promise yet always vulnerable to dysfunction. And even the best ones require a lot of maintenance. As Lucille Santos, a 61-year-old senior agent in North Haven, Connecticut, says, "My antennae are always up." Her partner, Allison Kaplan, is 28, and this is her first office job. "We need to be sure that we're asking the right questions and saying the right things to the clients and talent," says Santos. "In the beginning, Allison might have been a little timid about telling applicants they weren't dressed appropriately. I gave her some explicit suggestions, and she learned from watching me." Santos says Kaplan has taught her to relax a little bit more at work.

Randstad used to have an employee retention rate of 50 percent, which is the industry standard. In the past year, its rate has increased to 60 percent. "We have determined a clear connection between being in a unit and feeling more successful and productive," says HR chief Genia Spencer.

SOURCE: Excerpted from Susan Berfield, "Bridging the Generation Gap," *BusinessWeek*, September 17, 2007, downloaded from General Reference Center Gold, http://find.galegroup.com.

Questions

1. A sales agent for an employment agency such as Randstad would be seeking business clients to hire the agency's talent. Based on what you can learn from the information in this chapter, in the case, at Randstad's Web site (www.us.randstad.com), and from the Labor Department's O*NET database (http://online.onetcenter.org), draft a job description and job specifications for the sales agent's job.
2. What other information would you need to complete this job analysis? If you were an HR manager for Randstad, how would you go about getting that information?
3. How do you think the job-sharing arrangement at Randstad affects the efficiency of the sales agents' work? How do you think it affects motivation?

CASE: REDESIGNED WORK AT AIRBUS GETS THE A380 OFF THE GROUND

For Airbus, getting the A380 airborne in 2007 was a struggle, and not just because it's the world's largest passenger jet. Designing and building the aircraft required the talents of employees in different countries, using different computer systems, as well as parts from suppliers around the world. As the project fell behind schedule, with costs breaking the budget, the company had to reevaluate work flow and then redesign how the work would get done.

Airbus, an aircraft maker with headquarters in France and manufacturing and assembly facilities throughout Europe, had intended for the A380 to enter service in 2005. The aircraft is a complex piece of engineering, designed to be not only huge (seating about 550 passengers on two decks) but also the most fuel-efficient plane, as measured in fuel per passenger mile for a full plane. Producing it would require a great degree of cooperation in a company that had historically been highly decentralized. In the past, independent units in France, Germany, Britain, and Spain made various components to be assembled in Toulouse, France, and then flown to Hamburg, Germany, where interior parts such as seats were installed.

When the project got under way, coordination was more difficult than top management had predicted. The problems were especially evident in wiring the aircraft, a

project requiring 30,000 cables hidden behind walls to carry electricity to the plane's cockpit, cargo doors, lighting, and even the toilet flushers—everything on the plane requiring electrical power. Test flights in early 2005 showed that wiring needed to be modified, which meant that workers on two dozen planes that were already in production would have to make the changes in those planes. Airbus announced that the release of the plane would be delayed by six months.

A year later, engineers in Germany were still struggling to make all the changes to the wiring blueprints. By that point, 20 planes were in inventory in the Hamburg facility with temporary wiring. Airbus announced another six-month delay. Airbus's CEO put German engineer Rüdiger Fuchs in charge of A380 assembly in Germany, challenging him to create a more efficient work process.

Fuchs saw that a big part of the problem was lack of coordination. Separate teams were working on separate tasks, such as creating blueprints, obtaining materials, and manufacturing parts. For example, one team worked on the outer body and another on the interior cabin, but no team was assigned to the wiring between them. Also, the German engineers were using older design software than their French colleagues back at headquarters.

Realizing that under these conditions even the revised deadline would be impossible, Fuchs moved the engineers out of their offices and into the factories, where they could solve problems as they arose. Toward the end of the project, engineers were even working inside the jets, where they could advise assembly workers directly. At the end of each day, engineers and production managers met to discuss the day's accomplishments and problems. Those meetings reinforced the need for newer, more efficient design software, so a group of German engineers was moved to Toulouse, where they could learn the new software and work with French engineers on redesigning the parts. The cross-border teamwork, unprecedented for Airbus, began to see results. Finally, the first A380s were ready for take-off. Unfortunately, because the delays reduced sales, profits are still years away.

SOURCES: Daniel Michaels, "Airbus, Amid Turmoil, Revives Troubled Plane," *Wall Street Journal*, October 15, 2007, http://online.wsj.com; "The Giant on the Runway: The Airbus A380," *Economist*, October 13, 2007, downloaded from General Reference Center Gold, http://find.galegroup.com; and Harry Maurer and Christina Linblad, "More Snafus at Airbus," *Business-Week*, November 19, 2007, http://find.galegroup.com.

Questions

1. According to the information given in this case, what were the inputs, work activities, and outputs for producing A380 jets?
2. When Rüdiger Fuchs adjusted the engineers' work design so that some German engineers were working inside jets and others teamed up with colleagues in France, how did these changes affect the knowledge, skills, and abilities and other characteristics required for performing these engineers' jobs?
3. Suppose you had been an HR manager working at Airbus headquarters or in Hamburg when the production of the A380 was first delayed. Could you have helped the company meet its business goals? If so, how? If not, why not?

IT'S A WRAP!

www.mhhe.com/noefund3e is your source for **R**eviewing, **A**pplying, and **P**racticing the concepts you learned about in Chapter 4.

Review
- Chapter learning objectives
- Narrated lecture and iPod content

Application
- Manager's Hot Seat segment: "Virtual Workplace: Out of Office Reply"
- Video case and quiz: "Working Smart"
- Self-assessments Find Your Match: O*NET
- Web exercise: Comparative Job Analysis

Practice
- Chapter quiz

NOTES

1. Teach for America, "Teach for America Places Largest-Ever Corps, Expanding Its Impact to 26 Regions Nationwide," news release, August 15, 2007, www.teachforamerica.org; Lindsey Gerdes and Sophia Asare, "Teach for America Taps Titans," *BusinessWeek*, September 13, 2007, www.businessweek.com; C. Tejada, "Home Office: Millions Don't Leave Work at Work," *Wall Street Journal*, Interactive Edition, March 5, 2002; and C. Richards, "'Pink-Collar' Pressure," *Chicago Tribune*, March 6, 2002, sec. 8, pp. 1, 7.

2. D. Kiley, "The Toyota Way to No. 1," *BusinessWeek*, April 27, 2007, pp. 21–24; and Norman Bodek, "The Ninth Waste—Saying No," *Industry Week*, October 9, 2007, www.industryweek.com.

3. D. Shook, "Why Nike Is Dragging Its Feet," *Business-Week Online*, March 19, 2001; A. Bernstein, "Back-lash: Behind the Anxiety over Globalization," *BusinessWeek*, April 20, 2000, pp. 38-43; A. Bernstein, "Low Skilled Jobs: Do They Have to Move?" *BusinessWeek*, February 26, 2001.

4. J. R. Hollenbeck, H. Moon, A. Ellis, et al., "Structural Contingency Theory and Individual Differences: Examination of External and Internal Person-Team Fit," *Journal of Applied Psychology* 87 (2002), pp. 599–606.

5. C. Joinson, "Refocusing Job Descriptions," *HR Magazine*, January 2001, downloaded from Findarticles.com.

6. A. O'Reilly, "Skill Requirements: Supervisor-Subordinate Conflict," *Personnel Psychology* 26 (1973), pp. 75–80; J. Hazel, J. Madden, and R. Christal, "Agreement between Worker-Supervisor Descriptions of the Worker's Job," *Journal of Industrial Psychology* 2 (1964), pp. 71–79; and A. K. Weyman, "Investigating the Influence of Organizational Role on Perceptions of Risk in Deep Coal Mines," *Journal of Applied Psychology* 88 (2003), pp. 404–12.

7. L. E. Baranowski and L. E. Anderson, "Examining Rater Source Variation in Work Behavior to KSA Linkages," *Personnel Psychology* 58 (2005), pp. 1041–54.

8. U.S. Department of Labor, Employment and Training Administration, "O*NET in Action: Oklahoma," and "O*NET in Action: Manpower, Inc.," both accessed April 8, 2004, at www.doleta.gov/programs/onet/.

9. *PAQ Newsletter*, August 1989; and E. C. Dierdorff and M. A. Wilson, "A Meta-analysis of Job Analysis Reliability," *Journal of Applied Psychology* 88 (2003), pp. 635–46.

10. E. Fleishman and M. Reilly, *Handbook of Human Abilities* (Palo Alto, CA: Consulting Psychologists Press, 1992); E. Fleishman and M. Mumford, "Ability Requirements Scales," in *The Job Analysis Handbook for Business, Industry, and Government*, ed. S. Gael (New York: Wiley, 1988), pp. 917–35.

11. W. Cascio, *Applied Psychology in Personnel Management*, 4th ed. (Englewood Cliffs, NJ: Prentice Hall, 1991).

12. P. Wright and K. Wexley, "How to Choose the Kind of Job Analysis You Really Need," *Personnel*, May 1985, pp. 51–55.

13. M. K. Lindell, C. S. Clause, C. J. Brandt, and R. S. Landis, "Relationship between Organizational Context and Job Analysis Ratings," *Journal of Applied Psychology* 83 (1998), pp. 769–76.

14. S. Caudron, "Jobs Disappear when Work Becomes More Important," *Workforce*, January 2000, pp. 30–32.

15. R. Hackman and G. Oldham, *Work Redesign* (Boston: Addison-Wesley, 1980).

16. W. E. Byrnes, "Making the Job Meaningful All the Way Down the Line," *BusinessWeek*, May 1, 2006, p. 60.

17. M. A. Campion, G. J. Medsker, and A. C. Higgs, "Relations between Work Group Characteristics and Effectiveness: Implications for Designing Effective Work Groups," *Personnel Psychology* 46 (1993), pp. 823–50.

18. S. Greengard, "The Five-Alarm Job," *Workforce*, February 2004, pp. 43–48.

19. Karyn-Siobhan Robinson, "Where Did Everybody Go?" *HR Magazine*, May 2004, downloaded from Infotrac at http://web4.infotrac.galegroup.com.

20. Rachael King, "Working from Home: It's in the Details," *BusinessWeek*, February 12, 2007, pp. 39–40.

21. See, for example, S. Sonnentag and F. R. H. Zijistra, "Job Characteristics and Off-the-Job Activities as Predictors of Need for Recovery, Well-Being, and Fatigue," *Journal of Applied Psychology* 91 (2006), pp. 330–50.

22. D. May and C. Schwoerer, "Employee Health by Design: Using Employee Involvement Teams in Ergonomic Job Redesign," *Personnel Psychology* 47 (1994), pp. 861–86.

23. S. F. Brown, "International's Better Way to Build Trucks," *Fortune*, February 19, 2001, pp. 210k–210v.

24. N. W. Van Yperen and M. Hagerdoorn, "Do High Job Demands Increase Intrinsic Motivation or Fatigue or Both? The Role of Job Support and Social Control," *Academy of Management Journal* 46 (2003), pp. 339–48; and N. W. Van Yperen and O. Janssen, "Fatigued and Dissatisfied or Fatigued but Satisfied? Goal Orientations and Responses to High Job Demands," *Academy of Management Journal* 45 (2002), pp. 1161–71.

25. J. Baker, "From Open Doors to Gated Communities," *BusinessWeek*, September 8, 2003, p. 36.

26. Steve Ranger, "Email: The Root of Your Work Stress?" *Silicon.com*, August 13, 2007, http://hardware.silicon.com/desktops/.

27. L. E. LaBlanc, J. J. Hox, W. B. Schaufell, T. W. Taris, and M. C. W. Peters, "Take Care! The Evaluation of a Team-Based Burnout Intervention Program for Oncology Health Care Providers," *Journal of Applied Psychology* 92 (2007), pp. 213–27.

28. L. Landro, "Hospitals Combat Errors at the 'Hand-Off,'" *Wall Street Journal*, June 28, 2006, pp. D1–D2.

Acquiring and Preparing Human Resources

PART TWO

Planning for and Recruiting Human Resources

What Do I Need to Know?

After reading this chapter, you should be able to:

LO1 Discuss how to plan for human resources needed to carry out the organization's strategy.

LO2 Determine the labor demand for workers in various job categories.

LO3 Summarize the advantages and disadvantages of ways to eliminate a labor surplus and avoid a labor shortage.

LO4 Describe recruitment policies organizations use to make job vacancies more attractive.

LO5 List and compare sources of job applicants.

LO6 Describe the recruiter's role in the recruitment process, including limits and opportunities.

Introduction

Business news often contains stories of layoffs, as organizations seek cost savings or react to falling demand by cutting their workforce. Recently, automobile manufacturers reported the lowest U.S. sales volume in almost a decade.[1] Expecting slow demand to continue, the companies would not need to build as many vehicles as in the past. Chrysler, for example, announced that it would eliminate shifts at several of its U.S. manufacturing facilities. Such a plan generally involves laying off workers and not replacing any workers who leave voluntarily. In contrast, the situation is far different for accounting firms, which are actively competing to fill entry-level jobs with qualified candidates. Many major accounting firms recruit at colleges and even high schools, seeking interns to establish relationships with high-caliber students even before they are ready to start their careers.[2]

As these two examples show, trends and events that affect the economy also create opportunities and problems in obtaining human resources. When customer demand rises (or falls), organizations may need more (or fewer) employees. When the labor market changes—say, when more people go to college or when a sizable share of the population retires—the supply of qualified workers may grow, shrink, or change in nature. Organizations recently have had difficulty filling information technology jobs because the demand for people with these skills outstrips the supply. To prepare for and respond to these challenges, organizations engage in *human resource planning*—defined in Chapter 1 as identifying the numbers and types of employees the organization will require to meet its objectives.

This chapter describes how organizations carry out human resource planning. In the first part of the chapter, we lay out the steps that go into developing and implementing a human resource plan. Throughout each section, we focus especially on recent trends and practices, including downsizing, employing temporary workers, and outsourcing. The remainder of the chapter explores the process

chapter five

of recruiting. We describe the process by which organizations look for people to fill job vacancies and the usual sources of job candidates. Finally, we discuss the role of recruiters.

The Process of Human Resource Planning

Organizations should carry out human resource planning so as to meet business objectives and gain an advantage over competitors. To do this, organizations need a clear idea of the strengths and weaknesses of their existing internal labor force. They also must know what they want to be doing in the future—what size they want the organization to be, what products and services it should be producing, and so on. This knowledge helps them define the number and kinds of employees they will need. Human resource planning compares the present state of the organization with its goals for the future, then identifies what changes it must make in its human resources to meet those goals. The changes may include downsizing, training existing employees in new skills, or hiring new employees.

These activities give a general view of HR planning. They take place in the human resource planning process shown in Figure 5.1. The process consists of three stages: forecasting, goal setting and strategic planning, and program implementation and evaluation.

LO1 Discuss how to plan for human resources needed to carry out the organization's strategy.

Forecasting

The first step in human resource planning is **forecasting,** as shown in the top portion of Figure 5.1. In personnel forecasting, the HR professional tries to determine the supply of and demand for various types of human resources. The primary goal is to predict which areas of the organization will experience labor shortages or surpluses.

Forecasting supply and demand can use statistical methods or judgment. Statistical methods capture historic trends in a company's demand for labor. Under the right conditions, these methods predict demand and supply more precisely than a human forecaster can using subjective judgment. But many important events in the labor market have no precedent. When such events occur, statistical methods are of little use. To

forecasting
The attempts to determine the supply of and demand for various types of human resources to predict areas within the organization where there will be labor shortages or surpluses.

Figure 5.1

Overview of the Human Resource Planning Process

prepare for these situations, the organization must rely on the subjective judgments of experts. Pooling their "best guesses" is an important source of ideas about the future.

Forecasting the Demand for Labor

LO2 Determine the labor demand for workers in various job categories.

Usually, an organization forecasts demand for specific job categories or skill areas. After identifying the relevant job categories or skills, the planner investigates the likely demand for each. The planner must forecast whether the need for people with the necessary skills and experience will increase or decrease. There are several ways of making such forecasts.

trend analysis
Constructing and applying statistical models that predict labor demand for the next year, given relatively objective statistics from the previous year.

At the most sophisticated level, an organization might use **trend analysis,** constructing and applying statistical models that predict labor demand for the next year, given relatively objective statistics from the previous year. These statistics are called **leading indicators**—objective measures that accurately predict future labor demand. They might include measures of the economy (such as sales or inventory levels), actions of competitors, changes in technology, and trends in the composition of the workforce and overall population. For example, the demand for nurses in a community can historically be predicted by knowing the average age of community members. As the average age rises, so does the need for nurses. Studies based on these historical trends suggest that the U.S. economy will need 1.2 million more nurses in 2014.[3] On a more detailed scale, Wal-Mart uses past shopping patterns to predict how many employees will be needed to staff shifts in each of its stores on any given day and time.[4]

leading indicators
Objective measures that accurately predict future labor demand.

Statistical planning models are useful when there is a long, stable history that can be used to reliably detect relationships among variables. However, these models almost always have to be complemented with subjective judgments of experts. There are simply too many "once-in-a-lifetime" changes to consider, and statistical models cannot capture them.

Determining Labor Supply

Once a company has forecast the demand for labor, it needs an indication of the firm's labor supply. Determining the internal labor supply calls for a detailed analysis of how many people are currently in various job categories or have specific skills within the organization. The planner then modifies this analysis to reflect changes expected in the near future as a result of retirements, promotions, transfers, voluntary turnover, and terminations.

transitional matrix
A chart that lists job categories held in one period and shows the proportion of employees in each of those job categories in a future period.

One type of statistical procedure that can be used for this purpose is the analysis of a **transitional matrix.** This is a chart that lists job categories held in one period and shows the proportion of employees in each of those job categories in a future period. It answers two questions: "Where did people who were in each job category go?" and "Where did people now in each job category come from?" Table 5.1 is an example of a transitional matrix.

This example lists job categories for an auto parts manufacturer. The jobs listed at the left were held in 2004; the numbers at the right show what happened to the people in 2007. The numbers represent proportions. For example, .95 means 95 percent of the people represented by a row in the matrix. The column headings under 2007 refer to the row numbers. The first row is sales managers, so the numbers under column (1) represent people who became sales managers. Reading across the first row, we see that 95 of the people who were sales managers in 2004 are still sales managers in 2007. The other 5 percent correspond to position (8), "Not in organization," meaning the 5 percent of employees who are not still sales managers have left the organization. In

Table 5.1

Transitional Matrix: Example for an Auto Parts Manufacturer

2004	2007							
	(1)	(2)	(3)	(4)	(5)	(6)	(7)	(8)
(1) Sales manager	.95							.05
(2) Sales representative	.05	.60						.35
(3) Sales apprentice		.20	.50					.30
(4) Assistant plant manager				.90	.05			.05
(5) Production manager				.10	.75			.15
(6) Production assembler					.10	.80		.10
(7) Clerical							.70	.30
(8) Not in organization	.00	.20	.50	.00	.10	.20	.30	

the second row are sales representatives. Of those who were sales reps in 2004, 5 percent were promoted to sales manager, 60 percent are still sales reps, and 35 percent have left the organization. In row (3), half (50 percent) of sales apprentices are still in that job, but 20 percent are now sales reps and 30 percent have left the organization. This pattern of jobs shows a career path from sales apprentice to sales representative to sales manager. Of course, not everyone is promoted, and some of the people leave instead.

Reading down the columns provides another kind of information: the sources of employees holding the positions in 2007. In the first column, we see that most sales managers (95 percent) held that same job three years earlier. The other 5 percent were promoted from sales representative positions. Skipping over to column (3), half the sales apprentices on the payroll in 2007 held the same job three years before, and the other half were hired from outside the organization. This suggests that the organization fills sales manager positions primarily through promotions, so planning for this job would focus on preparing sales representatives. In contrast, planning to meet the organization's needs for sales apprentices would emphasize recruitment and selection of new employees.

Matrices such as this one are extremely useful for charting historical trends in the company's supply of labor. More important, if conditions remain somewhat constant, they can also be used to plan for the future. For example, if we believe that that we are going to have a surplus of labor in the production assembler job category in the next three years, we can plan to avoid layoffs. Still, historical data may not always reliably indicate future trends. Planners need to combine statistical forecasts of labor supply with expert judgments. For example, managers in the organization may see that a new training program will likely increase the number of employees qualified for new openings. Forecasts of labor supply also should take into account the organization's pool of skills. Many organizations include inventories of employees' skills in an HR database. When the organization forecasts that it will need new skills in the future, planners can consult the database to see how many existing employees have those skills.

As the average age of many workers in skilled trades grows, the coming demand for workers in many trades is expected to outstrip supply in the United States. There is a potential for employers in some areas to experience a labor shortage because of this. How can HR prepare for this reality? What should be done now to avoid the shortage?

Besides looking at the labor supply within the organization, the planner should examine trends in the external labor market. The planner should keep abreast of labor market forecasts, including the size of the labor market, the unemployment rate, and the kinds of people who will be in the labor market. For example, we saw in Chapter 2 that the U.S. labor market is aging and that immigration is an important source of new workers. Important sources of data on the external labor market include the *Occupational Outlook Quarterly* and the *Monthly Labor Review,* published by the Labor Department's Bureau of Labor Statistics. Details and news releases are available at the Web site of the Bureau of Labor Statistics (www.bls.gov).

LO3 Summarize the advantages and disadvantages of ways to eliminate a labor surplus and avoid a labor shortage.

Determining Labor Surplus or Shortage

Based on the forecasts for labor demand and supply, the planner can compare the figures to determine whether there will be a shortage or surplus of labor for each job category. Determining expected shortages and surpluses allows the organization to plan how to address these challenges.

Issues related to a labor surplus or shortage can pose serious challenges for the organization. Manufacturers, for example, expect to have difficulty filling skilled-trades positions such as jobs for ironworkers, machinists, plumbers, and welders. Demand for these jobs is strong and is likely to continue as important infrastructure such as bridges and tunnels ages. Also, the average age of tradespeople is rising above 55, and young people tend not to be attracted to these jobs, assuming, often incorrectly, that manufacturing-related jobs will be difficult to find or will not pay well.[5]

Goal Setting and Strategic Planning

The second step in human resource planning is goal setting and strategic planning, as shown in the middle of Figure 5.1. The purpose of setting specific numerical goals is to focus attention on the problem and provide a basis for measuring the organization's success in addressing labor shortages and surpluses. The goals should come directly from the analysis of labor supply and demand. They should include a specific figure indicating what should happen with the job category or skill area and a specific time-table for when the results should be achieved.

For each goal, the organization must choose one or more human resource strategies. A variety of strategies is available for handling expected shortages and surpluses of labor. The top of Table 5.2 shows major options for reducing an expected labor surplus, and the bottom of the table lists options for avoiding an expected labor shortage.

This planning stage is critical. The options differ widely in their expense, speed, and effectiveness. Options for reducing a labor surplus cause differing amounts of human suffering. The options for avoiding a labor shortage differ in terms of how easily the organization can undo the change if it no longer faces a labor shortage. For example, an organization probably would not want to handle every expected labor shortage by hiring new employees. The process is relatively slow and involves expenses to find and train new employees. Also, if the shortage becomes a surplus, the organization will have to consider laying off some of the employees. Layoffs involve another set of expenses, such as severance pay, and they are costly in terms of human suffering.

core competency
A set of knowledge and skills that make the organization superior to competitors and create value for customers.

Another consideration in choosing an HR strategy is whether the employees needed will contribute directly to the organization's success. Organizations are most likely to benefit from hiring and retaining employees who provide a **core competency**—that is, a set of knowledge and skills that make the organization superior to competitors and create value for customers. At a store, for example, core competencies include choosing

Table 5.2

HR Strategies for Addressing a Labor Shortage or Surplus

OPTIONS FOR REDUCING A SURPLUS		
OPTION	**SPEED OF RESULTS**	**AMOUNT OF SUFFERING CAUSED**
Downsizing	Fast	High
Pay reductions	Fast	High
Demotions	Fast	High
Transfers	Fast	Moderate
Work sharing	Fast	Moderate
Hiring freeze	Slow	Low
Natural attrition	Slow	Low
Early retirement	Slow	Low
Retraining	Slow	Low

OPTIONS FOR AVOIDING A SHORTAGE		
OPTION	**SPEED OF RESULTS**	**ABILITY TO CHANGE LATER**
Overtime	Fast	High
Temporary employees	Fast	High
Outsourcing	Fast	High
Retrained transfers	Slow	High
Turnover reductions	Slow	Moderate
New external hires	Slow	Low
Technological innovation	Slow	Low

downsizing
The planned elimination of large numbers of personnel with the goal of enhancing the organization's competitiveness.

merchandise that shoppers want and providing shoppers with excellent service. For other work that is not a core competency—say, cleaning the store and providing security—the organization may benefit from using HR strategies other than hiring full-time employees.

Organizations try to anticipate labor surpluses far enough ahead that they can freeze hiring and let natural attrition (people leaving on their own) reduce the labor force. Unfortunately for many workers, in the past decade, the typical way organizations have responded to a surplus of labor has been downsizing, which delivers fast results. Beyond the obvious economic impact, downsizing has a psychological impact that spills over and affects families, increasing the rates of divorce, child abuse, and drug and alcohol addiction.[6] To handle a labor shortage, organizations typically hire temporary employees or use outsourcing. Because downsizing, using temporary employees, and outsourcing are most common, we will look at each of these in greater detail in the following sections.

Downsizing

As we discussed in Chapter 2, **downsizing** is the planned elimination of large numbers of personnel with the goal of enhancing the organization's competitiveness. The primary reason organizations engage in downsizing is to promote future competitiveness. According to surveys, they do this by meeting four objectives:

1. *Reducing costs*—Labor is a large part of a company's total costs, so downsizing is an attractive place to start cutting costs.

Cold Stone Creamery employees give their company the competitive advantage with their "entertainment factor." The company is known to seek out employees who like to perform and then "audition" rather than interview potential employees.

2. *Replacing labor with technology*—Closing outdated factories, automating, or introducing other technological changes reduces the need for labor. Often, the labor savings outweigh the cost of the new technology.
3. *Mergers and acquisitions*—When organizations combine, they often need less bureaucratic overhead, so they lay off managers and some professional staff members.
4. *Moving to more economical locations*—Some organizations move from one area of the United States to another, especially from the Northeast, Midwest, and California to the South and the mountain regions of the West. Such moves are one reason that recent job growth has been strongest in Florida and Arizona. In contrast, Michigan, a state in which it is relatively expensive to operate, actually lost jobs during 2004, a period of national economic growth.[7] Other moves have shifted jobs to other countries, including Mexico, India, and China, where wages are lower.

Although the jury is still out on whether these downsizing efforts have enhanced performance, some indications are that the results have not lived up to expectations. According to a study of 52 Fortune 100 firms, most firms that announced a downsizing campaign showed worse, rather than better, financial performance in the years that followed.[8] The negative effect of downsizing was especially high among firms that engaged in high-involvement work practices, such as the use of teams and performance-related pay incentives. As a result, the more a company tries to compete through its human resources, the more layoffs hurt productivity.[9]

Why do so many downsizing efforts fail to meet expectations? There seem to be several reasons. First, although the initial cost savings give a temporary boost to profits, the long-term effects of an improperly managed downsizing effort can be negative. Downsizing leads to a loss of talent, and it often disrupts the social networks through which people are creative and flexible.[10] In a study of hospitals that cut costs by eliminating jobs across the board, the downsizing was followed by an increase in patient mortality rates. And within a year and a half, the costs had climbed to predownsizing levels.[11]

Also, many companies wind up rehiring. Downsizing campaigns often eliminate people who turn out to be irreplaceable. In one survey, 80 percent of the firms that had downsized later replaced some of the very people they had laid off. In one Fortune 100 firm, a bookkeeper making $9 an hour was let go. Later, the company realized she knew many things about the company that no one else knew, so she was hired back as a consultant—for $42 an hour.[12] Hiring back formerly laid-off workers has become so routine that many organizations track their laid-off employees, using software formerly used for tracking job applicants. If the organization ever faces a labor shortage, it can quickly contact these former workers and restore them to the payroll.[13]

Finally, downsizing efforts often fail because employees who survive the purge become self-absorbed and afraid to take risks. Motivation drops because any hope of future promotions—or any future—with the company dies. Many employees start looking for other employment opportunities. The negative publicity associated with a downsizing campaign can also hurt the company's image in the labor market, so it is harder to recruit employees later.

Many problems with downsizing can be reduced with better planning. Instead of slashing jobs across the board, successful downsizing makes surgical strategic cuts that improve the company's competitive position, and management addresses the problem of employees becoming demoralized. At Marlow Industries, planning for problems took the sting out of a downsizing effort that eliminated two-thirds of the company's U.S. workforce and moved work overseas, automated processes, and eliminated middle managers. Marlow's executives communicated extensively with the employees.

The company's president, Barry Nickerson, explained the company's finances and its plans to operate more profitably in the future, including its commitment to keeping the high-end manufacturing work in the United States. Within a few years, Marlow had survived the business downturn.[14]

Still, downsizing hardly guarantees an increase in an organization's competitiveness. Organizations should more carefully consider using all the other avenues for eliminating a labor surplus (shown in Table 5.2). Many of these take effect slowly, so organizations must improve their forecasting or be stuck with downsizing as their only viable option.

Early-Retirement Programs

Another popular way to reduce a labor surplus is with an early-retirement program. As we discussed in Chapter 2, the average age of the U.S. workforce is increasing. But even though many baby boomers are approaching traditional retirement age, early indications are that this group has no intention of retiring soon.[15] Reasons include improved health of older people, jobs becoming less physically demanding, concerns about the long-term viability of Social Security and pensions, and laws against age discrimination. Under the pressures associated with an aging labor force, many employers try to encourage older workers to leave voluntarily by offering a variety of early-retirement incentives. The more lucrative of these programs succeed by some measures. Research suggests that these programs encourage lower-performing older workers to retire.[16] Sometimes they work so well that too many workers retire.

Many organizations are moving from early-retirement programs to phased-retirement programs. In a *phased-retirement program,* the organization can continue to enjoy the experience of older workers while reducing the number of hours that these employees work, as well as the cost of those employees. This option also can give older employees the psychological benefit of easing into retirement, rather than being thrust entirely into a new way of life.[17]

Employing Temporary and Contract Workers

While downsizing has been a popular way to reduce a labor surplus, the most widespread methods for eliminating a labor shortage are hiring temporary and contract workers and outsourcing work. Employers may arrange to hire a temporary worker through an agency that specializes in linking employers with people who have the necessary skills. The employer pays the agency, which in turn pays the temporary worker. Employers also may contract directly with individuals, often professionals, to provide a particular service.

Temporary Workers

As we saw in Chapter 2, the federal government estimated that organizations are using over a million temporary workers. Temporary employment is popular with employers because it gives them flexibility they need to operate efficiently when demand for their products changes rapidly.

In addition to flexibility, temporary employment offers lower costs. Using temporary workers frees the employer from many administrative tasks and financial burdens associated with being the "employer of record." The cost of employee benefits, including health care, pension, life insurance, workers' compensation, and unemployment insurance, can account for 40 percent of payroll expenses for permanent employees. Assuming the agency pays for these benefits, a company using temporary workers may save money even if it pays the agency a higher rate for that worker than the usual wage paid to a permanent employee.

HR How To

USING TEMPORARY EMPLOYEES AND CONTRACTORS

Many full-time employees perceive temporary workers as a threat to their own job security. Such an attitude can interfere with cooperation and, in some cases, lead to outright sabotage if the situation is not well managed.

One way organizations should manage this situation is to complete any downsizing efforts before bringing in temporary or contract workers. Surviving a downsizing is almost like experiencing a death in the family. A decent time interval needs to occur before new temporary workers are introduced. Without the delay, the surviving employees will associate the downsizing effort (which was a threat) with the new temporary employees (who could be per-

ceived as outsiders brought in to replace old friends). If an upswing in demand follows a downsizing effort, the organization should probably begin meeting its expanded demand for labor by granting overtime to core employees. If the demand persists, the organization will be more certain that the upswing will last and future layoffs will be unnecessary. The extended stretches of overtime will eventually tax the full-time employees, so they will accept using temporary workers to help lessen their load.

The organization may also try to select "nonthreatening" temporary workers, especially those who enjoy temporary assignments for their variety or flexibility.

Many temporary-staffing firms attract people with this outlook.

Organizations that use temporary or contract workers must avoid treating them as second-class citizens. One way to do this is to ensure that the temporary agency provides temporaries with benefits that are comparable with those enjoyed by the organization's permanent workers. For example, one temporary agency, MacTemps, gives its workers long-term health coverage, full disability insurance, and complete dental coverage. This not only reduces the benefit gap between the temporary and permanent workers but also helps attract the best temporary workers in the first place.

Agencies that provide temporary employees also may handle some of the tasks associated with hiring. Small companies that cannot afford their own testing programs often get employees who have been tested by a temporary agency. Many temporary agencies also train employees before sending them to employers. This reduces employers' training costs and eases the transition for the temporary worker and employer.

Finally, temporary workers may offer value not available from permanent employees. Because the temporary worker has little experience at the employer's organization, this person brings an objective point of view to the organization's problems and procedures. Also, a temporary worker may have a great deal of experience in other organizations that can be applied to the current assignment.

To obtain these benefits, organizations need to overcome the disadvantages associated with temporary workers. For example, tension can develop between temporary and permanent employees. For suggestions on how to address this challenge, see the "HR How To" box.

Employee or Contractor?

Besides using a temporary-employment agency, a company can obtain workers for limited assignments by entering into contracts with them. If the person providing the services is an independent contractor, rather than an employee, the company does not pay employee benefits, such as health insurance and vacations. As with using temporary employees, the savings can be significant, even if the contractor works at a higher rate of pay.

FedEx Ground recently built up an efficient delivery system by signing on drivers to work as independent contractors. These contract drivers lease vans and buy uniforms from FedEx and take responsibility for the deliveries along a particular route. They are responsible for their business expenses, including gasoline and maintenance of their trucks. FedEx pays them according to the number of packages they deliver plus a bonus based on its own information about customer satisfaction. The payment method provides an incentive for the contractors to work hard and drum up new business. Some successful drivers have hired their own employees and leased additional trucks.[18]

This strategy carries risks, however. If the person providing the service is a contractor and not an employee, the company is not supposed to directly supervise the worker. The company can tell the contractor what criteria the finished assignment should meet but not, for example, where or what hours to work. This distinction is significant, because under federal law, if the company treats the contractor as an employee, the company has certain legal obligations, described in Part 4, related to matters such as overtime pay and withholding taxes. With regard to FedEx Ground, some drivers have become dissatisfied with their working arrangement and complained that they are actually employees. In courts in California, Montana, and New Jersey, judges found FedEx Ground drivers with contracts to be employees (the company appealed those rulings). The Internal Revenue Service has begun investigating these arrangements, to see whether FedEx management is exerting too much control. For FedEx, the challenge is to figure out whether it can continue an arrangement it says many drivers prefer, exert enough influence to ensure contractors meet its standards, and also meet the legal requirements for independent contractor status.[19]

When an organization wants to consider using independent contractors as a way to expand its labor force temporarily, human resource professionals can help by alerting the company to the need to verify that the arrangement will meet the legal requirements. A good place to start is with the advice to small businesses at the Internal Revenue Service Web site (www.irs.gov); search for "independent contractor" to find links to information and guidance. In addition, the organization may need to obtain professional legal advice.

Outsourcing

Instead of using a temporary or contract employee to fill a single job, an organization might want a broader set of services. Contracting with another organization to perform a broad set of services is called **outsourcing.** Organizations use outsourcing as a way to operate more efficiently and save money. They choose outsourcing firms that promise to deliver the same or better quality at a lower cost. One reason they can do this is that the outside company specializes in the service and can benefit from economies of scale (the economic principle that producing something in large volume tends to cost less for each additional unit than producing in small volume). This efficiency is often the attraction for outsourcing human resource functions such as payroll. Costs also are lower when the outsourcing firm is located in a part of the world where wages are relatively low. The labor forces of countries such as China, India, Jamaica, and those in Eastern Europe have been creating an abundant supply of labor for unskilled and low-skilled work.

The first uses of outsourcing emphasized manufacturing and routine tasks. However, technological advances in computer networks and transmission have speeded up the outsourcing process and have helped it spread beyond manufacturing areas and low-skilled jobs. For example, DuPont moved legal services associated with its $100 million asbestos case litigation to a team of lawyers working in the Philippines. The work is a combination of routine document handling and legal judgments such as determining the relevance of a document to the case. Salaries for lawyers and

outsourcing
Contracting with another organization to perform a broad set of services.

paralegals in the Philippines are about one-fifth the cost of their counterparts in the United States.[20]

Outsourcing may be a necessary way to operate as efficiently as competitors, but it does pose challenges. Quality-control problems, security violations, and poor customer service have sometimes wiped out the cost savings attributed to lower wages. To ensure success with an outsourcing strategy, companies should follow these guidelines:

- Look for experienced providers with adequate resources. Small overseas upstarts may promise more than they can deliver and take risks that a more established contractor would avoid.[21]
- Do not offshore any work that is proprietary or requires tight security.[22]
- Start small and monitor the work closely, especially in the beginning, when problems are most likely.[23]
- Look for opportunities to outsource work in areas that promote growth, for example, by partnering with experts who can help the organization tap new markets.[24]

Overtime and Expanded Hours

Organizations facing a labor shortage may be reluctant to hire employees, even temporary workers, or to commit to an outsourcing arrangement. Especially if the organization expects the shortage to be temporary, it may prefer an arrangement that is simpler and less costly. Under some conditions, these organizations may try to garner more hours from the existing labor force, asking them to go from part-time to full-time status or to work overtime.

A major downside of overtime is that the employer must pay nonmanagement employees one-and-a-half times their normal wages for work done overtime. Even so, employers see overtime pay as preferable to the costs of hiring and training new employees. The preference is especially strong if the organization doubts that the current higher level of demand for its products will last long.

For a short time at least, many workers appreciate the added compensation for working overtime. Over extended periods, however, employees feel stress and frustration from working long hours. Overtime therefore is best suited for short-term labor shortages.

Implementing and Evaluating the HR Plan

For whatever HR strategies are selected, the final stage of human resource planning involves implementing the strategies and evaluating the outcomes. This stage is represented by the bottom part of Figure 5.1. When implementing the HR strategy, the organization must hold some individual accountable for achieving the goals. That person also must have the authority and resources needed to accomplish those goals. It is also important that this person issue regular progress reports, so the organization can be sure that all activities occur on schedule and that the early results are as expected. The "Best Practices" box discusses one company's creative plan to attract video game developers.

Implementation at Electronic Data Systems involves using technology to make HR professionals aware of what skills the organization will need in the future, giving them time to prepare for change. The company has a database detailing employees' work histories and skills; over two-thirds of the 120,000 employees are in the database

Best Practices

A Stealthy HR Plan for Red 5 Studios

As founder of his start-up video game company, Red 5 Studios, Mark Kern was responsible for recruiting programmers. A year into Red 5's life, that effort was struggling. The company had posted want ads and hired recruiters, but not enough qualified candidates were expressing interest. Part of the problem was that although Kern and his core employees had a great reputation from creating the popular World of Warcraft games for a former employer, Red 5 was unknown; it had not yet released a game, and its plans were still largely secret.

To attract interest in his company, Kern decided to develop a creative recruiting plan. He and his 20 staff members came up with a list of top-notch game developers who had the experience and skills to fill key spots at Red 5.

The company sent each of them a package containing a box, which contained a smaller box, and a smaller box, down to a box containing an iPod Shuffle. Loaded on each iPod was a recorded message from Kern, explaining why the recipient should apply for a job at Red 5. A message engraved on each iPod gave the link to a private page of Red 5's Web site where the candidate could read the company's strategic plan.

Although the cost to reach each software developer was high, the effort was targeted to a precise group that Kern and his staff had researched ahead of time. The company paid about $50,000 for the whole effort, which Kern estimates would have been the cost for a recruiter to fill two major positions. More than 90 of the 100 prospects visited Red 5's Web site, and the company initially hired three of them. But the impact didn't stop there. The recruiting campaign generated excitement within the software industry, and a steady stream of résumés continued. Of 21 employees hired between the end of the recruiting campaign and fall 2007, 16 learned about Red 5 as a result of the iPod mailing. The company no longer bothers to pay for want ads at public sites, because it gets enough interested talent through its own Web site. Getting programmers to think of Red 5 as a viable employer is a game Kern has already won.

Sources: Simona Covel, "Start-Up Lures Talent with Creative Pitch," *Wall Street Journal*, June 4, 2007, downloaded from Factiva, http://integrate.factiva.com; and Ryan McCarthy, "'Help Wanted' Meets 'Buy It Now': Why More Companies Are Integrating Marketing and Recruiting," *Inc.*, November 2007, pp. 50–52.

so far. Employees enter the data themselves, using a Web-based system that allows them to select from pull-down menus and offers places to enter additional information. The information in the database includes knowledge of computer languages and certifications, as well as other education and work assignments completed. HR professionals compare information in the database against the company's five-year plan to identify any skills gaps. For example, EDS determined that 22,000 employees can program using COBOL, far more than the company expects to need. To solve this labor surplus, the company is preparing training programs in newer languages where the company has a labor shortage. Thus, the HR planning process is tied to the company's training activities.[25]

In evaluating the results, the most obvious step is checking whether the organization has succeeded in avoiding labor shortages or surpluses. Along with measuring these numbers, the evaluation should identify which parts of the planning process contributed to success or failure. In EDS's case, evaluation would include whether the company has a close match between the number of programmers who know each language and the number needed to program in that language. If there is a skills gap, the evaluation should consider whether the problem lies with the forecasts used to plan training or with the implementation. For example, are programmers signing up for training, do they know about the training, and is enough of the right kind of training available?

Applying HR Planning to Affirmative Action

As we discussed in Chapter 3, many organizations have a human resource strategy that includes affirmative action to manage diversity or meet government requirements. Meeting affirmative-action goals requires that employers carry out an additional level of human resource planning aimed at those goals. In other words, besides looking at its overall workforce and needs, the organization looks at the representation of subgroups in its labor force—for example, the proportion of women and minorities.

Affirmative-action plans forecast and monitor the proportion of employees who are members of various protected groups (typically, women and racial or ethnic minorities). The planning looks at the representation of these employees in the organization's job categories and career tracks. The planner can compare the proportion of employees who are in each group with the proportion each group represents in the labor market. For example, the organization might note that in a labor market that is 25 percent Hispanic, 60 percent of its customer service personnel are Hispanic. This type of comparison is called a **workforce utilization review.** The organization can use this process to determine whether there is any subgroup whose proportion in the relevant labor market differs substantially from the proportion in the job category.

workforce utilization review
A comparison of the proportion of employees in protected groups with the proportion that each group represents in the relevant labor market.

If the workforce utilization review indicates that some group—for example, African Americans—makes up 35 percent of the relevant labor market for a job category but that this same group constitutes only 5 percent of the employees actually in the job category at the organization, this is evidence of underutilization. That situation could result from problems in selection or from problems in internal movement (promotions or other movement along a career path). One way to diagnose the situation would be to use transitional matrices, such as the matrix shown in Table 5.1 earlier in this chapter.

The steps in a workforce utilization review are identical to the steps in the HR planning process that were shown in Figure 5.1. The organization must assess current utilization patterns, then forecast how they are likely to change in the near future. If these analyses suggest the organization is underutilizing certain groups and if forecasts suggest this pattern is likely to continue, the organization may need to set goals and timetables for changing. The planning process may identify new strategies for recruitment or selection. The organization carries out these HR strategies and evaluates their success.

LO4 Describe recruitment policies organizations use to make job vacancies more attractive.

Recruiting Human Resources

As the first part of this chapter shows, it is difficult to always predict exactly how many (if any) new employees the organization will have to hire in a given year in a given job category. The role of human resource recruitment is to build a supply of potential new hires that the organization can draw on if the need arises. In human resource management, **recruiting** consists of any practice or activity carried on by the organization with the primary purpose of identifying and attracting potential employees.[26] It thus creates a buffer between planning and the actual selection of new employees (the topic of the next chapter). The goals of recruiting (encouraging qualified people to apply for jobs) and selection (deciding which candidates would be the best fit) are different enough that they are most effective when performed separately, rather than combined as in a job interview that also involves selling candidates on the company.[27]

recruiting
Any activity carried on by the organization with the primary purpose of identifying and attracting potential employees.

Because of differences in companies' strategies, they may assign different degrees of importance to recruiting.[28] In general, however, all companies have to make decisions in three areas of recruiting: personnel policies, recruitment sources, and the characteristics

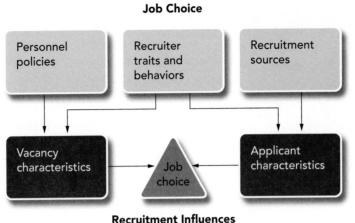

Figure 5.2

Three Aspects of Recruiting

and behavior of the recruiter. As shown in Figure 5.2, these aspects of recruiting have different effects on whom the organization ultimately hires. Personnel policies influence the characteristics of the positions to be filled. Recruitment sources influence the kinds of job applicants an organization reaches. And the nature and behavior of the recruiter affect the characteristics of both the vacancies and the applicants. Ultimately, an applicant's decision to accept a job offer—and the organization's decision to make the offer—depend on the match between vacancy characteristics and applicant characteristics.

The remainder of this chapter explores these three aspects of recruiting: personnel policies, recruitment sources, and recruiter traits and behaviors.

Personnel Policies

An organization's *personnel policies* are its decisions about how it will carry out human resource management, including how it will fill job vacancies. These policies influence the nature of the positions that are vacant. According to the research on recruitment, it is clear that characteristics of the vacancy are more important than recruiters or recruiting sources for predicting job choice.[29] Several personnel policies are especially relevant to recruitment:

- *Internal versus external recruiting*—Organizations with policies to "promote from within" try to fill upper-level vacancies by recruiting candidates internally—that is, finding candidates who already work for the organization. Opportunities for advancement make a job more attractive to applicants and employees. Decisions about internal versus external recruiting affect the nature of jobs, recruitment sources, and the nature of applicants, as we will describe later in the chapter.
- *Lead-the-market pay strategies*—Pay is an important job characteristic for almost all applicants. Organizations have a recruiting advantage if their policy is to take a "lead-the-market" approach to pay—that is, pay more than the current market wages for a job. Higher pay can also make up for a job's less desirable features, such as working on a night shift or in dangerous conditions. Organizations that compete for applicants based on pay may use bonuses, stock options, and other forms of pay besides wages and salaries. Chapters 11 and 12 will take a closer look at these and other decisions about pay.

Image advertising, such as in this campaign to recruit nurses, promotes a whole profession or organization as opposed to a specific job opening. This ad is designed to create a positive impression of the profession, which is now facing a shortage of workers.

employment at will
Employment principle that if there is no specific employment contract saying otherwise, the employer or employee may end an employment relationship at any time, regardless of cause.

due-process policies
Policies that formally lay out the steps an employee may take to appeal the employer's decision to terminate that employee.

LO5 List and compare sources of job applicants.

- *Employment-at-will policies*—Within the laws of the state where they are operating, employers have latitude to set polices about their rights in an employment relationship. A widespread policy follows the principle of **employment at will,** which holds that if there is no specific employment contract saying otherwise, the employer or employee may end an employment relationship at any time. An alternative is to establish extensive **due-process policies,** which formally lay out the steps an employee may take to appeal an employer's decision to terminate that employee. An organization's lawyers may advise the company to ensure that all recruitment documents say the employment is "at will," to protect the company from lawsuits about wrongful discharge. Management must decide how to weigh any legal advantages against the impact on recruitment. Job applicants are more attracted to organizations with due-process policies, which imply greater job security and concern for protecting employees, than to organizations with employment-at-will policies.[30]
- *Image advertising*—Besides advertising specific job openings, as discussed in the next section, organizations may advertise themselves as a good place to work in general.[31] Advertising designed to create a generally favorable impression of the organization is called *image advertising*. Image advertising is particularly important for organizations in highly competitive labor markets that perceive themselves as having a bad image.[32] Research suggests that the image of an organization's brand—for example, innovative, dynamic, or fun—influences the degree to which a person feels attracted to the organization.[33] This attraction is especially true if the person's own traits seem to match those of the organization. Also, job applicants seem to be particularly sensitive to issues of diversity and inclusion in image advertising, so organizations should ensure that their image advertisements reflect the broad nature of the labor market from which they intend to recruit.[34]

Recruitment Sources

Another critical element of an organization's recruitment strategy is its decisions about where to look for applicants. The total labor market is enormous and spread over the entire globe. As a practical matter, an organization will draw from a small fraction of that total market. The methods the organization chooses for communicating its labor needs and the audiences it targets will determine the size and nature of the labor market the organization taps to fill its vacant positions.[35] A person who responds to a job advertisement on the Internet is likely to be different from a person responding to a sign hanging outside a factory. The "Did You Know?" box presents some data on sources of recruitment. Each of the major sources from which organizations draw recruits has advantages and disadvantages.

Internal Sources

As we discussed with regard to personnel policies, an organization may emphasize internal or external sources of job applicants. Internal sources are employees who currently hold other positions in the organization. Organizations recruit existing

Did You Know?

In a survey of large, well-known businesses, respondents said about one-third of positions are filled with people who already work for the company and accept a promotion or transfer.

Sources: Gerry Crispin and Mark Mehler, "CareerXroads 6th Annual 2006 Sources of Hire Study," www.careerxroads.com; and Gerry Crispin and Mark Mehler, "Sources of Hire: The Good, the Bad and the In Between," *CareerXroads Update,* March 2007, http://www.careerxroads.com/news/updates/.

Sources of Hire

All External Sources, 66%

Internal Movement, 34%

Note: "Internal movement" refers to jobs filled from employees currently in the company who are referred by managers or receive promotions or transfers; "all external sources" refers to employees found using sources outside the company such as electronic recruiting from company or job Web sites, employment agencies, colleges and universities, walk-in applicants, newspaper ads, and referrals.

employees through **job posting,** or communicating information about the vacancy on company bulletin boards, in employee publications, on corporate intranets, and anywhere else the organization communicates with employees. Managers also may identify candidates to recommend for vacancies. Policies that emphasize promotions and even lateral moves to achieve broader career experience can give applicants a favorable impression of the organization's jobs. The use of internal sources also affects what kinds of people the organization recruits.

For the employer, relying on internal sources offers several advantages.[36] First, it generates applicants who are well known to the organization. In addition, these applicants are relatively knowledgeable about the organization's vacancies, which minimizes the possibility they will have unrealistic expectations about the job. Finally, filling vacancies through internal recruiting is generally cheaper and faster than looking outside the organization.

The value of a strong internal hiring system can be seen in the experience of Whirlpool. A few years ago, it was difficult for someone inside the company to know what jobs were available within the huge manufacturing conglomerate. The job-posting system was a paper-and-pencil process, organized regionally, so it was difficult and time-consuming to obtain information about positions out of state. The company replaced this ineffective system with a Web-based system that allows managers to enter information about open positions and lets employees enter their résumés. Both use a standardized format, so the software can search for key terms and locate matches. As Whirlpool began to fill over half of its open positions with internal hires, costs for recruiting and training fell by $1 million. The system also satisfies employees, who can use it for planning their careers.[37]

job posting
The process of communicating information about a job vacancy on company bulletin boards, in employee publications, on corporate intranets, and anywhere else the organization communicates with employees.

External Sources

Despite the advantages of internal recruitment, organizations often have good reasons to recruit externally.[38] For entry-level positions and perhaps for specialized upper-level positions, the organization has no internal recruits from which to draw. Also, bringing in outsiders may expose the organization to new ideas or new ways of doing business. An organization that uses only internal recruitment can wind up with a workforce whose members all think alike and therefore may be poorly suited to innovation.[39] So organizations often recruit through direct applicants and referrals, advertisements, employment agencies, schools, and Web sites. Figure 5.3 shows which of these sources are used most among large companies surveyed.

Direct Applicants and Referrals

Even without a formal effort to reach job applicants, an organization may hear from candidates through direct applicants and referrals. **Direct applicants** are people who apply for a vacancy without prompting from the organization. **Referrals** are people who apply because someone in the organization prompted them to do so. According to the survey results shown in Figure 5.3, the largest share (about one-fourth) of new employees hired by large companies came from referrals, and the next largest share (almost 21 percent)

direct applicants
People who apply for a vacancy without prompting from the organization.

referrals
People who apply for a vacancy because someone in the organization prompted them to do so.

Figure 5.3

External Recruiting Sources

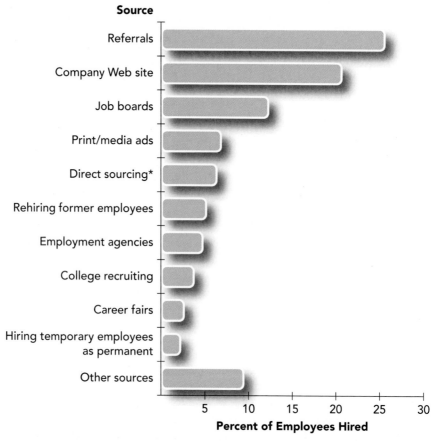

*Direct sourcing includes research by the employer, such as searching internal or public databases of résumés and other public records to identify and contact people who seem to be well-qualified but did not apply.

SOURCES: Gerry Crispin and Mark Mehler, "CareerXroads 6th Annual 2006 Sources of Hire Study," www.careerxroads.com; and Gerry Crispin and Mark Mehler, "Sources of Hire: The Good, the Bad and the In Between," *CareerXroads Update,* March 2007, http://www.careerxroads.com/news/updates/.

came from direct applications made at the employer's Web site.[40] These two sources of recruits share some characteristics that make them excellent pools from which to draw.

One advantage is that many direct applicants are to some extent already "sold" on the organization. Most have done some research and concluded there is enough fit between themselves and the vacant position to warrant submitting an application, a process called *self-selection*, which, when it works, eases the pressure on the organization's recruiting and selection systems. A form of aided self-selection occurs with referrals. Many job seekers look to friends, relatives, and acquaintances to help find employment. Using these social networks not only helps the job seeker but also simplifies recruitment for employers.[41] Current employees (who are familiar with the vacancy as well as the person they are referring) decide that there is a fit between the person and the vacancy, so they convince the person to apply for the job.

An additional benefit of using such sources is that it costs much less than formal recruiting efforts. Considering these combined benefits, referrals and direct applications are among the best sources of new hires. Some employers offer current employees financial incentives for referring applicants who are hired and perform acceptably on the job (for example, if they stay 180 days). Other companies such as Google and SAS play off their good reputations in the labor market to generate direct applications. SAS, a Cary, North Carolina–based developer of business systems, is so well-known in the software industry for its generous workplace benefits and challenging assignments that recruiting is a bargain—partly because so many people go to the company looking for jobs and partly because they tend to stick around when they are hired.[42]

The major downside of referrals is that they limit the likelihood of exposing the organization to fresh viewpoints. People tend to refer others who are like themselves. Furthermore, sometimes referrals contribute to hiring practices that are or that appear unfair, an example being **nepotism,** or the hiring of relatives. Employees may resent the hiring and rapid promotion of "the boss's son" or "the boss's daughter," or even the boss's friend.

nepotism
The practice of hiring relatives.

Advertisements in Newspapers and Magazines

Open almost any newspaper or magazine and you can find advertisements of job openings. These ads typically generate a less desirable group of applicants than direct applications or referrals, and do so at greater expense. However, few employers can fill all their vacancies purely through direct applications and referrals, so they usually need to advertise. Although many job searches today are conducted online, a recent survey of job hunters by the Conference Board found that about as many—71 percent—said they use newspaper ads as said they use online advertising.[43] Also, an employer can take many steps to increase the effectiveness of recruitment through advertising.

The person designing a job advertisement needs to answer two questions:

What do we need to say?
To whom do we need to say it?

With respect to the first question, an ad should give readers enough information to evaluate the job and its requirements, so they can make a well-informed judgment about their qualifications. Providing enough information may require long advertisements, which cost more. The employer should evaluate the additional costs against the costs of providing too little information: Vague ads generate a huge number of applicants, including many who are not reasonably qualified or would not accept the job if they learned more about it. Reviewing all these applications to eliminate unsuitable applicants is expensive. In practice, the people who write job advertisements tend to overstate the skills and experience required, perhaps generating too few qualified candidates. For example, some have blamed the shortage of qualified engineers in America on job advertising that requires experience with particular processes or software programs, rather than looking for broader abilities that can be transferred to new applications.[44]

Specifying whom to reach with the message helps the advertiser decide where to place the ad. The most common medium for advertising jobs is the classified section of local newspapers. These ads are relatively inexpensive yet reach many people in a specific geographic area who are currently looking for work (or at least interested enough to be reading the classifieds). On the downside, this medium offers little ability to target skill levels. Typically, many of the people reading classified ads are either over- or underqualified for the position. Also, people who are not looking for work rarely read the classifieds. These people may include candidates the organization could lure from their current employers. For reaching a specific part of the labor market, including certain skill levels and more people who are employed, the organization may get better results from advertising in professional or industry journals. Some employers also advertise on television—particularly cable television.[45]

Electronic Recruiting

In recent years, employers have shifted their spending on job advertisements away from print ads to online job advertising or a combination of the two. A recent survey by the Conference Board found that the number of online job ads rose by 24 percent over the previous year.[46] Online recruiting generally involves posting career information at company Web sites to address people who are interested in the particular company and posting paid advertisements at career services to attract people who are searching for jobs.

Most large companies and many smaller ones make career information available at their Web sites. To make that information easier to find, they may register a domain name with a ".jobs" extension, such as www.starbucks.jobs for a link to information about careers at Starbucks and www.unionpacific.jobs for information about careers at Union Pacific. To be an effective recruiting tool, corporate career information should move beyond generalities, offering descriptions of open positions and an easy way to submit a résumé. A user-friendly career site is not complicated. Basics include a prominent link to career information from the company's home page and additional links to career information for categories of candidates, such as college graduates, returning military personnel, or people in a particular profession. The user also should be able to link to information about the company to evaluate whether it will be a good fit with the candidates' interests and strengths. Candidates also appreciate an e-mail response that the company has received the résumé—especially a response that gives a timetable about further communications from the company.[47]

Accepting applications at the company Web site is not so successful for smaller and less well-known organizations, because fewer people are likely to visit the Web site. These organizations may get better results by going to the Web sites that are set up to attract job seekers, such as Monster, Yahoo HotJobs, and CareerBuilder, which attract a vast array of applicants. At these sites, job seekers submit standardized résumés. Employers can search the site's database for résumés that include specified key terms, and they can also submit information about their job opportunities, so that job seekers can search that information by key term. With both employers and job seekers submitting information to and conducting searches on them, these sites offer an efficient way to find matches between job seekers and job vacancies. However, a drawback is that the big job Web sites can provide too many leads of inferior quality because they are so huge and serve all job seekers and employers, not a select segment.

ONLINE RECRUITING GETS PERSONAL

When today's Internet users go online, they aren't satisfied just to read about a company: they want to interact with the company's people. For recruiting, that means companies are turning to Web tools that promote interaction.

One way companies are getting started is by asking for introductions to people who might have needed skills and connections. On social networking sites like Facebook and career-oriented site LinkedIn, they can make initial contact with people who are connected to someone the recruiter already knows. After that introduction, it is up to the recruiter to build a relationship online or set up a meeting. For example, Valerie Luther, founder of Creative Concepts, and her staff participate in social networking groups to gain exposure for the business and meet individuals who might be a good fit as employees.

Other companies set up shop virtually in the online role-playing community of Second Life. Dutch accounting firm Berk opened a virtual office in Second Life. Some of Berk's employees created avatars to interact with Second Life visitors who make an appointment to visit the company, telling them what it's like to be a Berk employee.

Sources: Deborah Perelman, "Leveraging Web 2.0 to Recruit," *eWeek,* November 2, 2007, www.careers. eweek.com; "Social Networks Are Good for Business, according to Creative Concepts," *Internet Wire,* October 24, 2007, downloaded from Business & Company Resource Center, http://galenet.galegroup. com; and Arvind Hickman, "Profession Logs On to Virtual Reality," *International Accounting Bulletin,* April 21, 2007, http://galenet.galegroup.com.

Because of this limitation of the large Web sites, smaller, more tailored Web sites called "niche boards" focus on certain industries, occupations, or geographic areas. Telecommcareers.net, for example, is a site devoted to, as the name implies, the telecommunications industry. CIO.com, a companion site to *CIO Magazine,* specializes in openings for chief information officers. In addition, companies can improve the effectiveness of online advertising by employing more interactive tools, such as social networking.

Public Employment Agencies

The Social Security Act of 1935 requires that everyone receiving unemployment compensation be registered with a local state employment office. These state employment offices work with the U.S. Employment Service (USES) to try to ensure that unemployed individuals eventually get off state aid and back on employer payrolls. To accomplish this, agencies collect information from the unemployed people about their skills and experience.

Employers can register their job vacancies with their local state employment office, and the agency will try to find someone suitable, using its computerized inventory of local unemployed individuals. The agency refers candidates to the employer at no charge. The organization can interview or test them to see if they are suitable for its vacancies. Besides offering access to job candidates at low cost, public employment agencies can be a useful resource for meeting certain diversity objectives. Laws often mandate that the agencies maintain specialized "desks" for minorities, disabled individuals, and war veterans. Employers that feel they currently are underutilizing any of these subgroups of the labor force may find the agencies to be an excellent source.

The government also provides funding to a variety of local employment agencies. For example, in Virginia, the Frederick County Job Training Agency receives funding from the federal, state, and county governments to help unemployed workers find and

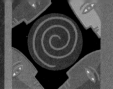

HR Oops!

Sneaky Recruiters

Imagine you're a busy executive, and your assistant whispers that a lawyer, reporter, or family member is on the phone, insisting to talk to you about some important confidential business. Worried, you stop what you're doing and take the call. The person on the line begins to tell you about a great opportunity for you to work at another company.

What's going on? The caller insists that the assistant must have misunderstood or that the message is so valuable but confidential that he or she simply had to be vague or confusing. What the caller is really doing is engaging in an unethical practice called "rusing," taking on a false identity to get the attention of an executive or other hard-to-reach employee. At least one company has even hired actors to play roles to get their phone calls put through to targeted managers.

Executive search consultants and trade groups criticize rusing as dishonest and unprofessional. And you have to wonder how well it works. Would you really want to place your future career in the hands of a recruiter who deceived you from the start?

Source: Joseph Daniel McCool, "Recruiters: 'Rusing' Their Way to the Top," *BusinessWeek,* September 20, 2007, www.businessweek.com.

Questions

1. If your company needed to fill an important position, would you, as an HR manager, want to hire a recruiting firm that used rusing? Why or why not?

2. Besides rusing, how else might a recruiter gain an audience with an executive?

prepare for new jobs. When the Von Hoffmann Corporation closed its Frederick plant to consolidate operations in Missouri and Iowa, the 165 employees didn't want to move. A career consultant at the Job Training Agency met with each of them to record their work history and goals. The laid-off workers also can use the agency to visit online job sites, mail résumés at no charge, and participate in classes on writing résumés and interviewing for a job. The Job Training Agency shares a building with the county's Office of Economic Development, in the hope that the development agency, which encourages businesses to locate in the county, can work with it to match employers and workers.[48]

Private Employment Agencies

In contrast to public employment agencies, which primarily serve the blue-collar labor market, private employment agencies provide much the same service for the white-collar labor market. Workers interested in finding a job can sign up with a private employment agency whether or not they are currently unemployed. Another difference between the two types of agencies is that private agencies charge the employers for providing referrals. Therefore, using a private employment agency is more expensive than using a public agency, but the private agency is a more suitable source for certain kinds of applicants.

For managers or professionals, an employer may use the services of a type of private agency called an *executive search firm (ESF)*. People often call these agencies "headhunters" because, unlike other employment agencies, they find new jobs for people almost exclusively already employed. For job candidates, dealing with executive search firms can be sensitive. Typically, executives do not want to advertise their availability, because it could trigger a negative reaction from their current employer. ESFs serve as a buffer, providing confidentiality between the employer and the recruit. That benefit may give an employer access to candidates it cannot recruit in other, more direct ways.

Colleges and Universities

Most colleges and universities have placement services that seek to help their graduates obtain employment. On-campus interviewing is the most important source of recruits for entry-level professional and managerial vacancies.[49] Organizations tend to focus especially on colleges that have strong reputations in areas for which they have critical needs—say, chemical engineering or public accounting.[50] The recruiting strategy at 3M includes concentrating on 25 to 30 selected universities. The company has a commitment to those selected universities and returns to them each year with new job openings. HR professionals make sure that the same person works with the same university year in and year out, to achieve "continuity of contact."[51]

One of the best ways for a company to establish a stronger presence on a campus is with a college internship program. Embassy Suites is one company that participates in such a program. How does this benefit the company and the students at the same time?

Many employers have found that successfully competing for the best students requires more than just signing up prospective graduates for interview slots. One of the best ways to establish a stronger presence on a campus is with a college internship program. Dun & Bradstreet funds a summer intern program for minority MBA students. D&B often hires these interns for full-time positions when they graduate.[52] Internship programs give an organization early access to potential applicants and let the organization assess their capabilities directly.

Another way of increasing the employer's presence on campus is to participate in university job fairs. In general, a job fair is an event where many employers gather for a short time to meet large numbers of potential job applicants. Although job fairs can be held anywhere (such as at a hotel or convention center), campuses are ideal locations because of the many well-educated, yet unemployed, individuals who are there. Job fairs are an inexpensive means of generating an on-campus presence. They can even provide one-on-one dialogue with potential recruits—dialogue that would be impossible through less interactive media, such as newspaper ads.

Evaluating the Quality of a Source

In general, there are few rules that say what recruitment source is best for a given job vacancy. Therefore, it is wise for employers to monitor the quality of all their recruitment sources. One way to do this is to develop and compare **yield ratios** for each source.[53] A yield ratio expresses the percentage of applicants who successfully move from one stage of the recruitment and selection process to the next. For example, the organization could find the number of candidates interviewed as a percentage of the total number of résumés generated by a given source (that is, number of interviews divided by number of résumés). A high yield ratio (large percentage) means that the source is an effective way to find candidates to interview. By comparing the yield ratios of different recruitment sources, HR professionals can determine which source is the best or most efficient for the type of vacancy.

yield ratio
A ratio that expresses the percentage of applicants who successfully move from one stage of the recruitment and selection process to the next.

Another measure of recruitment success is the *cost per hire*. To compute this amount, find the cost of using a particular recruitment source for a particular type of vacancy. Then divide that cost by the number of people hired to fill that type of vacancy. A low cost per hire means that the recruitment source is efficient; it delivers qualified candidates at minimal cost.

To see how HR professionals use these measures, look at the examples in Table 5.3. This table shows the results for a hypothetical organization that used five kinds of recruitment sources to fill a number of vacancies. For each recruitment source, the

TABLE 5.3

Results of a Hypothetical Recruiting Effort

	RECRUITING SOURCE					
	LOCAL UNIVERSITY	**RENOWNED UNIVERSITY**	**EMPLOYEE REFERRALS**	**NEWSPAPER AD**	**ONLINE JOB BOARD AD**	**EXECUTIVE SEARCH FIRMS**
Résumés generated	200	400	50	500	7000	20
Interview offers accepted	175	100	45	400	500	20
Yield ratio	**87%**	**25%**	**90%**	**80%**	**7%**	**100%**
Applicants judged acceptable	100	95	40	50	350	19
Yield ratio	**57%**	**95%**	**89%**	**12%**	**70%**	**95%**
Accept employment offers	90	10	35	25	200	15
Yield ratio	**90%**	**11%**	**88%**	**50%**	**57%**	**79%**
Cumulative yield ratio	90/200 **45%**	10/400 **3%**	35/50 **70%**	25/500 **5%**	200/7,000 **3%**	15/20 **75%**
Cost	$30,000	$50,000	$15,000	$20,000	$5,000	$90,000
Cost per hire	**$333**	**$5,000**	**$428**	**$800**	**$25**	**$6,000**

table shows four yield ratios and the cost per hire. To fill these jobs, the best two sources of recruits were local universities and employee referral programs. Newspaper ads generated the largest number of recruits (500 résumés). However, only 50 were judged acceptable, of which only half accepted employment offers, for a cumulative yield ratio of 25/500, or 5 percent. Recruiting at renowned universities generated highly qualified applicants, but relatively few of them ultimately accepted positions with the organization. Executive search firms produced the highest cumulative yield ratio. These generated only 20 applicants, but all of them accepted interview offers, most were judged acceptable, and 79 percent of these acceptable candidates took jobs with the organization. However, notice the cost per hire. The executive search firms charged $90,000 for finding these 15 employees, resulting in the largest cost per hire. In contrast, local universities provided modest yield ratios at the lowest cost per hire. Employee referrals provided excellent yield ratios at a slightly higher cost.

LO6 Describe the recruiter's role in the recruitment process, including limits and opportunities.

Recruiter Traits and Behaviors

As we showed in Figure 5.2, the third influence on recruitment outcomes is the recruiter, including this person's characteristics and the way he or she behaves. The recruiter affects the nature of both the job vacancy and the applicants generated. However, the recruiter often becomes involved late in the recruitment process. In many cases, by the time a recruiter meets some applicants, they have already made up their minds about what they desire in a job, what the vacant job has to offer, and their likelihood of receiving a job offer.[54]

Many applicants approach the recruiter with some skepticism. Knowing it is the recruiter's job to sell them on a vacancy, some applicants discount what the recruiter says, in light of what they have heard from other sources, such as friends, magazine articles, and professors. When candidates are already familiar with the company through knowing about its products, the recruiter's impact is especially weak.[55] For these and other reasons, recruiters' characteristics and behaviors seem to have limited impact on applicants' job choices.

Characteristics of the Recruiter

Most organizations must choose whether their recruiters are specialists in human resources or are experts at particular jobs (that is, those who currently hold the same kinds of jobs or supervise people who hold the jobs). According to some studies, applicants perceive HR specialists as less credible and are less attracted to jobs when recruiters are HR specialists.[56] The evidence does not completely discount a positive role for personnel specialists in recruiting. It does indicate, however, that these specialists need to take extra steps to ensure that applicants perceive them as knowledgeable and credible.

In general, applicants respond positively to recruiters whom they perceive as warm and informative. "Warm" means the recruiter seems to care about the applicant and to be enthusiastic about the applicant's potential to contribute to the organization. "Informative" means the recruiter provides the kind of information the applicant is seeking. The evidence of impact of other characteristics of recruiters—including their age, sex, and race—is complex and inconsistent.[57]

Behavior of the Recruiter

Recruiters affect results not only by providing plenty of information, but by providing the right kind of information. Perhaps the most-researched aspect of recruiting is the level of realism in the recruiter's message. Because the recruiter's job is to attract candidates, recruiters may feel pressure to exaggerate the positive qualities of the vacancy and to downplay its negative qualities. Applicants are highly sensitive to negative information. The highest-quality applicants may be less willing to pursue jobs when this type of information comes out.[58] But if the recruiter goes too far in a positive direction, the candidate can be misled and lured into taking a job that has been misrepresented. Then unmet expectations can contribute to a high turnover rate. When recruiters describe jobs unrealistically, people who take those jobs may come to believe that the employer is deceitful.[59]

Many studies have looked at how well **realistic job previews**—background information about jobs' positive and negative qualities—can get around this problem and help organizations minimize turnover among new employees. On the whole, the research suggests that realistic job previews have a weak and inconsistent effect on turnover.[60] Although recruiters can go overboard in selling applicants on the desirability of a job vacancy, there is little support for the belief that informing people about the negative characteristics of a job will "inoculate" them so that the negative features don't cause them to quit.[61]

realistic job preview
Background information about a job's positive and negative qualities.

Finally, for affecting whether people choose to take a job, but even more so, whether they stick with a job, the recruiter seems less important than an organization's personnel policies that directly affect the job's features (pay, security, advancement opportunities, and so on).

Enhancing the Recruiter's Impact

Nevertheless, although recruiters are probably not the most important influence on people's job choices, this does not mean recruiters cannot have an impact. Most recruiters receive little training.[62] If we were to determine what does matter to job candidates, perhaps recruiters could be trained in those areas.

Researchers have tried to find the conditions in which recruiters do make a difference. Such research suggests that an organization can take several steps to increase the positive impact that recruiters have on job candidates:

- Recruiters should provide timely feedback. Applicants dislike delays in feedback. They may draw negative conclusions about the organization (for starters, that the organization doesn't care about their application).
- Recruiters should avoid offensive behavior. They should avoid behaving in ways that might convey the wrong impression about the organization.[63] Figure 5.4 quotes applicants who felt they had extremely bad experiences with recruiters. Their statements provide examples of behaviors to avoid.

Figure 5.4

Recruits Who Were Offended by Recruiters

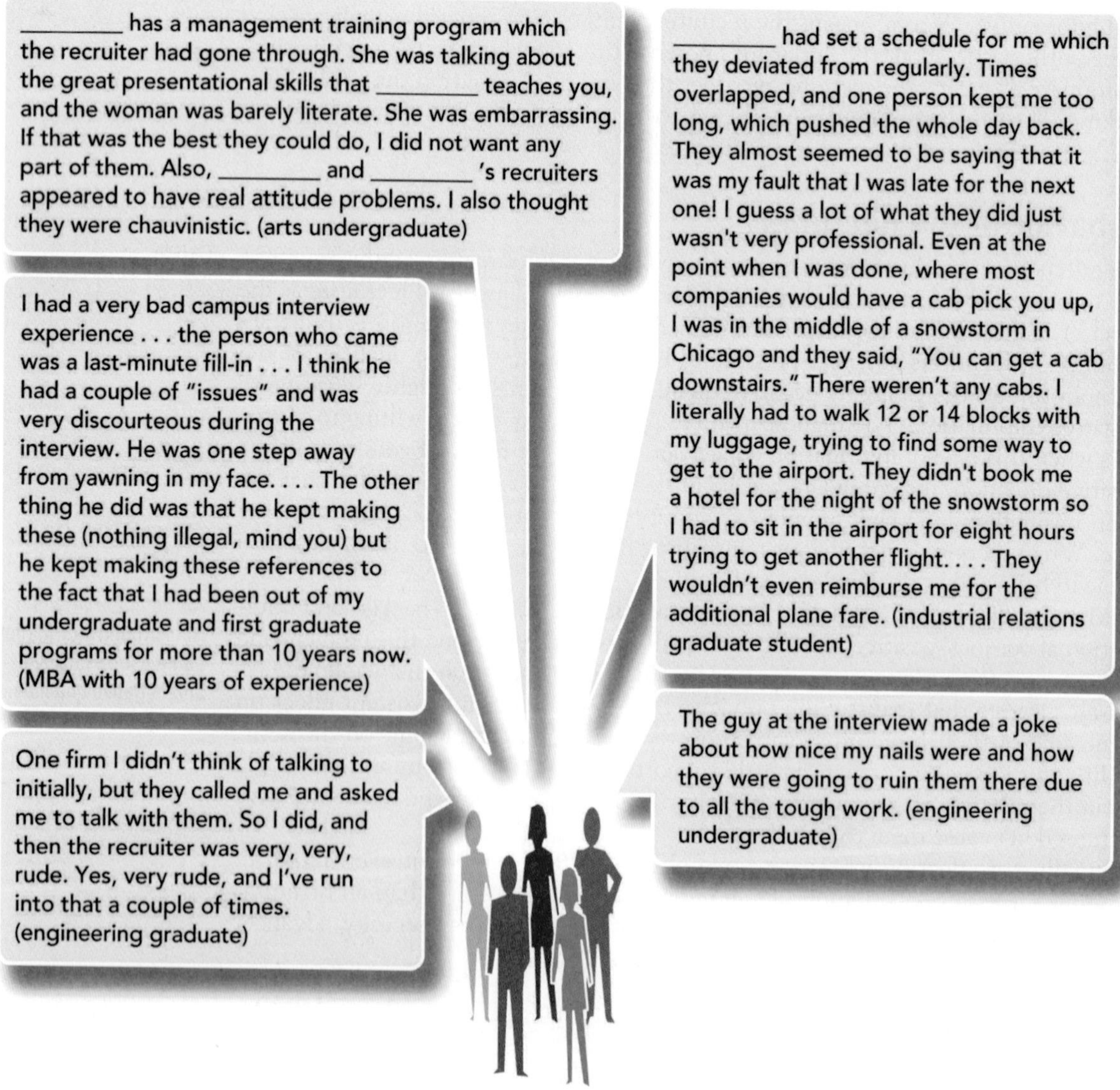

_____ has a management training program which the recruiter had gone through. She was talking about the great presentational skills that _____ teaches you, and the woman was barely literate. She was embarrassing. If that was the best they could do, I did not want any part of them. Also, _____ and _____ 's recruiters appeared to have real attitude problems. I also thought they were chauvinistic. (arts undergraduate)

I had a very bad campus interview experience . . . the person who came was a last-minute fill-in . . . I think he had a couple of "issues" and was very discourteous during the interview. He was one step away from yawning in my face. . . . The other thing he did was that he kept making these (nothing illegal, mind you) but he kept making these references to the fact that I had been out of my undergraduate and first graduate programs for more than 10 years now. (MBA with 10 years of experience)

One firm I didn't think of talking to initially, but they called me and asked me to talk with them. So I did, and then the recruiter was very, very, rude. Yes, very rude, and I've run into that a couple of times. (engineering graduate)

_____ had set a schedule for me which they deviated from regularly. Times overlapped, and one person kept me too long, which pushed the whole day back. They almost seemed to be saying that it was my fault that I was late for the next one! I guess a lot of what they did just wasn't very professional. Even at the point when I was done, where most companies would have a cab pick you up, I was in the middle of a snowstorm in Chicago and they said, "You can get a cab downstairs." There weren't any cabs. I literally had to walk 12 or 14 blocks with my luggage, trying to find some way to get to the airport. They didn't book me a hotel for the night of the snowstorm so I had to sit in the airport for eight hours trying to get another flight. . . . They wouldn't even reimburse me for the additional plane fare. (industrial relations graduate student)

The guy at the interview made a joke about how nice my nails were and how they were going to ruin them there due to all the tough work. (engineering undergraduate)

- The organization can recruit with teams rather than individual recruiters. Applicants view job experts as more credible than HR specialists, and a team can include both kinds of recruiters. HR specialists on the team provide knowledge about company policies and procedures.

Through such positive behavior, recruiters can give organizations a better chance of competing for talented human resources. In the next chapter, we will describe how an organization selects the candidates who best meet its needs.

THINKING ETHICALLY

WHEN EMPLOYEES LEAVE

The chapter described ways organizations can manage a labor surplus by downsizing or using temporary and contract workers. Layoffs are just one reason the average U.S. worker has an estimated 10.5 jobs between the ages of 18 and 40. Employees also leave voluntarily, especially when the demand for their skills is strong.

Just as there is advice for organizations laying off workers, some people offer advice to employees who leave voluntarily. Sylvia Ho, a contributing writer for Monster's career Web site, advises first of all that those who are leaving a job should not "burn their bridges." In other words, treat your soon-to-be-former boss and colleagues with the same respect you would use if you were planning to stick around. Careers take many twists and turns, and you can never be sure those relationships won't become important again in some way. She also advises that you keep in touch with those who have been important as mentors and business contacts, not just the people who were fun to know.

Despite all advice and good intentions, some employees do leave awkwardly. An employee who asked only to be known as Kathryn once had a job that seems to have come straight from *The Devil Wears Prada*. Upon graduation from college, where she had enjoyed art and worked on the school newspaper, she took a job as a personal assistant to the design director of a magazine. Before long, she was performing a series of what felt like mindless and thankless tasks. She believed she

should stick it out for a year, but eventually she couldn't resist interviewing for a position as a freelance designer at another magazine. Kathryn received a job offer but postponed it on the grounds her current boss would need plenty of notice. During a Christmas holiday, though, the situation came to a head. Kathryn's boss called her repeatedly and chastised her about a shipment to Scandinavia that was running late, while the prospective boss sent an e-mail cordially offering to move the start date at her convenience. The contrast was too much to ignore; Kathryn left the first job behind.

SOURCES: Sylvia Ho, "Leaving a Job Gracefully," Career Advice: On the Job, http://career-advice.monster.com, accessed March 20, 2008; and Elise Waxenberg, "How to Quit Your Job," *Fast Company*, December 19, 2007, www.fastcompany.com.

Questions

1. What ethical obligations does an organization have when downsizing?
2. Compare those obligations with the ethical obligations of an employee who leaves an organization voluntarily.
3. Consider the example of Kathryn. How would you have advised her to handle this situation? How would you have wanted to handle it if you were the employer?

SUMMARY

LO1 Discuss how to plan for human resources needed to carry out the organization's strategy.

The first step in human resource planning is personnel forecasting. Through trend analysis and good judgment, the planner tries to determine the supply of and demand for various human resources. Based on whether a surplus or a shortage is expected, the planner sets goals and creates a strategy for achieving

those goals. The organization then implements its HR strategy and evaluates the results.

LO2 Determine the labor demand for workers in various job categories.

The planner can look at leading indicators, assuming trends will continue in the future. Multiple regression can convert several leading indicators into a single prediction of labor needs. Analysis of a transitional matrix can help the planner identify which job categories can be filled internally and where high turnover is likely.

LO3   Summarize the advantages and disadvantages of ways to eliminate a labor surplus and avoid a labor shortage.

To reduce a surplus, downsizing, pay reductions, and demotions deliver fast results but at a high cost in human suffering that may hurt surviving employees' motivation and future recruiting. Also, the organization may lose some of its best employees. Transferring employees and requiring them to share work are also fast methods and the consequences in human suffering are less severe. A hiring freeze or natural attrition is slow to take effect but avoids the pain of layoffs. Early-retirement packages may unfortunately induce the best employees to leave and may be slow to implement; however, they, too, are less painful than layoffs. Retraining can improve the organization's overall pool of human resources and maintain high morale, but it is relatively slow and costly.

To avoid a labor shortage, requiring overtime is the easiest and fastest strategy, which can easily be changed if conditions change. However, overtime may exhaust workers and can hurt morale. Using temporary employees and outsourcing do not build an in-house pool of talent, but by these means staffing levels can be quickly and easily modified. Transferring and retraining employees require investment of time and money, but can enhance the quality of the organization's human resources; however, this may backfire if a labor surplus develops. Hiring new employees is slow and expensive but strengthens the organization if labor needs are expected to expand for the long term. Using technology as a substitute for labor can be slow to implement and costly, but it may improve the organization's long-term performance. New technology and hiring are difficult to reverse if conditions change.

LO4   Describe recruitment policies organizations use to make job vacancies more attractive.

Internal recruiting (promotions from within) generally makes job vacancies more attractive because candidates see opportunities for growth and advancement. Lead-the-market pay strategies make jobs economically desirable. Due-process policies signal that employers are concerned about employee rights. Image advertising can give candidates the impression that the organization is a good place to work.

LO5   List and compare sources of job applicants.

Internal sources, promoted through job postings, generate applicants who are familiar to the organization and motivate other employees by demonstrating opportunities for advancement. However, internal sources are usually insufficient for all of an organization's labor needs. Direct applicants and referrals tend to be inexpensive and to generate applicants who have self-selected; this source risks charges of unfairness, especially in cases of nepotism. Newspaper and magazine advertising reaches a wide audience and may generate many applications, although many are likely to be unsuitable. Electronic recruiting gives organizations access to a global labor market, tends to be inexpensive, and allows convenient searching of databases. Public employment agencies are inexpensive and typically have screened applicants. Private employment agencies charge fees but may provide many services. Another inexpensive channel is schools and colleges, which may give the employer access to top-notch entrants to the labor market.

LO6   Describe the recruiter's role in the recruitment process, including limits and opportunities.

Through their behavior and other characteristics, recruiters influence the nature of the job vacancy and the kinds of applicants generated. Applicants tend to perceive job experts as more credible than recruiters who are HR specialists. They tend to react more favorably to recruiters who are warm and informative. Recruiters should not mislead candidates. Realistic job previews are helpful but have a weak and inconsistent effect on job turnover compared with personnel policies and actual job conditions. Recruiters can improve their impact by providing timely feedback, avoiding behavior that contributes to a negative impression of the organization, and teaming up with job experts.

KEY TERMS

core competency, p. 122
direct applicants, p. 134
downsizing, p. 123
due-process policies, p. 132
employment at will, p. 132
forecasting, p. 119

job posting, p. 133
leading indicators, p. 120
nepotism, p. 135
outsourcing, p. 127
realistic job preview, p. 141
recruiting, p. 130

referrals, p. 134
transitional matrix, p. 120
trend analysis, p. 120
workforce utilization review,
   p. 130
yield ratio, p. 139

REVIEW AND DISCUSSION QUESTIONS

1. Suppose an organization expects a labor shortage to develop in key job areas over the next few years. Recommend general responses the organization could make in each of the following areas:
   a. Recruitment.
   b. Training.
   c. Compensation (pay and employee benefits).
2. Review the sample transitional matrix shown in Table 5.1. What jobs experience the greatest turnover (employees leaving the organization)? How might an organization with this combination of jobs reduce the turnover?
3. In the same transitional matrix, which jobs seem to rely the most on internal recruitment? Which seem to rely most on external recruitment? Why?
4. Why do organizations combine statistical and judgmental forecasts of labor demand, rather than relying on statistics or judgment alone? Give an example of a situation in which each type of forecast would be inaccurate.
5. Some organizations have detailed affirmative-action plans, complete with goals and timetables, for women and minorities, yet have no formal human resource plan for the organization as a whole. Why might this be the case? What does this practice suggest about the role of human resource management in these organizations?

6. Give an example of a personnel policy that would help attract a larger pool of job candidates. Give an example of a personnel policy that would likely reduce the pool of candidates. Would you expect these policies to influence the quality as well as the number of applicants? Why or why not?
7. Discuss the relative merits of internal versus external recruitment. Give an example of a situation in which each of these approaches might be particularly effective.
8. List the jobs you have held. How were you recruited for each of these? From the organization's perspective, what were some pros and cons of recruiting you through these methods?
9. Recruiting people for jobs that require international assignments is increasingly important for many organizations. Where might an organization go to recruit people interested in such assignments?
10. A large share of HR professionals have rated e-cruiting as their best source of new talent. What qualities of electronic recruiting do you think contribute to this opinion?
11. How can organizations improve the effectiveness of their recruiters?

BUSINESSWEEK CASE

BusinessWeek Netflix: Recruiting and Retaining the Best Talent

"I had the great fortune of doing a mediocre job at my first company," says Netflix founder Reed Hastings. He's talking about his 1990s startup, Pure Software, a wildly successful maker of debugging programs that, through a series of mergers, became part of IBM. Hastings says Pure, like many other outfits, went from being a heat-filled, everybody-wants-to-be-here place to a dronish, when-does-the-day-end sausage factory. "We got more bureaucratic as we grew," says Hastings.

After Pure, the Stanford-trained engineer spent two years thinking about how to ensure his next endeavor wouldn't suffer the same big-company creep.

The resulting sequel is Netflix, where Hastings is trying to revolutionize not only the way people rent movies but also how his managers work. Hastings pays his people lavishly, gives them unlimited vacations, and lets them structure their own compensation packages. In return, he expects ultra-high performance. His 400 salaried employees are expected to do the jobs of three or four people.

Hastings calls his approach "freedom and responsibility." And employees get all cinematic when describing the

vibe. Netflix is the workplace equivalent of *Ocean's 11*, says Todd S. Yellin, hired to perfect the site's movie-rating system. Hastings is Danny Ocean, the bright, charismatic leader who recruits the best in class, gives them a generous cut, and provides the flexibility to do what they do best, all while uniting them on a focused goal. The near-impossible mission: trying to become the leading purveyor of online movies.

Netflix is embroiled in a tough, two-front war: competing with Blockbuster for online supremacy in DVD rentals while inaugurating a digital streaming service to compete with the likes of Apple. That's one mighty gang of entrenched competitors. "There's usually room in a marketplace for more than one," says Wedbush Morgan Securities analyst Michael Pachter. "But in this case there really isn't."

Hastings is betting on Netflix's culture to get the company out of this corner. The plan includes continuing to increase what Hastings calls "talent density." Most companies go to great scientific lengths to ensure they are paying just enough to attract talent but not a dollar more than they need to. Netflix, which hands out salaries that are typically much higher than what is customary in Silicon

Valley, is unabashed in its we-pay-above-market swagger. "We're unafraid to pay high," says Hastings.

To ensure that the company is constantly nabbing A players, company talent hunters are told that money is no object. Each business group has what amounts to an internal boutique headhunting firm. Employees often recommend people they bonded with at work before.

Gibson Biddle, who runs the Web site, knew that Yellin, who had deep tech and film expertise, was the perfect guy to help Netflix improve how it recommends movies to customers on its site. Yellin had worked for Biddle at a family entertainment site. The snag was that Yellin, also a filmmaker, was finishing up his first feature film, *Brother's Shadow*, in Los Angeles. He also was allergic to anything corporate or publicly traded.

Impossible sell, right? But Netflix threw so much cash and flexibility at Yellin that he couldn't turn it down. During his first three months, he flew back and forth between L.A. and San Francisco doing his Netflix job and finishing his movie.

Pay is not tied to performance reviews, nor to some predetermined raise pool, but to the job market. Netflix bosses are constantly gleaning market compensation data from new hires and then amping up salaries when needed. And what happens when somebody doesn't live up to

expectations? "At most companies, average performers get an average raise," says Hastings. "At Netflix, they get a generous severance package."

Despite the luxe perks and killer culture, Hastings still has the battle of his career ahead. The Netflix people have "a huge competitive advantage because they are smart and they hire really well," says Pachter. "But that doesn't help you in the long run if your business model is flawed."

SOURCE: Excerpted from Michelle Conlin, "Netflix: Recruiting and Retaining the Best Talent," *BusinessWeek*, September 13, 2007, www.businessweek.com.

Questions

1. What are Netflix's personnel policies, as described in this case?
2. If Netflix's business strategy succeeds, it will need more employees from the competitive markets for programming and marketing talent. Of the options for avoiding a labor shortage (see Table 5.2), which do you think would be most effective for Netflix? Why?
3. Visit the careers section of Netflix's Web site (www.netflix.com/jobs). Is it easy to learn about jobs at the company? Does the site give a positive impression of the company as an employer? What, if any, improvements can you recommend?

CASE: THE HUNT FOR SEASONAL WORKERS CROSSES BORDERS

Every summer, High Sierra Pools needs lifeguards, and the Broadmoor Hotel in Colorado Springs adds 500 employees to its staff of 1,200 to handle the peak season. As the tourist season heats up on Cape Cod, Bubala's by the Bay needs extra restaurant workers. For these and other companies in the resort and hospitality industry, the seasonal rise in demand for workers creates an annual labor shortage.

The peak in the demand for labor is too steep to handle with overtime, and the type of work can't be outsourced to dishwashers or lifeguards in another location. The main option for employers is to find workers who want a summer job.

In the past, summer jobs were filled with high school and college students. Today, however, more students are looking for internships or jobs related to their career plans. Many high-schoolers are trying to improve their college prospects by taking courses or signing up for travel and service projects. Academic years now often start in August, so students aren't available through Labor Day. As a result, resort and pool owners have found it nearly impossible to fill seasonal jobs, even after boosting wages. High Sierra, for example, tried running newspaper ads in regions of the United States where unemployment was high, as well as recruiting students from swim teams. Such efforts largely failed.

The solution for High Sierra, the Broadmoor, Bubala's, and other seasonal employers has come from other countries. These companies have begun recruiting seasonal workers to come to the United States under a visa program called H-2B, which admits foreign workers for jobs lasting up to six months. Employers wishing to hire these workers must obtain approval by filing applications with the Department of Labor, Department of State, and Department of Homeland Security and must prove they cannot fill their jobs with American workers. To be considered for an H-2B visa, the foreign workers must show they have binding ties to their own countries so that they will return home when the visa expires.

High Sierra's first H-2B hires came from Germany. As economic conditions made it more attractive for young Germans to stay in Europe, the company began pushing its recruiting efforts farther east. Recently, High Sierra found most of its lifeguards in Bulgaria, the Czech Republic, Russia, and Kazakhstan. To recruit employees in these countries, the company's Web career pages are available in several languages (with links from the countries' flags). The career pages explain to young recruits and their parents how the company will help them with housing, health care, and other needs in America. In a recent year, half of the company's 500 temporary workers were foreigners.

These employees put in far more than half the needed hours, as they preferred to work 60 hours a week to earn overtime pay.

The Broadmoor's H-2B workers come mostly from Jamaica. Many return year after year, so they are already trained when they arrive. Jamaican workers also staff Bubala's by the Bay, working as sous chefs, line cooks, and dishwashers. The restaurant's general manager says, "We can't operate our business without these guys at all."

One downside of this option for combating a labor shortage is that it is subject to changing government policies. The federal government sets a limit, or cap, on the number of H-2B visas that may be issued each year. At the time this case was written, the number of H-2B visas that may be issued was 66,000 per year. Congress temporarily allowed businesses to obtain visas for returning workers who previously had received H-2B visas without counting those workers against the cap. However, that temporary provision expired. Businesses that relied on workers with H-2B visas have lobbied Congress to extend the provision for returning workers; but unless they succeed, they must find new solutions for their labor shortage if they cannot fill all their vacant positions before the visa cap is reached.

SOURCES: June Kronholz, "Why Filling Summer Jobs Is Tougher and Tougher," *Wall Street Journal*, July 6, 2007, http://online.wsj.com; Joan Johnson, "Competition Heating Up Summer Job Season in Colorado Springs," *Colorado Springs Business Journal*, June 29, 2007, downloaded from General Reference Center Gold, http://find.galegroup.com; Sarah Shemkus, "Cape Cod Employers Fear Changes in Visa Rules Could Reduce Seasonal Workforce," *Cape Cod Times*, October 5, 2007, http://find.galegroup.com; High Sierra Pools, "Lifeguards and Pool Managers" and "Sierra for Parents," High Sierra Web site, www.highsierrapools.com, accessed January 15, 2008; and U.S. Citizenship and Immigration Services, "Current Cap Count for Non-immigrant Worker Visas for Fiscal Year 2008," USCIS Employer Information, www.uscis.gov, accessed January 8, 2008.

Questions

1. If the companies described in this case cannot fill all vacant seasonal jobs with workers under H-2B visas, what other options are available for filling the jobs?
2. Which of the additional options, if any, would you recommend?
3. What additional recruiting strategies, besides the ones described in this case, would you recommend to High Sierra Pools?

 IT'S A WRAP!

www.mhhe.com/noefund3e is your source for Reviewing, Applying, and Practicing the concepts you learned about in Chapter 5.

Review
- Chapter learning objectives
- Narrated lecture and iPod content
- Test Your Knowledge: Recruitment Sources and Stages of the Strategic HRM Process

Application
- Manager's Hot Seat segment: "Diversity: Mediating Morality"
- Video case and quiz: "Balancing Act: Keeping Mothers on a Career Track"
- Self-Assessment: Improving Your Resume
- Web exercise: Texas Instrument's Fit Check

Practice
- Chapter quiz

NOTES

1. Rick Popely, "Fewest Vehicles Sold in Nine Years," *Chicago Tribune*, January 4, 2008, sec. 3, pp. 1, 4; and John D. Stoll and Neal E. Boudette, "December Slump in Vehicle Sales Augurs Ill for '08," *Wall Street Journal*, January 4, 2008, http://online.wsj.com.
2. N. Byrnes, "Get 'Em while They're Young," *BusinessWeek*, May 22, 2006, pp. 86–87; B. Leak, "The Draft Picks Get Younger," *BusinessWeek*, May 8, 2006, p. 96; and A. Singh, "Firms Court New Hires—in High School," *Wall Street Journal*, August 15, 2006, p. B5.
3. K. Doheny, "Nursing Is in Critical Condition," *Workforce Management*, October 9, 2006, pp. 39–41.
4. K. Maher, "Wal-Mart Seeks New Flexibility in Worker Shifts," *Wall Street Journal*, January 3, 2007, p. A1.
5. I. Brat, "Where Have All the Welders Gone, as Manufacturing and Repair Boom?" *Wall Street Journal*, August 15, 2006, pp. B2–B3.

6. M. Conlin, "Savaged by the Slowdown," *Business-Week*, September 17, 2001, pp. 74–77.
7. Matthew Benjamin, "Career Guide 2005," *U.S. News & World Report*, March 21, 2005, pp. 34–42.
8. K. P. DeMeuse, P. A. Vanderheiden, and T. J. Bergmann, "Announced Layoffs: Their Effect on Corporate Financial Performance," *Human Resource Management* 33 (1994), pp. 509–30.
9. C. D. Zatzick and R. D. Iverson, "High-Involvement Management and Workforce Reduction: Competitive Advantage or Disadvantage?" *Academy of Management Journal* 49 (2006), pp. 999–1015.
10. P. P. Shaw, "Network Destruction: The Structural Implications of Downsizing," *Academy of Management Journal* 43 (2000), pp. 101–12.
11. Jon E. Hilsenrath, "Adventures in Cost Cutting," *Wall Street Journal*, May 10, 2004, pp. R1, R3.
12. W. F. Cascio, "Downsizing: What Do We Know? What Have We Learned?" *Academy of Management Executive* 7 (1993), pp. 95–104.
13. J. Schu, "Internet Helps Keep Goodwill of Downsized Employees," *Workforce*, July 2001, p. 15.
14. Hilsenrath, "Adventures in Cost Cutting," p. R3.
15. Kathy Chu, "Older Workers Find New Favor among Employers," *Wall Street Journal*, September 1, 2004, p. D3.
16. S. Kim and D. Feldman, "Healthy, Wealthy, or Wise: Predicting Actual Acceptances of Early Retirement Incentives at Three Points in Time," *Personnel Psychology* 51 (1998), pp. 623–42.
17. D. Fandray, "Gray Matters," *Workforce*, July 2000, pp. 27–32.
18. Irwin Speizer, "Going to Ground," *Workforce Management*, December 2004, pp. 39–44.
19. Ibid.; and Monica Langley, "Drivers Deliver Trouble to FedEx by Seeking Employee Benefits," *Wall Street Journal*, January 7, 2005, pp. A1, A8.
20. P. Engardio, "Let's Offshore the Lawyers," *Business-Week*, September 18, 2006, pp. 42–43.
21. W. Zellner, "Lessons from a Faded Levi-Strauss," *BusinessWeek*, December 15, 2003, p. 44.
22. A. Meisler, "Think Globally, Act Rationally," *Workforce*, January 2004, pp. 40–45.
23. S. E. Ante, "Shifting Work Offshore? Outsourcer Beware," *BusinessWeek*, January 12, 2004, pp. 36–37.
24. P. Engardio, "The Future of Outsourcing," *Business-Week*, January 30, 2006, pp. 50–58.
25. Anne Freedman, "Filling the Gap," *Human Resource Executive*, January 2005, pp. 1, 22–30.
26. A. E. Barber, *Recruiting Employees* (Thousand Oaks, CA: Sage, 1998).
27. C. K. Stevens, "Antecedents of Interview Interactions, Interviewers' Ratings, and Applicants' Reactions," *Personnel Psychology* 51 (1998), pp. 55–85;

A. E. Barber, J. R. Hollenbeck, S. L. Tower, and J. M. Phillips, "The Effects of Interview Focus on Recruitment Effectiveness: A Field Experiment," *Journal of Applied Psychology* 79 (1994), pp. 886–96; and D. S. Chapman and D. I. Zweig, "Developing a Nomological Network for Interview Structure: Antecedents and Consequences of the Structured Selection Interview," *Personnel Psychology* 58 (2005), pp. 673–702.
28. J. D. Olian and S. L. Rynes, "Organizational Staffing: Integrating Practice with Strategy," *Industrial Relations* 23 (1984), pp. 170–83.
29. G. T. Milkovich and J. M. Newman, *Compensation* (Homewood, IL: Richard D. Irwin, 1990).
30. M. Leonard, "Challenges to the Termination-at-Will Doctrine," *Personnel Administrator* 28 (1983), pp. 49–56; C. Schowerer and B. Rosen, "Effects of Employment-at-Will Policies and Compensation Policies on Corporate Image and Job Pursuit Intentions," *Journal of Applied Psychology* 74 (1989), pp. 653–56.
31. M. Magnus, "Recruitment Ads at Work," *Personnel Journal* 64 (1985), pp. 42–63.
32. S. L. Rynes and A. E. Barber, "Applicant Attraction Strategies: An Organizational Perspective," *Academy of Management Review* 15 (1990), pp. 286–310; J. A. Breaugh, *Recruitment: Science and Practice* (Boston: PWS-Kent, 1992), p. 34.
33. J. E. Slaughter, M. J. Zickar, S. Highhouse, and D. C. Mohr, "Personality Trait Inferences about Organizations: Development of a Measure and Assessment of Construct Validity," *Journal of Applied Psychology* 89 (2004), pp. 85–103; and D. S. Chapman, K. L. Uggerslev, S. A. Carroll, K. A. Piasentin, and D. A. Jones, "Applicant Attraction to Organizations and Job Choice: A Meta-analytic Review of the Correlates of Recruiting Outcomes," *Journal of Applied Psychology* 90 (2005), pp. 928–44.
34. D. R. Avery, "Reactions to Diversity in Recruitment Advertising—Are Differences in Black and White?" *Journal of Applied Psychology* 88 (2003), pp. 672–79.
35. M. A. Conrad and S. D. Ashworth, "Recruiting Source Effectiveness: A Meta-Analysis and Reexamination of Two Rival Hypotheses," paper presented at the annual meeting of the Society of Industrial/Organizational Psychology, Chicago, 1986.
36. Breaugh, *Recruitment*.
37. L. G. Klaff, "New Internal Hiring Systems Reduce Cost and Boost Morale," *Workforce*, March 2004, pp. 76–78.
38. Breaugh, *Recruitment*, pp. 113–14.
39. R. S. Schuler and S. E. Jackson, "Linking Competitive Strategies with Human Resource Management Practices," *Academy of Management Executive* 1 (1987), pp. 207–19.

40. Gerry Crispin and Mark Mehler, "CareerXroads 6th Annual 2006 Sources of Hire Study," www.careerxroads.com.

41. C. R. Wanberg, R. Kanfer, and J. T. Banas, "Predictors and Outcomes of Networking Intensity among Job Seekers," *Journal of Applied Psychology* 85 (2000), pp. 491–503.

42. Patrick J. Kiger, "Burnishing Your Employment Brand: Part 2 of 2," *Workforce Management*, October 22, 2007, downloaded from General Reference Center Gold, http://find.galegroup.com.

43. Gina Ruiz, "Survey: Papers Still Important to Job Seekers," *Workforce Management*, December 11, 2006, p. 8.

44. S. Begley, "Behind 'Shortage' of Engineers: Employers Grow More Choosy," *Wall Street Journal*, November 16, 2005, pp. A1, A12.

45. Breaugh, *Recruitment*, p. 87.

46. Eric Benderoff, "Microsoft Takes on CareerBuilder Stake," *Chicago Tribune*, May 10, 2007, sec. 3, pp. 1, 6.

47. Martha Frase-Blunt, "Make a Good First Impression," *HR Magazine*, April 2004, downloaded from Infotrac at http://web2.infotrac.galegroup.com.

48. Amy Joyce, "When a Plant Closes, Job Agency Steps In," *Washington Post*, January 24, 2005, www.washingtonpost.com.

49. P. Smith, "Sources Used by Employers When Hiring College Grads," *Personnel Journal*, February 1995, p. 25.

50. J. W. Boudreau and S. L. Rynes, "Role of Recruitment in Staffing Utility Analysis," *Journal of Applied Psychology* 70 (1985), pp. 354–66.

51. D. Anfuso, "3M's Staffing Strategy Promotes Productivity and Pride," *Personnel Journal*, February 1995, pp. 28–34.

52. L. Winter, "Employers Go to School on Minority Recruiting," *Wall Street Journal*, December 15, 1992, p. B1.

53. R. Hawk, *The Recruitment Function* (New York: American Management Association, 1967).

54. C. K. Stevens, "Effects of Preinterview Beliefs on Applicants' Reactions to Campus Interviews," *Academy of Management Journal* 40 (1997), pp. 947–66.

55. C. Collins, "The Interactive Effects of Recruitment Practices and Product Awareness on Job Seekers' Employer Knowledge and Application Behaviors," *Journal of Applied Psychology* 92 (2007), pp. 180–90.

56. M. S. Taylor and T. J. Bergman, "Organizational Recruitment Activities and Applicants' Reactions at Different Stages of the Recruitment Process," *Personnel Psychology* 40 (1984), pp. 261–85; C. D. Fisher, D. R. Ilgen, and W. D. Hoyer, "Source Credibility, Information Favorability, and Job Offer Acceptance," *Academy of Management Journal* 22 (1979), pp. 94–103.

57. L. M. Graves and G. N. Powell, "The Effect of Sex Similarity on Recruiters' Evaluation of Actual Applicants: A Test of the Similarity-Attraction Paradigm," *Personnel Psychology* 48 (1995), pp. 85–98.

58. R. D. Tretz and T. A. Judge, "Realistic Job Previews: A Test of the Adverse Self-Selection Hypothesis," *Journal of Applied Psychology* 83 (1998), pp. 330–37.

59. P. Hom, R. W. Griffeth, L. E. Palich, and J. S. Bracker, "An Exploratory Investigation into Theoretical Mechanisms Underlying Realistic Job Previews," *Personnel Psychology* 51 (1998), pp. 421–51.

60. G. M. McEvoy and W. F. Cascio, "Strategies for Reducing Employee Turnover: A Meta-Analysis," *Journal of Applied Psychology* 70 (1985), pp. 342–53; S. L. Premack and J. P. Wanous, "A Meta-Analysis of Realistic Job Preview Experiments," *Journal of Applied Psychology* 70 (1985), pp. 706–19.

61. P. G. Irving and J. P. Meyer, "Reexamination of the Met-Expectations Hypothesis: A Longitudinal Analysis," *Journal of Applied Psychology* 79 (1995), pp. 937–49.

62. R. W. Walters, "It's Time We Become Pros," *Journal of College Placement* 12 (1985), pp. 30–33.

63. S. L. Rynes, R. D. Bretz, and B. Gerhart, "The Importance of Recruitment in Job Choice: A Different Way of Looking," *Personnel Psychology* 44 (1991), pp. 487–522.

Selecting Employees and Placing Them in Jobs

What Do I Need to Know?

After reading this chapter, you should be able to:

LO1 Identify the elements of the selection process.

LO2 Define ways to measure the success of a selection method.

LO3 Summarize the government's requirements for employee selection.

LO4 Compare the common methods used for selecting human resources.

LO5 Describe major types of employment tests.

LO6 Discuss how to conduct effective interviews.

LO7 Explain how employers carry out the process of making a selection decision.

Introduction

If you want successful employees, you should hire smart people, right? That's partly true, but a study recently reported in *Forbes* magazine suggests you might want to look for other qualities as well.[1] Using data gathered by the Bureau of Labor Statistics (BLS) over two decades, a Harvard researcher found that she could predict which people would earn the most by looking at their scores on a test that involves assigning codes to words. The test, developed by the armed services to identify people with clerical skills, doesn't require deep thought, just a willingness to try hard and persist until the job is done. When the BLS used this test to gather data on the 12,700 young people it tracked in its study, there was no reward for a high score. Those who did their best probably were inclined to try hard regardless of whether they would be rewarded—what we might call being conscientious. This study suggests that if you want successful employees, you should hire people who are both smart and conscientious. Hiring decisions are about finding the people who will be a good fit with the job and the organization. Any organization that appreciates the competitive edge provided by good people must take the utmost care in choosing its members. The organization's decisions about selecting personnel are central to its ability to survive, adapt, and grow. Selection decisions become especially critical when organizations face tight labor markets or must compete for talent with other organizations in the same industry. If a competitor keeps getting the best applicants, the remaining companies must make do with who is left.

This chapter will familiarize you with ways to minimize errors in employee selection and placement. The chapter starts by describing the selection process and how to evaluate possible methods for carrying out that process. It then takes an in-depth look at the most widely used methods: applications and résumés, employment tests, and interviews. The chapter ends by describing the process by which organizations arrive at a final selection decision.

chapter six

Selection Process

Through **personnel selection,** organizations make decisions about who will or will not be allowed to join the organization. Selection begins with the candidates identified through recruitment and attempts to reduce their number to the individuals best qualified to perform the available jobs. At the end of the process, the selected individuals are placed in jobs with the organization.

The process of selecting employees varies considerably from organization to organization and from job to job. At most organizations, however, selection includes the steps illustrated in Figure 6.1. First, a human resource professional reviews the applications received to see which meet the basic requirements of the job. For candidates who meet the basic requirements, the organization administers tests and reviews work samples to rate the candidates' abilities. Those with the best abilities are invited to the organization for one or more interviews. Often, supervisors and team members are involved in this stage of the process. By this point, the decision makers are beginning to form opinions about which candidates are most desirable. For the top few candidates, the organization should check references and conduct background checks to verify that the organization's information is correct. Then supervisors, teams, and other decision makers select a person to receive a job offer. In some cases, the candidate may negotiate with the organization regarding salary, benefits, and the like. If the candidate accepts the job, the organization places him or her in that job. The HR Oops! box highlights the importance of frequent contact with prospective employees.

How does an organization decide which of these elements to use and in what order? Some organizations simply repeat a selection process that is familiar. If members of the organization underwent job interviews, they conduct job interviews, asking familiar questions. However, what organizations *should* do is to create a selection process in support of its job descriptions. In Chapter 3, we explained that a job description identifies the knowledge, skills, abilities, and other characteristics required for successfully performing a job. The selection process should be set up in such a way that it lets the organization identify people who have the necessary KSAOs. The Federal Aviation Administration (FAA) has applied these principles to correct a pattern of hiring in which it was selecting many air-traffic controllers who could not pass the certification exam after they had been trained. The FAA began conducting research to learn which employment tests would identify people with the necessary skills: spatial (three-dimensional) thinking, strong memories, and ability to work well under time pressure.[2]

LO1 Identify the elements of the selection process.

personnel selection
The process through which organizations make decisions about who will or will not be allowed to join the organization.

Figure 6.1

Steps in the Selection Process

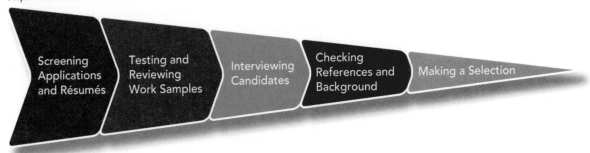

Screening Applications and Résumés

Testing and Reviewing Work Samples

Interviewing Candidates

Checking References and Background

Making a Selection

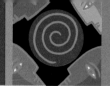

HR Oops!

Too Busy to Talk

Recently, a legal secretary looking for a new job visited a law firm, where she took employment tests and interviewed with the human resources director for an hour. She was told she would hear something by the next week, and she sent a thank-you note. A week later, she called, but no one returned her call. No one replied to her e-mail. She was happy when another firm offered her a job.

A Silicon Valley job hunter tops this story. She visited a prospective employer *eight* times to interview with various managers.

However, after all that time and all those introductions, no one at the company ever communicated with her by phone, letter, or e-mail to indicate anything about the company's hiring plans.

Hiring managers commenting on this lack of communication generally blame the sheer volume of work. Many companies receive thousands or hundreds of thousands of résumés and can't figure out how to reply to them all.

Sources: Liz Ryan, "The Courtesy of a Reply," *BusinessWeek,* January 29, 2007, downloaded from Business & Company Resource Center,

http://galenet.galegroup.com; and Amy Joyce, "Persistence Can Help Rescue a Résumé That's Lost in the Ether," *Washington Post,* January 7, 2007, www.washingtonpost.com.

Questions

1. Does it matter whether a company communicates with people it doesn't plan to hire? Why or why not?

2. Since electronic recruiting is generating a flood of job applicants, how could technology also help employers communicate with these applicants?

This kind of strategic approach to selection requires ways to measure the effectiveness of selection tools. From science, we have basic standards for this:

- The method provides *reliable* information.
- The method provides *valid* information.
- The information can be *generalized* to apply to the candidates.
- The method offers *high utility* (practical value).
- The selection criteria are *legal.*

LO2 Define ways to measure the success of a selection method.

reliability
The extent to which a measurement is free from random error.

Reliability

The **reliability** of a type of measurement indicates how free that measurement is from random error.[3] A reliable measurement therefore generates consistent results. Assuming that a person's intelligence is fairly stable over time, a reliable test of intelligence should generate consistent results if the same person takes the test several times. Organizations that construct intelligence tests should be able to provide (and explain) information about the reliability of their tests.

Usually, this information involves statistics such as *correlation coefficients*. These statistics measure the degree to which two sets of numbers are related. A higher correlation coefficient signifies a stronger relationship. At one extreme, a correlation coefficient of 1.0 means a perfect positive relationship—as one set of numbers goes up, so does the other. If you took the same vision test three days in a row, those scores would probably have nearly a perfect correlation. At the other extreme, a correlation of −1.0 means a perfect negative correlation—when one set of numbers goes up, the other goes down. In the middle, a correlation of 0 means there is no correlation at all. For example, the correlation (or relationship) between weather and intelligence would be at or near 0. A reliable test would be one for which scores by the same person (or people with similar attributes) have a correlation close to 1.0.

Validity

For a selection measure, **validity** describes the extent to which performance on the measure (such as a test score) is related to what the measure is designed to assess (such as job performance). Although we can reliably measure such characteristics as weight and height, these measurements do not provide much information about how a person will perform most kinds of jobs. Thus, for most jobs height and weight provide little validity as selection criteria. One way to determine whether a measure is valid is to compare many people's scores on that measure with their job performance. For example, suppose people who score above 60 words per minute on a keyboarding test consistently get high marks for their performance in data-entry jobs. This observation suggests the keyboarding test is valid for predicting success in that job.

As with reliability, information about the validity of selection methods often uses correlation coefficients. A strong positive (or negative) correlation between a measure and job performance means the measure should be a valid basis for selecting (or rejecting) a candidate. This information is important not only because it helps organizations identify the best employees but also because organizations can demonstrate fair employment practices by showing that their selection process is valid. The federal government's *Uniform Guidelines on Employee Selection Procedures* accept three ways of measuring validity: criterion-related, content, and construct validity.

validity
The extent to which performance on a measure (such as a test score) is related to what the measure is designed to assess (such as job performance).

Criterion-Related Validity

The first category, **criterion-related validity,** is a measure of validity based on showing a substantial correlation between test scores and job performance scores. In the example in Figure 6.2, a company compares two measures—an intelligence test and college grade point average—with performance as sales representative. In the left graph, which shows the relationship between the intelligence test scores and job performance, the points for the 20 sales reps fall near the 45-degree line. The correlation coefficient is near .90 (for a perfect 1.0, all the points would be on the 45-degree line). In the graph

criterion-related validity
A measure of validity based on showing a substantial correlation between test scores and job performance scores.

Figure 6.2

Criterion-Related Measurements of a Student's Aptitude

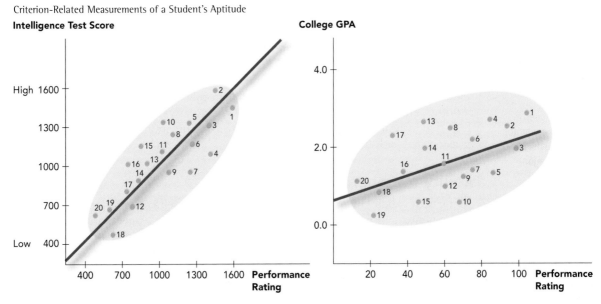

at the right, the points are scattered more widely. The correlation between college GPA and sales reps' performance is much lower. In this hypothetical example, the intelligence test is more valid than GPA for predicting success at this job.

Two kinds of research are possible for arriving at criterion-related validity:

predictive validation
Research that uses the test scores of all applicants and looks for a relationship between the scores and future performance of the applicants who were hired.

1. **Predictive validation**—This research uses the test scores of all applicants and looks for a relationship between the scores and future performance. The researcher administers the tests, waits a set period of time, and then measures the performance of the applicants who were hired.
2. **Concurrent validation**—This type of research administers a test to people who currently hold a job, then compares their scores to existing measures of job performance. If the people who score highest on the test also do better on the job, the test is assumed to be valid.

concurrent validation
Research that consists of administering a test to people who currently hold a job, then comparing their scores to existing measures of job performance.

Predictive validation is more time-consuming and difficult, but it is the best measure of validity. Job applicants tend to be more motivated to do well on the tests, and their performance on the tests is not influenced by their firsthand experience with the job. Also, the group studied is more likely to include people who perform poorly on the test—a necessary ingredient to accurately validate a test.[4]

Content and Construct Validity

content validity
Consistency between the test items or problems and the kinds of situations or problems that occur on the job.

Another way to show validity is to establish **content validity**—that is, consistency between the test items or problems and the kinds of situations or problems that occur on the job.[5] A test that is "content valid" exposes the job applicant to situations that are likely to occur on the job. It tests whether the applicant has the knowledge, skills, or ability to handle such situations. In the case of a company using tests for selecting a construction superintendent, tests with content validity included organizing a random list of subcontractors into the order they would appear at a construction site and entering a shed to identify construction errors that had intentionally been made for testing purposes.[6]

The usual basis for deciding that a test has content validity is through expert judgment. Experts can rate the test items according to whether they mirror essential functions of the job. Because establishing validity is based on the experts' subjective judgments, content validity is most suitable for measuring behavior that is concrete and observable.

construct validity
Consistency between a high score on a test and high level of a construct such as intelligence or leadership ability, as well as between mastery of this construct and successful performance of the job.

For tests that measure abstract qualities such as intelligence or leadership ability, establishment of validity may have to rely on **construct validity.** This involves establishing that tests really do measure intelligence, leadership ability, or other such "constructs," as well as showing that mastery of this construct is associated with successful performance of the job. For example, if you could show that a test measures something called "mechanical ability," and that people with superior mechanical ability perform well as assemblers, then the test has construct validity for the assembler job. Tests that measure a construct usually measure a combination of behaviors thought to be associated with the construct.

Ability to Generalize

generalizable
Valid in other contexts beyond the context in which the selection method was developed.

Along with validity in general, we need to know whether a selection method is valid in the context in which the organization wants to use it. A **generalizable** method applies not only to the conditions in which the method was originally developed—job, organization, people, time period, and so on. It also applies to other organizations, jobs, applicants, and so on. In other words, is a selection method that was valid in one context also valid in other contexts?

Gallup Helps Wesley Medical Center Find Practical Selection Methods

Typically, a hospital or other health care provider spends thousands of dollars a year to hire and train replacements for employees who quit. To address that problem, Wichita, Kansas–Wesley Medical Center asked Gallup Healthcare Group to help it use assessment tools to identify qualified prospects who would stick around.

Gallup's method identifies the talents of top performers and develops tools to recognize job candidates who have similar talents. For clients like Wesley, the consulting firm sets up a computerized system that gathers information from job seekers and guides HR staff through the selection process. Wesley first began using the method to select its nurses. Following success with that effort, the hospital began using similar methods for hiring all employees.

The system immediately compiles job candidates' responses, determines how well the candidate will fit a particular job's requirements, and reports whether scores indicate the candidate should be recommended, conditionally recommended, or not recommended. Experience with the selection of nurses has shown that those who were recommended by the system work with greater clinical accuracy, generate more favorable comments from patients, and have better work attendance than nurses who were conditionally recommended or not recommended. Such results deliver practical, measurable benefits to the hospital. The system is also more efficient, because all applicants go online to complete assessments that formerly took place in 45-minute phone calls. Don Morris, Wesley's vice president of human resources, says implementing Gallup's system was "a big investment initially," but the benefits outweigh those costs.

Sources: Andi Atwater, "Employee Screening Program Fits Wesley," *Wichita (Ks.) Eagle,* April 11, 2007, downloaded from General Reference Center Gold, http://find.galegroup.com; Gallup Inc., "Talent Acquisition," "Talent-Based Hiring," and "Nurse-Insight™," Gallup Consulting Web site, www.gallup.com/consulting/, accessed January 22, 2008; and Wesley Medical Center (WMC), "About Us," and "Employment," WMC Web site, www.wesleymc.com, accessed January 22, 2008.

Researchers have studied whether tests of intelligence and thinking skills (called *cognitivee ability*) can be generalized. The research has supported the idea that these tests are generalizable across many jobs. However, as jobs become more complex, the validity of many of these tests increases. In other words, they are most valid for complex jobs.[7]

NFL teams have been using cognitive tests to select players assuming that intelligence can be generalized to the job requirements of football teams, especially on teams that compete using complex offensive and defensive schemes. What other things, in addition to intelligence, would teams need to look for?

Practical Value

Not only should selection methods such as tests and interview responses accurately predict how well individuals will perform, but they should also produce information that actually benefits the organization. Being valid, reliable, and generalizable adds value to a method. Another consideration is the cost of using the selection method. Selection procedures such as testing and interviewing cost money. They should cost significantly less than the benefits of hiring the new employees. Methods that provide economic value greater than the cost of using them are said to have **utility.** For an example of an organization meeting these criteria with its selection methods, see the "Best Practices" box.

The choice of a selection method may differ according to the job being filled. If the job involves providing a product or service of high value to the organization, it is worthwhile to spend more to find a top performer. At a company where salespeople are responsible for closing million-dollar deals, the company will be willing to invest

utility
The extent to which something provides economic value greater than its cost.

more in selection decisions. At a fast-food restaurant, such an investment will not be worthwhile; the employer will prefer faster, simpler ways to select workers who ring up orders, prepare food, and keep the facility clean.

Legal Standards for Selection

LO3 Summarize the government's requirements for employee selection.

As we discussed in Chapter 3, the U.S. government imposes legal limits on selection decisions. The government requires that the selection process be conducted in a way that avoids discrimination and provides access to employees with disabilities. The laws described in Chapter 3 have many applications to the selection process:

- The Civil Rights Act of 1991 and the Age Discrimination in Employment Act of 1967 place requirements on the choice of selection methods. An employer that uses a neutral-appearing selection method that damages a protected group is obligated to show that there is a business necessity for using that method. For example, if an organization uses a test that eliminates many candidates from minority groups, the organization must show that the test is valid for predicting performance of that job. In this context, good performance does not include "customer preference" or "brand image" as a justification for adverse impact. For example, Abercrombie & Fitch was not able to justify its low rate of hiring nonwhite applicants on the basis that certain managers thought they lacked an "A&F look."[8]

- The Civil Rights Act of 1991 also prohibits preferential treatment in favor of minority groups. In the case of an organization using a test that tends to reject members of minority groups, the organization may not simply adjust minority applicants' scores upward. Such practices, besides being illegal, can interfere with motivation. According to research, when employees perceive selection decisions to be based partially on membership in some group (minority group or women), this perception undermines the confidence of members of the supposedly protected group. Their job performance suffers as well.[9]

- Equal employment opportunity laws affect the kinds of information an organization may gather on application forms and in interviews. As summarized in Table 6.1, the organization may not ask questions that gather information about a person's protected status, even indirectly. For example, requesting the dates a person attended high school and college could indirectly gather information about an applicant's age.

- The Americans with Disabilities Act (ADA) of 1991 requires employers to make "reasonable accommodation" to disabled individuals and restricts many kinds of questions during the selection process.[10] Under the ADA, preemployment questions may not investigate disabilities, but must focus on job performance. An interviewer may ask, "Can you meet the attendance requirements for this job?" but may not ask, "How many days did you miss work last year because you were sick?" Also, the employer may not, in making hiring decisions, use employment physical exams or other tests that could reveal a psychological or physical disability.

Along with equal employment opportunity, organizations must be concerned about candidates' privacy rights. The information gathered during the selection process may include information that employees consider confidential. Confidentiality is a particular concern when job applicants provide information online. Employers should collect data only at secure Web sites, and they may have to be understanding if online applicants are reluctant to provide data such as Social Security numbers, which hackers could use for identity theft.[11] For some jobs, background checks look at candidates' credit history. The Fair Credit Reporting Act requires employers to obtain a candidate's

Table 6.1

Permissible and Impermissible Questions for Applications and Interviews

PERMISSIBLE QUESTIONS	IMPERMISSIBLE QUESTIONS
What is your full name? Have you ever worked under a different name?	What was your maiden name? What's the nationality of your name?
Are you at least 18 years old?	How old are you?
Do you understand the job requirements? Are you able to perform this job, with or without reasonable accommodation?	What is your height? your weight? Do you have any disabilities? Have you been seriously ill? Please provide a photograph of yourself.
What languages do you speak? [Statement that employment is subject to verification of applicant's identity and employment eligibility under immigration laws]	What is your ancestry? Are you a citizen of the United States? Where were you born? How did you learn to speak that language?
What schools have you attended? What degrees have you earned? What was your major?	Is that school affiliated with [religious group]? When did you attend high school? [to learn applicant's age]
[No questions about religion]	What is your religion? What religious holidays do you observe?
Please provide the names of any relatives currently employed by this employer.	What is your marital status? Would you like to be addressed as Mrs., Ms., or Miss? Do you have any children?
Have you ever been convicted of a crime?	Have you ever been arrested?
Please give the name and address of a person we may contact in case of an emergency.	Please give the name and address of a relative we may contact in case of an emergency.
What organizations or groups do you belong to (excluding those that indicate members' race, religion, color, national origin, or ancestry)?	What organizations or groups do you belong to?

Note: This table provides examples and is not intended as a complete listing of permissible and impermissible questions. The examples are based on federal requirements; state laws vary and may affect these examples.

Sources: Examples based on "Legal and Illegal Preemployment Inquiries," Inc.com, *Human Resources Advice pages, www.inc. com, downloaded March 7, 2002; and S. Kahn, B. B. Brown, and M. Lanzarone,* Legal Guide to Human Resources *(Boston, MA: Warren, Gorham & Lamont, 1995).*

consent before using a third party to check the candidate's credit history or references. If the employer then decides to take an adverse action (such as not hiring) based on the report, the employer must give the applicant a copy of the report and summary of the applicant's rights *before* taking the action.

Another legal requirement is that employers hiring people to work in the United States must ensure that anyone they hire is eligible for employment in this country. Under the **Immigration Reform and Control Act of 1986,** employers must verify and maintain records on the legal rights of applicants to work in the United States. They do this by having applicants fill out the U.S. Citizenship and Immigration Services' Form I-9 and present documents showing their identity and eligibility to work. Employers must complete their portion of each Form I-9, check the applicant's documents, and

Immigration Reform and Control Act of 1986
Federal law requiring employers to verify and maintain records on applicants' legal rights to work in the United States.

SURFING THE TIDAL WAVE OF JOB APPLICATIONS

An online job posting or a career page on a company's Web site can stimulate a tidal wave of applications from serious and not-so-serious job hunters. Then comes the hard part: sifting through them to find a few candidates who might have what the company needs.

One solution is to post jobs at a service such as Protuo, which requires applicants to fill out a survey that is customized by the employer to ask about relevant experience, skills, work styles, and job preferences. Protuo screens out applications that aren't a good match. One Protuo client, Donovan Networks, reports that the process yields more suitable applicants, such as people who know about software development and have enough sales experience.

Big companies might contract with a firm that can tailor applications to the company's needs. Trend Micro's U.S. division uses a company called Trovix to analyze résumé data, identify relevant phrases, rank qualifications as specified by Trend Micro, and score candidates on how closely they match what the employer needs. For a management job, Trovix took just 20 minutes to pick the top 10 candidates from 700 résumés.

Sources: David H. Freedman, "The Monster Dilemma," *Inc.,* May 2007, pp. 77–78; and Michael Totty, "New Tools Emerge for Frazzled Recruiters," *Career Journal,* October 27, 2006, www.careerjournal.com.

retain the Form I-9 for at least three years. At the same time, assuming a person is eligible to work under this law, the law prohibits the employer from discriminating against the person on the basis of national origin or citizenship status.

An important principle of selection is to combine several sources of information about candidates, rather than relying solely on interviews or a single type of testing. The sources should be chosen carefully to relate to the characteristics identified in the job description. When organizations do this, they are increasing the validity of the decision criteria. They are more likely to make hiring decisions that are fair and unbiased. They also are more likely to choose the best candidates.

LO4 Compare the common methods used for selecting human resources.

Job Applications and Résumés

Nearly all employers gather background information on applicants at the beginning of the selection process. The usual ways of gathering background information are by asking applicants to fill out application forms and provide résumés. Organizations also verify the information by checking references and conducting background checks.

Asking job candidates to provide background information is inexpensive. The organization can get reasonably accurate information by combining applications and résumés with background checks and well-designed interviews.[12] A major challenge with applications and résumés is the sheer volume of work they generate for the organization. Human resource departments often are swamped with far more résumés than they can carefully review. The e-HRM box shows how software tools can help identify promising job candidates from hundreds of on-line applications a company can receive from an on-line job posting.

Application Forms

Asking each applicant to fill out an employment application is a low-cost way to gather basic data from many applicants. It also ensures that the organization has certain standard categories of information, such as mailing address and employment history, from each. Figure 6.3 is an example of an application form.

Figure 6.3

Sample Job Application Form

APPLICATION FOR EMPLOYMENT
An Equal Opportunity Employer

| FIRST NAME | MIDDLE NAME | LAST NAME | SOCIAL SECURITY NUMBER |

| LOCAL | STREET ADDRESS | CITY AND STATE | ZIP CODE | TELEPHONE |
| PERMANENT | STREET ADDRESS | CITY AND STATE | ZIP CODE | TELEPHONE |

ELECTRONIC MAIL ADDRESS

PLEASE ANSWER ALL ITEMS. IF NOT APPLICABLE, WRITE N/A.

ARE YOU A U.S. CITIZEN OR AUTHORIZED TO BE LEGALLY EMPLOYED ON AN ONGOING BASIS IN THE U.S. BASED ON YOUR VISA OR IMMIGRATION STATUS? ☐ YES ☐ NO

ARE YOU OVER 18 YEARS OF AGE? YES ☐ NO ☐

DO YOU CURRENTLY HAVE A NONIMMIGRANT U.S. VISA? ☐ YES ☐ NO   IF YES, PLEASE SPECIFY:

DO YOU HAVE ANY RELATIVES EMPLOYED HERE? ☐ NO ☐ YES
IF YES, GIVE NAME, RELATIONSHIP AND LOCATION WHERE THEY WORK

DO YOU HAVE ANY RELATIVES EMPLOYED BY THE COMPETITION? ☐ NO ☐ YES   WHAT COMPANY?

ARE YOU ABLE TO TRAVEL AS REQUIRED FOR THE POSITION SOUGHT? ☐ YES ☐ NO
ARE YOU WILLING TO RELOCATE? ☐ NO ☐ YES

ARE THERE GEOGRAPHICAL AREAS WHICH YOU WOULD PREFER OR REFUSE? ☐ NO ☐ YES   IF YES, PLEASE SPECIFY:

HAVE YOU EVER BEEN CONVICTED OR PLED GUILTY TO ANY FELONY OR MISDEMEANOR OTHER THAN FOR A MINOR TRAFFIC VIOLATION? ☐ NO ☐ YES
IF YES, STATE THE DATE(S) AND LOCATION(S):

WHEN | WHERE | NATURE OF OFFENSE(S)

WORK PREFERENCE

SPECIFIC POSITION FOR WHICH YOU ARE APPLYING

NUMBER OF YEARS OF RELATED EXPERIENCE

LIST COMPUTER SOFTWARE PACKAGES OR PROGRAMMING LANGUAGE SKILLS

STARTING SALARY EXPECTED | DATE AVAILABLE TO START WORK | HOW DID YOU HAPPEN TO APPLY FOR A POSITION HERE?

HAVE YOU EVER WORKED AT, OR APPLIED FOR WORK HERE BEFORE? ☐ NO ☐ YES
IF YES, WHEN? | WHERE?

LIST EMPLOYMENT REFERENCES HERE, IF NOT INCLUDED ON ATTACHED RESUME

TURN OVER

COMPLETE THIS SECTION IF INFORMATION IS NOT INCLUDED ON ATTACHED RESUME

EDUCATION (CIRCLE THE HIGHEST GRADE COMPLETED: ELEMENTARY 6 7 8   HIGH SCHOOL 1 2 3 4   COLLEGE 1 2 3 4 5 6 7 8

	NAME(S)	LOCATION(S)	MAJOR FIELDS OF STUDY AND PRINCIPAL PROFESSOR (OR ADVISOR)	GRADUATED ☐ YES ☐ NO	GRADE AVERAGE	DEGREE(S) RECEIVED	CLASS RANK ___ OUT OF ___
HIGH SCHOOL							OVERALL AND MAJOR GPA'S
COLLEGE							

ACADEMIC HONORS OR OTHER SPECIAL RECOGNITION

FOREIGN LANGUAGES READ | FOREIGN LANGUAGES SPOKEN

HAVE YOU TAKEN THE GMAT, GRE, SAT OR OTHER ACADEMIC ENTRANCE TEST(S) WITHIN THE LAST TEN YEARS? ☐ YES ☐ NO
IF YES, LIST TEST(S), DATE(S) AND HIGHEST SCORE(S).

	DATE TAKEN	SCORE(S)
SAT		TOTAL ___ VERBAL ___ MATHEMATICAL ___
ACT		TOTAL ___ ENGLISH ___ MATHEMATICS ___ READING ___ SCIENCE ___
GRE (GENERAL TEST)		TOTAL ___ VERBAL ___ QUANTITATIVE ___ ANALYTICAL ___
GMAT		TOTAL ___ VERBAL ___ MATH ___ AWA ___
OTHER		TOTAL ___

EMPLOYMENT AND MILITARY RECORD
LIST MOST RECENT FIRST. I AGREE TO FURNISH VERIFICATION IF REQUESTED. ATTACH RESUME. RESPOND BELOW IF INFORMATION IS NOT INCLUDED ON RESUME.

NAME AND ADDRESS OF EMPLOYER	POSITION HELD	PRIMARY RESPONSIBILITIES AND ACCOUNTABILITIES	SALARY START	SALARY FINISH	DATES FROM	DATES TO	REASON FOR LEAVING

ENCIRCLE THOSE EMPLOYERS YOU DO NOT WANT US TO CONTACT

TURN OVER

Employers can buy general-purpose application forms from an office supply store, or they can create their own forms to meet unique needs. Either way, employment applications include areas for applicants to provide several types of information:

- *Contact information*—The applicant's name, address, phone number, and e-mail address.
- *Work experience*—Companies the applicant worked for, job titles, and dates of employment.
- *Educational background*—High school, college, and universities attended and degree(s) awarded.
- *Applicant's signature*—Signature following a statement that the applicant has provided true and complete information.

The application form may include other areas for the applicant to provide additional information, such as specific work experiences, technical skills, or memberships in professional or trade groups. Also, including the date on an application is useful for keeping up-to-date records of job applicants. The application form should not request information that could violate equal employment opportunity standards. For example, questions about an applicant's race, marital status, or number of children would be inappropriate.

By reviewing application forms, HR personnel can identify which candidates meet minimum requirements for education and experience. They may be able to rank applicants—for example, giving applicants with 10 years' experience a higher ranking than applicants with 2 years' experience. In this way, the applications enable the organization to narrow the pool of candidates to a number it can afford to test and interview.

Résumés

The usual way that applicants introduce themselves to a potential employer is to submit a résumé. An obvious drawback of this information source is that applicants control the content of the information, as well as the way it is presented. This type of information is therefore biased in favor of the applicant and (although this is unethical) may not even be accurate. However, this inexpensive way to gather information does provide employers with a starting point. Organizations typically use résumés as a basis for deciding which candidates to investigate further.

As with employment applications, an HR staff member reviews the résumés to identify candidates meeting such basic requirements as educational background, related work performed, and types of equipment the person has used. Because résumés are created by the job applicants (or the applicants have at least approved résumés created by someone they hire), they also may provide some insight into how candidates communicate and present themselves. Employers tend to decide against applicants whose résumés are unclear, sloppy, or full of mistakes. On the positive side, résumés may enable applicants to highlight accomplishments that might not show up in the format of an employment application. Review of résumés is most valid when the content of the résumés is evaluated in terms of the elements of a job description.

Visit the text Web site www.mhhe.com/noefund3e for tips on writing an effective résumé.

References

Application forms often ask that applicants provide the names of several references. Applicants provide the names and phone numbers of former employers or others who can vouch for their abilities and past job performance. In some situations, the applicant may provide letters of reference written by those people. It is then up to the organization to have someone contact the references to gather information or verify the accuracy of the information provided by the applicant.

As you might expect, references are not an unbiased source of information. Most applicants are careful to choose references who will say something positive. In addition, former employers and others may be afraid that if they express negative opinions, they will be sued. Their fear is understandable. In 2003, a jury awarded $283,000 to a truck driver whose past employer told a would-be employer that he "was late most of the time, regularly missed two days a week, had a problem with authority and a poor work ethic."[13]

Usually the organization checks references after it has determined that the applicant is a finalist for the job. Contacting references for all applicants would be time-consuming, and it does pose some burden on the people contacted. Part of that burden is the risk of giving information that is seen as too negative or too positive. If the person who is a reference gives negative information, there is a chance the candidate will claim *defamation*, meaning the person damaged the applicant's reputation by making statements that cannot be proved truthful.[14] At the other extreme, if the person gives a glowing statement about a candidate, and the new employer later learns of misdeeds such as sexual misconduct or workplace violence, the new employer might sue the former employer for misrepresentation.[15]

Because such situations occasionally arise, often with much publicity, people who give references tend to give as little information as possible. Most organizations have policies that the human resource department will handle all requests for references and that they will only verify employment dates and sometimes the employee's final salary. In organizations without such a policy, HR professionals should be careful—and train managers to be careful—to stick to observable, job-related behaviors and to avoid broad opinions that may be misinterpreted. In spite of these drawbacks of references, the risks of not learning about significant problems in a candidate's past outweigh the possibility of getting only a little information. Potential employers should check references.

Background Checks

A background check is a way to verify that applicants are as they represent themselves to be. Unfortunately, not all candidates are open and honest. Others, even if honest, may find that the Internet makes it easy for potential employers to uncover information that reveals them in an unflattering light and may cost them a job. For more on this risk, see the "Did You Know?" box.

About 8 out of 10 large companies and over two-thirds of smaller organizations say they conduct criminal background checks. One of those businesses is Wal-Mart stores, which employs more U.S. workers than any other company. Wal-Mart uses private services, which check their databases to look for records of criminal offenses. The background checks are performed on applicants Wal-Mart has screened and identified as qualified for a position. If the background check shows a candidate has lied on his or her job application, the company will not hire that person. If the background check turns up a criminal conviction, Wal-Mart's policy is to evaluate each candidate individually, considering the nature and date of the offense and the responsibilities of the job for which the person is being considered.[16]

Verifying credentials and conducting background checks are more complicated when candidates are not U.S. citizens. Their education may include degrees from schools outside the United States. In such cases, the organization has to determine

Did You Know?

Employers Are Googling and Social Networking, Too

Sizable shares of college-level and executive recruiters say they use Internet search engines to learn about job applicants. Images that make you look unprofessional can cost you a job, but evidence of your commitment to a cause might help. Job hunters beware! Run a search on your name every now and then, and look for problems.

Sources: Kimberly Atkins and Ross Daly, "Search and Destroy," *Long Island Business News,* July 27,

2007, downloaded from General Reference Center Gold, http://find.galegroup.com; and Hope Viner Samborn, "Go Google Yourself!" *ABA Journal* 93 (August 2007), http://find.galegroup.com.

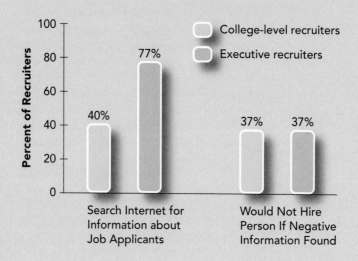

how the institution and the degree awarded compare with schools and degrees in the United States. Some companies, including Mobil Corporation, get around this issue by conducting their own screening tests for basic skills in reading and math. Other companies, such as the Knowledge Company in Fairfax, Virginia, use work sample tests. For example, an applicant for an engineering job would have to submit designs for a certain product, and experts evaluate the drawings. Criminal background checks also are difficult. Except for serious crimes, U.S. records contain little about crimes committed outside the United States. These and other hurdles can discourage U.S. employers from hiring foreign nationals. Organizations that overcome the hurdles therefore can gain an advantage in hiring the best of this talent.[17]

LO5 Describe major types of employment tests.

aptitude tests
Tests that assess how well a person can learn or acquire skills and abilities.

Employment Tests and Work Samples

When the organization has identified candidates whose applications or résumés indicate they meet basic requirements, the organization continues the selection process with this narrower pool of candidates. Often, the next step is to gather objective data through one or more employment tests. These tests fall into two broad categories:

1. **Aptitude tests** assess how well a person can learn or acquire skills and abilities. In the realm of employment testing, the best-known aptitude test is the General Aptitude Test Battery (GATB), used by the U.S. Employment Service.

162

Table 6.2

**Sources of Information
about Employment Tests**

Mental Measurements Yearbook	Descriptions and reviews of tests that are commercially available
Principles for the Validation and Use of Personnel Selection Procedures (Society for Industrial and Organizational Psychology)	Guide to help organizations evaluate tests
Standards for Educational and Psychological Tests (American Psychological Association)	Description of standards for testing programs
Tests: A Comprehensive Reference for Assessments in Psychology, Education, and Business	Descriptions of thousands of tests
Test Critiques	Reviews of tests, written by professionals in the field

2. **Achievement tests** measure a person's existing knowledge and skills. For example, government agencies conduct civil service examinations to see whether applicants are qualified to perform certain jobs.

Before using any test, organizations should investigate the test's validity and reliability. Besides asking the testing service to provide this information, it is wise to consult more impartial sources of information, such as the ones identified in Table 6.2.

achievement tests
Tests that measure a person's existing knowledge and skills.

Physical Ability Tests

Physical strength and endurance play less of a role in the modern workplace than in the past, thanks to the use of automation and modern technology. Even so, many jobs still require certain physical abilities or psychomotor abilities (those connecting brain and body, as in the case of eye-hand coordination). When these abilities are essential to job performance or avoidance of injury, the organization may use physical ability tests. These evaluate one or more of the following areas of physical ability: muscular tension, muscular power, muscular endurance, cardiovascular endurance, flexibility, balance, and coordination.[18]

Although these tests can accurately predict success at certain kinds of jobs, they also tend to exclude women and people with disabilities. As a result, use of physical ability tests can make the organization vulnerable to charges of discrimination. It is therefore important to be certain that the abilities tested for really are essential to job performance or that the absence of these abilities really does create a safety hazard.

Cognitive Ability Tests

Although fewer jobs require muscle power today, brainpower is essential for most jobs. Organizations therefore benefit from people who have strong mental abilities. **Cognitive ability tests**—sometimes called "intelligence tests"—are designed to measure such mental abilities as verbal skills (skill in using written and spoken language), quantitative skills (skill in working with numbers), and reasoning ability (skill in thinking through the answer to a problem). Many jobs require all of these cognitive skills, so employers often get valid information from general tests. Many reliable tests are commercially available. The tests are especially valid for complex jobs and for those requiring adaptability in changing circumstances.[19]

cognitive ability tests
Tests designed to measure such mental abilities as verbal skills, quantitative skills, and reasoning ability.

The evidence of validity, coupled with the relatively low cost of these tests, makes them appealing, except for one problem: concern about legal issues. These concerns arise from a historical pattern in which use of the tests has had an adverse impact on African Americans. Some organizations responded with *race norming*, establishing different norms for hiring members of different racial groups. Race norming poses its own problems, not the least of which is the negative reputation it bestows on the minority employees selected using a lower standard. In addition, the Civil Rights Act of 1991 forbids the use of race or sex norming. As a result, organizations that want to base selection decisions on cognitive ability must make difficult decisions about how to measure this ability while avoiding legal problems. One possibility is a concept called *banding*. This concept treats a range of scores as being similar, as when an instructor gives the grade of A to any student whose average test score is at least 90. All applicants within a range of scores, or band, are treated as having the same score. Then within the set of "tied" scores, employers give preference to underrepresented groups. This is a controversial practice, and some have questioned its legality.[20]

Job Performance Tests and Work Samples

Many kinds of jobs require candidates who excel at performing specialized tasks, such as operating a certain machine, handling phone calls from customers, or designing advertising materials. To evaluate candidates for such jobs, the organization may administer tests of the necessary skills. Sometimes the candidates take tests that involve a sample of work, or they may show existing samples of their work. Testing may involve a simulated work setting, perhaps in a testing center or in a computerized "virtual" environment.[21] Examples of job performance tests include tests of keyboarding speed and *in-basket tests*. An in-basket test measures the ability to juggle a variety of demands, as in a manager's job. The candidate is presented with simulated memos and phone messages describing the kinds of problems that confront a person in the job. The candidate has to decide how to respond to these messages and in what order. Examples of jobs for which candidates provide work samples include graphic designers and writers.

assessment center
A wide variety of specific selection programs that use multiple selection methods to rate applicants or job incumbents on their management potential.

Tests for selecting managers may take the form of an **assessment center**—a wide variety of specific selection programs that use multiple selection methods to rate applicants or job incumbents on their management potential. An assessment center typically includes in-basket tests, tests of more general abilities, and personality tests. Combining several assessment methods increases the validity of this approach.

Job performance tests have the advantage of giving applicants a chance to show what they can do, which leads them to feel that the evaluation was fair.[22] The tests also are job specific—that is, tailored to the kind of work done in a specific job. So they have a high level of validity, especially when combined with cognitive ability tests and a highly structured interview.[23] This advantage can become a disadvantage, however, if the organization wants to generalize the results of a test for one job to candidates for other jobs. The tests are more appropriate for identifying candidates who are generally able to solve the problems associated with a job, rather than for identifying which particular skills or traits the individual possesses.[24] Developing different tests for different jobs can become expensive. One way to save money is to prepare computerized tests that can be delivered online to various locations.

Personality Inventories

In some situations, employers may also want to know about candidates' personalities. For example, one way that psychologists think about personality is in terms of the

Code Jam NY 2006

"Big Five" traits: extroversion, adjustment, agreeableness, conscientiousness, and inquisitiveness (explained in Table 6.3). There is evidence that people who score high on conscientiousness tend to excel at work, especially when they also have high cognitive ability.[25] For people-related jobs like sales and management, extroversion and agreeableness also seem to be associated with success.[26] Strong social skills help conscientious people ensure that they get positive recognition for their hard work.[27]

The usual way to identify a candidate's personality traits is to administer one of the personality tests that are commercially available. The employer pays for the use of the test, and the organization that owns the test then scores the responses and provides a report about the test taker's personality. An organization that provides such tests should be able to discuss the test's validity and reliability. Assuming the tests are valid for the organization's jobs, they have advantages. Administering commercially available personality tests is simple, and these tests have generally not violated equal opportunity employment requirements.[28] On the downside, compared with intelligence tests, people are better at "faking" their answers to a personality test to score higher on desirable traits.[29] For example, people tend to score higher on conscientiousness when filling out job-related personality tests than when participating in research projects.[30] Ways to address this problem include using trained interviewers rather than surveys, collecting

		Table 6.3
1. Extroversion	Sociable, gregarious, assertive, talkative, expressive	**Five Major Personality Dimensions Measured by Personality Inventories**
2. Adjustment	Emotionally stable, nondepressed, secure, content	
3. Agreeableness	Courteous, trusting, good-natured, tolerant, cooperative, forgiving	
4. Conscientiousness	Dependable, organized, persevering, thorough, achievement-oriented	
5. Inquisitiveness	Curious, imaginative, artistically sensitive, broad-minded, playful	

information about the applicant from several sources, and letting applicants know that several sources will be used.[31]

A recent study found that 35 percent of U.S. organizations use personality tests when selecting personnel.[32] One reason is organizations' greater use of teamwork, where personality conflicts can be a significant problem. Traits such as agreeableness and conscientiousness have been associated with effective teamwork.[33] Bank of America uses personality tests that measure behaviors with questions such as "Were you most comfortable working with a large team, or one or two others, or on your own?" The bank says retention and productivity have improved since it started using the tests.[34]

Honesty Tests and Drug Tests

No matter what employees' personalities may be like, organizations want employees to be honest and to behave safely. Some organizations are satisfied to assess these qualities based on judgments from reference checks and interviews. Others investigate these characteristics more directly through the use of honesty tests and drug tests.

The most famous kind of honesty test is the polygraph, the so-called lie detector test. However, in 1988 the passage of the Polygraph Act banned the use of polygraphs for screening job candidates. As a result, testing services have developed paper-and-pencil honesty (or integrity) tests. Generally these tests ask applicants directly about their attitudes toward theft and their own experiences with theft. Most of the research into the validity of these tests has been conducted by the testing companies, but evidence suggests they do have some ability to predict such behavior as theft of the employer's property.[35]

As concerns about substance abuse have grown during recent decades, so has the use of drug testing. As a measure of a person's exposure to drugs, chemical testing has high reliability and validity. However, these tests are controversial for several reasons. Some people are concerned that they invade individuals' privacy. Others object from a legal perspective. When all applicants or employees are subject to testing, whether or not they have shown evidence of drug use, the tests might be an unreasonable search and seizure or a violation of due process. Taking urine and blood samples involves invasive procedures, and accusing someone of drug use is a serious matter.

Employers considering the use of drug tests should ensure that their drug-testing programs conform to some general rules:[36]

- Administer the tests systematically to all applicants for the same job.
- Use drug testing for jobs that involve safety hazards.
- Have a report of the results sent to the applicant, along with information about how to appeal the results and be retested if appropriate.
- Respect applicants' privacy by conducting tests in an environment that is not intrusive and keeping results confidential.

Another way organizations can avoid some of the problems with drug testing is to replace those tests with impairment testing of employees, also called *fitness-for-duty testing*. These testing programs measure whether a worker is alert and mentally able to perform critical tasks at the time of the test. The test does not investigate the cause of any impairment—whether the employee scores poorly because of illegal drugs, alcohol, prescription drugs, over-the-counter medicines, or simple fatigue. A typical impairment test looks like a video game. The employee looks into a dark viewport and tries to follow a randomly moving point of light with his or her eyes. The equipment analyzes the person's performance and compares it with a baseline to see whether the person is fit for duty at that moment. Results are available in as little as two minutes. Because the test measures involuntary physical response, employees cannot cheat (as some have done on urine or blood tests). These tests are expensive, so they are most appropriate for high-stakes industries, such as building aircraft or spacecraft, or making surgical equipment.[37]

Medical Examinations

Especially for physically demanding jobs, organizations may wish to conduct medical examinations to see that the applicant can meet the job's requirements. Employers may also wish to establish an employee's physical condition at the beginning of employment, so that there is a basis for measuring whether the employee has suffered a work-related disability later on. At the same time, as described in Chapter 3, organizations may not discriminate against individuals with disabilities who could perform a job with reasonable accommodations. Likewise, they may not use a measure of size or strength that discriminates against women, unless those requirements are valid in predicting the ability to perform a job. Furthermore, to protect candidates' privacy, medical exams must be related to job requirements and may not be given until the candidate has received a job offer. Therefore, organizations must be careful in how they use medical examinations. Many organizations make selection decisions first and then conduct the exams to confirm that the employee can handle the job, with any reasonable accommodations required. Limiting the use of medical exams in this way also holds down the cost of what tends to be an expensive process.

Interviews

Supervisors and team members most often get involved in the selection process at the stage of employment interviews. These interviews bring together job applicants and representatives of the employer to obtain information and evaluate the applicant's qualifications. While the applicant is providing information, he or she is also forming opinions about what it is like to work for the organization. Most organizations use interviewing as part of the selection process. In fact, this method is used more than any other.

LO6 Discuss how to conduct effective interviews.

Interviewing Techniques

Interview techniques include choices about the type of questions to ask and the number of people who conduct the interview. Several question types are possible:

- In a **nondirective interview,** the interviewer has great discretion in choosing questions. The candidate's reply to one question may suggest other questions to ask. Nondirective interviews typically include open-ended questions about the candidate's strengths, weaknesses, career goals, and work experience. Because these interviews give the interviewer wide latitude, their reliability is not great, and some interviewers ask questions that are not valid or even legal.

- A **structured interview** establishes a set of questions for the interviewer to ask. Ideally, the questions are related to job requirements and cover relevant knowledge, skills, and experiences. The interviewer is supposed to avoid asking questions that are not on the list. Although interviewers may object to being restricted, the results may be more valid and reliable than with a nondirective interview.

nondirective interview
A selection interview in which the interviewer has great discretion in choosing questions to ask each candidate.

structured interview
A selection interview that consists of a predetermined set of questions for the interviewer to ask.

When interviewing candidates, it's valid to ask about willingness to travel if that is part of the job. Interviewers might ask questions about previous business travel experiences and/or how interviewees handled situations requiring flexibility and self-motivation (qualities that would be an asset in someone who is traveling alone and solving business problems on the road).

situational interview
A structured interview in which the interviewer describes a situation likely to arise on the job, then asks the candidate what he or she would do in that situation.

behavior description interview (BDI)
A structured interview in which the interviewer asks the candidate to describe how he or she handled a type of situation in the past.

panel interview
Selection interview in which several members of the organization meet to interview each candidate.

- A **situational interview** is a structured interview in which the interviewer describes a situation likely to arise on the job and asks the candidate what he or she would do in that situation. This type of interview may have high validity in predicting job performance.[38]
- A **behavior description interview** is a situational interview in which the interviewer asks the candidate to describe how he or she handled a type of situation in the past. Questions about candidates' actual experiences tend to have the highest validity.[39]

The common setup for either a nondirected or structured interview is for an individual (an HR professional or the supervisor for the vacant position) to interview each candidate face to face. However, variations on this approach are possible. In a **panel interview,** several members of the organization meet to interview each candidate. A panel interview gives the candidate a chance to meet more people and see how people interact in that organization. It provides the organization with the judgments of more than one person, to reduce the effect of personal biases in selection decisions. Panel interviews can be especially appropriate in organizations that use teamwork. At the other extreme, some organizations conduct interviews without any interviewers; they use a computerized interviewing process. The candidate sits at a computer and enters replies to the questions presented by the computer. Such a format eliminates a lot of personal bias—along with the opportunity to see how people interact. Therefore, computer interviews are useful for gathering objective data, rather than assessing people skills.

Advantages and Disadvantages of Interviewing

The wide use of interviewing is not surprising. People naturally want to see prospective employees firsthand. As we noted in Chapter 1, the top qualities that employers seek in new hires include communication skills and interpersonal skills. Talking face to face can provide evidence of these skills. Interviews can give insights into candidates' personalities and interpersonal styles. They are more valid, however, when they focus on job knowledge and skill. Interviews also provide a means to check the accuracy of information on the applicant's résumé or job application. Asking applicants to elaborate about their experiences and offer details reduces the likelihood of a candidate being able to invent a work history.[40]

Despite these benefits, interviewing is not necessarily the most accurate basis for making a selection decision. Research has shown that interviews can be unreliable, low in validity,[41] and biased against a number of different groups.[42] Interviews are also costly. They require that at least one person devote time to interviewing each candidate, and the applicants typically have to be brought to one geographic location. Interviews are also subjective, so they place the organization at greater risk of discrimination complaints by applicants who were not hired, especially if those individuals were asked questions not entirely related to the job. The Supreme Court has held that subjective selection methods like interviews must be validated, using methods that provide criterion-related or content validation.[43]

HR How To

INTERVIEWING EFFECTIVELY

Interviewing is one HR function that almost all managers are involved with at some point. Here are some tips for conducting interviews that identify the best candidates:

- *Be prepared*—Make sure the place where you will interview is comfortable—for both the interviewer and job candidate—and that it is accessible to candidates who may have disabilities. Read the candidate's résumé and other paperwork ahead of time so that the interview can touch on information that has not already been provided. Prepare a list of questions, so you don't forget any important points.

- *Assign responsibilities*—Often, organizations arrange to have candidates interview with the future supervisor and co-workers. If the candidates will interview with more than one person, make the time spent in all the interviews valuable. Identify what each interviewer will try to assess, and choose questions relevant to that assessment.

- *Put the applicant at ease*—A nervous or cautious job candidate may not show his or her best qualities. Chat about casual matters for a minute or two, and be sure the candidate knows how your position relates to the job search or the position he or she is interviewing for.

- *Ask about past behaviors*—Talking about specific events makes it harder for a candidate to focus on guessing what the interviewer wants to hear, and the answers give clues about what the candidate will do in new situations. For example, a restaurant might ask prospective servers, "Tell me about your most angry customer and how you handled him or her," or "What did you do the last time you got mad at somebody?"

- Figure out what your best employees do, and ask questions that look for similar behaviors. If you want to hire the best, you have to know what makes some employees stand out.

- At the end of the interview, make sure the candidate knows what to expect next—for example, a phone call or additional interviews within the next week.

Sources: Gina LaVecchia Ragone, "Weeding Out the Wackos," *Restaurant Hospitality,* September 2007, downloaded from Business & Company Resource Center, http://galenet.galegroup.com; University of Michigan Recruiting and Employment Services, "Behavior/Skill-Based Interviewing," *Conducting a Successful Employee Selection Process,* http://www.hr.umich.edu/empserv/department/empsel/behavior.html, accessed January 16, 2008; and Leigh Buchanan, "No Further Questions," *Inc.,* July 2007, p. 120.

Organizations can avoid some of these pitfalls.[44] Human resource staff should keep the interviews narrow, structured, and standardized. The interview should focus on accomplishing a few goals, so that at the end of the interview, the organization has ratings on several observable measures, such as ability to express ideas. The interview should not try to measure abilities and skills—for example, intelligence—that tests can measure better. As noted earlier, situational interviews are especially effective for doing this. Organizations can prevent problems related to subjectivity by training interviewers and using more than one person to conduct interviews. Training typically includes focusing on the recording of observable facts, rather than on making subjective judgments, as well as developing interviewers' awareness of their biases.[45] Using a structured system for taking notes is helpful for limiting subjectivity and helping the interviewer remember and justify an evaluation later.[46] Finally, to address costs of interviewing, many organizations videotape interviews and send the tapes (rather than the applicants) from department to department. The above "HR How To" box provides more specific guidelines for successful interviewing.

Preparing to Interview

Organizations can reap the greatest benefits from interviewing if they prepare carefully. A well-planned interview should be standardized, comfortable for the participants, and focused on the job and the organization. The interviewer should have a quiet place in which to conduct interviews without interruption. This person should be trained in how to ask objective questions, what subject matter to avoid, and how to detect and handle his or her own personal biases or other distractions in order to fairly evaluate candidates.

The interviewer should have enough documents to conduct a complete interview. These should include a list of the questions to be asked in a structured interview, with plenty of space for recording the responses. When the questions are prepared, it is also helpful to determine how the answers will be scored. For example, if questions ask how interviewees would handle certain situations, consider what responses are best in terms of meeting job requirements. If the job requires someone who motivates others, then a response that shows motivating behavior would receive a higher score. The interviewer also should have a copy of the interviewee's employment application and résumé to review before the interview and refer to during the interview. If possible, the interviewer should also have printed information about the organization and the job. Near the beginning of the interview, it is a good idea to go over the job specifications, organizational policies, and so on, so that the interviewee has a clearer understanding of the organization's needs.

The interviewer should schedule enough time to review the job requirements, discuss the interview questions, and give the interviewee a chance to ask questions. To close, the interviewer should thank the candidate for coming and provide information about what to expect—for example, that the organization will contact a few finalists within the next two weeks or that a decision will be made by the end of the week.

LO7 Explain how employers carry out the process of making a selection decision.

Selection Decisions

After reviewing applications, scoring tests, conducting interviews, and checking references, the organization needs to make decisions about which candidates to place in which jobs. In practice, most organizations find more than one qualified candidate to fill an open position. The selection decision typically combines ranking based on objective criteria along with subjective judgments about which candidate will make the greatest contribution.

How Organizations Select Employees

The selection decision should not be a simple matter of whom the supervisor likes best or which candidate will take the lowest offer. Rather, the people making the selection should look for the best fit between candidate and position. In general, the person's performance will result from a combination of ability and motivation. Often, the selection is a choice among a few people who possess the basic qualifications. The decision makers therefore have to decide which of those people have the best combination of ability and motivation to fit in the position and in the organization as a whole.

multiple-hurdle model
Process of arriving at a selection decision by eliminating some candidates at each stage of the selection process.

The usual process for arriving at a selection decision is to gradually narrow the pool of candidates for each job. This approach, called the **multiple-hurdle model,** is based on a process such as the one shown earlier in Figure 6.1. Each stage of the process is a hurdle, and candidates who overcome a hurdle continue to the next stage of the process. For example, the organization reviews applications and/or résumés of all candidates, conducts some tests on those who meet minimum requirements, conducts initial interviews with those who had the highest test scores, follows up with additional interviews or testing, and then selects a candidate from the few who survived this process. Another, more expensive alternative is to take most applicants through all steps of the process and then to review all the scores to find the most desirable candidates. With this alternative, decision makers may use a **compensatory model,** in which a very high score on one type of assessment can make up for a low score on another.

Whether the organization uses a multiple-hurdle model or conducts the same assessments on all candidates, the decision maker(s) needs criteria for choosing among qualified candidates. An obvious strategy is to select the candidates who score highest on tests and interviews. However, employee performance depends on motivation as well as ability. It is possible that a candidate who scores very high on an ability test might be "overqualified"—that is, the employee might be bored by the job the organization needs to fill, and a less-able employee might actually be a better fit. Similarly, a highly motivated person might learn some kinds of jobs very quickly, potentially outperforming someone who has the necessary skills. Furthermore, some organizations have policies of developing employees for career paths in the organization. Such organizations might place less emphasis on the skills needed for a particular job and more emphasis on hiring candidates who share the organization's values, show that they have the people skills to work with others in the organization, and are able to learn the skills needed for advancement.

Finally, organizations have choices about who will make the decision. Usually a supervisor makes the final decision, often alone. This person may couple knowledge of the job with a judgment about who will fit in best with others in the department. The decision could also be made by a human resource professional using standardized, objective criteria. Especially in organizations that use teamwork, selection decisions may be made by a work team or other panel of decision makers.

> **compensatory model**
> Process of arriving at a selection decision in which a very high score on one type of assessment can make up for a low score on another.

Communicating the Decision

The human resource department is often responsible for notifying applicants about the results of the selection process. When a candidate has been selected, the organization should communicate the offer to the candidate. The offer should include the job responsibilities, work schedule, rate of pay, starting date, and other relevant details. If placement in a job requires that the applicant pass a physical examination, the offer should state that contingency. The person communicating the offer should also indicate a date by which the candidate should reply with an acceptance or rejection of the offer. For some jobs, such as management and professional positions, the candidate and organization may negotiate pay, benefits, and work arrangements before they arrive at a final employment agreement.

The person who communicates this decision should keep accurate records of who was contacted, when, and for which position, as well as of the candidate's reply. The HR department and the supervisor also should be in close communication about the job offer. When an applicant accepts a job offer, the HR department must notify the supervisor, so that he or she can be prepared for the new employee's arrival.

THINKING ETHICALLY

TECH WORKER SHORTAGE OR AGE DISCRIMINATION?

Companies that recruit engineers and computer scientists often complain about a shortage of talent. The companies recruit aggressively and lobby the federal government for more visas to bring in foreign workers with the necessary skills.

But some observers criticize this talk as merely pretending that the problem is about talent when the companies are really just trying to keep a lid on salaries. In this view, there are plenty of engineers and programmers; the problem is, many of them are experienced, commanding higher salaries than employers want to pay. They would rather hire a newly graduated employee or a foreign worker who would accept a lower salary.

For evidence, Professor Norm Matloff of the University of California, Davis, points to attrition rates—that is, the rate at which employees leave their chosen field. According to Matloff, only 57 percent of computer science graduates are working as programmers five years after graduating; ten years after that, only 34 percent remain. After 20 years, when these people are about 42 years old, that share is down to 19 percent. In civil engineering, a less high-tech field, the attrition rate is far lower. Looking at salaries, researchers at the University of California, Berkeley, found that pay in the semiconductor industry rose quickly for engineers in their 30s, then slowed and actually began falling for workers beyond age 50.

Employers counter that they want workers who are highly productive and familiar with the latest technology, and these often turn out to be the youngest candidates. Also, they say, older workers want higher-level jobs, and such jobs are just fewer in any organization.

SOURCE: Vivek Wadhwa, "High-Tech Hiring: Youth Matters," *BusinessWeek*, January 15, 2008, www.businessweek.com.

Questions

1. If a company tends to hire young engineers or programmers, is this necessarily age discrimination? Is it necessarily unethical? Why or why not?
2. Does an employer have an ethical obligation to recruit older workers? Does it have an ethical obligation to retain technical workers as they grow older (and more experienced)? Why or why not?
3. Suppose you are an HR manager at a company that employs computer programmers. In light of the trends described in this article, consider whether you can identify a business opportunity in taking the ethical high road in regard to your recruiting and selection processes. Summarize your recommendations for how the company should proceed.

SUMMARY

LO1 Identify the elements of the selection process.

Selection typically begins with a review of candidates' employment applications and résumés. The organization administers tests to candidates who meet basic requirements, and qualified candidates undergo one or more interviews. Organizations check references and conduct background checks to verify the accuracy of information provided by candidates. A candidate is selected to fill each vacant position. Candidates who accept offers are placed in the positions for which they were selected.

LO2 Define ways to measure the success of a selection method.

One criterion is reliability, which indicates the method is free from random error, so that measurements are consistent. A selection method should also be valid, meaning that performance on the measure (such as a test score) is related to what the measure is designed to assess (such as job performance). Criterion-related validity shows a correlation between test scores and job performance scores. Content validity shows consistency between the test items or problems and the kinds of situations or problems that occur on the job. Construct validity establishes that the test actually measures a specified construct, such as intelligence or leadership ability, which is presumed to be associated with success on the job. A selection method also should be generalizable, so that it applies to more than one specific situation. Each selection method should have utility, meaning it provides economic value greater than its cost. Finally, selection methods should meet the legal requirements for employment decisions.

LO3 Summarize the government's requirements for employee selection.

The selection process must be conducted in a way that avoids discrimination and provides access to persons with disabilities. This means selection methods must be valid for job performance, and scores may not be adjusted to discriminate against or give preference to any group. Questions may not gather information about a person's membership in a protected class, such as race, sex, or religion, nor may the employer investigate a person's disability status. Employers must respect candidates' privacy rights and ensure that they keep personal information confidential. They must obtain consent before conducting background checks and notify candidates about adverse decisions made as a result of background checks.

LO4 Compare the common methods used for selecting human resources.

Nearly all organizations gather information through employment applications and résumés. These methods are inexpensive, and an application form standardizes basic information received from all applicants. The information is not necessarily reliable, because each applicant provides the information. These methods are most valid when evaluated in terms of the criteria in a job description. References and background checks help to verify the accuracy of the information. Employment tests and work samples are more objective. To be legal, any test must measure abilities that actually are associated with successful job performance. Employment tests range from general to specific. General-purpose tests are relatively inexpensive and simple to administer. Tests should be selected to be related to successful job performance and avoid charges of discrimination. Interviews are widely used to obtain information about a candidate's interpersonal and communication skills and to gather more detailed information about a candidate's background. Structured interviews are more valid than unstructured ones. Situational interviews provide greater validity than general questions. Interviews are costly and may introduce bias into the selection process. Organizations can minimize the drawbacks through preparation and training.

LO5 Describe major types of employment tests.

Physical ability tests measure strength, endurance, psychomotor abilities, and other physical abilities. They can be accurate but can discriminate and are not always job related. Cognitive ability tests, or intelligence tests, tend to be valid, especially for complex jobs and those requiring adaptability. They

are a relatively low-cost way to predict job performance but have been challenged as discriminatory. Job performance tests tend to be valid but are not always generalizable. Using a wide variety of job performance tests can be expensive. Personality tests measure personality traits such as extroversion and adjustment. Research supports their validity for appropriate job situations, especially for individuals who score high on conscientiousness, extroversion, and agreeableness. These tests are relatively simple to administer and generally meet legal requirements. Organizations may use paper-and-pencil honesty tests, which can predict certain behaviors, including employee theft. Organizations may not use polygraphs to screen job candidates. Organizations may also administer drug tests (if all candidates are tested and drug use can be an on-the-job safety hazard). A more job-related approach is to use impairment testing. Passing a medical examination may be a condition of employment, but to avoid discrimination against persons with disabilities, organizations usually administer a medical exam only after making a job offer.

LO6 Discuss how to conduct effective interviews.

Interviews should be narrow, structured, and standardized. Interviewers should identify job requirements and create a list of questions related to the requirements. Interviewers should be trained to recognize their own personal biases and conduct objective interviews. Panel interviews can reduce problems related to interviewer bias. Interviewers should put candidates at ease in a comfortable place that is free of distractions. Questions should ask for descriptions of relevant experiences and job-related behaviors. The interviewers also should be prepared to provide information about the job and the organization.

LO7 Explain how employers carry out the process of making a selection decision.

The organization should focus on the objective of finding the person who will be the best fit with the job and organization. This includes an assessment of ability and motivation. Decision makers may use a multiple-hurdle model in which each stage of the selection process eliminates some of the candidates from consideration at the following stages. At the final stage, only a few candidates remain, and the selection decision determines which of these few is the best fit. An alternative is a compensatory model, in which all candidates are evaluated with all methods. A candidate who scores poorly with one method may be selected if he or she scores very high on another measure.

KEY TERMS

achievement tests, p. 163
aptitude tests, p. 162
assessment center, p. 164
behavior description interview
  (BDI), p. 168
cognitive ability tests, p. 163
compensatory model, p. 171
concurrent validation, p. 154

construct validity, p. 154
content validity, p. 154
criterion-related validity, p. 153
generalizable, p. 154
Immigration Reform and Control Act
  of 1986, p. 157
multiple-hurdle model, p. 170
nondirective interview, p. 167

panel interview, p. 168
personnel selection, p. 151
predictive validity, p. 154
reliability, p. 152
situational interview, p. 168
structured interview, p. 167
utility, p. 155
validity, p. 153

REVIEW AND DISCUSSION QUESTIONS

1. What activities are involved in the selection process? Think of the last time you were hired for a job. Which of those activities were used in selecting you? Should the organization that hired you have used other methods as well?
2. Why should the selection process be adapted to fit the organization's job descriptions?
3. Choose two of the selection methods identified in this chapter. Describe how you can compare them in terms of reliability, validity, ability to generalize, utility, and compliance with the law.
4. Why does predictive validation provide better information than concurrent validation? Why is this type of validation more difficult?
5. How do U.S. laws affect organizations' use of each of the employment tests? Interviews?
6. Suppose your organization needs to hire several computer programmers, and you are reviewing résumés you obtained from an online service. What kinds of information will you want to gather from the "work experience" portion of these résumés? What kinds of information will you want to gather from the "education" portion of these résumés? What methods would you use for verifying or exploring this information? Why would you use those methods?
7. For each of the following jobs, select the two kinds of tests you think would be most important to include in the selection process. Explain why you chose those tests.
   a. City bus driver.
   b. Insurance salesperson.

   c. Member of a team that sells complex high-tech equipment to manufacturers.
   d. Member of a team that makes a component of the equipment in (c).
8. Suppose you are a human resource professional at a large retail chain. You want to improve the company's hiring process by creating standard designs for interviews, so that every time someone is interviewed for a particular job category, that person answers the same questions. You also want to make sure the questions asked are relevant to the job and maintain equal employment opportunity. Think of three questions to include in interviews for each of the following jobs. For each question, state why you think it should be included.
   a. Cashier at one of the company's stores.
   b. Buyer of the stores' teen clothing line.
   c. Accounts payable clerk at company headquarters.
9. How can organizations improve the quality of their interviewing so that interviews provide valid information?
10. Some organizations set up a selection process that is long and complex. In some people's opinion, this kind of selection process not only is more valid but also has symbolic value. What can the use of a long, complex selection process symbolize to job seekers? How do you think this would affect the organization's ability to attract the best employees?

BUSINESSWEEK CASE

BusinessWeek Executives: Making It by Faking It

At least once or twice a year, businesspeople the world over are reminded of the high cost of a little exaggeration, a material omission, or an outright lie on a résumé and how a tangled web concerning one's background can lead to career catastrophe.

Consider the case of the MIT dean whose career track was halted when her employer realized that she hadn't graduated from a single one of the three institutions from which she had claimed to have earned degrees. Or any one of a string of business executives who learned the hard way that faking their way is no way of making their way into executive management.

Just ask headhunter Jude Werra. The president of Brookfield, Wisconsin–based Jude M. Werra & Associates has spent the better part of 25 years documenting executive résumé fraud, credentials inflation, and the misrepresentation of executive educational credentials. It's something that has kept Werra pretty busy over the years, given the prevalence of such management-level chicanery and the fact that so many ambitious and transition-minded individuals have convinced themselves that it's their credentials—real or otherwise—that matter most.

Werra's semiannual barometer of executive résumé deception hit a five-year high, based on his review of résumés he received during the first half of 2007. He figures that about 16 percent of executive résumés contain false academic claims and/or material omissions relating to educational experience.

And when you account for the fudging of claims of experience unrelated to academic degrees earned, it's easy to see why executive headhunters generally acknowledge that as many as one-third of management-level résumés contain errors, exaggerations, material omissions, and/or blatant falsehoods.

Some people will stop at almost nothing to get to where they want in their career. Still, Werra wonders why otherwise experienced executives would inflate their credentials or otherwise mislead with their résumé, in light of the potential career-ending consequences.

Given the alarming levels to which they do attempt to mislead, he constantly reminds hiring organizations that it's critical that they verify what they read on résumés, even at the executive level. What's even more alarming—and more prevalent than people falsifying their backgrounds and qualifications—is the number of hiring organizations that fail to conduct a rigorous background check on their new management recruits. Far too many organizations figure that checking a few references is enough.

And even the most thorough reference checks won't uncover false claims that predate those references' own professional interactions with the individual executive. It's quite possible that a fabrication of one's education, certifications, and experience is what got the executive his first management job many years ago, leaving the trail cold unless it's reopened during the course of a diligent background check.

When it comes to executive-level hiring that's going to cost the organization into the high six figures, at minimum, when you factor in headhunting fees, the new executive's salary, and benefits, it becomes a matter of caveat emptor [let the buyer beware].

A thorough background check is an important insurance policy for the recruiting process, and headhunters will tell you that your organization risks getting burned if an executive it hires has, at any time in his or her past, decided to assume the risks of playing with fire. Given the high cost of a bad executive hire, today's organizations simply can't afford not to do their homework.

SOURCE: Excerpted from Joseph Daniel McCool, "Executives: Making It by Faking It," *BusinessWeek*, October 4, 2007, www.businessweek.com.

Questions

1. Suppose you are an HR manager at a company that needs to fill an important management position. In what situations would a candidate's educational background be important? In what situations would a candidate's track record as a manager or leader be important?

2. If you are considering a candidate whose management track record is good, would it matter whether the candidate described his or her educational background accurately? Why or why not? What if the misrepresentations involved the candidate's work history? Would your opinion change?

3. The writer of this article expresses an opinion that the utility of background checks is high. Do you agree that employers should place more emphasis on background checks?

CASE: HOW GOOGLE CHOOSES EMPLOYEES

Finding the best engineers, programmers, and sales representatives is a challenge for any company, but it's especially tough for a company growing as fast as Google. In recent years, the company has doubled its ranks every year and has no plans to slow its hiring. More than 100,000 job applications pour into Google every month, and staffers have to sort through them to fill as many as 200 positions a week.

Early on, the company narrowed the pool of applicants by setting a very high bar on traditional measures such as academic success. For example, an engineer had to have made it through school with a 3.7 grade-point average. Such criteria helped the company find a manageable number of applicants to interview, but no one had really considered whether they were the most valid way to predict success at the company.

More recently, the company has tried to apply its quantitative excellence to the problem of making better selection decisions. First, it set out to measure which selection criteria were important. It did this by conducting a survey of employees who had been with Google for at least five months. These questions addressed a wide variety of characteristics, such as areas of technical expertise, workplace behavior, personality, and even some nonwork habits that might uncover something important about candidates. For example, perhaps subscribing to a certain magazine or owning a dog could be related to success at Google by indirectly measuring some important trait no one had thought to ask about. The results of the survey were compared with measures of successful performance, including performance appraisals, compensation, and organizational citizenship (behaving in ways that contribute to the company beyond what the job requires).

One important lesson of this effort was that academic performance was not the best predictor of success at Google. No single factor predicted success at every job, but a combination of factors could help predict success in particular positions.

From this information, Google compiled a set of questionnaires that were related to success in particular kinds of work at Google: engineering, sales, finance, and human resources. Now people who apply to work at Google go online to answer questions such as "Have you ever started a club or recreational group?" and "Compared to other people in your peer group, how would you describe the age at which you first got into (i.e., got excited about them, started using them, etc.) computers on a scale from 1 [much later than others] to 10 [much earlier than others]?" The data are analyzed by a series of formulas that compute scores from 1 to 100. The score predicts how well the applicant is expected to fit into the type of position at Google.

Michael Mumford, an expert in talent assessment at the University of Oklahoma, says that, in general, this approach to predicting performance is effective, but only when it relies on reasonable measures. So, starting a club might be a way to measure leadership behavior, but owning a dog (a measure Google abandoned) should be used only if the employer can find an explanation for why it is relevant.

SOURCE: Saul Hansell, "Google Answer to Filling Jobs Is an Algorithm," *New York Times*, January 3, 2007, www.nytimes.com; Yi-Wyn Yen and Michal Lev-Ram, "Help Wanted: Google," No. 1 on *100 Best Companies to Work For 2008*, *Fortune*, January 22, 2008, http://money.cnn.com; "Google Jobs," company Web site, http://www.google.com, accessed January 22, 2008.

Questions

1. Based on the information given, would you say that Google's use of questionnaires is a reliable, valid, and generalizable way to select employees? Why or why not?

2. How does this approach to selection contribute to making selection decisions that avoid illegal discrimination?

3. Besides the questionnaires, what other selection methods would you recommend that Google use? How would these improve selection decisions?

IT'S A WRAP!

www.mhhe.com/noefund3e is your source for Reviewing, Applying, and Practicing the concepts you learned about in Chapter 6.

Review
- Chapter learning objectives
- Narrated lecture and iPod content
- Test Your Knowledge: Reliability and Validity

Application
- Manager's Hot Seat segment: "Diversity in Hiring: Candidate Conundrum"
- Video case and quiz: "Job Market for Graduates"
- Self-assessments: Assessing How Personality Type Impacts Your Goal Setting Skills and Analyzing Behavioral Interviews
- Web exercise: National Association of Convenience Stores Employee Selection Tool

Practice
- Chapter quiz

NOTES

1. Ian Ayres and Barry Nalebuff, "For the Love of the Game," *Forbes*, March 12, 2007, downloaded from General Reference Center Gold, http://find.galegroup.com.

2. Scott McCartney, "The Air-Traffic Cops Go to School," *Wall Street Journal*, March 29, 2005, http://online.wsj.com.

3. J. C. Nunnally, *Psychometric Theory* (New York: McGraw-Hill, 1978).

4. N. Schmitt, R. Z. Gooding, R. A. Noe, and M. Kirsch, "Meta-Analysis of Validity Studies Published between 1964 and 1982 and the Investigation of Study Characteristics," *Personnel Psychology* 37 (1984), pp. 407–22.

5. C. H. Lawshe, "Inferences from Personnel Tests and Their Validity," *Journal of Applied Psychology* 70 (1985), pp. 237–38.

6. D. D. Robinson, "Content-Oriented Personnel Selection in a Small Business Setting," *Personnel Psychology* 34 (1981), pp. 77–87.

7. F. L. Schmidt and J. E. Hunter, "The Future of Criterion-Related Validity," *Personnel Psychology* 33 (1980), pp. 41–60; F. L. Schmidt, J. E. Hunter, and K. Pearlman, "Task Differences as Moderators of Aptitude Test Validity: A Red Herring," *Journal of Applied Psychology* 66 (1982), pp. 166–85; and R. L. Gutenberg, R. D. Arvey, H. G. Osburn, and R. P. Jeanneret, "Moderating Effects of Decision-Making/Information Processing Dimensions on Test Validities," *Journal of Applied Psychology* 68 (1983), pp. 600–8.

8. A. Meisler, "When Bad Things Happen to Hot Brands," *Workforce*, July 2003, pp. 20–21; see also A. Gutman, "Smith versus City of Jackson: Adverse Impact in the ADEA (Well Sort Of)," *Industrial Psychologist*, July 2005, pp. 31–32.

9. G. Flynn, "The Reverse Discrimination Trap," *Workforce*, June 2003, pp. 106–7; and M. E. Heilman, W. S. Battle, C. E. Keller, and R. A. Lee, "Type of Affirmative Action Policy: A Determinant of Reactions to Sex-Based Preferential Selection," *Journal of Applied Psychology* 83 (1998), pp. 190–205.

10. B. S. Murphy, "EEOC Gives Guidance on Legal and Illegal Inquiries under ADA," *Personnel Journal*, August 1994, p. 26.

11. Perri Capell, "When Applying for Jobs Online, You Can Skip Certain Questions," *Career Journal*, October 9, 2007, www.careerjournal.com.

12. T. W. Dougherty, D. B. Turban, and J. C. Callender, "Confirming First Impressions in the Employment Interview: A Field Study of Interviewer Behavior," *Journal of Applied Psychology* 79 (1994), pp. 659–65.

13. D. D. Hatch, "Bad Reference for Ex-employee Judged Defamatory," *Workforce*, December 2003, p. 20.

14. A. Ryan and M. Lasek, "Negligent Hiring and Defamation: Areas of Liability Related to Pre-employment Inquiries," *Personnel Psychology* 44 (1991), pp. 293–319.

15. A. Long, "Addressing the Cloud over Employee References: A Survey of Recently Enacted State Legislation," *William and Mary Law Review* 39 (October 1997), pp. 177–228.

16. Ann Zimmerman, "Wal-Mart to Probe Job Applicants," *Wall Street Journal*, August 12, 2004, pp. A3, A6.

17. C. J. Bachler, "Global Inpats—Don't Let Them Surprise You," *Personnel Journal*, June 1996, pp. 54–65; R. Horn, "Give Me Your Huddled . . . High-Tech Ph.D.s: Are High Skilled Foreigners Displacing U.S. Workers?" *BusinessWeek*, November 6, 1995, pp. 161–62; S. Greengard, "Gain the Edge in the Knowledge Race," *Personnel Journal*, August 1996, pp. 52–56.

18. L. C. Buffardi, E. A. Fleishman, R. A. Morath, and P. M. McCarthy, "Relationships between Ability Requirements and Human Errors in Job Tasks," *Journal of Applied Psychology* 85 (2000), pp. 551–64; J. Hogan, "Structure of Physical Performance in Occupational Tasks," *Journal of Applied Psychology* 76 (1991), pp. 495–507.

19. J. F. Salagado, N. Anderson, S. Moscoso, C. Bertuas, and F. De Fruyt, "International Validity Generalization of GMA and Cognitive Abilities: A European Community Meta-analysis," *Personnel Psychology* 56 (2003), pp. 573–605; M. J. Ree, J. A. Earles, and M. S. Teachout, "Predicting Job Performance: Not Much More than g," *Journal of Applied Psychology* 79 (1994), pp. 518–24; L. S. Gottfredson, "The g Factor in Employment," *Journal of Vocational Behavior* 29 (1986), pp. 293–96; J. E. Hunter and R. H. Hunter, "Validity and Utility of Alternative Predictors of Job Performance," *Psychological Bulletin* 96 (1984), pp. 72–98; Gutenberg et al., "Moderating Effects of Decision-Making/Information Processing Dimensions on Test Validities"; F. L. Schmidt, J. G. Berner, and J. E. Hunter, "Racial Differences in Validity of Employment Tests: Reality or Illusion," *Journal of Applied Psychology* 58 (1974), pp. 5–6; and J. A. LePine, J. A. Colquitt, and A. Erez, "Adaptability to Changing Task Contexts: Effects of General Cognitive Ability, Conscientiousness, and Openness to Experience," *Personnel Psychology* 53 (2000), pp. 563–93.

20. D. A. Kravitz and S. L. Klineberg, "Reactions to Versions of Affirmative Action among Whites, Blacks, and Hispanics," *Journal of Applied Psychology* (2000), pp. 597–611.

21. See, for example, C. Winkler, "Job Tryouts Go Virtual," *HRMagazine*, September 2006, pp. 10–15.

22. D. J. Schleiger, V. Venkataramani, F. P. Morgeson, and M. A. Campion, "So You Didn't Get the Job . . . Now What Do You Think? Examining Opportunity to Perform Fairness Perceptions," *Personnel Psychology* 59 (2006), pp. 559–90.

23. F. L. Schmidt and J. E. Hunter, "The Validity and Utility of Selection Methods in Personnel Psychology: Practical and Theoretical Implications of 85

Years of Research Findings," *Psychological Bulletin* 124 (1998), pp. 262–74.

24. W. Arthur, E. A. Day, T. L. McNelly, and P. S. Edens, "Meta-Analysis of the Criterion-Related Validity of Assessment Center Dimensions," *Personnel Psychology* 56 (2003), pp. 125–54; and C. E. Lance, T. A. Lambert, A. G. Gewin, F. Lievens, and J. M. Conway, "Revised Estimates of Dimension and Exercise Variance Components in Assessment Center Postexercise Dimension Ratings," *Journal of Applied Psychology* 89 (2004), pp. 377–85.

25. N. M. Dudley, K. A. Orvis, J. E. Lebieki, and J. M. Cortina, "A Meta-analytic Investigation of Conscientiousness in the Prediction of Job Performance: Examining the Intercorrelation and the Incremental Validity of Narrow Traits," *Journal of Applied Psychology* 91 (2006), pp. 40–57; W. S. Dunn, M. K. Mount, M. R. Barrick, and D. S. Ones, "Relative Importance of Personality and General Mental Ability on Managers' Judgments of Applicant Qualifications," *Journal of Applied Psychology* 79 (1995), pp. 500–9; P. M. Wright, K. M. Kacmar, G. C. McMahan, and K. Deleeuw, "$P = f(M \times A)$: Cognitive Ability as a Moderator of the Relationship between Personality and Job Performance," *Journal of Management* 21 (1995), pp. 1129–39.

26. M. Mount, M. R. Barrick, and J. P. Strauss, "Validity of Observer Ratings of the Big Five Personality Factors," *Journal of Applied Psychology* 79 (1994), pp. 272–80.

27. L. A. Witt and G. R. Ferris, "Social Skill as Moderator of the Conscientiousness–Performance Relationship: Convergent Results across Four Studies," *Journal of Applied Psychology* 88 (2003), pp. 809–20.

28. L. Joel, *Every Employee's Guide to the Law* (New York: Pantheon, 1993).

29. N. Schmitt and F. L. Oswald, "The Impact of Corrections for Faking on the Validity of Non-cognitive Measures in Selection Contexts," *Journal of Applied Psychology* (2006), pp. 613–21.

30. S. A. Birkland, T. M. Manson, J. L. Kisamore, M. T. Brannick, and M. A. Smith, "Faking on Personality Measures," *International Journal of Selection and Assessment* 14 (December 2006), pp. 317–35.

31. C. H. Van Iddekinge, P. H. Raymark, and P. L. Roth, "Assessing Personality with a Structured Employment Interview: Construct-Related Validity and Susceptibility to Response Inflation," *Journal of Applied Psychology* 90 (2005), pp. 536–52; R. Mueller-Hanson, E. D. Heggestad, and G. C. Thornton, "Faking and Selection: Considering the Use of Personality from Select-In and Select-Out Perspectives," *Journal of Applied Psychology* 88 (2003), pp. 348–55; and N. L. Vasilopoulos, J. M. Cucina, and J. M. McElreath, "Do

Warnings of Response Verification Moderate the Relationship between Personality and Cognitive Ability?" *Journal of Applied Psychology* 90 (2005), pp. 306–22.

32. E. Freudenheim, "Personality Testing Controversial, but Poised to Take Off," *Workforce Management*, August 14, 2006, p. 38.

33. V. Knight, "Personality Tests as Hiring Tools," *Wall Street Journal*, March 15, 2006, p. B1; G. L. Steward, I. S. Fulmer, and M. R. Barrick, "An Exploration of Member Roles as a Multilevel Linking Mechanism for Individual Traits and Team Outcomes," *Personnel Psychology* 58 (2005), pp. 343–65; and M. Mount, R. Ilies, and E. Johnson, "Relationship of Personality Traits and Counterproductive Work Behaviors: The Mediation Effects of Job Satisfaction," *Personnel Psychology* 59 (2006), pp. 591–622.

34. Barbara Rose, "Critics Wary as More Jobs Hinge on Personality Tests," *Chicago Tribune*, October 31, 2004, sec. 1, pp. 1, 15.

35. D. S. Ones, C. Viswesvaran, and F. L. Schmidt, "Comprehensive Meta-analysis of Integrity Test Validities: Findings and Implications for Personnel Selection and Theories of Job Performance," *Journal of Applied Psychology* 78 (1993), pp. 679–703; and H. J. Bernardin and D. K. Cooke, "Validity of an Honesty Test in Predicting Theft among Convenience Store Employees," *Academy of Management Journal* 36 (1993), pp. 1079–1106.

36. K. R. Murphy, G. C. Thornton, and D. H. Reynolds, "College Students' Attitudes toward Drug Test Programs," *Personnel Psychology* 43 (1990), pp. 615–31; and M. E. Paronto, D. M. Truxillo, T. N. Bauer, and M. C. Leo, "Drug Testing, Drug Treatment, and Marijuana Use: A Fairness Perspective," *Journal of Applied Psychology* 87 (2002), pp. 1159–66.

37. E. Beck, "Is the Time Right for Impairment Testing?" *Workforce*, February 2001, pp. 69–71; J. Farley, "Better than Caffeine," *USA Today*, March 9, 2001, p. C1; J. Hamilton, "A Video Game That Tells if Employees Are Fit for Work," *BusinessWeek*, June 3, 1991, pp. 34–35.

38. M. A. McDaniel, F. P. Morgeson, E. G. Finnegan, M. A. Campion, and E. P. Braverman, "Use of Situational Judgment Tests to Predict Job Performance: A Clarification of the Literature," *Journal of Applied Psychology* 86 (2001), pp. 730–40; J. Clavenger, G. M. Perreira, D. Weichmann, N. Schmitt, and V. S. Harvey, "Incremental Validity of Situational Judgment Tests," *Journal of Applied Psychology* 86 (2001), pp. 410–17.

39. M. A. Campion, J. E. Campion, and J. P. Hudson, "Structured Interviewing: A Note of Incremental Validity and Alternative Question Types," *Journal of

Applied Psychology 79 (1994), pp. 998–1002; E. D. Pulakos and N. Schmitt, "Experience-Based and Situational Interview Questions: Studies of Validity," *Personnel Psychology* 48 (1995), pp. 289–308; and A. P. J. Ellis, B. J. West, A. M. Ryan, and R. P. DeShon, "The Use of Impression Management Tactics in Structured Interviews: A Function of Question Type?" *Journal of Applied Psychology* 87 (2002), pp. 1200–8.

40. N. Schmitt, F. L. Oswald, B. H. Kim, M. A. Gillespie, L. J. Ramsey, and T. Y Yoo, "The Impact of Elaboration on Socially Desirable Responding and the Validity of Biodata Measures," *Journal of Applied Psychology* 88 (2003), pp. 979–88; and N. Schmitt and C. Kunce, "The Effects of Required Elaboration of Answers to Biodata Questions," *Personnel Psychology* 55 (2002), pp. 569–87.

41. Hunter and Hunter, "Validity and Utility of Alternative Predictors of Job Performance."

42. R. Pingitore, B. L. Dugoni, R. S. Tindale, and B. Spring, "Bias against Overweight Job Applicants in a Simulated Interview," *Journal of Applied Psychology* 79 (1994), pp. 184–90.

43. *Watson v. Fort Worth Bank and Trust,* 108 Supreme Court 2791 (1988).

44. M. A. McDaniel, D. L. Whetzel, F. L. Schmidt, and S. D. Maurer, "The Validity of Employment Interviews: A Comprehensive Review and Meta-Analysis," *Journal of Applied Psychology* 79 (1994), pp. 599–616; A. I. Huffcutt and W. A. Arthur, "Hunter and Hunter (1984) Revisited: Interview Validity for Entry-Level Jobs," *Journal of Applied Psychology* 79 (1994), pp. 184–90.

45. Y. Ganzach, A. N. Kluger, and N. Klayman, "Making Decisions from an Interview: Expert Measurement and Mechanical Combination," *Personnel Psychology* 53 (2000), pp. 1–21; G. Stasser and W. Titus, "Effects of Information Load and Percentage of Shared Information on the Dissemination of Unshared Information during Group Discussion," *Journal of Personality and Social Psychology* 53 (1987), pp. 81–93.

46. C. H. Middendorf and T. H. Macan, "Note-Taking in the Interview: Effects on Recall and Judgments," *Journal of Applied Psychology* 87 (2002), pp. 293–303.

Training Employees

Introduction

With 78,000 employees working in 294 offices in 48 countries, computer-chip maker Intel has to foster collaboration across many cultures and languages. Although English is widely used as a common language for international businesses, misunderstandings can arise, especially among people who usually speak a different language. Intel's solution is to offer a voluntary training program. Employees can take classes in Mandarin, Japanese, and Spanish at various offices throughout the United States. The classes help employees work with colleagues or clients from other countries. As the demand for language training increased, the company began planning similar programs for employees outside the United States. Intel also offers one-day classes that deliver basic information about other cultures' history and business practices so that employees can learn how to work effectively with people from those cultures. Company spokeswoman Tracy Koon explains, "You're not going to be an effective team if you are constantly offending the other members without knowing it." At Intel, the solution is training.[1]

Training consists of an organization's planned efforts to help employees acquire job-related knowledge, skills, abilities, and behaviors, with the goal of applying these on the job. A training program may range from formal classes to one-on-one mentoring, and it may take place on the job or at remote locations. No matter what its form, training can benefit the organization when it is linked to organizational needs and when it motivates employees.

This chapter describes how to plan and carry out an effective training program. We begin by discussing how to develop effective training in the context of the organization's strategy. Next, we discuss how organizations assess employees' training needs. We then review training methods and the process of evaluating a training program. The chapter concludes by discussing some special applications of training: orientation of new employees and the management of diversity.

chapter seven

Training Linked to Organizational Needs

The nature of the modern business environment makes training more important today than it ever has been. Rapid change, especially in the area of technology, requires that employees continually learn new skills. The new psychological contract, described in Chapter 2, has created the expectation that employees invest in their own career development, which requires learning opportunities. Growing reliance on teamwork creates a demand for the ability to solve problems in teams, an ability that often requires formal training. Finally, the diversity of the U.S. population, coupled with the globalization of business, requires that employees be able to work well with people who are different from them. Successful organizations often take the lead in developing this ability.

With training so essential in modern organizations, it is important to provide training that is effective. An effective training program actually teaches what it is designed to teach, and it teaches skills and behaviors that will help the organization achieve its goals. To achieve those goals, HR professionals approach training through **instructional design**—a process of systematically developing training to meet specified needs.[2]

A complete instructional design process includes the steps shown in Figure 7.1. It begins with an assessment of the needs for training—what the organization requires that its people learn. Next, the organization ensures that employees are ready for training in terms of their attitudes, motivation, basic skills, and work environment. The third step is to plan the training program, including the program's objectives, instructors, and methods. The organization then implements the program. Finally, evaluating the results of the training provides feedback for planning future training programs.

To carry out this process more efficiently and effectively, a growing number of organizations are using a **learning management system (LMS),** a computer application that automates the administration, development, and delivery of a company's training programs.[3] Managers and employees can use the LMS to identify training needs and enroll in courses. LMSs can make training programs more widely available and help companies reduce travel and other costs by providing online training. Administrative tools let managers track course enrollments and program completion. The system can be linked to the organization's performance management system to plan for and manage training needs, training outcomes, and associated rewards together.

Needs Assessment

Instructional design logically should begin with a **needs assessment,** the process of evaluating the organization, individual employees, and employees' tasks to determine what kinds of training, if any, are necessary. As this definition indicates, the needs assessment answers questions in three broad areas:[4]

1. *Organization*—What is the context in which training will occur?
2. *Person*—Who needs training?
3. *Task*—What subjects should the training cover?

L01 Discuss how to link training programs to organizational needs.

training
An organization's planned efforts to help employees acquire job-related knowledge, skills, abilities, and behaviors, with the goal of applying these on the job.

instructional design
A process of systematically developing training to meet specified needs.

learning management system (LMS)
A computer application that automates the administration, development, and delivery of training programs.

Figure 7.1

Stages of Instructional Design

Pfizer employees go through a representative training phase which teaches them about different Pfizer products and how to market them. Workers typically need to be trained in several processes to work in flexible manufacturing.

LO2 Explain how to assess the need for training.

needs assessment
The process of evaluating the organization, individual employees, and employees' tasks to determine what kinds of training, if any, are necessary.

The answers to these questions provide the basis for planning an effective training program.

A variety of conditions may prompt an organization to conduct a needs assessment. Management may observe that some employees lack basic skills or are performing poorly. Decisions to produce new products, apply new technology, or design new jobs should prompt a needs assessment because these changes tend to require new skills. The decision to conduct a needs assessment also may be prompted by outside forces, such as customer requests or legal requirements.

The outcome of the needs assessment is a set of decisions about how to address the issues that prompted the needs assessment. These decisions do not necessarily include a training program, because some issues should be resolved through methods other than training. For example, suppose a company uses delivery trucks to transport anesthetic gases to medical facilities, and a driver of one of these trucks mistakenly hooks up the supply line of a mild anesthetic from the truck to the hospital's oxygen system, contaminating the hospital's oxygen supply. This performance problem prompts a needs assessment. Whether or not the hospital decides to provide more training will depend partly on the reasons the driver erred. The driver may have hooked up the supply lines incorrectly because of a lack of knowledge about the appropriate line hookup, anger over a request for a pay raise being denied, or mislabeled valves for connecting the supply lines. Out of these three possibilities, only the lack of knowledge can be corrected through training. Other outcomes of a needs assessment might include plans for better rewards to improve motivation, better hiring decisions, and better safety precautions.

The remainder of this chapter discusses needs assessment and then what the organization should do when assessment indicates a need for training. The possibilities for action include offering existing training programs to more employees; buying or

Best Practices

Gentle Giant Moving

Lugging boxes and furniture between rooms and trucks may not sound like work that requires much training. But training is just what Gentle Giant Moving Company relies on to distinguish itself from the competition. The Somerville, Massachusetts–based moving and storage company breaks from the industry practice of laying off most employees after the summertime rush of moving contracts. Instead, during the slow months, it invests in training its workers.

The emphasis on training supports a strategy of being customer driven and team based. Gentle Giant emphasizes its goal of making moving a stress-free experience. That requires employees who know how to communicate, keep work on schedule, and fix any problems quickly. Many customers will pay a little extra for that kind of service. Being team based is also a way to maintain top-notch

service. Team members are expected to help each other improve. If an item is damaged, they are expected to be open about the problem and look for ways to avoid it in the future. Individuals' pay isn't cut to cover the cost of damage, as at other moving companies, because that tempts individuals to hide problems, which interferes with the focus on teamwork and service. All these policies and practices contribute to the company's mission of "making every customer a customer for life."

All employees start out with training in basic skills such as how to pack belongings and carry them safely. Where Gentle Giant stands out is in what comes later: training in customer relations, communication, problem solving, and project management. Learning these skills prepares employees to provide exceptional customer service, and it positions them to

take on greater responsibility, turning a summer job into a career in the moving industry.

Because Gentle Giant's employees know how to handle customers and problems, they resolve problems immediately, resulting in fewer complaints than other moving companies typically must handle. The career growth keeps many employees from quitting, which reduces the time and expense of hiring and training new people every spring. And it contributes to the company's overall business success. Gentle Giant has grown rapidly every year since its founding in 1980, with 80 percent of its business coming from repeat and referral customers.

Sources: Kelly K. Spors, "Top Small Workplaces 2007," *Wall Street Journal,* October 1, 2007, http://online.wsj.com; Timothy G. Habbershon, "All the Right Moves," *BusinessWeek,* September 19, 2005; and Gentle Giant Moving Co., "About Us," Gentle Giant Web site, www.gentlegiant.com, accessed January 28, 2008.

developing new training programs; and improving existing training programs. Before we consider the available training options, let's examine the elements of the needs assessment in more detail.

Organization Analysis

Usually, the needs assessment begins with the **organization analysis.** This is a process for determining the appropriateness of training by evaluating the characteristics of the organization. The organization analysis looks at training needs in light of the organization's strategy, resources available for training, and management's support for training activities.

Training needs will vary depending on whether the organization's strategy is based on growing or shrinking its personnel, whether it is seeking to serve a broad customer base or focusing on the specific needs of a narrow market segment, and various other strategic scenarios. An organization that concentrates on serving a niche market may need to continually update its workforce on a specialized skills set. A company that is cutting costs with a downsizing strategy may need to train employees who will be laid off in job search skills. The employees who remain following the downsizing may need cross-training so that they can handle a wider variety of responsibilities. For an example of a company where a commitment to training supports corporate strategy, see the "Best Practices" box.

organization analysis
A process for determining the appropriateness of training by evaluating the characteristics of the organization.

Anyone planning a training program must consider whether the organization has the budget, time, and expertise for training. For example, if the company is installing computer-based manufacturing equipment in one of its plants, it can ensure that it has the necessary computer-literate employees in one of three ways. If it has the technical experts on its staff, they can train the employees affected by the change. Or the company may use testing to determine which of its employees are already computer literate and then replace or reassign employees who lack the necessary skills. The third choice is to purchase training from an outside individual or organization.

Even if training fits the organization's strategy and budget, it can be viable only if the organization is willing to support the investment in training. Managers increase the success of training when they support it through such actions as helping trainees see how they can use their newly learned knowledge, skills, and behaviors on the job.[5] Conversely, the managers will be most likely to support training if the people planning it can show that it will solve a significant problem or result in a significant improvement, relative to its cost. Managers appreciate training proposals with specific goals, timetables, budgets, and methods for measuring success.

Person Analysis

person analysis
A process of determining individuals' needs and readiness for training.

Following the organizational assessment, needs assessment turns to the remaining areas of analysis: person and task. The **person analysis** is a process for determining individuals' needs and readiness for training. It involves answering several questions:

- Do performance deficiencies result from a lack of knowledge, skill, or ability? (If so, training is appropriate; if not, other solutions are more relevant.)
- Who needs training?
- Are these employees ready for training?

The answers to these questions help the manager identify whether training is appropriate and which employees need training. In certain situations, such as the introduction of a new technology or service, all employees may need training. However, when needs assessment is conducted in response to a performance problem, training is not always the best solution.

The person analysis is therefore critical when training is considered in response to a performance problem. In assessing the need for training, the manager should identify all the variables that can influence performance. The primary variables are the person's ability and skills, his or her attitudes and motivation, the organization's input (including clear directions, necessary resources, and freedom from interference and distractions), performance feedback (including praise and performance standards), and positive consequences to motivate good performance. Of these variables, only ability and skills can be affected by training. Therefore, before planning a training program, it is important to be sure that any performance problem results from a deficiency in knowledge and skills. Otherwise, training dollars will be wasted, because the training is unlikely to have much effect on performance.

The person analysis also should determine whether employees are ready to undergo training. In other words, the employees to receive training not only should require additional knowledge and skill, but must be willing and able to learn. (After our discussion of the needs assessment, we will explore the topic of employee readiness in greater detail.)

Task Analysis

The third area of needs assessment is **task analysis,** the process of identifying the tasks, knowledge, skills, and behaviors that training should emphasize. Usually, task analysis is conducted along with person analysis. Understanding shortcomings in performance usually requires knowledge about the tasks and work environment as well as the employee.

To carry out the task analysis, the HR professional looks at the conditions in which tasks are performed. These conditions include the equipment and environment of the job, time constraints (for example, deadlines), safety considerations, and performance standards. These observations form the basis for a description of work activities, or the tasks required by the person's job. For a selected job, the analyst interviews employees and their supervisors to prepare a list of tasks performed in that job. Then the analyst validates the list by showing it to employees, supervisors, and other subject-matter experts and asking them to complete a questionnaire about the importance, frequency, and difficulty of the tasks. Table 7.1 is an example of a task analysis questionnaire for an electrical maintenance worker. For each task listed, the subject-matter expert uses the scales to rate the task's importance, frequency, and difficulty.

The information from these questionnaires is the basis for determining which tasks will be the focus of the training. The person or committee conducting the needs assessment must decide what levels of importance, frequency, and difficulty signal a need for training. Logically, training is most needed for tasks that are important, frequent, and at least moderately difficult. For each of these tasks, the analysts must

task analysis
The process of identifying and analyzing tasks to be trained for.

LO3 Explain how to assess employees' readiness for training.

Table 7.1

Sample Items from a Task Analysis Questionnaire

Job: Electrical Maintenance Worker			
		Task Performance Ratings	
Task #s	**Task Description**	**Frequency of Performance**	**Importance**	**Difficulty**
199-264	Replace a light bulb	0 1 2 3 4 5	0 1 2 3 4 5	0 1 2 3 4 5
199-265	Replace an electrical outlet	0 1 2 3 4 5	0 1 2 3 4 5	0 1 2 3 4 5
199-266	Install a light fixture	0 1 2 3 4 5	0 1 2 3 4 5	0 1 2 3 4 5
199-267	Replace a light switch	0 1 2 3 4 5	0 1 2 3 4 5	0 1 2 3 4 5
199-268	Install a new circuit breaker	0 1 2 3 4 5	0 1 2 3 4 5	0 1 2 3 4 5
		Frequency of Performance 0=never 5=often	**Importance** 1=negligible 5=extremely high	**Difficulty** 1=easiest 5=most difficult

Source: E. F. Holton III and C. Bailey, "Top-to-Bottom Curriculum Redesign," Training and Development, March 1995, pp. 40–44. Reprinted with permission of Training and Development.

identify the knowledge, skills, and abilities required to perform the task. This information usually comes from interviews with subject-matter experts, such as employees who currently hold the job.

Readiness for Training

readiness for training
A combination of employee characteristics and positive work environment that permit training.

Effective training requires not only a program that addresses real needs, but also a condition of employee readiness. **Readiness for training** is a combination of employee characteristics and positive work environment that permit training. The necessary employee characteristics include ability to learn the subject matter, favorable attitudes toward the training, and motivation to learn. A positive work environment is one that encourages learning and avoids interfering with the training program.

Employee Readiness Characteristics

To be ready to learn, employees need basic learning skills, especially *cognitive ability*, which includes being able to use written and spoken language, solve math problems, and use logic to solve problems. Ideally, the selection process identified job candidates with enough cognitive ability to handle not only the requirements for doing a job but also the training associated with that job. However, recent forecasts of the skill levels of the U.S. workforce indicate that many companies will have to work with employees who lack basic skills.[6] For example, they may have to provide literacy training or access to classes teaching basic skills before some employees can participate in job-related training.

Employees learn more from training programs when they are highly motivated to learn—that is, when they really want to learn the content of the training program.[7] Employees tend to feel this way if they believe they are able to learn, see potential benefits from the training program, are aware of their need to learn, see a fit between the training and their career goals, and have the basic skills needed for participating in the program. Managers can influence a ready attitude in a variety of ways. For example, they can provide feedback that encourages employees, establish rewards for learning, and communicate with employees about the organization's career paths and future needs.

Work Environment

Readiness for training also depends on two broad characteristics of the work environment: situational constraints and social support.[8] *Situational constraints* are the limits on training's effectiveness that arise from the situation or the conditions within the organization. Constraints can include a lack of money for training, lack of time for training or practicing, and failure to provide proper tools and materials for learning or applying the lessons of training. Conversely, trainees are likely to apply what they learn if the organization gives them opportunities to use their new skills and if it rewards them for doing so.[9]

Social support refers to the ways the organization's people encourage training, including giving trainees praise and encouraging words, sharing information about participating in training programs, and expressing positive attitudes toward the organization's training programs. Table 7.2 summarizes some ways in which managers can support training.

Support can also come from employees' peers. The organization can formally provide peer support by establishing groups of employees who meet regularly to discuss their progress. For example, group members can share how they coped with challenges related

Table 7.2

**What Managers Should
Do to Support Training**

Understand the content of the training.
Know how training relates to what you need employees to do.
In performance appraisals, evaluate employees on how they apply training to their jobs.
Support employees' use of training when they return to work.
Ensure that employees have the equipment and technology needed to use training.
Prior to training, discuss with employees how they plan to use training.
Recognize newly trained employees who use training content.
Give employees release time from their work to attend training.
Explain to employees why they have been asked to attend training.
Give employees feedback related to skills or behavior they are trying to develop.

Source: Based on A. Rossett, "That Was a Great Class, but . . . " Training and Development, July 1997, p. 21.

to what they learned. Schlumberger, which provides oil field services, sets up online "communities of practice," where geologists, physicists, managers, engineers, and other employees around the world can trade knowledge to solve problems.[10] Another way to encourage peer support is for the human resource department or others to publish a newsletter with articles relevant to training, perhaps including interviews with employees who successfully applied new skills. Finally, the organization can assign experienced employees as mentors to trainees, providing advice and support.

Planning the Training Program

L04 Describe how to plan an effective training program.

Decisions about training are often the responsibility of a specialist in the organization's training or human resources department. When the needs assessment indicates a need for training and employees are ready to learn, the person responsible for training should plan a training program that directly relates to the needs identified. Planning begins with establishing objectives for the training program. Based on those objectives, the planner decides who will provide the training, what topics the training will cover, what training methods to use, and how to evaluate the training.

Objectives of the Program

Formally establishing objectives for the training program has several benefits. First, a training program based on clear objectives will be more focused and more likely to succeed. In addition, when trainers know the objectives, they can communicate them to the employees participating in the program. Employees learn best when they know what the training is supposed to accomplish. Finally, down the road, establishing objectives provides a basis for measuring whether the program succeeded, as we will discuss later in this chapter.

Effective training objectives have several characteristics:

- They include a statement of what the employee is expected to do, the quality or level of performance that is acceptable, and the conditions under which the employee is to apply what he or she learned (for instance, physical conditions, mental stresses, or equipment failure).[11]
- They include performance standards that are measurable.
- They identify the resources needed to carry out the desired performance or outcome. Successful training requires employees to learn but also employers to provide the necessary resources.

Did You Know?

Many Companies Outsource Training Tasks

A recent survey of U.S.-based corporations found that over half were outsourcing the instruction of training courses. Four out of ten said they used outside experts to create custom content.

Source: "Training 2007 Industry Report," *Training,* November/December 2007, pp. 8–24.

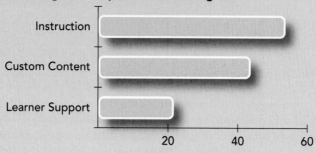

Percentage of Companies Outsourcing Task

A related issue at the outset is who will participate in the training program. Some training programs are developed for all employees of the organization or all members of a team. Other training programs identify individuals who lack desirable skills or have potential to be promoted, then provide training in the areas of need that are identified for the particular employees. When deciding whom to include in training, the organization has to avoid illegal discrimination. The organization should not—intentionally or unintentionally—exclude members of protected groups, such as women, minorities, and older employees. During the training, all participants should receive equal treatment, such as equal opportunities for practice. In addition, the training program should provide reasonable accommodation for trainees with disabilities. The kinds of accommodations that are appropriate will vary according to the type of training and type of disability. One employee might need an interpreter, whereas another might need to have classroom instruction provided in a location accessible to wheelchairs.

In-House or Contracted Out?

An organization can provide an effective training program, even if it lacks expertise in training. As shown in the "Did You Know?" box, many organizations use outside experts to develop and instruct training courses. Many companies and consultants provide training services to organizations. Community colleges often work with employers to train employees in a variety of skills.

To select a training service, an organization can mail several vendors a *request for proposal (RFP)*, which is a document outlining the type of service needed, the type and number of references needed, the number of employees to be trained, the date by which the training is to be completed, and the date by which proposals should be received. A complete RFP also indicates funding for the project and the process by which the organization will determine its level of satisfaction. Putting together a request for proposal is time-consuming but worthwhile because it helps the organization clarify its objectives, compare vendors, and measure results.

Vendors that believe they are able to provide the services outlined in the RFP submit proposals that provide the types of information requested. The organization reviews the proposals to eliminate any vendors that do not meet requirements and to compare the vendors that do qualify. They check references and select a candidate, based on the proposal and the vendor's answers to questions about its experience, work samples, and evidence that its training programs meet objectives.

The cost of purchasing training from a contractor can vary substantially. In general, it is much costlier to purchase specialized training that is tailored to the organization's unique requirements than to participate in a seminar or training course that teaches general skills or knowledge. According to estimates by consultants, preparing a training program can take 10 to 20 hours for each hour of instruction. Highly technical content that requires the developer to meet often with experts in the subject can take 50 percent longer.[12]

Even in organizations that send employees to outside training programs, someone in the organization may be responsible for coordinating the overall training program. Called *training administration*, this is typically the responsibility of a human resources professional. Training administration includes activities before, during, and after training sessions.

Choice of Training Methods

Whether the organization prepares its own training programs or buys training from other organizations, it is important to verify that the content of the training relates directly to the training objectives. Relevance to the organization's needs and objectives ensures that training money is well spent. Tying training content closely to objectives also improves trainees' learning, because it increases the likelihood that the training will be meaningful and helpful.

After deciding on the goals and content of the training program, planners must decide how the training will be conducted. As we will describe in the next section, a wide variety of methods is available. Training methods fall into the broad categories described in Table 7.3: presentation, hands-on, and group-building methods.[13]

Training programs may use these methods alone or in combination. In general, the methods used should be suitable for the course content and the learning abilities of the participants. The following section explores the options in greater detail.

METHOD	TECHNIQUES	APPLICATIONS
Presentation methods: trainees receive information provided by others	Lectures, workbooks, CD-ROMs, DVDs, podcasts, Web sites	Conveying facts or comparing alternatives
Hands-on methods: trainees are actively involved in trying out skills	On-the-job training, simulations, role-plays, computer games	Teaching specific skills; showing how skills are related to job or how to handle interpersonal issues
Group-building methods: trainees share ideas and experiences, build group identities, learn about interpersonal relationships and the group	Group discussions, experiential programs, team training	Establishing teams or work groups; managing performance of teams or work groups

Table 7.3

Categories of Training Methods

Percentage of Student Hours Delivered by Each Training Method

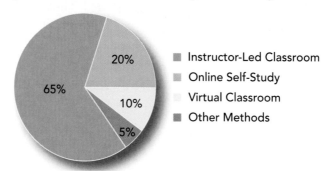

■ Instructor-Led Classroom

■ Online Self-Study

Virtual Classroom

■ Other Methods

SOURCE: *"Training* 2007 Industry Report," *Training,* November/December 2007, pp. 8–24.

LO5 Compare widely used training methods.

Training Methods

A wide variety of methods is available for conducting training. Figure 7.2 shows the percentage of learner hours delivered to employees by each of several methods: instructor-led classrooms, online self-study, virtual classrooms, and other methods, including workbooks and videos. These other methods are being phased out at most companies as more and more training moves to Internet applications. As a result, today most training programs are taking place in classrooms or online.[14]

Classroom Instruction

At school, we tend to associate learning with classroom instruction, and that type of training is most widely used in the workplace, too. Classroom instruction typically involves a trainer lecturing a group. Trainers often supplement lectures with slides, discussions, case studies, question-and-answer sessions, and role playing. Actively involving trainees enhances learning.

When the course objectives call for presenting information on a specific topic to many trainees, classroom instruction is one of the least expensive and least time-consuming ways to accomplish that goal. Learning will be more effective if trainers enhance lectures with job-related examples and opportunities for hands-on learning.

Modern technology has expanded the notion of the classroom to classes of trainees scattered in various locations. With *distance learning,* trainees at different locations attend programs online, using their computers to view lectures, participate in discussions, and share documents. Technology applications in distance learning may include videoconferencing, e-mail, instant messaging, document-sharing software, and Web cameras. General Mills uses these virtual classrooms at its smaller facilities, where offering a class on site is not cost-effective. Employees can sign up for online courses about specific products, general technical skills, and work functions such as maintenance procedures.[15]

Distance learning provides many of the benefits of classroom training without the cost and time of travel to a shared classroom. The major disadvantage of distance learning is that interaction between the trainer and audience may be limited. To overcome this hurdle, distance learning usually provides a communications link between trainees and trainer. Also, on-site instructors or facilitators should be available to answer questions and moderate question-and-answer sessions.

Audiovisual Training

Presentation methods need not require trainees to attend a class. Trainees can also work independently, using course material prepared on CDs and DVDs or in workbooks. Audiovisual techniques such as overhead transparencies, PowerPoint or other presentation software, and videos or audio clips can also supplement classroom instruction.

Some technologies make audiovisual training available as podcasts on portable devices such as PDAs and iPods or other portable audio players. As video-enabled devices become more widespread, the use of video files is likely to grow. At Capital One, employees enrolled in training courses receive iPods. They can download programs on topics such as leadership, conflict management, and customer service. To make the audio programs more engaging, some are written in the format of a radio call-in show. In classroom programs, role-play and other exercises are recorded and then made available for download to trainees' iPods.[16] Challenges of using podcasts for learning include ensuring that employees know when and how to use the technology, encouraging collaboration and interaction among trainees, and ensuring that employees can obtain the necessary downloads from their particular location and with their mobile device.[17]

Mobile technology is useful not only for entertainment, but can also be used for employees who travel and need to be in touch with the office. iPods and Personal Digital Assistants also give employees the ability to listen to and participate in training programs at their own leisure.

Users of audiovisual training often have some control over the presentation. They can review material and may be able to slow down or speed up the lesson. Videos can show situations and equipment that cannot be easily demonstrated in a classroom. Another advantage of audiovisual presentations is that they give trainees a consistent presentation, not affected by an individual trainer's goals and skills. The problems associated with these methods may include their trying to present too much material, poorly written dialogue, overuse of features such as humor or music, and drama that distracts from the key points. A well-written and carefully produced video can overcome these problems.

Computer-Based Training

Although almost all organizations use classroom training, new technologies are gaining in popularity as technology improves and becomes cheaper. With computer-based training, participants receive course materials and instruction distributed over the Internet or on CD-ROM. Often, these materials are interactive, so participants can answer questions and try out techniques, with course materials adjusted according to participants' responses. Online training programs may allow trainees to submit questions via e-mail and to participate in online discussions. Multimedia capabilities enable computers to provide sounds, images, and video presentations, along with text.

Computer-based training is generally less expensive than putting an instructor in a classroom of trainees. The low cost to deliver information gives the company flexibility in scheduling training, so that it can fit around work requirements. Training can be delivered in smaller doses, so material is easier to remember.[18] Trainees often appreciate the multimedia capabilities, which appeal to several senses, and the opportunity to actively participate in learning and apply it to situations on the job. Finally, it is easier to customize computer-based training for individual learners.

COMPUTERS REV UP TRAINING AT DETROIT DIESEL

The toughest training challenge for Detroit Diesel, which makes engines for commercial trucks, is motivating independent service technicians to keep up with new product developments so that they can correctly diagnose and fix problems. The company had formerly combined classroom training with service bulletins. But classes in which experts learned alongside new technicians were dull for the former group and confusing for the latter, and the bulletins mainly sat in e-mail in-boxes.

Detroit Diesel's solution was to use computer-based training tools.

The company posted about three dozen Web-based courses online, organized by engine type. Technicians, based on their career goals and the needs at their location, choose which courses to access. Classroom training is offered only to technicians who have already completed the relevant online coursework. That frees instructors to focus on the strengths of classroom training, such as collaboration and hands-on work.

Technical bulletins are now posted online, along with an optional quiz. A quiz might not seem motivating, but technicians who

take them become eligible to receive rewards from Detroit Diesel. Also, the company places random calls asking technicians questions about the bulletins. If they answer correctly, their company earns a prize.

With computers, Detroit Diesel has increased the amount of interaction in its training program—and with that, the enthusiasm of its trainees.

Source: Sarah Boehle, "Powering Lifelong Learning: Detroit Diesel's Tech Training," *Training Top 125,* January 2, 2008, www.trainingmag.com.

Current applications of computer-based training can extend its benefits:

e-learning
Receiving training via the Internet or the organization's intranet.

- **E-learning** involves receiving training via the Internet or the organization's intranet, typically through some combination of Web-based training modules, distance learning, and virtual classrooms. E-learning uses electronic networks for delivering and sharing information, and it offers tools and information for helping trainees improve performance. Training programs may include links to other online information resources and to trainees and experts for collaboration on problem solving. The e-learning system may also process enrollments, test and evaluate participants, and monitor progress.

- *Electronic performance support systems (EPSSs)* provide access to skills training, information, and expert advice when a problem occurs on the job.[19] As employees need to learn new skills, they can use the EPSS, which gives them access to the particular information they need, such as detailed instructions on how to perform an unfamiliar task. Using an EPSS is faster and more relevant than attending classes, even classes offered online.

The best e-learning combines the advantages of the Internet with the principles of a good learning environment. It takes advantage of the Web's dynamic nature and ability to use many positive learning features, including hyperlinks to other training sites and content, control by the trainee, and ability for trainees to collaborate.

on-the-job training (OJT)
Training methods in which a person with job experience and skill guides trainees in practicing job skills at the workplace.

On-the-Job Training

Although people often associate training with classrooms, much learning occurs while employees are performing their jobs. **On-the-job training (OJT)** refers to training methods in which a person with job experience and skill guides trainees in practicing

APPRENTICESHIP	INTERNSHIP
Bricklayer	Accountant
Carpenter	Doctor
Electrician	Journalist
Plumber	Lawyer
Printer	Nurse
Welder	

Table 7.4

Typical Jobs for Apprentices and Interns

job skills at the workplace. This type of training takes various forms, including apprenticeships and internships.

An **apprenticeship** is a work-study training method that teaches job skills through a combination of structured on-the-job training and classroom training. The OJT component of an apprenticeship involves the apprentice assisting a certified tradesperson (a journeyman) at the work site. Typically, the classroom training is provided by local trade schools, high schools, and community colleges. Under state and federal guidelines, apprenticeship programs must require at least 144 hours of classroom instruction plus 2,000 hours (one year) of on-the-job experience.[20] Some apprenticeship programs are sponsored by individual companies, others by employee unions. As shown in the left column of Table 7.4, most apprenticeship programs are in the skilled trades, such as plumbing, carpentry, and electrical work. For trainees, a major advantage of apprenticeship is the ability to earn an income while learning a trade. In addition, training through an apprenticeship is usually effective because it involves hands-on learning and extensive practice. At its manufacturing facility in Toledo, Ohio, Libbey Glass has apprenticeship programs in mold making, machine repair, millwrighting, and maintenance repair.[21] The program develops employees who are open to change, enables Libbey to use employees rather than outsource work, helps the company attract ambitious workers, and lets the company tailor training and work experiences to meet its specific needs.

An **internship** is on-the-job learning sponsored by an educational institution as a component of an academic program. The sponsoring school works with local employers to place students in positions where they can gain experience related to their area of study. For example, in Cedar Rapids, Iowa, Kirkwood Community College participates in an organization called Workplace Learning Connection, which finds students internships at hundreds of local companies.[22] High school students who pass a screening by the Workplace Learning Connection participate in semester-long internships. Many interns hope the internship will not only teach them about a workplace but also lead to a job offer. Brian Whitlatch interned at the Iowa 80 Truck Stop, where he helped mechanics work on trucks. He worked without pay as an intern, but he received course credit and, three weeks before graduation, a job offer. Many internships prepare students for professions such as those listed in the right column of Table 7.4.

To be effective, OJT programs should include several characteristics:

- The organization should issue a policy statement describing the purpose of OJT and emphasizing the organization's support for it.
- The organization should specify who is accountable for conducting OJT. This accountability should be included in the relevant job descriptions.
- The organization should review OJT practices at companies in similar industries.
- Managers and peers should be trained in OJT principles.

apprenticeship
A work-study training method that teaches job skills through a combination of on-the-job training and classroom training.

internship
On-the-job learning sponsored by an educational institution as a component of an academic program.

- Employees who conduct OJT should have access to lesson plans, checklists, procedure manuals, training manuals, learning contracts, and progress report forms.
- Before conducting OJT with an employee, the organization should assess the employee's level of basic skills.[23]

Simulations

simulation
A training method that represents a real-life situation, with trainees making decisions resulting in outcomes that mirror what would happen on the job.

A **simulation** is a training method that represents a real-life situation, with trainees making decisions resulting in outcomes that mirror what would happen on the job. Simulations enable trainees to see the impact of their decisions in an artificial, risk-free environment. They are used for teaching production and process skills as well as management and interpersonal skills. Simulations used in training include call centers stocked with phones and reference materials, as well as mockups of houses used for training cable installers.

Simulators must have elements identical to those found in the work environment. The simulator needs to respond exactly as equipment would under the conditions and response given by the trainee. For this reason, simulators are expensive to develop and need constant updating as new information about the work environment becomes available. Still, they are an excellent training method when the risks of a mistake on the job are great. Trainees do not have to be afraid of the impact of wrong decisions when using the simulator, as they would be with on-the-job training. Also, trainees tend to be enthusiastic about this type of learning and to learn quickly, and the lessons are generally related very closely to job performance. Given these benefits, this training method is likely to become more widespread as its development costs fall into a range more companies can afford.[24]

avatars
Computer depictions of trainees, which the trainees manipulate in an online role-play.

When simulations are conducted online, trainees often participate by creating **avatars,** or computer depictions of themselves, which they manipulate onscreen to play roles as workers or other participants in a job-related situation. Trainees at CDW Corporation use avatars to participate in mock interviews with customers. Employees of Loews Corporation use avatars to learn how to participate in meetings more effectively. As their avatar participates or remains silent during the simulated meetings, the program computes a score of their effectiveness.[25]

virtual reality
A computer-based technology that provides an interactive, three-dimensional learning experience.

Virtual reality is a computer-based technology that provides an interactive, three-dimensional learning experience. Using specialized equipment or viewing the virtual model on a computer screen, trainees move through the simulated environment and interact with its components.[26] Devices relay information from the environment to the trainees' senses. For example, audio interfaces, gloves that provide a sense of touch, treadmills, or motion platforms create a realistic but artificial environment. Devices also communicate information about the trainee's movements to a computer. Virtual reality is a feature of the simulated environment of the advanced manufacturing courses in Motorola's Pager Robotic Assembly facility. Employees wear a head-mounted display that lets them view a virtual world of lab space, robots, tools, and the assembly operation. The trainees hear the sounds of using the real equipment. The equipment responds as if trainees were actually using it in the factory.[27]

Business Games and Case Studies

Training programs use business games and case studies to develop employees' management skills. A case study is a detailed description of a situation that trainees study and discuss. Cases are designed to develop higher-order thinking skills, such as the ability to analyze and evaluate information. They also can be a safe way to encourage trainees to take appropriate risks, by giving them practice in weighing and acting on uncertain outcomes. There are many sources of case studies, including Harvard Business School, the Darden Business School at the University of Virginia, and McGraw-Hill publishing company.

With business games, trainees gather information, analyze it, and make decisions that influence the outcome of the game. For instance, legendary motorcycle maker Harley-Davidson uses a business game to help prospective dealers understand how dealerships make money. Each round of the game challenges teams to manage a Harley dealership and compete against each other as they face a different business situation—new products, a change in interest rates, or a crisis such as a fire at the business.[28] Games stimulate learning because they actively involve participants and mimic the competitive nature of business. A realistic game may be more meaningful to trainees than presentation techniques such as classroom instruction.

Training with case studies and games requires that participants come together to discuss the cases or the progress of the game. This requires face-to-face or electronic meetings. Also, participants must be willing to be actively involved in analyzing the situation and defending their decisions.

Behavior Modeling

Research suggests that one of the most effective ways to teach interpersonal skills is through behavior modeling.[29] This involves training sessions in which participants observe other people demonstrating the desired behavior, then have opportunities to practice the behavior themselves. For example, a training program could involve several days of four-hour sessions, each focusing on one interpersonal skill, such as communicating or coaching. At the beginning of each session, participants hear the reasons for using the key behaviors; then they watch a video of a model performing the key behaviors. They practice through role-playing and receive feedback about their performance. In addition, they evaluate the performance of the model in the video and discuss how they can apply the behavior on the job.

Experiential Programs

To develop teamwork and leadership skills, some organizations enroll their employees in a form of training called **experiential programs.** In experiential programs, participants learn concepts and then apply them by simulating the behaviors involved and analyzing the activity, connecting it with real-life situations.[30] In France, some businesses are signing up their managers to attend cooking schools, where they whip up a gourmet meal together. Jacques Bally, who works for a school run by one of France's top chefs, says cooking is a great way to learn teamwork: "It's like in any squad, everyone is responsible for playing their part; they have their own tasks but a common objective—and if they want to eat in the end, then they have to get the meal ready."[31]

Experiential training programs should follow several guidelines. A program should be related to a specific business problem. Participants should feel challenged and move outside their comfort zones but within limits that keep their motivation strong and help them understand the purpose of the program.

One form of experiential program, called **adventure learning,** uses challenging, structured outdoor activities, which may include difficult sports such as dogsledding

experiential programs
Training programs in which participants learn concepts and apply them by simulating behaviors involved and analyzing the activity, connecting it with real-life situations.

adventure learning
A teamwork and leadership training program based on the use of challenging, structured outdoor activities.

One of the most important features of organizations today is teamwork. Experiential programs include team-building exercises like wall climbing and rafting to help build trust and cooperation among employees.

or mountain climbing. Other activities may be structured tasks like climbing walls, completing rope courses, climbing ladders, or making "trust falls" (in which each trainee stands on a table and falls backward into the arms of other group members).

The impact of adventure learning programs has not been rigorously tested, but participants report they gained a greater understanding of themselves and the ways they interact with their co-workers. One key to the success of such programs may be that the organization insist that entire work groups participate together. This encourages people to see, discuss, and correct the kinds of behavior that keep the group from performing well.

Before requiring employees to participate in experiential programs, the organization should consider the possible drawbacks. Because these programs are usually physically demanding and often require participants to touch each other, companies face certain risks. Some employees may be injured or may feel that they were sexually harassed or that their privacy was invaded. Also, the Americans with Disabilities Act (discussed in Chapter 3) raises questions about requiring employees with disabilities to participate in physically demanding training experiences.

Team Training

A possible alternative to experiential programs is team training, which coordinates the performance of individuals who work together to achieve a common goal. An organization may benefit from providing such training to groups when group members must share information and group performance depends on the performance of the individual group members. Examples include the military, nuclear power plants, and commercial airlines. In those work settings, much work is performed by crews, groups, or teams. Success depends on individuals' coordinating their activities to make decisions, perhaps in dangerous situations.

Ways to conduct team training include cross-training and coordination training.[32] In **cross-training,** team members understand and practice each other's skills so that they are prepared to step in and take another member's place. In a factory, for example, production workers could be cross-trained to handle all phases of assembly. This enables the company to move them to the positions where they are most needed to complete an order on time.

cross-training
Team training in which team members understand and practice each other's skills so that they are prepared to step in and take another member's place.

Coordination training trains the team in how to share information and decisions to obtain the best team performance. This type of training is especially important for commercial aviation and surgical teams. Both of these kinds of teams must monitor different aspects of equipment and the environment at the same time sharing information to make the most effective decisions regarding patient care or aircraft safety and performance.

coordination training
Team training that teaches the team how to share information and make decisions to obtain the best team performance.

To improve the performance of its ramp employees, United Airlines arranged for them to attend Pit Instruction & Training, near Charlotte, North Carolina. The training program uses a quarter-mile racetrack and pit road to train NASCAR pit crews, but it also provides team training to companies that want their teams to work as efficiently together as a NASCAR pit crew. In United's training program, the ramp workers actually work on race cars—changing tires, filling gas tanks, and so on. The trainers take videos, time them, and deliver feedback on their performance as they face challenges such as staff shortages or a parking spot strewn with lug nuts. The goal is for the ramp workers to develop skills in organizing, communicating, and standardizing their work.[33]

Training may also target the skills needed by the teams' leaders. **Team leader training** refers to training people in the skills necessary for team leadership. For example, the training may be aimed at helping team leaders learn to resolve conflicts or coordinate activities.

team leader training
Training in the skills necessary for effectively leading the organization's teams.

Action Learning

Another form of group building is **action learning.** In this type of training, teams or work groups get an actual problem, work on solving it and commit to an action plan, and are accountable for carrying out the plan.[34] Typically, 6 to 30 employees participate in action learning; sometimes the participants include customers and vendors. Another arrangement is to bring together employees from various functions affected by the problem. ATC, a public transportation services management company in Illinois, used action learning to help boost profitability by reducing operating costs. Employees were divided into Action Workout Teams to identify ways of reducing costs and to brainstorm effective solutions. Teams of five to seven employees met once a week for a couple of hours for up to two months. The teams studied problems and issues such as overtime, preventive maintenance, absenteeism, parts inventory, and inefficient safety-inspection procedures. The teams assigned priorities to their ideas, developed action plans, tried their ideas, and measured the outcomes, eventually saving the company more than $1.8 million.[35]

action learning
Training in which teams get an actual problem, work on solving it and commit to an action plan, and are accountable for carrying it out.

The effectiveness of action learning has not been formally evaluated. This type of training seems to result in a great deal of learning, however, and employees are able to apply what they learn because action learning involves actual problems the organization is facing. The group approach also helps teams identify behaviors that interfere with problem solving.

LO6 Summarize how to implement a successful training program.

Implementing the Training Program: Principles of Learning

Learning permanently changes behavior. For employees to acquire knowledge and skills in the training program and apply what they have learned in their jobs, the training program must be implemented in a way that applies what we know about how people learn. Researchers have identified a number of ways employees learn best.[36] Table 7.5 summarizes ways that training can best encourage learning. In general, effective training communicates learning objectives clearly, presents information in distinctive and memorable ways, and helps trainees link the subject matter to their jobs.

Employees are most likely to learn when training is linked to their current job experiences and tasks.[37] There are a number of ways trainers can make this link. Training sessions should present material using familiar concepts, terms, and examples. As far as possible, the training context—such as the physical setting or the images presented on a computer—should mirror the work environment. Along with physical elements, the context should include emotional elements. In the earlier example of training store personnel to handle upset customers, the physical context is more relevant if it includes trainees acting out scenarios of personnel dealing with unhappy customers. The role-play interaction between trainees adds emotional realism and further enhances learning.

Table 7.5

Ways That Training Helps Employees Learn

TRAINING ACTIVITY	WAYS TO PROVIDE TRAINING ACTIVITY
Communicate the learning objective.	Demonstrate the performance to be expected. Give examples of questions to be answered.
Use distinctive, attention-getting messages.	Emphasize key points. Use pictures, not just words.
Limit the content of training.	Group lengthy material into chunks. Provide a visual image of the course material. Provide opportunities to repeat and practice material.
Guide trainees as they learn.	Use words as reminders about sequence of activities. Use words and pictures to relate concepts to one another and to their context.
Elaborate on the subject.	Present the material in different contexts and settings. Relate new ideas to previously learned concepts. Practice in a variety of contexts and settings.
Provide memory cues.	Suggest memory aids. Use familiar sounds or rhymes as memory cues.
Transfer course content to the workplace.	Design the learning environment so that it has elements in common with the workplace. Require learners to develop action plans that apply training content to their jobs. Use words that link the course to the workplace.
Provide feedback about performance.	Tell trainees how accurately and quickly they are performing their new skill. Show how trainees have met the objectives of the training.

Source: Adapted from R. M. Gagne, "Learning Processes and Instruction," Training Research Journal 1 (1995/96), pp. 17–28.

To fully understand and remember the content of the training, employees need a chance to demonstrate and practice what they have learned. Trainers should provide ways to actively involve the trainees, have them practice repeatedly, and have them complete tasks within a time that is appropriate in light of the learning objectives. Practice requires physically carrying out the desired behaviors, not just describing them. Practice sessions could include role-playing interactions, filling out relevant forms, or operating machinery or equipment to be used on the job. The more the trainee practices these activities, the more comfortable he or she will be in applying the skills on the job. People tend to benefit most from practice that occurs over several sessions, rather than one long practice session.[38] For complex tasks, it may be most effective to practice a few skills or behaviors at a time, then combine them in later practice sessions.

Trainees need to understand whether or not they are succeeding. Therefore, training sessions should offer feedback. Effective feedback focuses on specific behaviors and is delivered as soon as possible after the trainees practice or demonstrate what they have learned.[39] One way to do this is to videotape trainees, then show the video while indicating specific behaviors that do or do not match the desired outcomes of the training. Feedback should include praise when trainees show they have learned material, as well as guidance on how to improve.

Well-designed training helps people remember the content. Training programs need to break information into chunks that people can remember. Research suggests that people can attend to no more than four to five items at a time. If a concept or procedure involves more than five items, the training program should deliver information in shorter sessions or chunks.[40] Other ways to make information more memorable include presenting it with visual images and practicing some tasks enough that they become automatic.

Written materials should have an appropriate reading level. A simple way to assess **readability**—the difficulty level of written materials—is to look at the words being used and at the length of sentences. In general, it is easiest to read short sentences and simple, standard words. If training materials are too difficult to understand, several adjustments can help. The basic approach is to rewrite the material looking for ways to simplify it.

readability
The difficulty level of written materials.

- Substitute simple, concrete words for unfamiliar or abstract words.
- Divide long sentences into two or more short sentences.
- Divide long paragraphs into two or more short paragraphs.
- Add checklists (like this one) and illustrations to clarify the text.

Another approach is to substitute video, hands-on learning, or other nonwritten methods for some of the written material. A longer-term solution is to use tests to identify employees who need training to improve their reading levels and to provide that training first.

Measuring Results of Training

LO7 Evaluate the success of a training program.

After a training program ends, or at intervals during an ongoing training program, organizations should ensure that the training is meeting objectives. The stage to prepare for evaluating a training program is when the program is being developed. Along with designing course objectives and content, the planner should identify how to measure achievement of objectives. Depending on the objectives, the evaluation can use one or more of the measures shown in Figure 7.3: trainee

Figure 7.3

Measures of Training Success

transfer of training
On-the-job use of
knowledge, skills, and
behaviors learned in
training.

satisfaction with the program, knowledge or abilities gained, use of new skills and behavior on the job (transfer of training), and improvements in individual and organizational performance. The usual way to measure whether participants have acquired information is to administer tests on paper or electronically. Trainers or supervisors can observe whether participants demonstrate the desired skills and behaviors. Surveys measure changes in attitude. Changes in company performance have a variety of measures, many of which organizations keep track of for preparing performance appraisals, annual reports, and other routine documents in order to demonstrate the final measure of success shown in Figure 7.3: return on investment.

Evaluation Methods

Evaluation of training should look for **transfer of training,** or on-the-job use of knowledge, skills, and behaviors learned in training. Transfer of training requires that employees actually learn the content of the training program and that the necessary conditions are in place for employees to apply what they learned. Thus, the assessment can look at whether employees have an opportunity to perform the skills related to the training. The organization can measure this by asking employees three questions about specific training-related tasks:

1. Do you perform the task?
2. How many times do you perform the task?
3. To what extent do you perform difficult and challenging learned tasks?

Frequent performance of difficult training-related tasks would signal great opportunity to perform. If there is low opportunity to perform, the organization should conduct further needs assessment and reevaluate readiness to learn. Perhaps the organization does not fully support the training activities in general or the employee's supervisor does not provide opportunities to apply new skills. Lack of transfer can also mean that employees have not learned the course material. The organization might offer a refresher course to give trainees more practice. Another reason for poor transfer of training is that the content of the training may not be important for the employee's job.

Assessment of training also should evaluate training *outcomes*, that is, what (if anything) has changed as a result of the training. The relevant training outcomes are the ones related to the organization's goals for the training and its overall performance. Possible outcomes include the following:

- Information such as facts, techniques, and procedures that trainees can recall after the training.
- Skills that trainees can demonstrate in tests or on the job.
- Trainee and supervisor satisfaction with the training program.
- Changes in attitude related to the content of the training (for example, concern for safety or tolerance of diversity).
- Improvements in individual, group, or company performance (for example, greater customer satisfaction, more sales, fewer defects).

Training is a significant part of many organizations' budgets. Therefore, economic measures are an important way to evaluate the success of a training program. Businesses that invest in training want to achieve a high *return on investment*—the monetary benefits of the investment compared to the amount invested, expressed as a percentage. For example, IBM's e-learning program for new managers, Basic Blue, costs $8,708 per manager.[41] The company has measured an improvement in each new manager's performance worth $415,000. That gives IBM a benefit of $415,000 − $8,708 = $406,292 for each manager. This is an extremely large return on investment: $406,292/$8,708 = 46.65, or 4,665 percent! In other words, for every $1 IBM invests in Basic Blue, it receives almost $47.

For any of these methods, the most accurate but most costly way to evaluate the training program is to measure performance, knowledge, or attitudes among all employees before the training and then train only part of the employees. After the training is complete, the performance, knowledge, or attitudes are again measured, and the trained group is compared with the untrained group. A simpler but less accurate way to assess the training is to conduct the pretest and posttest on all trainees, comparing their performance, knowledge, or attitudes before and after the training. This form of measurement does not rule out the possibility that change resulted from something other than training (for example, a change in the compensation system). The simplest approach is to use only a posttest. Of course, this type of measurement does not enable accurate comparisons, but it may be sufficient, depending on the cost and purpose of the training.

Applying the Evaluation

The purpose of evaluating training is to help with future decisions about the organization's training programs. Using the evaluation, the organization may identify a need to modify the training and gain information about the kinds of changes needed. The organization may decide to expand on successful areas of training and cut back on training that has not delivered significant benefits.

At the Mayo Clinic, evaluation of training for new managers helped the organization select the most cost-effective method. Mayo had determined that new managers needed training in management skills. Coaching would be more expensive than classes, but would it be more effective? The organization tried both forms of training with two test groups of managers. Then it assessed trainees' satisfaction with the program and the managers' knowledge and performance after the program. There was no statistically significant difference in these measures between the two groups, so Mayo decided to proceed with the less costly method, classroom training.[42]

Applications of Training

Two training applications that have become widespread among U.S. companies are orientation of new employees and training in how to manage workforce diversity.

Orientation of New Employees

Many employees receive their first training during their first days on the job. This training is the organization's **orientation** program—its training designed to prepare

LO8 Describe training methods for employee orientation and diversity management.

orientation
Training designed to prepare employees to perform their jobs effectively, learn about their organization, and establish work relationships.

Table 7.6

Content of a Typical Orientation Program

Company-level information
Company overview (e.g., values, history, mission)
Key policies and procedures
Compensation
Employee benefits and services
Safety and accident prevention
Employee and union relations
Physical facilities
Economic factors
Customer relations

Department-level information
Department functions and philosophy
Job duties and responsibilities
Policies, procedures, rules, and regulations
Performance expectations
Tour of department
Introduction to department employees

Miscellaneous
Community
Housing
Family adjustment

Source: J. L. Schwarz and M. A. Weslowski, "Employee Orientation: What Employers Should Know," Journal of Contemporary Business Issues, Fall 1995, p. 48. Used with permission.

employees to perform their job effectively, learn about the organization, and establish work relationships. Organizations provide for orientation because, no matter how realistic the information provided during employment interviews and site visits, people feel shock and surprise when they start a new job.[43] Also, employees need to become familiar with job tasks and learn the details of the organization's practices, policies, and procedures.

The objectives of orientation programs include making new employees familiar with the organization's rules, policies, and procedures. Table 7.6 summarizes the content of a typical orientation program. Such a program provides information about the overall company and about the department in which the new employee will be working. The topics include social as well as technical aspects of the job. Miscellaneous information helps employees from out of town learn about the surrounding community. The "HR How To" box offers tips for developing effective orientation programs.

At Randstad North America, a staffing services company, orientation for new staffing agents takes place over 16 weeks. To get basic facts about their job, new employees use online resources, while classroom instruction focuses on understanding the Randstad culture. District managers give presentations on the company's culture, job expectations, selling, performance, and bonus plans. Trainees shadow more experienced co-workers, and managers provide coaching. The company credits this orientation program with enabling agents to increase sales by $4 million.[44]

HR How To

DEVELOPING AN ORIENTATION PROGRAM THAT WORKS

There is so much to know about working at any organization that, for the developer of training programs, it can be tempting to dump all that information into new employees' laps. But consider that "orientation" is simpler; it's just about getting pointed in the right direction. How can you move new employees from feeling dazed to being clear about where to go?

- **Start where employees are**— Tell them who you are, how your job relates to theirs, and how the location of the orientation relates to where they will be working.

- **Keep it simple**—Hold off on the piles of forms and manuals as long as possible. Can employees sign up for insurance later, online?

- **Allow for conversation**—Set aside some time for one-on-one conversation. That's when employees' real concerns and questions are apt to surface.

- **Encourage participation**—Use role-playing, games, and other interactive methods. Trainees will learn more if they aren't limited to listening.

- **Help employees communicate**—Try to think of all the jargon—technical terms and abbreviations—your company uses, and make a glossary. Employees can check it again and again without embarrassment.

- **Help employees remember**—A credit union gives each new employee a deck of flashcards detailing the organization's

products and industry regulations. Employees appreciate the opportunity to review the facts over and over at their convenience.

- **Learn from experience**—Pay attention to which questions keep coming up during orientation sessions. Prepare a list of frequently asked questions and answers. At the end of each session, ask trainees what did and didn't help, and take notes so that you can improve the training next time.

Sources: Liz Ryan, "Orientation from the Ground Up," *BusinessWeek,* August 27, 2007, downloaded from General Reference Center Gold, http://find. galegroup.com; and Sarah Boehle, "WSECU Uses Evaluation to Enhance Training," *Training,* December 4, 2007, www.trainingmag.com.

Orientation programs may combine various training methods such as printed and audiovisual materials, classroom instruction, on-the-job training, and e-learning. Decisions about how to conduct the orientation depend on the type of material to be covered and the number of new employees, among other factors.

Diversity Training

In response to Equal Employment Opportunity laws and market forces, many organizations today are concerned about managing diversity—creating an environment that allows all employees to contribute to organizational goals and experience personal growth. This kind of environment includes access to jobs as well as fair and positive treatment of all employees. Chapter 3 described how organizations manage diversity by complying with the law. Besides these efforts, many organizations provide training designed to teach employees attitudes and behaviors that support the management of diversity, such as appreciation of cultural differences and avoidance of behaviors that isolate or intimidate others.

Training designed to change employee attitudes about diversity and/or develop skills needed to work with a diverse workforce is called **diversity training.** These programs generally emphasize either attitude awareness and change or behavior change.

diversity training
Training designed to change employee attitudes about diversity and/or develop skills needed to work with a diverse workforce.

Diversity training programs, like the one conducted by Harvard Pilgrim Health Care, are designed to teach employees attitudes and behaviors that support the management of diversity. Why is it important for companies to provide this type of training?

Programs that focus on attitudes have objectives to increase participants' awareness of cultural and ethnic differences, as well as differences in personal characteristics and physical characteristics (such as disabilities). These programs are based on the assumption that people who become aware of differences and their stereotypes about those differences will be able to avoid letting stereotypes influence their interactions with people. Many of these programs use video and experiential exercises to increase employees' awareness of the negative emotional and performance effects of stereotypes and resulting behaviors on members of minority groups. A risk of these programs is that they may actually reinforce stereotypes by focusing on differences rather than similarities among co-workers.[45] But it is generally held that greater awareness has a positive effect.

Programs that focus on behavior aim at changing the organizational policies and individual behaviors that inhibit employees' personal growth and productivity. Sometimes these programs identify incidents that discourage employees from working up to their potential. Employees work in groups to discuss specific promotion opportunities or management practices that they believe were handled unfairly. Another approach is to teach managers and employees basic rules of behavior in the workplace.[46] Trainees may be more positive about receiving this type of training than other kinds of diversity training. Finally, some organizations provide diversity training in the form of *cultural immersion,* sending employees directly into communities where they have to interact with persons from different cultures, races, and nationalities. Participants might talk with community members, work in community organizations, or learn about events that are significant to the community they visit. Pepsi addresses behavior change at the highest level of the organization. Senior executives are assigned to be sponsors for specific employee groups, including African Americans, Latinos, Asians, women, white males, women of color, disabled employees, and employees who are gay, lesbian, or transgendered. The executives are responsible for understanding the needs of their assigned group, for identifying talent, and for mentoring at least three of these employees.[47]

Although many organizations have used diversity training, few have provided programs lasting more than a day, and few have researched their long-term effectiveness.[48] The little research that exists on the subject has provided no support for a direct link between diversity programs and business success, but there is evidence that some characteristics make diversity training more effective.[49] Most important, the training should be tied to business objectives, such as understanding customers. The support and involvement of top management, and the involvement of managers at all levels, also are important. Diversity training should emphasize learning behaviors and skills, not blaming employees. Finally, the program should be well structured, deliver rewards for performance, and include a way to measure the success of the training. The "HR Oops!" box highlights how effectively managing diversity goes beyond just diversity training.

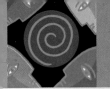

HR Oops!

Training without Results

If diversity training works, companies using it should have more managers from groups that experience discrimination. But in a study by three sociologists, most companies that introduced diversity training saw no significant change in the number of women and minority managers.

At the companies studied, talking about differences did not make people value diversity, at least not enough to promote women and minorities. However, assigning mentors to female and minority employees helped. Making managers responsible for achieving diversity targets made a bigger difference. And doing all three had the most impact.

An example shows the problem with focusing on training alone. A law firm trying to attract and retain more female attorneys provided training to foster respect for female colleagues. The trainers did their assignment, but no one was assigned to look for the real problem: the firm routinely assigned big clients to its male attorneys. For a successful career, the female attorneys needed polite colleagues less than they did experience with key clients.

Sources: Alana Conner Snibbe, "Diversity Training Doesn't Work," *Stanford Social Innovation Review,* Winter 2007, www.allbusiness.com; Lisa Takeuchi, "The Diversity Delusion," *Time,* May 7, 2007, downloaded from General Reference Center Gold, http://find.galegroup.com; and A. Kalev, F. Dobbin, and E. Kelly, "Best Practices or Best Guesses? Assessing the Efficacy of Corporate Affirmative Action and Diversity Policies," *American Sociological Review* 71 (2006), pp. 589–617.

Questions

1. In the example of the law firm, what step(s) in the training process did the firm skip before it set up training?

2. What business goals can a diversity training program reasonably be expected to achieve? How can it be made more goal-oriented?

THINKING ETHICALLY

CAN YOU TEACH PEOPLE TO BE ETHICAL?

This chapter looked at training as a way to ensure that employees have a variety of skills and abilities, such as knowing how to perform the tasks involved in a particular trade and being able to work constructively with a diverse group of people. Some organizations also provide training to help their employees make ethical decisions.

Best Buy Company uses training to help its employees live up to the company's code of ethics, adopted in 2000. Each year Best Buy's 140,000 U.S. and Canadian employees participate in the ethics training. At first, says chief ethics officer Kathleen Edmond, the training took place "out of context," unrelated to issues employees were actually facing. Edmond revised the program so that each year's lessons focus on specific work issues. Ethics training starts with all new employees, who receive a trainer-delivered presentation about the overall ethics program. Later, store employees receive the annual training via computers. Training is also linked to rewards; one-fifth of the score in employees' performance reviews is based on their demonstration of Best Buy's ethical principles and values. During their performance review, employees discuss how they put the values in practice while on the job.

SOURCE: Based on Jean Thilmany, "Supporting Ethical Employees," *HRMagazine,* September 2007, downloaded from General Reference Center Gold, http://find.galegroup.com.

Questions

1. To make ethical decisions, what skills and abilities do you need? What else do you need besides skills and abilities?

2. Do you think the ethics training described here will help make Best Buy employees more ethical? Explain.

3. Suppose you became responsible for providing ethics training at Best Buy. What additional ideas from the chapter or your own experience would you want to apply to the program described here?

SUMMARY

LO1 Discuss how to link training programs to organizational needs.

Organizations need to establish training programs that are effective. In other words, they teach what they are designed to teach, and they teach skills and behaviors that will help the organization achieve its goals. Organizations create such programs through instructional design. This process begins with a needs assessment. The organization then ensures readiness for training, including employee characteristics and organizational support. Next, the organization plans a training program, implements the program, and evaluates the results.

LO2 Explain how to assess the need for training.

Needs assessment consists of an organization analysis, person analysis, and task analysis. The organization analysis determines the appropriateness of training by evaluating the characteristics of the organization, including its strategy, resources, and management support. The person analysis determines individuals' needs and readiness for training. The task analysis identifies the tasks, knowledge, skills, and behaviors that training should emphasize. It is based on examination of the conditions in which tasks are performed, including equipment and environment of the job, time constraints, safety considerations, and performance standards.

LO3 Explain how to assess employees' readiness for training.

Readiness for training is a combination of employee characteristics and positive work environment that permit training. The necessary employee characteristics include ability to learn the subject matter, favorable attitudes toward the training, and motivation to learn. A positive work environment avoids situational constraints such as lack of money and time. In a positive environment, both peers and management support training.

LO4 Describe how to plan an effective training program.

Planning begins with establishing objectives for the training program. These should define an expected performance or outcome, the desired level of performance, and the conditions under which the performance should occur. Based on the objectives, the planner decides who will provide the training, what topics the training will cover, what training methods to use, and how to evaluate the training. Even when organizations purchase outside training, someone in the organization, usually a member of the HR department, often is responsible for training administration.

The training methods selected should be related to the objectives and content of the training program. Training methods may include presentation methods, hands-on methods, or group-building methods.

LO5 Compare widely used training methods.

Classroom instruction is most widely used and is one of the least expensive and least time-consuming ways to present information on a specific topic to many trainees. It also allows for group interaction and may include hands-on practice. Audiovisual and computer-based training need not require that trainees attend a class, so organizations can reduce time and money spent on training. Computer-based training may be interactive and may provide for group interaction. On-the-job training methods such as apprenticeships and internships give trainees firsthand experiences. A simulation represents a real-life situation, enabling trainees to see the effects of their decisions without dangerous or expensive consequences. Business games and case studies are other methods for practicing decision-making skills. Participants need to come together in one location or collaborate online. Behavior modeling gives trainees a chance to observe desired behaviors, so this technique can be effective for teaching interpersonal skills. Experiential and adventure learning programs provide an opportunity for group members to interact in challenging circumstances but may exclude members with disabilities. Team training focuses a team on achievement of a common goal. Action learning offers relevance, because the training focuses on an actual work-related problem.

LO6 Summarize how to implement a successful training program.

Implementation should apply principles of learning. In general, effective training communicates learning objectives, presents information in distinctive and memorable ways, and helps trainees link the subject matter to their jobs. Employees are most likely to learn when training is linked to job experiences and tasks. Employees learn best when they demonstrate or practice what they have learned and when they receive feedback that helps them improve. Trainees remember information better when it is broken into small chunks, presented with visual images, and practiced many times. Written materials should be easily readable by trainees.

LO7 Evaluate the success of a training program.

Evaluation of training should look for transfer of training by measuring whether employees are performing the tasks taught in the training program. Assessment of training also should evaluate training outcomes, such as change in attitude, ability to perform a new skill, and recall of facts or behaviors taught in the training program. Training should result in improvement in the group's or organization's outcomes, such as customer satisfaction or sales. An economic measure of training success is return on investment.

LO8 Describe training methods for employee orientation and diversity management.

Employee orientation is training designed to prepare employees to perform their job effectively, learn about the organization, and establish work relationships. Organizations provide for orientation because, no matter how realistic the information provided during employment interviews and site visits, people feel shock and surprise when they start a new job, and they need to learn the details of how to perform the job. A typical orientation program includes information about the overall company and the department in which the new employee will be working, covering social as well as technical aspects of the job. Orientation programs may combine several training methods, from printed materials to on-the-job training to e-learning. Diversity training is designed to change employee attitudes about diversity and/or develop skills needed to work with a diverse workforce. Evidence regarding these programs suggests that diversity training is most effective if it is tied to business objectives, has management support, emphasizes behaviors and skills, and is well structured with a way to measure success.

KEY TERMS

action learning, p. 197
adventure learning, p. 195
apprenticeship, p.193
avatars, p. 194
coordination training, p.197
cross-training, p. 197
diversity training, p. 203
e-learning, p. 192
experiential programs, p. 195

instructional design, p.181
internship, p. 193
learning management system (LMS), p. 181
needs assessment, p. 182
on-the-job training (OJT), p. 192
organization analysis, p. 183
orientation, p. 201
person analysis, p. 184

readability, p. 199
readiness for training, p. 186
simulation, p. 194
task analysis, p. 185
team leader training, p. 197
training, p. 181
transfer of training, p. 200
virtual reality, p. 194

REVIEW AND DISCUSSION QUESTIONS

1. "Melinda!" bellowed Toran to the company's HR specialist, "I've got a problem, and you've got to solve it. I can't get people in this plant to work together as a team. As if I don't have enough trouble with our competitors and our past-due accounts, now I have to put up with running a zoo. You're responsible for seeing that the staff gets along. I want a training proposal on my desk by Monday." Assume you are Melinda.
   a. Is training the solution to this problem? How can you determine the need for training?
   b. Summarize how you would conduct a needs assessment.
2. How should an organization assess readiness for learning? In Question 1, how do Toran's comments suggest readiness (or lack of readiness) for learning?
3. Assume you are the human resource manager of a small seafood company. The general manager has told you that customers have begun complaining about the quality of your company's fresh fish. Currently, training consists of senior fish cleaners showing new employees how to perform the job. Assuming your needs assessment indicates a need for training, how would you plan a training program? What steps should you take in planning the program?
4. Many organizations turn to e-learning as a less-expensive alternative to classroom training. What are some other advantages of substituting e-learning for classroom training? What are some disadvantages?
5. Suppose the managers in your organization tend to avoid delegating projects to the people in their groups. As a result, they rarely meet their goals. A training needs analysis indicates that an appropriate solution is training in management skills. You have identified two outside training programs that are consistent with your goals. One program involves experiential programs, and the other is an interactive computer program. What are the strengths and

weaknesses of each technique? Which would you choose? Why?

6. Consider your current job or a job you recently held. What types of training did you receive for the job? What types of training would you like to receive? Why?

7. A manufacturing company employs several maintenance employees. When a problem occurs with the equipment, a maintenance employee receives a description of the symptoms and is supposed to locate and fix the source of the problem. The company recently installed a new, complex electronics system. To prepare its maintenance workers, the company provided classroom training. The trainer displayed electrical drawings of system components and posed problems about the system. The trainer would point to a component in a drawing and ask, "What would happen if this component were faulty?" Trainees would study the diagrams, describe the likely symptoms, and discuss how to repair the problem. If you were responsible for this company's training, how would you evaluate the success of this training program?

8. In Question 7, suppose the maintenance supervisor has complained that trainees are having difficulty troubleshooting problems with the new electronics system. They are spending a great deal of time on problems with the system and coming to the supervisor with frequent questions that show a lack of understanding. The supervisor is convinced that the employees are motivated to learn the system, and they are well qualified. What do you think might be the problems with the current training program? What recommendations can you make for improving the program?

9. Who should be involved in orientation of new employees? Why would it not be appropriate to provide employee orientation purely online?

10. Why do organizations provide diversity training? What kinds of goals are most suitable for such training?

BUSINESSWEEK CASE

BusinessWeek IBM's Management Games: No Fooling Around

Thunder crashes, lightning flashes, and a camera zooms in on a shadowy, futuristic-looking, gray-and-black office. The camera follows a female avatar in slacks and a button-down shirt as she jogs from one cubicle to the next, up a spiral staircase, and across a high gangplank as dramatic classical music plays in the background. This YouTube trailer could easily be a plug for a new shoot-'em-up video game or a slasher flick. Instead, it's promoting a video game called Innov8, which IBM began selling in September 2007.

IBM says it received dozens of calls from potential customers after showing the video clip at a recent conference for clients. Designed to help tech managers better understand the roles of businesspeople, and vice versa, players go into a virtual business unit to test their hand at ventures such as redesigning a call center, opening a brokerage account, or processing an insurance claim.

Why is one of the world's most buttoned-down organizations encouraging its people and customers to play games? IBM says that the skills honed playing massive multiplayer dragon-slaying games like World of Warcraft can be useful when managing modern multinationals. The company says its research supports that claim.

IBM tracked the leadership qualities of gamers with the help of Seriosity (a company that develops enterprise software inspired by multiplayer games), Stanford, and MIT. IBM also surveyed more than 200 game-playing managers at the company over a seven-month period.

The IBM researchers found that those who are deeply immersed in online worlds that link millions of players, such as World of Warcraft, were ideally suited to manage in the new millennium. They were particularly savvy at gathering information from far-flung sources, determining strategic risks, failing fast, and moving on to the new challenge quickly.

One of the key findings from the research, says Thomas Malone, an MIT professor of management and Seriosity board member, is that companies need to create more opportunities for flexible, project-oriented leadership. In fast-paced games, people can jump in to manage a team for as little as 10 minutes, if they have the needed skills for the task at hand. "Games make leaders from lemmings," says Tony O'Driscoll, an IBM learning strategist and one of the authors of the study. "Since leadership happens quickly and easily in online games, otherwise reserved players are more likely to try on leadership roles."

The study points out that games can become "management flight simulators" of sorts, letting employees manage a global workforce in cyberspace before they do so in the real world. More than half of the managers surveyed said playing massive multiplayer games had helped them lead at work. Three-quarters of those surveyed believed that specific game tools, such as expressive avatars that can communicate via body language, as well as by voice and typing, would help manage remote employees in the real world.

IBM, of course, has every reason to stress the importance of online gaming. It's trying to fashion itself as the go-to consultant for business games, working with more than 250 clients. For now, IBM's challenge is convincing companies that online games are more than just a frivolous pursuit. IBM also is pouring millions into developing what it calls "the 3D Internet," in the hope that corporate gaming will become the next lucrative online frontier.

SOURCE: Excerpted from Aili McConnon, "IBM's Management Games: No Fooling Around," *BusinessWeek*, June 15, 2007, downloaded from General Reference Center Gold, http://find.galegroup.com.

Questions

1. In an organization that wants to use Innov8 for management or sales training, how could you assess readiness for training?
2. What are some strengths and weaknesses of this training method? What other training methods would you combine with online gaming to prepare managers to lead?
3. How could you assess whether using Innov8 to train managers is improving leadership at your company?

CASE: TRAINING FOR EXCELLENCE AT WEGMANS FOOD MARKETS

Wegmans Food Markets, a regional supermarket chain based in Rochester, New York, is one of the top 75 U.S. supermarkets in terms of sales volume and is widely respected in the industry. It has appeared on *Fortune*'s list of the 100 Best Companies to Work For every year since the magazine began compiling the list. Observers agree that training is a big reason why the company stands out.

Wegmans uses a blended approach to training, combining classroom sessions with on-the-job learning. CEO Danny Wegman points out, "We're a food business, so learning with the five senses is very important to us." That means a lot of the training must be hands on.

Training content includes practical matters such as product knowledge, food safety, and the ways to cook and bake. But the company also wants to ensure that employees learn the value it places on superior customer service and working toward common goals in a cooperative, friendly spirit. To convey values, training approaches must bring people face-to-face so that they can see attitudes and behaviors—in Danny Wegman's words, "that we mean what we say and we live what we say." Trainees hear stories about employees showing that they care about their customers. They also see a spirit of caring when they see experienced employees step forward to help a new employee puzzled by a problem.

Learning to sell follows from these earlier lessons. This vision of training assumes that people who understand what they are selling and who care about customers will naturally be able to sell by providing value to the customers through their knowledge and positive attitude. This understanding of sales is consistent with the company's strategy of competing on the basis of quality and service. Wegman offers an example: "If a customer doesn't know how to cook an artichoke, no matter how cheap it is, it doesn't do any good to buy it." In contrast, an employee who can discuss artichoke preparation with customers can build demand for artichokes.

Jo Natale, a company spokeswoman, says the training increases motivation as well as skill. Employees with in-depth product knowledge "want to learn about new cooking techniques," explains Natale. She adds, "They want to share that knowledge with customers and one another."

Wegmans also operates a youth apprenticeship program. About 250 teens work in teams on a project addressing a need of the department in which they work. The teamwork helps them not only learn about the business but also practice the company's values. The young employees make presentations and experience what it feels like to be listened to respectfully.

Wegmans measures the success of its training based on whether a store's sales are growing. In fact, sales and profit growth are primary ways the company measures the performance of the company's director of training and development. This motivates HR leadership to keep the training program focused on business benefits.

SOURCES: Tony Bingham and Pat Galagan, "A Higher Level of Learning," *T&D*, September 2005, www.astd.org; Wegmans, "Wegmans Food Markets, Inc.: An Overview," *News Room: Company Overview*, www.wegmans.com, last updated April 2007; Wegmans, "Why We're Proud *PLUS* the Top 10 Reasons to Work Here!" *Employment: Who We Are*, www.wegmans.com, accessed April 20, 2007; and Deborah Alexander, "Wegmans Charisma: Groceries, with Love," *Rochester (N.Y.) Democrat and Chronicle*, April 20, 2007, www.democratandchronicle.com.

Questions

1. How is training at Wegmans related to its organizational needs?
2. According to the case, how does Wegmans measure the success of its training? What other measures might be important?
3. Do you think e-learning might be an appropriate training method at Wegmans? Why or why not? For what aspects of training might it be most beneficial?

IT'S A WRAP!

www.mhhe.com/noefund3e is your source for Reviewing, Applying, and Practicing the concepts you learned about in Chapter 7.

Review	**Application**	**Practice**
• Chapter learning objectives	• Manager's Hot Seat segment: "Working in Teams: Cross-Functional Dysfunction"	• Chapter quiz
• Narrated lecture and iPod content	• Video case and quiz: "Johnson & Johnson eUniversity"	
• Test Your Knowledge: Training Methods	• Self-assessment: Evaluate Your Own Training Needs	
	• Web exercise: Online Learning Courses	

NOTES

1. G. Weber, "Intel's Internal Approach," *Workforce Management* 83 (2004), p. 49; and K. Kranhold, D. Bileklan, M. Karnitschnig, and G. Parker, "Lost in Translation," *Wall Street Journal*, May 18, 2004, pp. B1, B6.

2. R. Noe, *Employee Training and Development*, 4th ed. (New York: Irwin/McGraw-Hill, 2008).

3. "Learning Management Systems: An Executive Summary," *Training*, March 2002, p. 4.

4. I. L. Goldstein, E. P. Braverman, and H. Goldstein, "Needs Assessment," in *Developing Human Resources*, ed. K. N. Wexley (Washington, DC: Bureau of National Affairs, 1991), pp. 5-35–5-75.

5. J. Z. Rouillier and I. L. Goldstein, "Determinants of the Climate for Transfer of Training" (presented at Society of Industrial/Organizational Psychology meetings, St. Louis, MO, 1991); J. S. Russell, J. R. Terborg, and M. L. Powers, "Organizational Performance and Organizational Level Training and Support," *Personnel Psychology* 38 (1985), pp. 849–63; H. Baumgartel, G. J. Sullivan, and L. E. Dunn, "How Organizational Climate and Personality Affect the Payoff from Advanced Management Training Sessions," *Kansas Business Review* 5 (1978), pp. 1–10.

6. Jill Casner-Lotto et al., *Are They Really Ready to Work?* (New York: Conference Board; Washington, DC: Corporate Voices for Working Families; Tucson, AZ: Partnership for 21st Century Skills; Alexandria, VA: Society for Human Resource Management, 2006), available at www.infoedge.com; R. Davenport, "Eliminate the Skills Gap," *T&D*, February 2006, pp. 26–34; M. Schoeff, "Amid Calls to Bolster U.S. Innovation, Experts Lament Paucity of Basic Math Skills," *Workforce Management*, March 2006, pp. 46–49.

7. R. A. Noe, "Trainees' Attributes and Attitudes: Neglected Influences on Training Effectiveness," *Academy of Management Review* 11 (1986), pp. 736–49; T. T. Baldwin, R. T. Magjuka, and B. T. Loher, "The Perils of Participation: Effects of Choice on Trainee Motivation and Learning," *Personnel Psychology* 44 (1991), pp. 51–66; S. I. Tannenbaum, J. E. Mathieu, E. Salas, and J. A. Cannon-Bowers, "Meeting Trainees' Expectations: The Influence of Training Fulfillment on the Development of Commitment, Self-Efficacy, and Motivation," *Journal of Applied Psychology* 76 (1991), pp. 759–69.

8. L. H. Peters, E. J. O'Connor, and J. R. Eulberg, "Situational Constraints: Sources, Consequences, and Future Considerations," in *Research in Personnel and Human Resource Management*, eds. K. M. Rowland and G. R. Ferris (Greenwich, CT: JAI Press, 1985), vol. 3, pp. 79–114; E. J. O'Connor, L. H. Peters, A. Pooyan, J. Weekley, B. Frank, and B. Erenkranz, "Situational Constraints' Effects on Performance, Affective Reactions, and Turnover: A Field Replication and Extension," *Journal of Applied Psychology* 69 (1984), pp. 663–72; D. J. Cohen, "What Motivates Trainees?" *Training and Development Journal*, November 1990, pp. 91–93; Russell, Terborg, and Powers, "Organizational Performance."

9. J. B. Tracey, S. I. Trannenbaum, and M. J. Kavanaugh, "Applying Trade Skills on the Job: The Importance of the Work Environment," *Journal of Applied Psychology* 80 (1995), pp. 239–52; P. E. Tesluk, J. L. Farr, J. E. Mathieu, and R. J. Vance, "Generalization of Employee Involvement Training to the Job Setting: Individuals and Situational Effects," *Personnel Psychology* 48 (1995), pp. 607–32; J. K. Ford, M. A.

Quinones, D. J. Sego, and J. S. Sorra, "Factors Affecting the Opportunity to Perform Trained Tasks on the Job," *Personnel Psychology* 45 (1992), pp. 511–27.

10. S. Allen, "Water Cooler Wisdom," *Training*, August 2005, pp. 30–34.

11. B. Mager, *Preparing Instructional Objectives*, 2nd ed. (Belmont, CA: Lake, 1984); B. J. Smith and B. L. Delahaye, *How to Be an Effective Trainer*, 2nd ed. (New York: Wiley, 1987).

12. R. Zemke and J. Armstrong, "How Long Does It Take? (The Sequel)," *Training*, May 1997, pp. 69–79.

13. C. Lee, "Who Gets Trained in What?" *Training*, October 1991, pp. 47–59; W. Hannum, *The Application of Emerging Training Technology* (San Diego, CA: University Associates, 1990); B. Filipczak, "Make Room for Training," *Training*, October 1991, pp. 76–82; A. P. Carnevale, L. J. Gainer, and A. S. Meltzer, *Workplace Basics Training Manual* (San Francisco: Jossey-Bass, 1990).

14. "*Training 2007 Industry Report*," *Training*, November/December 2007, pp. 8–24.

15. "Training Top 100 Best Practices 2006: General Mills," *Training*, March 2006, p. 61.

16. M. Weinstein, "Ready or Not, Here Comes Podcasting," *Training*, January 2006, pp. 22–23; D. Sussman, "Now Hear This," *T&D*, September 2005, pp. 53–54; and J. Pont, "Employee Training on iPod Playlist," *Workforce Management*, August 2005, p. 18.

17. E. Wagner and P. Wilson, "Disconnected," *T&D*, December 2005, pp. 40–43.

18. G. Yohe, "The Best of Both?" *Human Resource Executive*, March 6, 2002, pp. 35, 38–39.

19. G. Stevens and E. Stevens, "The Truth about EPSS," *Training and Development* 50 (1996), pp. 59–61.

20. O. Crosby, "Apprenticeships: Career Training, Credentials—and a Paycheck in Your Pocket," *Occupational Outlook Quarterly*, Summer 2002, downloaded from FindArticles at www.findarticles.com.

21. M. Rowh, "The Rise of the Apprentice," *Human Resource Executive*, January 2006, pp. 38–43.

22. J. Bailey, "Community College Can Help Small Firms with Job Training," *Wall Street Journal*, February 19, 2002, http://online.wsj.com.

23. W. J. Rothwell and H. C. Kanzanas, "Planned OJT Is Productive OJT," *Training and Development Journal*, October 1990, pp. 53–56.

24. C. Cornell, "Better than the Real Thing?" *Human Resource Executive*, August 2005, pp. 34–37; E. Frauenheim, "Can Video Games Win Points as Teaching Tools?" *Workforce Management*, April 10, 2006, pp. 12–14; S. Boehle, "Simulations: The Next Generation of E-Learning," *Training*, January 2005, pp. 22–31; and J. Borzo, "Almost Human," *Wall Street Journal*, May 24, 2004, pp. R1, R10.

25. Borzo, "Almost Human"; and J. Hoff, "My Virtual Life," *BusinessWeek*, May 1, 2006, pp. 72–78.

26. N. Adams, "Lessons from the Virtual World," *Training*, June 1995, pp. 45–48.

27. Ibid.

28. "Business War Games," *Training*, December 2002, p. 18.

29. G. P. Latham and L. M. Saari, "Application of Social Learning Theory to Training Supervisors through Behavior Modeling," *Journal of Applied Psychology* 64 (1979), pp. 239–46.

30. D. Brown and D. Harvey, *An Experiential Approach to Organizational Development* (Englewood Cliffs, NJ: Prentice Hall, 2000); and J. Schettler, "Learning by Doing," *Training*, April 2002, pp. 38–43.

31. K. Willsher, "French Firms Drop Bungee for Bouillon," *Guardian Unlimited*, February 25, 2005, www.guardian.co.uk.

32. C. Clements, R. J. Wagner, and C. C. Roland, "The Ins and Outs of Experiential Training," *Training and Development*, February 1995, pp. 52–56.

33. S. Carey, "Racing to Improve," *Wall Street Journal*, March 24, 2006, pp. B1, B6.

34. P. Froiland, "Action Learning," *Training*, January 1994, pp. 27–34.

35. "A Team Effort," *Training*, September 2002, p. 18.

36. C. E. Schneier, "Training and Development Programs: What Learning Theory and Research Have to Offer," *Personnel Journal*, April 1974, pp. 288–93; M. Knowles, "Adult Learning," in *Training and Development Handbook*, 3rd ed., ed. R. L. Craig (New York: McGraw-Hill, 1987), pp. 168–79; R. Zemke and S. Zemke, "30 Things We Know for Sure about Adult Learning," *Training*, June 1981, pp. 45–52; B. J. Smith and B. L. Delahaye, *How to Be an Effective Trainer*, 2nd ed. (New York: Wiley, 1987).

37. K. A. Smith-Jentsch, F. G. Jentsch, S. C. Payne, and E. Salas, "Can Pretraining Experiences Explain Individual Differences in Learning?" *Journal of Applied Psychology* 81 (1996), pp. 110–16.

38. W. McGehee and P. W. Thayer, *Training in Business and Industry* (New York: Wiley, 1961).

39. R. M. Gagne and K. L. Medsker, *The Condition of Learning* (Fort Worth, TX: Harcourt-Brace, 1996).

40. J. C. Naylor and G. D. Briggs, "The Effects of Task Complexity and Task Organization on the Relative Efficiency of Part and Whole Training Methods," *Journal of Experimental Psychology* 65 (1963), pp. 217–24.

41. K. Mantyla, *Blended E-Learning* (Alexandria, VA: ASTD, 2001).

42. D. Sussman, "Strong Medicine Required," *T&D*, November 2005, pp. 34–38.

43. M. R. Louis, "Surprise and Sense Making: What Newcomers Experience in Entering Unfamiliar

Organizational Settings," *Administrative Science Quarterly* 25 (1980), pp. 226–51.

44. D. Sussman, "Getting Up to Speed," *T&D*, December 2005, pp. 49–51.

45. S. M. Paskoff, "Ending the Workplace Diversity Wars," *Training*, August 1996, pp. 43–47; H. B. Karp and N. Sutton, "Where Diversity Training Goes Wrong," *Training*, July 1993, pp. 30–34.

46. Paskoff, "Ending the Workplace Diversity Wars."

47. C. Terhune, "Pepsi, Vowing Diversity Isn't Just Image Polish, Seeks Inclusive Culture," *Wall Street Journal*, April 19, 2005, p. B1.

48. S. Rynes and B. Rosen, "A Field Study of Factors Affecting the Adoption and Perceived Success of Diversity Training," *Personnel Psychology* 48 (1995), pp. 247–70.

49. S. Rynes and B. Rosen, "What Makes Diversity Programs Work?" *HR Magazine*, October 1994, pp. 67–73; Rynes and Rosen, "A Field Survey of Factors Affecting the Adoption and Perceived Success of Diversity Training"; J. Gordon, "Different from What? Diversity as a Performance Issue," *Training*, May 1995, pp. 25–33; T. Kochan, K. Bezrukova, R. Ely, S. Jackson, A. Joshi, K. Jehn, J. Leonard, D. Levine, and D. Thomas, "The Effects of Diversity on Business Performance: Report of the Diversity Research Network," *Human Resource Management* 42 (2003), pp. 8–21; and F. Hansen, "Diversity's Business Case Just Doesn't Add Up," *Workforce*, June 2003, pp. 29–32.

Assessing Performance and Developing Employees

PART THREE

Managing Employees' Performance

What Do I Need to Know?

After reading this chapter, you should be able to:

LO1 Identify the activities involved in performance management.

LO2 Discuss the purposes of performance management systems.

LO3 Define five criteria for measuring the effectiveness of a performance management system.

LO4 Compare the major methods for measuring performance.

LO5 Describe major sources of performance information in terms of their advantages and disadvantages.

LO6 Define types of rating errors, and explain how to minimize them.

LO7 Explain how to provide performance feedback effectively.

LO8 Summarize ways to produce improvement in unsatisfactory performance.

LO9 Discuss legal and ethical issues that affect performance management.

Introduction

The Zoological Society of San Diego had a problem. Its employees often didn't know whether they were doing a good job. Even worse, the organization didn't have a consistent method to rate job performance, and managers faced no consequences if they did not give formal appraisals. To remedy the situation, the Zoological Society set up a formal system so that each employee has individual goals that are tied to the organization's objectives, such as visitor satisfaction and revenue. Managers use a Web-based computer system to rate employees on their progress in meeting goals and on specific areas of competence, such as teamwork and communications. Employees use online journals to record their accomplishments, so managers have easy access to that data. Managers must rate employees twice a year and then discuss the reports face-to-face with each employee. Employees appreciate the clear feedback—and the raises they get if they perform well.[1]

Setting goals, rating performance, and discussing performance, as the Zoological Society's managers do, are all parts of performance management. **Performance management** is the process through which managers ensure that employees' activities and outputs contribute to the organization's goals. This process requires knowing what activities and outputs are desired, observing whether they occur, and providing feedback to help employees meet expectations. In the course of providing feedback, managers and employees may identify performance problems and establish ways to resolve those problems.

In this chapter we examine a variety of approaches to performance management. We begin by describing the activities involved in managing performance, then discuss the purpose of carrying out this process. Next, we discuss specific approaches to performance management, including the strengths and weaknesses of each approach. We also look at various sources of performance information. The next section explores

chapter eight

the kinds of errors that commonly occur during the assessment of performance, as well as ways to reduce those errors. Then we describe ways of giving performance feedback effectively and intervening when performance must improve. Finally, we summarize legal and ethical issues affecting performance management.

The Process of Performance Management

Although many employees have come to dread the annual "performance appraisal" meeting, at which a boss picks apart the employee's behaviors and apparent attitudes from the past year, performance management can potentially deliver many benefits. Effective performance management can tell top performers that they are valued, encourage communication between managers and their employees, establish uniform standards for evaluating employees, and help the organization identify its strongest and weakest performers. According to the Hay Group, companies on its Global Most Admired list, which it prepares for *Fortune* magazine, have chief executive officers who understand that performance measurement helps the organization motivate people and link performance to rewards.[2] Many of these executives report that performance measurement encourages employees to cooperate and helps the company focus on smooth operations, customer loyalty, and employee development.

To meet these objectives, performance management includes several activities. As shown in Figure 8.1, these are defining performance, measuring performance, and feeding back performance information. First, the organization specifies which aspects of performance are relevant to the organization. These decisions are based on the job analysis, described in Chapter 4. Next, the organization measures the relevant aspects of performance by conducting performance appraisals. Finally, through performance feedback sessions, managers give employees information about their performance so they can adjust their behavior to meet the organization's goals. When there are performance problems, the feedback session should include efforts to identify and resolve the underlying problems. In addition, performance feedback can come through the organization's rewards, as described in Chapter 12.

Using this performance management process helps managers and employees focus on the organization's goals. Unfortunately, as described in the "Did You Know?" box, this is an area in which many organizations need to improve.

Computer software is available to help managers at various stages of performance management. Software can help managers customize performance measurement forms. The manager uses the software to establish a set of performance standards for each job. The manager rates each employee according to the predetermined standards, and the software provides a report that compares the employee's performance to the standards and identifies the employee's strengths and weaknesses. Other software offers help with diagnosing performance problems. This type of software asks questions—for example, Does the employee work under time pressure? The answers suggest reasons for performance problems and ways the manager can help the employee improve.

performance management
The process through which managers ensure that employees' activities and outputs contribute to the organization's goals.

LO1 Identify the activities involved in performance management.

Figure 8.1

Stages of the Performance Management Process

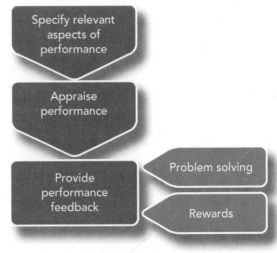

Performance Management Needs to Be Managed

Slightly more than half of HR executives say their performance management systems are effectively linked to business results.

Source: Fay Hansen, "Lackluster Performance," *Workforce Management,* November 5, 2007, pp. 39–45.

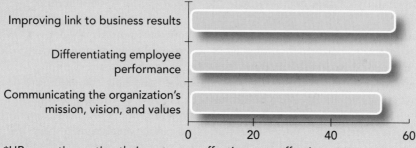

Percentage of executives' rating system effective for meeting goal*:

- Improving link to business results
- Differentiating employee performance
- Communicating the organization's mission, vision, and values

(0, 20, 40, 60)

*HR executives rating their system as effective, very effective, or extremely effective.

L02 Discuss the purposes of performance management systems.

Purposes of Performance Management

Organizations establish performance management systems to meet three broad purposes: strategic, administrative, and developmental. *Strategic purpose* means effective performance management helps the organization achieve its business objectives. It does this by helping to link employees' behavior with the organization's goals. Performance management starts with defining what the organization expects from each employee. It measures each employee's performance to identify where those expectations are and are not being met. This enables the organization to take corrective action, such as training, incentives, or discipline. Performance management can achieve its strategic purpose only when measurements are truly linked to the organization's goals and when the goals and feedback about performance are communicated to employees. Just Born, the company that makes Peeps and Mike and Ike candy, meets the strategic purpose of performance management. Its system has employees and managers meet to agree on several personal objectives through which each employee will help meet the objectives of his or her department. Together, they identify whatever training the employee needs and meet regularly to discuss the employee's progress in meeting the objectives.[3]

The *administrative purpose* of a performance management system refers to the ways in which organizations use the system to provide information for day-to-day decisions about salary, benefits, and recognition programs. Performance management can also support decision making related to employee retention, termination for poor behavior, and hiring or layoffs. Because performance management supports these administrative decisions, the information in a performance appraisal can have a great impact on the future of individual employees. Managers recognize this, which is the reason they may feel uncomfortable conducting performance appraisals when the appraisal information is negative and, therefore, likely to lead to a layoff, disappointing pay increase, or other negative outcome.

Finally, performance management has a *developmental purpose*, meaning that it serves as a basis for developing employees' knowledge and skills. Even employees who are

Aetna Shapes Up Performance Management

Aetna, a major provider of health, life, and disability insurance, has more than 34,000 employees. Those staff members work with employers, health-care providers, patients, public officials, and each other to fulfill the company's mission of "helping people achieve health and financial security." Several years ago, the company was struggling and losing money, and part of the problem was performance management. Its approach to appraising performance was fragmented—in an industry that depends heavily on the skills and knowledge of its workers, managers didn't know what they were doing.

Under a new executive team, Aetna began to build a superior performance management system. When it is time for a manager to review an employee's performance, the manager goes online

to open a secure "dashboard," where the manager rates the employee's skills and competencies, using objective criteria, such as knowledge of a particular programming language, as well as subjective criteria. The company has identified 43 tasks and abilities managers rate for each position. Employees also rank themselves, and managers discuss any differences in face-to-face meetings.

The dashboard helps the manager evaluate training needs; likewise, if employees see that they fall short in some area, they can use the system to identify training opportunities. Overall ratings on a 5-point scale for each employee help managers identify high performers who should be offered more incentives to stick around. Employees who score 5, indicating they far exceed expectations, are considered good candidates for a promotion.

The Web-based system makes it easier for managers to evaluate performance and turn in reports on time. It's also easier to show employees how their work contributes to the organization's goals. Aetna requires executives to set companywide goals at the end of each year, and then divisions, teams, and individuals set supporting goals. A recent survey found that 83 percent of employees said they understand how they "contribute to the successful implementation of Aetna's strategic/operational goals." Four years before, the share who understood was just 59 percent.

Sources: Michael Myser, "Bosses Get a Helping Hand," *Business 2.0,* July 2007, downloaded from General Reference Center Gold, http://find.galegroup.com; Mary K. Pratt, "No More Job Reviews," *Computerworld,* April 2, 2007, http://find.galegroup.com; and Aetna, "Aetna At-A-Glance: Aetna Facts," Aetna Web site, www.aetna.com, accessed January 28, 2008.

meeting expectations can become more valuable when they hear and discuss performance feedback. Effective performance feedback makes employees aware of their strengths and of the areas in which they can improve. Discussing areas in which employees fall short can help the employees and their manager uncover the source of problems and identify steps for improvement. Although discussing weaknesses may feel uncomfortable, it is necessary when performance management has a developmental purpose.

The "Best Practices" box describes a company with a performance management system that can meet its strategic, administrative, and developmental purposes.

Criteria for Effective Performance Management

In Chapter 6, we saw that there are many ways to predict performance of a job candidate. Similarly, there are many ways to measure the performance of an employee. For performance management to achieve its goals, its methods for measuring performance must be good. Selecting these measures is a critical part of planning a performance management system. Several criteria determine the effectiveness of performance measures:

LO3 Define five criteria for measuring the effectiveness of a performance management system.

- *Fit with strategy*—A performance management system should aim at achieving employee behavior and attitudes that support the organization's strategy, goals, and culture. If a company emphasizes customer service, then its performance management system should define the kinds of behavior that contribute to good customer service.

Figure 8.2

Contamination and
Deficiency of a Job
Performance Measure

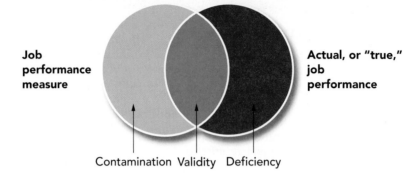

Job performance measure

Actual, or "true," job performance

Contamination   Validity   Deficiency

Performance appraisals should measure whether employees are engaging in those behaviors. Feedback should help employees improve in those areas. When an organization's strategy changes, human resource personnel should help managers assess how the performance management system should change to serve the new strategy.

- *Validity*—As we discussed in Chapter 6, *validity* is the extent to which a measurement tool actually measures what it is intended to measure. In the case of performance appraisal, validity refers to whether the appraisal measures all the relevant aspects of performance and omits irrelevant aspects of performance. Figure 8.2 shows two sets of information. The circle on the left represents all the information in a performance appraisal; the circle on the right represents all relevant measures of job performance. The overlap of the circles contains the valid information. Information that is gathered but irrelevant is "contamination." Comparing salespeople based on how many calls they make to customers could be a contaminated measure. Making a lot of calls does not necessarily improve sales or customer satisfaction, unless every salesperson makes only well-planned calls. Information that is not gathered but is relevant represents a deficiency of the performance measure. For example, suppose a company measures whether employees have good attendance records but not whether they work efficiently. This limited performance appraisal is unlikely to provide a full picture of employees' contribution to the company. Performance measures should minimize both contamination and deficiency.
- *Reliability*—With regard to a performance measure, reliability describes the consistency of the results that the performance measure will deliver. *Interrater reliability* is consistency of results when more than one person measures performance. Simply asking a supervisor to rate an employee's performance on a scale of 1 to 5 would likely have low interrater reliability; the rating will differ depending on who is scoring the employees. *Test-retest reliability* refers to consistency of results over time. If a performance measure lacks test-retest reliability, determining whether an employee's performance has truly changed over time will be impossible.
- *Acceptability*—Whether or not a measure is valid and reliable, it must meet the practical standard of being acceptable to the people who use it. For example, the people who use a performance measure must believe that it is not too time-consuming. Likewise, if employees believe the measure is unfair, they will not use the feedback as a basis for improving their performance.
- *Specific feedback*—A performance measure should specifically tell employees what is expected of them and how they can meet those expectations. Being specific helps performance management meet the goals of supporting strategy and developing employees. If a measure does not specify what an employee must do to help the organization achieve its goals, it does not support the strategy. If the measure fails to point out employees' performance problems, they will not know how to improve.

Methods for Measuring Performance

Organizations have developed a wide variety of methods for measuring performance. Some methods rank each employee to compare employees' performance. Other methods break down the evaluation into ratings of individual attributes, behaviors, or results. Many organizations use a measurement system that includes a variety of the preceding measures, as in the case of applying total quality management to performance management. Table 8.1 compares these methods in terms of our criteria for effective performance management.

LO4 Compare the major methods for measuring performance.

Making Comparisons

The performance appraisal method may require the rater to compare one individual's performance with that of others. This method involves some form of ranking, in which some employees are best, some are average, and others are worst. The usual techniques for making comparisons are simple ranking, forced distribution, and paired comparison.

Simple ranking requires managers to rank employees in their group from the highest performer to the poorest performer. In a variation of this approach, *alternation*

simple ranking
Method of performance measurement that requires managers to rank employees in their group from the highest performer to the poorest performer.

Table 8.1

Basic Approaches to Performance Measurement

APPROACH	CRITERIA				
	FIT WITH STRATEGY	VALIDITY	RELIABILITY	ACCEPTABILITY	SPECIFICITY
Comparative	Poor, unless manager takes time to make link	Can be high if ratings are done carefully	Depends on rater, but usually no measure of agreement used	Moderate; easy to develop and use but resistant to normative standard	Very low
Attribute	Usually low; requires manager to make link	Usually low; can be fine if developed carefully	Usually low; can be improved by specific definitions of attributes	High; easy to develop and use	Very low
Behavioral	Can be quite high	Usually high; minimizes contamination and deficiency	Usually high	Moderate; difficult to develop, but accepted well for use	Very high
Results	Very high	Usually high; can be both contaminated and deficient	High; main problem can be test–retest— depends on timing of measure	High; usually developed with input from those to be evaluated	High regarding results, but low regarding behaviors necessary to achieve them
Quality	Very high	High, but can be both contaminated and deficient	High	High; usually developed with input from those to be evaluated	High regarding results, but low regarding behaviors necessary to achieve them

ranking, the manager works from a list of employees. First, the manager decides which employee is best and crosses that person's name off the list. From the remaining names, the manager selects the worst employee and crosses off that name. The process continues with the manager selecting the second best, second worst, third best, and so on, until all the employees have been ranked. The major downside of ranking involves validity. To state a performance measure as broadly as "best" or "worst" doesn't define what exactly is good or bad about the person's contribution to the organization. Ranking therefore raises questions about fairness.

Another way to compare employees' performance is with the **forced-distribution method.** This type of performance measurement assigns a certain percentage of employees to each category in a set of categories. For example, the organization might establish the following percentages and categories:

forced-distribution method
Method of performance measurement that assigns a certain percentage of employees to each category in a set of categories.

- Exceptional—5 percent
- Exceeds standards—25 percent
- Meets standards—55 percent
- Room for improvement—10 percent
- Not acceptable—5 percent

The manager completing the performance appraisal would rate 5 percent of his or her employees as exceptional, 25 percent as exceeding standards, and so on. A forced-distribution approach works best if the members of a group really do vary this much in terms of their performance. It overcomes the temptation to rate everyone high in order to avoid conflict. Research simulating some features of forced rankings found that they improved performance when combined with goals and rewards, especially in the first few years, when the system eliminated the poorest performers.[4] However, a manager who does very well at selecting, motivating, and training employees will have a group of high performers. This manager would have difficulty assigning employees to the bottom categories. In that situation, saying that some employees require improvement or are "not acceptable" not only will be inaccurate, but will hurt morale.

paired-comparison method
Method of performance measurement that compares each employee with each other employee to establish rankings.

Another variation on rankings is the **paired-comparison method.** This approach involves comparing each employee with each other employee to establish rankings. Suppose a manager has five employees, Allen, Barbara, Caitlin, David, and Edgar. The manager compares Allen's performance to Barbara's and assigns one point to whichever employee is the higher performer. Then the manager compares Allen's performance to Caitlin's, then to David's, and finally to Edgar's. The manager repeats this process with Barbara, comparing her performance to Caitlin's, David's, and Edgar's. When the manager has compared every pair of employees, the manager counts the number of points for each employee. The employee with the most points is considered the top-ranked employee. Clearly, this method is time-consuming if a group has more than a handful of employees. For a group of 15, the manager must make 105 comparisons.

In spite of the drawbacks, ranking employees offers some benefits. It counteracts the tendency to avoid controversy by rating everyone favorably or near the center of the scale. Also, if some managers tend to evaluate behavior more strictly (or more leniently) than others, a ranking system can erase that tendency from performance scores. Therefore, ranking systems can be useful for supporting decisions about how to distribute pay raises or layoffs. Some ranking systems are easy to use, which makes them acceptable to the managers who use them. A major drawback of rankings is that they often are not linked to the organization's goals. Also, a simple ranking system leaves the basis for the ranking open to interpretation. In that case, the rankings are not helpful for employee development and may hurt morale or result in legal challenges.

Rating Individuals

Instead of focusing on arranging a group of employees from best to worst, performance measurement can look at each employee's performance relative to a uniform set of standards. The measurement may evaluate employees in terms of attributes (characteristics or traits) believed desirable. Or the measurements may identify whether employees have *behaved* in desirable ways, such as closing sales or completing assignments. For both approaches, the performance management system must identify the desired attributes or behaviors, then provide a form on which the manager can rate the employee in terms of those attributes or behaviors. Typically, the form includes a rating scale, such as a scale from 1 to 5, where 1 is the worst performance and 5 is the best.

Rating Attributes

The most widely used method for rating attributes is the **graphic rating scale.** This method lists traits and provides a rating scale for each trait. The employer uses the scale to indicate the extent to which the employee being rated displays the traits. The rating scale may provide points to circle (as on a scale going from 1 for poor to 5 for excellent), or it may provide a line representing a range of scores, with the manager marking a place along the line. Figure 8.3 shows an example of a graphic rating scale that uses a set of ratings from 1 to 5. A drawback of this approach is that it leaves to the particular manager the decisions about what is "excellent knowledge" or "commendable judgment" or "poor interpersonal skills." The result is low reliability, because managers are likely to arrive at different judgments.

graphic rating scale
Method of performance measurement that lists traits and provides a rating scale for each trait; the employer uses the scale to indicate the extent to which an employee displays each trait.

Figure 8.3

Example of a Graphic Rating Scale

The following areas of performance are significant to most positions. Indicate your assessment of performance on each dimension by circling the appropriate rating.

PERFORMANCE DIMENSION	RATING				
	DISTINGUISHED	EXCELLENT	COMMENDABLE	ADEQUATE	POOR
Knowledge	5	4	3	2	1
Communication	5	4	3	2	1
Judgment	5	4	3	2	1
Managerial skill	5	4	3	2	1
Quality performance	5	4	3	2	1
Teamwork	5	4	3	2	1
Interpersonal skills	5	4	3	2	1
Initiative	5	4	3	2	1
Creativity	5	4	3	2	1
Problem solving	5	4	3	2	1

Figure 8.4

Example of a Mixed-Standard Scale

Three traits being assessed:		Levels of performance in statements:		
Initiative (INTV)		High (H)		
Intelligence (INTG)		Medium (M)		
Relations with others (RWO)		Low (L)		

Instructions: Please indicate next to each statement whether the employee's performance is above (+), equal to (0), or below (−) the statement.

INTV	H	1.	This employee is a real self-starter. The employee always takes the initiative and his/her superior never has to prod this individual.	+
INTG	M	2.	While perhaps this employee is not a genius, s/he is a lot more intelligent than many people I know.	+
RWO	L	3.	This employee has a tendency to get into unnecessary conflicts with other people.	0
INTV	M	4.	While generally this employee shows initiative, occasionally his/her superior must prod him/her to complete work.	+
INTG	L	5.	Although this employee is slower than some in understanding things, and may take a bit longer in learning new things, s/he is of average intelligence.	+
RWO	H	6.	This employee is on good terms with everyone. S/he can get along with people even when s/he does not agree with them.	−
INTV	L	7.	This employee has a bit of a tendency to sit around and wait for directions.	+
INTG	H	8.	This employee is extremely intelligent, and s/he learns very rapidly.	−
RWO	M	9.	This employee gets along with most people. Only very occasionally does s/he have conflicts with others on the job, and these are likely to be minor.	−

Scoring Key:

STATEMENTS			SCORE
HIGH	MEDIUM	LOW	
+	+	+	7
0	+	+	6
−	+	+	5
−	0	+	4
−	−	+	3
−	−	0	2
−	−	−	1

Example score from preceding ratings:

	STATEMENTS			SCORE
	HIGH	MEDIUM	LOW	
Initiative	+	+	+	7
Intelligence	0	+	+	6
Relations with others	−	−	0	2

mixed-standard scales
Method of performance measurement that uses several statements describing each trait to produce a final score for that trait.

To get around this problem, some organizations use **mixed-standard scales,** which use several statements describing each trait to produce a final score for that trait. The manager scores the employee in terms of how the employee compares to each statement. Consider the sample mixed-standard scale in Figure 8.4. To create this scale, the organization determined that the relevant traits are initiative, intelligence, and relations with others. For each trait, sentences were written to describe a person having a high level of that trait, a medium level, and a low level. The sentences for the traits were rearranged so that the nine statements about the three traits are mixed together. The manager who uses this scale reads each sentence, then indicates whether the employee performs above (+), at (0), or below (−) the level described. The key in the middle section of Figure 8.4 tells how to use the pluses, zeros, and minuses to score performance. Someone who excels at every level of performance (pluses for high, medium, and low performance) receives a score of 7 for that trait. Someone who fails to live up to every description of performance (minuses for high, medium, and low) receives a score of 1 for that trait. The bottom of Figure 8.4 calculates the scores for the ratings used in this example.

An employee's performance measurement differs from job to job. For example, a car dealer's performance is measured by the dollar amount of sales, the number of new customers, and customer satisfaction surveys. How would the performance measurements of a car dealer differ from those of a company CEO?

Rating attributes is the most popular way to measure performance in organizations. In general, attribute-based performance methods are easy to develop and can be applied to a wide variety of jobs and organizations. If the organization is careful to identify which attributes are associated with high performance, and to define them carefully on the appraisal form, these methods can be reliable and valid. However, appraisal forms often fail to meet this standard. In addition, measurement of attributes is rarely linked to the organization's strategy. Furthermore, employees tend perhaps rightly to be defensive about receiving a mere numerical rating on some attribute. How would you feel if you were told you scored 2 on a 5-point scale of initiative or communication skill? The number might seem arbitrary, and it doesn't tell you how to improve.

Rating Behaviors

One way to overcome the drawbacks of rating attributes is to measure employees' behavior. To rate behaviors, the organization begins by defining which behaviors are associated with success on the job. Which kinds of employee behavior help the organization achieve its goals? The appraisal form asks the manager to rate an employee in terms of each of the identified behaviors.

One way to rate behaviors is with the **critical-incident method.** This approach requires managers to keep a record of specific examples of the employee acting in ways that are either effective or ineffective. Here's an example of a critical incident in the performance evaluation of an appliance repairperson:

> A customer called in about a refrigerator that was not cooling and was making a clicking noise every few minutes. The technician prediagnosed the cause of the problem and checked his truck for the necessary parts. When he found he did not have them, he checked the parts out from inventory so that the customer's refrigerator would be repaired on his first visit and the customer would be satisfied promptly.

critical-incident method
Method of performance measurement based on managers' records of specific examples of the employee acting in ways that are either effective or ineffective.

This incident provides evidence of the employee's knowledge of refrigerator repair and concern for efficiency and customer satisfaction. Evaluating performance in this specific way gives employees feedback about what they do well and what they do poorly. The manager can also relate the incidents to how the employee is helping the company achieve its goals. Keeping a daily or weekly log of critical incidents requires significant effort, however, and managers may resist this requirement. Also, critical incidents may be unique, so they may not support comparisons among employees.

Figure 8.5

Task-BARS Rating
Dimension: Patrol Officer

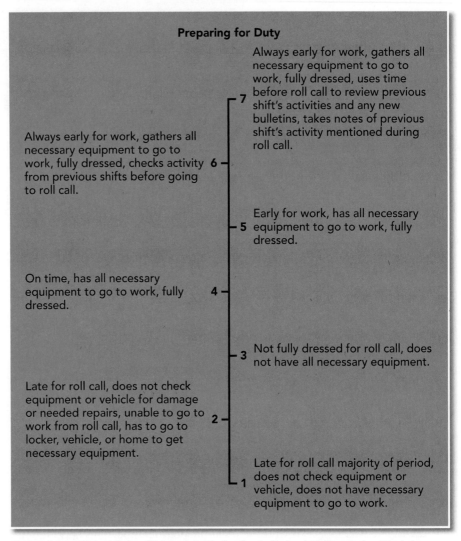

Preparing for Duty

Always early for work, gathers all necessary equipment to go to work, fully dressed, uses time before roll call to review previous shift's activities and any new bulletins, takes notes of previous shift's activity mentioned during roll call. — 7

Always early for work, gathers all necessary equipment to go to work, fully dressed, checks activity from previous shifts before going to roll call. — 6

Early for work, has all necessary equipment to go to work, fully dressed. — 5

On time, has all necessary equipment to go to work, fully dressed. — 4

Not fully dressed for roll call, does not have all necessary equipment. — 3

Late for roll call, does not check equipment or vehicle for damage or needed repairs, unable to go to work from roll call, has to go to locker, vehicle, or home to get necessary equipment. — 2

Late for roll call majority of period, does not check equipment or vehicle, does not have necessary equipment to go to work. — 1

SOURCE: Adapted from R. Harvey, "Job Analysis," in *Handbook of Industrial & Organizational Psychology,* 2nd ed., ed. M. Dunnette and L. Hough (Palo Alto, CA: Consulting Psychologists Press, 1991), p. 138.

behaviorally anchored rating scale (BARS)
Method of performance measurement that rates behavior in terms of a scale showing specific statements of behavior that describe different levels of performance.

A **behaviorally anchored rating scale (BARS)** builds on the critical-incidents approach. The BARS method is intended to define performance dimensions specifically, using statements of behavior that describe different levels of performance.[5] (The statements are "anchors" of the performance levels.) The scale in Figure 8.5 shows various performance levels for the behavior of "preparing for duty." The statement at the top (rating 7) describes the highest level of preparing for duty. The statement at the bottom describes behavior associated with poor performance. These statements are based on data about past performance. The organization gathers many critical incidents representing effective and ineffective performance, then classifies them from most to least effective. When experts about the job agree the statements clearly represent levels of performance, they are used as anchors to guide the rater. Although BARS can improve interrater reliability, this method can bias the manager's memory. The statements used as anchors can help managers remember similar behaviors, at the expense of other critical incidents.[6]

Figure 8.6

Example of a Behavioral Observation Scale

Overcoming Resistance to Change				
Directions: Rate the frequency of each behavior from 1 (Almost Never) to 5 (Almost Always).				
	Almost Never			Almost Always
1. Describes the details of the change to employees.	1	2	3	4	5
2. Explains why the change is necessary.	1	2	3	4	5
3. Discusses how the change will affect the employee.	1	2	3	4	5
4. Listens to the employee's concerns.	1	2	3	4	5
5. Asks the employee for help in making the change work.	1	2	3	4	5
6. If necessary, specifies the date for a follow-up meeting to respond to the employee's concerns.	1	2	3	4	5

Score: Total number of points = _____

Performance

Points	Performance Rating
6–10	Below adequate
11–15	Adequate
16–20	Full
21–25	Excellent
26–30	Superior

Scores are set by management.

A **behavioral observation scale (BOS)** is a variation of a BARS. Like a BARS, a BOS is developed from critical incidents.[7] However, while a BARS discards many examples in creating the rating scale, a BOS uses many of them to define all behaviors necessary for effective performance (or behaviors that signal ineffective performance). As a result, a BOS may use 15 behaviors to define levels of performance. Also, a BOS asks the manager to rate the frequency with which the employee has exhibited the behavior during the rating period. These ratings are averaged to compute an overall performance rating. Figure 8.6 provides a simplified example of a BOS for measuring the behavior "overcoming resistance to change."

A major drawback of this method is the amount of information required. A BOS can have 80 or more behaviors, and the manager must remember how often the employee exhibited each behavior in a 6- to 12-month rating period. This is taxing enough for one employee, but managers often must rate 10 or more employees. Even so, compared to BARS and graphic rating scales, managers and employees have said they prefer BOS for ease of use, providing feedback, maintaining objectivity, and suggesting training needs.[8]

Another approach to assessment builds directly on a branch of psychology called *behaviorism*, which holds that individuals' future behavior is determined by their past experiences—specifically, the ways in which past behaviors have been reinforced.

behavioral observation scale (BOS)
A variation of a BARS which uses all behaviors necessary for effective performance to rate performance at a task.

**organizational
behavior modification
(OBM)**
A plan for managing
the behavior of
employees through a
formal system of
feedback and
reinforcement.

People tend to repeat behaviors that have been rewarded in the past. Providing feedback and reinforcement can therefore modify individuals' future behavior. Applied to behavior in organizations, **organizational behavior modification (OBM)** is a plan for managing the behavior of employees through a formal system of feedback and reinforcement. Specific OBM techniques vary, but most have four components:[9]

1. Define a set of key behaviors necessary for job performance.
2. Use a measurement system to assess whether the employee exhibits the key behaviors.
3. Inform employees of the key behaviors, perhaps in terms of goals for how often to exhibit the behaviors.
4. Provide feedback and reinforcement based on employees' behavior.

OBM techniques have been used in a variety of settings. For example, a community mental health agency used OBM to increase the rates and timeliness of critical job behaviors by showing employees the connection between job behaviors and the agency's accomplishments.[10] This process identified job behaviors related to administration, record keeping, and service provided to clients. Feedback and reinforcement improved staff performance. OBM also increased the frequency of safety behaviors in a processing plant.[11]

Behavioral approaches such as organizational behavior modification and rating scales can be very effective. These methods can link the company's goals to the specific behavior required to achieve those goals. Behavioral methods also can generate specific feedback, along with guidance in areas requiring improvements. As a result, these methods tend to be valid. The people to be measured often help in developing the measures, so acceptance tends to be high as well. When raters are well trained, reliability also tends to be high. However, behavioral methods do not work as well for complex jobs in which it is difficult to see a link between behavior and results or there is more than one good way to achieve success.[12]

Measuring Results

Performance measurement can focus on managing the objective, measurable results of a job or work group. Results might include sales, costs, or productivity (output per worker or per dollar spent on production), among many possible measures. Two of the most popular methods for measuring results are measurement of productivity and management by objectives.

Productivity is an important measure of success, because getting more done with a smaller amount of resources (money or people) increases the company's profits. Productivity usually refers to the output of production workers, but it can be used more generally as a performance measure. To do this, the organization identifies the products—set of activities or objectives—it expects a group or individual to accomplish. At a repair shop, for instance, a product might be something like "quality of repair." The next step is to define how to measure production of these products. For quality of repair, the repair shop could track the percentage of items returned because they still do not work after a repair and the percentage of quality-control inspections passed. For each measure, the organization decides what level of performance is desired. Finally, the organization sets up a system for tracking these measures and giving employees feedback about their performance in terms of these measures. This type of performance measurement can be time-consuming to set up, but research suggests it can improve productivity.[13]

Table 8.2

Management by Objectives: Two Objectives for a Bank

KEY RESULT AREA	OBJECTIVE	% COMPLETE	ACTUAL PERFORMANCE
Loan portfolio management	Increase portfolio value by 10% over the next 12 months	90	Increased portfolio value by 9% over the past 12 months
Sales	Generate fee income of $30,000 over the next 12 months	150	Generated fee income of $45,000 over the past 12 months

Management by objectives (MBO) is a system in which people at each level of the organization set goals in a process that flows from top to bottom, so employees at all levels are contributing to the organization's overall goals. These goals become the standards for evaluating each employee's performance. An MBO system has three components:[14]

1. Goals are specific, difficult, and objective. The goals listed in the second column of Table 8.2 provide two examples for a bank.
2. Managers and their employees work together to set the goals.
3. The manager gives objective feedback through the rating period to monitor progress toward the goals. The two right-hand columns in Table 8.2 are examples of feedback given after one year.

MBO can have a very positive effect on an organization's performance. In 70 studies of MBO's performance, 68 showed that productivity improved.[15] The productivity gains tended to be greatest when top management was highly committed to MBO. Also, because staff members are involved in setting goals, it is likely that MBO systems effectively link individual employees' performance with the organization's overall goals.

In general, evaluation of results can be less subjective than other kinds of performance measurement. This makes measuring results highly acceptable to employees and managers alike. Results-oriented performance measurement is also relatively easy to link to the organization's goals. However, measuring results has problems with validity, because results may be affected by circumstances beyond each employee's performance. Also, if the organization measures only final results, it may fail to measure significant aspects of performance that are not directly related to those results. If individuals focus only on aspects of performance that are measured, they may neglect significant skills or behaviors. For example, if the organization measures only productivity, employees may not be concerned enough with customer service. The outcome may be high efficiency (costs are low) but low effectiveness (sales are low, too).[16] Finally, focusing strictly on results does not provide guidance on how to improve.

Total Quality Management

The principles of *total quality management*, introduced in Chapter 2, provide methods for performance measurement and management. Total quality management (TQM) differs from traditional performance measurement in that it assesses both individual performance and the system within which the individual works. This assessment is a process through which employees and their customers work together to set standards and measure performance, with the overall goal being to improve customer satisfaction. In this sense, an employee's customers may be inside or outside the organization;

management by objectives (MBO) A system in which people at each level of the organization set goals in a process that flows from top to bottom, so employees at all levels are contributing to the organization's overall goals; these goals become the standards for evaluating each employee's performance.

Coaches provide feedback to their team just as managers provide feedback to their employees. Feedback is important so that individuals know what they are doing well and what areas they may need to work on.

a "customer" is whoever uses the goods or services produced by the employee. The feedback aims at helping employees continuously improve the satisfaction of their customers. The focus on continuously improving customer satisfaction is intended to avoid the pitfall of rating individuals on outcomes, such as sales or profits, over which they do not have complete control.

With TQM, performance measurement essentially combines measurements of attributes and results. The feedback in TQM is of two kinds: (1) subjective feedback from managers, peers, and customers about the employee's personal qualities such as cooperation and initiative; and (2) objective feedback based on the work process. The second kind of feedback comes from a variety of methods called *statistical quality control*. These methods use charts to detail causes of problems, measures of performance, or relationships between work-related variables. Employees are responsible for tracking these measures to identify areas where they can avoid or correct problems. Because of the focus on systems, this feedback may result in changes to a work process, rather than assuming that a performance problem is the fault of an employee. The TQM system's focus has practical benefits, but it does not serve as well to support decisions about work assignments, training, or compensation.

LO5 Describe major sources of performance information in terms of their advantages and disadvantages.

Sources of Performance Information

All the methods of performance measurement require decisions about who will collect and analyze the performance information. To qualify for this task, a person should have an understanding of the job requirements and the opportunity to see the employee doing the job. The traditional approach is for managers to gather information about their employees' performance and arrive at performance ratings. However, many sources are possible. Possibilities of information sources include managers, peers, subordinates, self, and customers.

Using just one person as a source of information poses certain problems. People tend to like some people more than others, and those feelings can bias how an employee's efforts are perceived. Also, one person is likely to see an employee in a limited number of situations. A supervisor, for example, cannot see how an employee behaves when the supervisor is not watching—for example, when a service technician is at the customer's facility. To get as complete an assessment as possible, some organizations combine information from most or all of the possible sources, in what is called a **360-degree performance appraisal.**

Managers

The most-used source of performance information is the employee's manager. For example, Burlington Northern Santa Fe Corporation improved its performance management process by holding leaders accountable for setting annual goals, creating individual development plans, providing feedback and coaching to employees, and self-evaluation. An online performance management system supports the process. The company's executive team creates the overall company objectives, which cascade down to each department and employee, so each employee can see how he or she contributes to the company's success. Managers and employees can go online to see how they and the department are progressing on the objectives. This system encourages managers to give their employees the communication, feedback, and coaching they need.[17]

It is usually safe for organizations to assume that supervisors have extensive knowledge of the job requirements and that they have enough opportunity to observe their employees. In other words, managers possess the basic qualifications for this responsibility. Another advantage of using managers to evaluate performance is that they have an incentive to provide accurate and helpful feedback, because their own success depends so much on their employees' performance.[18] Finally, when managers try to observe employee behavior or discuss performance issues in the feedback session, their feedback can improve performance, and employees tend to perceive the appraisal as accurate.[19]

Still, in some situations, problems can occur with using supervisors as the source of performance information. For employees in some jobs, the supervisor does not have enough opportunity to observe the employee performing job duties. A sales manager with many outside salespeople cannot be with the salespeople on many visits to customers. Even if the sales manager does make a point of traveling with salespeople for a few days, they are likely to be on their best behavior while the manager is there. The manager cannot observe how they perform at other times.

360-degree performance appraisal Performance measurement that combines information from the employee's managers, peers, subordinates, self, and customers.

Performance management is critical for executing a talent management system and involves one-on-one contact with managers to ensure that proper training and development are taking place.

MEASURING EMPLOYEE NETWORKS

Asking employees, not how well they did, but with whom they worked generates another kind of performance data: the extent to which employees collaborate. In today's organizations, which are concerned with teamwork, this information helps managers assess which employees are playing a key role in sharing knowledge. To conduct this network analysis, the organization has each employee list the people he or she relies on most. Follow-up questions help the employee describe the extent to which these interpersonal contacts cross departmental lines and touch different levels of the hierarchy. A computer analyzes the results to create visual reports of the networks created by these interactions.

A lab manager at TRW used network analysis to learn about his employees' contributions. The manager noticed that a scientist who had been hired because of his expertise showed very few connections to others in the group. Another employee had less status but was at the center of a virtual web of links. The manager investigated and learned that the first scientist was unhelpful and impatient with others. The second went out of her way to help colleagues solve problems. As she developed her network, she was able to steer colleagues to those who knew the most on any given topic.

Sources: Mike Reid and Christian Gray, "Online Social Networks, Virtual Communities, Enterprises, and Information Professionals: Part 2, Stories," *Searcher*, October 2007, downloaded from General Reference Center Gold, http://find.galegroup.com; and Rob Cross and Sally Colella, "Building Vibrant Employee Networks," *HRMagazine*, December 2004, http://find.galegroup.com.

Peers

Another source of performance information is the employee's peers or co-workers. Peers are an excellent source of information about performance in a job where the supervisor does not often observe the employee. Examples include law enforcement and sales. For these and other jobs, peers may have the most opportunity to observe the employee in day-to-day activities. Peers have expert knowledge of job requirements. They also bring a different perspective to the evaluation and can provide extremely valid assessments of performance.[20]

Peer evaluations obviously have some potential disadvantages. Friendships (or rivalries) have the potential to bias ratings. Research, however, has provided little evidence that this is a problem.[21] Another disadvantage is that when the evaluations are done to support administrative decisions, peers are uncomfortable with rating employees for decisions that may affect themselves. Generally, peers are more favorable toward participating in reviews to be used for employee development.[22]

The "e-HRM" box shows how employee social networks can be a valuable source in evaluating teamwork, collaboration, and knowledge sharing.

Subordinates

For evaluating the performance of managers, subordinates are an especially valuable source of information. Subordinates—the people reporting to the manager—often have the best chance to see how well a manager treats employees. Dell, for example, asks employees to rate their manager in terms of measures such as whether the employee receives ongoing performance feedback and whether the supervisor "is effective at managing people."[23]

Subordinate evaluations have some potential problems because of the power relationships involved. Subordinates are reluctant to say negative things about the person to whom they report; they prefer to provide feedback anonymously. Managers, however, have a more positive reaction to this type of feedback when the subordinates are identified. When feedback forms require that the subordinates identify themselves, they tend to give the manager higher ratings.[24] Another problem is that when managers receive ratings from their subordinates, the employees have more power, so managers tend to emphasize employee satisfaction, even at the expense of productivity. This issue arises primarily when the evaluations are used for administrative decisions. Therefore, as with peer evaluations, subordinate evaluations are most appropriate for developmental purposes. To protect employees, the process should be anonymous and use at least three employees to rate each manager.

Self

No one has a greater chance to observe the employee's behavior on the job than does the employee himself or herself. Self-ratings are rarely used alone, but they can contribute valuable information. A common approach is to have employees evaluate their own performance before the feedback session. This activity gets employees thinking about their performance. Areas of disagreement between the self-appraisal and other evaluations can be fruitful topics for the feedback session.

The obvious problem with self-ratings is that individuals have a tendency to inflate assessments of their performance. Especially if the ratings will be used for administrative decisions, exaggerating one's contributions has practical benefits. Also, social psychologists have found that, in general, people tend to blame outside circumstances for their failures while taking a large part of the credit for their successes. Supervisors can soften this tendency by providing frequent feedback, but because people tend to perceive situations this way, self-appraisals are not appropriate as the basis for administrative decisions.[25]

Customers

Services are often produced and consumed on the spot, so the customer is often the only person who directly observes the service performance and may be the best source of performance information. Many companies in service industries have introduced customer evaluations of employee performance. Marriott Corporation provides a customer satisfaction card in every room and mails surveys to a random sample of its hotel customers. Whirlpool's Consumer Services Division conducts mail and telephone surveys of customers after factory technicians have serviced their appliances. These surveys allow the company to evaluate an individual technician's customer-service behaviors while in the customer's home.

Using customer evaluations of employee performance is appropriate in two situations.[26] The first is when an employee's job requires direct service to the customer or linking the customer to other services within the organization. Second, customer evaluations are appropriate when the organization is interested in gathering information to determine what products and services the customer wants. That is, customer evaluations contribute to the organization's goals by enabling HRM to support the organization's marketing activities. In this regard, customer evaluations are useful both for evaluating an employee's performance and for helping to determine whether the organization can improve customer service by making changes in HRM activities such as training or compensation.

The weakness of customer surveys for performance measurement is their expense. The expenses of a traditional survey can add up to hundreds of dollars to evaluate one individual. Many organizations therefore limit the information gathering to short periods once a year.

Errors in Performance Measurement

LO6 Define types of rating errors, and explain how to minimize them.

As we noted in the previous section, one reason for gathering information from several sources is that performance measurements are not completely objective, and errors can occur. People observe behavior, and they have no practical way of knowing all the circumstances, intentions, and outcomes related to that behavior, so they interpret what they see. In doing so, observers make a number of judgment calls, and in some situations may even distort information on purpose. Therefore, fairness in rating performance and interpreting performance appraisals requires that managers understand the kinds of distortions that commonly occur.

Types of Rating Errors

Several kinds of errors and biases commonly influence performance measurements:

- People often tend to give a higher evaluation to people they consider similar to themselves. Most of us think of ourselves as effective, so if others are like us, they must be effective, too. Research has demonstrated that this effect is strong. Unfortunately, it is sometimes wrong, and when similarity is based on characteristics such as race or sex, the decisions may be discriminatory.[27]
- If the rater compares an individual, not against an objective standard, but against other employees, *contrast errors* occur. A competent performer who works with exceptional people may be rated lower than competent, simply because of the contrast.
- Raters make *distributional errors* when they tend to use only one part of a rating scale. The error is called *leniency* when the reviewer rates everyone near the top, *strictness* when the rater favors lower rankings, and *central tendency* when the rater puts everyone near the middle of the scale. Distributional errors make it difficult to compare employees rated by the same person. Also, if different raters make different kinds of distributional errors, scores by these raters cannot be compared.
- Raters often let their opinion of one quality color their opinion of others. For example, someone who speaks well might be seen as helpful or talented in other areas, simply because of the overall good impression created by this one quality. Or someone who is occasionally tardy might be seen as lacking in motivation. When the bias is in a favorable direction, this is called the *halo error*. When it involves negative ratings, it is called the *horns error*. Halo error can mistakenly tell employees they don't need to improve in any area, while horns error can cause employees to feel frustrated and defensive.

Ways to Reduce Errors

Usually people make these errors unintentionally, especially when the criteria for measuring performance are not very specific. Training can reduce rating errors.[28] Raters can be trained how to avoid rating errors.[29] Prospective raters watch videos whose scripts or storylines are designed to lead them to make specific rating errors. After rating the fictional employees in the videos, raters discuss their rating decisions and how such errors affected their rating decisions. Training programs offer tips for avoiding the errors in the future.

Another training method for raters focuses on the complex nature of employee performance.[30] Raters learn to look at many aspects of performance that deserve their attention. Actual examples of performance are studied to bring out various performance dimensions and the standards for those dimensions. This training aims to help raters evaluate employees' performance more thoroughly and accurately.

Political Behavior in Performance Appraisals

Unintentional errors are not the only cause of inaccurate performance measurement. Sometimes the people rating performance distort an evaluation on purpose to advance their personal goals. This kind of appraisal politics is unhealthy especially because the resulting feedback does not focus on helping employees contribute to the organization's goals. High-performing employees who are rated unfairly will become frustrated, and low-performing employees who are overrated will be rewarded rather than encouraged to improve. Therefore, organizations try to identify and discourage appraisal politics.

Several characteristics of appraisal systems and company culture tend to encourage appraisal politics. Appraisal politics are most likely to occur when raters are accountable to the employee being rated, the goals of rating are not compatible with one another, performance appraisal is directly linked to highly desirable rewards, top executives tolerate or ignore distorted ratings, and senior employees tell newcomers company "folklore" that includes stories about distorted ratings.

Political behavior occurs in every organization. Organizations can minimize appraisal politics by establishing an appraisal system that is fair. Some ways to promote fairness are to involve managers and employees in developing the system, use consistent standards for evaluating different employees, require that feedback be timely and complete, allow employees to challenge their evaluation, and communicate expectations about performance standards, evaluations, and rewards.[31] The organization can also help managers give accurate and fair appraisals by training them to use the appraisal process, encouraging them to recognize accomplishments that the employees themselves have not identified, and fostering a climate of openness in which employees feel they can be honest about their weaknesses.[32]

Giving Performance Feedback

Once the manager and others have measured an employee's performance, this information must be given to the employee. Only after the employee has received feedback can he or she begin to plan how to correct any shortcomings. Although the feedback stage of performance management is essential, it is uncomfortable to managers and employees. Delivering feedback feels to the manager as if he or she is standing in judgment of others—a role few people enjoy. Receiving criticism feels even worse. Fortunately, managers can do much to smooth the feedback process and make it effective.

LO7 Explain how to provide performance feedback effectively.

Scheduling Performance Feedback

Performance feedback should be a regular, expected management activity. The custom or policy at many organizations is to give formal performance feedback once a year. But annual feedback is not enough. One reason is that managers are responsible for correcting performance deficiencies as soon as they occur. If the manager notices a problem with an employee's behavior in June, but the annual appraisal is scheduled for November, the employee will miss months of opportunities for improvement.

When giving performance feedback, do it in an appropriate meeting place. Meet in a setting that is neutral and free of distractions. What other factors are important for a feedback session?

Another reason for frequent performance feedback is that feedback is most effective when the information does not surprise the employee. If an employee has to wait for up to a year to learn what the manager thinks of his work, the employee will wonder whether he is meeting expectations. Employees should instead receive feedback so often that they know what the manager will say during their annual performance review.

Preparing for a Feedback Session

Managers should be well prepared for each formal feedback session. The manager should create the right context for the meeting. The location should be neutral. If the manager's office is the site of unpleasant conversations, a conference room may be more appropriate. In announcing the meeting to an employee, the manager should describe it as a chance to discuss the role of the employee, the role of the manager, and the relationship between them. Managers should also say (and believe) that they would like the meeting to be an open dialogue.

Managers should also enable the employee to be well prepared. The manager should ask the employee to complete a self-assessment ahead of time. The self-assessment requires employees to think about their performance over the past rating period and to be aware of their strengths and weaknesses, so they can participate more fully in the discussion. Even though employees may tend to overstate their accomplishments, the self-assessment can help the manager and employee identify areas for discussion. When the purpose of the assessment is to define areas for development, employees may actually understate their performance. Also, differences between the manager's and the employee's rating may be fruitful areas for discussion. As discussed in the "HR How To" box, the content of the feedback session and the type of language used can determine the success of this meeting.

Conducting the Feedback Session

During the feedback session, managers can take any of three approaches. In the "tell-and-sell" approach, managers tell the employees their ratings and then justify those ratings. In the "tell-and-listen" approach, managers tell employees their ratings and then let the employees explain their side of the story. In the "problem-solving" approach, managers and employees work together to solve performance problems in an atmosphere of respect and encouragement. Not surprisingly, research demonstrates that the problem-solving approach is superior. Perhaps surprisingly, most managers rely on the tell-and-sell approach.[33] Managers can improve employee satisfaction with the feedback process by letting employees voice their opinions and discuss performance goals.[34]

The content of the feedback should emphasize behavior, not personalities. For example, "You did not meet the deadline" can open a conversation about what needs

HR How To

Employees and managers often dread feedback sessions, because criticism feels uncomfortable. To smooth the way, managers should deliver a balance of praise and criticism that accurately reflects how well the employee has performed. In general, the most effective criticism is brief and focused on problem solving—if the manager needs to criticize, that part of the discussion should include ideas for improvement. The manager also should be prepared to discuss how the organization can support improvement and provide necessary resources, perhaps additional training or clearer directions. Another way to remove some of the sting from criticism is to discuss it in the context of the organization's commitment to continuous improvement—if it is, in fact, committed to that goal.

Managers should avoid vague language like "OK" or "satisfactory." Instead, they should talk about specific behaviors. Also, the employee should know the specific standards or objectives he or she is expected to meet; this makes it easier to describe the employee's performance in meaningful ways by referring to the standards.

Don't wait until the performance appraisal to let employees know how they are doing. Managers should give frequent, brief feedback about specific situations as they occur. When a manager later recalls these situations during the feedback session, the employee won't be surprised. Instead, the employee will already know that those performance areas are important, and the appraisal can focus more time on how the employee can improve, what the manager can do to help, and which short-term and long-term goals are most important for development and career advancement.

Finally, when new employees come on board, managers can ask them about their desire for feedback. They can ask whether the new employees would like to hear from the manager when they are falling short of expectations and when they are performing well. Employees desire this type of information. Putting that desire into words provides a foundation for later feedback discussions. During the feedback session, the manager can acknowledge that criticism or even praise might feel uncomfortable, but that the manager is simply providing the information that the employee previously agreed is important. This acknowledgment may not make feedback easy to receive, but it reminds the manager and employee that feedback is simply meant to be useful—and important—information.

Sources: David K. Lindo, "Can You Answer Their Questions?" *Supervision,* January 2007, downloaded from General Reference Center Gold, http://find.galegroup.com; Michael H. Smith, "Performance Review Anxiety," *Recorder,* April 18, 2007, http://find.galegroup.com; and Kerry Sulkowicz, "Straight Talk at Review Time," *BusinessWeek,* September 10, 2007, http://find.galegroup.com.

to change, but "You're not motivated" may make the employee feel defensive and angry. The feedback session should end with goal setting and a decision about when to follow up.

Finding Solutions to Performance Problems

When performance evaluation indicates that an employee's performance is below standard, the feedback process should launch an effort to correct the problem. Even when the employee is meeting current standards, the feedback session may identify areas in which the employee can improve in order to contribute more to the organization in a current or future job. In sum, the final, feedback stage of performance management involves identifying areas for improvement and ways to improve performance in those areas.

As shown in Figure 8.7, the most effective way to improve performance varies according to the employee's ability and motivation. In general, when employees have

LO8 Summarize ways to produce improvement in unsatisfactory performance.

Figure 8.7

Improving Performance

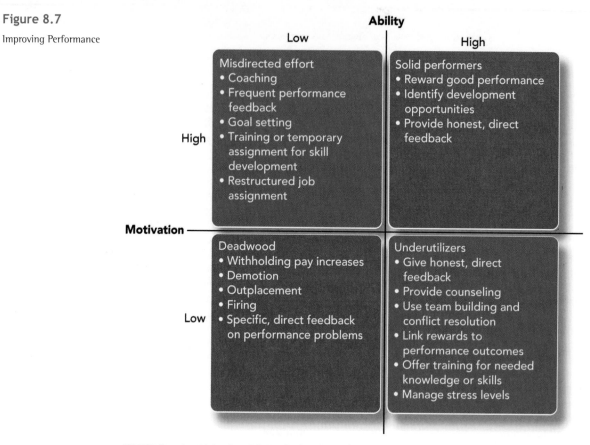

SOURCE: Based on M. London, *Job Feedback* (Mahwah, NJ: Lawrence Erlbaum Associates, 1997), pp. 96–97. Used by permission.

high levels of ability and motivation, they perform at or above standards. But when they lack ability, motivation, or both, corrective action is needed. The type of action called for depends on what the employee lacks:

- *Lack of ability*—When a motivated employee lacks knowledge, skills, or abilities in some area, the manager may offer coaching, training, and more detailed feedback. Sometimes it is appropriate to restructure the job so the employee can handle it.
- *Lack of motivation*—Managers with an unmotivated employee can explore ways to demonstrate that the employee is being treated fairly and rewarded adequately. The solution may be as simple as more positive feedback (praise). Employees may need a referral for counseling or help with stress management.
- *Lack of both*—Performance may improve if the manager directs the employee's attention to the significance of the problem by withholding rewards or providing specific feedback. If the employee does not respond, the manager may have to demote or terminate the employee.

The "HR Oops!" Box asks for your opinion on the impact of rewarding poorly performing managers.

As a rule, employees who combine high ability with high motivation are solid performers. As Figure 8.7 indicates, managers should by no means ignore these employees

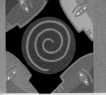

HR Oops!

Rewarding Poor Performance

When the problem performer is somebody's boss, what should an organization do? Poor leaders not only fail to accomplish their own goals but also can demoralize everyone who reports to them. Respondents to an informal online poll complained that as a result of having a difficult boss, they were experiencing nightmares, exhaustion, depression, and other problems. So how did the respondents' organizations manage this performance problem? Surprisingly, the majority said their manager was rewarded. Over 60 percent of the respondents said their employer either failed to intervene or actually gave the boss a promotion.

Perhaps management in these situations did see that the boss was not leading the group effectively. Decision makers may have preferred to move the boss out of the way—even if that move involved a promotion.

Sources: Rachel Breitman, "Bad Bosses Get Promoted, Not Punished?" *Yahoo News,* August 3, 2007, http://news.yahoo.com; and Anthony Erickson, James B. Shaw, and Zha Agabe, "An Empirical Investigation of the Antecedents, Behaviors, and Outcomes of Bad Leadership," *Journal of Leadership Studies* 1, no. 3 (November 2007), pp. 26–43, abstract at http://www3.interscience.wiley.com.

Questions

1. Why do you think an organization might promote someone who manages ineffectively? What are the consequences?

2. How can an organization better manage this type of performance problem?

on the grounds of leaving well enough alone. Rather, such employees are likely to appreciate opportunities for further development. Rewards and direct feedback help to maintain these employees' high motivation levels.

Legal and Ethical Issues in Performance Management

LO9 Discuss legal and ethical issues that affect performance management.

In developing and using performance management systems, human resource professionals need to ensure that these systems meet legal requirements, such as the avoidance of discrimination. In addition, performance management systems should meet ethical standards, such as protection of employees' privacy.

Legal Requirements for Performance Management

Because performance measures play a central role in decisions about pay, promotions, and discipline, employment-related lawsuits often challenge an organization's performance management system. Lawsuits related to performance management usually involve charges of discrimination or unjust dismissal.

Discrimination claims often allege that the performance management system discriminated against employees on the basis of their race or sex. Many performance measures are subjective, and measurement errors, such as those described earlier in the chapter, can easily occur. The Supreme Court has held that the selection guidelines in the federal government's *Uniform Guidelines on Employee Selection Procedures* also apply to performance measurement.[35] In general, these guidelines (discussed in Chapters 3 and 6) require that organizations avoid using criteria such as race and age as a basis for employment decisions. This requires overcoming widespread rating errors. A substantial body of evidence has shown that white and black raters tend to give higher ratings to members of their own racial group, even after rater training.[36] In addition, evidence suggests that this tendency is strongest when one group is only a small percentage of the total work group. When the vast majority of the group is male, females receive lower ratings; when the minority is male, males receive lower ratings.[37]

With regard to lawsuits filed on the grounds of unjust dismissal, the usual claim is that the person was dismissed for reasons besides the ones that the employer states. Suppose an employee who works for a defense contractor discloses that the company defrauded the government. If the company fires the employee, the employee might argue that the firing was a way to punish the employee for blowing the whistle. In this type of situation, courts generally focus on the employer's performance management system, looking to see whether the firing could have been based on poor performance. To defend itself, the employer would need a performance management system that provides evidence to support its employment decisions.

To protect against both kinds of lawsuits, it is important to have a legally defensible performance management system.[38] Such a system would be based on valid job analyses, as described in Chapter 4, with the requirements for job success clearly communicated to employees. Performance measurement should evaluate behaviors or results, rather than traits. The organization should use multiple raters (including self-appraisals) and train raters in how to use the system. The organization should provide for a review of all performance ratings by upper-level managers and set up a system for employees to appeal when they believe they were evaluated unfairly. Along with feedback, the system should include a process for coaching or training employees to help them improve, rather than simply dismissing poor performers.

Electronic Monitoring and Employee Privacy

Computer technology now supports many performance management systems. Organizations often store records of employees' performance ratings, disciplinary actions, and work-rule violations in electronic databases. Many companies use computers to monitor productivity and other performance measures electronically. Illiana Financial Credit Union in Calumet City, Illinois, uses a fingerprint recognition system to track when its tellers and loan officers arrive and leave. The system prevents employees from exaggerating the hours they work. Automated Waste Disposal, based in Danbury, Connecticut, installed global positioning system (GPS) devices in its garbage trucks and sales vehicles. The location information management receives discourages the drivers from wasting time by idling or getting "lost."[39]

Although electronic monitoring can improve productivity, it also generates privacy concerns. Critics point out that an employer should not monitor employees when it has no reason to believe anything is wrong. They complain that monitoring systems threaten to make the workplace an electronic sweatshop in which employees are treated as robots, robbing them of dignity. Some note that employees' performance should be measured by accomplishments, not just time spent at a desk or workbench. Electronic systems should not be a substitute for careful management. When monitoring is necessary, managers should communicate the reasons for using it. Monitoring may be used more positively to gather information for coaching employees and helping them develop their skills. Finally, organizations must protect the privacy of performance measurements, as they must do with other employee records.

THINKING ETHICALLY

DO FINANCIAL GOALS GET MANAGERS IN TROUBLE?

The owners of a corporation naturally expect the company's managers and employees to work to increase the company's value (often expressed in terms of its stock price). Other basic financial goals for a business are to increase profits through greater sales or lower costs. But can a company's people focus on those goals too much?

In some situations, employees complain that pressure to meet difficult short-term targets causes them to make choices that are less than ideal for the long-term—and are sometimes unethical. Consider what recently happened at Dell. An investigation by the company's audit committee found evidence of accounting adjustments over several years that appeared to be designed to show that the company had met its quarterly financial goals. These adjustments, which usually were made near the end of a quarter, shifted the timing of when income or expenses were recognized, appearing to make the company's performance better than it was. Some of the changes were approved or requested by senior executives at Dell. The audit committee also found situations where the employees of business units gave auditors information that was incomplete or incorrect. The Securities and Exchange Commission launched an investigation to determine whether some of these actions violated the law, and Dell announced that it would be adjusting the financial statements to correct misinformation. The company's top management also promised to introduce controls that would prevent such manipulation of data in the future.

Source: "Dell to Restate Earnings, Reveals Accounting Troubles" *Information Week*, August 16, 2007, downloaded from General Reference Center Gold, http://find.galegroup.com.

Questions

1. Who benefits when a company's employees are focused on making the company more profitable?
2. Do goals related to short-term profits—for this month or this quarter—ever conflict with longer-term goals? Explain. Do these goals conflict with ethical standards? Explain.
3. Imagine that you are an HR manager at Dell. How can you help the company avoid similar ethical and legal problems in the future?

SUMMARY

LO1 Identify the activities involved in performance management.

Performance management is the process through which managers ensure that employees' activities and outputs contribute to the organization's goals. The organization begins by specifying which aspects of performance are relevant to the organization. Next, the organization measures the relevant aspects of performance through performance appraisal. Finally, in performance feedback sessions, managers provide employees with information about their performance so they can adjust their behavior to meet the organization's goals. Feedback includes efforts to identify and solve problems.

LO2 Discuss the purposes of performance management systems.

Organizations establish performance management systems to meet three broad purposes. Effective performance management helps the organization with strategic purposes, that is, meeting business objectives. It does this by helping to link employees' behavior with the organization's goals. The administrative purpose of performance management is to provide information for day-to-day decisions about salary, benefits, recognition, and retention or termination. The developmental purpose of performance management is using the system as a basis for developing employees' knowledge and skills.

LO3 Define five criteria for measuring the effectiveness of a performance management system.

Performance measures should fit with the organization's strategy by supporting its goals and culture. Performance measures should be valid, so they measure all the relevant aspects of performance and do not measure irrelevant aspects of performance. These measures should also provide interrater and test-retest reliability, so that appraisals are consistent among raters and over time. Performance measurement systems should be acceptable to the people who use them or receive feedback from them. Finally, a performance measure should specifically tell employees what is expected of them and how they can meet those expectations.

LO4   Compare the major methods for measuring performance.

Performance measurement may use ranking systems such as simple ranking, forced distribution, or paired comparisons to compare one individual's performance with that of other employees. These methods may be time-consuming, and they will be seen as unfair if actual performance is not distributed in the same way as the ranking system requires. However, ranking counteracts some forms of rater bias and helps distinguish employees for administrative decisions. Other approaches involve rating employees' attributes, behaviors, or outcomes. Rating attributes is relatively simple but not always valid, unless attributes are specifically defined. Rating behaviors requires a great deal of information, but these methods can be very effective. They can link behaviors to goals, and ratings by trained raters may be highly reliable. Rating results, such as productivity or achievement of objectives, tends to be less subjective than other kinds of rating, making this approach highly acceptable. Validity may be a problem because of factors outside the employee's control. This method also tends not to provide much basis for determining how to improve. Focusing on quality can provide practical benefits but is not as useful for administrative and developmental decisions.

LO5   Describe major sources of performance information in terms of their advantages and disadvantages.

Performance information may come from an employee's self-appraisal and from appraisals by the employee's supervisor, employees, peers, and customers. Using only one source makes the appraisal more subjective. Organizations may combine many sources into a 360-degree performance appraisal. Gathering information from each employee's manager may produce accurate information, unless the supervisor has little opportunity to observe the employee. Peers are an excellent source of information about performance in a job where the supervisor does not often observe the employee. Disadvantages are that friendships (or rivalries) may bias ratings and peers may be uncomfortable with the role of rating a friend. Subordinates often have the best chance to see how a manager treats employees. Employees may be reluctant to contribute honest opinions about a supervisor unless they can provide information anonymously. Self-appraisals may be biased, but they do come from the person with the most knowledge of the employee's behavior on the job, and they provide a basis for discussion in feedback sessions, opening up fruitful comparisons and areas of disagreement between the self-appraisal and other appraisals. Customers may be an excellent source of performance information, although obtaining customer feedback tends to be expensive.

LO6   Define types of rating errors, and explain how to minimize them.

People observe behavior often without a practical way of knowing all the relevant circumstances and outcomes, so they necessarily interpret what they see. A common tendency is to give higher evaluations to people we consider similar to ourselves. Other errors involve using only part of the rating scale: Giving all employees ratings at the high end of the scale is called leniency error. Rating everyone at the low end of the scale is called strictness error. Rating all employees at or near the middle is called central tendency. The halo error refers to rating employees positively in all areas because of strong performance observed in one area. The horns error is rating employees negatively in all areas because of weak performance observed in one area. Ways to reduce rater error are training raters to be aware of their tendencies to make rating errors and training them to be sensitive to the complex nature of employee performance so they will consider many aspects of performance in greater depth. Politics also may influence ratings. Organizations can minimize appraisal politics by establishing a fair appraisal system, involving managers and employees in developing the system, allowing employees to challenge evaluations, communicating expectations, and fostering a climate of open discussion.

LO7   Explain how to provide performance feedback effectively.

Performance feedback should be a regular, scheduled management activity, so that employees can correct problems as soon as they occur. Managers should prepare by establishing a neutral location, emphasizing that the feedback session will be a chance for discussion and asking the employee to prepare a self-assessment. During the feedback session, managers should strive for a problem-solving approach and encourage employees to voice their opinions and discuss performance goals. The manager should look for opportunities to praise and should limit criticism. The discussion should focus on behavior and results rather than on personalities.

LO8   Summarize ways to produce improvement in unsatisfactory performance.

For an employee who is motivated but lacks ability, the manager should provide coaching and training, give detailed feedback about performance, and consider restructuring the job. For an employee who has ability but lacks motivation, the manager should investigate whether outside problems are a distraction and if so, refer the employee for help. If the problem has to do with the employee's not feeling appreciated or rewarded, the manager should try to deliver more praise and evaluate whether additional pay and other rewards are appropriate. For an employee lacking both ability and motivation, the manager should consider whether the employee is a good fit for the position. Specific feedback or withholding rewards may spur improvement, or the employee may have to be demoted or terminated. Solid employees who are high in ability and motivation will continue so and may be able to contribute even more if the manager provides appropriate direct feedback, rewards, and opportunities for development.

LO9 Discuss legal and ethical issues that affect performance management.

Lawsuits related to performance management usually involve charges of discrimination or unjust dismissal. Managers must make sure that performance management systems and decisions treat employees equally, without regard to their race, sex, or other protected status. Organizations can do this by establishing and using valid performance measures and by training raters to evaluate performance accurately. A system is more likely to be legally defensible if it is based on behaviors and results, rather than on traits, and if multiple raters evaluate each person's performance. The system should include a process for coaching or training employees to help them improve, rather than simply dismissing poor performers. An ethical issue of performance management is the use of electronic monitoring. This type of performance measurement provides detailed, accurate information, but employees may find it demoralizing, degrading, and stressful. They are more likely to accept it if the organization explains its purpose, links it to help in improving performance, and keeps the performance data private.

KEY TERMS

360-degree performance appraisal, p. 229
behavioral observation scale (BOS), p. 225
behaviorally anchored rating scale (BARS), p. 224

critical-incident method, p. 223
forced-distribution method, p. 220
graphic rating scale, p. 221
management by objectives (MBO), p. 227
mixed-standard scales, p. 222

organizational behavior modification (OBM), p. 226
paired-comparison method, p. 220
performance management, p. 215
simple ranking, p. 219

REVIEW AND DISCUSSION QUESTIONS

1. How does a complete performance management system differ from the use of annual performance appraisals?
2. Give two examples of an administrative decision that would be based on performance management information. Give two examples of developmental decisions based on this type of information.
3. How can involving employees in the creation of performance standards improve the effectiveness of a performance management system? (Consider the criteria for effectiveness listed in the chapter.)
4. Consider how you might rate the performance of three instructors from whom you are currently taking a course. (If you are currently taking only one or two courses, consider this course and two you recently completed.)
   a. Would it be harder to *rate* the instructors' performance or to *rank* their performance? Why?
   b. Write three items to use in rating the instructors—one each to rate them in terms of an attribute, a behavior, and an outcome.

c. Which measure in (*b*) do you think is most valid? Most reliable? Why?
d. Many colleges use questionnaires to gather data from students about their instructors' performance. Would it be appropriate to use the data for administrative decisions? Developmental decisions? Other decisions? Why or why not?
5. Imagine that a pet supply store is establishing a new performance management system to help employees provide better customer service. Management needs to decide who should participate in measuring the performance of each of the store's salespeople. From what sources should the store gather information? Why?
6. Would the same sources be appropriate if the store in Question 5 used the performance appraisals to support decisions about which employees to promote? Explain.
7. Suppose you were recently promoted to a supervisory job in a company where you have worked for two

years. You genuinely like almost all your co-workers, who now report to you. The only exception is one employee, who dresses more formally than the others and frequently tells jokes that embarrass you and the other workers. Given your preexisting feelings for the employees, how can you measure their performance fairly and effectively?

8. Continuing the example in Question 7, imagine that you are preparing for your first performance feedback session. You want the feedback to be effective—that is, you want the feedback to result in improved performance. List five or six steps you can take to achieve your goal.

9. Besides giving employees feedback, what steps can a manager take to improve employees' performance?

10. Suppose you are a human resource professional helping to improve the performance management system of a company that sells and services office equipment. The company operates a call center that takes calls from customers who are having problems with their equipment. Call center employees are supposed to

verify that the problem is not one the customer can easily handle (for example, equipment that will not operate because it has come unplugged). Then, if the problem is not resolved over the phone, the employees arrange for service technicians to visit the customer. The company can charge the customer only if a service technician visits, so performance management of the call center employees focuses on productivity—how quickly they can complete a call and move on to the next caller. To measure this performance efficiently and accurately, the company uses electronic monitoring.

a. How would you expect the employees to react to the electronic monitoring? How might the organization address the employees' concerns?

b. Besides productivity in terms of number of calls, what other performance measures should the performance management system include?

c. How should the organization gather information about the other performance measures?

BUSINESSWEEK CASE

BusinessWeek   ## The Employee is Always Right

Vineet Nayar, CEO of Indian outsourcer HCL Technologies, needs to work on his time management skills. Last year, his team rated him 3.6 out of 5 for how well he keeps projects running on schedule. That was among Nayar's lowest scores from the 81 managers who rated him, and everybody at HCL knows it.

Nayar's grades, along with ratings for the top 20 managers at HCL, are published on the company's intranet for anyone who wants to see them. Employees also have the capability to see their own supervisors' scores. While many companies have "360-degree reviews," HCL may be the only one in the world that broadcasts the results throughout the organization. That has created no shortage of workplace angst. "There was this whole picture of me that [emerged] as a heavy taskmaster," says R. Srikrishna, who runs HCL's U.S. infrastructure services division, of his early results. "It was very unsettling the first time."

The public grading of managers is just one of several unconventional steps HCL has taken over the past two years to build a more democratic workplace. While plenty of CEOs utter bromides about "servant leadership" and say their most important job is supporting employees, Nayar is more willing than most to back up his words with actions. In fast-growing India, the challenge of attracting and retaining workers has prompted a pile-on of perks, from fattened paychecks to corporate campuses decked out with multiplexes and bowling alleys. Because HCL Technologies, the fifth-largest of India's info-tech outsourcers,

arrived late to the software services game, it has had to work even harder to build cachet among recruits. And its growth plans are staggering: In the next year, HCL expects to add about 10,000 more employees to its workforce of 45,600.

So far, Nayar's methods appear to be having an impact. HCL's once-troubling attrition rate, which at 20.4 percent was among the highest in the industry when Nayar took over as president in 2005, has dropped three quarters in a row, to 17.2 percent (though it is still higher than that of many rivals). The progress is no small achievement in a country where young engineers, as marketing manager Krishnan Chatterjee puts it, can be like "coin-operated machines," disregarding corporate culture and jumping ship wherever there's more pay.

In addition to the shared 360 ratings, Nayar has other tools that force the company to respond quickly to employee concerns. On HCL's intranet, Nayar publicly posts responses to every question left by HCLites, as they call themselves. He spends about seven hours answering the 50 or so questions he gets each week, often on Sunday mornings at home. HCL has developed a one-stop online "smart service desk," where workers file complaints about any issue, whether it's the freezing air conditioning or the size of their bonus.

Even though HCL employees were the primary beneficiaries of Nayar's innovations, some were initially skeptical. "People did not really believe that this program would make a difference," says 27-year-old Anisha Khanna. Just 10 percent of the engineers in her department showed up at Nayar's early speeches. Others worried how it would look if they got negative ratings by their underlings. (All employees who take the time to rate managers above them can get access to their scores.) But workers learned to trust the system, in large part because Nayar makes it clear the feedback isn't used to determine bonuses or promotions. Enough employees have gotten comfortable with the public feedback that HCL expanded it for 2007. Now workers can see results not only of their managers but also of peers they rate.

Source: Excerpted from Jena McGregor, "The Employee Is Always Right," *BusinessWeek*, November 19, 2007, downloaded from General Reference Center Gold, http://find.galegroup.com.

Questions

1. Based on the information given, discuss how well HCL's performance management system addresses the strategic, administrative, and developmental purposes of performance management.
2. The reviews described in this case are ratings. What are the strengths and weaknesses of this method? What other methods, besides ratings, would you recommend for HCL to use for evaluating performance?
3. What are some risks of posting the rating results on HCL's intranet, where they are accessible to employees? How would you recommend that the company address these risks?

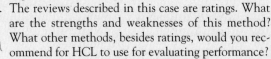

CASE: A PERFORMANCE MANAGEMENT OVERHAUL FOR WAYNE FARMS

Wayne Farms, headquartered in Oakwood, Georgia, describes itself as the "fourth largest vertically integrated poultry processor in the United States." "Vertically integrated" means it handles all the work of bringing chicken to its customers—from raising chickens, to processing nearly 2 billion pounds of their meat in its 13 facilities, to selling raw and cooked chicken to restaurant chains and food manufacturers such as Campbell Soup Company and Jack in the Box. The effort requires expertise in a variety of fields, including agriculture, veterinary science, engineering, sales, and accounting, as well as many meat-processing jobs.

Competition for cost-conscious poultry buyers is stiff. Wayne Farms' strategy is to stand out through innovation. Wayne's president, Elton Maddox, describes innovation as "a way of life" for the privately held company. Innovation is obvious in areas such as new-product development and processing plants designed with food safety in mind. But behind the scenes, innovation has also reshaped the company's performance management system.

A few years ago, when David Malfitano was hired as vice president of human resources, he reviewed how performance management was being done at Wayne Farms. He discovered a system in which employees were supposed to be rated annually on a 5-point scale. Oddly, he found that one out of five employees was being rated 2, and all the rest were rated 3. Could it be that no one in the company was doing more than meeting expectations? Was no one doing excellent work—or poor work? Such questions were difficult to answer, because each employee's review was done on his or her hiring anniversary, so the company had no snapshot of overall performance on any one date.

Malfitano started by focusing on a system that would give the company "a real picture of performance." He required all managers to deliver performance appraisals of their employees at the beginning of the company's fiscal year. Then he followed up to be sure he had a complete response.

Malfitano considered addressing the unusual pattern of ratings by establishing a forced distribution. But based on his experience with a previous company, he doubted that the method would be effective. Instead, he applied a method similar to compensation decisions. Before the company grants raises, managers must identify which employees are in the top 20 percent of their group and which are in the bottom 10 percent. With pressure to keep costs down, only top-scoring employees receive raises, but those raises are as large as 8 percent.

Changing the way managers think about employee ratings is difficult. Malfitano meets with each manager to review the ratings they assign and to coach them on how to talk with employees about their appraisal results. So far, only a few employee ratings have shifted to a 1 or 4, but Malfitano sees a trend toward "honest feedback" and toward a clearer link between performance and pay.

Sources: Fay Hansen, "Lackluster Performance," *Workforce Management*, November 5, 2007, pp. 39–45; Wayne Farms, "Company Information," www.waynefarmsllc.com, accessed January 28, 2008; Ann Bagel, "All Things Unequaled," *Poultry*, October–November 2005, pp. 36–39; and "Wayne Farms LLC Company Profile," *Yahoo Finance*, accessed January 28, 2008.

Questions

1. At Wayne Farms, employees are rated on a 5-point scale, but all employees had been rated either 2 or 3. What rating errors by managers might explain this pattern?
2. Could it be that managers weren't making rating errors, but all Wayne Farms employees actually were performing at a level 2 or 3? If so, why would the performance management system still need to be improved? What purposes of performance management has it been failing to achieve?
3. Besides coaching managers to use all five points of the rating scale and deliver better feedback, how else should Malfitano consider reforming the performance management system at Wayne Farms? What other aspects of performance management should he consider?

IT'S A WRAP!

www.mhhe.com/noefund3e is your source for Reviewing, Applying, and Practicing the concepts you learned about in Chapter 8.

Review
- Chapter learning objectives
- Narrated lecture and iPod content
- Test Your Knowledge: Appraisal Methods and Potential Errors in the Rating Process

Application
- Manager's Hot Seat segment: "Project Management: Steering the Committee"
- Video case and quiz: "Now Who's Boss?"
- Self-assessment: Conduct an Assessment of Your Job or Project
- Web exercise: Visit HRNet

Practice
- Chapter quiz

NOTES

1. T. Henneman, "Employee Performance Management: What's Gnu at the Zoo?" *Workforce Management Online*, September 2006, http://www.workforce.com.
2. "Measuring People Power," *Fortune*, October 2, 2000.
3. M. Sallie-Dosunmu, "Born to Grow," *T&D*, May 2006, pp. 33–37.
4. S. Scullen, P. Bergey, and L. Aiman-Smith, "Forced Choice Distribution Systems and the Improvement of Workforce Potential: A Baseline Simulation," *Personnel Psychology* 58 (2005), pp. 1–32.
5. P. Smith and L. Kendall, "Retranslation of Expectations: An Approach to the Construction of Unambiguous Anchors for Rating Scales," *Journal of Applied Psychology* 47 (1963), pp. 149–55.
6. K. Murphy and J. Constans, "Behavioral Anchors as a Source of Bias in Rating," *Journal of Applied Psychology* 72 (1987), pp. 573–77; M. Piotrowski, J. Barnes-Farrel, and F. Estig, "Behaviorally Anchored Bias: A Replication and Extension of Murphy and Constans," *Journal of Applied Psychology* 74 (1989), pp. 823–26.
7. G. Latham and K. Wexley, *Increasing Productivity through Performance Appraisal* (Boston: Addison-Wesley, 1981).
8. U. Wiersma and G. Latham, "The Practicality of Behavioral Observation Scales, Behavioral Expectation Scales, and Trait Scales," *Personnel Psychology* 39 (1986), pp. 619–28.
9. D. C. Anderson, C. Crowell, J. Sucec, K. Gilligan, and M. Wikoff, "Behavior Management of Client Contacts in a Real Estate Brokerage: Getting Agents to Sell More," *Journal of Organizational Behavior Management* 4 (2001), pp. 580–90; and F. Luthans and R. Kreitner, *Organizational Behavior Modification and Beyond* (Glenview, IL: Scott-Foresman, 1975).
10. K. L. Langeland, C. M. Jones, and T. C. Mawhinney, "Improving Staff Performance in a Community Mental Health Setting: Job Analysis, Training, Goal Setting, Feedback, and Years of Data," *Journal of Organizational Behavior Management* 18 (1998), pp. 21–43.
11. J. Komaki, R. Collins, and P. Penn, "The Role of Performance Antecedents and Consequences in Work Motivation," *Journal of Applied Psychology* 67 (1982), pp. 334–40.
12. S. Snell, "Control Theory in Strategic Human Resource Management: The Mediating Effect of Administrative Information," *Academy of Management Journal* 35 (1992), pp. 292–327.
13. R. Pritchard, S. Jones, P. Roth, K. Stuebing, and S. Ekeberg, "The Evaluation of an Integrated Approach to Measuring Organizational Productivity," *Personnel Psychology* 42 (1989), pp. 69–115.
14. G. Odiorne, *MOBII: A System of Managerial Leadership for the 80s* (Belmont, CA: Pitman, 1986).
15. R. Rodgers and J. Hunter, "Impact of Management by Objectives on Organizational Productivity," *Journal of Applied Psychology* 76 (1991), pp. 322–26.
16. P. Wright, J. George, S. Farnsworth, and G. McMahan, "Productivity and Extra-role Behavior: The Effects of Goals and Incentives on Spontaneous Helping," *Journal of Applied Psychology* 78, no. 3 (1993), pp. 374–81.
17. K. Ellis, "Developing for Dollars," *Training*, May 2003, pp. 34–39.
18. R. Heneman, K. Wexley, and M. Moore, "Performance Rating Accuracy: A Critical Review," *Journal of Business Research* 15 (1987), pp. 431–48.
19. T. Becker and R. Klimoski, "A Field Study of the Relationship between the Organizational Feedback Environment and Performance," *Personnel Psychology* 42

(1989), pp. 343–58; H. M. Findley, W. F. Giles, and K. W. Mossholder, "Performance Appraisal and Systems Facets: Relationships with Contextual Performance," *Journal of Applied Psychology* 85 (2000), pp. 634–40.

20. K. Wexley and R. Klimoski, "Performance Appraisal: An Update," in *Research in Personnel and Human Resource Management*, vol. 2, ed. K. Rowland and G. Ferris (Greenwich, CT: JAI Press, 1984).

21. F. Landy and J. Farr, *The Measurement of Work Performance: Methods, Theory, and Applications* (New York: Academic Press, 1983).

22. G. McEvoy and P. Buller, "User Acceptance of Peer Appraisals in an Industrial Setting," *Personnel Psychology* 40 (1987), pp. 785–97.

23. A. Pomeroy, "Agent of Change," *HRMagazine*, May 2005, pp. 52–56.

24. D. Antonioni, "The Effects of Feedback Accountability on Upward Appraisal Ratings," *Personnel Psychology* 47 (1994), pp. 349–56.

25. R. Steel and N. Ovalle, "Self-Appraisal Based on Supervisor Feedback," *Personnel Psychology* 37 (1984), pp. 667–85; and L. E. Atwater, "The Advantages and Pitfalls of Self-Assessment in Organizations," in *Performance Appraisal: State of the Art in Practice*, ed. J. W. Smither (San Francisco: Jossey-Bass, 1998), pp. 331–65.

26. J. Bernardin, C. Hagan, J. Kane, and P. Villanova, "Effective Performance Management: A Focus on Precision, Customers, and Situational Constraints," in *Performance Appraisal: State of the Art in Practice*, pp. 3–48.

27. K. Wexley and W. Nemeroff, "Effects of Racial Prejudice, Race of Applicant, and Biographical Similarity on Interviewer Evaluations of Job Applicants," *Journal of Social and Behavioral Sciences* 20 (1974), pp. 66–78.

28. D. Smith, "Training Programs for Performance Appraisal: A Review," *Academy of Management Review* 11 (1986), pp. 22–40.

29. G. Latham, K. Wexley, and E. Pursell, "Training Managers to Minimize Rating Errors in the Observation of Behavior," *Journal of Applied Psychology* 60 (1975), pp. 550–55.

30. E. Pulakos, "A Comparison of Rater Training Programs: Error Training and Accuracy Training," *Journal of Applied Psychology* 69 (1984), pp. 581–88.

31. S. W. Gilliland and J. C. Langdon, "Creating Performance Management Systems That Promote Perceptions of Fairness," in *Performance Appraisal: State of the Art in Practice*, pp. 209–43.

32. S. W. J. Kozlowski, G. T. Chao, and R. F. Morrison, "Games Raters Play: Politics, Strategies, and Impression Management in Performance Appraisal," in *Performance Appraisal: State of the Art in Practice*, pp. 163–205.

33. K. Wexley, V. Singh, and G. Yukl, "Subordinate Participation in Three Types of Appraisal Interviews," *Journal of Applied Psychology* 58 (1973), pp. 54–57; K. Wexley, "Appraisal Interview," in *Performance Assessment*, ed. R. A. Berk (Baltimore: Johns Hopkins University Press, 1986), pp. 167–85.

34. D. Cederblom, "The Performance Appraisal Interview: A Review, Implications, and Suggestions," *Academy of Management Review* 7 (1982), pp. 219–27; B. D. Cawley, L. M. Keeping, and P. E. Levy, "Participation in the Performance Appraisal Process and Employee Reactions: A Meta-analytic Review of Field Investigations," *Journal of Applied Psychology* 83, no. 3 (1998), pp. 615–63; and W. Giles and K. Mossholder, "Employee Reactions to Contextual and Session Components of Performance Appraisal," *Journal of Applied Psychology* 75 (1990), pp. 371–77.

35. *Brito v. Zia Co.*, 478 F.2d 1200 (10th Cir. 1973).

36. K. Kraiger and J. Ford, "A Meta-Analysis of Ratee Race Effects in Performance Rating," *Journal of Applied Psychology* 70 (1985), pp. 56–65.

37. P. Sackett, C. DuBois, and A. Noe, "Tokenism in Performance Evaluation: The Effects of Work Group Representation on Male-Female and White-Black Differences in Performance Ratings," *Journal of Applied Psychology* 76 (1991), pp. 263–67.

38. G. Barrett and M. Kernan, "Performance Appraisal and Terminations: A Review of Court Decisions since *Brito v. Zia* with Implications for Personnel Practices," *Personnel Psychology* 40 (1987), pp. 489–503; H. Feild and W. Holley, "The Relationship of Performance Appraisal System Characteristics to Verdicts in Selected Employment Discrimination Cases," *Academy of Management Journal* 25 (1982), pp. 392–406; J. M. Werner and M. C. Bolino, "Explaining U.S. Courts of Appeals Decisions Involving Performance Appraisal: Accuracy, Fairness, and Validation," *Personnel Psychology* 50 (1997), pp. 1–24; and J. A. Segal, "86 Your Performance Appraisal Process," *HR Magazine*, October 2000, pp. 199–202.

39. D. Onley, "Technology Gives Big Brother Capability," *HRMagazine*, July 2005, pp. 99–102.

Developing Employees for Future Success

What Do I Need to Know?

After reading this chapter, you should be able to:

LO1 Discuss how development is related to training and careers.

LO2 Identify the methods organizations use for employee development.

LO3 Describe how organizations use assessment of personality type, work behaviors, and job performance to plan employee development.

LO4 Explain how job experiences can be used for developing skills.

LO5 Summarize principles of successful mentoring programs.

LO6 Tell how managers and peers develop employees through coaching.

LO7 Identify the steps in the process of career management.

LO8 Discuss how organizations are meeting the challenges of the "glass ceiling," succession planning, and dysfunctional managers.

Introduction

As we noted in Chapter 1, employees' commitment to their organization depends on how their managers treat them. To "win the war for talent" managers must be able to identify high-potential employees, make sure the organization uses the talents of these people, and reassure them of their value, so that they do not become dissatisfied and leave the organization. Managers also must be able to listen. Although new employees need strong direction, they expect to be able to think independently and be treated with respect. In all these ways, managers provide for **employee development**—the combination of formal education, job experiences, relationships, and assessment of personality and abilities to help employees prepare for the future of their careers. Human resource management establishes a process for employee development that prepares employees to help the organization meet its goals.

This chapter explores the purpose and activities of employee development. We begin by discussing the relationships among development, training, and career management. Next, we look at development approaches, including formal education, assessment, job experiences, and interpersonal relationships. The chapter emphasizes the types of skills, knowledge, and behaviors that are strengthened by each development method, so employees and their managers can choose appropriate methods when planning for development. The third section of the chapter describes the steps of the career management process, emphasizing the responsibilities of employee and employer at each step of the process. The chapter concludes with a discussion of special challenges related to employee development—the so-called glass ceiling, succession planning, and dysfunctional managers.

Training, Development, and Career Management

Organizations and their employees must constantly expand their knowledge, skills, and behavior to meet customer needs and compete in today's demanding and rapidly changing business environment. More and more companies operate internationally, requiring that employees understand different cultures and customs. More companies organize work in terms of projects or customers, rather than specialized functions, so employees need to acquire a broad range of technical and interpersonal skills. Many companies expect employees at all levels to perform roles once reserved for management. Modern organizations are expected to provide development opportunities to employees without regard to their sex, race, ethnic background, or age, so that they have equal opportunity for advancement. In this climate, organizations are placing greater emphasis on training and development. To do this, organizations must understand development's relationship to training and career management.

> **employee development**
> The combination of formal education, job experiences, relationships, and assessment of personality and abilities to help employees prepare for the future of their careers.

> **LO1** Discuss how development is related to training and careers.

Development and Training

The definition of development indicates that it is future oriented. Development implies learning that is not necessarily related to the employee's current job.[1] Instead, it prepares employees for other positions in the organization and increases their ability to move into jobs that may not yet exist.[2] Development also may help employees prepare for changes in their current jobs, such as changes resulting from new technology, work designs, or customers. So development is about preparing for change in the form of new jobs, new responsibilities, or new requirements.

In contrast, training traditionally focuses on helping employees improve performance of their current jobs. Many organizations have focused on linking training programs to business goals. In these organizations, the distinction between training and development is more blurred. Table 9.1 summarizes the traditional differences.

Development for Careers

The concept of a career has changed in recent years. In the traditional view, a career consists of a sequence of positions within an occupation or organization.[3] For example, an academic career might begin with a position as a university's adjunct professor. It continues with appointment to faculty positions as assistant professor, then associate professor, and finally full professor. An engineer might start as a staff engineer, then with greater experience earn promotions to the positions of advisory engineer, senior engineer, and vice president of engineering. In these examples, the career resembles a set of stairs from the bottom of a profession or organization to the top.

Recently, however, changes such as downsizing and restructuring have become the norm, so the concept of a career has become more fluid. Today's employees are more likely to have a **protean career,** one that frequently changes based on changes in the person's interests, abilities, and values and in the work environment. For example, an

> **protean career**
> A career that frequently changes based on changes in the person's interests, abilities, and values and in the work environment.

	TRAINING	DEVELOPMENT
Focus	Current	Future
Use of work experiences	Low	High
Goal	Preparation for current job	Preparation for changes
Participation	Required	Voluntary

> **Table 9.1**
> **Training versus Development**

HR How To

PROVIDING DEVELOPMENT OPPORTUNITIES TO FUTURE LEADERS

In any organization, the top managers are likely to leave at some point, either to retire or to pursue new challenges. And in a growing organization, additional leadership spots are likely to open up. One way organizations meet the need for new leaders is by identifying their high-potential employees and getting them ready to lead. Here are some ideas for getting that job done well:

- *Decide which employees have high potential for leadership—* High potential—being able to learn how to lead—is different from performing well at a job. The salesperson who sells the most won't necessarily be the best vice president of sales. An intern who can persuade senior employees to help might be pure gold. Assessments, described later in this chapter, can help organizations identify high-potential employees. Don't simply assume that the most vocal employees are the talented ones.

- *Provide top-management support—*Managers will be more committed to supporting leadership development if the organization rewards them for identifying and giving opportunities to high-potential employees. At companies with a stellar reputation for employee development, such as General Electric and McDonald's, the CEO personally reviews top employees' development progress.

- *Build relationships—*High-potential employees should have opportunities to work closely with the organization's current leaders, not just their immediate supervisor. Consider developing teams of high-potential employees, not just individuals.

- *Let high-potential employees know the organization is interested in helping them develop and move up—*Otherwise, they might leave the company, not seeing an opportunity for career growth. At the same time, to avoid disappointments and misunderstandings, the organization should not appear to be promising promotions. Also, provide plenty of feedback along the way so that employees know how well they are doing.

- *Provide development opportunities—*Support the development of high-potential employees not only through their participation in training courses or education programs (such as executive MBA programs) but also through job experiences (such as special projects and temporary assignments). This not only gives the organization an opportunity to see whether employees have what it takes for management positions but also gives the employees a chance to stretch their skills and determine their interest in leadership.

- *Allow room for mistakes—*If the development program is providing real challenges, employees will sometimes fall short. Focus on what the employee can learn from the experience.

Sources: Holly Dolezalek, "Got High Potentials?" *Training* (January–February 2007), downloaded from General Reference Center Gold, http://find.galegroup.com; and Geoff Colvin, "Leader Machines," *Fortune*, October 1, 2007, http://find.galegroup.com.

engineer might decide to take a sabbatical from her job to become a manager with Engineers without Borders, so she can develop managerial skills and decide whether she likes managing. As in this example, employees in protean careers take responsibility for managing their careers. This practice is consistent with the modern *psychological contract* described in Chapter 2. Employees look for organizations to provide, not job security and a career ladder to climb, but instead development opportunities and flexible work arrangements. The "HR How To" box discusses how organizations can provide development opportunities.

To remain marketable, employees must continually develop new skills. Fewer of today's careers involve repetitive tasks, and more rely on an expanding base of knowledge.[4] Jobs are less likely to last a lifetime, so employees have to prepare for newly created positions. Beyond knowing job requirements, employees need to understand the business in which they are working and be able to cultivate valuable relationships with co-workers, managers, suppliers, and customers. Learning such skills requires useful job experiences as well as effective training programs.

These relationships and experiences often take an employee along a career path that is far different from the traditional steps upward through an organization or profession. Although such careers will not disappear, more employees will follow a spiral career path in which they cross the boundaries between specialties and organizations. As organizations provide for employee development (and as employees take control of their own careers), they will need to (1) determine their interests, skills, and weaknesses and (2) seek development experiences involving jobs, relationships, and formal courses. As discussed later in the chapter, organizations can meet these needs through a system for *career management* or *development planning*. Career management helps employees select development activities that prepare them to meet their career goals. It helps employers select development activities in line with their human resource needs.

Approaches to Employee Development

Children's Healthcare of Atlanta, a medical organization specializing in pediatric care, focuses development efforts on high-performing employees who have the potential to become managers. These employees complete a full day of assessment that includes taking a personality test and participating in a business simulation in which they take the role of managers. Each year they also attend five workshops, where they learn about leading change, developing a business strategy, and creating a personal vision. They work in teams to solve a practical problem affecting Children's, and they receive coaching to help them set and achieve their own goals.[5]

L02 Identify the methods organizations use for employee development.

The many approaches to employee development fall into four broad categories: formal education, assessment, job experiences, and interpersonal relationships.[6] Figure 9.1 summarizes these four methods. Many organizations combine these approaches, as in the previous example of Children's Healthcare.

Formal Education

Organizations may support employee development through a variety of formal educational programs, either at the workplace or off-site. These may include workshops designed specifically for the organization's employees, short courses offered by consultants or universities, university programs offered to employees who live on campus during the program, and executive MBA programs (which enroll managers to meet on weekends or evenings to earn a master's degree in business administration). These programs may involve lectures by business experts, business games and simulations,

Figure 9.1

Four Approaches to Employee Development

experiential programs, and meetings with customers. Chapter 7 described most of these training methods, including their pros and cons.

Many companies, including Bank of Montreal and General Electric, operate training and development centers that offer seminars and longer-term programs. The Bank of Montreal operates its own Institute for Learning, featuring classrooms, a presentation hall, and guest accommodations for out-of-town employees. Programs include training in management leadership, risk management, and project management, as well as courses toward an MBA degree.[7] General Electric has one of the oldest and best-known management development centers, the John F. Welch Leadership Center in Crotonville, New York. Each year, GE managers choose employees with high performance and potential and send them to Crotonville for management development programs combining coursework and job experiences.[8]

Independent institutions offering executive education include Harvard, the Wharton School of Business, the University of Michigan, and the Center for Creative Leadership. A growing number of companies and universities are using distance learning (discussed in Chapter 7) to reach executive audiences. For example, Duke University's Fuqua School of Business offers an electronic executive MBA program. Besides attending traditional classes, students use personal computers to view lectures on CD-ROM, download study aids, discuss lectures, and work on team projects online.

Another trend in executive education is for employers and the education provider to create short courses with content designed specifically for the audience. MetLife worked with Babson College to develop a course in which faculty members discuss business principles and then invite corporate executives to discuss how the principles work in MetLife and the insurance industry. Small teams of class participants work on related class projects and develop recommendations for company executives. MetLife has implemented 82 percent of these projects.[9]

Assessment

LO3 Describe how organizations use assessment of personality type, work behaviors, and job performance to plan employee development.

assessment
Collecting information and providing feedback to employees about their behavior, communication style, or skills.

Another way to provide for employee development is **assessment**—collecting information and providing feedback to employees about their behavior, communication style, or skills.[10] Information for assessment may come from the employees, their peers, managers, and customers. The most frequent uses of assessment are to identify employees with managerial potential to measure current managers' strengths and weaknesses. Organizations also use assessment to identify managers with potential to move into higher-level executive positions. Organizations that assign work to teams may use assessment to identify the strengths and weaknesses of individual team members and the effects of the team members' decision-making and communication styles on the team's productivity.

For assessment to support development, the information must be shared with the employee being assessed. Along with that assessment information, the employee needs suggestions for correcting skill weaknesses and for using skills already learned. The suggestions might be to participate in training courses or develop skills through new job experiences. Based on the assessment information and available development opportunities, employees should develop action plans to guide their efforts at self-improvement.

Organizations vary in the methods and sources of information they use in developmental assessment. Many organizations appraise performance. Organizations with sophisticated development systems use psychological tests to measure employees' skills, personality types, and communication styles. They may collect self, peer, and manager ratings of employees' behavior and style of working with others. The tools used for these assessment methods include the Myers-Briggs Type Indicator, assessment centers, the Benchmarks assessment, performance appraisal, and 360-degree feedback.

Myers-Briggs Type Indicator®

The most popular psychological inventory for employee development is the **Myers-Briggs Type Indicator (MBTI)®**. This assessment identifies individuals' preferences for source of energy, means of information gathering, way of decision making, and lifestyle. The assessment consists of more than 100 questions about how the person feels or prefers to behave in different situations (such as "Are you usually a good 'mixer' or rather quiet and reserved?). The assessment describes these individuals' preferences in the four areas:

One way to develop employees is to begin with an assessment which may consist of assigning an activity to a team and seeing who brings what skills and strengths to the team. How can this assessment help employees?

1. The *energy* dichotomy indicates where individuals gain interpersonal strength and vitality, measured as their degree of introversion or extroversion. Extroverted types (E) gain energy through interpersonal relationships. Introverted types (I) gain energy by focusing on inner thoughts and feelings.
2. The *information-gathering* dichotomy relates to the preparations individuals make before making decisions. Individuals with a Sensing (S) preference tend to gather the facts and details to prepare for a decision. Intuitive types (N) tend to focus less on the facts and more on possibilities and relationships among them.
3. In *decision making*, individuals differ in the amount of consideration they give to their own and others' values and feelings, as opposed to the hard facts of a situation. Individuals with a Thinking (T) preference try always to be objective in making decisions. Individuals with a Feeling (F) preference tend to evaluate the impact of the alternatives on others, as well as their own feelings; they are more subjective.
4. The *lifestyle* dichotomy describes an individual's tendency to be either flexible or structured. Individuals with a Judging (J) preference focus on goals, establish deadlines, and prefer to be conclusive. Individuals with a Perceiving (P) preference enjoy surprises, are comfortable with changing a decision, and dislike deadlines.

Myers-Briggs Type Indicator (MBTI)® Psychological inventory that identifies individuals' preferences for source of energy, means of information gathering, way of decision making, and lifestyle, providing information for team building and leadership development.

The alternatives for each of the four dichotomies result in 16 possible combinations, the personality types summarized in Table 9.2. Of course people are likely to be mixtures of these types, but the point of the assessment is that certain types predominate in individuals.

As a result of their psychological types, people develop strengths and weaknesses. For example, individuals who are Introverted, Sensing, Thinking, and Judging (known as ISTJs) tend to be serious, quiet, practical, orderly, and logical. They can organize tasks, be decisive, and follow through on plans and goals. But because they do not

Table 9.2

Personality Types Used in the Myers-Briggs Type Indicator (MBTI)® Assessment

	SENSING TYPES (S)		INTUITIVE TYPES (N)	
	THINKING (T)	**FEELING (F)**	**FEELING (F)**	**THINKING (T)**
Introverts (I) Judging (J)	**ISTJ** Quiet, serious, earn success by thoroughness and dependability. Practical, matter-of-fact, realistic, and responsible. Decide logically what should be done and work toward it steadily, regardless of distractions. Take pleasure in making everything orderly and organized—their work, their home, their life. Value traditions and loyalty.	**ISFJ** Quiet, friendly, responsible, and conscientious. Committed and steady in meeting their obligations. Thorough, painstaking, and accurate. Loyal, considerate, notice and remember specifics about people who are important to them, concerned with how others feel. Strive to create an orderly and harmonious environment at work and at home.	**INFJ** Seek meaning and connection in ideas, relationships, and material possessions. Want to understand what motivates people and are insightful about others. Conscientious and committed to their firm values. Develop a clear vision about how best to serve the common good. Organized and decisive in implementing their vision.	**INTJ** Have original minds and great drive for implementing their ideas and achieving their goals. Quickly see patterns in external events and develop long-range explanatory perspectives. When committed, organize a job and carry it through. Skeptical and independent, have high standards of competence and performance—for themselves and others.
Perceiving (P)	**ISTP** Tolerant and flexible, quiet observers until a problem appears, then act quickly to find workable solutions. Analyze what makes things work and readily get through large amounts of data to isolate the core of practical problems. Interested in cause and effect, organize facts using logical principles, value efficiency.	**ISFP** Quiet, friendly, sensitive, and kind. Enjoy the present moment, what's going on around them. Like to have their own space and to work within their own time frame. Loyal and committed to their values and to people who are important to them. Dislike disagreements and conflicts, do not force their opinions or values on others.	**INFP** Idealistic, loyal to their values and to people who are important to them. Want an external life that is congruent with their values. Curious, quick to see possibilities, can be catalysts for implementing ideas. Seek to understand people and to help them fulfill their potential. Adaptable, flexible, and accepting unless a value is threatened.	**INTP** Seek to develop logical explanations for everything that interests them. Theoretical and abstract, interested more in ideas than in social interaction. Quiet, contained, flexible, and adaptable. Have unusual ability to focus in depth to solve problems in their area of interest. Skeptical, sometimes critical, always analytical.

have the opposite preferences (Extroversion, Intuition, Feeling, and Perceiving), ISTJs have several weaknesses. They may have difficulty responding to unexpected opportunities, appear to their colleagues to be too task-oriented or impersonal, and make decisions too fast.

Applying this kind of information about employees' preferences or tendencies helps organizations understand the communication, motivation, teamwork, work styles, and leadership of the people in their groups. For example, salespeople or executives who want to communicate better can apply what they learn about their own personality styles and the way other people perceive them. For team development, the MBTI® inventory can help teams match team members with assignments based on their preferences and thus improve problem solving.[11] The team could assign brainstorming (idea-generating) tasks to employees with an Intuitive preference and evaluation of the ideas to employees with a Sensing preference.

People who take the MBTI® inventory find it a positive experience and say it helps them change their behavior. However, MBTI® inventory scores are not necessarily stable over time. Studies in which the MBTI® inventory was administered at two different times found that as few as one-fourth of those who took the assessment were classified as exactly the same type the second time. Still, the MBTI® inventory is a valuable tool for understanding communication styles and the ways people prefer to interact with others. It is not appropriate for measuring job performance, however, or as the only means of evaluating promotion potential.[12]

SENSING TYPES (S)		INTUITIVE TYPES (N)	
THINKING (T)	FEELING (F)	FEELING (F)	THINKING (T)
Extroverts (E) **Perceiving (P)**	**ESTP** Flexible and tolerant, they take a pragmatic approach focused on immediate results. Theories and conceptual explanations bore them—they want to act energetically to solve the problem. Focus on the here-and-now, spontaneous, enjoy each moment that they can be active with others. Enjoy material comforts and style. Learn best through doing.	**ESFP** Outgoing, friendly, and accepting. Exuberant lovers of life, people, and material comforts. Enjoy working with others to make things happen. Bring common sense and a realistic approach to their work, and make work fun. Flexible and spontaneous, adapt readily to new people and environments. Learn best by trying a new skill with other people.	**ENFP** Warmly enthusiastic and imaginative. See life as full of possibilities. Make connections between events and information very quickly, and confidently proceed based on the patterns they see. Want a lot of affirmation from others, and readily give appreciation and support. Spontaneous and flexible, often rely on their ability to improvise and their verbal fluency.	**ENTP** Quick, ingenious, stimulating, alert, and outspoken. Resourceful in solving new and challenging problems. Adept at generating conceptual possibilities and then analyzing them strategically. Good at reading other people. Bored by routine, will seldom do the same thing the same way, apt to turn to one new interest after another.
Judging (J)	**ESTJ** Practical, realistic, matter-of-fact. Decisive, quickly move to implement decisions. Organize projects and people to get things done, focus on getting results in the most efficient way possible. Take care of routine details. Have a clear set of logical standards, systematically follow them and want others to also. Forceful in implementing their plans.	**ESFJ** Warmhearted, conscientious, and cooperative. Want harmony in their environment, work with determination to establish it. Like to work with others to complete tasks accurately and on time. Loyal, follow through even in small matters. Notice what others need in their day-by-day lives and try to provide it. Want to be appreciated for who they are and for what they contribute.	**ENFJ** Warm, empathetic, responsive, and responsible. Highly attuned to the emotions, needs, and motivations of others. Find potential in everyone, want to help others fulfill their potential. May act as catalysts for individual and group growth. Loyal, responsive to praise and criticism. Sociable, facilitate others in a group, and provide inspiring leadership.	**ENTJ** Frank, decisive, assume leadership readily. Quickly see illogical and inefficient procedures and policies, develop and implement comprehensive systems to solve organizational problems. Enjoy long-term planning and goal setting. Usually well informed, well read, enjoy expanding their knowledge and passing it on to others. Forceful in presenting their ideas.

Assessment Centers

At an **assessment center,** multiple raters or evaluators (assessors) evaluate employees' performance on a number of exercises.[13] An assessment center is usually an off-site location such as a conference center. Usually 6 to 12 employees participate at one time. The primary use of assessment centers is to identify whether employees have the personality characteristics, administrative skills, and interpersonal skills needed for managerial jobs. Organizations also use them to determine whether employees have the skills needed for working in teams.

The types of exercises used in assessment centers include leaderless group discussions, interviews, in-baskets, and role-plays.[14] In a **leaderless group discussion,** a team of five to seven employees is assigned a problem and must work together to solve it within a certain time period. The problem may involve buying and selling supplies, nominating a subordinate for an award, or assembling a product. Interview questions typically cover each employee's work and personal experiences, skill strengths and weaknesses, and career plans. In-basket exercises, discussed as a selection method in Chapter 6, simulate the administrative tasks of a manager's job, using a pile of documents for the employee to handle. In role-plays, the participant takes the part of a manager or employee in a situation involving the skills to be assessed. For example, a participant might be given the role of a manager who must discuss performance problems with an employee, played by someone who works for the assessment center. Other exercises in assessment centers might include interest and aptitude tests to evaluate an employee's vocabulary, general mental ability, and reasoning skills. Personality tests may be used to determine employees' ability get along with others, tolerance for uncertainty, and other traits related to success as a manager or team member.

assessment center
An assessment process in which multiple raters or evaluators (assessors) evaluate employees' performance on a number of exercises, usually as they work in a group at an off-site location.

leaderless group discussion
An assessment center exercise in which a team of five to seven employees is assigned a problem and must work together to solve it within a certain time period.

The assessors are usually managers who have been trained to look for employee behaviors that are related to the skills being assessed. Typically, each assessor observes and records one or two employees' behaviors in each exercise. The assessors review their notes and rate each employee's level of skills (for example, 5 = high level of leadership skills, 1 = low level of leadership skills). After all the employees have completed the exercises, the assessors discuss their observations of each employee. They compare their ratings and try to agree on each employee's rating for each of the skills.

As we mentioned in Chapter 6, research suggests that assessment center ratings are valid for predicting performance, salary level, and career advancement.[15] Assessment centers may also be useful for development because of the feedback that participants receive about their attitudes, skill strengths, and weaknesses.[16]

Benchmarks

Benchmarks
A measurement tool that gathers ratings of a manager's use of skills associated with success in managing.

A development method that focuses on measuring management skills is an instrument called **Benchmarks.** This measurement tool gathers ratings of a manager's use of skills associated with success in managing. The items measured by Benchmarks are based on research into the lessons that executives learn in critical events of their careers.[17] Items measure the 16 skills and perspectives listed in Table 9.3, including how well managers

Table 9.3

Skills Related to Success as a Manager

Resourcefulness	Can think strategically, engage in flexible problem solving, and work effectively with higher management.
Doing whatever it takes	Has perseverance and focus in the face of obstacles.
Being a quick study	Quickly masters new technical and business knowledge.
Building and mending relationships	Knows how to build and maintain working relationships with co-workers and external parties.
Leading subordinates	Delegates to subordinates effectively, broadens their opportunities, and acts with fairness toward them.
Compassion and sensitivity	Shows genuine interest in others and sensitivity to subordinates' needs.
Straightforwardness and composure	Is honorable and steadfast.
Setting a developmental climate	Provides a challenging climate to encourage subordinates' development.
Confronting problem subordinates	Acts decisively and fairly when dealing with problem subordinates.
Team orientation	Accomplishes tasks through managing others.
Balance between personal life and work	Balances work priorities with personal life so that neither is neglected.
Decisiveness	Prefers quick and approximate actions to slow and precise ones in many management situations.
Self-awareness	Has an accurate picture of strengths and weaknesses and is willing to improve.
Hiring talented staff	Hires talented people for the team.
Putting people at ease	Displays warmth and a good sense of humor.
Acting with flexibility	Can behave in ways that are often seen as opposites.

Source: Adapted with permission from C. D. McCauley, M. M. Lombardo, and C. J. Usher, "Diagnosing Management Development Needs: An Instrument Based on How Managers Develop," Journal of Management 15 (1989), pp. 389–403.

deal with subordinates, acquire resources, and create a productive work climate. Research has found that managers who have these skills are more likely to receive positive performance evaluations, be considered promotable, and be promoted.[18]

To provide a complete picture of managers' skills, the managers' supervisors, their peers, and the managers themselves all complete the instrument. The results include a summary report, which the organization provides to the manager so he or she can see the self-ratings in comparison to the ratings by others. Also available with this method is a development guide containing examples of experiences that enhance each skill and ways successful managers use the skill.

Performance Appraisals and 360-Degree Feedback

As we stated in Chapter 8, *performance appraisal* is the process of measuring employees' performance. This information can be useful for employee development under certain conditions.[19] The appraisal system must tell employees specifically about their performance problems and ways to improve their performance. Employees must gain a clear understanding of the differences between current performance and expected performance. The appraisal process must identify causes of the performance discrepancy and develop plans for improving performance. Managers must be trained to deliver frequent performance feedback and must monitor employees' progress in carrying out their action plans.

A recent trend in performance appraisals, also discussed in Chapter 8, is *360-degree feedback*—performance measurement by the employee's supervisor, peers, employees, and customers. Often the feedback involves rating the individual in terms of work-related behaviors. For development purposes, the rater would identify an area of behavior as a strength of that employee or an area requiring further development. The results presented to the employee show how he or she was rated on each item and how self-evaluations differ from other raters' evaluations. The individual reviews the results, seeks clarification from the raters, and sets specific development goals based on the strengths and weaknesses identified.[20]

Consider how Capital One, a consumer credit company, uses 360-degree feedback.[21] The company developed assessments based on specific competencies, so raters evaluate those areas of performance, concentrating on three or four strengths or areas requiring development. The questions seek comments, which often provide specific information about what aspect of the competency needs to be improved. Using the ratings and comments, the company can tailor coaching and training to fit each person's needs. In this way, the company links feedback from the 360-degree assessment to employee development plans.

There are several benefits of 360-degree feedback. Organizations collect multiple perspectives of managers' performance, allowing employees to compare their own personal evaluations with the views of others. This method also establishes formal communications about behaviors and skill ratings between employees and their internal and external customers. Several studies have shown that performance improves and behavior changes as a result of participating in upward feedback and 360-degree feedback systems.[22] The change is greatest in people who received lower ratings from others than what they gave themselves. The 360-degree feedback system is most likely to be effective if the rating instrument enables reliable or consistent ratings, assesses behaviors or skills that are job related, and is easy to use. Also, the system should ensure raters' confidentiality, and managers should receive and act on the feedback.[23]

Best Practices

Career Paths Go Everywhere at Alaska Wildland Adventures

Alaska Wildland Adventures, which operates eco-friendly tours in Alaska, has just 12 year-round employees and fewer than 100 seasonal workers in the summertime. With such a small staff, it can be difficult for workers to see much of a future at the company. That doesn't prevent the Girdwood, Alaska, company from hanging on to its best people. It stands out by letting its people tackle any assignment they can handle and move up to greater responsibility when positions become open.

A good example is the company's general manager, Kyle Kelley. In the 1990s, he started out by taking an internship as a safari driver. Later he became a natural-history guide and then moved up to safari manager, program director, and operations manager. As employees like Kelley move up through the ranks, they develop a broad understanding of how the company works. This prepares them to move from job to job and eventually handle management responsibility.

One reason that the company can be so flexible with job assignments is that it is so small. If a task needs to be done, others can easily see the need, and somebody jumps in to help. In addition, managers can get to know employees and learn about their career goals. Jackie Collins, for instance, started out as a receptionist, but it soon became evident that when a customer called, Collins was skillful at answering questions. Managers began giving her marketing duties. Eventually, she was officially assigned to marketing—first part-time and then full-time as she grew into the job.

Another way that Alaska Wildland Adventures develops its people is to give them information and wide authority to make decisions. Owner Kirk Hoessle shares the company's financial data, so they can know when the company is succeeding and learn what its financial limits are. Employees share the responsibility for deciding on the company's holiday schedule. Like taking on other responsibilities, decision making helps shape employees for leadership jobs.

Sources: Kelly K. Spors, "Top Small Workplaces 2007," *Wall Street Journal*, October 1, 2007, http://online.wsj.com; Winning Workplaces, "Survival of the Fittest," Success Stories, www.winningworkplaces.org, accessed January 30, 2008; and Alaska Wildland Adventures, "Our Company History," www.alaskawildland.com, accessed January 30, 2008.

There are potential limitations of 360-degree feedback. This method demands a significant amount of time for raters to complete the evaluations. If raters, especially subordinates or peers, provide negative feedback, some managers might try to identify and punish them. A facilitator is needed to help interpret results. Finally, simply delivering ratings to a manager does not provide ways for the manager to act on the feedback (for example, development planning, meeting with raters, or taking courses). As noted earlier, any form of assessment should be accompanied by suggestions for improvement and development of an action plan.

LO4 Explain how job experiences can be used for developing skills.

job experiences
The combination of relationships, problems, demands, tasks, and other features of an employee's jobs.

Job Experiences

Most employee development occurs through **job experiences**[24]—the combination of relationships, problems, demands, tasks, and other features of an employee's jobs. Using job experiences for employee development assumes that development is most likely to occur when the employee's skills and experiences do not entirely match the skills required for the employee's current job. To succeed, employees must stretch their skills. In other words, they must learn new skills, apply their skills and knowledge in new ways, and master new experiences.[25] For example, companies that want to prepare employees to expand overseas markets are assigning them to a variety of international jobs. To learn how a small company successfully uses job experiences to develop employees, see the "Best Practices" box.

Most of what we know about development through job experiences comes from a series of studies conducted by the Center for Creative Leadership.[26] These studies asked executives to identify key career events that made a difference in their managerial styles and the lessons they learned from these experiences. The key events included job assignments (such as fixing a failed operation), interpersonal relationships (getting along with supervisors), and types of transitions (situations in which the manager at first lacked the necessary background). Through job experiences like these, managers learn how to handle common challenges, prove themselves, lead change, handle pressure, and influence others.

The usefulness of job experiences for employee development varies depending on whether the employee views the experiences as positive or negative sources of stress. When employees view job experiences as positive stressors, the experiences challenge them and stimulate learning. When they view job experiences as negative stressors, employees may suffer from high levels of harmful stress. Of the job demands studied, managers were most likely to experience negative stress from creating change and overcoming obstacles (adverse business conditions, lack of management support, lack of personal support, or a difficult boss). Research suggests that all of the job demands except obstacles are related to learning.[27] Organizations should offer job experiences that are most likely to increase learning, and they should consider the consequences of situations that involve negative stress.

Although the research on development through job experiences has focused on managers, line employees also can learn through job experiences. Organizations may, for example, use job experiences to develop skills needed for teamwork, including conflict resolution, data analysis, and customer service. These experiences may occur when forming a team and when employees switch roles within a team.

Various job assignments can provide for employee development. The organization may enlarge the employee's current job or move the employee to different jobs. Lateral moves include job rotation, transfer, or temporary assignment to another organization. The organization may also use downward moves or promotions as a source of job experience. Figure 9.2 summarizes these alternatives.

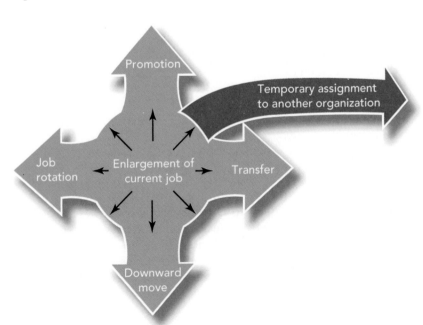

Figure 9.2

How Job Experiences Are Used for Employee Development

Job Enlargement

As Chapter 4 stated in the context of job design, *job enlargement* involves adding challenges or new responsibilities to employees' current jobs. Examples include completing a special project, switching roles within a work team, or researching new ways to serve customers. An engineering employee might join a task force developing new career paths for technical employees. The work on the project could give the engineer a leadership role through which the engineer learns about the company's career development system while also practicing leadership skills to help the task force reach its goals. In this way, job enlargement not only makes a job more interesting but also creates an opportunity for employees to develop new skills.

Job Rotation

Another job design technique that can be applied to employee development is *job rotation*, moving employees through a series of job assignments in one or more functional areas. Regions Financial has job rotation programs in information technology (IT) and regional banking. Employees in the bank's IT program rotate through six IT departments to work on special projects. In regional banking, employees receive training as they rotate through the positions of teller, financial service representative, and branch sales manager.[28]

Job rotation helps employees gain an appreciation for the company's goals, increases their understanding of different company functions, develops a network of contacts, and improves problem-solving and decision-making skills.[29] Job rotation also helps employees increase their salary and earn promotions faster. However, job rotation poses some problems for employees and the organization. Knowing they will be rotated to another job may give the employees a short-term perspective on problems and their solutions. Employees may feel less satisfied and motivated because they have difficulty developing specialized skills and leave the position too soon to fulfill any challenging assignments. The rotation of employees through a department may hurt productivity and increase the workload of those who remain after employees are rotated out. Job rotation is most likely to succeed when it meets certain conditions:[30]

- Job rotation is used for developing skills as well as gaining experience for management careers.
- Employees understand specifically what skills rotation is to develop.
- The organization uses job rotation for all levels and types of employees.
- Job rotation is linked with the career management process so employees know what development needs each assignment addresses.
- The organization manages the timing of rotations to maximize their benefits and minimize their costs.
- All employees have equal opportunities for job rotation, regardless of their demographic group.

Transfers, Promotions, and Downward Moves

transfer
Assignment of an employee to a position in a different area of the company, usually in a lateral move.

Most companies use upward, downward, and lateral moves as an option for employee development. In a **transfer,** the organization assigns an employee to a position in a different area of the company. Transfers do not necessarily increase job responsibilities or compensation. They are usually lateral moves, that is, moves to a job with a similar level of responsibility. They may involve relocation to another part of the country or even to another country.

Relocation can be stressful because of the demands of moving, especially when family members are affected. People have to find new housing, shopping, health care, and leisure facilities, and they often lack the support of nearby friends and family. These stresses come at the same time the employee must learn the expectations and responsibilities associated with the new position. Because transfers can provoke anxiety, many companies have difficulty getting employees to accept them. Employees most willing to accept transfers tend to be those with high career ambitions and beliefs that the organization offers a promising future and that accepting the transfer will help the company succeed.[31]

A **downward move** occurs when an employee is given less responsibility and authority. The organization may demote an employee because of poor performance or move the employee to a lower-level position in another function so that the employee can develop different skills. The temporary cross-functional move is the most common way to use downward moves for employee development. For example, engineers who want to move into management often take lower-level positions, such as shift supervisor, to develop their management skills.

Working outside one's home country is the most important job experience that can develop an employee for a career in the global economy.

Many employees have difficulty associating transfers and downward moves with development; these changes may feel more like forms of punishment. Employees often decide to leave an organization rather than accept such a change, and then the organization must bear the costs of replacing those employees. Employees will be more likely to accept transfers and downward moves as development opportunities if the organization provides information about the change and its possible benefits and involves the employee in planning the change. Employees are also more likely to be positive about such a recommendation if the organization provides clear performance objectives and frequent feedback. Employers can encourage an employee to relocate by providing financial assistance with the move, information about the new location and job, and help for family members, such as identifying schools, child care and elder care options, and job search assistance for the employee's spouse.[32]

A **promotion** involves moving an employee into a position with greater challenges, more responsibility, and more authority than in the previous job. Usually promotions include pay increases. Because promotions improve the person's pay, status, and feelings of accomplishment, employees are more willing to accept promotions than lateral or downward moves. Even so, employers can increase the likelihood that employees will accept promotions by providing the same kind of information and assistance that are used to support transfers and downward moves. Organizations can more easily offer promotions if they are profitable and growing. In other conditions, opportunities for promoting employees may be limited.

downward move
Assignment of an employee to a position with less responsibility and authority.

promotion
Assignment of an employee to a position with greater challenges, more responsibility, and more authority than in the previous job, usually accompanied by a pay increase.

Temporary Assignments with Other Organizations

In some cases, an employer may benefit from the skills an employee can learn at another organization. The employer may encourage the employee to participate in an

externship
Employee development through a full-time temporary position at another organization.

externship—a full-time temporary position at another organization. Mercer Management, a consulting firm, uses externships to develop employees who want experience in a specific industry.[33] Mercer Management promises to employ the externs after their assignments end. One employee with several years' experience as a Mercer consultant became vice president of Internet services for Crayola. He had been consulting on an Internet project for the company and wanted to implement his recommendations, rather than just give them to the client and move on to another project. He started working at Crayola while remaining employed by Mercer Management, though his pay comes from Crayola. Mercer believes that employees who participate in its externship program will remain committed to the consulting firm because they have a chance to learn and grow professionally without the demands of a job search.

sabbatical
A leave of absence from an organization to renew or develop skills.

Temporary assignments can include a **sabbatical**—a leave of absence from an organization to renew or develop skills. Employees on sabbatical often receive full pay and benefits. Sabbaticals let employees get away from the day-to-day stresses of their jobs and acquire new skills and perspectives. Sabbaticals also allow employees more time for personal pursuits such as writing a book or spending more time with family members. Fallon Worldwide, an advertising agency, offers a sabbatical program called Dreamcatchers to staff members who want to work on a project or travel. Dreamcatchers was developed to help the agency avoid employee burnout and loss of creative edge. Employees have taken time off to write novels, to kayak, and to motorcycle through the Alps. Fallon matches employee contributions of up to $1,000 annually for two years and offers up to two extra weeks of paid vacation. The agency's partners believe the program has helped them retain key employees and recruit new ones, as well as meet the goal of recharging creativity.[34] How employees spend their sabbaticals varies from company to company. Some employees may work for a nonprofit service agency; others may study at a college or university or travel and work on special projects in non-U.S. subsidiaries of the company.

Interpersonal Relationships

Employees can also develop skills and increase their knowledge about the organization and its customers by interacting with a more experienced organization member. Two types of relationships used for employee development are mentoring and coaching.

LO5 Summarize principles of successful mentoring programs.

Mentors

mentor
An experienced, productive senior employee who helps develop a less-experienced employee (a protégé).

A **mentor** is an experienced, productive senior employee who helps develop a less experienced employee, called the *protégé*. Most mentoring relationships develop informally as a result of interests or values shared by the mentor and protégé. According to research, the employees most likely to seek and attract a mentor have certain personality characteristics: emotional stability, ability to adapt their behavior to the situation, and high needs for power and achievement.[35] Mentoring relationships also can develop as part of the organization's planned effort to bring together successful senior employees with less-experienced employees.

One major advantage of formal mentoring programs is that they ensure access to mentors for all employees, regardless of gender or race. Another advantage is that participants in a company-sponsored mentoring program know what is expected of them.[36] However, in an artificially created relationship, mentors may have difficulty providing counseling and coaching.[37] Mentoring programs tend to be most successful when they are voluntary and participants understand the details of the program. Rewarding managers for employee development is also important, because it signals that mentoring and other development activities are worthwhile. In addition, the organization should carefully select mentors based on their interpersonal and technical skills, train them for the role, and evaluate whether the program has met its objectives.[38]

Information technology can help organizations meet some of these guidelines. For example, videoconferencing may be a good substitute if the mentor and protégé cannot meet face-to-face. Databases can store information about potential mentors' characteristics, and the protégé can use a search engine to locate mentors who best match the qualities he or she is looking for. Wyndham Hotels and

Rick Pitino, head basketball coach at Louisville, is known for being a good mentor. His track record proves it; many former assistants and players have become college head coaches after working with him.

Resorts uses a Web-based matching system. The protégé generates a list of available mentors with specified qualities and has seven days to contact one of the mentors and arrange a meeting. The system, which also sends participants reminders of their regular meetings, has tripled the participation in Wyndham's mentoring program.[39]

Mentors and protégés can both benefit from a mentoring relationship. Protégés receive career support, including coaching, protection, sponsorship, challenging assignments, and visibility among the organization's managers. They also receive benefits of a positive relationship—a friend and role model who accepts them, has a positive opinion toward them, and gives them a chance to talk about their worries. Employees with mentors are also more likely to be promoted, earn higher salaries, and have more influence within their organization.[40] Acting as a mentor gives managers a chance to develop their interpersonal skills and increase their feelings that they are contributing something important to the organization. Working with a technically trained protégé on matters such as new research in the field may also increase the mentor's technical knowledge.

So that more employees can benefit from mentoring, some organizations use *group mentoring programs*, which assign four to six protégés to a successful senior employee. A potential advantage of group mentoring is that protégés can learn from each other as well as from the mentor. The leader helps protégés understand the organization, guides them in analyzing their experiences, and helps them clarify career directions. Each member of the group may complete specific assignments, or the group may work together on a problem or issue.

Coaching

A **coach** is a peer or manager who works with an employee to motivate the employee, help him or her develop skills, and provide reinforcement and feedback. Coaches may play one or more of three roles:[41]

LO6 Tell how managers and peers develop employees through coaching.

coach
A peer or manager who works with an employee to motivate the employee, help him or her develop skills, and provide reinforcement and feedback.

1. Working one-on-one with an employee, as when giving feedback.
2. Helping employees learn for themselves—for example, helping them find experts and teaching them to obtain feedback from others.
3. Providing resources such as mentors, courses, or job experiences.

At Wachovia Corporation, the leadership development program includes coaching of each participant by an executive from another division. The coach helps the manager interpret the results of 360-degree reviews and set goals for improvement.[42]

Research suggests that coaching helps managers improve by identifying areas for improvement and setting goals.[43] Coaching is most likely to succeed if coaches are empathetic, supportive, practical, and self-confident but don't act infallible or try to tell others what to do.[44] To benefit from coaching, employees need to be open-minded and interested in the process.

L07 Identify the steps in the process of career management.

Systems for Career Management

Employee development is most likely to meet the organization's needs if it is part of a human resource system of career management. In practice, organizations' career management systems vary. Some rely heavily on informal relationships, while others are sophisticated programs. As shown in Figure 9.3, a basic career management system involves four steps: self-assessment, reality check, goal setting, and action planning. At each step, both the employee and the organization have responsibilities. The system is most likely to be beneficial if it is linked to the organization's objectives and needs, has support from top management, and is created with employee participation.[45] Human resource professionals can also contribute to the system's success by ensuring that it is linked to other HR practices such as performance management, training, and recruiting. The "e-HRM" box shows how talent management software can benefit employees' career management.

Figure 9.3

Steps and Responsibilities in the Career Management Process

	Self-assessment	**Reality check**	**Goal setting**	**Action planning**
Employee responsibility	Identify opportunities and needs to improve.	Identify what needs are realistic to develop.	Identify goal and method to determine goal progress.	Identify steps and timetable to reach goal.
Company responsibility	Provide assessment information to identify strengths, weaknesses, interests, and values.	Communicate performance evaluation, where employee fits in long-range plans of the company, changes in industry, profession, and workplace.	Ensure that goal is specific, challenging, and attainable; commit to help employee reach the goal.	Identify resources employee needs to reach goal, including courses, work experiences, relationships.

TALENT MANAGEMENT SOFTWARE

The right software can help organizations connect their career management to other HR functions. A growing number of companies are turning to talent management systems. This type of computer system gathers knowledge on experience areas and performance data for a company's employees and makes the data available for selection and training decisions. Managers can track the number of employees joining and leaving particular divisions or jobs, using the analysis to help them spot areas where they need to step up recruiting or prepare employees for promotion. By searching for particular types of experience or knowledge, they can identify which employees are likely candidates for development or new assignments.

At United Parcel Service, public relations supervisor Diana Hatcher used the company's talent management system to determine that she could qualify for a promotion in two years if she gained experience in another area of her department. Armed with that information, Hatcher went to her boss to arrange for the needed experience. Hatcher believes performance appraisals at UPS are now more helpful because they provide information that can enable employees to progress in their careers. Her boss agrees.

Source: Sarah E. Needleman, "Demand Rises for Talent-Management Software," *Wall Street Journal*, January 15, 2008, http://online.wsj.com.

Self-Assessment

In discussing the methods of employee development, we highlighted several assessment tools. Such tools may be applied to the first stage of career development, **self-assessment.** This is the use of information by employees to determine their career interests, values, aptitudes, and behavioral tendencies. The employee's responsibility is to identify opportunities and personal areas needing improvement. The organization's responsibility is to provide assessment information for identifying strengths, weaknesses, interests, and values.

Self-assessment tools often include psychological tests such as the Myers-Briggs Type Inventory (described earlier in the chapter), the Strong-Campbell Interest Inventory, and the Self-Directed Search. The Strong-Campbell inventory helps employees identify their occupational and job interests. The Self-Directed Search identifies employees' preferences for working in different kinds of environments—sales, counseling, and so on. Tests may also help employees identify the relative values they place on work and leisure activities. Self-assessment tools can include exercises such as the one in Figure 9.4. This type of exercise helps an employee consider his or her current career status, future plans, and the fit between the career and the employee's current situation and resources. Some organizations provide counselors to help employees in the self-assessment process and to interpret the results of psychological tests. Completing the self-assessment can help employees identify a development need. Such a need can result from gaps between current skills or interests and the type of work or position the employee has or wants.

These benefits are realized at Lockheed Martin when employees complete assessments using My LM Career Assessment, a system available on the company's intranet.

self-assessment
The use of information by employees to determine their career interests, values, aptitudes, behavioral tendencies, and development needs.

Figure 9.4

Sample Self-Assessment Exercise

Step 1: Where am I?
Examine current position of life and career.
Think about your life from past and present to the future. Draw a time line to represent important events.

Step 2: Who am I?
Examine different roles.
Using 3" × 5" cards, write down one answer per card to the question "Who am I?"

Step 3: Where would I like to be, and what would I like to happen?
Begin setting goals.
Consider your life from present to future. Write an autobiography answering these questions:
• What do you want to have accomplished?
• What milestones do you want to achieve?
• What do you want to be remembered for?

Step 4: An ideal year in the future
Identify resources needed.
Consider a one-year period in the future. Answer these questions:
• If you had unlimited resources, what would you do?
• What would the ideal environment look like?
• Does the ideal environment match Step 3?

Step 5: An ideal job
Create current goal.
In the present, think about an ideal job for you with your available resources. Describe your role, resources, and type of training or education needed.

Step 6: Career by objective inventory
Summarize current situation.
• What gets you excited each day?
• What do you do well? What are you known for?
• What do you need to achieve your goals?
• What could interfere with reaching your goals?
• What should you do now to move toward reaching your goals?
• What is your long-term career objective?

SOURCE: Based on J. E. McMahon and S. K. Merman, "Career Development," in *The ASTD Training and Development Handbook,* 4th ed., ed. R. L. Craig (New York: McGraw-Hill, 1996), pp. 679–97. Reproduced with permission.

Employees take a career inventory that identifies their career interests and skills so that they can begin to identify steps necessary for a successful career. The company encourages employees to discuss the results with their manager or mentor or with human resource representatives.[46]

Reality Check

reality check
Information employers give employees about their skills and knowledge and where these assets fit into the organization's plans.

In the next step of career management, the **reality check,** employees receive information about their skills and knowledge and where these assets fit into the organization's plans. The employee's responsibility is to identify what skills she or he could realistically develop in light of the opportunities available. The organization's responsibility is to communicate the performance evaluation and the opportunities available to the employee, given the organization's long-range plans. Opportunities might include promotions and transfers.

Usually the employer conducts the reality check as part of a performance appraisal or as the feedback stage of performance management. In well-developed career management systems, the manager may hold separate discussions for performance feedback and career development.

Goal Setting

Based on the information from the self-assessment and reality check, the employee sets short- and long-term career objectives. These goals usually involve one or more of the following categories:

- Desired positions, such as becoming sales manager within three years.
- Level of skill to apply—for example, to use one's budgeting skills to improve the unit's cash flow problems.
- Work setting—for example, to move to corporate marketing within two years.
- Skill acquisition, such as learning how to use the company's human resource information system.

As in these examples, the goals should be specific, and they should include a date by which the goal is to be achieved. It is the employee's responsibility to identify the goal and the method of determining her or his progress toward that goal.

Usually the employee discusses the goals with his or her manager. The organization's responsibilities are to ensure that the goal is specific, challenging, and attainable and to help the employee reach the goal. At candy maker Just Born, employees involved in the company's Career Development Process define future job interests, identify the necessary experiences for obtaining those jobs, and set short- and long-term goals. Each employee discusses these goals with his or her manager, who can suggest changes or support the goals as written.[47]

Action Planning

During the final step, employees prepare an action plan for how they will achieve their short- and long-term career goals. The employee is responsible for identifying the steps and timetable to reach the goals. The employer should identify resources needed, including courses, work experiences, and relationships.

Action plans may involve any one or a combination of the development methods discussed earlier in the chapter—training, assessment, job experiences, or the help of a mentor or coach. The approach used depends on the particular developmental needs and career objectives. For example, suppose the program manager in an information systems department uses feedback from performance appraisals to determine that he needs greater knowledge of project management software. The manager plans to increase that knowledge by reading articles (formal education), meeting with software vendors, and contacting the vendors' customers to ask them about the software they have used (job experiences). The manager and his supervisor agree that six months will be the target date for achieving the higher level of knowledge through these activities.

The outcome of action planning often takes the form of a career development plan. Figure 9.5 is an example of a development plan for a product manager. Development plans usually include descriptions of strengths and weaknesses, career goals, and development activities for reaching each goal.

Figure 9.5

Career Development Plan

Name:	**Title:** Project Manager	**Immediate Manager:**

Competencies

Please identify your three greatest strengths and areas for improvement.

Strengths

- Strategic thinking and execution (confidence, command skills, action orientation)
- Results orientation (competence, motivating others, perseverance)
- Spirit for winning (building team spirit, customer focus, respect colleagues)

Areas for Improvement

- Patience (tolerance of people or processes and sensitivity to pacing)
- Written communications (ability to write clearly and succinctly)
- Overly ambitious (too much focus on successful completion of projects rather than developing relationships with individuals involved in the projects)

Career Goals

Please describe your overall career goals.

- **Long-term:** Accept positions of increased responsibility to a level of general manager (or beyond). The areas of specific interest include but are not limited to product and brand management, technology and development, strategic planning, and marketing.
- **Short-term:** Continue to improve my skills in marketing and brand management while utilizing my skills in product management, strategic planning, and global relations.

Next Assignments

Identify potential next assignments (including timing) that would help you develop toward your career goals.

- Manager or director level in planning, development, product, or brand management. Timing estimated to be Spring 2009.

Training and Development Needs

List both training and development activities that will either help you develop in your current assignment or provide overall career development.

- Master's degree classes will allow me to practice and improve my written communications skills. The dynamics of my current position, teamwork, and reliance on other individuals allow me to practice patience and to focus on individual team members' needs along with the success of the projects.

Employee _____ **Date** _____
Immediate Manager _____ **Date** _____
Mentor _____ **Date** _____

Development-Related Challenges

LO8 Discuss how organizations are meeting the challenges of the "glass ceiling," succession planning, and dysfunctional managers.

A well-designed system for employee development can help organizations face three widespread challenges: the glass ceiling, succession planning, and dysfunctional behavior by managers.

The Glass Ceiling

As we mentioned in Chapter 1, women and minorities are rare in the top level of U.S. corporations. Observers of this situation have noted that it looks as if an invisible barrier is keeping women and minorities from reaching the top jobs, a barrier that has come to be known as the **glass ceiling.** For example, a recent census of the board membership of *Fortune* 500 companies found that just 15.6 percent of their officers were women, and 74 of the companies had no female corporate officers.[48]

Indra Nooyi became the first woman CEO of PepsiCo in 2006. Her success at the company gives her the distinction of being one of the women to break through the glass ceiling.

The glass ceiling is likely caused by a lack of access to training programs, appropriate developmental job experiences, and developmental relationships such as mentoring.[49] According to research, women and men have equal access to job experiences involving transitions or creating change.[50] But male managers receive significantly more assignments involving great responsibility (high stakes, managing business diversity, handling external pressure) than female managers of similar ability and managerial level. Also, female managers report experiencing more challenge due to lack of personal support (which, as we saw earlier in the chapter, is related to harmful stress). With regard to developmental relationships, women and minorities often have trouble finding mentors. They may not participate in the organization's, profession's, or community's "old boys' network." Also, managers in the organization may prefer to interact with people who have similar status or may avoid interacting with certain people because of discomfort or negative stereotypes.[51]

glass ceiling
Circumstances resembling an invisible barrier that keep most women and minorities from attaining the top jobs in organizations.

Organizations can use development systems to help break through the glass ceiling. Managers making developmental assignments need to carefully consider whether stereotypes are influencing the types of assignments men and women receive. A formal process for regularly identifying development needs and creating action plans can make these decisions more objective.

An organization that is actively working to eliminate the glass ceiling is insurance company Cigna. Women being developed for leadership at Cigna are rotated through supervisory jobs in different business units and assigned a mentor. They attend management training run by senior executives. Cigna, which has a relatively high proportion of executive and senior management women (24 percent), has seen a dramatic decline in the turnover rate among its female executives.[52]

Succession Planning

Organizations have always had to prepare for the retirement of their leaders, but the need is more intense than ever. The aging of the workforce means that a greater share of employees are reaching retirement age. Many organizations are fueling the trend by downsizing through early-retirement programs. As positions at the top of organizations become vacant, many organizations have determined that their middle managers are fewer and often unprepared for top-level responsibility. This situation has raised awareness of the need for **succession planning**—the process of identifying and tracking high-potential employees who will be able to fill top management positions when they become vacant.

succession planning
The process of identifying and tracking high-potential employees who will be able to fill top management positions when they become vacant.

Succession planning offers several benefits.[53] It forces senior management to regularly and thoughtfully review the company's leadership talent. It ensures that top-level management talent is available. It provides a set of development experiences that managers must complete to be considered for top management positions, so the organization does not promote managers before they are ready. Succession planning systems also help attract and retain ambitious managerial employees by providing development opportunities. Although succession planning is important, the "HR Oops!" box suggests that not all companies take it seriously.

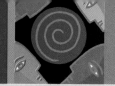

HR Oops!

Forgetting to Plan for HR

Succession planning is an important human resource function, so you might expect that HR divisions would be leading the way in this practice. But even as HR executives help other divisions prepare for their leaders' eventual departure, a recent study found that only 8 out of 100 companies were doing succession planning for the leaders of human resources. Edward Lawler, director of the Center for Effective Organizations at the University of Southern California, commented that the situation sounds too much like the "old story about the cobbler's children who don't have shoes." In other words, too many HR leaders are so busy helping the rest of the organization that they don't have time to take care of their own "family," their division.

Some observers conclude that HR divisions neglect succession planning because HR leadership is not seen as crucial for corporate leadership and success. That thinking runs counter to recent arguments that HR practices are essential for long-term success.

Source: Patrick J. Kiger, "Knowing It All: All-Around Players," *Workforce Management*, June 25, 2007, downloaded from General Reference Center Gold, http://find.galegroup.com.

Questions

1. What long-run consequences would you predict in an organization that fails to engage in succession planning for HR leaders?

2. What arguments would you make to support better HR planning in an organization you were advising? How would you back up your arguments?

Succession planning focuses on *high-potential employees*, that is, employees the organization believes can succeed in higher-level business positions such as general manager of a business unit, director of a function (such as marketing or finance), or chief executive officer.[54] A typical approach to development of high-potential employees is to have them complete an individual development program including education, executive mentoring and coaching, and rotation through job assignments. Job assignments are based on the successful career paths of the managers whom the high-potential employees are preparing to replace. High-potential employees may also receive special assignments, such as making presentations and serving on committees and task forces.

Research shows that an effective program for developing high-potential employees has three stages:[55]

1. *Selection of high-potential employees*—Organizations may select outstanding performers and employees who have completed elite academic programs, such as earning a master's degree in business administration from a prestigious university. They may also use the results of psychological tests such as assessment centers.

2. *Developmental experiences*—As employees participate in developmental experiences, the organization identifies those who succeed in the experiences. The organization looks for employees who continue to show qualities associated with success in top jobs, such as communication skills, leadership talent, and willingness to make sacrifices for the organization. Employees who display these qualities continue to be considered high-potential employees.

3. *Active involvement with the CEO*—High-potential employees seen by top management as fitting into the organization's culture and having personality characteristics necessary for representing the company become actively involved with the chief executive officer. The CEO exposes these employees to the organization's key people and gives them a greater understanding of the organization's culture. The development of high-potential employees is a slow process. Reaching stage 3 may take 15 to 20 years.

Figure 9.6 breaks this process into seven steps. It begins with identifying the positions to be planned for and the employees to be included in the plan. Planning should also include establishing position requirements and deciding how to measure employees' potential for being able to fill those requirements. The organization also needs to develop a process for reviewing the existing talent. The next step is to link succession planning with other human resource systems. Finally, the organization needs a way to provide employees with feedback about career paths available to them and how well they are progressing toward their goals.

A good example of succession planning is the system at WellPoint, a health care company headquartered in Thousand Oaks, California, with operations across the United States. WellPoint has a Web-based corporate database that identifies employees for management jobs throughout the company and tracks the development of employee talent. The succession-planning system includes 600 managers and executives, with detailed information on possible candidates, including performance evaluations, summaries of accomplishments at the company, self-evaluations and career goals, and personal information such as willingness to relocate. Standards are used to identify each candidate's strengths and identify the best candidates for promotion. Managers and the human resource team can use the system to identify and evaluate candidates for every management position in the company. They can also track the development of promising candidates and identify areas where further development is needed. In areas where development needs exceed management talent, WellPoint sets up additional training programs. This use of succession planning has helped WellPoint fill most of its management jobs with current employees, reduce employee turnover, and shorten the time needed to fill management jobs.[56]

Figure 9.6

Process for Developing a Succession Plan

Identify Positions to Plan For

Identify Employees to Include

Define Job Requirements

Measure Employee Potential

Review and Plan to Meet Development Needs

Link Succession Planning with Other HR Systems

Provide Feedback to Employees

SOURCE: Based on B. Dowell, "Succession Planning," in *Implementing Organizational Interventions*, ed. J. Hedge and E. Pulaskos (San Francisco: Jossey-Bass, 2002), pp. 78–109.

Dysfunctional Managers

A manager who is otherwise competent may engage in some behaviors that make him or her ineffective or even "toxic"—someone who stifles good ideas and drives away employees. These dysfunctional behaviors include insensitivity to others, inability to be a team player, arrogance, poor conflict management skills, inability to meet business objectives, and inability to adapt to change.[57] For example, a manager who has strong technical knowledge but is abrasive and discourages

Bad Bosses Take a Toll

A study at Florida State University surveyed 700 people in a variety of jobs and found that many employees feel poorly treated by their boss. These employees said they feel exhausted, nervous, and stressed, and they keep their work involvement to a minimum. Here are some of the behaviors they complained about:

Source: Brent Kallestad, "Survey: Bad Bosses Common, Problematic," *Yahoo News,* January 1, 2007, http://news.yahoo.com.

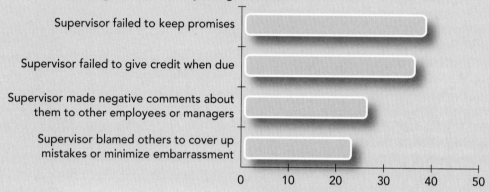

Percentage of workers reporting behavior:

employees from contributing their ideas is likely to have difficulty motivating employees and may alienate people inside and outside the organization. The "Did You Know?" box identifies some dysfunctional behaviors that many employees complain about.

When a manager is an otherwise valuable employee and is willing to improve, the organization may try to help him or her change the dysfunctional behavior. The usual ways to provide this type of development include assessment, training, and counseling. A middle manager at PG&E, an energy company, treated her colleagues in a way that alienated them and was hurting her career. PG&E hired a coach to work with her. The coach videotaped her as she role-played an actual clash she had had with another manager. As she and the coach reviewed the videotape, the manager could see that her behavior was aloof, abrasive, cold, and condescending. The coach helped the manager to understand the downside of this approach and to relate to her colleagues more constructively.[58]

Development programs for managers with dysfunctional behavior may include specialized programs such as one called Individual Coaching for Effectiveness (ICE). The ICE program includes diagnosis, coaching, and support activities tailored to each manager's needs.[59] Psychologists conduct the diagnosis, coach and counsel the manager, and develop action plans for implementing new skills on the job. Research suggests that managers who participate in programs like ICE improve their skills and are less likely to be terminated.[60] One possible conclusion is that organizations can benefit from offering development opportunities to valuable employees with performance problems, not just to star performers.

THINKING ETHICALLY

MENTORING TO DEVELOP ETHICAL EMPLOYEES

According to business professor Linda Treviño, ethical behavior in organizations depends less on formal training programs than on such management practices as ethical leadership. Perhaps most important is creating an environment in which employees believe people are treated fairly. Managers can foster such an environment by responding positively when employees raise ethical and other concerns. They can also build ethical leadership by rewarding ethical behavior in managers and by placing ethical managers in positions where they can mentor others.

In recent years, mentoring has become especially critical in companies' financial divisions. Several high-profile scandals involving misleading financial reports have brought greater regulation and public scrutiny, especially aimed at the chief financial officer (CFO) and his or her staff. Whereas CFOs were once valued primarily for their quantitative skills, today they need a broader range of ethical skills. In particular, they must be role models for ethical behavior, mentoring the organization's other financial experts. With these greater demands, the average length of service for a CFO is now just 30 months.

SOURCES: Linda Treviño, "The Key Role of HR in Organizational Ethics," Ethics Resource Center, 2007, www.ethics.org, accessed March 21, 2008; and Cynthia Jamison, "Struggling to Survive," *Strategic Finance*, April 2007, downloaded from General Reference Center Gold, http://find.galegroup.com.

Questions

1. In general, how might a senior executive mentor junior employees in behaving ethically?
2. If you were an employee who contributed to preparing an organization's financial statements, would having a CFO who places a high priority on ethical behavior help you meet high ethical standards? Why or why not?
3. How might an HR department help to develop financial executives who are ethical leaders and mentors?

SUMMARY

LO1 Discuss how development is related to training and careers.

Employee development is the combination of formal education, job experiences, relationships, and assessment of personality and abilities to help employees prepare for the future of their careers. Training is more focused on improving performance in the current job, but training programs may support employee development. In modern organizations, the concept of a career is fluid—a protean career that changes along with changes in a person's interests, abilities, and values and changes in the work environment. To plan and prepare for a protean career requires active career management, which includes planning for employee development.

LO2 Identify the methods organizations use for employee development.

Organizations may use formal educational programs at the workplace or off-site, such as workshops, university courses and degree programs, company-sponsored training, or programs offered by independent institutions. Organizations may use the assessment process to help employees identify strengths and areas requiring further development. Assessment can help the organization identify employees with managerial potential or identify areas in which teams need to develop. Job experiences help employees develop by stretching their skills as they meet new challenges. Interpersonal relationships with a more experienced member of the organization—often in the role of mentor or coach—can help employees develop their understanding of the organization and its customers.

LO3 Describe how organizations use assessment of personality type, work behaviors, and job performance to plan employee development.

Organizations collect information and provide feedback to employees about their behavior, communication style, and skills. The information may come from the employees, their peers, managers, and customers. Many organizations use performance appraisals as a source of assessment information. Appraisals may take the form of 360-degree feedback. Some organizations use psychological tests designed for this purpose, including the MBTI® inventory and the Benchmarks assessment. Assessment centers combine a variety of methods to provide assessment information. Managers must share the assessments, along with suggestions for improvement.

LO4 Explain how job experiences can be used for developing skills.

Job experiences contribute to development through a combination of relationships, problems, demands, tasks, and other features of an employee's jobs. The assumption is that development is most likely to occur when the employee's skills and experiences do not entirely match the skills required for the employee's current job, so employees must stretch to meet the demands of the new assignment. The impact varies according to whether the employee views the experience as a positive or negative source of stress. Job experiences that support employee development may include job enlargement, job rotations, transfers, promotions, downward moves, and temporary assignments with other organizations.

LO5   Summarize principles of successful mentoring programs.

A mentor is an experienced, productive senior employee who helps develop a less-experienced employee. Although most mentoring relationships develop informally, organizations can link mentoring to development goals by establishing a formal mentoring program. A formal program also provides a basis for ensuring that all eligible employees are included. Mentoring programs tend to be most successful when they are voluntary and participants understand the details of the program. The organization should reward managers for employee development, carefully select mentors based on interpersonal and technical skills, train them for the role, and evaluate whether the program has met its objectives.

LO6   Tell how managers and peers develop employees through coaching.

A coach is a peer or manager who works with an employee to motivate the employee, help him or her develop skills, and provide reinforcement and feedback. Coaches should be prepared to take on one or more of three roles: working one-on-one with an employee, helping employees learn for themselves, and providing resources, such as mentors, courses, or job experiences.

LO7   Identify the steps in the process of career management.

First, during self-assessment, employees use information to determine their career interests, values, aptitudes, and behavioral tendencies, looking for opportunities and areas needing improvement. Self-assessment tools often include psychological tests or exercises that ask about career status and plans. The second step is the reality check, during which the organization communicates information about the employee's skills and knowledge and how these fit into the organization's plan. The employee then sets goals and discusses them with his or her manager, who ensures that the goals are specific, challenging, and attainable. Finally, the employee works with his or her manager to create an action plan for development activities that will help the employee achieve the goals.

LO8   Discuss how organizations are meeting the challenges of the "glass ceiling," succession planning, and dysfunctional managers.

The glass ceiling is a barrier that has been observed preventing women and minorities from achieving top jobs in an organization. Development programs can ensure that these employees receive access to development resources such as coaches, mentors, and developmental job assignments. Succession planning ensures that the organization prepares qualified employees to fill management jobs as managers retire. It focuses on applying employee development to high-potential employees. Effective succession planning includes methods for selecting these employees, providing them with developmental experiences, and getting the CEO actively involved with employees who display qualities associated with success as they participate in the developmental activities. For dysfunctional managers who have the potential to contribute to the organization, the organization may offer development targeted at correcting the areas of dysfunction. Typically, the process includes collecting information about the manager's personality, skills, and interests; providing feedback, training, and counseling; and ensuring that the manager can apply new, functional behaviors on the job.

KEY TERMS

assessment, p. 250
assessment center, p. 253
Benchmarks, p. 254
coach, p. 261
downward move, p. 259
employee development, p. 247
externship, p. 260

glass ceiling, p. 267
job experiences, p. 256
leaderless group discussion, p. 253
mentor, p. 260
Myers-Briggs Type Indicator (MBTI)®, p. 251
promotion, p. 259

protean career, p. 247
reality check, p. 264
sabbatical, p. 260
self-assessment, p. 263
succession planning, p. 267
transfer, p. 258

REVIEW AND DISCUSSION QUESTIONS

1. How does development differ from training? How does development support career management in modern organizations?

2. What are the four broad categories of development methods? Why might it be beneficial to combine all of these methods into a formal development program?

3. Recommend a development method for each of the following situations, and explain why you chose that method.
   a. An employee recently promoted to the job of plant supervisor is having difficulty motivating employees to meet quality standards.
   b. A sales manager annoys salespeople by dictating every detail of their work.
   c. An employee has excellent leadership skills but lacks knowledge of the financial side of business.
   d. An organization is planning to organize its production workers into teams for the first time.

4. A company that markets sophisticated business management software systems uses sales teams to help customers define needs and to create systems that meet those needs. The teams include programmers, salespeople who specialize in client industries, and software designers. Occasionally sales are lost as a result of conflict or communication problems among team members. The company wants to improve the effectiveness of these teams, and it wants to begin with assessment. How can the teams use 360-degree feedback and psychological tests to develop?

5. In an organization that wants to use work experiences as a method of employee development, what basic options are available? Which of these options would be most attractive to you as an employee? Why?

6. Many employees are unwilling to relocate because they like their current community and family members prefer not to move. Yet preparation for management requires that employees develop new skills, strengthen areas of weakness, and be exposed to new aspects of the organization's business. How can an organization change an employee's current job to develop management skills?

7. Many people feel that mentoring relationships should occur naturally, in situations where senior managers feel inclined to play that role. What are some advantages of setting up a formal mentoring program, rather than letting senior managers decide how and whom to help?

8. What are the three roles of a coach? How is a coach different from a mentor? What are some advantages of using someone outside the organization as a coach? Some disadvantages?

9. Why should organizations be interested in helping employees plan their careers? What benefits can companies gain? What are the risks?

10. What are the manager's roles in a career management system? Which role do you think is most difficult for the typical manager? Which is the easiest role? List reasons why managers might resist becoming involved in career management.

11. What is the glass ceiling? What are the possible consequences to an organization that has a glass ceiling? How can employee development break the glass ceiling? Can succession planning help? Explain.

12. Why might an organization benefit from giving employee development opportunities to a dysfunctional manager, rather than simply dismissing the manager? Do these reasons apply to nonmanagement employees as well?

BUSINESSWEEK CASE

BusinessWeek Toyota's All-Out Drive to Stay Toyota

How's this for strange? Toyota Motor, the company that has the rest of the auto industry running scared, is worried. As new hires pour in and top executives approach retirement, the company fears it might lose the culture of frugality, discipline, and constant improvement that has been vital to its success. So management has launched a slew of education initiatives and even uses a business school in Tokyo to teach Toyota to be, well, more like Toyota.

Peek under the hood at Toyota, and you start to understand why management is worried. Rapid growth has forced this most Japanese of companies to rely more and more on *gaijin* (foreigners) overseas. Top brass—the ones who transformed a lean upstart into a global powerhouse—are nearing retirement, to be replaced by a generation that has never had a bad day at the office. And in the past three years, Toyota has hired 40,000 workers new to the company's culture.

When Steve St. Angelo was hired from General Motors in 2005, the executive immediately found himself back on the assembly line for several weeks. It didn't matter that he had spent almost 10 years at a plant in Fremont, California, jointly owned by GM and Toyota, where the Toyota Way has been alive and well for decades. The company figured an outsider hired to a management job—a rarity at Toyota—would need schooling in the basics. "They assumed I knew nothing about Toyota's production system," says St. Angelo, who in June was promoted to North American manufacturing boss.

Just in case St. Angelo forgets any of his Toyota training, he has someone watching his back. His retired predecessor, Gary Convis, still gets paid to advise him. That's an idea Toyota imported from Japan, where the company asks retiring engineers to stick around to mentor young employees. The ranks of these old-timers are growing rapidly as the company tries to safeguard its culture. Last year, Toyota rehired 650 of the 1,200 skilled workers eligible for retirement in Japan and will soon have 3,000 of these folks on its payroll.

Even lifers get the treatment. Randy Pflughaupt has worked at the company since 1982 and this summer was promoted to U.S. marketing chief for the flagship brand. With the promotion, he was handed a stack of books and binders telling him all about the Toyota Way and was packed off to the Toyota Institute in rural Mikkabi, Japan, for a week of indoctrination. "Why does a 25-year veteran go to training? I could take it personally," Pflughaupt jokes. "It's to remind me that I don't have all the answers."

There's another, more stressful step that growing numbers of newly minted executives must endure: finding a problem Toyota faces and coming up with a solution, which will be presented to company president Katsuaki Watanabe. Pflughaupt is figuring out how marketers can analyze the effectiveness of different media—print, television,

Web—in various regions. He'll be graded not just on his solution but on whether he used an eight-step method that's part of the Toyota Way to figure it out.

In Japan, a management school called Globis instructs white-collar staffers in the company's philosophy. The aim is to apply the same principles that have worked in manufacturing to other areas of the business. One lesson teaches office workers to apply the "five whys"—a tenet of the Toyota Production System that tells engineers to ask continually why a problem is occurring until they can think of no new answers. Toyota "may soon become the number one automaker in the world, but they still have a strong sense of urgency," says Yoshito Hori, chief executive of Globis.

SOURCE: Excerpted from David Welch and Ian Rowley, "Toyota's All-Out Drive to Stay Toyota," *BusinessWeek*, November 27, 2007, downloaded from General Reference Center Gold, http://find.galegroup.com.

Questions

1. Which of the four approaches to employee development (see Figure 9.1) are described in this case? Do you see any approaches that are missing?
2. What advantages and disadvantages can you identify in Toyota's use of retired employees to coach people who are new in their positions?
3. Do you think these development programs contribute to Toyota's strength as an automaker committed to continuous improvement and high quality? If you were an HR executive at a different auto company, would you suggest using similar approaches to development? Why or why not?

CASE: ACCOUNTING FOR TALENT AT ERNST & YOUNG

In the accounting profession, women and men alike have been finding excellent opportunities to start a career with a major firm. However, in a classic case of the glass ceiling, women make up half the entry-level jobs but just one-fifth of most firms' partners. Firms are concerned, not just out of fear they will be slapped with a discrimination lawsuit, but because accounting is a competitive market. More and more experienced accountants are retiring while demand for accounting and related services is rising. The best firms want to find—and keep—the best people.

Ernst & Young has found that attractive career paths are an important way to keep female accountants. At the time when their male colleagues may be moving to the management fast track, many female accountants are juggling work with the need to care for children or elderly parents. Traditionally, firms have avoided assigning top clients to accountants who want to limit their hours. Ernst & Young has begun defining career opportunities more

flexibly, offering reduced schedules, flexible hours, and telecommuting. So that these career options are as interesting as those offered to people on traditional schedules, the firm established leadership teams to ensure that assignments given to high-potential women and minorities include top clients.

Keeping employees on the payroll offers another advantage: The firm's managers have more time to spot the best talent. Ernst & Young has begun to capitalize on this advantage by getting its partners more involved in the process. It asked them to identify the skills needed for various roles, so the firm can offer assessments of these skills. Staffers can see what skills they have and those they need to acquire to qualify for senior positions. Employees can sign up for training programs in areas where they need improvement.

The firm makes a special effort to develop female and minority employees identified as having high potential.

Members of the executive board are assigned to serve as mentors to high-potential employees. Not only do the mentors offer the wisdom of their experience, but the mentoring relationship also makes the female and minority candidates more visible when the firm is looking for candidates to take on important assignments. The high-potential employees also complete a 360-degree assessment and work with a coach from outside the company.

Billie Williamson, a senior partner at Ernst & Young who is charged with the firm's gender-equity strategy, identified an important challenge in these mentoring relationships: The firm's partners, usually male, sometimes were unsure *how* to mentor or coach female accountants. So Williamson's efforts include helping the partners develop in that role. For example, she advises partners to invite women along to meetings, rather than expecting them to speak up and ask to attend, as men more often do. Some of the partners have worried about how women will react to negative feedback. Williamson encourages them to be direct about such matters as appropriate, professional attire. She frankly addresses fears that female protégés might cry in response to criticism, pointing out the importance of constructive criticism—and the likelihood that tears will pass quickly if the mentor simply waits patiently.

Along with mentors' worries, Williamson helps uncover their unspoken expectations. In one situation, a manager had more talented women than openings for partner. When Williamson suggested offering transfers to

some of them, the manager admitted he hadn't thought to ask because he assumed the women's husbands would object to moving. Williamson replied by suggesting he let the candidates address those concerns themselves. The manager tried and soon reported to Williamson that he had a win-win situation: a new senior manager who was delighted to relocate and pursue a career that offered a future as a partner at Ernst & Young.

SOURCES: Carol Hymowitz, "Coaching Men on Mentoring Women Is Ernst & Young Partner's Mission," *Wall Street Journal*, June 14, 2007, http://online.wsj.com; "Leadership Drivers," *Training*, June 1, 2007, downloaded from General Reference Center Gold, http://find.galegroup.com; Joe Cavaluzzi, "Women Are Not on Par(tner) with Male Colleagues," *Crain's New York Business*, September 24, 2007, http://find.galegroup.com; and "Accounting for Good People: Talent Management," *Economist*, July 21, 2007, http://find.galegroup.com.

Questions

1. Why is breaking the glass ceiling a significant business consideration for Ernst & Young?
2. Which approaches to development does Ernst & Young use to address the challenge of the glass ceiling?
3. How well does Ernst & Young's approach to development fulfill the steps and responsibilities of the career management process (see Figure 9.3)? Besides the efforts described in the case, what else should Ernst & Young and its accountants do to fulfill all these steps and responsibilities?

IT'S A WRAP!

www.mhhe.com/noefund3e is your source for Reviewing, Applying, and Practicing the concepts you learned about in Chapter 9.

Review
- Chapter learning objectives
- Narrated lecture and iPod content
- Test Your Knowledge: Mentoring

Application
- Manager's Hot Seat segment: "Personal Disclosure: Confession Coincidence"
- Video case and quiz: "Patagonia"
- Self-assessment: Employee Development
- Web exercise: Leadership programs at GE

Practice
- Chapter quiz

NOTES

1. M. London, *Managing the Training Enterprise* (San Francisco: Jossey-Bass, 1989).
2. R. W. Pace, P. C. Smith, and G. E. Mills, *Human Resource Development* (Englewood Cliffs, NJ: Prentice Hall, 1991); W. Fitzgerald, "Training versus Development," *Training and Development Journal*, May 1992, pp. 81–84; R. A. Noe, S. L. Wilk, E. J. Mullen, and J. E. Wanek, "Employee Development: Issues in Construct Definition and Investigation of Antecedents," in *Improving Training Effectiveness in Work Organizations*, ed. J. K. Ford (Mahwah, NJ: Lawrence Erlbaum, 1997), pp. 153–89.

3. J. H. Greenhaus and G. A. Callanan, *Career Management*, 2nd ed. (Fort Worth, TX: Dryden Press, 1994); and D. Hall, *Careers in and out of Organizations* (Thousand Oaks, CA: Sage, 2002).

4. M. B. Arthur, P. H. Claman, and R. J. DeFillippi, "Intelligent Enterprise, Intelligent Careers," *Academy of Management Executive* 9 (1995), pp. 7–20; and C. Ansberry, "A New Blue-Collar World," *Wall Street Journal*, June 30, 2003, p. B1.

5. M. Weinstein, "Teaching the Top," *Training*, February 2005, pp. 30–33.

6. R. Noe, *Employee Training and Development*, 4th ed. (New York: McGraw-Hill Irwin, 2008).

7. C. Waxer, "Bank of Montreal Opens Its Checkbook in the Name of Employee Development," *Workforce Management*, October 24, 2005, pp. 46–48.

8. R. Knight, "GE's Corporate Boot Camp cum Talent Spotting Venue," *Financial Times Business Education*, March 20, 2006, p. 2; and J. Durett, "GE Hones Its Leaders at Crotonville," *Training*, May 2006, pp. 25–27.

9. I. Speizer, "Custom Fit," *Workforce Management*, March 2005, pp. 57–63.

10. A. Howard and D. W. Bray, *Managerial Lives in Transition: Advancing Age and Changing Times* (New York: Guilford, 1988); J. Bolt, *Executive Development* (New York: Harper Business, 1989); J. R. Hinrichs and G. P. Hollenbeck, "Leadership Development," in *Developing Human Resources*, pp. 5-221–5-237.

11. A. Thorne and H. Gough, *Portraits of Type* (Palo Alto, CA: Consulting Psychologists Press, 1993).

12. D. Druckman and R. A. Bjork, eds., *In the Mind's Eye: Enhancing Human Performance* (Washington, DC: National Academy Press, 1991); M. H. McCaulley, "The Myers-Briggs Type Indicator and Leadership," in *Measures of Leadership*, ed. K. E. Clark and M. B. Clark (West Orange, NJ: Leadership Library of America, 1990), pp. 381–418.

13. G. C. Thornton III and W. C. Byham, *Assessment Centers and Managerial Performance* (New York: Academic Press, 1982); L. F. Schoenfeldt and J. A. Steger, "Identification and Development of Management Talent," in *Research in Personnel and Human Resource Management*, ed. K. N. Rowland and G. Ferris (Greenwich, CT: JAI Press, 1989), vol. 7, pp. 151–81.

14. Thornton and Byham, *Assessment Centers and Managerial Performance*.

15. P. G. W. Jansen and B. A. M. Stoop, "The Dynamics of Assessment Center Validity: Results of a Seven-Year Study," *Journal of Applied Psychology* 86 (2001), pp. 741–53; and D. Chan, "Criterion and Construct Validation of an Assessment Centre," *Journal of Occupational and Organizational Psychology* 69 (1996), pp. 167–81.

16. R. G. Jones and M. D. Whitmore, "Evaluating Developmental Assessment Centers as Interventions," *Personnel Psychology* 48 (1995), pp. 377–88.

17. C. D. McCauley and M. M. Lombardo, "Benchmarks: An Instrument for Diagnosing Managerial Strengths and Weaknesses," in *Measures of Leadership*, pp. 535–45; and Center for Creative Leadership, "Benchmarks®—Overview," www.ccl.org, accessed March 28, 2006.

18. C. D. McCauley, M. M. Lombardo, and C. J. Usher, "Diagnosing Management Development Needs: An Instrument Based on How Managers Develop," *Journal of Management* 15 (1989), pp. 389–403.

19. S. B. Silverman, "Individual Development through Performance Appraisal," in *Developing Human Resources*, pp. 5-120–5-151.

20. B. Pfau and I. Kay, "Does 360-Degree Feedback Negatively Affect Company Performance?" *HR Magazine* 47 (2002), pp. 54–59; J. F. Brett and L. E. Atwater, "360-Degree Feedback: Accuracy, Reactions, and Perceptions of Usefulness," *Journal of Applied Psychology* 86 (2001), pp. 930–42.

21. A. Freedman, "The Evolution of 360s," *Human Resource Executive*, December 2002, pp. 47–51.

22. L. Atwater, P. Roush, and A. Fischthal, "The Influence of Upward Feedback on Self- and Follower Ratings of Leadership," *Personnel Psychology* 48 (1995), pp. 35–59; J. F. Hazucha, S. A. Hezlett, and R. J. Schneider, "The Impact of 360-Degree Feedback on Management Skill Development," *Human Resource Management* 32 (1993), pp. 325–51; J. W. Smither, M. London, N. Vasilopoulos, R. R. Reilly, R. E. Millsap, and N. Salvemini, "An Examination of the Effects of an Upward Feedback Program over Time," *Personnel Psychology* 48 (1995), pp. 1–34; J. Smither and A. Walker, "Are the Characteristics of Narrative Comments Related to Improvements in Multirater Feedback Ratings over Time?" *Journal of Applied Psychology* 89 (2004), pp. 575–81; and J. Smither, M. London, and R. Reilly, "Does Performance Improve Following Multisource Feedback? A Theoretical Model, Meta-analysis, and Review of Empirical Findings," *Personnel Psychology* 58 (2005), pp. 33–66.

23. D. Bracken, "Straight Talk about Multirater Feedback," *Training and Development*, September 1994, pp. 44–51.

24. M. W. McCall Jr., *High Flyers* (Boston: Harvard Business School Press, 1998).

25. R. S. Snell, "Congenial Ways of Learning: So Near yet So Far," *Journal of Management Development* 9 (1990), pp. 17–23.

26. M. McCall, M. Lombardo, and A. Morrison, *Lessons of Experience* (Lexington, MA: Lexington Books, 1988); M. W. McCall, "Developing Executives through Work Experiences," *Human Resource Planning* 11 (1988),

pp. 1–11; M. N. Ruderman, P. J. Ohlott, and C. D. McCauley, "Assessing Opportunities for Leadership Development," in *Measures of Leadership*, pp. 547–62; and C. D. McCauley, L. J. Estman, and P. J. Ohlott, "Linking Management Selection and Development through Stretch Assignments," *Human Resource Management* 34 (1995), pp. 93–115.

27. C. D. McCauley, M. N. Ruderman, P. J. Ohlott, and J. E. Morrow, "Assessing the Developmental Components of Managerial Jobs," *Journal of Applied Psychology* 79 (1994), pp. 544–60.

28. "Training Top 100 Best Practices: Regions Financial," *Training*, March 2006, p. 61.

29. M. London, *Developing Managers* (San Francisco: Jossey-Bass, 1985); M. A. Camion, L. Cheraskin, and M. J. Stevens, "Career-Related Antecedents and Outcomes of Job Rotation," *Academy of Management Journal* 37 (1994), pp. 1518–42; and London, *Managing the Training Enterprise*.

30. L. Cheraskin and M. Campion, "Study Clarifies Job Rotation Benefits," *Personnel Journal*, November 1996, pp. 31–38.

31. R. A. Noe, B. D. Steffy, and A. E. Barber, "An Investigation of the Factors Influencing Employees' Willingness to Accept Mobility Opportunities," *Personnel Psychology* 41 (1988), pp. 559–80; S. Gould and L. E. Penley, "A Study of the Correlates of Willingness to Relocate," *Academy of Management Journal* 28 (1984), pp. 472–78; J. Landau and T. H. Hammer, "Clerical Employees' Perceptions of Intraorganizational Career Opportunities," *Academy of Management Journal* 29 (1986), pp. 385–405; and J. M. Brett and A. H. Reilly, "On the Road Again: Predicting the Job Transfer Decision," *Journal of Applied Psychology* 73 (1988), pp. 614–20.

32. J. M. Brett, "Job Transfer and Well-Being," *Journal of Applied Psychology* 67 (1992), pp. 450–63; F. J. Minor, L. A. Slade, and R. A. Myers, "Career Transitions in Changing Times," in *Contemporary Career Development Issues*, eds. R. F. Morrison and J. Adams (Hillsdale, NJ: Lawrence Erlbaum, 1991), pp. 109–20; C. C. Pinder and K. G. Schroeder, "Time to Proficiency Following Job Transfers," *Academy of Management Journal* 30 (1987), pp. 336–53; and G. Flynn, "Heck No—We Won't Go!" *Personnel Journal*, March 1996, pp. 37–43.

33. R. E. Silverman, "Mercer Tries to Keep Employees through Its 'Externship' Program," *Wall Street Journal*, November 7, 2000, p. B18.

34. E. Jossi, "Taking Time Off from Advertising," *Workforce*, April 2002, p. 15.

35. D. B. Turban and T. W. Dougherty, "Role of Protégé Personality in Receipt of Mentoring and Career Success," *Academy of Management Journal* 37 (1994), pp. 688–702; and E. A. Fagenson, "Mentoring: Who Needs It? A Comparison of Protégés' and Nonprotégés' Needs for Power, Achievement, Affiliation, and Autonomy," *Journal of Vocational Behavior* 41 (1992), pp. 48–60.

36. A. H. Geiger, "Measures for Mentors," *Training and Development Journal*, February 1992, pp. 65–67.

37. K. E. Kram, *Mentoring at Work: Developmental Relationships in Organizational Life* (Glenview, IL: Scott-Foresman, 1985); L. L. Phillips-Jones, "Establishing a Formalized Mentoring Program," *Training and Development Journal* 2 (1983), pp. 38–42; K. Kram, "Phases of the Mentoring Relationship," *Academy of Management Journal* 26 (1983), pp. 608–25; G. T. Chao, P. M. Walz, and P. D. Gardner, "Formal and Informal Mentorships: A Comparison of Mentoring Functions and Contrasts with Nonmentored Counterparts," *Personnel Psychology* 45 (1992), pp. 619–36; and C. Wanberg, E. Welsh, and S. Hezlett, "Mentoring Research: A Review and Dynamic Process Model," in *Research in Personnel and Human Resources Management*, eds. J. Martocchio and G. Ferris (New York: Elsevier Science, 2003), pp. 39–124.

38. L. Eby, M. Butts, A. Lockwood, and A. Simon, "Protégés' Negative Mentoring Experiences: Construct Development and Nomological Validation," *Personnel Psychology* 57 (2004), pp. 411–47; and M. Boyle, "Most Mentoring Programs Stink—but Yours Doesn't Have To," *Training*, August 2005, pp. 12–15.

39. E. Tahmincioglu, "Looking for a Mentor? Technology Can Help Make the Right Match," *Workforce Management*, December 2004, pp. 63–65; and D. Owens, "Virtual Mentoring," *HRMagazine*, March 2006, pp. 105–107.

40. R. A. Noe, D. B. Greenberger, and S. Wang, "Mentoring: What We Know and Where We Might Go," in *Research in Personnel and Human Resources Management*, eds. G. Ferris and J. Martocchio (New York: Elsevier Science, 2002), vol. 21, pp. 129–74; and T. D. Allen, L. T. Eby, M. L. Poteet, E. Lentz, and L. Lima, "Career Benefits Associated with Mentoring for Protégés: A Meta-Analysis," *Journal of Applied Psychology* 89 (2004), pp. 127–36.

41. D. B. Peterson and M. D. Hicks, *Leader as Coach* (Minneapolis: Personnel Decisions, 1996).

42. H. Johnson, "The Ins and Outs of Executive Coaching," *Training*, May 2004, pp. 36–41.

43. J. Smither, M. London, R. Flautt, Y. Vargas, and L. Kucine, "Can Working with an Executive Coach Improve Multisource Ratings over Time? A Quasi-experimental Field Study," *Personnel Psychology* 56 (2003), pp. 23–44.

44. J. Toto, "Untapped World of Peer Coaching," *T&D*, April 2006, pp. 69–71.

45. B. Baumann, J. Duncan, S. E. Former, and Z. Leibowitz, "Amoco Primes the Talent Pump," *Personnel Journal*, February 1996, pp. 79–84.

46. M. Weinstein, "Flying High," *Training*, March 2006, pp. 36–38; and Lockheed Martin Web site, www.lockheedmartin.com.

47. M. Sallie-Dosunmu, "Born to Grow," *T&D*, May 2006, pp. 34–37.

48. Catalyst, "2007 Census: Corporate Offices and Top Earners," Catalyst Web site, www.catalystwomen.org, accessed February 1, 2008.

49. P. J. Ohlott, M. N. Ruderman, and C. D. McCauley, "Gender Differences in Managers' Developmental Job Experiences," *Academy of Management Journal* 37 (1994), pp. 46–67; and D. Mattioli, "Programs to Promote Female Managers Win Citations," *Wall Street Journal*, January 30, 2007, p. B7.

50. L. A. Mainiero, "Getting Anointed for Advancement: The Case of Executive Women," *Academy of Management Executive* 8 (1994), pp. 53–67; J. S. Lublin, "Women at Top Still Are Distant from CEO Jobs," *Wall Street Journal*, February 28, 1995, pp. B1, B5; P. Tharenov, S. Latimer, and D. Conroy, "How Do You Make It to the Top? An Examination of Influences on Women's and Men's Managerial Advancements," *Academy of Management Journal* 37 (1994), pp. 899–931.

51. U.S. Department of Labor, *A Report on the Glass Ceiling Initiative* (Washington, DC: Labor Department, 1991); R. A. Noe, "Women and Mentoring: A Review and Research Agenda," *Academy of Management Review* 13 (1988), pp. 65–78; and B. R. Ragins and J. L. Cotton, "Easier Said than Done: Gender Differences in Perceived Barriers to Gaining a Mentor," *Academy of Management Journal* 34 (1991), pp. 939–51.

52. E. Tahmincioglu, "When Women Rise," *Workforce Management*, September 2004, pp. 26–32.

53. W. J. Rothwell, *Effective Succession Planning*, 2nd ed. (New York: AMACOM, 2001).

54. B. E. Dowell, "Succession Planning," in *Implementing Organizational Interventions*, eds. J. Hedge and E. D. Pulakos (San Francisco: Jossey-Bass, 2002), pp. 78–109.

55. C. B. Derr, C. Jones, and E. L. Toomey, "Managing High-Potential Employees: Current Practices in Thirty-Three U.S. Corporations," *Human Resource Management* 27 (1988), pp. 273–90; K. M. Nowack, "The Secrets of Succession," *Training and Development* 48 (1994), pp. 49–54; and J. S. Lublin, "An Overseas Stint Can Be a Ticket to the Top," *Wall Street Journal*, January 29, 1996, pp. B1, B2.

56. P. Kiger, "Succession Planning Keeps WellPoint Competitive," *Workforce*, April 2002, pp. 50–54; and E. Fravenheim, "Succession Progression," *Workforce Management*, January 2006, pp. 31–34.

57. M. W. McCall Jr. and M. M. Lombardo, "Off the Track: Why and How Successful Executives Get Derailed," *Technical Report*, no. 21 (Greensboro, NC: Center for Creative Leadership, 1983); and E. V. Veslo and J. B. Leslie, "Why Executives Derail: Perspectives across Time and Cultures," *Academy of Management Executive* 9 (1995), pp. 62–72.

58. J. Lublin, "Did I Just Say That?! How You Can Recover from Foot-in-Mouth," *Wall Street Journal*, June 18, 2002, p. B1.

59. L. W. Hellervik, J. F. Hazucha, and R. J. Schneider, "Behavior Change: Models, Methods, and a Review of Evidence," in *Handbook of Industrial and Organizational Psychology*, 2nd ed., eds. M. D. Dunnette and L. M. Hough (Palo Alto, CA: Consulting Psychologists Press, 1992), vol. 3, pp. 823–99.

60. D. B. Peterson, "Measuring and Evaluating Change in Executive and Managerial Development," paper presented at the annual conference of the Society for Industrial and Organizational Psychology, Miami, 1990.

Separating and Retaining Employees

What Do I Need to Know?

After reading this chapter, you should be able to:

LO1 Distinguish between involuntary and voluntary turnover, and describe their effects on an organization.

LO2 Discuss how employees determine whether the organization treats them fairly.

LO3 Identify legal requirements for employee discipline.

LO4 Summarize ways in which organizations can fairly discipline employees.

LO5 Explain how job dissatisfaction affects employee behavior.

LO6 Describe how organizations contribute to employees' job satisfaction and retain key employees.

Introduction

Keeping productive employees can be a challenge when work and family demands collide. Recently, *Wall Street Journal* reporters talked to some of the nation's top female executives about their career success, and one issue that came up repeatedly was time pressure. Although work and family obligations have caused many women to rethink promising careers, the women who were interviewed had found ways to cope and prosper. Melanie Healey, president of Global Health and Feminine Care at Procter & Gamble, recalled that she had her first child while working in Mexico for an executive who routinely put in 16-hour days. At Healey's request, she and her boss agreed on a set of goals for her to accomplish on her own terms, while leaving each evening at six o'clock. In the end, Healey was so successful that her boss tried to recruit her when he left for a position at another company.

Sheryl Sandberg, a Google vice president, encountered a similar situation from the manager's perspective. A top employee was expecting a baby, and Sandberg encouraged her to stay with the company, opening a discussion on how to make that happen. The woman said that what would matter would be for Sandberg to stop sending her e-mail late at night. If 11:30 P.M. was the best time for Sandberg to work, she needed to realize that a response could wait until the next day.[1] Such efforts to communicate and establish a flexible work environment can be essential for retaining high-performing employees.

Every organization recognizes that it needs satisfied, loyal customers. In addition, success requires satisfied, loyal employees. Research provides evidence that retaining employees helps retain customers and increase sales.[2] Organizations with low turnover and satisfied employees tend to perform better.[3] On the other side of the coin, organizations have to act when an employee's performance consistently falls short. Sometimes terminating a poor performer is the only way to show fairness, ensure quality, and maintain customer satisfaction.

chapter ten

This chapter explores the dual challenges of separating and retaining employees. We begin by distinguishing involuntary and voluntary turnover, describing how each affects the organization. Next we explore the separation process, including ways to manage this process fairly. Finally, we discuss measures the organization can take to encourage employees to stay. These topics provide a transition between Parts 3 and 4. The previous chapters in Part 3 considered how to assess and improve performance, and this chapter describes measures to take depending on whether performance is high or low. Part 4 discusses pay and benefits, both of which play an important role in employee retention.

LO1 Distinguish between involuntary and voluntary turnover, and describe their effects on an organization.

involuntary turnover
Turnover initiated by an employer (often with employees who would prefer to stay).

voluntary turnover
Turnover initiated by employees (often when the organization would prefer to keep them).

Managing Voluntary and Involuntary Turnover

Organizations must try to ensure that good performers want to stay with the organization and that employees whose performance is chronically low are encouraged—or forced—to leave. Both of these challenges involve *employee turnover*, that is, employees leaving the organization. When the organization initiates the turnover (often with employees who would prefer to stay), the result is **involuntary turnover.** Examples include terminating an employee for drug use or laying off employees during a downturn. Most organizations use the word *termination* to refer only to a discharge related to a discipline problem, but some organizations call any involuntary turnover a termination. When the employees initiate the turnover (often when the organization would prefer to keep them), it is **voluntary turnover.** Employees may leave to retire or to take a job with a different organization.

In general, organizations try to avoid the need for involuntary turnover and to minimize voluntary turnover, especially among top performers. Both kinds of turnover are costly, as summarized in Table 10.1. Replacing workers is expensive, and new employees need time to learn their jobs and build teamwork skills.[4] In addition, people today are more ready to sue a former employer if they feel they were unfairly discharged. The prospect of workplace violence also raises the risk associated with discharging employees. Effective human resource management can help the organization minimize both kinds of turnover, as well as carry it out effectively when necessary. Despite a company's best efforts at personnel selection, training, and compensation, some employees will fail to meet performance requirements or will violate company policies. When this happens, organizations need to apply a discipline program that could ultimately lead to discharging the individual.

For a number of reasons, discharging employees can be very difficult. First, the decision has legal aspects that can affect the organization. Historically, if the organization and employee do not have a specific employment contract, the employer or employee may end the employment relationship at any time. This is the *employment-at-will doctrine*, described in Chapter 5. This doctrine has eroded significantly, however.

Table 10.1

Costs Associated with Turnover

INVOLUNTARY TURNOVER	VOLUNTARY TURNOVER
Recruiting, selecting, and training replacements	Recruiting, selecting, and training replacements
Lost productivity	Lost productivity
Lawsuits	Loss of talented employees
Workplace violence	

Employees who have been terminated sometimes sue their employers for wrongful discharge. Some judges have considered that there could be an implied employment contract if employees meet certain criteria such as length of employment, promotions, raises, or favorable performance appraisals—even when the organization has a handbook that says there is an employment-at-will relationship.[5] In a typical lawsuit for wrongful discharge, the former employee tries to establish that the discharge violated either an implied agreement or public policy (for example, firing an employee for refusing to do something illegal). Most employers settle these claims out of court. Even though few former employees win wrongful-discharge suits, and employers usually win when they appeal, the cost of defending the lawsuit can be hundreds of thousands of dollars.[6]

Along with the financial risks of dismissing an employee, there are issues of personal safety. Distressing as it is that some former employees go to the courts, far worse are the employees who react to a termination decision with violence. Violence in the workplace has become a major organizational problem. Although any number of organizational actions or decisions may incite violence among employees, the "nothing else to lose" aspect of an employee's dismissal makes the situation dangerous, especially when the nature of the work adds other risk factors.[7]

Retaining top performers is not always easy either, and recent trends have made this more difficult than ever. Today's psychological contract, in which workers feel responsibility for their own careers rather than loyalty to a particular employer, makes voluntary turnover more likely. Also, competing organizations are constantly looking at each other's top performers; in a tight labor market, "poaching talent" has become an art form.[8]

Employee Separation

Because of the critical financial and personal risks associated with employee dismissal, it is easy to see why organizations must develop a standardized, systematic approach to discipline and discharge. These decisions should not be left solely to the discretion of individual managers or supervisors. Policies that can lead to employee separation should be based on principles of justice and law, and they should allow for various ways to intervene.

Principles of Justice

The sensitivity of a system for disciplining and possibly terminating employees is obvious, and it is critical that the system be seen as fair. Employees form conclusions about the system's fairness based on the system's outcomes and procedures and the way managers treat employees when carrying out those procedures. Figure 10.1 summarizes these principles as outcome fairness, procedural justice, and interactional justice. Outcome fairness involves the ends of a discipline process, while procedural and interactional justice focus on the means to those ends. Not only is behavior in accord with these principles ethical, but research has also linked the last two categories of justice with employee satisfaction and productivity.[9]

People's perception of **outcome fairness** depends on their judgment that the consequences of a decision to employees are just. As shown in Figure 10.1, one employee's consequences should be consistent with other employees' consequences. Suppose several employees went out to lunch, returned drunk, and were reprimanded. A few weeks later, another employee was fired for being drunk at work. Employees might well conclude that

LO2 Discuss how employees determine whether the organization treats them fairly.

outcome fairness
A judgment that the consequences given to employees are just.

Figure 10.1

Principles of Justice

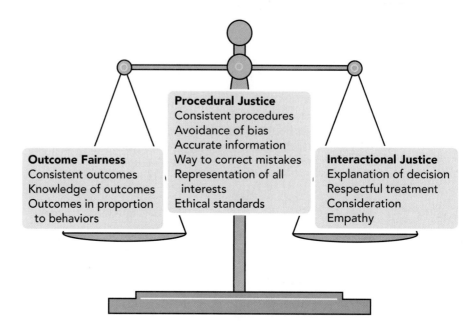

Procedural Justice
Consistent procedures
Avoidance of bias
Accurate information
Way to correct mistakes
Representation of all
   interests
Ethical standards

Outcome Fairness
Consistent outcomes
Knowledge of outcomes
Outcomes in proportion
   to behaviors

Interactional Justice
Explanation of decision
Respectful treatment
Consideration
Empathy

outcomes are not fair because they are inconsistent. Another basis for outcome fairness is that everyone should know what to expect. Organizations promote outcome fairness when they clearly communicate policies regarding the consequences of inappropriate behavior. Finally, the outcome should be proportionate to the behavior. Terminating an employee for being late to work, especially if this is the first time the employee is late, would seem out of proportion to the offense in most situations. Employees' sense of outcome fairness usually would reserve loss of a job for the most serious offenses.

procedural justice
A judgment that fair methods were used to determine the consequences an employee receives.

People's perception of **procedural justice** is their judgment that fair methods were used to determine the consequences an employee receives. Figure 10.1 shows six principles that determine whether people perceive procedures as fair. The procedures should be consistent from one person to another, and the manager using them should suppress any personal biases. The procedures should be based on accurate information, not rumors or falsehoods. The procedures should also be correctable, meaning the system includes safeguards, such as channels for appealing a decision or correcting errors. The procedures should take into account the concerns of all the groups affected—for example, by gathering information from employees, customers, and managers. Finally, the procedures should be consistent with prevailing ethical standards, such as concerns for privacy and honesty.

interactional justice
A judgment that the organization carried out its actions in a way that took the employee's feelings into account.

A perception of **interactional justice** is a judgment that the organization carried out its actions in a way that took the employee's feelings into account. It is a judgment about the ways that managers interact with their employees. A disciplinary action meets the standards of interactional justice if the manager explains to the employee how the action is procedurally just. The manager should listen to the employee. The manager should also treat the employee with dignity and respect and should empathize with the employee's feelings. Even when a manager discharges an employee for doing something wrong, the manager can speak politely and state the reasons for the action. These efforts to achieve interactional justice are especially important when managing an employee who has a high level of hostility and is at greater risk of responding with violence.[10] The "HR Oops!" box shows examples of poor separation practices.

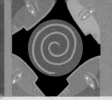

HR Oops!

An Awkward Good-Bye

Meeting the standards of justice when terminating an employee is difficult, because managers are as uncomfortable as anyone else when they have to deliver bad news. As a result, some organizations handle separation in ways that employees find infuriating.

When an electronics retailer cut 400 jobs, it notified the laid-off workers by sending them an e-mail message saying their position had been eliminated. Workers were told to meet with their manager that morning to discuss their severance pay. In another instance, a salesperson in London received a text message from her employer saying she was no longer needed.

Other managers don't even deliver the bad news themselves. They hire a contractor. A consulting firm that provides HR services in California's Bay Area recently assigned one of its people to meet with 20 software engineers whose positions were being moved to China. On behalf of her client, she told them about their severance pay and escorted them from the building.

Sources: Amy Joyce, "Fired via E-mail, and Other Tales of Poor Exits," *Washington Post,* September 10, 2006, www.washingtonpost.com; "RadioShack Lays Off Employees via E-mail," *USA Today,* August 30, 2006, updated March 2, 2007, www.usatoday.com; and Max Chafkin, "Meet Rebecca: She's Here to Fire You," *Inc.,* November 2007, pp. 25–26.

Questions

1. How do these examples meet or fail to meet the principles of justice shown in Figure 10.1?

2. How could these companies and managers better fulfill the principles of justice?

Legal Requirements

The law gives employers wide latitude in hiring and firing, but employers must meet certain requirements. They must avoid wrongful discharge and illegal discrimination. They also must meet standards related to employees' privacy and adequate notice of layoffs.

L03 Identify legal requirements for employee discipline.

Wrongful Discharge

As we noted earlier in the chapter, discipline practices must avoid the charge of wrongful discharge. First, this means the discharge may not violate an implied agreement. Terminating an employee may violate an implied agreement if the employer had promised the employee job security or if the action is inconsistent with company policies. An example might be that an organization has stated that an employee with an unexcused absence will receive a warning for the first violation, but an angry supervisor fires an employee for being absent on the day of an important meeting.

Another reason a discharge may be considered wrongful is that it violates public policy. Violations of public policy include terminating the employee for refusing to do something illegal, unethical, or unsafe. Suppose an employee refuses to dump chemicals into the sewer system; firing that employee could be a violation of public policy. It is also a violation of public policy to terminate an employee for doing what the law requires—for example, cooperating with a government investigation, reporting illegal behavior by the employer, or reporting for jury duty.

HR professionals can help organizations avoid (and defend against) charges of wrongful discharge by establishing and communicating policies for handling misbehavior. They should define unacceptable behaviors and identify how the organization will respond to them. Managers should follow these procedures consistently and document precisely the reasons for disciplinary action. In addition, the organization should train managers to avoid making promises that imply job security (for example, "As long as you keep up that level of performance, you'll have a job with us"). Finally, in writing and reviewing employee handbooks, HR professionals should avoid any statements that could be interpreted as employment contracts. When there is any doubt about a statement, the organization should seek legal advice.

Discrimination

Another benefit of a formal discipline policy is that it helps the organization comply with equal employment opportunity requirements. As in other employment matters, employers must make decisions without regard to individuals' age, sex, race, or other protected status. If two employees steal from the employer but one is disciplined more harshly than the other, the employee who receives the harsher punishment could look for the cause in his or her being of a particular race, country of origin, or some other group. Evenhanded, carefully documented discipline can avoid such claims.

Employees' Privacy

The courts also have long protected individuals' privacy in many situations. At the same time, employers have legitimate reasons for learning about some personal matters, especially when behavior outside the workplace can affect productivity, workplace safety, and employee morale. Employers therefore need to ensure that the information they gather and use is relevant to these matters. For example, safety and security make it legitimate to require drug testing of all employees holding jobs such as police officer, firefighter, and airline flight crew.[11] (Governments at the federal, state, and local levels have many laws affecting drug-testing programs, so it is wise to get legal advice before planning such tests.)

Organizations such as day care facilities and schools must protect employees' right to privacy in their lives and on the job while balancing the need to protect children from harm.

Privacy issues also surface when employers wish to search or monitor employees on the job. An employer that suspects theft by employees or drug use on the job may wish to search employees for evidence. In general, random searches of areas such as desks, lockers, and toolboxes are permissible, so long as the employer can justify that there is probable cause for the search and the organization has work rules that provide for searches.[12] Employers can act fairly and minimize the likelihood of a lawsuit by publicizing the search policy, applying it consistently, asking for the employee's consent before the search begins, and conducting the search discreetly. Also, when a search is a random check, it is important to clarify that no one has been accused of misdeeds.[13]

No matter how sensitively the organization gathers information leading to disciplinary actions, it should also consider privacy issues when deciding who will see the information.[14] In general, it is advisable to share the information only with people who have a business need to see it—for example, the employee's supervisor, union officials, and in some cases, co-workers. Letting outsiders know the reasons

Ensure that information is relevant.
Publicize information-gathering policies and consequences.
Request consent before gathering information.
Treat employees consistently.
Conduct searches discreetly.
Share information only with those who need it.

Table 10.2

Measures for Protecting Employees' Privacy

for terminating an employee can embarrass the employee, who might file a defamation lawsuit. HR professionals can help organizations avoid such lawsuits by working with managers to determine fact-based explanations and to decide who needs to see these explanations.

Table 10.2 summarizes these measures for protecting employees' privacy.

Notification of Layoffs

Sometimes terminations are necessary not because of individuals' misdeeds, but because the organization determines that for economic reasons it must close a facility. An organization that plans such broad-scale layoffs may be subject to the Workers' Adjustment Retraining and Notification Act. This federal law requires that organizations with more than 100 employees give 60 days' notice before any closing or layoff that will affect at least 50 full-time employees. If employers covered by this law do not give notice to the employees (and their union, if applicable), they may have to provide back pay and fringe benefits and pay penalties as well. Several states and cities have similar laws, and the federal law contains a number of exemptions. Therefore, it is important to seek legal advice before implementing a plant closing.

LO4 Summarize ways in which organizations can fairly discipline employees.

Progressive Discipline

Organizations look for methods of handling problem behavior that are fair, legal, and effective. A popular principle for responding effectively is the **hot-stove rule.** According to this principle, discipline should be like a hot stove: The glowing or burning stove gives warning not to touch. Anyone who ignores the warning will be burned. The stove has no feelings to influence which people it burns, and it delivers the same burn to any touch. Finally, the burn is immediate. Like the hot stove, an organization's discipline should give warning and have consequences that are consistent, objective, and immediate. The "HR How To" box offers suggestions for putting these principles into practice.

The principles of justice suggest that the organization prepare for problems by establishing a formal discipline process in which the consequences become more serious if the employee repeats the offense. Such a system is called **progressive discipline.** A typical progressive discipline system identifies and communicates unacceptable behaviors and responds to a series of offenses with the actions shown in Figure 10.2—spoken and then written warnings, temporary suspension, and finally, termination. This process fulfills the purpose of discipline by teaching employees what is expected of them and creating a situation in which employees must try to do what is expected. It seeks to prevent misbehavior (by publishing rules) and to correct, rather than merely punish, misbehavior.

Such procedures may seem exasperatingly slow, especially when the employee's misdeeds hurt the team's performance. In the end, however, if an employee must be

hot-stove rule
Principle of discipline that says discipline should be like a hot stove, giving clear warning and following up with consistent, objective, immediate consequences.

progressive discipline
A formal discipline process in which the consequences become more serious if the employee repeats the offense.

HR How To

ANTIDOTES FOR TOXIC EMPLOYEES

A "toxic" employee is someone whose abrasive personality, lack of effort, or confusion about what needs to be done makes co-workers dislike the person and interferes with work. Such a person makes everyone else's job unpleasant, and the whole group's motivation and performance may suffer. One company tried calculating the cost of the abusive behavior by a top salesperson; they found her impact on staff turnover, need for intervention, and other measures cost the company about $160,000 a year.

For managers, the first challenge is to be aware that such an employee is on the payroll. The rest of the group may not think it is wise to complain to the boss. So the first step in the cure for toxic employees is to find out the reasons for a tense atmosphere or an isolated team member. The manager might say, "This team seems uncomfortable about something. Would you please let me know what you think might be wrong?"

If the evidence points to a problem employee, justice and productivity both require action. Ignoring a problem sends a message that the manager isn't leading and that the team's effectiveness isn't a priority. Instead, the toxic employee seems to be more important than everyone else on the team.

In confronting a toxic employee, a manager can start by discussing whether the problem can be solved without dismissing the employee. Some useful questions are, "Do you understand the standards you are supposed to meet?" and "What training or what else do you need to improve?" The manager should also verify that the employee understands the consequences of not improving.

If the employee does not make the changes, then the manager should consider the pros and cons of dismissing the employee. Asking a toxic employee to leave frees the manager to hire a replacement who will contribute to the team. Many managers have found that a tremendous amount of energy went to coping with a toxic employee, and without him or her, all the team's work becomes easier. Nancy Traversy, founder of publisher Barefoot Books, says she learned that many workers suffer as a result of one toxic employee, so "I learned to focus my compassion on the rest of the team."

Sources: Liz Ryan, "The Toxic Employee," *Business-Week,* November 1, 2007, www.businessweek.com; Michaela Cavallaro, "Questions for Problem Employees," *Restaurant Business,* July 2007, p. 17; "Ask Inc.," November 2007, pp. 69–70; and Robert Sutton, "Building the Civilized Workplace," *McKinsey Quarterly,* May 2007, www.mckinseyquarterly.com.

discharged, careful use of the procedure increases other employees' belief that the organization is fair and reduces the likelihood that the problem employee will sue (or at least that the employee will win in court). For situations in which misbehavior is dangerous, the organization may establish a stricter policy, even terminating an employee for the first offense. In that case, it is especially important to communicate the procedure—not only to ensure fairness but also to prevent the dangerous misbehavior.

Figure 10.2

Progressive Discipline Responses

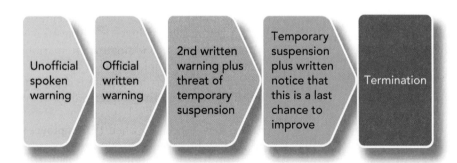

Creating a formal discipline process is a primary responsibility of the human re-source department. The HR professional should consult with supervisors and manag-ers to identify unacceptable behaviors and establish rules and consequences for violating the rules. The rules should cover disciplinary problems such as the following behaviors encountered in many organizations:

- Tardiness
- Absenteeism
- Unsafe work practices
- Poor quantity or quality of work
- Sexual harassment of co-workers
- Coming to work impaired by alcohol or drugs
- Theft of company property
- Cyberslacking (conducting personal business online during work hours)

For each infraction, the HR professional would identify a series of responses, such as those in Figure 10.2. In addition, the organization must communicate these rules and consequences in writing to every employee. Ways of publishing rules include pre-senting them in an employee handbook, posting them on the company's intranet, and displaying them on a bulletin board. Supervisors should be familiar with the rules, so that they can discuss them with employees and apply them consistently.

Along with rules and a progression of consequences for violating the rules, a pro-gressive discipline system should have requirements for documenting the rules, of-fenses, and responses. For issuing an unofficial warning about a less-serious offense, it may be enough to have a witness present. Even then, a written record would be help-ful in case the employee repeats the offense in the future. The organization should provide a document for managers to file, recording the nature and date of the offense, the specific improvement expected, and the consequences of the offense. It is also helpful to indicate how the offense affects the performance of the individual em-ployee, others in the group, or the organization as a whole. These documents are im-portant for demonstrating to a problem employee why he or she has been suspended or terminated. They also back up the organization's actions if it should have to defend a lawsuit. Following the hot-stove rule, the supervisor should complete and discuss the documentation immediately after becoming aware of the offense. A copy of the records should be placed in the employee's personnel file. The organization may have a policy of removing records of warnings after a period such as six months, on the grounds that the employee has learned from the experience.

As we noted in the earlier discussion of procedural justice, the discipline system should provide an opportunity to hear every point of view and to correct errors. Be-fore discussing and filing records of misbehavior, it is important for the supervisor to investigate the incident. The employee should be made aware of what he or she is said to have done wrong and should have an opportunity to present his or her version of events. Anyone who witnessed the misdeed also should have a chance to describe what happened. In general, employees who belong to a union have a right to the pres-ence of a union representative during a formal investigation interview if they request representation.[15]

Besides developing these policies, HR professionals have a role in carrying out pro-gressive discipline.[16] In meetings to announce disciplinary actions, it is wise to include two representatives of the organization. Usually, the employee's supervisor presents the information, and a representative from the HR department acts as a witness. This person can help the meeting stay on track and, if necessary, can later confirm what

Figure 10.3

Typical Stages of Alternative Dispute Resolution

happened during the meeting. Especially at the termination stage of the process, the employee may be angry, so it is helpful to be straightforward but polite. The supervisor should state the reason for the meeting, the nature of the problem behavior, and the consequences. Listening to the employee is important, but because an investigation was already conducted, there is no purpose to arguing. When an employee is suspended or terminated, the organization should designate a person to escort the employee from the building to protect the organization's people and property.

Alternative Dispute Resolution

Sometimes problems are easier to solve when an impartial person helps to create the solution. Therefore, at various points in the discipline process, the employee or organization might want to bring in someone to help with problem solving. Rather than turning to the courts every time an outsider is desired, more and more organizations are using **alternative dispute resolution (ADR).** A variety of ADR techniques show promise for resolving disputes in a timely, constructive, cost-effective manner.

In general, a system for alternative dispute resolution proceeds through the four stages shown in Figure 10.3:

1. **Open-door policy**—Based on the expectation that two people in conflict should first try to arrive at a settlement together, the organization has a policy of making managers available to hear complaints. Typically, the first "open door" is that of the employee's immediate supervisor, and if the employee does not get a resolution from that person, the employee may appeal to managers at higher levels. This policy works only to the degree that managers who hear complaints listen and are able to act.
2. **Peer review**—If the people in conflict cannot reach an agreement, they take their conflict to a panel composed of representatives from the organization at the same levels as the people in the dispute. The panel hears the case and tries to help the parties arrive at a settlement. To set up a panel to hear disputes as they arise, the organization may assign managers to positions on the panel and have employees elect nonmanagement panel members.
3. **Mediation**—If the peer review does not lead to a settlement, a neutral party from outside the organization hears the case and tries to help the people in conflict arrive at a settlement. The process is not binding, meaning the mediator cannot force a solution.
4. **Arbitration**—If mediation fails, a professional arbitrator from outside the organization hears the case and resolves it by making a decision. Most arbitrators are experienced employment lawyers or retired judges. The employee and employer both have to accept this person's decision.

alternative dispute resolution (ADR)
Methods of solving a problem by bringing in an impartial outsider but not using the court system.

open-door policy
An organization's policy of making managers available to hear complaints.

peer review
Process for resolving disputes by taking them to a panel composed of representatives from the organization at the same levels as the people in the dispute.

mediation
Nonbinding process in which a neutral party from outside the organization hears the case and tries to help the people in conflict arrive at a settlement.

arbitration
Binding process in which a professional arbitrator from outside the organization (usually a lawyer or judge) hears the case and resolves it by making a decision.

Each stage reflects a somewhat broader involvement of people outside the dispute. The hope is that the conflict will be resolved at earlier stages, where the costs, time, and embarrassing publicity are lowest. However, even the arbitration stage tends to be much faster, simpler, and more private than a lawsuit.[17]

Experience shows that ADR can effectively save time and money. Over a four-year period of using ADR, Houston-based Kellogg, Brown and Root experienced a 90 percent drop in its legal fees. Of 2,000 disputes, only 30 ever reached the stage of binding arbitration.[18]

Employee Assistance Programs

While ADR is effective in dealing with problems related to performance and disputes between people at work, many of the problems that lead an organization to want to terminate an employee involve drug or alcohol abuse. In these cases, the organization's discipline program should also incorporate an **employee assistance program (EAP).** An EAP is a referral service that employees can use to seek professional treatment for emotional problems or substance abuse. EAPs began in the 1950s with a focus on treating alcoholism, and in the 1980s they expanded into drug treatment. Today, many are now fully integrated into employers' overall health benefits plans, where they refer employees to covered mental health services.

EAPs vary widely, but most share some basic elements. First, the programs are usually identified in official documents published by the employer, such as employee handbooks. Supervisors (and union representatives when workers belong to a union) are trained to use the referral service for employees whom they suspect of having health-related problems. The organization also trains employees to use the system to refer themselves when necessary. The organization regularly evaluates the costs and benefits of the program, usually once a year.

The variations among EAPs make evaluating these programs especially important. For example, the treatment for alcoholism varies widely, including hospitalization and participation in Alcoholics Anonymous (AA). General Electric performed an experiment to compare the outcomes of these treatments, and it found that employees who were hospitalized tended to fare the best in a two-year follow-up.[19] Another study looked at the costs and benefits of treating depression in white- and blue-collar employees of 16 large companies. The depressed employees who received the more aggressive intervention, including phone calls encouraging them to seek help, missed fewer days of work, were more likely to remain employed, and were more likely to recover. Their treatment, which could include prescriptions and therapy sessions conducted over the phone, cost far less than disease-related expenses such as time off work and employee turnover.[20]

Outplacement Counseling

An employee who has been discharged is likely to feel angry and confused about what to do next. If the person feels there is nothing to lose and nowhere else to turn, the potential for violence or a lawsuit is greater than most organizations are willing to tolerate. This concern is one reason many organizations provide **outplacement counseling,** which tries to help dismissed employees manage the transition from one job to another. Organizations also may address ongoing poor performance with discussion about whether the employee is a good fit for the current job. Rather than simply firing the poor performer, the supervisor may encourage this person to think about leaving. In this situation, the availability of outplacement counseling may help the employee decide to

employee assistance program (EAP)
A referral service that employees can use to seek professional treatment for emotional problems or substance abuse.

outplacement counseling
A service in which professionals try to help dismissed employees manage the transition from one job to another.

look for another job. This approach may protect the dignity of the employee who leaves and promote a sense of fairness.

Some organizations have their own staff for conducting outplacement counseling. Other organizations have contracts with outside providers to help with individual cases. Either way, the goals for outplacement programs are to help the former employee address the psychological issues associated with losing a job—grief, depression, and fear—while at the same time helping the person find a new job.

Outplacement counseling tries to help people realize that losing a job is not the end of the world and that other opportunities exist. For many people, losing a job can be a learning experience that plants the seed for future success. For example, after John Morgridge was fired from his job with Honeywell, he applied his skills to building computer network maker Cisco Systems, which became an industry leader.

Although this was a success story for Morgridge, letting this talented manager go certainly spelled a lost opportunity for Honeywell. Retaining people who can contribute knowledge and talent is essential to business success. Therefore, the remainder of this chapter explores issues related to retaining employees.

Job Withdrawal

job withdrawal
A set of behaviors with which employees try to avoid the work situation physically, mentally, or emotionally.

Organizations need employees who are fully engaged and committed to their work. Therefore, retaining employees goes beyond preventing them from quitting. The organization needs to prevent a broader negative condition, called **job withdrawal**—or a set of behaviors with which employees try to avoid the work situation physically, mentally, or emotionally. Job withdrawal results when circumstances such as the nature of the job, supervisors and co-workers, pay levels, or the employee's own disposition cause the employee to become dissatisfied with the job. As shown in Figure 10.4, this job dissatisfaction produces job withdrawal. Job withdrawal may take the form of behavior change, physical job withdrawal, or psychological withdrawal. Some researchers believe employees engage in the three forms of withdrawal behavior in that order, while others think they select from these behaviors to address the particular sources of job dissatisfaction they experience.[21] Although the specifics of these models vary, the consensus is that withdrawal behaviors are related to one another and are at least partially caused by job dissatisfaction.[22]

Job Dissatisfaction

LO5 Explain how job dissatisfaction affects employee behavior.

Many aspects of people and organizations can cause job dissatisfaction, and managers and HR professionals need to be aware of them because correcting them can increase job satisfaction and prevent job withdrawal. The causes of job dissatisfaction

Figure 10.4

Job Withdrawal Process

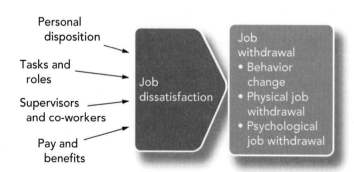

identified in Figure 10.4 fall into four categories: personal dispositions, tasks and roles, supervisors and co-workers, and pay and benefits.

Personal Dispositions

Job dissatisfaction is a feeling experienced by individuals, so it is not surprising that many researchers have studied individual personality differences to see if some kinds of people are more disposed to be dissatisfied with their jobs. Several personal qualities have been found to be associated with job dissatisfaction, including negative affectivity and negative self-evaluations.

Negative affectivity means pervasive low levels of satisfaction with all aspects of life, compared with other people's feelings. People with negative affectivity experience feelings such as anger, contempt, disgust, guilt, fear, and nervousness more than other people do, at work and away.[23] They tend to focus on the negative aspects of themselves and others.[24] Not surprisingly, people with negative affectivity tend to be dissatisfied with their jobs, even after changing employers or occupations.[25]

Core self-evaluations are bottom-line opinions individuals have of themselves and may be positive or negative. People with a positive core self-evaluation have high self-esteem, believe in their ability to accomplish their goals, and are emotionally stable. They also tend to experience job satisfaction.[26] Part of the reason for their satisfaction is that they tend to seek out and obtain jobs with desirable characteristics, and when they are in a situation they dislike, they are more likely to seek change in socially acceptable ways.[27] In contrast, people with negative core self-evaluations tend to blame other people for their problems, including their dissatisfying jobs. They are less likely to work toward change; they either do nothing or act aggressively toward the people they blame.[28]

Tasks and Roles

As a predictor of job dissatisfaction, nothing surpasses the nature of the task itself.[29] Many aspects of a task have been linked to dissatisfaction. Of particular significance are the complexity of the task, the degree of physical strain and exertion required, and the value the employee places on the task.[30] In general, employees (especially women) are bored and dissatisfied with simple, repetitive jobs.[31] People also are more dissatisfied with jobs requiring a great deal of physical strain and exertion. Because automation has removed much of the physical strain associated with jobs, employers often overlook this consideration. Still, many jobs remain physically demanding. Finally, employees feel dissatisfied if their work is not related to something they value.

Employees not only perform specific tasks but also have roles within the organization.[32] A person's **role** consists of the set of behaviors that people expect of a person in that job. These expected behaviors include the formally defined duties of the job but also much more. Sometimes things get complicated or confusing. Co-workers, supervisors, and customers have expectations for how the employee should behave often going far beyond a formal job description and having a large impact on the employee's work satisfaction. Several role-related sources of dissatisfaction are the following:

- **Role ambiguity** is uncertainty about what the organization and others expect from the employee in terms of what to do or how to do it. Employees suffer when they are unclear about work methods, scheduling, and performance criteria, perhaps because others hold different ideas about these. Employees particularly want to know how the organization will evaluate their performance. When they aren't sure, they become dissatisfied.[33]

role
The set of behaviors that people expect of a person in a particular job.

role ambiguity
Uncertainty about what the organization expects from the employee in terms of what to do or how to do it.

Military reservists who are sent overseas often experience role conflict among *three* roles: soldier, family member, and civilian employee. Overseas assignments often intensify role conflicts.

role conflict
An employee's recognition that demands of the job are incompatible or contradictory.

role overload
A state in which too many expectations or demands are placed on a person.

- **Role conflict** is an employee's recognition that demands of the job are incompatible or contradictory; a person cannot meet all the demands. For example, a company might bring together employees from different functions to work on a team to develop a new product. Team members feel role conflict when they realize that their team leader and functional manager have conflicting expectations of them. Also, many employees may feel conflict between work roles and family roles. A role conflict may be triggered by an organization's request that an employee take an assignment overseas. Foreign assignments can be highly disruptive to family members, and the resulting role conflict is the top reason that people quit overseas assignments.[34]

- **Role overload** results when too many expectations or demands are placed on a person. (The opposite situation is *role underload*.) After an organization downsizes, it may expect so much of the remaining employees that they experience role overload. A recent study found that many middle- and upper-level managers were working more than 60 hours a week. Such heavy work requirements not only overload individuals but may lay a foundation for role conflict.[35]

Supervisors and Co-workers

Negative behavior by managers and peers in the workplace can produce tremendous dissatisfaction. Research by the Corporate Leadership Council found that employees who said they planned to leave their jobs most often said it was because managers acted as if they did not value the employees.[36] Some organizations have substantially reduced turnover by removing a supervisor who lacks interpersonal skills—a problem they could have prevented in the first place by selecting supervisors for more than their technical skills.[37] In other cases, conflicts between employees left unaddressed by management may cause job dissatisfaction severe enough to lead to withdrawal or departure. Research suggests that turnover is higher when employees do not feel that their values and beliefs fit with their work group's values and beliefs.[38]

Pay and Benefits

For all the concern with positive relationships and interesting work, it is important to keep in mind that employees definitely care about their earnings. A job is the primary source of income and financial security for most people. Pay also is an indicator of status within the organization and in society at large, so it contributes to some people's self-worth. For all these reasons, satisfaction with pay is significant for retaining employees. Decisions about pay and benefits are so important and complex that the chapters of the next part of this book are devoted to this topic.

With regard to job satisfaction, the pay level—that is, the amount of income associated with each job—is especially important. Employers seeking to lure away another organization's employees often do so by offering higher pay. Benefits, such as insurance and vacation time, are also important, but employees often have difficulty measuring their worth. Therefore, although benefits influence job satisfaction, employees may not always consider them as much as pay itself.

Behavior Change

A reasonable expectation is that an employee's first response to dissatisfaction would be to try to change the conditions that generate the dissatisfaction. As the employee tries to bring about changes in policy or personnel, the efforts may involve confrontation and conflict with the employee's supervisor. In an organization where employees are represented by a union, as we will discuss in Chapter 14, more grievances may be filed.

From the manager's point of view, the complaints, confrontations, and grievances may feel threatening. On closer inspection, however, this is an opportunity for the manager to learn about and solve a potentially important problem. Don McAdams, a manager at Johnsonville Foods, recalls an incident in which one particular employee had been very critical of the company's incentive system. McAdams listened to the employee's concerns and asked him to head a committee charged with developing a better incentive system. The employee became so enthusiastic about the project that he was the one who presented the system to the employees. His history of criticizing the old system gave him great credibility with the other employees, so he became a force for constructive change.[39]

In this example, the result was positive because the organization responded to legitimate concerns. When employees cannot work with management to make changes, they may look for help from outside the organization. Some employees may engage in *whistle-blowing*, taking their charges to the media in the hope that if the public learns about the situation, the organization will be forced to change. From the organization's point of view, whistle-blowing is harmful because of the negative publicity.

Another way employees may go outside the organization for help is to file a lawsuit. This way to force change is available if the employee is disputing policies on the grounds that they violate state and federal laws, such as those forbidding employment discrimination or requiring safe working conditions. Defending a lawsuit is costly, both financially and in terms of the employer's image, whether the organization wins or loses. Most employers would prefer to avoid lawsuits and whistle-blowing. Keeping employees satisfied is one way to do this.

Physical Job Withdrawal

If behavior change has failed or seems impossible, a dissatisfied worker may physically withdraw from the job. Options for physically leaving a job range from arriving late to calling in sick, requesting a transfer, or leaving the organization altogether. Even while they are on the job, employees may withdraw by not actually working, as described in the "Did You Know?" box. All these options are costly to the employer.

Finding a new job is rarely easy and can take months, so employees often are cautious about quitting. Employees who would like to quit may be late for work. Tardiness

Workers Waste an Hour a Day

A poll of U.S. workers asked them to estimate how much of their workday do they spend not doing anything productive. On average, they said they waste 1 hour a day, and they guessed that their co-workers waste 1.44 hours.

Source: Joseph Carroll, "U.S. Workers Say They Waste about an Hour at Work Each Day," Gallup News Service, September 6, 2007, www.gallup.com.

How many hours per workday do you personally waste (don't do anything productive)?

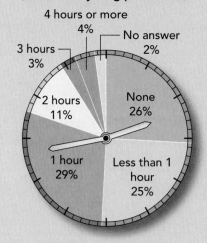

4 hours or more
4%

No answer
2%

3 hours
3%

2 hours
11%

None
26%

1 hour
29%

Less than 1 hour
25%

is costly because late employees are not contributing for part of the day. Especially when work is done by teams, the tardiness creates difficulties that spill over and affect the entire team's ability to work. Absenteeism is even more of a problem. According to a recent survey, employers spent 15 cents out of every payroll dollar to make up for absent workers.[40]

An employee who is dissatisfied because of circumstances related to the specific job—for example, an unpleasant workplace or unfair supervisor—may be able to resolve that problem with a job transfer. If the source of the dissatisfaction is organizational policies or practices, such as low pay scales, the employee may leave the organization altogether. These forms of physical job withdrawal contribute to high turnover rates for the department or organization. As a result, the organization faces the costs of replacing the employees, as well as lost productivity until replacement employees learn the jobs.

Organizations need to be concerned with their overall turnover rates as well as the nature of the turnover in terms of who is staying and who is leaving. For example, companies' top performers tend to be among the hardest employees to keep.[41] Also, among managers, women and minorities often have higher turnover rates. Many leave because they see little opportunity for promotions. Chapter 9 discussed how organizations are addressing this problem through career management and efforts to break the glass ceiling.

Psychological Withdrawal

Employees need not leave the company in order to withdraw from their jobs. Especially if they have been unable to find another job, they may psychologically remove themselves. They are physically at work, but their minds are elsewhere.

Psychological withdrawal can take several forms. If an employee is primarily dissatisfied with the job itself, the employee may display a very low level of job involvement. **Job involvement** is the degree to which people identify themselves with their jobs. People with a high level of job involvement consider their work an important part of their life. Doing well at work contributes to their sense of who they are (their *self-concept*). For a dissatisfied employee with low job involvement, performing well or poorly does not affect the person's self-concept.

When an employee is dissatisfied with the organization as a whole, the person's organizational commitment may be low. **Organizational commitment** is the degree to which an employee identifies with the organization and is willing to put forth effort on its behalf.[42] Employees with high organizational commitment will stretch themselves to help the organization through difficult times. Employees with low organizational commitment are likely to leave at the first opportunity for a better job. They have a strong intention to leave, so like employees with low job involvement, they are hard to motivate.

job involvement
The degree to which people identify themselves with their jobs.

organizational commitment
The degree to which an employee identifies with the organization and is willing to put forth effort on its behalf.

Job Satisfaction

Clearly, organizations want to prevent withdrawal behaviors. As we saw in Figure 10.4, the driving force behind job withdrawal is dissatisfaction. To prevent job withdrawal, organizations therefore need to promote **job satisfaction,** a pleasant feeling resulting from the perception that one's job fulfills or allows for the fulfillment of one's important job values.[43] Several aspects of job satisfaction are:

LO6 Describe how organizations contribute to employees' job satisfaction and retain key employees.

job satisfaction
A pleasant feeling resulting from the perception that one's job fulfills or allows for the fulfillment of one's important job values.

- Job satisfaction is related to a person's values, defined as "what a person consciously or unconsciously desires to obtain."
- Different employees have different views of which values are important, so the same circumstances can produce different levels of job satisfaction.
- Job satisfaction is based on perception, not always on an objective and complete measurement of the situation. Each person compares the job situation to his or her values, and people are likely to differ in what they perceive.

In sum, values, perceptions, and ideas of what is important are the three components of job satisfaction. People will be satisfied with their jobs as long as they perceive that their jobs meet their important values. As shown in Figure 10.5, organizations can contribute to job satisfaction by addressing the four sources of job dissatisfaction we identified earlier: personal dispositions, job tasks and roles, supervisors and co-workers, and pay and benefits.

Personal Dispositions

In our discussion of job withdrawal, we noted that sometimes personal qualities of the employee, such as negative affectivity and negative core self-evaluation, are associated with job dissatisfaction. This linkage suggests employee selection in the first instance plays a role in raising overall levels of employee satisfaction. People making the selection decisions should look for evidence of whether employees are

Figure 10.5

Increasing Job Satisfaction

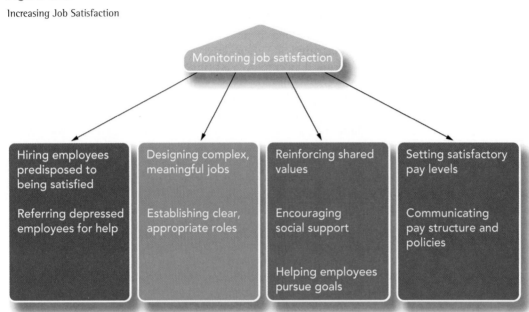

predisposed to being satisfied.[44] Interviews should explore employees' satisfaction with past jobs. If an applicant says he was dissatisfied with his past six jobs, what makes the employer think the person won't be dissatisfied with the organization's vacant position?

Employers also should recognize that dissatisfaction with other facets of life can spill over into the workplace. A worker who is having problems with a family member may attribute some of the negative feelings to the job or organization. Of course, managers should not try to become clinical psychologists for their employees and applicants. Still, when employees express negativity and dissatisfaction in many areas, managers should consider that the employee may be clinically depressed.[45] The manager should suggest that the employee contact the organization's employee assistance program or his or her physician. Depression is a common condition, but most cases can be managed with proper care. As a reasonable accommodation under the Americans with Disabilities Act, the employer may need to grant the employee time off or a flexible schedule to accommodate treatment.

Tasks and Roles

Organizations can improve job satisfaction by making jobs more complex and meaningful, as we discussed in Chapter 4. Some of the methods available for this approach to job design are job enrichment and job rotation. Organizations also can increase satisfaction by developing clear and appropriate job roles. To learn how a public relations firm applied these methods successfully, see the "Best Practices" box.

Job Complexity

Not only can job design add to enriching complexity, but employees themselves sometimes take measures to make their work more interesting. Some employees bring

Best Practices

Satisfying Jobs at Corporate Ink are PR-Worthy

Usually a public relations firm is seeking good news for its clients, but Corporate Ink Public Relations generated plenty of good PR for itself. The Newton, Massachusetts, company was named by the *Wall Street Journal* as one of the top small workplaces in the United States, primarily because it structures work in a way that employees appreciate.

At Corporate Ink, all of the 12 employees are directly involved in making important decisions. Each employee is placed in charge of some area, such as maintaining the database or seeing that employees get the training they need. Junior staff members have real responsibility for managing accounts, rather than simply focusing on clerical tasks that would be the norm at other firms.

All employees attend—and are expected to participate in—the company's strategy meetings.

Even when the company had to make dramatic cutbacks during the economic slowdown in 2001, it called the employees together to participate in the decision making. They agreed they would rather cut salaries than lose any of the company's talent. Amy Bermar, Corporate Ink's founder and president, went along with their decision and took a 30 percent pay cut herself. The group intensified its focus on quality and came through the difficult period stronger than ever.

Even the company's sabbatical program contributes to making jobs more interesting. Employees who have been with the company for at least four years are eligible to take three weeks off to pursue any interest. While an employee is on sabbatical, the remaining employees stretch their skills by taking on the absent worker's duties.

Of course, this level of responsibility can seem overwhelming if people are not managed well. When new employees join Corporate Ink, a more experienced employee is assigned to act as a mentor. In addition, employees set goals for their job, so they can measure how well they are doing. New staffers participate in informal monthly meetings with Bermar, who shares her expertise in landing new clients, pitching stories, and handling bad news for clients. The result is that employees feel excited about their work and committed to the company.

Source: Kelly K. Spors, "Top Small Workplaces 2007," *Wall Street Journal,* October 1, 2007, http://online.wsj.com; Winning Workplaces, "Navigating the 'Cut Salaries or Cut Staff' Quandary," Success Stories, 2006, www.winningworkplaces.org, accessed February 13, 2008; Corporate Ink, "About Us: Working Here," www.corporateink.com, accessed February 13, 2008; and Scott S. Smith, "Taking the Lead," *Impact,* August 2007, downloaded at www.corporateink.com/about-us/in-the-news.html.

personal music players with headsets to work, so they can listen to music or radio shows while they are working. Many supervisors disapprove, worrying that the headsets will interfere with the employees' ability to provide good customer service. However, in simple jobs with minimal customer contact (like processing paperwork or entering data into computers), research suggests that personal headsets can improve performance. One study examined the use of stereo headsets by workers in 32 jobs at a large retailing company. The stereo-using group outperformed the no-stereo group on simple jobs (like invoice processor) but performed worse than the stereo-free group on complex jobs (such as accountant).[46]

Meaningful Work

When it comes to generating satisfaction, the most important aspect of work is the degree to which it is meaningfully related to workers' core values. People sign on to help charitable causes for little or no pay simply because of the value they place on making a difference in the world. A similar kind of motivation can exist in businesses. Genentech, for example, focuses on developing and testing "big ideas" related to life-and-death treatments in health care. The company selects employees who

Appropriate tasks and roles include safety precautions, especially when work could involve risks to workers' health and safety.

have a passion for this type of challenge, and it gives them wide latitude to pursue their goals. This approach has helped Genentech attract top scientists and dramatically increase its revenues.[47]

Clear and Appropriate Roles

Organizations can do much to avoid role-related sources of dissatisfaction. They can define roles, clearly spelling out work methods, schedules, and performance measures. They can be realistic about the number of hours required to complete job requirements. When jobs require overtime hours, the employer must be prepared to comply with laws requiring overtime pay, as well as to help employees manage the conflict between work and family roles.

To help employees manage role conflict, employers have turned to a number of family-friendly policies. These policies may include provisions for child care, elder care, flexible work schedules, job sharing, telecommuting, and extended parental leaves.[48] Although these programs create some headaches for managers in terms of scheduling work and reporting requirements, they increase employees' commitment to the organization.[49] Organizations with family-friendly policies also have enjoyed improvements in performance, especially at companies that employ a large percentage of women.[50] Chapter 13 discusses such benefits in greater detail.

Organizations should also pay attention to the fit between job titles and roles, especially as more and more Americans feel overworked. One consequence of this perception is lawsuits seeking overtime pay. The Fair Labor Standards Act exempts managers and professionals from its requirement that the company pay overtime to employees who work more than a 40-hour week. Increasingly, employees are complaining that they have been misclassified as managers and should be treated as nonexempt workers. Their job titles sound like managerial jobs, but their day-to-day activities involve no supervision. IBM, for example, recently reclassified more than 7,500 technical support workers following settlement of a lawsuit charging they had illegally been denied overtime pay. The company had considered them exempt because they are highly skilled professionals, but the employees argued their jobs did not give them enough decision-making authority or creative latitude for that classification.[51]

role analysis technique
A process of formally identifying expectations associated with a role.

Because role problems rank just behind job problems in creating job dissatisfaction, some interventions aim directly at role elements. One of these is the **role analysis technique,** a process of formally identifying expectations associated with a role. The technique follows the steps shown in Figure 10.6. The *role occupant* (the person who fills a role) and each member of the person's *role set* (people who directly interact with this employee) each write down their expectations for the role. They meet to discuss their expectations and develop a preliminary list of the role's duties and behaviors, trying to resolve any conflicts among expectations. Next, the role occupant lists what he or she expects of others in the set, and the group meets again to reach a consensus on these expectations. Finally, the group modifies its preliminary list and reaches a consensus on the occupant's role. This process may uncover instances of overload and underload, and the group tries to trade off requirements to develop more balanced roles.

Supervisors and Co-workers

The two primary sets of people in an organization who affect job satisfaction are co-workers and supervisors. A person may be satisfied with these people for one of three reasons:

1. The people share the same values, attitudes, and philosophies. Most individuals find this very important, and many organizations try to foster a culture of shared values. Even when this does not occur across the whole organization, values shared between workers and their supervisor can increase satisfaction.[52]
2. The co-workers and supervisor may provide social support, meaning they are sympathetic and caring. Social support greatly increases job satisfaction, whether the support comes from supervisors or co-workers.[53] Turnover is also lower among employees who experience support from other members of the organization.[54]
3. The co-workers or supervisor may help the person attain some valued outcome. For example, they can help a new employee figure out what goals to pursue and how to achieve them.[55]

Because a supportive environment reduces dissatisfaction, many organizations foster team building both on and off the job (such as with softball or bowling leagues). The idea is that playing together as a team will strengthen ties among group members and develop relationships in which individuals feel supported by one another. Organizations also are developing their managers' mentoring skills and helping to set up these beneficial relationships.[56] (Mentoring was described in Chapter 9.) At Lockheed Martin, turnover plummeted among jobs targeted by a mentoring program.[57]

Pay and Benefits

Organizations recognize the importance of pay in their negotiations with job candidates. HR professionals can support their organizations in this area by repeatedly monitoring pay levels in their industry and for the professions or trades they employ. As we noted in Chapter 5 and will discuss further in Chapter 11, organizations make decisions about whether to match or exceed the industry averages. Also, HR professionals can increase job satisfaction by communicating to employees the value of their benefits.

Two other aspects of pay satisfaction influence job satisfaction. One is satisfaction with pay structure—the way the organization assigns different pay levels to different levels and job categories. A manager of a sales force, for example, might be satisfied with her pay level until she discovers that some of the sales representatives she supervises are earning more than she is. The other important aspect of pay satisfaction is pay raises. People generally expect that their pay will increase over time. They will be satisfied if their expectations are met or dissatisfied if raises fall short of expectations. HR professionals can contribute to these sources of job satisfaction by helping to communicate the reasoning behind the organization's pay structure and pay raises. For example, sometimes economic conditions force an organization to limit pay raises. If employees understand the circumstances (and recognize that the same conditions are likely to be affecting other employers), they may feel less dissatisfied.

Figure 10.6

Steps in the Role Analysis Technique

Members of role set write expectations for role

Members of role set discuss expectations

Preliminary list of role's duties and behaviors

Role occupant lists expectations for others in role set

Members of role set discuss expectations and reach consensus on occupant's role

Modified list of role's duties and behaviors

Co-worker relationships can contribute to job satisfaction, and organizations therefore try to provide opportunities to build positive relationships. Would a strong sense of teamwork and friendship help you enjoy your work more?

Monitoring Job Satisfaction

Employers can better retain employees if they are aware of satisfaction levels, so they can make changes if employees are dissatisfied. The usual way to measure job satisfaction is with some kind of survey. A systematic, ongoing program of employee surveys should be part of the organization's human resource strategy. This program allows the organization to monitor trends and prevent voluntary turnover. For example, if satisfaction with promotion opportunities has been falling over several years, the trend may signal a need for better career management (a topic of Chapter 9). An organizational change, such as a merger, also might have important consequences for job satisfaction. In addition, ongoing surveys give the organization a way to measure whether policies adopted to improve job satisfaction and employee retention are working. Organizations can also compare results from different departments to identify groups with successful practices that may apply elsewhere in the organization. Another benefit is that some scales provide data that organizations can use to compare themselves to others in the same industry. This information will be valuable for creating and reviewing human resource policies that enable organizations to attract and retain employees in a competitive job market. Finally, conducting surveys gives employees a chance to be heard, so the practice itself can contribute to employee satisfaction.

To obtain a survey instrument, an excellent place to begin is with one of the many established scales. The validity and reliability of many satisfaction scales have been tested, so it is possible to compare the survey instruments. The main reason for the organization to create its own scale would be that it wants to measure satisfaction with aspects of work that are specific to the organization (such as satisfaction with a particular health plan).

A widely used measure of job satisfaction is the Job Descriptive Index (JDI). The JDI emphasizes specific aspects of satisfaction—pay, the work itself, supervision, co-workers, and promotions. Figure 10.7 shows several items from the JDI scale. Other scales measure general satisfaction, using broad questions such as "All in all, how satisfied are you with your job?"[58] Some scales avoid language altogether, relying on pictures. The faces scale in Figure 10.8 is an example of this type of measure. Other scales exist for measuring more specific aspects of satisfaction. For example, the Pay Satisfaction Questionnaire (PSQ) measures satisfaction with specific aspects of pay, such as pay levels, structure, and raises.[59]

Figure 10.7

Example of Job Descriptive Index (JDI)

Instructions: Think of your present work. What is it like most of time? In the blank beside each word given below, write

___Y___ for "Yes" if it describes your work
___N___ for "No" if it does NOT describe your work
___?___ if you cannot decide

Work Itself	Pay	Promotion Opportunities
_____ Routine	_____ Less than I deserve	_____ Dead-end job
_____ Satisfying	_____ Highly paid	_____ Unfair policies
_____ Good	_____ Insecure	_____ Based on ablility

Supervision	Co-workers
_____ Impolite	_____ Intelligent
_____ Praises good work	_____ Responsible
_____ Doesn't supervise enough	_____ Boring

SOURCE: W. K. Balzar, D. C. Smith, D. E. Kravitz, S. E. Lovell, K. B. Paul, B. A. Reilly, and C. E. Reilly, *User's Manual for the Job Descriptive Index (JDI)* (Bowling Green, OH: Bowling Green State University, 1990).

Job Satisfaction from the Faces Scale
Consider all aspects of your job. Circle the face that best describes your feelings about your job in general.

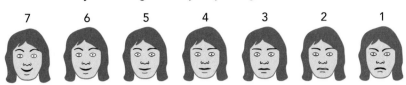

SOURCE: From R. B. Dunham and J. B. Herman, *Journal of Applied Psychology* 60 (1975), pp. 629–31. Reprinted with permission.

Figure 10.8

Example of a Simplified, Nonverbal Measure of Job Satisfaction

For a more sophisticated analysis of employee satisfaction, the researchers can sort responses according to groups of employees. For example, IndyMac Bank, a California mortgage lender, found a surprise in the relationship between performance and satisfaction as measured by employee turnover.[60] As expected, higher-performing employees tended to be satisfied and stay with the company, but a subgroup of those employees was actually *more* likely to quit. The company rated employees' performance on a 100-point scale, and all employees at 85 or above were considered to exceed expectations. However, the company's performance awards—grants of stock—went only to employees who rated at 90 or above. Employees who scored at 85 to 89 on the rating scale were noticeably less satisfied than employees who scored high enough to receive a stock grant, suggesting that the company's reward system might not meet some of the criteria of fairness described earlier in this chapter. The survey at IndyMac launched a reevaluation of the bank's HR practices such as stock grants.

In spite of surveys and other efforts to retain employees, some employees inevitably will leave the organization. This presents another opportunity to gather information for retaining employees: the **exit interview**—a meeting of the departing employee with the employee's supervisor and/or a human resource specialist to discuss the employee's reasons for leaving. A well-conducted exit interview can uncover reasons why employees leave and perhaps set the stage for some of them to return. HR professionals can help make exit interviews more successful by arranging for the employee to talk to someone from the HR department (rather than the departing employee's supervisor) in a neutral location.[61] Questions should start out open-ended and general, to give the employee a chance to name the source of the dissatisfaction.

A recruiter armed with information about what caused a specific person to leave may be able to negotiate a return when the situation changes. And when several exiting employees give similar reasons for leaving, management should consider whether this indicates a need for change. In the war for talent, the best way to manage retention is to engage in a battle for every valued employee, even when it looks as if the battle has been lost.

exit interview
A meeting of a departing employee with the employee's supervisor and/or a human resource specialist to discuss the employee's reasons for leaving.

THINKING ETHICALLY

CAN FAIRNESS PREVENT DISSATISFACTION?

Workers traditionally dread management plans to improve productivity, because the changes have so often focused on getting people to work harder without necessarily earning greater rewards. So when Sport Chalet launched a productivity improvement effort for its warehouse workers, managers knew that employee satisfaction would be a key issue. An initiative based on fairness paved the way to actually get workers excited about being the best.

The 45-store regional retailer consolidates most of its warehousing in a California distribution center.

There, employees focus on transferring products to stores as quickly as they are needed for sale. As Sport Chalet added stores, it wanted to expand its capacity to serve them with its existing distribution center, rather than bearing the significant expense of opening a new one. So management called a meeting and explained to all the employees that it was going to try boosting productivity by measuring what workers were already doing, identifying best practices, and setting standards. Steve Belardi, vice president of logistics, explained that the effort would be "fact based," so performance would never be measured according to supervisors' subjective judgments. And whenever employees exceeded standards, they would be rewarded.

Employees immediately recognized that the system emphasized fairness. They appreciated that more sophisticated measurements and targets would be objective, so anyone could earn the performance rewards. As the new measurement process went forward, results were posted, so employees received timely feedback on how they were doing. If they wanted to earn a bonus—or be best at what they do—they could easily see whether they qualified. Employee buy-in to the productivity initiative was evident quickly, as employees used their break time to check the numbers posted on the break room bulletin boards.

SOURCE: John Kerr, "Clocking Performance," *Logistics Management*, April 1, 2007, downloaded from General Reference Center Gold, http://find.galegroup.com.

Questions

1. For a company launching an effort to improve productivity, why is employee satisfaction important? What consequences could result from neglecting this issue?
2. What measures of fairness could Sport Chalet's employees apply to the company's plans for improving productivity? From the evidence given, would you say the company treated these employees ethically?
3. Imagine that you are an HR manager for a company that plans to conduct time and motion studies to improve productivity. Suggest how you might help the company launch the program in a way that treats employees ethically. What business advantages are associated with this concern for ethics?

SUMMARY

LO1 Distinguish between involuntary and voluntary turnover, and describe their effects on an organization.

Involuntary turnover occurs when the organization requires employees to leave, often when they would prefer to stay. Voluntary turnover occurs when employees initiate the turnover, often when the organization would prefer to keep them. Both are costly because of the need to recruit, hire, and train replacements. Involuntary turnover can also result in lawsuits and even violence.

LO2 Discuss how employees determine whether the organization treats them fairly.

Employees draw conclusions based on the outcomes of decisions regarding them, the procedures applied, and the way managers treat employees when carrying out those procedures. Outcome fairness is a judgment that the consequences are just. The consequences should be consistent, expected, and in proportion to the significance of the behavior. Procedural justice is a judgment that fair methods were used to determine the consequences. The procedures should be consistent, unbiased, based on accurate information, and correctable. They should take into account the viewpoints of everyone involved, and they should be consistent with prevailing ethical standards. Interactional justice is a judgment that the organization carried out its actions in a way that took the employee's feelings into account—for example, by listening to the employee and treating the employee with dignity.

LO3 Identify legal requirements for employee discipline.

Employee discipline should not result in wrongful discharge, such as a termination that violates an implied contract or public policy. Discipline should be administered evenhandedly, without discrimination. Discipline should respect individual employees' privacy. Searches and surveillance should be for a legitimate business purpose, and employees should know about and consent to them. Reasons behind disciplinary actions should be shared only with those who need to know them. When termination is part of a plant closing, employees should receive the legally required notice, if applicable.

LO4 Summarize ways in which organizations can fairly discipline employees.

Discipline should follow the principles of the hot-stove rule, meaning discipline should give warning and have consequences that are consistent, objective, and immediate. A system that can meet these requirements is progressive discipline, in which rules are established and communicated, and increasingly severe consequences follow each violation of the rules. Usually, consequences range from a spoken warning through written warnings, suspension, and termination. These actions should be documented in writing. Organizations also may resolve problems through alternative dispute resolution, including an open-door policy, peer review, mediation, and arbitration. When performance problems seem to result from substance abuse or mental illness, the manager may refer the employee to an employee assistance program. When a manager terminates an employee or encourages an employee to leave, outplacement counseling may smooth the process.

LO5   Explain how job dissatisfaction affects employee behavior.

Circumstances involving the nature of a job, supervisors and co-workers, pay levels, or the employee's own disposition may produce job dissatisfaction. When employees become dissatisfied, they may engage in job withdrawal. This may include behavior change, as employees try to bring about changes in policy and personnel through inside action or through whistle-blowing or lawsuits. Physical job withdrawal may range from tardiness and absenteeism to job transfer or leaving the organization altogether. Especially when employees cannot find another job, they may psychologically withdraw by displaying low levels of job involvement and organizational commitment.

LO6   Describe how organizations contribute to employees' job satisfaction and retain key employees.

Organizations can try to identify and select employees who have personal dispositions associated with job satisfaction. They can make jobs more complex and meaningful—for example, through job enrichment and job rotation. They can use methods such as the role analysis technique to make roles clear and appropriate. They can reinforce shared values and encourage social support among employees. They can try to establish satisfactory pay levels and communicate with employees about pay structure and pay raises. Monitoring job satisfaction helps organizations identify which of these actions are likely to be most beneficial.

KEY TERMS

alternative dispute resolution (ADR), p. 288
arbitration, p. 288
employee assistance program (EAP), p. 289
exit interview, p. 301
hot-stove rule, p. 285
interactional justice, p. 282
involuntary turnover, p. 280

job involvement, p. 295
job satisfaction, p. 295
job withdrawal, p. 290
mediation, p. 288
open-door policy, p. 288
organizational commitment, p. 295
outcome fairness, p. 281
outplacement counseling, p. 289

peer review, p. 288
procedural justice, p. 282
progressive discipline, p. 285
role, p. 291
role ambiguity, p. 291
role analysis technique, p. 298
role conflict, p. 292
role overload, p. 292
voluntary turnover, p. 280

REVIEW AND DISCUSSION QUESTIONS

1. Give an example of voluntary turnover and an example of involuntary turnover. Why should organizations try to reduce both kinds of turnover?
2. A member of a restaurant's serving staff is chronically late to work. From the organization's point of view, what fairness issues are involved in deciding how to handle this situation? In what ways might the employee's and other servers' ideas of fairness be different?
3. For the situation in Question 2, how would a formal discipline policy help the organization address issues of fairness?
4. The progressive discipline process described in this chapter is meant to be fair and understandable, but it tends to be slow. Try to think of two or three offenses that should result in immediate discharge, rather than follow all the steps of progressive discipline. Explain

why you selected these offenses. If the dismissed employee sued, do you think the organization would be able to defend its action in court?
5. A risk of disciplining employees is that some employees retaliate. To avoid that risk, what organizational policies might encourage low-performing employees to leave while encouraging high-performing employees to stay? (Consider the sources of employee satisfaction and dissatisfaction discussed in this chapter.)
6. List forms of behavior that can signal job withdrawal. Choose one of the behaviors you listed, and describe how you would respond if an otherwise valuable employee whom you supervised engaged in this kind of behavior.
7. What are the four factors that influence an employee's job dissatisfaction (or satisfaction)? Which of these do you

think an employer can most easily change? Which would be the most expensive to change?

8. The section on principles of justice used noncompete agreements as an example. How would you expect the use of noncompete agreements to affect voluntary turnover? How might the use of these agreements affect job withdrawal and job satisfaction? Besides requiring noncompete agreements, how could an organization reduce the likelihood of employees leaving to work for competitors? Would these other methods have a better effect on employee satisfaction?

9. Consider your current job or a job you recently held. Overall, were you satisfied or dissatisfied with that job? How did your level of satisfaction or dissatisfaction affect your behavior on the job? Is your own experience consistent with this chapter's models of job withdrawal and job satisfaction?

10. Suppose you are an HR professional who convinced your company's management to conduct a survey of employee satisfaction. Your budget was limited, and you could not afford a test that went into great detail. Rather, you investigated overall job satisfaction and learned that it is low, especially among employees in three departments. You know that management is concerned about spending a lot for HR programs because sales are in a slump, but you want to address the issue of low job satisfaction. Suggest some ways you might begin to make a difference, even with a small budget. How will you convince management to try your ideas?

11. Why are exit interviews important? Should an organization care about the opinions of people who are leaving? How are those opinions relevant to employee separation and retention?

BUSINESSWEEK CASE

BusinessWeek Shirking Working: The War on Hooky

When it comes to your underlings, do you look the other way when the poor souls fake a sick day so they can loll about? Such a luxury may soon be a relic of the analog past. The corporate cost slashers have a fresh target in their sights: the absent employee. Some companies are instituting tough policies to combat hooky. Others are limiting the amount of time you can take off before unpaid leave kicks in. And then there are those using brawny human resources software that mines worker data and analyzes no-shows.

Employers have long been clueless about the magnitude of the absentee problem. Now, though, armed with new research about absenteeism's productivity costs (an estimated $74 billion lost annually), sophisticated tracking software from companies such as Kronos, and stern directives from chief financial officers (CFOs), more human resources departments are starting to confront the problem.

Consider that 85 percent of labor costs pay for actual work. The rest goes to what HR wonks call "nonproductive time" and what the rest of us call vacation, caring for a sick child, or nursing a hangov—ahem—cold. Legitimate absences are one thing. But absence abuse—what HR consultants portray as a stealthy, bottom-line killer—is on the rise, with employees collecting disability, vacation, health insurance benefits, or personal days to which they aren't entitled. And as companies push workers harder, workers are pushing back—by taking advantage of every last moment of time off.

The new climate was evident last year when word came of Wal-Mart's revamped absence policy. It mandates that workers will have to call an automated 1-800 number instead of notifying their managers, who can be subjective. It also doles out demerits for leaving work early or arriving

for work 10 minutes late—barring something as extreme as a terrorist attack or a co-worker's funeral. Four unauthorized absences, and disciplinary actions begin. Wal-Mart declined to comment.

While the chance to save money is welcome to CFOs, to some employees the new crackdown smacks of Big Brother. After he was out sick for two days, Stanley Straughter, a Delphi laborer in Rochester, New York, was asked to sign a waiver releasing his medical information to the company. Straughter, citing privacy concerns, refused and was fired, he claims. The Equal Employment Opportunity Commission, which says such requests for medical information for absent employees are standard at Delphi, has since filed suit against the automotive supplier on Straughter's behalf. Delphi declined to comment.

Although theirs may be among the most draconian measures, Wal-Mart and Delphi are not the only ones putting worker whereabouts under the microscope. Dell, Georgia-Pacific, and Southwest Airlines are just a few of the companies availing themselves of the services of consultants who are rebranding "lost time" into the new science of "absence management." Southwest says new software that tracks the under-the-wing crew has saved the company $2 million annually in reduced administrative costs. The carrier plans to roll out automated absence tracking for headquarters staff in 2008.

Analyzing absenteeism isn't just leading the corporate cops to malingerers and chronic Mondays-off types. Workforce intelligence is also providing insights into undetected management problems. At one manufacturing company, a group of employees loathed their manager's style. The sentiment went unnoticed by top executives until a software program created by Convergys started scouring the department's data and found it had a high absence rate compared with other units. At that point, Convergys performed an "intervention" with the manager's employees: confidential focus groups where the workers could vent. Once the company attended to the problems, attendance rose.

SOURCE: Michell Conlin, "Shirking Working: The War on Hooky," *BusinessWeek*, November 12, 2007, downloaded from General Reference Center Gold, http://find.galegroup.com.

Questions

1. This case presents examples from Wal-Mart, Delphi, and an unnamed manufacturing company. Evaluate whether the company's actions in each example met the principles of justice described in this chapter.
2. For each example, describe one other action the company could take to reduce absences in a way that meets the principles of justice.
3. This case emphasizes methods for discouraging the behavior of absenteeism, rather than improving worker satisfaction in the hope that improved attendance will follow. If you were a manager, in what situations would you focus on detecting and punishing absenteeism, and when would you emphasize employee satisfaction? Why?

CASE: IS EMPLOYEE PRIVACY GOING UP IN SMOKE?

Scott Rodrigues had worked at Scott's Miracle-Gro Company for less than a year when he was fired for failing a drug test. But rather than detecting some illegal substance such as cocaine or marijuana, Rodrigues's drug test detected nicotine in his system. In other words, Miracle-Gro fired Rodrigues for smoking cigarettes.

Scott's Miracle-Gro Company is at the forefront of firms taking extreme steps to curtail rising health care costs. Among its most controversial measures: a "no tobacco" policy. Smokers have more health problems, so insuring them is more expensive. As a result, the company has a policy of not employing smokers. Rodrigues, however, hired a lawyer to challenge the decision in court.

Miracle-Gro's health assessment program delves into other behaviors. Employees are asked not only whether they smoke cigarettes but also whether they chew tobacco, drink alcohol, suffer from high cholesterol or high blood pressure, are depressed, experience stressful family relationships, and more. The company began investigating such matters after management became convinced that its workforce was in such bad physical shape that the costs it was incurring for health care expenses were destroying its ability to compete. Between 1999 and 2003, for example, Miracle-Gro's health care expenditures had doubled.

Other companies have faced similar concerns. Delta Airlines, for example, determined that its health care expenses were rising 10 percent a year, with much of the cost attributable to a small percentage of its workers. Most employers that run the numbers come to a similar conclusion: a small percentage of workers drive a big percentage of costs—and predicting which workers are in this group is easy. The valid predictors are the very measures that Miracle-Gro screens for.

Employers that want to address these health concerns have to weigh the advantages against concern for protecting employees' privacy. Many of the harmful behaviors, such as smoking, excessive drinking, and poor diet, occur outside work and do not directly affect work performance. So, asking about these behaviors feels highly intrusive to many employees.

Employers have to make decisions regarding how to balance privacy concerns with cost concerns and how much pressure to place on employees whose lifestyle puts them at risk. Although financial benefits are often the driving force behind these programs, employees' quality of life on and off the job also is affected.

While Scott Rodrigues was suing Miracle-Gro over its decision to fire him, another employee, Joe Pellegrini, was celebrating the fact that the same company program had saved his life. Although Pellegrini had been physically fit, his health assessment showed he had a high level of cholesterol, so the company required him to see a physician. That trip to the doctor revealed a 95 percent blockage in a heart valve—a condition that was likely to have killed him within a few days. Far from being offended by the privacy issues, Pellegrini is grateful that Miracle-Gro forced him to see a doctor.

SOURCE: M. Colin, "Get Healthy—or Else," *BusinessWeek*, February 26, 2007, pp. 58–69; J. Marquez, "Being Healthy May Be Its Own Reward, but a Little Cash Can Also Help Keep Workers Fit," *Workforce Management*, September 2005, pp. 66–69; and V. Leo, "Wellness—or Orwellness?" *BusinessWeek*, March 19, 2007, p. 82.

Questions

1. Does the no-smoking policy at Scott's Miracle-Gro Company meet the principles of justice described in this chapter? If not, what could the company do to reduce unfairness without significantly increasing costs?
2. What specific aspects of job satisfaction does Miracle-Gro's policy affect? How could the policy be modified to improve job satisfaction?
3. Suppose you work in the HR department of a company considering a no-smoking policy. You have been asked to recommend the responses that managers should take if one of their employees is found to have been smoking. What would you recommend?

IT'S A WRAP!

www.mhhe.com/noefund3e is your source for **R**eviewing, **A**pplying, and **P**racticing the concepts you learned about in Chapter 10.

Review	Application	Practice
• Chapter learning objectives	• Manager's Hot Seat segment: "Whistle-Blowing: Code Red or Red Ink?"	• Chapter quiz
• Narrated lecture and iPod content		
• Test Your Knowledge: Styles of Handling Conflict	• Video case and quiz: "Finding and Keeping the Best Employees at SAS"	
	• Self-Assessments: Take a sample employee survey and answer the assessment "What Is Your Preferred Conflict Handling Style"	
	• Web exercise: Cyberspace and Employee Satisfaction	

NOTES

1. "View from the Top," *Wall Street Journal*, November 19, 2007, http://online.wsj.com; and Carol Hymowitz, "Women Get Better at Forming Networks to Help Their Climb," *Wall Street Journal*, November 19, 2007, http://online.wsj.com.

2. J. D. Shaw, M. K. Duffy, J. L. Johnson, and D. E. Lockhart, "Turnover, Social Capital Losses, and Performance," *Academy of Management Journal* 48 (2005), pp. 594–606; and R. Batt, "Managing Customer Services: Human Resource Practices, Quit Rates, and Sales Growth," *Academy of Management Journal* 45 (2002), pp. 587–97.

3. D. J. Koys, "The Effects of Employee Satisfaction, Organizational Citizenship Behavior, and Turnover on Organizational Effectiveness: A Unit-Level Longitudinal Study," *Personnel Psychology* 54 (2001), pp. 101–14; R. Batt, "Managing Customer Services: Human Resource Practices, Quit Rates, and Sales Growth," *Academy of Management Journal* 45 (2002), pp. 587–97; and M. Boyle, "Happy People, Happy Returns," *Fortune*, January 22, 2007, p. 100.

4. K. M. Kacmer, M. C. Andrews, D. L. Van Rooy, R. C. Steilberg, and S. Cerrone, "Sure Everyone Can Be Replaced . . . but at What Cost? Turnover as a Predictor of Unit-Level Performance," *Academy of Management Journal* 49 (2006), pp. 133–44; J. D. Shaw, N. Gupta, and J. E. Delery, "Alternative Conceptualizations of the Relationship between Voluntary Turnover and Organizational Performance," *Academy of Management Journal* 48 (2005), pp. 50–68; and J. Lublin, "Keeping Clients by Keeping Workers," *Wall Street Journal*, November 20, 2006, p. B1.

5. M. Heller, "A Return to At-Will Employment," *Workforce*, May 2001, pp. 42–46.

6. M. Orey, "Fear of Firing," *BusinessWeek*, April 23, 2007, pp. 52–62.

7. M. M. Le Blanc and K. Kelloway, "Predictors and Outcomes of Workplace Violence and Aggression," *Journal of Applied Psychology*, 87, 2002, pp. 444–53.

8. F. Hanson, "'Poaching' Can Be Pricey, but Benefits May Outweigh Costs," *Workforce Management*, January 30, 2006, pp. 37–39.

9. B. J. Tepper, "Relationship among Supervisors' and Subordinates' Procedural Justice Perceptions and Organizational Citizenship Behaviors," *Academy of Management Journal* 46 (2003), pp. 97–105; and T. Simons and Q. Roberson, "Why Managers Should Care about Fairness: The Effects of Aggregate Justice Perception on Organizational Outcomes," *Journal of Applied Psychology* 88 (2003), pp. 432–43.

10. T. A. Judge, B. A. Scott, and R. Ilies, "Hostility, Job Attitudes and Workplace Deviance: A Test of a Multilevel Model," *Journal of Applied Psychology* 91 (2006), pp. 126–38.

11. *Harmon v. Thornburgh*, CA, DC No. 88-5265 (July 30, 1989); *Treasury Employees Union v. Von Raab*, U.S. Sup. Ct. No. 86-18796 (March 21, 1989); *City of Annapolis v. United Food & Commercial Workers Local 400*, Md. Ct. App. No. 38 (November 6, 1989); *Skinner v. Railway Labor Executives Association*, U.S. Sup. Ct. No. 87-1555 (March 21, 1989); and *Bluestein v. Skinner*, 908 F.2d 451, 9th Cir. (1990).

12. D. J. Hoekstra, "Workplace Searches: A Legal Overview," *Labor Law Journal* 47, no. 2 (February 1996), pp. 127–38.

13. G. Henshaw and K. Youmans, "Employee Privacy in the Workplace and an Employer's Right to Conduct Workplace Searches and Surveillance," *SHRM Legal Report*, Spring 1990, pp. 1–5; B. K. Repa, *Your Rights in the Workplace* (Berkeley, CA: Nolo Press, 1997).

14. J. Schramm, "Privacy at Work," *HRMagazine*, April 2005, downloaded from Infotrac at http://web1.infotrac.galegroup.com; M. Denis and J. Andes, "Defamation—Do You Tell Employees Why a Co-worker Was Discharged?" *Employee Relations Law Journal* 16, no. 4 (Spring 1991), pp. 469–79; R. S. Soderstrom and J. R. Murray, "Defamation in Employment: Suits by At-Will Employees," *FICC Quarterly*, Summer 1992, pp. 395–426; and R. J. Posch Jr., "Your Personal Exposure for Interoffice Communications," *Direct Marketing* 61 (August 1998).

15. N. Orkin and M. Heise, "Weingarten through the Looking Glass," *Labor Law Journal* 48, no. 3 (March 1997), pp. 157–63.

16. K. Karl and C. Sutton, "A Review of Expert Advice on Employment Termination Practices: The Experts Don't Always Agree," in *Dysfunctional Behavior in Organizations*, eds. R. Griffin, A. O'Leary-Kelly, and J. Collins (Stanford, CT: JAI Press, 1998).

17. "Arbitration's Popularity Still Growing," *HRNext*, March 18, 2002, www.hrnext.com; and J. Howard-Martin, "Arbitration Can Speed Resolution of Grievances," *USA Today*, March 26, 2002, http://careers.usatoday.com.

18. S. Caudron, "Blowing the Whistle on Employee Disputes," *Workforce*, May 1997, pp. 50–57.

19. S. Johnson, "Results, Relapse Rates Add to Cost of Non-Hospital Treatment," *Employee Benefit Plan Review* 46 (1992), pp. 15–16.

20. "Treating Employees' Depression Can Benefit Bottom Line, Study Says," *Wall Street Journal*, September 25, 2007, http://online.wsj.com.

21. D. W. Baruch, "Why They Terminate," *Journal of Consulting Psychology* 8 (1944), pp. 35–46; J. G. Rosse, "Relations among Lateness, Absence and Turnover: Is There a Progression of Withdrawal?" *Human Relations* 41 (1988), pp. 517–31; C. Hulin, "Adaptation, Persistence and Commitment in Organizations," in *Handbook of Industrial & Organizational Psychology*, 2nd ed., eds. M. D. Dunnette and L. M. Hough (Palo Alto, CA: Consulting Psychologists Press, 1991), pp. 443–50; and C. Hulin, M. Roznowski, and D. Hachiya, "Alternative Opportunities and Withdrawal Decisions," *Psychological Bulletin* 97 (1985), pp. 233–50.

22. D. A. Harrison, D. A. Newman, and P. L. Roth, "How Important Are Job Attitudes? Meta-analytic Comparisons of Integrative Behavioral Outcomes and Time Sequences," *Academy of Management Journal* 49 (2006), pp. 305–25.

23. D. Watson, L. A. Clark, and A. Tellegen, "Development and Validation of Brief Measures of Positive and Negative Affect: The PANAS Scales," *Journal of Personality and Social Psychology* 54 (1988), pp. 1063–70.

24. T. A. Judge, E. A. Locke, C. C. Durham, and A. N. Kluger, "Dispositional Effects on Job and Life Satisfaction: The Role of Core Evaluations," *Journal of Applied Psychology* 83 (1998), pp. 17–34.

25. B. M. Staw, N. E. Bell, and J. A. Clausen, "The Dispositional Approach to Job Attitudes: A Lifetime Longitudinal Test," *Administrative Science Quarterly* 31 (1986), pp. 56–78; B. M. Staw and J. Ross, "Stability in the Midst of Change: A Dispositional Approach to Job Attitudes," *Journal of Applied Psychology* 70 (1985), pp. 469–80; and R. P. Steel and J. R. Rentsch, "The Dispositional Model of Job Attitudes Revisited: Findings of a 10-Year Study," *Journal of Applied Psychology* 82 (1997), pp. 873–79.

26. T. A. Judge and J. E. Bono, "Relationship of Core Self-Evaluation Traits—Self-Esteem, Generalized Self-Efficacy, Locus of Control, and Emotional Stability—with Job Satisfaction and Job Performance: A Meta-Analysis," *Journal of Applied Psychology* 86 (2001), pp. 80–92.

27. T. A. Judge, J. E. Bono, and E. A. Locke, "Personality and Job Satisfaction: The Mediating Role of Job Characteristics," *Journal of Applied Psychology* 85 (2000), pp. 237–49.

28. S. C. Douglas and M. J. Martinko, "Exploring the Role of Individual Differences in the Prediction of Workplace Aggression," *Journal of Applied Psychology* 86 (2001), pp. 547–59.

29. B. A. Gerhart, "How Important Are Dispositional Factors as Determinants of Job Satisfaction? Implications for Job Design and Other Personnel Programs," *Journal of Applied Psychology* 72 (1987), pp. 493–502.

30. E. F. Stone and H. G. Gueutal, "An Empirical Derivation of the Dimensions along Which Characteristics of Jobs Are Perceived," *Academy of Management Journal* 28 (1985), pp. 376–96.

31. L. W. Porter and R. M. Steers, "Organizational Work and Personal Factors in Employee Absenteeism and Turnover," *Psychological Bulletin* 80 (1973), pp. 151–76; and S. Melamed, I. Ben-Avi, J. Luz, and M. S. Green, "Objective and Subjective Work Monotony: Effects on Job Satisfaction, Psychological Distress, and Absenteeism in Blue Collar Workers," *Journal of Applied Psychology* 80 (1995), pp. 29–42.

32. D. R. Ilgen and J. R. Hollenbeck, "The Structure of Work: Job Design and Roles," in *Handbook of Industrial & Organizational Psychology*, 2nd ed.

33. J. A. Breaugh and J. P. Colihan, "Measuring Facets of Job Ambiguity: Construct Validity Evidence," *Journal of Applied Psychology* 79 (1994), pp. 191–201.

34. M. A. Shaffer and D. A. Harrison, "Expatriates' Psychological Withdrawal from Interpersonal Assignments: Work, Non-work, and Family Influences," *Personnel Psychology* 51 (1998), pp. 87–118.

35. J. M. Brett and L. K. Stroh, "Working 61 Plus Hours a Week: Why Do Managers Do It?" *Journal of Applied Psychology* 88 (2003), pp. 67–78; and V. S. Major, K. J. Klein, and M. G. Ehrhart, "Work Time, Work

Interference with Family, and Psychological Distress," *Journal of Applied Psychology* 87 (2002), pp. 427–36.

36. S. M. Lilienthal, "Screen and Glean," *Workforce*, October 2000, downloaded from FindArticles.com.

37. P. Lattman, "Does Thank You Help Keep Associates?" *Wall Street Journal*, January 24, 2007; and S. Aryee, Z. X. Chen, L. Y. Sun, and Y. A. Debrah, "Antecedents and Outcomes of Abusive Supervision: Test of a Trickle-Down Model," *Journal of Applied Psychology* 92 (2007), pp. 191–201.

38. J. M. Sacco and N. Schmitt, "A Dynamic Multi-level Model of Demographic Diversity and Misfit Effects," *Journal of Applied Psychology* 90 (2005), pp. 203–31; and R. E. Ployhart, J. A. Weekley, and K. Baughman, "The Structure and Function of Human Capital Emergence: A Multilevel Examination of the Attraction–Selection–Attrition Model," *Academy of Management Journal* 49 (2006), pp. 661–77.

39. J. Cook, "Positively Negative," *Human Resource Executive*, June 15, 2001, pp. 101–4.

40. S. F. Gale, "Sickened by Costs of Absenteeism, Companies Look for Solutions," *Workforce*, September 2003, pp. 72–75.

41. J. Sullivan, "Not All Turnover Is Equal," *Workforce Management*, May 21, 2007, p. 42.

42. R. T. Mowday, R. M. Steers, and L. W. Porter, "The Measurement of Organizational Commitment," *Journal of Vocational Behavior* 14 (1979), pp. 224–47.

43. E. A. Locke, "The Nature and Causes of Job Dissatisfaction," in *The Handbook of Industrial & Organizational Psychology*, ed. M. D. Dunnette (Chicago: Rand McNally, 1976), pp. 901–69.

44. N. A. Bowling, T. A. Beehr, S. H. Wagner, and T. M. Libkuman, "Adaptation-Level Theory, Opponent Process Theory, and Dispositions: An Integrated Approach to the Stability of Job Satisfaction," *Journal of Applied Psychology* 90 (2005), pp. 1044–53.

45. E. Tanouye, "Depression Takes Annual Toll of $70 Billion on Employers," *Wall Street Journal*, June 13, 2001, p. 1; E. Tanouye, "Mental Illness in the Workplace Afflicts Bosses, Can Affect Business," *Wall Street Journal*, June 13, 2001, pp. 1–2; and J. Vennochi, "When Depression Comes to Work," *Working Woman*, August 1995, pp. 43–51.

46. G. R. Oldham, A. Cummings, L. J. Mischel, J. M. Schmidtke, and J. Zhou, "Listen While You Work? Quasi-experimental Relations between Personal-Stereo Headset Use and Employee Work Responses," *Journal of Applied Psychology* 80 (1995), pp. 547–64.

47. B. Morris, "The Best Place to Work Now," *Fortune*, January 20, 2006, pp. 79–86.

48. B. Kaye, "Wake Up and Smell the Coffee: People Flock to Family Friendly," *BusinessWeek Online*, January 28, 2001, pp. 1–2.

49. G. Flynn, "The Legalities of Flextime," *Workforce*, October 2001, pp. 62–66; G. Weber, "Flexible Jobs Mean Fewer Absences," *Workforce*, November 2003, pp. 26–28; and M. Hammers, "Babies Deliver a Loyal Workforce," *Workforce*, April 2003, p. 52.

50. J. E. Perry-Smith, "Work Family Human Resource Bundles and Perceived Organizational Performance," *Academy of Management Journal* 43 (2000), pp. 801–15; and M. M. Arthur, "Share Price Reactions to Work-Family Initiatives: An Institutional Perspective," *Academy of Management Journal* 46 (2003), pp. 497–505.

51. Brian Bergstein, "IBM Riles Employees with Base Pay Cuts," *Yahoo News*, January 23, 2008, http://news.yahoo.com.

52. B. M. Meglino, E. C. Ravlin, and C. L. Adkins, "A Work Values Approach to Corporate Culture: A Field Test of the Value Congruence Process and Its Relationship to Individual Outcomes," *Journal of Applied Psychology* 74 (1989), pp. 424–33.

53. G. C. Ganster, M. R. Fusilier, and B. T. Mayes, "Role of Social Support in the Experience of Stress at Work," *Journal of Applied Psychology* 71 (1986), pp. 102–11.

54. R. Eisenberger, F. Stinghamber, C. Vandenberghe, I. L. Sucharski, and L. Rhoades, "Perceived Supervisor Support: Contributions to Perceived Organizational Support and Employee Retention," *Journal of Applied Psychology* 87 (2002), pp. 565–73.

55. R. T. Keller, "A Test of the Path-Goal Theory of Leadership with Need for Clarity as a Moderator in Research and Development Organizations," *Journal of Applied Psychology* 74 (1989), pp. 208–12.

56. S. C. Payne and A. H. Huffman, "A Longitudinal Examination of the Influence of Mentoring on Organizational Commitment and Turnover," *Academy of Management Journal* 48 (2005), pp. 158–68.

57. A. Fisher, "Have You Outgrown Your Job?" *Fortune*, August 21, 2006, pp. 46–54.

58. R. P. Quinn and G. L. Staines, *The 1977 Quality of Employment Survey* (Ann Arbor, MI: Survey Research Center, Institute for Social Research, University of Michigan, 1979).

59. T. Judge and T. Welbourne, "A Confirmatory Investigation of the Dimensionality of the Pay Satisfaction Questionnaire," *Journal of Applied Psychology* 79 (1994), pp. 461–66.

60. P. Babcock, "Find What Workers Want," *HRMagazine*, April 2005, www.shrm.org/hrmagazine.

61. H. E. Allerton, "Can Teach Old Dogs New Tricks," *Training & Development*, November 2000, downloaded from FindArticles.com.

Compensating Human Resources

Chapter 11
Establishing a Pay Structure

Chapter 12
Recognizing Employee Contributions with Pay

Chapter 13
Providing Employee Benefits

PART FOUR

Establishing a Pay Structure

Introduction

Competition among law firms to get the best new lawyers has been so stiff that salaries have been rising year after year. Traditionally, firms pay them according to their years out of school; the longer the associates have been working, the more they earn. So when a company raises associate salaries, it is raising them for everyone—an expensive move. Recently, however, some law firms have broken that mold and are tying pay more closely to what each associate contributes to the firm. For example, in San Diego, the firm Luce, Forward, Hamilton & Scripps set up 14 pay levels related to the associate's productivity (some work more hours than others) and practice area (some types of legal work are more profitable than others). Some recruiters question whether the new system will seem less fair, identifying some lawyers as having a less-valuable practice. The firm argues that its pay levels offer a wider range of opportunities for lawyers who might prefer to work fewer hours or in a less-profitable area. With the new system, hiring these lawyers becomes affordable.[1]

From the employer's point of view, pay is a powerful tool for meeting the organization's goals. Pay has a large impact on employee attitudes and behaviors. It influences which kinds of employees are attracted to (and remain with) the organization. By rewarding certain behaviors, it can align employees' interests with the organization's goals. Employees care about policies affecting earnings because the policies affect the employees' income and standard of living. Besides the level of pay, employees care about its fairness compared with what others earn. Also, employees consider pay a sign of status and success. They attach great importance to pay decisions when they evaluate their relationship with their employer. For these reasons, organizations must carefully manage and communicate decisions about pay.

At the same time, pay is a major cost. Its share of total costs varies widely, but across all industries, pay averages almost one-fourth of a company's revenues.[2] Some companies spend 40 percent or more of their revenues on paying employees. Managers have to keep this cost reasonable.

This chapter describes how managers weigh the importance and costs of pay to arrive at a structure for compensation and levels of pay for different jobs. We first define the basic decisions in terms of pay structure and pay level. Next, we look at several considerations that influence these decisions: legal requirements related to pay, economic forces, the nature of the organization's jobs, and employees' judgments about the fairness of pay levels. We describe methods for evaluating jobs and market data to arrive at a pay structure. We then summarize alternatives to the usual focus on jobs. The chapter closes with a look at two issues of current importance—pay for employees on leave to serve in the military and pay for executives.

Decisions about Pay

LO1 Identify the kinds of decisions involved in establishing a pay structure.

Because pay is important both in its effect on employees and on account of its cost, organizations need to plan what they will pay employees in each job. An unplanned approach, in which each employee's pay is independently negotiated, will likely result in unfairness, dissatisfaction, and rates that are either overly expensive or so low that positions are hard to fill. Organizations therefore make decisions about two aspects of pay structure: job structure and pay level. **Job structure** consists of the relative pay for different jobs within the organization. It establishes relative pay among different functions and different levels of responsibility. For example, job structure defines the difference in pay between an entry-level accountant and an entry-level assembler, as well as the difference between an entry-level accountant, the accounting department manager, and the organization's comptroller. **Pay level** is the average amount (including wages, salaries, and bonuses) the organization pays for a particular job. Together, job structure and pay levels establish a **pay structure** that helps the organization achieve goals related to employee motivation, cost control, and the ability to attract and retain talented human resources. The "Best Practices" box describes the pay structure of a department of the Volusia County, Florida, government in terms of its organizational objectives.

job structure
The relative pay for different jobs within the organization.

pay level
The average amount (including wages, salaries, and bonuses) the organization pays for a particular job.

pay structure
The pay policy resulting from job structure and pay-level decisions.

The organization's job structure and pay levels are policies of the organization, rather than the amount a particular employee earns. For example, an organization's pay structure could include the range of pay that a person may earn in the job of entry-level accountant. An individual accountant could be earning an amount anywhere within that range. Typically, the amount a person earns depends on the individual's qualifications, accomplishments, and experience. The individual's pay may also depend partly on how well the organization performs. This chapter focuses on the organization's decisions about pay structure, and the next chapter will explore decisions that affect the amount of pay an individual earns.

Especially in an organization with hundreds or thousands of employees, it would be impractical for managers and the human resource department to make an entirely unique decision about each employee's pay. The decision would have to weigh so many factors that this approach would be expensive, difficult, and often unsatisfactory. Establishing a pay structure simplifies the process of making decisions about individual employees' pay by grouping together employees with similar jobs. As shown in Figure 11.1, human resource professionals develop this pay structure based on legal requirements, market forces, and the organization's goals, such as attracting a high-quality workforce and meeting principles of fairness.

Best Practices

Logical Pay Structure for Volusia County Fleet Management

Local governments need vehicles such as fire trucks, police cars, pickup trucks for maintenance workers, and cars for official business. Volusia County, located on Florida's east coast, has a fleet of over 2,100 vehicles and related equipment such as excavators, lawn mowers, and even boats. Its fleet management division is charged with maintaining these vehicles, keeping them fueled, and replacing them as they age. This work requires mechanics, inventory control specialists, and a small staff of office assistants.

Finding and keeping skilled mechanics can be difficult. The fleet management division meets the challenge by providing its 50 mechanics a career path tied to pay increases. The division structures pay for mechanics in

four levels, and everyone sees them spelled out in the division's Technician Progression Agreement. To advance from one level to the next, mechanics need to obtain specified National Institute for Automotive Service Excellence (ASE) certifications and complete at least 1,550 billable hours of work per year. Because mechanics know the requirements and report their billable hours each month, they can easily tell whether they are on track for a promotion to the next pay level.

Along with this basic structure, mechanics know they can earn more by doing exceptional work. Every year, they know what their goals are and what percentage of raise is associated with achieving those goals. Their performance is measured in annual reviews. They

also can earn bonuses for exceptional performance.

These pay practices not only keep mechanics working for the county but have also helped drive the team toward excellence. The division was named one of the nation's top 100 fleets by *Fleet Equipment,* an industry trade magazine. A top fleet must meet many requirements, including recognition of employee performance, creativity and collaboration, high-quality and efficient performance, and competitive pricing.

Sources: Bruce Adams, "A Top 100 Tale," *Fleet Equipment,* January 2007, pp. 38–39; Volusia County Government Fleet Management Division Web site and strategic business plan for 2007, http://volusia.org/fleet/, accessed February 21, 2008; and Rachael Jackson, "Volusia County's Fleet-Management Division Earns Top National Recognition," *Orlando Sentinel,* November 22, 2007, downloaded from General Reference Center Gold, http://find.galegroup.com.

Figure 11.1

Issues in Developing a Pay Structure

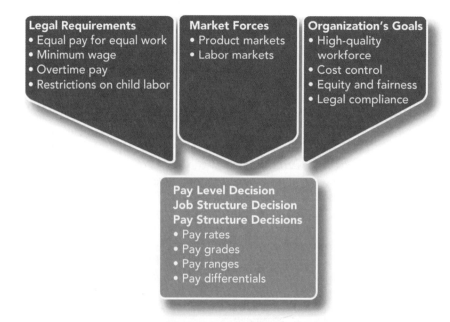

Legal Requirements
• Equal pay for equal work
• Minimum wage
• Overtime pay
• Restrictions on child labor

Market Forces
• Product markets
• Labor markets

Organization's Goals
• High-quality workforce
• Cost control
• Equity and fairness
• Legal compliance

Pay Level Decision
Job Structure Decision
Pay Structure Decisions
• Pay rates
• Pay grades
• Pay ranges
• Pay differentials

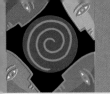

HR Oops!

Women Don't Ask

Years ago, female doctoral students at a big university complained that their male counterparts landed teaching positions, while all the women remained as lowlier teaching assistants. An investigation found that the reason was simply that the men had asked for the positions and the women had not. Further research found one reason why women in general tend to earn less than men on average: the men were more likely to ask for higher pay, while women were more likely to accept the amount offered. As salaries rose from a smaller starting amount, the women never caught up.

At organizations seeking to treat women equally, the solution seemed obvious: train women to ask for more. But still more research has found that the results are more complicated. In a series of studies, women who asked for more were viewed more negatively than men who did the same. The exception? When a woman was dealing with another woman.

Source: Shankar Vedantam, "Salary, Gender and the Social Cost of Haggling," *Washington Post,* July 30, 2007, www.washingtonpost.com.

Questions

1. Hiring a female candidate for less pay than a male candidate has an obvious financial advantage for the employer. What risks or negative consequences could occur as well?

2. If women see a social cost to asking for more pay, how can an employer treat women fairly when making decisions about pay and promotions?

Legal Requirements for Pay

Government regulation affects pay structure in the areas of equal employment opportunity, minimum wages, pay for overtime, and prevailing wages for federal contractors. All of an organization's decisions about pay should comply with the applicable laws.

LO2 Summarize legal requirements for pay policies.

Equal Employment Opportunity

Under the laws governing Equal Employment Opportunity, described in Chapter 3, employers may not base differences in pay on an employee's age, sex, race, or other protected status. Any differences in pay must instead be tied to such business-related considerations as job responsibilities or performance. The goal is for employers to provide *equal pay for equal work*. Job descriptions, job structures, and pay structures can help organizations demonstrate that they are upholding these laws.

These laws do not guarantee equal pay for men and women, whites and minorities, or any other groups, because so many legitimate factors, from education to choice of occupation, affect a person's earnings. In fact, numbers show that women and racial minorities in the United States tend to earn less than white men. Among full-time workers in 2006, women on average earned 81 cents for every dollar earned by men, while black workers on average earned 80 cents for every dollar earned by white workers and Hispanic workers earned closer to 70 cents per dollar earned by whites.[3] Even when these figures are adjusted to take into account education, experience, and occupation, the earnings gap does not completely close.[4] The "HR Oops!" box suggests other reasons for differences in pay for men and women performing similar jobs.

Two employees who do the same job cannot be paid different wages because of gender, race, or age. It would be illegal to pay these two employees differently because one is male and the other is female. Only if there are differences in their experience, skills, seniority, or job performance are there legal reasons why their pay might be different.

One explanation for historical lower pay for women has been that employers have undervalued work performed by women—in particular, placing a lower value on occupations traditionally dominated by women. Some policy makers have proposed a remedy for this called equal pay for *comparable worth*. This policy uses job evaluation (described later in the chapter) to establish the worth of an organization's jobs in terms of such criteria as their difficulty and their importance to the organization. The employer then compares the evaluation points awarded to each job with the pay for each job. If jobs have the same number of evaluation points, they should be paid equally. If they are not, pay of the lower-paid job is raised to meet the goal of comparable worth.

Comparable-worth policies are controversial. From an economic standpoint, the obvious drawback of such a policy is that raising pay for some jobs places the employer at an economic disadvantage relative to employers that pay the market rate. In addition, a free-market economy assumes people will take differences in pay into account when they choose a career. The courts allow organizations to defend themselves against claims of discrimination by showing that they pay the going market rate.[5] Businesses are reluctant to place themselves at an economic disadvantage, but many state governments adjust pay to achieve equal pay for comparable worth. Also, at both private and government organizations, policies designed to shatter the "glass ceiling" (discussed in Chapter 9) can help to address the problem of unequal pay.

Minimum Wage

minimum wage
The lowest amount that employers may pay under federal or state law, stated as an amount of pay per hour.

In the United States, employers must pay at least the **minimum wage** established by law. (A *wage* is the rate of pay per hour.) At the federal level, the 1938 **Fair Labor Standards Act (FLSA)** establishes a minimum wage that is $6.55 per hour as of July 2008 and $7.25 per hour as of July 2009. The FLSA also permits a lower "training wage," which employers may pay to workers under the age of 20 for a period of up to 90 days. This subminimum wage is approximately 85 percent of the minimum wage. Some states have laws specifying minimum wages; in these states, employers must pay whichever rate is higher.

Fair Labor Standards Act (FLSA)
Federal law that establishes a minimum wage and requirements for overtime pay and child labor.

From the standpoint of social policy, an issue related to the minimum wage is that it tends to be lower than the earnings required for a full-time worker to rise above the poverty level. A number of cities have therefore passed laws requiring a so-called *living wage*, essentially a minimum wage based on the cost of living in a particular region.

Overtime Pay

Another requirement of the FLSA is that employers must pay higher wages for overtime, defined as hours worked beyond 40 hours per week. The overtime rate under the FLSA is one and a half times the employee's usual hourly rate, including any bonuses and piece-rate payments (amounts paid per item produced). The overtime rate applies to the hours worked beyond 40 in one week. Time worked includes not

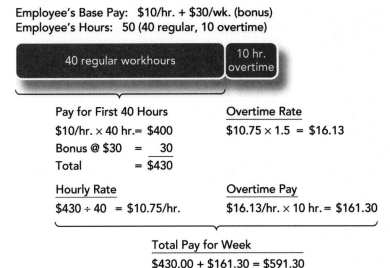

Figure 11.2

Computing Overtime Pay

only hours spent on production or sales but also time on such activities as attending required classes, cleaning up the work site, or traveling between work sites. Figure 11.2 shows how this applies to an employee who works 50 hours to earn a base rate of $10 per hour plus a weekly bonus of $30. The overtime pay is based on the base pay ($400) plus the bonus ($30), for a rate of $10.75 per hour. For each of the 10 hours of overtime, the employee would earn $16.13, so the overtime pay is $161.30 ($16.13 times 10). When employees are paid per unit produced or when they receive a monthly or quarterly bonus, those payments must be converted into wages per hour, so that the employer can include these amounts when figuring the correct overtime rate.

Overtime pay is required, whether or not the employer specifically asked or expected the employee to work more than 40 hours.[6] In other words, if the employer knows the employee is working overtime but does not pay time and a half, the employer may be violating the FLSA.

Not everyone is eligible for overtime pay. Under the FLSA, executive, professional, administrative, and highly compensated white-collar employees are considered **exempt employees,** meaning employers need not pay them one and a half times their regular pay for working more than 40 hours per week. Exempt status depends on the employee's job responsibilities, salary level (at least $455 per week), and "salary basis," meaning that the employee is paid a given amount regardless of the number of hours worked or quality of the work.[7] Paying an employee on a salary basis means the organization expects that this person can manage his or her own time to get the work done, so the employer may deduct from the employee's pay only in certain limited circumstances, such as disciplinary action or for unpaid leave for personal reasons. Additional exceptions apply to certain occupations, including outside salespersons, teachers, and computer professionals (if they earn at least $27.63 per hour). Thus, the standards are fairly complicated. For more details about the standards for exempt employees, contact the Wage and Hour Division of the Labor Department's Employment Standards Administration or refer to its Web site at www.dol.gov/esa.

exempt employees
Managers, outside salespeople, and any other employees not covered by the FLSA requirement for overtime pay.

Any employee who is not in one of the exempt categories is called a **nonexempt employee.** Most workers paid on an hourly basis are nonexempt and therefore subject to the laws governing overtime pay. However, paying a salary does not necessarily mean a job is exempt.

Child Labor

In the early years of the Industrial Revolution, employers could pay low wages by hiring children. The FLSA now sharply restricts the use of child labor, with the aim of protecting children's health, safety, and educational opportunities.[8] The restrictions apply to children younger than 18. Under the FLSA, children aged 16 and 17 may not be employed in hazardous occupations defined by the Department of Labor, such as mining, meatpacking, and certain kinds of manufacturing using heavy machinery. Children aged 14 and 15 may work only outside school hours, in jobs defined as nonhazardous, and for limited time periods. A child under age 14 may not be employed in any work associated with interstate commerce, except work performed in a nonhazardous job for a business entirely owned by the child's parent or guardian. A few additional exemptions from this ban include acting, baby-sitting, and delivering newspapers to consumers.

Besides the FLSA, state laws also restrict the use of child labor. Many states have laws requiring working papers or work permits for minors, and many states restrict the number of hours or times of day that minors aged 16 and older may work. Before hiring any workers under the age of 18, employers must ensure they are complying with the child labor laws of their state, as well as the FLSA requirements for their industry.

Prevailing Wages

Two additional federal laws, the Davis-Bacon Act of 1931 and the Walsh-Healy Public Contracts Act of 1936, govern pay policies of federal contractors. Under these laws, federal contractors must pay their employees at rates at least equal to the prevailing wages in the area. The calculation of prevailing rates must be based on 30 percent of the local labor force. Typically, the rates are based on relevant union contracts. Pay earned by union members tends to be higher than the pay of non-union workers in similar jobs, so the effect of these laws is to raise the lower limit of pay an employer can offer.

These laws do not cover all companies. Davis-Bacon covers construction contractors that receive more than $2,000 in federal money. Walsh-Healy covers all government contractors receiving $10,000 or more in federal funds.

Economic Influences on Pay

An organization cannot make spending decisions independent of the economy. Organizations must keep costs low enough that they can sell their products profitably, yet they must be able to attract workers in a competitive labor market. Decisions about how to respond to the economic forces of product markets and labor markets limit an organization's choices about pay structure.

Product Markets

The organization's *product market* includes organizations that offer competing goods and services. In other words, the organizations in a product market are competing to serve the same customers. To succeed in their product markets, organizations must be able to sell their goods and services at a quantity and price that will bring them a sufficient profit. They may try to win customers by being superior in a number of areas, including quality, customer service, and price. An important influence on price is the cost to produce the goods and services for sale. As we mentioned earlier, the cost of labor is a significant part of an organization's costs.

If an organization's labor costs are higher than those of its competitors, it will be under pressure to charge more than competitors charge for similar products. If one company spends $50 in labor costs to make a product and its competitor spends only $35, the second company will be more profitable unless the first company can justify a higher price to customers. This is one reason U.S. automakers have had difficulty competing against Japanese companies. The labor-related expenses per vehicle for a U.S. company are over $1,000 higher than for Japanese car makers operating in the United States.[9]

Product markets place an upper limit on the pay an organization will offer. This upper limit is most important when labor costs are a large part of an organization's total costs and when the organization's customers place great importance on price. Organizations that want to lure top-quality employees by offering generous salaries therefore have to find ways to automate routine activities (so that labor is a smaller part of total costs) or to persuade customers that high quality is worth a premium price. Organizations under pressure to cut labor costs may respond by reducing staff levels, freezing pay levels, postponing hiring decisions, or requiring employees to bear more of the cost of benefits such as insurance premiums.

Labor Markets

Besides competing to sell their products, organizations must compete to obtain human resources in *labor markets*. In general, workers prefer higher-paying jobs and avoid employers that offer less money for the same type of job. In this way, competition for labor establishes the minimum an organization must pay to hire an employee for a particular job. If an organization pays less than the minimum, employees will look for jobs with other organizations.

An organization's competitors in labor markets typically include companies with similar products and companies in other industries that hire similar employees. For example, a truck transportation firm would want to know the pay earned by truck drivers at competing firms as well as truck drivers for manufacturers that do their own shipping, drivers for moving and storage companies, and drivers for stores that provide delivery services. In setting pay levels for its bookkeepers and administrative assistants, the company would probably define its labor market differently, because bookkeepers and administrative assistants work for most kinds of businesses. The company would likely look for data on the earnings of bookkeepers and administrative assistants in the region. For all these jobs, the company wants to know what others are paying so that it will pay enough to attract and keep qualified employees.

There is currently a strong demand for nurses in the labor market. What this means for hospitals is that they have to pay competitive wages and other perks to attract and retain staff. How does this differ from the current airline industry's labor market?

Did You Know?

Tech Workers Out-Earn Managers

Looking at broad occupational categories, people in technology-related jobs are some of the nation's top earners. The pay rates are for the *median* worker in each category (half the employees earn more and half earn less).

Source: U.S. Census Bureau, *Statistical Abstract of the United States: 2008,* Table 627, www.census.gov.

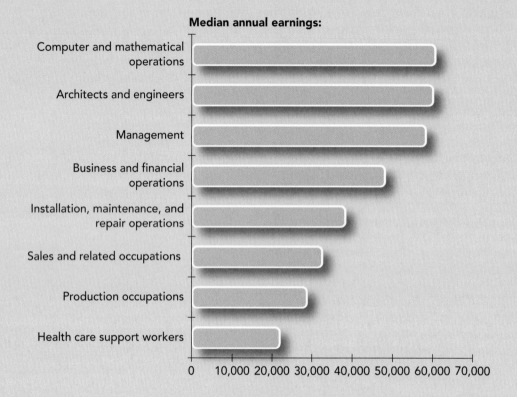

Median annual earnings:

The "Did You Know?" box compares average pay levels for some broad occupational categories in the United States.

Another influence on labor markets is the *cost of living*—the cost of a household's typical expenses, such as house payments, groceries, medical care, and gasoline. In some parts of the country, the cost of living is higher than in others, so the local labor markets there will likely demand higher pay. Also, over time, the cost of living tends to rise. When the cost of living is rising rapidly, labor markets demand pay increases. The federal government tracks trends in the nation's cost of living with a measure called the Consumer Price Index (CPI). Following and studying changes in the CPI can help employers prepare for changes in the demands of the labor market.

Pay Level: Deciding What to Pay

Although labor and product markets limit organizations' choices about pay levels, there is a range within which organizations can make decisions.[10] The size of this range depends on the details of the organization's competitive environment. If many workers are competing for a few jobs, employers will have more choice. Similarly, employers can be more flexible about pay policies if they use technology and work design to get better results from employees than their competitors do.

When organizations have a broad range in which to make decisions about pay, they can choose to pay at, above, or below the rate set by market forces. Economic theory holds that the most profitable level, all things being equal, would be at the market rate. Often, however, all things are not equal from one employer to another. For instance, an organization may gain an advantage by paying above the market rate if it uses the higher pay as one means to attract top talent and then uses these excellent employees' knowledge to be more innovative, produce higher quality, or work more efficiently.

This approach is based on the view of employees as resources. Higher pay may be an investment in superior human resources. Having higher labor costs than your competitors is not necessarily bad if you also have the best and most effective work-force, which produces more products of better quality. Pay policies are one of the most important human resource tools for encouraging desired employee behaviors and discouraging undesired behaviors. Therefore, organizations must evaluate pay as more than a cost, but also as an investment that can generate returns in attract-ing, retaining, and motivating a high-quality workforce. For this reason, paying above the going rate may be advantageous for an organization that empowers em-ployees or that cannot closely watch employees (as with repair technicians who travel to customers). Those employers might use high pay to attract and retain top candidates and to motivate them to do their best because they want to keep their high-paying jobs.[11]

Gathering Information about Market Pay

To compete for talent, organizations use **benchmarking,** a procedure in which an organization compares its own practices against those of successful competitors. In terms of compensation, benchmarking involves the use of pay surveys. These provide information about the going rates of pay at competitors in the organization's product and labor markets. An organization can conduct its own surveys, but the federal government and other organizations make a great deal of data available already.

benchmarking
A procedure in which an organization compares its own practices against those of successful competitors.

Pay surveys are available for many kinds of industries (product markets) and jobs (labor markets). The primary collector of this kind of data in the United States is the Bureau of Labor Statistics, which conducts an ongoing National Compensation Survey measuring wages, salaries, and benefits paid to the nation's employees. The "HR How To" box provides guidelines for using the BLS Web site as a source of wage data. The Society for Human Resource Management, the American Management Association, and many industry, trade, and professional groups also collect wage and salary data. Employers should check with the relevant groups to see what surveys are available. Consulting firms also will provide data, including the results of international surveys, and can tailor data to the organiza-tion's particular needs.

Human resource professionals need to determine whether to gather data focusing on particular industries or on job categories. Industry-specific data are especially rele-vant for jobs with skills that are specific to the type of product. For jobs with skills that can be transferred to companies in other industries, surveys of job classifications will be more relevant.

HR How To

A convenient source of data on hourly wages is the wage query system of the Bureau of Labor Statistics (BLS). This federal agency makes data available at its Web site on an interactive basis. The data come from the BLS's National Compensation Survey. The user specifies the category of data desired, and the BLS provides tables of data almost instantly. Here's how to use the BLS system.

Visit the BLS Web site (www. bls.gov) and click on the link to Wages, Earnings, and Benefits. Find and click on the link to the National Compensation Survey (NCS). On the NCS Web page, click on "Get Detailed NCS Statistics" and then on "Create Customized Tables (one screen)" for wages. In the pop-up window that opens, you can enter a geographic area and a general or specific occupation, including different work levels for certain occupations. The search engine will provide the hourly wage for the occupation and area you specified.

You can also start by using the map to select an area. The National Compensation Survey gathers data from selected areas of the United States, designed to be representative of the entire country. Wage data cover about 90 areas, including most metropolitan areas. You can select one of these areas, or one of nine broad geographic regions, or the entire United States. When you select an area, the system allows you to select from the occupations for which the BLS has published data in that area.

The survey data cover hundreds of occupations, grouped into more general categories. For example, at the most specific level, you could look at civil engineers. More broadly, you could look at all engineers, or at the larger grouping of engineers, architects, and surveyors. Still more broadly, you could request data for all professional specialty occupations, which is part of the yet-broader group called professional specialty and technical occupations. This category is part of white-collar occupations, which is part of the "all occupations" group. You should select the most specific grouping that covers the occupation you want to investigate. If you select occupation first, you can then select geographic areas for which the database includes data on that occupation.

After selecting an occupation, you may select a work level. This describes the level of such work features as knowledge required and the scope, complexity, and demands of the job. For instance, you could look only at data for entry-level or senior accountants, rather than all accountants. Some occupations, including artists, athletes, and announcers, are not classified by work level.

Click on the Get Data link to submit the request to the BLS. The system immediately processes the request and presents the table (or tables) on your computer screen.

Source: Bureau of Labor Statistics Web site, www.bls.gov, February 22, 2008.

L04 Describe how employees evaluate the fairness of a pay structure.

Employee Judgments about Pay Fairness

In developing a pay structure, it is important to keep in mind employees' opinions about fairness. After all, one of the purposes of pay is to motivate employees, and they will not be motivated by pay if they think it is unfair.

Judging Fairness

Employees evaluate their pay relative to the pay of other employees. Social scientists have studied this kind of comparison and developed *equity theory* to describe how people make judgments about fairness.[12] According to equity theory, people measure outcomes such as pay in terms of their inputs. For example, an employee might think of her pay in terms of her master's degree, her 12 years of experience, and her 60-hour workweeks. To decide whether a level of pay is equitable, the person compares her ratio of outcomes and inputs with other people's outcome/input

Equity: Pay Seems Fair   **Inequity: Pay Seems Unfair**

Figure 11.3

Opinions about
Fairness: Pay Equity

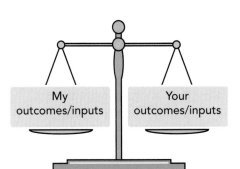

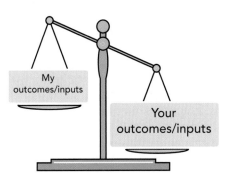

ratios, as shown in Figure 11.3. The person in the previous example might notice that an employee with less education or experience is earning more than she is (unfair) or that an employee who works 80 hours a week is earning more (fair). In general, employees compare their pay and contributions against several yardsticks:

- What they think employees in other organizations earn for doing the same job.
- What they think other employees holding different jobs within the organization earn for doing work at the same or different levels.
- What they think other employees in the organization earn for doing the same job as theirs.

Employees' conclusions about equity depend on what they choose as a standard of comparison. The results can be surprising. For example, some organizations have set up two-tier wage systems as a way to cut labor costs without cutting employees' existing salaries. Typically, employers announce these programs as a way to avoid moving jobs out of the country or closing down altogether. In a two-tier wage system, existing employees continue on at their current (upper-tier) pay rate while new employees sign on for less pay (the lower tier). One might expect reaction among employees in the lower tier that the pay structure is unfair. But a study of these employees found that they were *more* satisfied than the top-tier employees.[13] The lower-tier employees were not comparing their pay with that of the upper-tier employees but with the other alternatives they saw for themselves: lower-paying jobs or unemployment.

The ways employees respond to their impressions about equity can have a great impact on the organization. Typically, if employees see their pay as equitable, their attitudes and behavior continue unchanged. If employees see themselves as receiving an advantage, they usually rethink the situation to see it as merely equitable. But if employees conclude that they are underrewarded, they are likely to make up the difference in one of three ways. They might put forth less effort (reducing their inputs), find a way to increase their outcomes (for example, stealing), or withdraw by leaving the organization or refusing to cooperate. Employees' beliefs about fairness also influence their willingness to accept transfers or promotions. For example, if a job change involves more work, employees will expect higher pay.

Communicating Fairness

Equity theory tells organizations that employees care about their pay relative to what others are earning and that these feelings are based on what the employees *perceive* (what they notice and form judgments about). An organization can do much to contribute to what employees know and, as a result, what they perceive. If the organization researches salary levels and concludes that it is paying its employees generously, it should communicate this. If the employees do not know what the organization learned from its research, they may reach an entirely different conclusion about their pay. For example, to slow rapid growth in the wages it pays to U.S. workers, Toyota has shifted from using U.S. auto industry wages as its standard. The company now compares its wages with the prevailing wages in the state where each plant is located. Toyota has to educate its employees about this change and convince them that it is a fair way to compare wages.[14]

Employers must also recognize that employees know much more about what other employers pay now than they did before the Internet became popular. In the past, when gathering wage and salary data was expensive and difficult, employers had more leeway in negotiating with individual employees. Today's employees can go to Web sites like jobstar.org or salary.com to find hundreds of links to wage and salary data. For a fee, executive search firms provide data, such as the information at www.futurestep.com, operated by Korn/Ferry. Resources like these give employees information about what other workers are earning, along with the expectation that information will be shared. This means employers will face increased pressure to clearly explain their pay policies.

Managers play the most significant role in communication because they interact with their employees each day. The HR department should prepare them to explain why the organization's pay structure is designed as it is and to judge whether employee concerns about the structure indicate a need for change. A common issue is whether to reclassify a job because its content has changed. If an employee takes on more responsibility, the employee will often ask the manager for help in seeking more pay for the job.

Job Structure: Relative Value of Jobs

LO5 Explain how organizations design pay structures related to jobs.

Along with market forces and principles of fairness, organizations consider the relative contribution each job should make to the organization's overall performance. In general, an organization's top executives have a great impact on the organization's performance, so they tend to be paid much more than entry-level workers. Executives at the same level of the organization—for example, the vice president of marketing and the vice president of information systems—tend to be paid similar amounts. Creation of a pay structure requires that the organization develop an internal structure showing the relative contribution of its various jobs.

job evaluation
An administrative procedure for measuring the relative internal worth of the organization's jobs.

One typical way of doing this is with a **job evaluation,** an administrative procedure for measuring the relative worth of the organization's jobs. Usually, the organization does this by assembling and training a job evaluation committee, consisting of people familiar with the jobs to be evaluated. The committee often includes a human resource specialist and, if its budget permits, may hire an outside consultant.

To conduct a job evaluation, the committee identifies each job's *compensable factors,* meaning the characteristics of a job that the organization values and chooses to pay for. As shown in Table 11.1, an organization might value the experience and

Table 11.1

Job Evaluation of Three Jobs with Three Factors

JOB TITLE	COMPENSABLE FACTORS			
	EXPERIENCE	EDUCATION	COMPLEXITY	TOTAL
Computer operator	40	30	40	110
Computer programmer	40	50	65	155
Systems analyst	65	60	85	210

education of people performing computer-related jobs, as well as the complexity of those jobs. Other compensable factors might include working conditions and responsibility. Based on the job attributes defined by job analysis (discussed in Chapter 4), the jobs are rated for each factor. The rater assigns each factor a certain number of points, giving more points to factors when they are considered more important and when the job requires a high level of that factor. Often the number of points comes from one of the *point manuals* published by trade groups and management consultants. If necessary, the organization can adapt the scores in the point manual to the organization's situation or even develop its own point manual. As in the example in Table 11.1, the scores for each factor are totaled to arrive at an overall evaluation for each job.

Job evaluations provide the basis for decisions about relative internal worth. According to the sample assessments in Table 11.1, the job of systems analyst is worth almost twice as much to this organization as the job of computer operator. Therefore, the organization would be willing to pay almost twice as much for the work of a systems analyst as it would for the work of a computer operator.

The organization may limit its pay survey to jobs evaluated as *key jobs*. These are jobs that have relatively stable content and are common among many organizations, so it is possible to obtain survey data about what people earn in these jobs. Organizations can make the process of creating a pay structure more practical by defining key jobs. Research for creating the pay structure is limited to the key jobs that play a significant role in the organization. Pay for the key jobs can be based on survey data, and pay for the organization's other jobs can be based on the organization's job structure. A job with a higher evaluation score than a particular key job would receive higher pay than that key job.

Popular actors, such as Leonardo DiCaprio, are evaluated by their impact on box office receipts and other revenues and then compensated based on these evaluations.

Pay Structure: Putting It All Together

As we described in the first section of this chapter, the pay structure reflects decisions about how much to pay (pay level) and the relative value of each job (job structure). The organization's pay structure should reflect what the organization knows about market forces, as well as its own unique goals and the relative contribution of each job to achieving the goals. By balancing this external and internal information, the organization's goal is to set levels of pay that employees will consider equitable and motivating. Organizations typically apply the information by establishing some combination of pay rates, pay grades, and pay ranges. Within this structure, they may state the pay in terms of a rate per hour, commonly called an **hourly wage;** a rate of pay for each unit produced, known as a **piecework rate;** or a rate of pay per month or year, called a **salary.**

hourly wage
Rate of pay for each hour worked.

piecework rate
Rate of pay for each unit produced.

salary
Rate of pay for each week, month, or year worked.

Pay Rates

If the organization's main concern is to match what people are earning in comparable jobs, the organization can base pay directly on market research into as many of its key jobs as possible. To do this, the organization looks for survey data for each job title. If it finds data from more than one survey, it must weight the results based on their quality

Figure 11.4

Pay Policy Lines

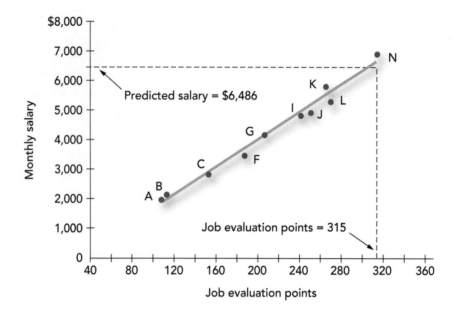

pay policy line
A graphed line showing the mathematical relationship between job evaluation points and pay rate.

and relevance. The final number represents what the competition pays. In light of that knowledge, the organization decides what it will pay for the job.

The next step is to determine salaries for the nonkey jobs, for which the organization has no survey data. Instead, the person developing the pay structure creates a graph like the one in Figure 11.4. The vertical axis shows a range of possible pay rates, and the horizontal axis measures the points from the job evaluation. The analyst plots points according to the job evaluation and pay rate for each key job. Finally, the analyst fits a line, called a **pay policy line,** to the points plotted. (This can be done statistically on a computer, using a procedure called regression analysis.) Mathematically, this line shows the relationship between job evaluation and rate of pay. Thus, the line slopes upward from left to right, and if higher-level jobs are especially valuable to the organization, the line may curve upward to indicate even greater pay for high-level jobs. Using this line, the analyst can estimate the market pay level for a given job evaluation. Looking at the graph gives approximate numbers, or the regression analysis will provide an equation for calculating the rate of pay. For example, using the pay policy line in Figure 11.4, a job with 315 evaluation points would have a predicted salary of $6,486 per month.

The pay policy line reflects the pay structure in the market, which does not always match rates in the organization (see key job F in Figure 11.4). Survey data may show that people in certain jobs are actually earning significantly more or less than the amount shown on the pay policy line. For example, some kinds of expertise are in short supply. People with that expertise can command higher salaries, because they can easily leave one employer to get higher pay somewhere else. Suppose, in contrast, that local businesses have laid off many warehouse employees. Because so many of these workers are looking for jobs, organizations may be able to pay them less than the rate that job evaluation points would suggest.

When job structure and market data conflict in these ways, organizations have to decide on a way to resolve the two. One approach is to stick to the job evaluations and pay according to the employees' worth to the organization. Organizations that do so will be paying more or less than they have to, so they will likely have more difficulty competing for customers or employees. A way to moderate this approach is to consider the importance of each position to the organization's goals.[15] If a position is critical for meeting the organization's goals, paying more than competitors pay may be worthwhile.

At the other extreme, the organization could base pay entirely on market forces. However, this approach also has some practical drawbacks. One is that employees may conclude that pay rates are unfair. Two vice presidents or two supervisors will expect to receive similar pay because their responsibilities are similar. If the differences between their pay are large, because of different market rates, the lower-paid employee will likely be dissatisfied. Also, if the organization's development plans include rotating managers through different assignments, the managers will be reluctant to participate if managers in some departments receive lower pay. Organizations therefore must weigh all the objectives of their pay structure to arrive at suitable rates.

Pay Grades

A large organization could have hundreds or even thousands of different jobs. Setting a pay rate for each job would be extremely complex. Therefore, many organizations group jobs into **pay grades**—sets of jobs having similar worth or content, grouped together to establish rates of pay. For example, the organization could establish five pay grades, with the same pay available to employees holding any job within the same grade.

pay grades
Sets of jobs having similar worth or content, grouped together to establish rates of pay.

A drawback of pay grades is that grouping jobs will result in rates of pay for individual jobs that do not precisely match the levels specified by the market and the organization's job structure. Suppose, for example, that the organization groups together its senior accountants (with a job evaluation of 255 points) and its senior systems analysts (with a job evaluation of 270 points). Surveys might show that the market rate of pay for systems analysts is higher than that for accountants. In addition, the job evaluations give more points to systems analysts. Even so, for simplicity's sake, the organization pays the same rate for the two jobs because they are in the same pay grade. The organization would have to pay more than the market requires for accountants or pay less than the market rate for systems analysts (so it would probably have difficulty recruiting and retaining them).

Pay Ranges

Usually, organizations want some flexibility in setting pay for individual jobs. They want to be able to pay the most valuable employees the highest amounts and to give rewards for performance, as described in the next chapter. Flexibility also helps the organization balance conflicting information from market surveys and job evaluations. Therefore, pay structure usually includes a **pay range** for each job or pay grade. In other words, the organization establishes a minimum, maximum, and midpoint of pay for employees holding a particular job or a job within a particular pay grade. Employees holding the same job may receive somewhat different pay, depending on where their pay falls within the range.

pay range
A set of possible pay rates defined by a minimum, maximum, and midpoint of pay for employees holding a particular job or a job within a particular pay grade.

A typical approach is to use the market rate or the pay policy line as the midpoint of a range for the job or pay grade. The minimum and maximum values for the range may also be based on market surveys of those amounts. Pay ranges are most common for white-collar jobs and for jobs that are not covered by union contracts. Figure 11.5 shows an example of pay ranges based on the pay policy line in Figure 11.4. Notice that the jobs are grouped into five pay grades, each with its own pay range. In this

Figure 11.5

Sample Pay Range Structure

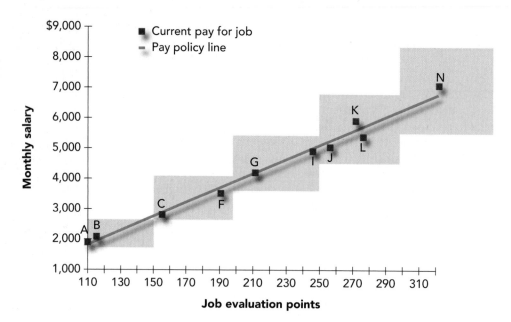

example, the range is widest for employees who are at higher levels in terms of their job evaluation points. That is because the performance of these higher-level employees will likely have more effect on the organization's performance, so the organization needs more latitude to reward them. For instance, as discussed earlier, the organization may want to select a higher point in the range to attract an employee who is more critical to achieving the organization's goals.

Usually pay ranges overlap somewhat, so that the highest pay in one grade is somewhat higher than the lowest pay in the next grade. Overlapping ranges gives the organization more flexibility in transferring employees among jobs, because transfers need not always involve a change in pay. On the other hand, the less overlap, the more important it is to earn promotions in order to keep getting raises. Assuming the organization wants to motivate employees through promotions (and assuming enough opportunities for promotion are available), the organization will want to limit the overlap from one level to the next.

Pay Differentials

In some situations organizations adjust pay to reflect differences in working conditions or labor markets. For example, an organization may pay extra to employees who work the night shift, because night hours are less desirable for most workers. Similarly, organizations may pay extra to employees in locations where living expenses are higher. These adjustments are called **pay differentials.**

pay differential
Adjustment to a pay rate to reflect differences in working conditions or labor markets.

A survey of businesses in the United States found that over half have a formal or informal policy of providing pay differentials based on geographic location.[16] These differentials are intended as a way to treat employees fairly, without regard to where they work. The most common approach is to move an employee higher in the pay structure to compensate for higher living costs. For instance, the American Chamber of Commerce Research Association estimates that the cost of living in New York City is more than twice that of the average metropolitan area. An organization with employees in New York City and in an average U.S. city might pay its New York office manager substantially more than its office manager in the average city. This pay policy can become expensive for organizations that must operate in high-cost locations. Also, organizations need to handle the delicate issue of how to pay employees transferred to lower-cost areas.

Alternatives to Job-Based Pay

The traditional and most widely used approach to developing a pay structure focuses on setting pay for jobs or groups of jobs.[17] This emphasis on jobs has some limitations. The precise definition of a job's responsibilities can contribute to an attitude that some activities "are not in my job description," at the expense of flexibility, innovation, quality, and customer service. Also, the job structure's focus on higher pay for higher status can work against an effort at empowerment. Organizations may avoid change because it requires repeating the time-consuming process of creating job descriptions and related paperwork. Another change-related problem is that when the organization needs a new set of knowledge, skills, and abilities, the existing pay structure may be rewarding the wrong behaviors. Finally, a pay structure that rewards employees for winning promotions may discourage them from gaining valuable experience through lateral career moves.

Organizations have responded to these problems with a number of alternatives to job-based pay structures. Some organizations have found greater flexibility through **delayering,** or reducing the number of levels in the organization's job structure. By combining more assignments into a single layer, organizations give managers more flexibility in making assignments and awarding pay increases. These broader groupings often are called *broad bands*. In the 1990s, IBM changed from a pay structure with 5,000 job titles and 24 salary grades to one with 1,200 jobs and 10 bands. When IBM began using broad bands, it replaced its point-factor job evaluation system with an approach based on matching jobs to descriptions. Figure 11.6 shows descriptions of several job characteristics used by IBM. Job descriptions are assigned to the band whose characteristics best match those in the job description. Broad bands reduce the opportunities for promoting employees, so organizations that eliminate layers in their job descriptions must find other ways to reward employees.

Another way organizations have responded to the limitations of job-based pay has been to move away from the link to jobs and toward pay structures that reward employees based on their knowledge and skills.[18] **Skill-based pay systems** are pay structures that set pay according to the employees' level of skill or knowledge and what they are capable of doing. Paying for skills makes sense at organizations where changing technology requires employees to continually widen and deepen their knowledge. For example, modern machinery often requires that operators know how to program and monitor computers to perform a variety of tasks. Skill-based pay also supports efforts to empower employees and enrich jobs because it encourages employees to add to their knowledge so they can make decisions in many areas. In this way, skill-based pay helps organizations become more flexible and innovative. More generally, skill-based pay can encourage a climate of learning and adaptability and give employees a broader view of how the organization functions. These changes should help employees use their knowledge and ideas more productively. A field study of a manufacturing plant found that changing to a skill-based pay structure led to better quality and lower labor costs.[19]

Of course, skill-based pay has its own disadvantages.[20] It rewards employees for acquiring skills but does not provide a way to ensure that employees can use their new skills. The result may be that the organization is paying employees more for learning skills

Night hours are less desirable for most workers. Therefore, some companies pay a differential for night work to compensate them.

LO6 Describe alternatives to job-based pay.

delayering
Reducing the number of levels in the organization's job structure.

skill-based pay systems
Pay structures that set pay according to the employees' levels of skill or knowledge and what they are capable of doing.

Figure 11.6

IBM's New Job Evaluation Approach

Below is an abbreviated schematic illustration of the new—and simple—IBM job evaluation approach:

POSITION REFERENCE GUIDE

Band	Skills Required	Leadership/Contribution	Scope/Impact
1			
2			
3			
4			
5			
6			
7			
8			
9			
10			

Both the bands and the approach are global. In the U.S., bands 1–5 are nonexempt; bands 6–10 are exempt. Each cell in the table contains descriptive language about key job characteristics. Position descriptions are compared to the chart and assigned to bands on a "best fit" basis. There are no points or scoring mechanisms. Managers assign employees to bands by selecting a position description that most closely resembles the work being done by an employee using an online position description library.

Factors: Leadership/Contribution

Band 06: Understand the mission of the professional group and vision in own area of competence.

Band 07: Understand the departmental mission and vision.

Band 08: Understand departmental/functional mission and vision.

Band 09: Has vision of functional or unit mission.

Band 10: Has vision of overall strategies.

That's it!

SOURCE: A. S. Richter, "Paying the People in Black at Big Blue," *Compensation and Benefits Review*, May–June 1998, pp. 51–59. Reprinted with permission of Sage Publications, Inc.

that the employer is not benefiting from. The challenge for HRM is to design work so that the work design and pay structure support one another. Also, if employees learn skills very quickly, they may reach the maximum pay level so quickly that it will become difficult to reward them appropriately. Skill-based pay does not necessarily provide an alternative to the bureaucracy and paperwork of traditional pay structures, because it requires records related to skills, training, and knowledge acquired. Finally, gathering market data about skill-based pay is difficult, because most wage and salary surveys are job-based.

Pay Structure and Actual Pay

L07 Summarize how to ensure that pay is actually in line with the job structure.

Usually, the human resource department is responsible for establishing the organization's pay structure. But building a structure is not the end of the organization's decisions about pay structure. The structure represents the organization's policy, but what the organization actually does may be different. As part of its management responsibility, the HR department therefore should compare actual pay to the pay structure, making sure that policies and practices match.

A common way to do this is to measure a *compa-ratio*, the ratio of average pay to the midpoint of the pay range. Figure 11.7 shows an example. Assuming the organization

ONLINE PAYROLL SYSTEMS

Besides making decisions about pay structure, HR departments have to decide how to administer pay plans, including activities such as gathering data on timesheets, deducting taxes, and issuing paychecks. Most companies have automated these activities, or they pay a service that uses the necessary software. Now more companies are also putting their payroll systems online.

With online payroll processing, employees can enter payroll data, prepare checks, and generate tax reports from any secure location. This capability is especially useful in organizations where employees work in many locations. Those employees can submit their timesheets electronically, making the information immediately available.

Organizations can also make HR functions more efficient by giving employees access to data related to their own pay. Employees can go online to check their tax withholding status, print a copy of a pay stub, or look up their pay range. Ideally, the system also can share information with the organization's accounting software.

Source: Wayne Schulz, "Have Payroll, Will Travel," *Accounting Technology,* November 2007, downloaded from General Reference Center Gold, http://find.galegroup.com.

has pay grades, the organization would find a compa-ratio for each pay grade: the average paid to all employees in the pay grade divided by the midpoint for the pay grade. If the average equals the midpoint, the compa-ratio is 1. More often, the compa-ratio is somewhat above 1 (meaning the average pay is above the midpoint for the pay grade) or below 1 (meaning the average pay is below the midpoint).

Assuming that the pay structure is well planned to support the organization's goals, the compa-ratios should be close to 1. A compa-ratio greater than 1 suggests that the organization is paying more than planned for human resources and may have difficulty keeping costs under control. A compa-ratio less than 1 suggests that the organization is underpaying for human resources relative to its target and may have difficulty attracting and keeping qualified employees. When compa-ratios are more or less than 1, the numbers signal a need for the HR department to work with managers to identify whether to adjust the pay structure or the organization's pay practices. The compa-ratios may indicate that the pay structure no longer reflects market rates of pay. Or maybe performance appraisals need to be more accurate, as discussed in Chapter 8. The "e-HRM" box shows how online payroll systems can make it easier for companies to process payroll.

Pay Grade: 1
Midpoint of Range: $2,175 per month

Salaries of Employees in Pay Grade

Employee 1	$2,306
Employee 2	$2,066
Employee 3	$2,523
Employee 4	$2,414

Compa-Ratio

$$\frac{\text{Average}}{\text{Midpoint}} = \frac{\$2,327.25}{\$2,175.00} = 1.07$$

Average Salary of Employees
$2,306 + $2,066 + $2,523 + $2,414 = $9,309
$9,309 ÷ 4 = $2,327.25

Figure 11.7

Finding a Compa-Ratio

LO8 Discuss issues related to paying employees serving in the military and paying executives.

Current Issues Involving Pay Structure

An organization's policies regarding pay structure greatly influence employees' and even the general public's opinions about the organization. Issues affecting pay structure therefore can hurt or help the organization's reputation and ability to recruit, motivate, and keep employees. Recent issues related to pay structure include decisions about paying employees on active military duty and decisions about how much to pay the organization's top executives.

Pay during Military Duty

As we noted in Chapter 3, the Uniformed Services Employment and Reemployment Rights Act (USERRA) requires employers to make jobs available to their workers when they return after fulfilling military duties for up to five years. During the time these employees are performing their military service, the employer faces decisions related to paying these people. The armed services pay service members during their time of duty, but military pay often falls short of what they would earn in their civilian jobs. Some employers have chosen to support their employees by paying the difference between their military and civilian earnings for extended periods. Surveys have found that during the military actions in Afghanistan and Iraq, about half of U.S. employers have provided compensation to Reservists on active duty.[21] Some make up the full difference in pay, while others might provide health insurance. Wachovia Corporation goes further, paying full salaries for employees called to active duty. The financial-services firm does this as an expression of its culture and values and as a way to encourage employees to return following their deployment.

Policies to make up the difference between military pay and civilian pay are costly. The employer is paying employees while they are not working for the organization, and it may have to hire temporary employees as well. This challenge has posed a significant hardship on some employers since 2002, as hundreds of thousands of Reservists and National Guard members have been mobilized. Even so, as the nation copes with this challenge, hundreds of employers have decided that maintaining positive relations with employees—and the goodwill of the American public—makes the expense worthwhile.

Pay for Executives

The media have drawn public attention to the issue of executive pay. The issue attracts notice because of the very high pay that the top executives of major U.S. companies have received in recent years. A significant form of executive compensation comes in the form of company stock (a type of compensation discussed in the next chapter). In recent years, as shown in Figure 11.8, the total compensation paid to executives of large companies was typically more than $6 million, of which about $2.5 million was in the form of salary plus bonus. Interestingly, at the five companies that had the highest shareholder returns in 2006, the median compensation was less than $5 million, and at the five companies with the lowest shareholder returns, CEOs earned more than $12 million.[22]

Although these high amounts apply to only a small proportion of the total workforce, the issue of executive pay is relevant to pay structure in terms of equity theory. As we discussed earlier in the chapter, employees draw conclusions about the fairness of pay by making comparisons among employees' inputs and outcomes. By many comparisons, U.S. CEOs' pay is high. CEO pay in the United States is roughly twice that of CEOs in Canada, Mexico, France, and Germany, and it is between three and four times the compensation paid to CEOs in Japan and Korea.[23] According to equity

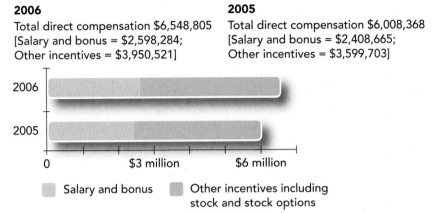

2006
Total direct compensation $6,548,805
[Salary and bonus = $2,598,284;
Other incentives = $3,950,521]

2005
Total direct compensation $6,008,368
[Salary and bonus = $2,408,665;
Other incentives = $3,599,703]

Figure 11.8

Median CEO
Compensation at 350
Large U.S. Corporations

SOURCE: Data from Joann S. Lublin, "The Pace of Pay Gains: A Survey Overview," *Wall Street Journal*, April 9, 2007, http://online.wsj.com.

theory, employees would see this as fair if the U.S. CEOs also do more for their organizations than CEOs in other countries do. The situation becomes more complex for international organizations, where executives compare their pay to other executives in the same country, as well as to other executives in the same organization.

Another way to think about the equity of CEO pay is to compare it with the pay of other employees in the organization. Chief executives of large U.S. businesses earn almost 40 times as much as manufacturing employees in their companies. This multiple is one and a half to four times that enjoyed by CEOs in Canada, France, Japan, and Korea.[24] Again, equity theory would consider not only the size of executive pay relative to pay for other employees but also the amount the CEOs contribute. An organization's executives potentially have a much greater effect on the organization's performance than other employees have. But if they do not seem to contribute 40 times more, employees will see the compensation as unfair.

Top executives help to set the tone or culture of the organization, and employees at all levels are affected by behavior at the top. As a result, the equity of executive pay can affect more employees than, say, equity among warehouse workers or sales clerks. One study that investigated this issue compared the pay of rank-and-file employees and executives in various business units.[25] In business units where the difference in pay was greater, customer satisfaction was lower. The researchers speculated that employees thought pay was inequitable and adjusted their behavior to provide lower inputs by putting forth less effort to satisfy customers. To avoid this type of situation, organizations need to plan not only *how much* to pay managers and executives, but also *how* to pay them. In the next chapter, we will explore many of the options available.

THINKING ETHICALLY

SHOULD SERVERS' TIPS HELP PAY RESTAURANTS' BILLS?

When you use a credit card to pay for your meal in a restaurant, the card company typically charges the restaurant a fee of 1.5 to 3 percent of the total bill. If you add your tip to the amount you charge, the fee is applied to the tip as well. So if you pay $50 for a meal

and add a $10 tip, a 3 percent fee would be $1.80. Many restaurants recover part of that fee from the server by deducting part of the processing fee from their tip income. In this example, 3 percent of the $10 tip would be 30 cents withheld from that server's tips. The practice is legal under federal law, but a few states prohibit such deductions.

Restaurants explain that practice by pointing out that food costs have been rising, cutting into profits, and that employees are paid fairly. Nikki Hickman, controller for Specialty Restaurants Corporation, says, "Most servers look at themselves as being self-employed," so they consider the deduction for processing fees their "cost of doing business." Specialty Restaurants takes the deduction from tips in states where it is allowed.

In some parts of the country, the practice has generated publicity and controversy. OSI Restaurant Partners recently started deducting fees from tips earned by servers at its Illinois and Arkansas restaurants, but servers and customers started complaining. One server in Arkansas told local media that the policy would reduce her tip income by about $800 a year. Some customers who learned about the policy complaints on their credit slips and paid tips in cash. As a result, the chain dropped the practice.

SOURCE: Dina Berta, "Garnishing of Tips to Pay Charge Card Fees Sparks Controversy," *Nation's Restaurant News*, February 18, 2008, downloaded from General Reference Center Gold, http://find.galegroup.com.

Questions

1. How well do you think the policy of deducting a share of transaction fees from tips meets a restaurant's business, legal, and fairness requirements for pay?
2. Is it ethical for business to expect employees will help cover business expenses? What do you think about the argument that servers think of themselves as "self-employed"?
3. Suppose you are an HR manager for a restaurant chain. The company is concerned about rising food costs and wants to evaluate its pay policy to look for cost savings. What ethical criteria do you want to emphasize as you do so?

SUMMARY

LO1 Identify the kinds of decisions involved in establishing a pay structure.

Organizations make decisions to define a job structure, or relative pay for different jobs within the organization. They establish relative pay for different functions and different levels of responsibility for each function. Organizations also must establish pay levels, or the average paid for the different jobs. These decisions are based on the organization's goals, market data, legal requirements, and principles of fairness. Together, job structure and pay level establish a pay structure policy.

LO2 Summarize legal requirements for pay policies.

To meet the standard of equal employment opportunity, employers must provide equal pay for equal work, regardless of an employee's age, race, sex, or other protected status. Differences in pay must relate to factors such as a person's qualifications or market levels of pay. Under the Fair Labor Standards Act (FLSA), the employer must pay at least the minimum wage established by law. Some state and local governments have established higher minimum wages. The FLSA also requires overtime pay—at one and a half times the employee's regular pay rate, including bonuses—for hours worked beyond 40 in each week. Managers, professionals, and outside salespersons are exempt from the overtime pay requirement. Employers must meet FLSA requirements concerning child labor. Federal contractors also must meet requirements to pay at least the prevailing wage in the area where their employees work.

LO3 Discuss how economic forces influence decisions about pay.

To remain competitive, employers must meet the demands of product and labor markets. Product markets seek to buy at the lowest price, so organizations must limit their costs as much as possible. In this way, product markets place an upper limit on the pay an employer can afford to offer. Labor markets consist of workers who want to earn as much as possible. To attract and keep workers, employers must pay at least the going rate in their labor markets. Organizations make decisions about whether to pay at, above, or below the pay rate set by these market forces. Paying above the market rate may make the organization less competitive in product markets but give it an advantage in labor markets. The organization benefits only if it can attract the best candidates and provide the systems that motivate and enable them to do their best work. Organizations that pay below the market rate need creative practices for recruiting and training workers so that they can find and keep enough qualified people.

LO4 Describe how employees evaluate the fairness of a pay structure.

According to equity theory, employees think of their pay relative to their inputs, such as training, experience, and effort. To decide whether their pay is equitable, they compare their outcome (pay)/input ratio with other people's outcome/input ratios. Employees make these comparisons with people doing the same job in other organizations and with people doing the same or different jobs in the same organization. If employees conclude that their outcome/input ratio is less than the comparison person's, they conclude that their pay is unfair and may engage in behaviors to create a situation they think is fair.

LO5 Explain how organizations design pay structures related to jobs.

Organizations typically begin with a job evaluation to measure the relative worth of their jobs. A job evaluation committee identifies each job's compensable factors and rates each factor. The committee may use a point manual to assign an appropriate number of points to each job. The committee can research market pay levels for key jobs, then identify appropriate rates of pay for other jobs, based on their number of points relative to the key jobs. The organization can do this with a pay policy line, which plots a salary for each job. The organization can combine jobs into several groups, called pay grades. For each pay grade or job, the organization typically establishes a pay range, using the market rate or pay policy line as the midpoint. Differences in working conditions or labor markets sometimes call for the use of pay differentials to adjust pay levels.

LO6 Describe alternatives to job-based pay.

To obtain more flexibility, organizations may reduce the levels in the organization's job structure. This process of delayering creates broad bands of jobs with a pay range for each. Other organizations reward employees according to their knowledge and skills. They establish skill-based pay systems, or structures that set pay according to the employees' level of knowledge and what they are capable of doing. This encourages employees to be more flexible and adapt to changing technology. However, if the organization does not also provide systems in which employees can apply new skills, it may be paying them for skills they do not actually use.

LO7 Summarize how to ensure that pay is actually in line with the pay structure.

The human resource department should routinely compare actual pay with the pay structure to see that policies and practices match. A common way to do this is to measure a compa-ratio for each job or pay grade. The compa-ratio is the ratio of average pay to the midpoint of the pay range. Assuming the pay structure supports the organization's goals, the compa-ratios should be close to 1. When compa-ratios are more or less than 1, the HR department should work with managers to identify whether to adjust the pay structure or the organization's pay practices.

LO8 Discuss issues related to paying employees serving in the military and paying executives.

The Uniformed Services Employment and Reemployment Rights Act requires employers to make jobs available to any of their employees who leave to fulfill military duties for up to five years. While these employees are performing their military service, many are earning far less. To demonstrate their commitment to these employees and to earn the public's goodwill, many companies pay the difference between their military and civilian earnings, even though this policy is costly. Executive pay has drawn public scrutiny because top executive pay is much higher than average workers' pay. The great difference is an issue in terms of equity theory. Chief executive officers have an extremely large impact on the organization's performance, but critics complain that when performance falters, executive pay does not decline as fast as the organization's profits or stock price. Top executives help to set the organization's tone or culture, and employees at all levels are affected by the behavior of the people at the top. Therefore, employees' opinions about the equity of executive pay can have a large effect on the organization's performance.

KEY TERMS

benchmarking, p. 319
delayering, p. 327
exempt employees, p. 315
Fair Labor Standards Act (FLSA), p. 314
hourly wage, p. 323
job evaluation, p. 322

job structure, p. 311
minimum wage, p. 314
nonexempt employees, p. 316
pay differential, p. 326
pay grades, p. 325
pay level, p. 311
pay policy line, p. 324

pay range, p. 325
pay structure, p. 311
piecework rate, p. 323
salary, p. 323
skill-based pay systems, p. 327

REVIEW AND DISCUSSION QUESTIONS

1. In setting up a pay structure, what legal requirements must an organization meet? Which of these do you think would be most challenging for a small start-up business? Why?

2. In gathering data for its pay policies, what product markets would a city's hospital want to use as a basis for comparison? What labor markets would be relevant? How might the labor markets for surgeons be different from the labor markets for nursing aides?

3. Why might an organization choose to pay employees more than the market rate? Why might it choose to pay less? What are the consequences of paying more or less than the market rate?

4. Suppose you work in the HR department of a manufacturing company that is planning to enrich jobs by having production workers work in teams and rotate through various jobs. The pay structure will have to be adjusted to fit this new work design. How would you expect the employees to evaluate the fairness of their pay in their redesigned jobs? In terms of equity theory, what comparisons would they be likely to make?

5. Summarize the way organizations use information about jobs as a basis for a pay structure.

6. Imagine that you manage human resources for a small business. You have recently prepared a report on the market rate of pay for salespeople, and the company's owner says the market rate is too high. The company cannot afford this level of pay, and furthermore, paying that much would cause salespeople to earn more than most of the company's managers. Suggest three possible measures the company might take to help resolve this conflict.

7. What are the advantages of establishing pay ranges, rather than specific pay levels, for each job? What are the drawbacks of this approach?

8. Suppose the company in Question 1 wants to establish a skills-based pay structure. What would be some advantages of this approach? List the issues the company should be prepared to address in setting up this system. Consider the kinds of information you will need and the ways employees may react to the new pay structure.

9. Why do some employers subsidize the pay of military reserve members called up to active duty? If the military instead paid these people the wage they command in the civilian market (that is, the salary they earn at their regular jobs), who would bear the cost? When neither the reserve members' employers nor the military pays reserve members their civilian wage, reserve members and their families bear the cost. In your opinion, who *should* bear this cost—employers, taxpayers, or service members (or someone else)?

10. Do you think U.S. companies pay their chief executives too much? Why or why not?

BUSINESSWEEK CASE

BusinessWeek Wage Wars

There's a place in Reno, Nevada, that practically mints money. It's not one of the many casinos in town. It is a law firm nestled in the foothills of the Sierra Nevadas. From a utilitarian office, with a view of horses grazing in a neighbor's paddock, attorney Mark R. Thierman pursues a practice that in recent years has won his clients hundreds of millions of dollars from some of the biggest names in Corporate America.

A Harvard Law School grad, Thierman spent the first 20 years of his career as a management-side labor attorney and self-described union buster. But in the mid-1990s he brought a series of cases on behalf of workers in California and established himself as a trailblazer in what had long been a sleepy, neglected area of the law. Thierman sues companies for violating "wage and hour" rules, typically claiming they have failed to pay overtime to workers who deserve it. Because wage and hour laws have been so widely violated, undetonated legal mines remain buried in countless companies, according to defense and plaintiffs' lawyers alike. No one tracks precise figures, but lawyers on both sides estimate that over the last few years companies have collectively paid out more than $1 billion annually to resolve these claims.

In overtime cases, Depression-era laws aimed at factories and textile mills are being applied in a 21st-century economy. Generally, workers with jobs that require independent judgment have not been entitled to overtime pay. But with businesses embracing efficiency and quality-control initiatives, more and more tasks, even in offices, are becoming standardized, tightly choreographed routines. Then there's technology: In an always-on, telecommuting world, when does the workday begin and end?

The bulk of Thierman's cases involve claims of misclassification. In the case he settled against Starbucks in 2003, Thierman contended that merely giving employees the title of store manager or assistant manager doesn't make them "executives," who are exempt from overtime. A majority of their work, he argued, was making lattes and Frappucinos, just like the lower-ranking, and overtime-eligible, baristas. This is the same approach he is pressing against a wide range of other companies on behalf of employees who would widely be viewed as white-collar. His focus is on what they actually do, not on their job titles, income, or academic degrees. "You don't have to be stupid to get overtime," Thierman says. "In fact, you're stupid if you don't get overtime."

Computer workers of various stripes, for example, have commonly not been paid for their extra hours. In a sop to the IT industry, lawmakers exempted such employees, who tend to be well educated, well paid, and have a culture of working virtually around the clock. The companies argued that they would otherwise not be able to remain competitive with foreign rivals. But under California law, the exemption applies only for workers whose primary function involves "the exercise of discretion and independent judgment." In numerous lawsuits, Thierman and other attorneys have alleged that legions of systems engineers, help desk staff, and customer service personnel do no such thing. Already the settlements are rolling in. Siebel Systems agreed to pay $27.5 million to about 800 software engineers, and IBM is forking over $65 million to technical and customer support workers.

In some lawsuits, Thierman has made off-the-clock claims on behalf of lower-wage employees. In a suit on behalf of employees of Hollywood Video stores, a movie rental chain, he alleged workers had to boot up the computer before they could punch in, and had to punch out before they could close the register for the night and do the store tally. Nearly all the cases faced by Wal-Mart are off-the-clock claims, with allegations that employees worked through lunch breaks without pay or were forced to punch out when the store closed but then continue with tasks such as restocking shelves.

SOURCE: Excerpted from Michael Orey, "Wage Wars," *BusinessWeek*, October 1, 2007, downloaded from General Reference Center Gold, http://find.galegroup.com.

Questions

1. In today's fast-paced, high-tech, quality-driven business environment, is tracking employees' hours and paying overtime a reasonable requirement? Why or why not?
2. How can a carefully planned pay structure help an organization comply with legal requirements for overtime pay?
3. If you worked in the HR department of a software company that is concerned about ensuring it is complying with requirements for overtime pay, what actions would you recommend that the company take?

CASE: WHEN EMPLOYEES ARE CALLED TO SERVE

The Defense Department's Employer Support of the Guard and Reserve Division recently honored some companies for exceptional support to employees who are members of the National Guard and Army Reserve. These companies are nominated by employees for supporting them when they were called up to active duty.

Creative Healthcare Solutions has just 18 employees, but it swung into action when marketing consultant Thomas Weikert announced that he had to report for duty in about a week. The marketing firm ensured that Weikert's deployment would not be a financial hardship for his family, providing differential pay to make up for the lower military pay, as well as continuing his benefits during his absence. The company also sent care packages for Weikert while he was deployed, including an iPod and other items. Employees in other locations even arranged a trip to Atlanta to take Weikert's sons to a hockey game. After a one-year tour of duty during which he helped Iraqi and U.S. leaders plan the surge of forces around Baghdad, Weikert returned home safely and resumed his work for Creative Healthcare Solutions.

A larger company that has won the award is Sodexho USA, a food service company. When any of its 125,000 employees are called up for duty, Sodexho offers a pay differential and continues their employee benefits. Like Creative Healthcare Solutions, Sodexho also arranges for care packages.

These two winners are among many companies that extend pay and other benefits to employees who are called to active duty. Verizon Communications, for example, has paid a salary differential and continued benefit plans for the more than 1,300 employees who have been called to active duty since September 11, 2001. Other companies that offer a pay differential include Lockheed Martin, Exxon Mobil, and Texas Instruments. American Express and Merrill Lynch offer full pay.

Why do companies pay for employees who are not at work? Some say that support for service members is consistent with their values of patriotism or concern for employees' well-being. Another reason is that taking care of employees during their military duty makes them more likely to return to the company when that service ends.

Some employees are more likely to get differential pay. Since the point is to make up the difference between civilian and military pay, the differential only applies to employees who earn more in their civilian job, typically middle-income earners who hold technical or professional positions. Top-level managers rarely belong to the Army Reserves or National Guard. Lower-level employees may actually earn more in the military than in their civilian jobs.

Differential pay does pose some administrative challenges. Like military pay, the income is taxable. However, under current IRS rules, the employer does not treat the person as being on the payroll, so taxes are not withheld from differential pay. Employees need to be educated to set aside some of their earnings to pay their taxes or else to have extra taxes withheld from their military pay.

SOURCES: Carolyn Hirschman, "Supporting the Troops," *HRMagazine*, July 2007, downloaded from General Reference Center Gold, http://find.galegroup.com; Samantha Sault, "Good Company: The Businesses That Do More for Their Citizen Soldiers," *Weekly Standard*, September 12, 2007, http://find.galegroup.com; Gerry J. Gilmore, "Reservist Cites Healthcare Marketing Firm's Superb Support," news release, U.S. Department of Defense, www.defenselink.mil, August 29, 2007; "Sodexho USA Receives Freedom Award from U.S. Dept. of Defense," *Nation's Restaurant News*,

October 22, 2007, p. 42; and Elizabeth H. Manning and Carol Kelly, "Fortune 500 Survey," *The Officer*, December 2006, pp. 68–76.

Questions

1. Do the companies described in this case seem to have a solid business argument for paying differentials and other benefits to Reservists when they are called to active duty? Why or why not?
2. Applying the principles of equity theory, how well do these pay policies meet the criteria for fairness?
3. Imagine you are an HR manager in a company that has decided to create a formal policy for paying wage differentials and offering benefits to Army Reserve and National Guard members who are called to active duty.
   a. Summarize the message(s) you would communicate about this policy to the employees eligible for this pay.
   b. Summarize what you would communicate to all employees about this policy.

IT'S A WRAP!

www.mhhe.com/noefund3e is your source for Reviewing, Applying, and Practicing the concepts you learned about in Chapter 11.

Review
- Chapter learning objectives
- Narrated lecture and iPod content

Application
- Manager's Hot Seat segment: "Negotiation: Thawing the Salary Freeze"
- Video case and quiz: "Gender Gap: Why Do Women Make Less than Men?"
- Self-Assessment: Test your expectation of salary brackets
- Web Exercise: Experiment with salary calculators

Practice
- Chapter quiz

NOTES

1. Kellie Schmitt, "Luce Rethinks Associate Pay System," *Recorder*, January 14, 2008, downloaded from General Reference Center Gold, http://find.galegroup.com.
2. Saratoga Institute, *2000 Human Capital Benchmarking Report* (Santa Clara, CA: Saratoga Institute, 2000); and Saratoga/PriceWaterhouseCoopers, *Key Trends in Human Capital: A Global Perspective, 2006*, PriceWaterhouseCoopers UK Web site, Publications page, www.pwc.co.uk.
3. Bureau of Labor Statistics, *Women in the Labor Force: A Databook*, 2007 ed., Current Population Surveys, www.bls.gov/cps/wlf-databook2007.htm.
4. B. Morris, K. Bonamici, S. M. Kaufman, and P. Neering, "How Corporate America Is Betraying Women," *Fortune*, January 10, 2005, downloaded from Infotrac at http://web6.infotrac.galegroup.com; B. Gerhart, "Gender Differences in Current and Starting Salaries: The Role of Performance, College Major, and Job Title," *Industrial and Labor Relations Review* 43 (1990), pp. 418–33; and G. G. Cain, "The Economic Analysis of Labor Market Discrimination: A Survey," in *Handbook of Labor Economics*, eds. O. Ashenfelter and R. Layard (New York: North-Holland, 1986), pp. 694–785.

5. S. L. Rynes and G. T. Milkovich, "Wage Surveys: Dispelling Some Myths about the 'Market Wage,'" *Personnel Psychology* 39 (1986), pp. 71–90; and G. T. Milkovich and J. Newman, *Compensation* (Homewood, IL: BPI/Irwin, 1993).

6. U.S. Department of Labor, Employment Standards Division, "Overtime Requirements of the FLSA," Fact Sheet 23, www.dol.gov/esa, accessed May 19, 2005.

7. M. M. Clark, "Step by Step," *HRMagazine,* February 2005, downloaded from Infotrac at http://web6. infotrac.galegroup.com.

8. U.S. Department of Labor, Employment Standards Administration, "Child Labor Provisions of the Fair Labor Standards Act (FLSA) for Nonagricultural Occupations," Fact Sheet 43, Labor Department Web site, www.dol.gov, downloaded August 15, 2002.

9. J. McCracken, "Desperate to Cut Costs, Ford Gets Union's Help,"*Wall Street Journal,* March 2, 2007.

10. B. Gerhart and G. T. Milkovich, "Organizational Differences in Managerial Compensation and Financial Performance," *Academy of Management Journal* 33 (1990), pp. 663–91; and E. L. Groshen, "Why Do Wages Vary among Employers?" *Economic Review* 24 (1988), pp. 19–38.

11. G. A. Akerlof, "Gift Exchange and Efficiency-Wage Theory: Four Views," *American Economic Review* 74 (1984), pp. 79–83; and J. L. Yellen, "Efficiency Wage Models of Unemployment," *American Economic Review* 74 (1984), pp. 200–5.

12. J. S. Adams, "Inequity in Social Exchange," in *Advances in Experimental Social Psychology,* ed. L. Berkowitz (New York: Academic Press, 1965); P. S. Goodman, "An Examination of Referents Used in the Evaluation of Pay," *Organizational Behavior and Human Performance* 12 (1974), pp. 170–95; and J. B. Miner," *Theories of Organizational Behavior* (Hinsdale, IL: Dryden Press, 1980).

13. P. Capelli and P. D. Sherer, "Assessing Worker Attitudes under a Two-Tier Wage Plan," *Industrial and Labor Relations Review* 43 (1990), pp. 225–44.

14. J. Roberson, "Toyota Sweats U.S. Labor Costs," *Detroit Free Press,* February 8, 2007.

15. J. P. Pfeffer and A. Davis-Blake, "Understanding Organizational Wage Structures: A Resource Dependence Approach," *Academy of Management Journal* 30 (1987), pp. 437–55.

16. Runzheimer International, *1997–1998 Survey of Geographic Pay Differential Policies and Practices* (Rochester, WI: Runzheimer, 1998).

17. This section draws freely on B. Gerhart and R. D. Bretz, "Employee Compensation," in *Organization and Management of Advanced Manufacturing,* eds. W. Karwowski and G. Salvendy (New York: Wiley, 1994), pp. 81–101.

18. E. E. Lawler III, *Strategic Pay* (San Francisco: Jossey-Bass, 1990); G. Ledford, "3 Cases on Skill-Based Pay: An Overview," *Compensation and Benefits Review,* March–April 1991, pp. 11–23; and G. E. Ledford, "Paying for the Skills, Knowledge, Competencies of Knowledge Workers," *Compensation and Benefits Review,* July–August 1995, p. 55.

19. B. C. Murray and B. Gerhart, "An Empirical Analysis of a Skill-Based Pay Program and Plant Performance Outcomes," *Academy of Management Journal* 41, no. 1 (1998), pp. 68–78.

20. Ibid.; N. Gupta, D. Jenkins, and W. Curington, "Paying for Knowledge: Myths and Realities," *National Productivity Review,* Spring 1986, pp. 107–23; and J. D. Shaw, N. Gupta, A. Mitra, and G. E. Ledford, "Success and Survival of Skill-Based Pay Plans," *Journal of Management* 31 (2005), pp. 28–49.

21. B. Leonard, "Data Indicate Strong Employer Support for Activated Reservists," *HRMagazine,* October 2003, downloaded from Infotrac at http://web4. infotrac.galegroup.com; and Carolyn Hirschman, "Supporting the Troops," *HRMagazine,* July 2007, downloaded from General Reference Center Gold, http://find.galegroup.com.

22. Joann S. Lublin, "The Pace of Pay Gains: A Survey Overview," *Wall Street Journal,* April 9, 2007, http:// online.wsj.com.

23. Towers Perrin, *2005–2006 Worldwide Total Remuneration* (Stamford, CT: Towers Perrin, 2006).

24. Ibid.

25. D. M. Cowherd and D. I. Levine, "Product Quality and Pay Equity between Lower-Level Employees and Top Management: An Investigation of Distributive Justice Theory," *Administrative Science Quarterly* 37 (1992), pp. 302–20.

Recognizing Employee Contributions with Pay

What Do I Need to Know?

After reading this chapter, you should be able to:

LO1 Discuss the connection between incentive pay and employee performance.

LO2 Describe how organizations recognize individual performance.

LO3 Identify ways to recognize group performance.

LO4 Explain how organizations link pay to their overall performance.

LO5 Describe how organizations combine incentive plans in a "balanced scorecard."

LO6 Summarize processes that can contribute to the success of incentive programs.

LO7 Discuss issues related to performance-based pay for executives.

Introduction

The 7,500 employees of Jamba Juice Company know how to earn more money. They know that their pay raises depend on how well they performed their jobs the previous year. Supervisors rank employees according to whether their performance was outstanding, above requirements, meeting requirements, or below requirements. Those in the top category receive the largest raises. Those rated as performing below requirements receive no raise at all, and they don't have a chance to earn a bonus. According to Russ Testa, Jamba Juice's vice president of human resources, this pay system is a practical matter of allocating the company's money to the company's best employees: "If you're devoting dollars to underperformers, that simply means you're taking away from your high performers."[1] Employees consider the process fair because they understand how their performance will be measured and how it will affect their pay.

The pay earned by each Jamba Juice employee depends on the starting pay for a particular job (the topic of the preceding chapter) and pay raises tied to the employee's performance. In this chapter we focus on using pay to recognize and reward employees' contributions to the organization's success. Employees' pay does not depend solely on the jobs they hold. Instead, organizations vary the amount paid according to differences in performance of the individual, group, or whole organization, as well as differences in employee qualities such as seniority and skills.[2]

In contrast to decisions about pay structure, organizations have wide discretion in setting performance-related pay, called **incentive pay.** Organizations can tie incentive pay to individual performance, profits, or many other measures of success. They select incentives based on their costs, expected influence on performance, and fit with the organization's broader HR and company policies and goals. These decisions are significant. A study of 150 organizations found that the way organizations paid employees was strongly associated with their level of profitability.[3]

chapter twelve

This chapter explores the choices available to organizations with regard to incentive pay. First, the chapter describes the link between pay and employee performance. Next, we discuss ways organizations provide a variety of pay incentives to individuals. The following two sections describe pay related to group and organizational performance. We then explore the organization's processes that can support the use of incentive pay. Finally, we discuss incentive pay for the organization's executives.

incentive pay
Forms of pay linked to an employee's performance as an individual, group member, or organization member.

Incentive Pay

Along with wages and salaries, many organizations offer *incentive pay*—that is, pay specifically designed to energize, direct, or control employees' behavior. The "Did You Know?" box illustrates the popularity of this type of pay. Incentive pay is influential because the amount paid is linked to certain predefined behaviors or outcomes. For example, as we will see in this chapter, an organization can pay a salesperson a *commission* for closing a sale, or the members of a production department can earn a *bonus* for meeting a monthly production goal. Usually, these payments are in addition to wages and salaries. Knowing they can earn extra money for closing sales or meeting departmental goals, the employees often try harder or get more creative than they might without the incentive pay. In addition, the policy of offering higher pay for higher performance may make an organization attractive to high performers when it is trying to recruit and retain these valuable employees.[4]

LO1 Discuss the connection between incentive pay and employee performance.

For incentive pay to motivate employees to contribute to the organization's success, the pay plans must be well designed. In particular, effective plans meet the following requirements:

- Performance measures are linked to the organization's goals.
- Employees believe they can meet performance standards.
- The organization gives employees the resources they need to meet their goals.
- Employees value the rewards given.
- Employees believe the reward system is fair.
- The pay plan takes into account that employees may ignore any goals that are not rewarded.

Since incentive pay is linked to particular outcomes or behaviors, the organization is encouraging employees to demonstrate those chosen outcomes and behaviors. As obvious as that may sound, the implications are more complicated. If incentive pay is extremely rewarding, employees may focus on only the performance measures rewarded under the plan and ignore measures that are not rewarded. Suppose an organization pays managers a bonus when employees are satisfied; this policy may interfere with other management goals. A manager who doesn't quite know how to inspire employees to do their best might be tempted to fall back on overly positive performance appraisals, letting work slide to keep everyone happy. Similarly, many call centers pay employees based on how many calls they handle, as an incentive to work quickly and efficiently. However, speedy call handling does not necessarily foster good customer relationships. As we will see in this chapter, organizations may combine a number of incentives so employees do not focus on one measure to the exclusion of others.

Attitudes that influence the success of incentive pay include whether employees value the rewards and think the pay plan is fair. Offering money as an incentive avoids the pitfall of inappropriate rewards. An insurance company in California once rewarded salespeople with tickets to a Christmas program at a nearby cathedral.

Most Companies Use Incentive Pay

Most large companies use some form of variable (incentive) pay, and they are spending almost 12 cents out of every dollar on this category of compensation. As recently as 1991, only about half of companies had a variable-pay plan for a majority of their employees.

Source: Hewitt Associates, "Hewitt Study: While Salary Increases in 2008 Remain Modest, Variable Pay Awards Reach Record High," news release, August 21, 2007, www.hewittassociates.com.

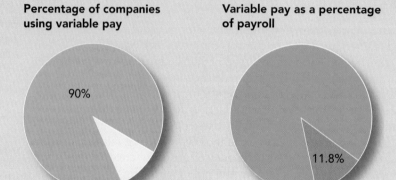

Percentage of companies using variable pay

90%

Variable pay as a percentage of payroll

11.8%

One-third of the salespeople were Jewish, and they were more than unenthusiastic—they were offended.[5] Although most, if not all, employees value pay, it is important to remember that earning money is not the only reason people try to do a good job. As we discuss in other chapters (see Chapters 4, 8, and 13), people also want interesting work, appreciation for their efforts, flexibility, and a sense of belonging to the work group—not to mention the inner satisfaction of work well done. Therefore, a complete plan for motivating and compensating employees has many components, from pay to work design to developing managers so they can exercise positive leadership.

With regard to the fairness of incentive pay, the preceding chapter described equity theory, which explains how employees form judgments about the fairness of a pay structure. The same process applies to judgments about incentive pay. In general, employees compare their efforts and rewards with other employees', considering a plan to be fair when the rewards are distributed according to what the employees contribute.

The remainder of this chapter identifies elements of incentive pay systems. We consider each option's strengths and limitations with regard to these principles. The many kinds of incentive pay fall into three broad categories: incentives linked to individual, group, or organizational performance. Choices from these categories should consider not only their strengths and weaknesses, but also their fit with the organization's goals. The choice of incentive pay may affect not only the level of motivation but also the kinds of employees who are attracted to and stay with the organization. For example, there is some evidence that organizations with team-based rewards will tend to attract employees who are more team-oriented, while rewards tied to individual performance make an organization more attractive to those who think and act independently, as individuals.[6]

Pay for Individual Performance

Organizations may reward individual performance with a variety of incentives:

- Piecework rates
- Standard hour plans
- Merit pay
- Individual bonuses
- Sales commissions

LO2 Describe how organizations recognize individual performance.

Piecework Rates

As an incentive to work efficiently, some organizations pay production workers a **piecework rate,** a wage based on the amount they produce. The amount paid per unit is set at a level that rewards employees for above-average production volume. For example, suppose that on average, assemblers can finish 10 components in an hour. If the organization wants to pay its average assemblers $8 per hour, it can pay a piecework rate of $8/hour divided by 10 components/hour, or $.80 per component. An assembler who produces the average of 10 components per hour earns an amount equal to $8 per hour. An assembler who produces 12 components in an hour would earn $.80 $\times$ 12, or $9.60 each hour. This is an example of a **straight piecework plan,** because the employer pays the same rate per piece, no matter how much the worker produces.

A variation on straight piecework is **differential piece rates** (also called *rising* and *falling differentials*), in which the piece rate depends on the amount produced. If the worker produces more than the standard output, the piece rate is higher. If the worker produces at or below the standard, the amount paid per piece is lower. In the preceding example, the differential piece rate could be $1 per component for components exceeding 12 per hour and $.80 per component for up to 12 components per hour.

In one study, the use of piece rates increased production output by 30 percent—more than any other motivational device evaluated.[7] An obvious advantage of piece rates is the direct link between how much work the employee does and the amount the employee earns. This type of pay is easy to understand and seems fair to many people, if they think the production standard is reasonable. In spite of their advantages, piece rates are relatively rare for several reasons.[8] Most jobs, including those of managers, have no physical output, so it is hard to develop an appropriate performance measure. This type of incentive is most suited for very routine, standardized jobs with output that is easy to measure. For complex jobs or jobs with hard-to-measure outputs, piecework plans do not apply very well. Also, unless a plan is well designed to include performance standards, it may not reward employees for focusing on quality or customer satisfaction if it interferes with the day's output. In Figure 12.1, the employees quickly realize they can earn huge bonuses by writing software "bugs" and then fixing them, while writing bug-free software affords no chance to earn bonuses. More seriously, a bonus based on number of faucets produced gives production workers no incentive to stop a manufacturing line to correct a quality-control problem. Production-oriented goals may do nothing to encourage employees to learn new skills or cooperate with others. Therefore, individual incentives such as these may be a poor incentive in an organization that wants to encourage teamwork. They may not be helpful in an organization with complex jobs, employee empowerment, and team-based problem solving.

piecework rate
A wage based on the amount workers produce.

straight piecework plan
Incentive pay in which the employer pays the same rate per piece, no matter how much the worker produces.

differential piece rates
Incentive pay in which the piece rate is higher when a greater amount is produced.

Figure 12.1

How Incentives Sometimes "Work"

SOURCE: DILBERT reprinted by permission of United Features Syndicate, Inc.

Standard Hour Plans

standard hour plan
An incentive plan that pays workers extra for work done in less than a preset "standard time."

Another quantity-oriented incentive for production workers is the **standard hour plan,** an incentive plan that pays workers extra for work done in less than a preset "standard time." The organization determines a standard time to complete a task, such as tuning up a car engine. If the mechanic completes the work in less than the standard time, the mechanic receives an amount of pay equal to the wage for the full standard time. Suppose the standard time for tuning up an engine is 2 hours. If the mechanic finishes a tune-up in 1½ hours, the mechanic earns 2 hours' worth of pay in 1½ hours. Working that fast over the course of a week could add significantly to the mechanic's pay.

In terms of their pros and cons, standard hour plans are much like piecework plans. They encourage employees to work as fast as they can, but not necessarily to care about quality or customer service. Also, they only succeed if employees want the extra money more than they want to work at a pace that feels comfortable.

Merit Pay

merit pay
A system of linking pay increases to ratings on performance appraisals.

Almost all organizations have established some program of **merit pay**—a system of linking pay increases to ratings on performance appraisals. (Chapter 8 described the content and use of performance appraisals.) To make the merit increases consistent, so they will be seen as fair, many merit pay programs use a *merit increase grid*, such as the sample for Merck, the giant drug company, in Table 12.1. As the table shows, the decisions about merit pay are based on two factors: the individual's performance rating and the individual's compa-ratio (pay relative to average pay, as defined in Chapter 11). This system gives the biggest pay increases to the best performers and to those whose pay is relatively low for their job. At the highest extreme, an exceptional employee earning 80 percent of the average pay for his job could receive a 15 percent merit raise. An employee rated as having "room for improvement" would receive a raise only if that employee was earning relatively low pay for the job (compa-ratio of .95 or less).

By today's standards, all of these raises are large, because they were created at a time when inflation was strong and economic forces demanded big pay increases to keep up with the cost of living. The range of percentages for a policy used today would be lower. Organizations establish and revise merit increase grids in light of changing economic conditions. When organizations revise pay ranges, employees have new compa-ratios. A higher pay range would result in lower compa-ratios, causing employees to become

TABLE 12.1

Sample Merit Increase Grid

	SUGGESTED MERIT INCREASE PERCENTAGE			
PERFORMANCE RATING	**COMPA-RATIO 80.00–95.00**	**COMPA-RATIO 95.01–110.00**	**COMPA-RATIO 110.01–120.00**	**COMPA-RATIO 120.01–125.00**
EX (Exceptional within Merck)	13–15%	12–14%	9–11%	To maximum of range
WD (Merck Standard with Distinction)	9–11	8–10	7–9	—
HS (High Merck Standard)	7–9	6–8	—	—
RI (Merck Standard Room for Improvement)	5–7	—	—	—
NA (Not Adequate for Merck)	—	—	—	—

Source: K. J. Murphy, "Merck & Co., Inc. (B)," Boston: Harvard Business School, Case 491-006. Copyright © 1990 by the President & Fellows of Harvard College. Reprinted with permission.

eligible for bigger merit increases. An advantage of merit pay is therefore that it makes the reward more valuable by relating it to economic conditions.

A drawback is that conditions can shrink the available range of increases. During recent years, budgets for merit pay increases were about 3 to 5 percent of pay, so average performers could receive a 4 percent raise, and top performers perhaps as much as 6 percent. The 2-percentage-point difference, after taxes and other deductions, would amount to only a few dollars a week on a salary of $40,000 per year. Over an entire career, the bigger increases for top performers can grow into a major change, but viewed on a year-by-year basis, they are not much of an incentive to excel.[9] As Figure 12.2 shows, companies typically spread merit raises fairly evenly across all employees. However, experts advise making pay increases twice as great for top performers as for average employees—and not rewarding the poor performers with a raise at all.[10] Imagine if the raises given to the bottom two categories in Figure 12.2 instead went toward 7 percent raises for the top performers. This type of decision signals that excellence is rewarded.

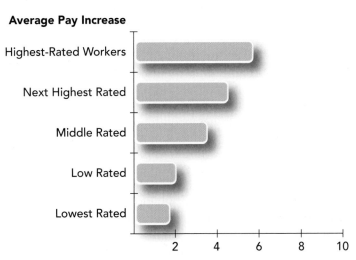

Average Pay Increase

- Highest-Rated Workers
- Next Highest Rated
- Middle Rated
- Low Rated
- Lowest Rated

2   4   6   8   10

Figure 12.2

Ratings and Raises: Underrewarding the Best

Note: Experts advise that the top category should receive twice as much as the middle category.

Another advantage of merit pay is that it provides a method for rewarding performance in all of the dimensions measured in the organization's performance management system. If that system is appropriately designed to measure all the important job behaviors, then the merit pay is linked to the behaviors the organization desires. This link seems logical, although so far there is little research showing the effectiveness of merit pay.[11]

A drawback of merit pay, from the employer's standpoint, is that it can quickly become expensive. Managers at a majority of organizations rate most employees' performance in the top two categories (out of four or five).[12] Therefore, the majority of employees are eligible for the biggest merit increases, and their pay rises rapidly. This cost is one reason that some organizations have established guidelines about the percentage of employees that may receive the top rating, as discussed in Chapter 8. Another correction might be to use 360-degree performance feedback (discussed in Chapter 9), but so far, organizations have not used multisource data for pay decisions.[13]

Another drawback of merit pay is that it makes assumptions that may be misleading. Rewarding employees for superior performance ratings assumes that those ratings depend on employees' ability and motivation. But performance may actually depend on forces outside the employee's control, such as managers' rating biases, the level of cooperation from co-workers, or the degree to which the organization gives employees the authority, training, and resources they need. Under these conditions, employees will likely conclude that the merit pay system is unfair.

Quality guru W. Edwards Deming also criticizes merit pay for discouraging teamwork. In Deming's words, "Everyone propels himself forward, or tries to, for his own good, on his own life preserver. The organization is the loser."[14] For example, if employees in the purchasing department are evaluated based on the number or cost of contracts they negotiate, they may have little interest in the quality of the materials they buy, even when the manufacturing department is having quality problems. In reaction to such problems, Deming advocated the use of group incentives. Another alternative is for merit pay to include ratings of teamwork and cooperation. Some employers ask co-workers to provide such ratings.

Performance Bonuses

Like merit pay, performance bonuses reward individual performance, but bonuses are not rolled into base pay. The employee must re-earn them during each performance period. In some cases, the bonus is a one-time reward. Bonuses may also be linked to objective performance measures, rather than subjective ratings.

Bonuses for individual performance can be extremely effective and give the organization great flexibility in deciding what kinds of behavior to reward. For example, as we saw in Chapter 2, Continental Airlines pays employees a quarterly bonus for ranking in the top three airlines for on-time arrivals, a measure of service quality. In many cases, employees receive bonuses for meeting such routine targets as sales or production numbers. Such bonuses encourage hard work. But an organization that focuses on growth and innovation may get better results from rewarding employees for learning new skills than from linking bonuses to mastery of existing jobs.

Adding to this flexibility, organizations also may motivate employees with one-time bonuses. For example, when one organization acquires another, it usually wants to retain certain valuable employees in the organization it is buying. Therefore, it is common for organizations involved in an acquisition to pay *retention bonuses*—one-time incentives paid in exchange for remaining with the company—to top managers, engineers, top-performing salespeople, and information technology specialists. When Wachovia Securities announced its merger with A. G. Edwards & Sons, it arranged to pay retention bonuses to A. G. Edwards brokers who remained with the company one month after completion of the merger. Some left, but most were still there when Wachovia issued the checks five months later.[15]

Sales Commissions

A variation on piece rates and bonuses is the payment of **commissions,** or pay calculated as a percentage of sales. For instance, a furniture salesperson might earn commissions equaling 6 percent times the price of the furniture the person sells during the period. Selling a $2,000 couch would add $120 to the salesperson's commissions for the period. At most organizations, commissions range from 5 percent to 20 percent of sales.[16]

> **commissions**
> Incentive pay calculated as a percentage of sales.

Some salespeople earn a commission in addition to a base salary; others earn only commissions—a pay arrangement called a *straight commission plan.* Straight commissions are common among insurance and real estate agents and car salespeople. Other salespeople earn no commissions at all, but a straight salary. Paying most or all of a salesperson's compensation in the form of salary frees the salesperson to focus on developing customer goodwill. Paying most or all of a salesperson's compensation in the form of commissions encourages the salesperson to focus on closing sales. In this way, differences in salespeople's compensation directly influence how they spend their time, how they treat customers, and how much the organization sells.

Many car salespeople earn a straight commission, meaning that 100% of their pay comes from commission instead of a salary. What type of individual might enjoy a job like this?

The nature of salespeople's compensation also affects the kinds of people who will want to take and keep sales jobs with the organization. Hard-driving, ambitious, risk-taking salespeople might enjoy the potential rewards of a straight commission plan. An organization that wants salespeople to concentrate on listening to customers and building relationships might want to attract a different kind of salesperson by offering more of the pay in the form of a salary. Basing part or all of a salesperson's pay on commissions assumes that the organization wants to attract people with some willingness to take risks—probably a reasonable assumption about people whose job includes talking to strangers and encouraging them to spend money.

Pay for Group Performance

Employers may address the drawbacks of individual incentives by including group incentives in the organization's compensation plan. To win group incentives, employees must cooperate and share knowledge so that the entire group can meet its performance targets. Common group incentives include gainsharing, bonuses, and team awards.

> **LO3** Identify ways to recognize group performance.

> **gainsharing**
> Group incentive program that measures improvements in productivity and effectiveness and distributes a portion of each gain to employees.

Gainsharing

Organizations that want employees to focus on efficiency may adopt a **gainsharing** program, which measures increases in productivity and effectiveness and distributes a portion of each gain to employees. For example, if a factory enjoys a productivity gain worth $30,000, half the gain might be the company's share. The other $15,000 would be distributed among the employees in the factory. Knowing that they can enjoy a financial benefit from helping the company be more productive, employees supposedly will look for ways to work more efficiently and improve the way the factory operates.

Gainsharing addresses the challenge of identifying appropriate performance measures for complex jobs. For example, how would a hospital measure the production of its nurses—in terms of satisfying patients, keeping costs down, or completing a number of tasks? Each of these measures oversimplifies the complex responsibilities involved in nursing care. Even for simpler jobs, setting acceptable standards and measuring performance can be complicated. Gainsharing frees employees to determine how to improve their own and their group's performance. It also broadens employees' focus beyond their individual interests. But in contrast to profit sharing, discussed later, it keeps the performance measures within a range of activity that most employees believe they can influence. Organizations can enhance the likelihood of a gain by providing a means for employees to share knowledge and make suggestions, as we will discuss in the last section of this chapter.

Gainsharing is most likely to succeed when organizations provide the right conditions. Among the conditions identified, the following are among the most common:[17]

- Management commitment.
- Need for change or strong commitment to continuous improvement.
- Management acceptance and encouragement of employee input.
- High levels of cooperation and interaction.
- Employment security.
- Information sharing on productivity and costs.
- Goal setting.
- Commitment of all involved parties to the process of change and improvement.
- Performance standard and calculation that employees understand and consider fair and that is closely related to managerial objectives.
- Employees who value working in groups.

Scanlon plan
A gainsharing program in which employees receive a bonus if the ratio of labor costs to the sales value of production is below a set standard.

A popular form of gainsharing is the **Scanlon plan,** developed in the 1930s by Joseph N. Scanlon, president of a union local at Empire Steel and Tin Plant in Mansfield, Ohio. The Scanlon plan gives employees a bonus if the ratio of labor costs to the sales value of production is below a set standard. To keep this ratio low enough to earn the bonus, workers have to keep labor costs to a minimum and produce as much as possible with that amount of labor. Figure 12.3 provides an example. In this example, the standard is a ratio of 20/100, or 20 percent, and the workers produced parts worth $1.2 million. To meet the standard, the labor costs should be less than 20 percent of $1.2 million, or $240,000. Since the actual labor costs were $210,000, the workers will get a gainsharing bonus based on the $30,000 difference between the $240,000 target and the actual cost.

Typically, an organization does not pay workers all of the gain immediately. First, the organization keeps a share of the gain to improve its own bottom line. A portion of the remainder goes into a reserve account. This account offsets losses in any months when the gain is negative (that is, when costs rise

Figure 12.3

Finding the Gain in a Scanlon Plan

$$\text{Target Ratio: } \frac{\text{Labor Costs}}{\text{Sales Value of Production}} = \frac{20}{100}$$

Sales Value of Production: $1,200,000

$$\text{Goal: } \frac{20}{100} \times \$1,200,000 = \$240,000$$

Actual: $210,000

Gain: $240,000 − $210,000 = $30,000

SOURCE: EXAMPLE adapted from B. Graham-Moore and Timothy L. Ross, *Gainsharing: Plans for Improving Performance* (Washington, DC: Bureau of National Affairs, 1990), p. 57.

or production falls). At the end of the year, the organization closes out the account and distributes any remaining surplus. If there were a loss at the end of the year, the organization would absorb it.

Group Bonuses and Team Awards

In contrast to gainsharing plans, which typically reward the performance of all employees at a facility, bonuses for group performance tend to be for smaller work groups.[18] These bonuses reward the members of a group for attaining a specific goal, usually measured in terms of physical output. Team awards are similar to group bonuses, but they are more likely to use a broad range of performance measures, such as cost savings, successful completion of a project, or even meeting deadlines.

Group members that meet a sales goal or a product development team that meets a deadline or successfully launches a product may be rewarded with a bonus for group performance. What are some advantages and disadvantages of group bonuses?

Both types of incentives have the advantage that they encourage group or team members to cooperate so that they can achieve their goal. However, depending on the reward system, competition among individuals may be replaced by competition among groups. Competition may be healthy in some situations, as when groups try to outdo one another in satisfying customers. On the downside, competition may also prevent necessary cooperation among groups. To avoid this, the organization should carefully set the performance goals for these incentives so that concern for costs or sales does not obscure other objectives, such as quality, customer service, and ethical behavior.

Pay for Organizational Performance

Two important ways organizations measure their performance are in terms of their profits and their stock price. In a competitive marketplace, profits result when an organization is efficiently providing products that customers want at a price they are willing to pay. Stock is the owners' investment in a corporation; when the stock price is rising, the value of that investment is growing. Rather than trying to figure out what performance measures will motivate employees to do the things that generate high profits and a rising stock price, many organizations offer incentive pay tied to those organizational performance measures. The expectation is that employees will focus on what is best for the organization.

LO4 Explain how organizations link pay to their overall performance.

These organization-level incentives can motivate employees to align their activities with the organization's goals. For example, when Harry Kraemer joined Baxter International as chief financial officer, he observed that the executives in charge of the company's divisions operated so independently that Baxter lacked focus. To align the executives' efforts, Kraemer directed the company to change its incentive pay policy. Instead of relying on bonuses linked to divisional results, Baxter encouraged managers to purchase the company's stock and later began granting stock options to all employees.[19]

Linking incentives to the organization's profits or stock price exposes employees to a high degree of risk. Profits and stock price can soar very high very fast, but they can also fall. The result is a great deal of uncertainty about the amount of incentive pay each employee will receive in each period. Therefore, these kinds of incentive pay are likely to be most effective in organizations that emphasize growth and innovation, which tend to need employees who thrive in a risk-taking environment.[20]

HR Oops!

Too Much Risk, Too Little Reward

A survey by HR consulting firm Towers Perrin found that setting up a variable-pay program such as profit sharing is not necessarily linked to better performance. Also, most of the companies that use these plans don't even know they have a problem, because they do not have a method to measure whether the programs are giving them a good return on investment.

One change the plans are making is shifting risks to employees. If the company has a good year, employees enjoy a big profit-sharing check. But if sales slow down, expenses rise, and profits fall, the company does not have to pay them as much. The problem with that, according to Ravin Jesuthasan of Towers Perrin, is that "you can't keep transferring risk to employees without also transferring control." In other words, if pay is related to profits, then employees need to have control over the factors that lead to high profits. Otherwise, employees will simply become indifferent to or frustrated with the profit-sharing plan.

Source: Fay Hansen, "Control and Customization," *Workforce Management,* November 5, 2007, p. 42.

Questions

1. Broadly speaking, what are some of the conditions, forces, and company actions that contribute to high profits? What are some of the conditions, forces, and company actions that hurt profits?

2. Which of these factors can a salesperson control? Which can an engineer control? Which can be controlled by a production supervisor and a production worker?

The "HR Oops!" box discusses why employees can become frustrated with pay linked to organizational performance.

Profit Sharing

profit sharing
Incentive pay in which payments are a percentage of the organization's profits and do not become part of the employees' base salary.

Under **profit sharing,** payments are a percentage of the organization's profits and do not become part of the employees' base salary. For example, General Motors provides for profit sharing in its contract with its workers' union, the United Auto Workers. Depending on how large GM's profits are in relation to its total sales for the year, at least 6 percent of the company's profits are divided among the workers according to how many hours they worked during the year.[21] The formula for computing and dividing the profit-sharing bonus is included in the union contract.

Organizations use profit sharing for a number of reasons. It may encourage employees to think more like owners, taking a broad view of what they need to do in order to make the organization more effective. They are more likely to cooperate and less likely to focus on narrow self-interests. Also, profit sharing has the practical advantage of costing less when the organization is experiencing financial difficulties. If the organization has little or no profit, this incentive pay is small or nonexistent, so employers may not need to rely as much on layoffs to reduce costs.[22]

Does profit sharing help organizations perform better? The evidence is not yet clear. Although research supports a link between profit-sharing payments and profits, researchers have questioned which of these causes the other.[23] For example, Ford, Chrysler, and GM have similar profit-sharing plans in their contracts with the United Auto Workers, but the payouts are not always similar. In one year, the average worker received $4,000 from Ford, $550 from GM, and $8,000 from Chrysler. Since the plans are similar, something other than the profit sharing must have made Ford and Chrysler more profitable than GM.

Differences in payouts, as in the preceding example, raise questions not only about the effectiveness of the plans, but about equity. Assuming workers at Ford, Chrysler, and GM have similar jobs, they would expect to receive similar profit-sharing checks. In the year of this example, GM workers might have seen their incentive pay as highly inequitable unless GM could show how Chrysler workers did more to earn their big checks. Employees also may feel that small profit-sharing checks are unfair because they have little control over profits. If profit sharing is offered to all employees but most employees think only management decisions about products, price, and marketing have much impact on profits, they will conclude that there is little connection between their actions and their rewards. In that case, profit-sharing plans will have little impact on employee behavior. This problem is even greater when employees have to wait months before profits are distributed. The time lag between high-performance behavior and financial rewards is simply too long to be motivating.

An organization setting up a profit-sharing plan should consider what to do if profits fall. If the economy slows and profit-sharing payments disappear along with profits, employees may become discouraged or angry. Mission Controls Automation counters this problem with open sharing of information and a commitment to avoid layoffs whenever possible. The engineering firm, located in Costa Mesa, California, gives employees profit-sharing payments when business is profitable. When economic conditions sour, employees understand what is happening and how they can make a difference. Management calls everyone together for twice-a-year financial meetings to explain the company's performance, and employees elect representatives to the company's board of directors.[24] The open sharing of information supports the profit-sharing incentive at Mission Controls because employees understand the connection between what they are doing and how well the company performs—as well as the impact of the business cycle—so the program seems fair. For more ideas on how to set up a profit-sharing plan that effectively motivates employees, see the "HR How To" box.

Given the limitations of profit-sharing plans, one strategy is to use them as a component of a pay system that includes other kinds of pay more directly linked to individual behavior. This increases employees' commitment to organizational goals while addressing concerns about fairness.

Stock Ownership

While profit-sharing plans are intended to encourage employees to "think like owners," a stock ownership plan actually makes employees part owners of the organization. Like profit sharing, employee ownership is intended as a way to encourage employees to focus on the success of the organization as a whole. The drawbacks of stock ownership as a form of incentive pay are similar to those of profit sharing. Specifically, it may not have a strong effect on individuals' motivation. Employees may not see a strong link between their actions and the company's stock price, especially in larger organizations. The link between pay and performance is even harder to appreciate because the financial benefits mostly come when the stock is sold—typically when the employee leaves the organization.

Ownership programs usually take the form of *stock options* or *employee stock ownership plans*. These are illustrated in Figure 12.4.

Stock Options

One way to distribute stock to employees is to grant them **stock options**—the right to buy a certain number of shares of stock at a specified price. (Purchasing the stock is called *exercising* the option.) Suppose that in 2005 a company's employees received

stock options
Rights to buy a certain number of shares of stock at a specified price.

MOTIVATING WITH A PROFIT-SHARING PLAN

When London-based Happy Computers, an information technology training company, switched from individual bonuses to a profit-sharing plan, employees began thinking about how they could work together better for the entire company's benefit. That change surprised and pleased the company's chief executive. In fact, careful planning can deliver such happy results and avoid the pitfalls of profit-sharing and other incentive plans.

Here are some ideas for setting up a profit-sharing plan that motivates employees:

- *Get supervisors on board—* Make sure they understand how the profit-sharing plan works and how they can lead their people to contribute to high profits. Find out what training they need, and make sure they get it.
- *Make sure employees understand how the plan works—* Give them opportunities to air their concerns and ask questions. Be prepared for questions about the plan's fairness. Tell employees what goals they must reach and what the percentage payouts will be for meeting or exceeding the goals.
- *Identify the behaviors and results that contribute to greater profits—*Set group and individual goals that lead to these behaviors and results. Ensure that employees and their supervisors have the training and resources necessary for meeting their goals.
- *Make sure managers understand that they contribute to the profit-sharing goals by encouraging their employees and keeping them focused on their goals—*Some may need training in effective performance management.
- *Consider linking rewards to the department's or division's performance, if profits can be assigned to the group—*That gives employees a sense that they have more control over the results, rather than depending on every division of a large company.
- *Make the rewards big enough to matter—*One expert recommends profit-sharing payments that are 20 to 33 percent of the employee's base salary.
- *Time the profit-sharing payments for maximum effect—*That may involve splitting the payout into two checks, delivered six months apart, so that employees have an incentive to stick around to enjoy the full reward.

Sources: Phil Shohet, "Inventive Incentive," *Accountancy Age,* October 18, 2007; and "Employee Engagement: How to Avoid the Pitfalls of Performance Payments," *Employee Benefits,* June 12, 2007, both downloaded from General Reference Center Gold, http://find.galegroup.com.

options to purchase the company's stock at $10 per share. The employees will benefit if the stock price rises above $10 per share, because they can pay $10 for something (a share of stock) that is worth more than $10. If in 2010 the stock is worth $30, they can exercise their options and buy stock for $10 a share. If they want to, they can sell their stock for the market price of $30, receiving a gain of $20 for each share of stock.

Figure 12.4

Types of Pay for Organizational Performance

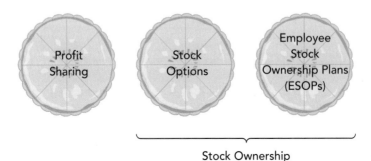

Of course, stock prices can also fall. If the 2010 stock price is only $8, the employees would not bother to exercise the options.

Traditionally, organizations have granted stock options to their executives. During the 1990s, many organizations pushed eligibility for options further down in the organization's structure. Wal-Mart and PepsiCo are among the large companies that have granted stock options to employees at all levels. Stock values were rising so fast during the 1990s that options were extremely rewarding for a time.

Some studies suggest that organizations perform better when a large percentage of top and middle managers are eligible for long-term incentives such as stock options. This evidence is consistent with the idea of encouraging employees to think like owners.[25] It is not clear whether these findings would hold up for lower-level employees. They may see much less opportunity to influence the company's performance in the stock market.

Recent scandals have drawn attention to another challenge of using stock options as incentive pay. As with other performance measures, employees may focus so much on stock price that they lose sight of other goals, including ethical behavior. Ideally, managers would bring about an increase in stock price by adding value in terms of efficiency, innovation, and customer satisfaction. But there are other, unethical ways to increase stock price by tricking investors into thinking the organization is more valuable and more profitable than it actually is. Hiding losses and inflating the recorded value of revenues are just two of the ways some companies have boosted stock prices, enriching managers until these misdeeds come to light. Also, officials at some companies, including Apple, Monster, and McAfee, have been charged with "backdating" options granted to executives. This practice involves changing the date and/or price in the original option agreement so that the option holder can buy stock at a bargain price—making the backdated option profitable or more profitable. At the same time, backdating eliminates or reduces the incentive to improve the stock's performance. If backdating of options is kept secret, those who do it may be guilty of falsifying financial statements, which is unethical and may be illegal.[26]

employee stock ownership plan (ESOP) An arrangement in which the organization distributes shares of stock to all its employees by placing it in a trust.

Employee Stock Ownership Plans

While stock options are most often used with top management, a broader arrangement is the **employee stock ownership plan (ESOP).** In an ESOP, the organization distributes shares of stock to its employees by placing the stock into a trust managed on the employees' behalf. Employees receive regular reports on the value of their stock, and when they leave the organization, they may sell the stock to the organization or (if it is a publicly traded company) on the open market.

ESOPs are the most common form of employee ownership, with the number of employees in such plans increasing from over 3 million in 1980 to more than 11 million in 2008 in the United States.[27] Figure 12.5 shows the growth in the number of ESOPs in the United States. One reason for ESOPs' popularity is that earnings of the trust holdings are exempt from income taxes.

ESOPs raise a number of issues. On the negative side, they carry a significant risk for employees. By law, an ESOP must invest at least 51 percent of its assets in the company's own stock (in contrast to other kinds of stock

Figure 12.5

Number of ESOPS

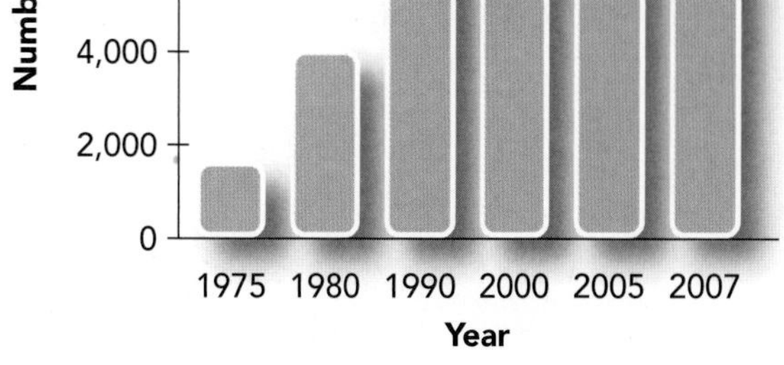

SOURCE: National Center for Employee Ownership, "A Statistical Profile of Employee Ownership," Research & Statistics page of NCEO Web site, updated February 2008, www.nceo.org.

Best Practices

Van Meter Industrial's Employees Act Like Owners

At Van Meter Industrial, employees own every share of the company's stock. And each year, employees receive more shares, worth a few weeks' pay. Van Meter, an electrical-parts distributor, offers this type of incentive to encourage employees to act like owners, focused on the company's long-term success.

Several years ago, however, managers realized that the incentive might not be working as intended. At a companywide meeting, an employee grumbled that he didn't care about the stock and would rather receive something more practical, say, "a couple hundred bucks" in bonus money to spend as he liked. Mick Slinger, the company's chief financial officer, was startled. He had been watching Van Meter's stock price rise year after year, matching the inflation rate. He realized that while this steady climb looked valuable to him, many employees didn't fully realize what it meant to be an employee owner.

So under Slinger's leadership, the company began to educate its employees about company ownership. The first step was to set up a 12-member employee committee to learn about the ESOP and then share their knowledge. The committee studied enrollment procedures and the schedule for becoming fully vested in the plan. They met with employees at other employee-owned companies to learn how they were benefiting from their ESOPs. Then the committee members began visiting Van Meter's facilities to have informal discussions about the program. They developed practical, concrete lessons. For example, they pointed out that after 10 years, the rising value of company stock can make it worth five years' earnings—equivalent to working for 10 years and getting 15 years' pay. Management learned that employees more readily understand that focus—that a contribution equals 9½ weeks' pay instead of 18 percent of salary.

Van Meter also built employee enthusiasm by treating the ESOP as a significant benefit. In the past, after employees had been with the company for six months, they simply were told they were enrolled and that details of the ESOP were included in the information packets they had received when they joined the company. Now enrollment in the plan is celebrated with a jacket bearing the slogan "I am in," coupled with training in employee ownership.

Perhaps most important, the education also shows employees how their actions can cut costs, speed up debt collection, and boost the bottom line, adding to the worth of their stock. Employees meet once a month to talk about how they have helped to save the company money. Results are posted on Van Meter's Web site for any employee to read.

In the years since Van Meter began showing its employees how to think like owners, its stock price has jumped. Also, its employee turnover has dropped from 18 percent to just 8 percent.

Source: Simona Covel, "How to Get Workers to Think and Act like Owners," *Wall Street Journal*, February 7, 2008, http://online.wsj.com.

---

funds that hold a wide diversity of companies). Problems with the company's performance therefore can take away significant value from the ESOP. Many companies set up ESOPs to hold retirement funds, so these risks directly affect employees' retirement income. Adding to the risk, funds in an ESOP are not guaranteed by the Pension Benefit Guarantee Corporation (described in Chapter 13). Sometimes employees use an ESOP to buy their company when it is experiencing financial problems; this is a highly risky investment.

Still, ESOPs can be attractive to employers. Along with tax and financing advantages, ESOPs give employers a way to build pride in and commitment to the organization. Employees have a right to participate in votes by shareholders (if the stock is registered on a national exchange, such as the New York Stock Exchange).[28] This means employees participate somewhat in corporate-level decision making. Still, the overall level of participation in decisions appears to vary significantly among organizations with ESOPs. Some research suggests that the benefits of ESOPs are greatest when employee participation is greatest.[29] For an example of a company that uses ESOPs effectively, see the "Best Practices" box.

Balanced Scorecard

As the preceding descriptions indicate, any form of incentive pay has advantages and disadvantages. For example, relying exclusively on merit pay or other individual incentives may produce a workforce that cares greatly about meeting those objectives but competes to achieve them at the expense of cooperating to achieve organizational goals. Relying heavily on profit sharing or stock ownership may increase cooperation but do little to motivate day-to-day effort or to attract and retain top individual performers. Because of this, many organizations design a mix of pay programs. The aim is to balance the disadvantages of one type of incentive pay with the advantages of another type.

One way of accomplishing this goal is to design a **balanced scorecard**—a combination of performance measures directed toward the company's long- and short-term goals and used as the basis for awarding incentive pay. A corporation would have financial goals to satisfy its stockholders (owners), quality- and price-related goals to satisfy its customers, efficiency goals to ensure better operations, and goals related to acquiring skills and knowledge for the future to fully tap into employees' potential. Different jobs would contribute to those goals in different ways. For example, an engineer could develop products that better meet customer needs and can be produced more efficiently. The engineer could also develop knowledge of new technologies in order to contribute more to the organization in the future. A salesperson's goals would include measures related to sales volume, customer service, and learning about product markets and customer needs. Organizations customize their balanced scorecards according to their markets, products, and objectives. The scorecards of a company that is emphasizing low costs and prices would be different from the scorecards of a company emphasizing innovative use of new technology.

LO5 Describe how organizations combine incentive plans in a "balanced scorecard."

balanced scorecard A combination of performance measures directed toward the company's long- and short-term goals and used as the basis for awarding incentive pay.

Tellabs is one company that uses a balanced scorecard. The company conducts quarterly meetings at which employees learn how their performance will be evaluated according to the scorecard. The company also makes this information available on the intranet.

Table 12.2

Sample Balanced Scorecard for a Production Manager

PERFORMANCE MEASURE	TARGET INCENTIVE PER MONTH	PERFORMANCE LEVEL	% TARGET EARNED
INCENTIVE SCHEDULE			
Financial • Return on capital employed	$ 1,000	20%+ 16–20% 12–16% Below 12%	150% 100% 50% 0%
Customer • Product returns	$ 400	1 in: 1,000 + 900–999 800–899 Below 800	1 150% 100% 50% 0%
Internal • Cycle time reduction (%)	$ 300	9%+ 6–9% 3–6% 0–3%	150% 100% 50% 0%
Learning and growth • Voluntary employee turnover	$ 300	Below 5% 5–8% 8–12%	150% 100% 50%
Total	$ 2,000		

Source: Adapted from F. C. McKenzie and M. P. Shilling, "Avoiding Performance Traps: Ensuring Effective Incentive Design and Implementation," Compensation and Benefits Review, July–August 1998, pp. 57–65. Reprinted with permission of Sage Publications, Inc.

Table 12.2 shows the kinds of information that go into a balanced scorecard. This scorecard for a manager in a manufacturing company includes four performance measures. The financial performance measure is return on capital employed (that is, profits divided by capital used during the period). A higher percentage means the capital (money and equipment) generated more profits. The measure of customer satisfaction is product returns. If customers return 1 product out of 1,000, they are better satisfied than if they return 1 product out of 800. The measure of internal operations is the percentage by which the manager's group reduces *cycle time*, the amount of time required to complete the group's process, such as fulfilling an order or getting a new product into production. Finally, the manager's objective for learning and growth in the group is to reduce voluntary turnover among employees. This goal assumes that the manager can develop a more experienced, valuable group of employees by reducing turnover.

For each of these goals, the balanced scorecard assigns a target incentive payment for the manager to earn and four levels of performance. If the manager achieves the top level of performance, the manager will earn 150 percent of the target incentive. The payout would fall to 100 percent of the incentive for achieving the second level of performance, 50 percent of the incentive for achieving the third level, and nothing for achieving the bottom level. In this example, the manager's target incentive is $2,000 per time period (e.g., per month), but the manager could earn $3,000 per period for exceeding all of the performance objectives—or nothing for failing to achieve all of the objectives.

Not only does the balanced scorecard combine the advantages of different incentive-pay plans, it helps employees understand the organization's goals. By communicating the balanced scorecard to employees, the organization shows employees information about what its goals are and what it expects employees to accomplish. In Table 12.2, for example, the organization indicates not only that the manager should meet the four performance objectives but also that it is especially concerned with the financial target, because half the incentive is based on this one target.

Processes That Make Incentives Work

As we explained in Chapter 11, communication and employee participation can contribute to a belief that the organization's pay structure is fair. In the same way, the process by which the organization creates and administers incentive pay can help it use incentives to achieve the goal of motivating employees. The monetary rewards of gainsharing, for example, can substantially improve productivity,[30] but the organization can set up the process to be even more effective. In a study of an automotive parts plant, productivity rose when the gainsharing plan added employee participation in the form of monthly meetings with managers to discuss the gainsharing plan and ways to increase productivity. A related study asked employees what motivated them to participate actively in the plan (for example, by making suggestions for improvement). According to employees, other factors besides the pay itself were important—especially the ability to influence and control the way their work was done.[31]

LO6 Summarize processes that can contribute to the success of incentive programs.

Participation in Decisions

Employee participation in pay-related decisions can be part of a general move toward employee empowerment. If employees are involved in decisions about incentive pay plans and employees' eligibility for incentives, the process of creating and administering these plans can be more complex.[32] There is also a risk that employees will make decisions that are in their interests at the expense of the organization's interests. However, employees have hands-on knowledge about the kinds of behavior that can help the organization perform well, and they can see whether individuals are displaying that behavior.[33] Therefore, in spite of the potential risks, employee participation can contribute to the success of an incentive plan. This is especially true when monetary incentives encourage the monitoring of performance and when the organization fosters a spirit of trust and cooperation.

Communication

Along with empowerment, communicating with employees is important. It demonstrates to employees that the pay plan is fair. Also, when employees understand the requirements of the incentive pay plan, the plan is more likely to influence their behavior as desired.

It is particularly important to communicate with employees when changing the plan. Employees tend to feel concerned about changes. Pay is a frequent topic of rumors and assumptions based on incomplete information, partly because of pay's importance to employees. When making any changes, the human resource department should determine the best ways to communicate the reasons for the change. Some organizations rely heavily on videotaped messages from the chief executive officer. Other means of communication include brochures that show examples of how

FINANCIAL EDUCATION ONLINE

Employees get the most value from—and appreciation of—their benefits if they understand how to manage their financial assets. As employers are coming to appreciate this fact, they are also recognizing that online training is an efficient and convenient way to deliver a financial education.

For example, GlaxoSmithKline offers financial education at each of its locations. For its diverse workforce, the pharmaceutical company supplements face-to-face seminars with online instruction and downloadable presentations. This method of training is especially useful for employees who work at home or frequently travel.

Along with recorded training presentations on DVDs and podcasts, online training offers the power of the computer for showing employees how to get the most out of their earnings. Online modeling tools can show employees how the value of their stock can grow over time if they don't sell it immediately. Or employees can see how the power of compound interest can make their bonus or profit-sharing check grow if they invest it in various ways.

Sources: "Best Practice: Face Up to Provision of Multi-Site Financial Education," *Employee Benefits,* February 8, 2008; and "Financial Education: Cache of Literacy," *Employee Benefits,* October 8, 2007, both downloaded from General Reference Center Gold, http://find.galegroup.com.

employees will be affected. The human resource department may also conduct small-group interviews to learn about employees' concerns, then address those concerns in the communications effort.

L07 Discuss issues related to performance-based pay for executives.

Incentive Pay for Executives

Because executives have a much stronger influence over the organization's performance than other employees do, incentive pay for executives warrants special attention. Assuming that incentives influence performance, decisions about incentives for executives should have a great impact on how well the executives and the organization perform. Along with overall pay levels for executives (discussed in Chapter 11), organizations need to create incentive plans for this small but important group of employees.

To encourage executives to develop a commitment to the organization's long-term success, executive compensation often combines short-term and long-term incentives. *Short-term incentives* include bonuses based on the year's profits, return on investment, or other measures related to the organization's goals. Sometimes, to gain tax advantages, the actual payment of the bonus is deferred (for example, by making it part of a retirement plan). *Long-term incentives* include stock options and stock purchase plans. The rationale for these long-term incentives is that executives will want to do what is best for the organization because that will cause the value of their stock to grow.

Each year *BusinessWeek* publishes a list of top executives who did the most for their pay (that is, their organizations performed best) and those who did the least. The performance of the latter group has prompted much of the negative attention that executive pay has received. The problem seems to be that in some organizations, the chief executive's pay is high every year, regardless of the organization's profitability or performance in the stock market. In terms of people's judgments about equity, it seems fairer if high-paid executives must show results to justify their pay levels.

Table 12.3

**Balanced Scorecard for
Whirlpool Executives**

TYPE OF VALUE CREATION	MEASURES
Shareholder value	Economic value added Earnings per share Cash flow Total cost productivity
Customer value	Quality Market share Customer satisfaction
Employee value	High-performance culture index High-performance culture deployment Training and development diversity

Source: E. L. Gubman, The Talent Solution *(New York: McGraw-Hill, 1998).*

A corporation's shareholders—its owners—want the corporation to encourage managers to act in the owners' best interests. They want managers to care about the company's profits and stock price, and incentive pay can encourage this interest. One way to achieve these goals is to tie a large share of executives' pay to performance. In a *BusinessWeek* survey, almost 80 percent of chief executives' pay came in the form of stock options and other incentive pay based on long-term performance objectives. Another study has found that relying on such long-term incentives is associated with greater profitability.[34]

Performance Measures for Executives

The balanced-scorecard approach is useful in designing executive pay. Whirlpool, for example, has used a balanced scorecard that combines measures of whether the organization is delivering value to shareholders, customers, and employees. These measures are listed in Table 12.3. Rewarding achievement of a variety of goals in a balanced scorecard reduces the temptation to win bonuses by manipulating financial data.

Regulators and shareholders have pressured companies to do a better job of linking executive pay and performance. The Securities and Exchange Commission (SEC) has required companies to more clearly report executive compensation levels and the company's performance relative to that of competitors. These reporting requirements shine a light on situations where executives of poorly performing companies receive high pay, so companies feel more pressure to link pay to performance. Some forms of incentive pay also have tax advantages. Under the Omnibus Budget Reconciliation Act of 1993, companies may not deduct executive pay that exceeds $1 million, but performance-related pay (including stock options) is exempt, so it is deductible even over $1 million.

Warren Buffet must be doing something right. The billionaire once was ranked by *BusinessWeek* magazine as being the top executive who gave shareholders the most for their pay.

Ethical Issues

Incentive pay for executives lays the groundwork for significant ethical issues. When an organization links pay to its stock performance, executives need the ethical backbone to be honest about their company's performance even when dishonesty or clever shading of the truth offers the tempting potential for large earnings. As recent scandals involving WorldCom, Enron, Global Crossing, and other companies have shown, the results can be disastrous when unethical behavior comes to light.

Among these issues is one we have already touched on in this chapter: the difficulty of setting performance measures that encourage precisely the behavior desired. In the case of incentives tied to stock performance, executives may be tempted to inflate the stock price in order to enjoy bonuses and valuable stock options. The intent is for the executive to boost stock value through efficient operations, technological innovation, effective leadership, and so on. Unfortunately, individuals at some companies determined that they could obtain faster results through accounting practices that stretched the norms in order to present the company's performance in the best light. When such practices are discovered to be misleading, stock prices plunge and the company's reputation is damaged, sometimes beyond repair.

A related issue when executive pay includes stock or stock options is insider trading. When executives are stockholders, they have a dual role as owners and managers. This places them at an advantage over others who want to invest in the company. An individual, a pension fund, or other investors have less information about the company than its managers do—for example, whether product development is proceeding on schedule, whether a financing deal is in the works, and so on. An executive who knows about these activities could therefore reap a windfall in the stock market by buying or selling stock based on knowledge about the company's future. The SEC places strict limits on this "insider trading," but some executives have violated these limits. In the worst cases executives have sold stock, secretly knowing their company was failing, before the stock price collapsed. The losers are the employees, retirees, and other investors who hold the now-worthless stock.

As recent news stories have reminded us, linking pay to stock price can reward unethical behavior, at least in the short term and at least in the minds of a handful of executives. Yet, given the motivational power of incentive pay, organizations cannot afford to abandon incentives for their executives. These temptations are among the reasons that executive positions demand individuals who maintain the highest ethical standards.

THINKING ETHICALLY

CAN EMPLOYEE STOCK OWNERSHIP SHAPE VALUES?

IMA Financial Group is entirely owned by its employees. The insurance brokerage's president, Bob Reiter, says making every employee an owner "has a profound impact not only on the way we operate but on how our clients feel." The company hopes that its shared ownership will build employees' dedication to its mission, which is to "protect profits and make a difference." That difference is defined as improvements in the lives of IMA's clients, employees, and community.

Reiter says IMA employees benefit from a climate of respect and trust in an organization focused less on the competition than on ways to improve what it does. Clients benefit from service that goes beyond selling to help them manage their risk. And the community benefits from IMA's commitment to service projects and a foundation that supports local charities. Recently, for all these efforts, IMA Group's Colorado office won a Colorado Ethics in Business Alliance Award.

SOURCE: Rebecca Cole, "IMA Financial Group," *ColoradoBiz*, 16th Annual Colorado Ethics in Business Alliance Awards, March 2008, downloaded from General Reference Center Gold, http://find.galegroup.com.

Questions

1. How does this description of IMA's conduct compare with your own understanding of business ethics?
2. IMA president Bob Reiter explains employees' commitment to the company's values as being partly the result of their owning shares of IMA's

stock. In what ways might employee stock ownership plans contribute to ethical conduct? In what circumstances would stock ownership plans effectively promote ethical conduct?

3. Could an employee stock ownership plan also contribute to *unethical* conduct in an organization? Why or why not?

SUMMARY

LO1 Discuss the connection between incentive pay and employee performance.

Incentive pay is pay tied to individual performance, profits, or other measures of success. Organizations select forms of incentive pay to energize, direct, or control employees' behavior. It is influential because the amount paid is linked to predefined behaviors or outcomes. To be effective, incentive pay should encourage the kinds of behavior that are most needed, and employees must believe they have the ability to meet the performance standards. Employees must value the rewards, have the resources they need to meet the standards, and believe the pay plan is fair.

LO2 Describe how organizations recognize individual performance.

Organizations may recognize individual performance through such incentives as piecework rates, standard hour plans, merit pay, sales commissions, and bonuses for meeting individual performance objectives. Piecework rates pay employees according to the amount they produce. Standard hour plans pay workers extra for work done in less than a preset "standard time." Merit pay links increases in wages or salaries to ratings on performance appraisals. Bonuses are similar to merit pay, because they are paid for meeting individual goals, but they are not rolled into base pay, and they usually are based on achieving a specific output, rather than subjective performance ratings. A sales commission is incentive pay calculated as a percentage of sales closed by a salesperson.

LO3 Identify ways to recognize group performance.

Common group incentives include gainsharing, bonuses, and team awards. Gainsharing programs, such as Scanlon plans, measure increases in productivity and distribute a portion of each gain to employees. Group bonuses reward the members of a group for attaining a specific goal, usually measured in terms of physical output. Team awards are more likely to use a broad range of performance measures, such as cost savings, successful completion of a project, or meeting a deadline.

LO4 Explain how organizations link pay to their overall performance.

Incentives for meeting organizational objectives include profit sharing and stock ownership. Profit-sharing plans pay workers a percentage of the organization's profits; these payments do not become part of the employees' base salary. Stock ownership incentives may take the form of stock options or employee stock ownership plans. A stock option is the right to buy a certain number of shares at a specified price. The employee benefits by exercising the option at a price lower than the market price, so the employee benefits when the company's stock price rises. An employee stock ownership plan (ESOP) is an arrangement in which the organization distributes shares of its stock to employees by placing the stock in a trust managed on the employees' behalf. When employees leave the organization, they may sell their shares of the stock.

LO5 Describe how organizations combine incentive plans in a "balanced scorecard."

A balanced scorecard is a combination of performance measures directed toward the company's long- and short-term goals and used as the basis for awarding incentive pay. Typically, it includes financial goals to satisfy stockholders, quality- and price-related goals for customer satisfaction, efficiency goals for improved operations, and goals related to acquiring skills and knowledge for the future. The mix of pay programs is intended to balance the disadvantages of one type of incentive with the advantages of another type. The balanced scorecard also helps employees to understand and care about the organization's goals.

LO6 Summarize processes that can contribute to the success of incentive programs.

Communication and participation in decisions can contribute to employees' feeling that the organization's incentive pay plans are fair. Employee participation in pay-related decisions can be part of a general move toward employee empowerment. Employees may put their own interests first in developing the plan, but they also have firsthand insight into the kinds of behavior that can contribute to organizational goals. Communicating with employees is important because it demonstrates that the pay plan is fair and helps them understand what is expected of them. Communication is especially important when the organization is changing its pay plan.

LO7 Discuss issues related to performance-based pay for executives.

Because executives have such a strong influence over the organization's performance, incentive pay for them receives special attention. Executive pay usually combines long-term and short-term incentives. By motivating executives, these incentives can significantly affect the organization's performance. The size of incentives should be motivating but also meet standards for equity. Performance measures should encourage behavior that is in the organization's best interests, including ethical behavior. Executives need ethical standards that keep them from insider trading or deceptive practices designed to manipulate the organization's stock price.

KEY TERMS

REVIEW AND DISCUSSION QUESTIONS

1. With some organizations and jobs, pay is primarily wages or salaries, and with others, incentive pay is more important. For each of the following jobs, state whether you think the pay should emphasize base pay (wages and salaries) or incentive pay (bonuses, profit sharing, and so on). Give a reason for each.
   a. An accountant at a manufacturing company.
   b. A salesperson for a software company.
   c. A chief executive officer.
   d. A physician in a health clinic.

2. Consider your current job or a job that you have recently held. Would you be most motivated in response to incentives based on your individual performance, your group's performance, or the organization's overall performance (profits or stock price)? Why?

3. What are the pros and cons of linking incentive pay to individual performance? How can organizations address the negatives?

4. Suppose you are a human resource professional at a company that is setting up work teams for production and sales. What group incentives would you recommend to support this new work arrangement?

5. Why do some organizations link incentive pay to the organization's overall performance? Is it appropriate to use stock performance as an incentive for employees at all levels? Why or why not?

6. Stock options have been called the pay program that "built Silicon Valley," because of their key role as incentive pay for employees in high-tech companies. They were popular during the 1990s, when the stock market was rising rapidly. Since then, stock prices have fallen.
   a. How would you expect this change to affect employees' attitudes toward stock options as incentive pay?
   b. How would you expect this change to affect the effectiveness of stock options as an incentive?

7. Based on the balanced scorecard in Table 12.2, what would be the total incentive paid to a manager if the group's return on capital employed was 12 percent, customers returned 1 product out of every 1,200 products delivered, cycle time was reduced by 5 percent, and employee turnover was 4 percent? (For each measure, find the performance level, then multiply the corresponding percentage by the target incentive to find the incentive earned.)

8. Why might a balanced scorecard like the one in Question 7 be more effective than simply using merit pay for a manager?

9. How can the way an organization creates and carries out its incentive plan improve the effectiveness of that plan?

10. In a typical large corporation, the majority of the chief executive's pay is tied to the company's stock price. What are some benefits of this pay strategy? Some risks? How can organizations address the risks?

BUSINESSWEEK CASE

BusinessWeek The Billion-Dollar Losers

Big-name U.S. CEOs have taken a bath, but not the kind that leaves you feeling warm and relaxed. As the bears took over Wall Street, chief executives, rewarded handsomely in years past with stock options, have seen the value of their holdings plummet.

Market forces have chewed up the portfolios of even the savviest chief executives. Financial information provider Capital IQ estimates that since October 2007, five CEOs of major U.S. companies have lost more than $1 billion through holdings of their companies' stock: Larry Ellison of Oracle, Michael Dell of Dell, Micky Arison of Carnival Corporation, Jeffrey Bezos of Amazon.com, and Rupert Murdoch of News Corporation.

More than 20 CEOs have lost more than $100 million. The pain is widespread, too. Of the 450 major-company CEOs analyzed, only about 60 escaped the last three months without losses. The markets were so difficult that only five of that group were able to achieve what these CEOs would typically take for granted—gains of more than $10 million each.

The U.S. economy's troubles began in the financial sector during the summer of 2007, as bad mortgage debt caused havoc in the credit markets. As a result, some of the biggest losers are CEOs in the financial sector. Countrywide Financial CEO Angelo Mozilo has seen his stock lose nearly two-thirds of its value, costing him more than $100 million. (Mozilo will step down as Countrywide's chief after the planned acquisition of the company by Bank of America is completed.) Subprime debt has also devastated the holdings of CEOs of bond insurers.

Don't reach for the Kleenex just yet. Despite recent market turbulence, CEOs are still quite wealthy in company stock. Capital IQ identified 16 CEOs who still own more than $1 billion in their firm's shares and 73 who own more than $100 million.

In the past, base salary was a much larger part of executive compensation, but starting in the 1990s, corporate boards began to add a lot more stock to pay packages. Shareholder groups had argued that the interests of CEOs and shareholders weren't properly aligned. By paying CEOs in stock or stock options, "the concept is they get paid for the performance of the organization overall," says Don Lindner of WorldatWork, a human resources nonprofit.

But this doesn't always work perfectly. When the economy is booming and the stock market is rising, even lackluster CEOs get rewarded. But now, while a recession threatens, CEOs of even top performers are hurt. For example, Amazon.com's Bezos doubled profits in 2007, yet he lost $1.6 billion since October of that year.

The list of CEOs includes a variety of executives who have somehow found a way to make money in a tough market. Their outperformance usually reflects extraordinary circumstances: surprisingly strong results that bucked an industry trend, or an outlook that suddenly turned from poor to favorable.

Of course, in today's volatile markets, the current winners could wind up in the company of their unlucky brethren in a heartbeat.

SOURCE: Excerpted from Ben Steverman, "The Billion-Dollar Losers," *BusinessWeek*, February 4, 2008, downloaded from General Reference Center Gold, http://find.galegroup.com.

Questions

1. According to the case, when stock prices in general are falling, the value of most CEOs' compensation drops, whether or not particular CEOs are effective. How do you think this affects CEOs' incentive to perform well? (For example, consider including other forms of performance-related pay.)
2. The opposite is true, too: when the stock market is rising, most CEOs' compensation is growing, even if the CEOs are doing a mediocre or poor job. How can a compensation package that emphasizes stock be adjusted to keep executives motivated?
3. In employee-owned companies—notably, those using ESOPs—all the employee-owners see their earnings rise and fall with the stock market. If you were an HR manager at an employee-owned company, how would you recommend that the company handle the possible effects on employees' motivation?

CASE: XCEL ENERGY PAYS FOR EMPLOYEES WHO EXCEL

The management of Xcel Energy, an electricity and natural-gas utility based in Minneapolis and serving eight states, believes in linking rewards to performance. For example, an incentive plan called Xpress Ideas pays employees an immediate bonus for submitting beneficial suggestions.

The company's employees loved the idea; in one year alone, they submitted 6,133 suggestions, and most of them were implemented—and rewarded.

The downside of this plan is that Xcel Energy hadn't set up a system for measuring whether the rewards were worth the money—more than $427,000 for the 6,133 ideas. So the company is trying to tie future rewards more closely to its strategy by focusing more on merit bonuses paid for a combination of individual, group, and corporate performance. The company's strategy is to be a top utility by "continuously improving our operations to be the lowest cost, most reliable and most environmentally sound energy provider."

If Xcel can excel at its merit-pay program, it will be far ahead of the average company. Typically, corporations try to keep everyone satisfied by spreading a rather small pool of merit pay fairly evenly across all employees. Recently, the average share of the payroll budget devoted to merit pay was just 4 percent. With a budget that size, at many companies, a top performer might get a bonus that is just 2 percentage points higher than that of an average worker. The average and poor workers might be happy, but the best people might actually be annoyed.

One way Xcel is addressing this challenge is to channel more of the merit-pay budget to nonmanagement employees. Managers' merit increases are limited to 2 percent, freeing more money for everyone else. Then it is urging managers to give bigger raises and bonuses to the best employees. Chief financial officer Ben Fowke says this arrangement is intended to "send a signal about how you can be rewarded if you're a performer."

Xcel is also considering a long-term incentive plan for nonmanagement employees. Managers already can earn bonuses in the form of stock shares. The company may extend the stock plan to employees who are not managers.

As Xcel develops these programs, it is keeping issues of fairness in mind. An unfair compensation arrangement will fail as an incentive for good performance. One outcome is that when rising health care costs forced Xcel to begin deducting more for health insurance from employees' paychecks, the company also cut some perks for its executives, including medical coverage without a deductible, free financial planning, and home security systems. Michael Connelly, Xcel's vice president of human resources, explains the decision this way: "Employees understand that executives are going to be paid more, but they also respond well when they see a company being consistent in its actions."

SOURCE: Roy Harris, "Just Rewards," *CFO*, February 2007, pp. 71–74; and Xcel Energy, "About Us," Xcel Web site, www.xcelenergy.com, accessed February 25, 2008.

Questions

1. Based on the information given, do you agree with management's conclusion that merit pay can support Xcel's strategy better than paying for suggestions? Why or why not?

2. How might Xcel continue to encourage suggestions as it aligns incentive pay more closely with its strategy? How do you think employees might react to these changes?

3. Imagine that Xcel has asked you to be a consultant advising on how to improve its merit pay system. Make three suggestions for ensuring that merit pay at Xcel is effective as an incentive.

IT'S A WRAP!

www.mhhe.com/noefund3e is your source for **R**eviewing, **A**pplying, and **P**racticing the concepts you learned about in Chapter 12.

Review
- Chapter learning objectives
- Narrated lecture and iPod content
- Test Your Knowledge: Reinforcement Theory

Application
- Video case and quiz: "A Motivation Convention in Chicago"
- Self-Assessment: Test your money-talk skills
- Web Exercise: Inform yourself on compensation and benefits management

Practice
- Chapter quiz

NOTES

1. S. J. Wells, "No Results, No Raise," *HRMagazine*, May 2005, downloaded from Infotrac at http://web6.infotrac.galegroup.com.

2. This chapter draws freely on several literature reviews: B. Gerhart and G. T. Milkovich, "Employee Compensation: Research and Practice," in *Handbook*

of *Industrial and Organizational Psychology*, 2nd ed., eds. M. D. Dunnette and L. M. Hough (Palo Alto, CA: Consulting Psychologists Press, 1992), vol. 3; and B. Gerhart and S. L. Rynes, *Compensation: Theory, Evidence, and Strategic Implications* (Thousand Oaks, CA: Sage, 2003).

3. B. Gerhart and G. T. Milkovich, "Organizational Differences in Managerial Compensation and Financial Performance," *Academy of Management Journal* 33 (1990), pp. 663–91.

4. G. T. Milkovich and A. K. Wigdor, *Pay for Performance* (Washington, DC: National Academy Press, 1991); Gerhart and Milkovich, "Employee Compensation"; C. Trevor, B. Gerhart, and J. W. Boudreau, "Voluntary Turnover and Job Performance: Curvilinearity and the Moderating Influences of Salary Growth and Promotions," *Journal of Applied Psychology* 82 (1997), pp. 44–61; Salamin and P. W. Horm, "In Search of the Elusive U-Shaped Performance-Turnover Relationship: Are High Performing Swiss Bankers More Likely to Quit?" *Journal of Applied Psychology* 90 (2005), pp. 1204–16; and C. B. Cadsby, F. Song, and F. Tapon, "Sorting and Incentive Effects of Pay-for-Performance: An Experimental Investigation," *Academy of Management Journal* 50 (2007), pp. 387–405.

5. E. Tahmincioglu, "Gifts That Gall, Part 1 of 2," *Workforce Management*, April 2004, downloaded from Infotrac at http://web7.infotrac.galegroup.com.

6. R. D. Bretz, R. A. Ash, and G. F. Dreher, "Do People Make the Place? An Examination of the Attraction-Selection-Attrition Hypothesis," *Personnel Psychology* 42 (1989), pp. 561–81; T. A. Judge and R. D. Bretz, "Effect of Values on Job Choice Decisions," *Journal of Applied Psychology* 77 (1992), pp. 261–71; and D. M. Cable and T. A. Judge, "Pay Performance and Job Search Decisions: A Person-Organization Fit Perspective," *Personnel Psychology* 47 (1994), pp. 317–48.

7. E. A. Locke, D. B. Feren, V. M. McCaleb, K. N. Shaw, and A. T. Denny, "The Relative Effectiveness of Four Methods of Motivating Employee Performance," in *Changes in Working Life*, eds. K. D. Duncan, M. M. Gruenberg, and D. Wallis (New York: Wiley, 1980), pp. 363–88.

8. Gerhart and Milkovich, "Employee Compensation."

9. E. E. Lawler III, "Pay for Performance: A Strategic Analysis," in *Compensation and Benefits*, ed. L. R. Gomez-Mejia (Washington, DC: Bureau of National Affairs, 1989); A. M. Konrad and J. Pfeffer, "Do You Get What You Deserve? Factors Affecting the Relationship between Productivity and Pay," *Administrative Science Quarterly* 35 (1990), pp. 258–85; J. L. Medoff and K. G. Abraham, "Are Those Paid More Really More Productive? The Case of Experience," *Journal of Human Resources* 16 (1981), pp. 186–216;

and K. S. Teel, "Are Merit Raises Really Based on Merit?" *Personnel Journal* 65, no. 3 (1986), pp. 88–95.

10. F. Hansen, "Lackluster Performance," *Workforce Management*, November 5, 2007, pp. 38–45; and Jack Welch and Suzy Welch, "Give Till It Doesn't Hurt," *BusinessWeek*, February 11, 2008, downloaded from General Reference Center Gold, http://find.galegroup.com.

11. R. D. Bretz, G. T. Milkovich, and W. Read, "The Current State of Performance Appraisal Research and Practice," *Journal of Management* 18 (1992), pp. 321–52; R. L. Heneman, "Merit Pay Research," *Research in Personnel and Human Resource Management* 8 (1990), pp. 203–63; and Milkovich and Wigdor, *Pay for Performance*.

12. Bretz et al., "Current State of Performance Appraisal Research."

13. S. L. Rynes, B. Gerhart, and L. Parks, "Personnel Psychology: Performance Evaluation and Compensation," *Annual Review of Psychology* (2005).

14. W. E. Deming, *Out of the Crisis* (Cambridge, MA: Center for Advanced Engineering Study, Massachusetts Institute of Technology, 1986), p. 110.

15. T. Chapelle, "Payday to Test Loyalty to the New Wachovia," *On Wall Street*, November 1, 2007, downloaded from General Reference Center Gold, http://find.galegroup.com.

16. J. Bennett, "A Career on Commission Can Be a Hard Sell," *Chicago Tribune*, March 24, 2002, sec. 5, p. 5.

17. T. L. Ross and R. A. Ross, "Gainsharing: Sharing Improved Performance," in *The Compensation Handbook*, 3rd ed., eds. M. L. Rock and L. A. Berger (New York: McGraw-Hill, 1991).

18. T. M. Welbourne and L. R. Gomez-Mejia, "Team Incentives in the Workplace," in *The Compensation Handbook*, 3rd ed.

19. D. Harbrecht, "Baxter's Harry Kraemer: 'I Don't Golf,'" *BusinessWeek Online*, March 28, 2002, www.xcelenergy.com (interview with Harry Kraemer Jr.).

20. L. R. Gomez-Mejia and D. B. Balkin, *Compensation, Organizational Strategy, and Firm Performance* (Cincinnati: South-Western, 1992).

21. J. A. Fossum, *Labor Relations* (New York: McGraw-Hill, 2002).

22. This idea has been referred to as the "share economy." See M. L. Weitzman, "The Simple Macroeconomics of Profit Sharing," *American Economic Review* 75 (1985), pp. 937–53. For supportive research, see the following studies: J. Chelius and R. S. Smith, "Profit Sharing and Employment Stability," *Industrial and Labor Relations Review* 43 (1990), pp. 256S–73S; B. Gerhart and L. O. Trevor, "Employment Stability under Different Managerial Compensation Systems," working paper (Cornell University Center for Advanced Human Resource

Studies, 1995); D. L. Kruse, "Profit Sharing and Employment Variability: Microeconomic Evidence on the Weitzman Theory," *Industrial and Labor Relations Review* 44 (1991), pp. 437–53.

23. Gerhart and Milkovich, "Employee Compensation"; M. L. Weitzman and D. L. Kruse, "Profit Sharing and Productivity," in *Paying for Productivity*, ed. A. S. Blinder (Washington, DC: Brookings Institution, 1990); D. L. Kruse, *Profit Sharing: Does It Make a Difference?* (Kalamazoo, MI: Upjohn Institute, 1993); and M. Magnan and S. St.-Onge, "The Impact of Profit Sharing on the Performance of Financial Services Firms," *Journal of Management Studies* 42 (2005), pp. 761–91.

24. Jan Norman, "Engineering Firm Makes Layoffs the Last Option," *Orange County Register,* March 23, 2005, downloaded from Infotrac at http://web7.infotrac.galegroup.com.

25. Gerhart and Milkovich, "Organizational Differences in Managerial Compensation."

26. Arik Hesseldahl, "The SEC Subpoenas Jobs over Backdating," *BusinessWeek Online,* September 21, 2007, downloaded from General Reference Center Gold, http://find.galegroup.com; and S. Reisinger, "It's What You Know," *Corporate Counsel,* January 2008, p. 17 (interview with John Villa). See also S. Reisinger, "Feds Look to Send First GC to Trial on Backdating," *Fulton County Daily Report,* January 23, 2008, http://find.galegroup.com.

27. National Center for Employee Ownership, "A Statistical Profile of Employee Ownership," Research & Statistics page of NCEO Web site, updated February 2008, www.nceo.org.

28. M. A. Conte and J. Svejnar, "The Performance Effects of Employee Ownership Plans," in *Paying for Productivity,* pp. 245–94.

29. Ibid.; T. H. Hammer, "New Developments in Profit Sharing, Gainsharing, and Employee Ownership," in *Productivity in Organizations,* eds. J. P. Campbell, R. J. Campbell, et al. (San Francisco: Jossey-Bass, 1988); and K. J. Klein, "Employee Stock Ownership and Employee Attitudes: A Test of Three Models," *Journal of Applied Psychology* 72 (1987), pp. 319–32.

30. R. T. Kaufman, "The Effects of Improshare on Productivity," *Industrial and Labor Relations Review* 45 (1992), pp. 311–22; M. H. Schuster, "The Scanlon Plan: A Longitudinal Analysis," *Journal of Applied Behavioral Science* 20 (1984), pp. 23–28; and J. A. Wagner III, P. Rubin, and T. J. Callahan, "Incentive Payment and Nonmanagerial Productivity: An Interrupted Time Series Analysis of Magnitude and Trend," *Organizational Behavior and Human Decision Processes* 42 (1988), pp. 47–74.

31. C. R. Gowen III and S. A. Jennings, "The Effects of Changes in Participation and Group Size on Gainsharing Success: A Case Study," *Journal of Organizational Behavior Management* 11 (1991), pp. 147–69.

32. D. I. Levine and L. D. Tyson, "Participation, Productivity, and the Firm's Environment," in *Paying for Productivity.*

33. T. Welbourne, D. Balkin, and L. Gomez-Mejia, "Gainsharing and Mutual Monitoring: A Combined Agency–Organizational Justice Interpretation," *Academy of Management Journal* 38 (1995), pp. 881–99.

34. Gerhart and Milkovich, "Organizational Differences in Managerial Compensation."

Providing Employee Benefits

Introduction

Patagonia has a long and strong reputation for caring about the environment and helping customers enjoy nature while using its top-quality recreational gear and clothing. The Ventura, California–based company carries out its mission to build the best products while reducing its environmental impact through dedicated people who deliver results. Most are drawn to Patagonia by its mission. Pay rates are, at best, only slightly above the market rate, but generous benefits help to keep talented employees on board. All Patagonia employees, full- and part-time, receive a full health insurance package, and the headquarters boasts an on-site day care center. In addition, the company will pay employees for a sabbatical of up to two months that is spent working for environmental groups.[1]

Like Patagonia's employees, employees at almost every organization receive more than dollars and cents in exchange for their efforts. They also receive a package of **employee benefits**—compensation in forms other than cash. Besides the use of corporate fitness centers, examples include paid vacation time, employer-paid health insurance, and pension plans, among a wide range of possibilities.

This chapter describes the contents of an employee benefits package and the way organizations administer employee benefits. We begin by discussing the important role of benefits as a part of employee compensation. The following sections define major types of employee benefits: benefits required by law, paid leave, insurance policies, retirement plans, and other benefits. We then discuss how to choose which of these alternatives to include in an employee benefits package so that it contributes to meeting the organization's goals. The next section summarizes the regulations affecting how employers design and administer benefits programs. Finally, we explain why and how organizations should effectively communicate with employees about their benefits.

chapter thirteen

The Role of Employee Benefits

As a part of the total compensation paid to employees, benefits serve functions similar to pay. Benefits contribute to attracting, retaining, and motivating employees. The variety of possible benefits also helps employers tailor their compensation to the kinds of employees they need. Different employees look for different types of benefits. Employers need to examine their benefits package regularly to see whether they meet the needs of today. At the same time, benefits packages are more complex than pay structures, so benefits are harder for employees to understand and appreciate. Even if employers spend large sums on benefits, if employees do not understand how to use them or why they are valuable, the cost of the benefits will be largely wasted.[2] Employers need to communicate effectively so that the benefits succeed in motivating employees. As the "HR Oops!" box highlights, it's important to know what benefits employees value.

Employees have come to expect that benefits will help them maintain economic security. Social Security contributions, pensions, and retirement savings plans help employees prepare for their retirement. Insurance plans help to protect employees from unexpected costs such as hospital bills. This important role of benefits is one reason that benefits are subject to government regulation. Some benefits, such as Social Security, are required by law. Other regulations establish requirements that benefits must meet to obtain the most favorable tax treatment. Later in the chapter, we will describe some of the most significant regulations affecting benefits.

Even though many kinds of benefits are not required by law, they have become so common that today's employees expect them. Many employers find that attracting qualified workers requires them to provide medical and retirement benefits of some sort. A large employer without such benefits would be highly unusual and would have difficulty competing in the labor market. Still, the nature of the benefits package changes over time, as we will discuss at various points throughout the chapter.

Like other forms of compensation, benefits impose significant costs. On average, out of every dollar spent on compensation, 30 cents or more go to benefits. As Figure 13.1 shows, this share has grown over the past decades. These numbers indicate that an organization managing its labor costs must pay careful attention to the cost of its employee benefits.

Why do organizations pay a growing share of compensation in the form of benefits? It would be simpler to pay all compensation in cash and let employees buy their own insurance and contribute to their own savings plans. That arrangement would also give employees greater control over what their compensation buys. However, several forces have made benefits a significant part of compensation packages. One is that laws require employers to provide certain benefits, such as contributions to Social Security and unemployment insurance. Also, tax laws can make benefits favorable to employees. For example, employees do not pay income taxes on most benefits they receive, but they pay income taxes on cash compensation. Therefore, an employee who receives a $1,000 raise "takes home" less than the full $1,000, but an employee who receives an additional $1,000 worth of benefits receives the full benefits. Another cost advantage of paying benefits is that employers, especially large ones, often can get a better deal on insurance or other programs than employees can obtain on their own. Finally, some employers assemble creative benefits packages that set them apart in the

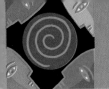

HR Oops!

Thankless Employees

One manager was so committed to motivating his employees that he took them out to lunch every week—a substantial investment of time and money. At first, employees seemed to appreciate the attention. But after a while, they began take the outings for granted and stopped thanking him. Soon the manager wondered why he even bothered.

Of course, it's always courteous to say thank you, but this case also brings up an important business question: Is the manager making careful choices about how to reward employees effectively?

If the employees don't appreciate the reward, then the reward is not effective.

One change the manager might make would be to investigate what his employees value. Maybe they would rather have the same amount of money or time to use as they choose. If the lunchtime outings are simply an opportunity to discuss work, it might be better to hold the meetings during working hours. Finally, the frequency of the meetings raises a red flag; 50 lunches a year likely feels less and less like a privilege and more and more like a routine. The lesson? Before you

offer a benefit, make sure your employees want it.

Source: "Ask Inc.," Inc., July 2007, pp. 56–57.

Questions

1. Do you think you would appreciate having lunch with your manager once a week? Why or why not? Do you think this manager was realistic to assume his employees would appreciate this benefit?

2. Suggest one way for this manager to make the lunch benefit more valuable.

competition for talent. For example, International Business Machines and Texas Instruments offer an online course that helps employees cope with the demands of being a caregiver for an ill family member, while Pitney Bowes and Marriott International offer insurance that pays the full cost of drugs for chronic conditions like asthma and high blood pressure.[3]

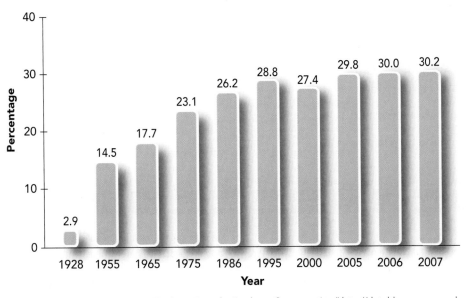

Figure 13.1

Benefits as a Percentage of Total Compensation

SOURCE: Bureau of Labor Statistics, "Employer Costs for Employee Compensation," http://data.bls.gov, accessed March 6, 2008.

Benefits Required by Law

LO2 Summarize the types of employee benefits required by law.

The federal and state governments require various forms of social insurance to protect workers from the financial hardships of being out of work. In general, Social Security provides support for retired workers, unemployment insurance assists laid-off workers, and workers' compensation insurance provides benefits and services to workers injured on the job. Employers must also provide unpaid leave for certain family and medical needs. Because these benefits are required by law, employers cannot gain an advantage in the labor market by offering them, nor can they design the nature of these benefits. Rather, the emphasis must be on complying with the details of the law. Table 13.1 summarizes legally required benefits.

Social Security
The federal Old Age, Survivors, Disability, and Health Insurance (OASDHI) program, which combines old age (retirement) insurance, survivor's insurance, disability insurance, hospital insurance (Medicare Part A), and supplementary medical insurance (Medicare Part B) for the elderly.

Social Security

In 1935 the federal Social Security Act established old-age insurance and unemployment insurance. Congress later amended the act to add survivor's insurance (1939), disability insurance (1956), hospital insurance (Medicare Part A, 1965), and supplementary medical insurance (Medicare Part B, 1965) for the elderly. Together, the law and its amendments created what is now the Old Age, Survivors, Disability, and Health Insurance (OASDHI) program, informally known as **Social Security.** This program covers over 90 percent of U.S. employees. The main exceptions are railroad and federal, state, and local government employees, who often have their own plans.

Kathleen Casey-Kirschling was the first of the baby boomers to begin receiving Social Security benefits. The widening gap between those contributing to the system and those receiving benefits is a major concern.

Workers who meet eligibility requirements receive the retirement benefits according to their age and earnings history. If they elect to begin receiving benefits at full retirement age, they can receive full benefits, or if they elect to begin receiving benefits at age 62, they receive benefits at a permanently reduced level. The full retirement age rises with birth year: a person born in 1940 reaches full retirement age at 65 years and 6 months, and a person born in 1960 or later reaches full retirement age at 67. The benefit amount rises with the person's past earnings, but the level goes up very little after a certain level. In 2008, the maximum monthly benefit was $2,185. The government increases the payments each year according to the growth in the consumer price index. Also, spouses of covered earners receive benefits, even if they have no covered earnings. They receive either the benefit associated with their own earnings or one-half of the amount received by the covered earner, whichever is greater.

Table 13.1

Benefits Required by Law

BENEFIT	EMPLOYER REQUIREMENT
Social Security	Flat payroll tax on employees and employers
Unemployment insurance	Payroll tax on employers that depends on state requirements and experience rating
Workers' compensation insurance	Provide coverage according to state requirements. Premiums depend on experience rating
Family and medical leave	Up to 12 weeks of unpaid leave for childbirth, adoption, or serious illness

Benefits may be reduced if the worker is still earning wages above a maximum, called the *exempt amount*. In 2008, the exempt amount was $13,560 for beneficiaries under the full retirement age. A beneficiary in that age range who earns more than the exempt amount sees a reduction in his or her benefit. The amount of the reduction is $1 for every $2 the person earns above the exempt amount. For example a 63-year-old who earned $15,560 in 2008 would have earned $2,000 above the exempt amount, so the person's Social Security benefits would be reduced by $1,000. During the year a worker reaches full retirement age, the maximum untaxed earnings are $36,120 (in 2008), and benefits are reduced $1 for every $3 in earnings. Beginning in the month they reach full retirement age, workers face no reduction in benefits for earning above the exempt amount. For workers below that age, the penalty increases the incentive to retire or at least reduce the number of hours worked. Adding to this incentive, Social Security benefits are free from federal income taxes and free from state taxes in about half the states.

Employers and employees share the cost of Social Security through a payroll tax. The percentage is set by law and has changed from time to time. In 2008, employers and employees each paid a tax of 7.65 percent on the first $102,000 of the employee's earnings, with 6.2 percent of earnings going to OASDI and 1.45 percent going to Medicare (Part A). For earnings above $102,000, only the 1.45 percent for Medicare is assessed.

Unemployment Insurance

Along with OASDHI, the Social Security Act of 1935 established a program of **unemployment insurance.** This program has four objectives related to minimizing the hardships of unemployment. It provides payments to offset lost income during involuntary unemployment, and it helps unemployed workers find new jobs. The payment of unemployment insurance taxes gives employers an incentive to stabilize employment. And providing workers with income during short-term layoffs preserves investments in worker skills because workers can afford to wait to return to their employer, rather than start over with another organization. Technically, the federal government left it to each state's discretion to establish an unemployment insurance program. At the same time, the Social Security Act created a tax incentive structure that quickly led every state to establish the program.

unemployment insurance
A federally mandated program to minimize the hardships of unemployment through payments to unemployed workers, help in finding new jobs, and incentives to stabilize employment.

Most of the funding for unemployment insurance comes from federal and state taxes on employers. The federal tax rate is currently 0.8 percent of the first $7,000 of each employee's wages. The state tax rate varies. For a new employer, rates range from 1 percent to 6 percent, and the taxable wage base ranges from $7,000 to $32,200, so the amount paid depends a great deal on where the company is located.[4] Also, some states charge new employers whatever rate is the average for their industry, so the amount of tax paid in those states also depends on the type of business.

No state imposes the same tax rate on every employer in the state. The size of the unemployment insurance tax imposed on each employer depends on the employer's **experience rating**—the number of employees the company laid off in the past and the cost of providing them with unemployment benefits. Employers with a history of laying off a large share of their workforces pay higher taxes than those with few layoffs. In some states, an employer with very few layoffs may pay no state tax. In contrast, an employer with a poor experience rating could pay a tax as high as 5.4 to 12.27 percent, depending on the state. The use of experience ratings gives employers some control over the cost of unemployment insurance. Careful human resource planning can minimize layoffs and keep their experience rating favorable.

experience rating
The number of employees a company has laid off in the past and the cost of providing them with unemployment benefits.

To receive benefits, workers must meet four conditions:

1. They meet requirements demonstrating they had been employed (often 52 weeks or four quarters of work at a minimum level of pay).
2. They are available for work.
3. They are actively seeking work. This requirement includes registering at the local unemployment office.
4. They were not discharged for cause (such as willful misconduct), did not quit voluntarily, and are not out of work because of a labor dispute (such as a union member on strike).

Workers who meet these conditions receive benefits at the level set by the state—typically about half the person's previous earnings—for a period of 26 weeks. States with a sustained unemployment rate above a particular threshold or significantly above recent levels also offer extended benefits for up to 13 weeks. Sometimes Congress funds emergency extended benefits. All states have minimum and maximum weekly benefit levels.

Workers' Compensation

workers' compensation
State programs that provide benefits to workers who suffer work-related injuries or illnesses, or to their survivors.

Decades ago, workers who suffered work-related injury or illness had to bear the cost unless they won a lawsuit against their employer. Those who sued often lost the case because of the defenses available to employers. Today, the states have passed **workers' compensation** laws, which help workers with the expenses resulting from job-related accidents and illnesses.[5] These laws operate under a principle of *no-fault liability*, meaning that an employee does not need to show that the employer was grossly negligent in order to receive compensation, and the employer is protected from lawsuits. The employer loses this protection if it intentionally contributes to a dangerous workplace. Employees are not eligible if their injuries are self-inflicted or if they result from intoxication or "willful disregard of safety rules."[6]

About 9 out of 10 U.S. workers are covered by state workers' compensation laws, with the level of coverage varying from state to state. The benefits fall into four major categories: (1) disability income, (2) medical care, (3) death benefits, and (4) rehabilitative services. The amount of income varies from state to state but is typically two-thirds of the worker's earnings before the disability. The benefits are tax free.

The states differ in terms of how they fund workers' compensation insurance. Some states have a single state fund. Most states allow employers to purchase coverage from private insurance companies. Most also permit self-funding by employers. The cost of the workers' compensation insurance depends on the kinds of occupations involved, the state where the company is located, and the employer's experience rating. Premiums for low-risk occupations may be less than 1 percent of payroll. For some of the most hazardous occupations, the cost may be as high as 100 percent of payroll. Costs also vary from state to state, so that one state's program requires higher premiums than another state's program. As with unemployment insurance, unfavorable experience ratings lead to higher premiums. Organizations can minimize the cost of this benefit by keeping workplaces safe and making employees and their managers conscious of safety issues, as discussed in Chapter 3.

Unpaid Family and Medical Leave

Family and Medical Leave Act (FMLA)
Federal law requiring organizations with 50 or more employees to provide up to 12 weeks of unpaid leave after childbirth or adoption; to care for a seriously ill family member; or for an employee's own serious illness.

In the United States, unpaid leave is required by law for certain family needs. Specifically, the **Family and Medical Leave Act (FMLA)** of 1993 requires organizations with 50 or more employees within a 75-mile radius to provide as much as 12 weeks of unpaid leave after childbirth or adoption; to care for a seriously ill child, spouse, or parent; or for an employee's own serious illness. Employers must also guarantee these employees the same or a comparable job when they return to work. The law does not cover employees who have less than one year of service, work fewer than 25 hours per week, or are among the organization's 10 percent highest paid. The 12 weeks of unpaid leave amount to a smaller benefit than is typical of Japan and most countries in Western Europe. Japan and West European nations typically require paid family leave.

Experience with the Family and Medical Leave Act suggests that a majority of those opting for this benefit fail to take the full 12 weeks. In about one out of four situations, employees take their leave intermittently, over periods of days or even hours, creating a significant record-keeping task.[7] Other employees, especially female executives, are simply keeping parental leaves under FMLA to a minimum, less than the available 12 weeks. Many are eager to return to their careers, and others fear that staying away for three months would damage their career opportunities.[8] Of course, another reason for not taking the full 12 weeks is that not everyone can afford three months without pay, especially when responsible for the expenses that accompany childbirth, adoption, or serious illness.

When employees experience pregnancy and childbirth, employers must also comply with the Pregnancy Discrimination Act, described in Chapter 3. If an employee is temporarily unable to perform her job due to pregnancy, the employer must treat her in the same way as any other temporarily disabled employee. For example, the employer may provide modified tasks, alternative assignments, disability leave, or leave without pay.

Optional Benefits Programs

Other types of benefits are optional. These include various kinds of insurance, retirement plans, and paid leave. Figure 13.2 shows the percentage of full-time workers receiving the most common employee benefits. (Part-time workers often receive fewer benefits.) The most widely offered benefits are paid leave for vacations and holidays, life and medical insurance, and retirement plans. In general, benefits packages at smaller companies tend to be more limited than at larger companies.

Benefits such as health insurance often extend to employees' dependents. Traditionally, these benefits have covered employees, their spouses, and dependent children. Today, many employers also cover *domestic partners,* defined either by local law or by the companies themselves. Typically, a domestic partner is an adult nonrelative who lives with the employee in a relationship defined as permanent and financially interdependent. Some local governments provide for registration of domestic partners. Organizations offering coverage to domestic partners generally require that the partners sign a document stating they meet the requirements for a domestic partnership. Benefits provided to domestic partners do not have the same tax advantages as benefits provided to spouses. The partner's benefits are taxed as wages of the employee receiving the benefits.

Paid Leave

The major categories of paid leave are vacations, holidays, and sick leave. Employers also should establish policies for other situations that may require time off. Organizations often provide for paid leave for jury duty, funerals of family members, and military duty. Some organizations provide for other paid leave, such as time off to

LO3 Describe the most common forms of paid leave.

Figure 13.2

Percentage of Full-Time Workers with Access to Selected Benefit Programs

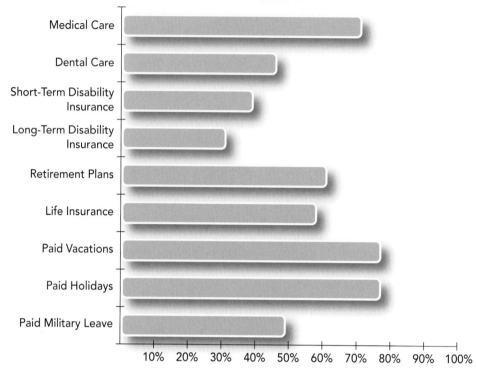

SOURCE: Bureau of Labor Statistics, "National Compensation Survey: Employee Benefits in Private Industry in the United States, March 2007," August 2007, http://stats.bls.gov.

vote or to donate blood. Establishing policies communicates the organization's values, clarifies what employees can expect, and prevents situations in which unequal treatment leads to claims of unfairness.

At first blush, paid vacation, holidays, sick leave, and other paid leave may not seem to make economic sense. The employer pays the employee for time spent not working, so the employer receives nothing in return for the pay. Some employers may see little direct advantage. This may be the reason that Western European countries require a minimum number of paid vacation days, with new employees receiving 30 days off in many countries. The United States, in contrast, has no such legal requirement. It is up to U.S. employers to decide whether paid leave has a payoff in recruiting and retaining employees. At U.S. companies, paid vacation is typically two weeks or less a year for the first few years (see the "Did You Know?" box). To receive as much vacation as European employees, U.S. workers must typically stay with an employer for more than 20 years.[9]

Paid holidays are time off on specified days in addition to vacation time. In Western Europe and the United States, employees typically have about 10 paid holidays each year, regardless of length of service. The most common paid holidays in the United States are New Year's Day, Memorial Day, Independence Day, Labor Day, Thanksgiving Day, and Christmas Day.

Sick leave programs pay employees for days not worked because of illness. The amount of sick leave is often based on length of service, so that it accumulates over time—for example, one day added to sick leave for each month of service. Employers must decide how many sick days to grant and whether to let them continue accumulating year after year. If sick days accumulate without limit, employees can

Did You Know?

U.S. Workers Take Short Vacations

On average, workers in the United States are allowed 14 days of vacation, but they typically take only 11 days.

Source: David Futrelle, "What Goes On beyond the Cubicle Wall," *Money,* December 2007, downloaded from General Reference Center Gold, http://find.galegroup.com.

Average number of vacation days allowed

Average number of vacation days taken

"save" them in case of disability. If an employee becomes disabled, the employee can use up the accumulated sick days, receiving full pay rather than smaller payments from disability insurance, discussed later. Some employers let sick days accumulate for only a year, and unused sick days "disappear" at year-end. This may provide an unintended incentive to use up sick days. Some healthy employees may call in sick near the end of the year so that they can obtain the benefit of the paid leave before it disappears. Employers may counter this tendency by paying employees for some or all of their unused sick days at year-end or when the employees retire or resign.

An organization's policies for time off may include other forms of paid and unpaid leave. For a workforce that values flexibility, the organization may offer paid *personal days*, days off that employees may schedule according to their personal needs, with the supervisor's approval. Typically, organizations offer a few personal days in addition

Paid time off is a way for employees to enjoy time with their families and to refresh their bodies and spirits. Is paid time off an important criteria for you when accepting a position?

to sick leave. *Floating holidays* are paid holidays that vary from year to year. The organization may schedule floating holidays so that they extend a Tuesday or Thursday holiday into a long weekend. Organizations may also give employees discretion over the scheduling of floating holidays.

The most flexible approach to time off is to grant each employee a bank of *paid time off*, in which the employer pools personal days, sick days, and vacation days for employees to use as the need or desire arises. This flexibility is especially attractive to younger workers, who tend to rate work/life balance as one of the most important sources of job satisfaction. The flexibility also fits with the U.S. trend toward more frequent but shorter vacations.

Employers should also establish policies for leaves without pay—for example, leaves of absence to pursue nonwork goals or to meet family needs. Unpaid leave is an employee benefit because the employee usually retains seniority and benefits during the leave.

LO4 Identify the kinds of insurance benefits offered by employers.

Group Insurance

As we noted earlier, rates for group insurance are typically lower than for individual policies. Also, insurance benefits are not subject to income tax, as wages and salaries are. When employees receive insurance as a benefit, rather than higher pay so they can buy their own insurance, employees can get more for their money. Because of this, most employees value group insurance. The most common types of insurance offered as employee benefits are medical, life, and disability insurance.

Medical Insurance

For the average person, the most important benefit by far is medical insurance.[10] As Figure 13.2 shows, about seven out of every ten full-time employees receive medical benefits. The policies typically cover three basic types of medical expenses: hospital expenses, surgical expenses, and visits to physicians. Some employers offer additional coverage, such as dental care, vision care, birthing centers, and prescription drug programs. Under the Mental Health Parity Act of 1996, health insurance plans offered to employees must have the same maximum dollar benefits for covered mental illness as for other medical and surgical benefits. Some states have stricter requirements than the federal law. However, insurance plans can and do impose other restrictions on mental health care, such as limits on the number of days of hospitalization, and some employers avoid the restrictions by offering insurance without any mental health coverage.[11]

Consolidated Omnibus Budget Reconciliation Act (COBRA)
Federal law that requires employers to permit employees or their dependents to extend their health insurance coverage at group rates for up to 36 months following a qualifying event, such as a layoff, reduction in hours, or the employee's death.

Employers that offer medical insurance must meet the requirements of the **Consolidated Omnibus Budget Reconciliation Act (COBRA)** of 1985. This federal law requires employers to permit employees to extend their health insurance coverage at group rates for up to 36 months following a "qualifying event." Qualifying events include termination (except for gross misconduct), a reduction in hours that leads to loss of health insurance, and the employee's death (in which case the surviving spouse or dependent child would extend the coverage). To extend the coverage, the employee or the surviving spouse or dependent must pay for the insurance, but the payments are at the group rate. These employees and their families must have access to the same services as those who did not lose their health insurance.

Figure 13.3

Health Care Costs in
Various Countries

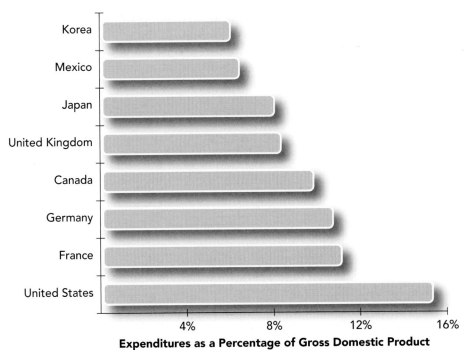

Expenditures as a Percentage of Gross Domestic Product

SOURCE: Organization for Economic Cooperation and Development, "Demography and Health: Health Spending and Resources," *OECD in Figures 2007,* www.oecd.org.

As we will discuss later in the chapter, health insurance is a significant and fast-growing share of benefits costs at U.S. organizations. Figure 13.3 shows that the United States spends much more of its total wealth on health care than other countries do. Most Western European countries have nationalized health systems, but the majority of Americans with coverage for health care expenses get it through their own or a family member's employer. As a result, a growing number of employees whose employers cannot afford this benefit are left without insurance to cover health care expenses.

Employers have looked for ways to control the cost of health care coverage while keeping this valuable benefit. They have used variations of managed care, employee-driven savings, and promotion of employee wellness:

- With *managed care*, the insurer plays a role in decisions about health care, aimed at avoiding unnecessary procedures. The insurer may conduct claims review, studying claims to determine whether procedures are effective for the type of illness or injury. Patients may be required to obtain approval before hospital admissions, and the insurer may require alternatives to hospital stays—for example, outpatient surgery or home health care.
- A **health maintenance organization (HMO)** is a health care plan that requires patients to receive their medical care from the HMO's health care professionals, who are often paid a flat salary, and provides all services on a prepaid basis. In other words, the premiums paid for the HMO cover all the patient's visits and procedures, without an additional payment from the patient. By paying physicians a salary, rather than a fee for each service, the HMO hopes to remove any incentive to provide more services than the patients really need. HMO coverage tends to cost less than traditional health insurance. The downside is that employees sometimes complain cost-control incentives work so well that they are denied access to services they actually need.

health maintenance organization (HMO)
A health care plan that requires patients to receive their medical care from the HMO's health care professionals, who are often paid a flat salary, and provides all services on a prepaid basis.

preferred provider organization (PPO)
A health care plan that contracts with health care professionals to provide services at a reduced fee and gives patients financial incentives to use network providers.

flexible spending account
Employee-controlled pretax earnings set aside to pay for certain eligible expenses such as health care expenses during the same year.

employee wellness program (EWP)
A set of communications, activities, and facilities designed to change health-related behaviors in ways that reduce health risks.

- A **preferred provider organization (PPO)** is a health care plan that contracts with health care professionals to provide services at a reduced fee. Often, the PPO does not require employees to use providers in the network, but it pays a larger share of the cost of services from PPO providers. For example, the employee might pay 10 percent of the cost of a test by an in-network provider and 20 percent if the employee goes out of the PPO network. PPOs have quickly grown to become the most widely used health plan among U.S. employers. Recent data found that among workers with health insurance, about two-thirds were enrolled in a PPO; most of the remainder—almost one-fourth—were in an HMO.[12]

- With a **flexible spending account,** employees set aside a portion of pretax earnings to pay for eligible expenses. In particular, a *medical savings account* lets employees use their pretax savings to pay for qualified health care expenses (for example, payment of premiums). To avoid taxation, the money in the account must meet IRS requirements. Contributions to this account may not exceed $5,000 per year and must be designated in advance. The money in the account may be spent on health care expenses of the employee and employee's dependents during the plan year. At the end of the year, any remaining funds in the account revert to the employer. The major advantage of flexible spending accounts is that the money in the account is not taxed, so employees will have more take-home pay. But if they do not use all the money in the flexible spending account, they lose the amount they do not spend. Therefore, employees are most likely to benefit from a flexible spending account if they have predictable health care expenses, such as insurance premiums.

- *Consumer-driven health plans* (CDHPs) are intended to provide health coverage in a way that gets employees involved as consumers making decisions to lower costs. A CDHP typically brings together three elements: insurance with a high deductible, a medical savings account in which the employer contributes to employee-controlled accounts for paying expenses below the deductible, and health education aimed at helping employees improve their health and thus lower their need for health care. Whole Foods Market is one of the few companies that have offered this type of plan so far. But many others are investigating the idea, and some, including Quest Diagnostics and Lockheed Martin, have offered this type of plan as one option for employees.[13]

- An **employee wellness program (EWP)** is a set of communications, activities, and facilities designed to change health-related behaviors in ways that reduce health risks. Typically, an EWP aims at specific health risks, such as high blood pressure, high cholesterol levels, smoking, and obesity, by encouraging preventive measures such as exercise and good nutrition. *Passive* programs provide information and services, but no formal support or motivation to use the program. Examples include health education (such as lunchtime courses) and fitness facilities. *Active* wellness programs assume that behavior change requires support and reinforcement along with awareness and opportunity. Such a program may include counselors who tailor programs to individual employees' needs, take baseline measurements (for example, blood pressure and weight), and take follow-up measures for comparison to the baseline. In general, passive health education programs cost less than fitness facilities and active wellness programs.[14] All these variations

Tom Johnson runs on a treadmill at the Western & Southern Financial Group headquarters building in Cincinnati. The company is encouraging employees to reduce their health risks as insurance costs climb. Can you think of firms that offer other unique benefits to reduce health risks?

Best Practices

Wellness Matters at Worthington Industries

Back in the 1980s, when the idea of an employee wellness program was still a novelty, Worthington Industries signed on. The metals manufacturer set up a gym at its headquarters so that employees could easily get some exercise. Soon after, Worthington started offering free classes in yoga, step aerobics, and cardio fitness. In 1995, the company expanded its facilities, building a complete wellness center, where employees could visit a doctor, have lab tests performed, and pick up a prescription.

But facilities alone weren't enough. In 2003, the cost of health insurance was still on the rise, and CEO John McConnell decided employees needed further incentives to take care of their health. So the company launched a program called Healthy Choices, aimed at targeting employees' individual health challenges. Of course, not

everyone is excited about the opportunity to lose weight or lower their blood pressure, so Worthington provides incentives. Anyone who participates in the Healthy Choices program receives up to $50 a month to offset part of their health insurance premiums.

Healthy Choices coaches employees toward achieving a variety of health goals, such as smoking cessation, better eating habits, and getting more exercise. In the first two years that the company began offering the program, its health insurance claims were a total of $2.5 million lower. That savings is more than twice the amount the company spent to offer Healthy Choices.

As spectacular as those results may sound, they are hardly unique to Worthington Industries. Research has found that companies using wellness programs can see their insurance

claims drop by 15 percent, saving millions of dollars at a large company. These programs are most likely to work if, as at Worthington, they have the support of the company's leadership and deliver incentives for participating. Finally, companies should support—and avoid sabotaging—their wellness program by encouraging wellness throughout the workplace. Simple measures, such as installing a bike rack for commuters, encouraging stretch breaks, and ordering fruit instead of doughnuts to serve at meetings, can keep employees on track toward improving their health.

Source: Lisa Takeuchi Cullen, "The Company Doctor," *Time,* June 25, 2007, Global Business section, p. 4; Andrew Sykes, "The Secrets to Success in Wellness Programs: Leadership, Incentives, Healthy Workplace," *Industry Week,* January 1, 2008, www.industryweek.com: "Awards," Worthington Industries Web site, www.worthingtonindustries.com, accessed March 11, 2008.

have had success in reducing risk factors associated with cardiovascular disease (obesity, high blood pressure, smoking, lack of exercise), but the follow-up method is most successful. The "Best Practices" box discusses one company's experiences with its wellness program.

Life Insurance

Employers may provide life insurance to employees or offer the opportunity to buy coverage at low group rates. With a *term life insurance* policy, if the employee dies during the term of the policy, the employee's beneficiaries receive a payment called the death benefit. In policies purchased as an employee benefit, the usual death benefit is twice the employee's yearly pay. The policies may provide additional benefits for accidental death and dismemberment (loss of a body part such as a hand or foot). Along with a basic policy, the employer may give employees the option of purchasing additional coverage, usually at a nominal cost.

Disability Insurance

Employees risk losing their incomes if a disability makes them unable to work. Disability insurance provides protection against this loss of income. Typically, **short-term disability**

short-term disability insurance
Insurance that pays a percentage of a disabled employee's salary as benefits to the employee for six months or less.

long-term disability insurance
Insurance that pays a percentage of a disabled employee's salary after an initial period and potentially for the rest of the employee's life.

contributory plan
Retirement plan funded by contributions from the employer and employee.

noncontributory plan
Retirement plan funded entirely by contributions from the employer.

LO5 Define the types of retirement plans offered by employers.

defined-benefit plan
Pension plan that guarantees a specified level of retirement income.

insurance provides benefits for six months or less. **Long-term disability insurance** provides benefits after that initial period, potentially for the rest of the disabled employee's life. Disability payments are a percentage of the employee's salary—typically 50 to 70 percent. Payments under short-term plans may be higher. Often the policy sets a maximum amount that may be paid each month. Because its limits make it more affordable, short-term disability coverage is offered by more employers. Fewer than half of employers offer long-term plans.

In planning an employee benefits package, the organization should keep in mind that Social Security includes some long-term disability benefits. To manage benefits costs, the employer should ensure that the disability insurance is coordinated with Social Security and any other programs that help workers who become disabled.

Long-Term Care Insurance

The cost of long-term care, such as care in a nursing home, can be devastating. Today, with more people living to an advanced age, many people are concerned about affording long-term care. Some employers address this concern by offering long-term care insurance. These policies provide benefits toward the cost of long-term care and related medical expenses.

Retirement Plans

Despite the image of retired people living on their Social Security checks, Figure 13.4 shows that those checks amount to less than half of a retired person's income. Among persons over age 65, pensions provided a significant share of income in 2006. Employers have no obligation to offer retirement plans beyond the protection of Social Security, but most offer some form of pension or retirement savings plan. About half of employees working for private businesses (that is, nongovernment jobs) have employer-sponsored retirement plans. These plans are most common for higher-earning employees. Among employees earning the top one-fifth of incomes, almost three-quarters have a pension plan, and about one out of six employees in the bottom fifth have pensions.[15] Retirement plans may be **contributory plans,** meaning they are funded by contributions from the employer and employee, or **noncontributory plans,** meaning all the contributions come from the employer.

Defined-Benefit Plans

Employers have a choice of using retirement plans that define the amount to be paid out after retirement or plans that define the amount the employer will invest each year. A **defined-benefit plan** guarantees a specified level of retirement income. Usually the amount of this defined benefit is calculated for each employee based on the employee's years of service, age, and earnings level (for example, the average of the employee's five highest-earnings years). These calculations typically result in pension payments that range from 20 percent of final salary for an employee who is relatively young and has few years of service to 35 percent of the final salary of an older employee who has spent many years with the organization. Using

Figure 13.4

Sources of Income for Persons 65 and Older

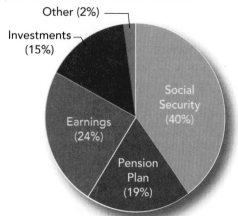

SOURCE: Employee Benefit Research Institute, "Fast Facts from EBRI," no. 69, December 12, 2007, www.ebri.org.

years of service as part of the basis for calculating benefits gives employees an incentive to stay with the organization as long as they can, so it can help to reduce voluntary turnover.

Defined-benefit plans must meet the funding requirements of the **Employee Retirement Income Security Act (ERISA)** of 1974. This law increased the responsibility of pension plan trustees to protect retirees, established certain rights related to vesting (earning a right to receive the pension) and *portability* (being able to move retirement savings when changing employers), and created the **Pension Benefit Guarantee Corporation (PBGC).** The PBGC is the federal agency that insures retirement benefits and guarantees retirees a basic benefit if the employer experiences financial difficulties. To fund the PBGC, employers must make annual contributions of $33 per fund participant. Plans that are *underfunded*— meaning the employer does not contribute enough to the plan each year to meet future obligations—must pay an additional premium tied to the amount by which the plan is underfunded.[16] The PBGC's protection applies to the pensions of 44 million workers.

With a defined-benefit plan, the employer sets up a pension fund to invest the contributions. As required by ERISA, the employer must contribute enough for the plan to cover all the benefits to be paid out to retirees. Defined-benefit plans protect employees from the risk that the pension fund will not earn as much as expected. If the pension fund earns less than expected, the employer makes up the difference from other sources. If the employer experiences financial difficulties so that it must end or reduce employee pension benefits, the PBGC provides a basic benefit, which does not necessarily cover the full amount promised by the employer's pension plan. The PBGC establishes a maximum; in 2007, it was the lesser of $1/_{12}$ of an employee's annual gross income or $3,712 per month.

Defined-Contribution Plans

An alternative to defined benefits is a **defined-contribution plan,** which sets up an individual account for each employee and specifies the size of the investment into that account, rather than the amount to be paid out upon retirement. The amount the retiree receives will depend on the account's performance. Many kinds of defined-contribution plans are available, including the following:

- *Money purchase plan*—The employer specifies a level of annual contributions (for example, 10 percent of salary). The contributions are invested, and when the employee retires, he or she is entitled to receive the amount of the contributions plus the investment earnings. ("Money purchase" refers to the fact that when employees retire, they often buy an annuity with the money, rather than taking it as a lump sum.)
- *Profit-sharing and employee stock ownership plans*—As we saw in Chapter 12, incentive pay may take the form of profit sharing and employee stock ownership plans (ESOPs). These payments may be set up so that the money goes into retirement plans. By defining its contributions in terms of stock or a share of profits, the organization has more flexibility to contribute less dollar value in lean years and more in good years.
- *Section 401(k) plans*—Employees contribute a percentage of their earnings, and employers may make matching contributions. The amount employees contribute is not taxed as part of their income until they receive it from the plan. The federal government limits the amount that may be contributed each year. The limit for

Employee Retirement Income Security Act (ERISA)
Federal law that increased the responsibility of pension plan trustees to protect retirees, established certain rights related to vesting and portability, and created the Pension Benefit Guarantee Corporation.

Pension Benefit Guarantee Corporation (PBGC)
Federal agency that insures retirement benefits and guarantees retirees a basic benefit if the employer experiences financial difficulties.

defined-contribution plan
Retirement plan in which the employer sets up an individual account for each employee and specifies the size of the investment into that account.

2007 and 2008 was $15,500; it may increase by up to $500 a year through 2010, depending on the inflation rate. The contribution limits are higher for persons 50 and older.[17]

These plans free employers from the risks that investments will not perform as well as expected. They put the responsibility for wise investing squarely on the shoulders of each employee. A defined-contribution plan is also easier to administer. The employer need not calculate payments based on age and service, and payments to the PBGC are not required. Considering the advantages to employers, it is not surprising that a growing share of retirement plans are defined-contribution plans. Three decades ago, the majority of workers with pension plans had defined-benefit plans, and less than one-fourth had defined-contribution plans. Today, following a steady decline in the number of defined-benefit plans and a steady rise in the number of defined-contribution plans, that pattern is reversed.[18] Still, many organizations offer both kinds of retirement plans.

When retirement plans make individual employees responsible for investment decisions, the employees need information about retirement planning. Retirement savings plans often give employees much control over decisions about when and how much to invest. Many employees do not appreciate the importance of beginning to save early in their careers. As Figure 13.5 shows, an employee who invests $3,000 a year ($250 a month) between the ages of 21 and 29 will have far more at age 65 than an employee who invests the same amount between ages 31 and 39. Another important lesson is to diversify investments. Based on investment performance between 1946 and 1990, stocks earned an average of 11.4 percent per year, bonds earned 5.1 percent, and bank savings accounts earned 5.3 percent. But in any given year, one of these types of investments might outperform the other. And within the categories of stocks and bonds, it is important to invest in a wide variety of companies. If one company performs poorly, the investments in other companies might perform better.

However, studies of investment decisions by employees have found that many employees hold a sizable share of their retirement savings in stock of the company they work for, and few have followed basic guidelines for diversifying investments among stocks, bonds, and savings accounts according to their age and investment needs.[19] To help employees handle such risks, some organizations provide financial planning as a separate benefit, offer an option to have a professional invest the funds in a 401(k) plan, or direct funds into default investments geared toward the needs of employees at different life stages. For example, when a Portland, Oregon, developer called Classic American Homes found that its employees made poor investments, such as moving into risky real estate funds *after* real estate prices had been rising, the company began offering just one fund that combines 60 percent stocks and 40 percent bonds.

In spite of these challenges, defined-contribution plans also offer an advantage to employees in today's highly mobile workforce. They do not penalize employees for changing jobs. With these plans, retirement earnings are less related to the number of years an employee stays with a company.

Figure 13.5

Value of Retirement Savings Invested at Different Ages

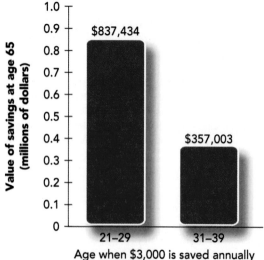

Note: Investment portfolio consists of 60 percent stocks, 30 percent bonds, and 10 percent cash (e.g., money-market funds, bank savings accounts), assuming average rates of return based on historical rates from 1946 to 1990.

Cash Balance Plans

An increasingly popular way to combine the advantages of defined-benefit plans and defined-contribution plans is to use a **cash balance plan.** This type of retirement plan consists of individual accounts, as in a 401(k) plan. But in contrast to a 401(k), all the contributions come from the employer. Usually, the employer contributes a percentage of the employee's salary, say, 4 or 5 percent. The money in the cash balance plan earns interest according to a predetermined rate, such as the rate paid on U.S. Treasury bills. Employers guarantee this rate as in a defined-benefit plan. This arrangement helps employers plan their contributions and helps employees predict their retirement benefits. If employees change jobs, they generally can roll over the balance into an individual retirement account.

A switch from traditional defined benefit plans to cash balance plans, like any major change, requires employers to consider the effects on employees as well as on the organization's bottom line. Defined-benefit plans are most generous to older employees with many years of service, and cash balance plans are most generous to young employees who will have many years ahead in which to earn interest. For an organization with many experienced employees, switching from a defined-benefit plan can produce great savings in pension benefits. In that case, the older workers are the greatest losers, unless the organization adjusts the program to retain their benefits. After IBM switched to a cash-benefit plan, a group of employees filed an age discrimination lawsuit. IBM won the lawsuit on appeal, and the Pension Protection Act of 2006 seeks to clarify the legal requirements of such plans. As a result, some companies may renew their interest in cash balance plans, but IBM has decided to focus on its 401(k) plan.

cash balance plan
Retirement plan in which the employer sets up an individual account for each employee and contributes a percentage of the employee's salary; the account earns interest at a predefined rate.

Government Requirements for Vesting and Communication

Along with requirements for funding defined-benefit plans, ERISA specifies a number of requirements related to eligibility for benefits and communication with employees. ERISA guarantees employees that when they become participants in a pension plan and work a specified number of years, they earn a right to a pension upon retirement. These rights are called **vesting rights.** Employees whose contributions are *vested* have met the requirements (enrolling and length of service) to receive a pension at retirement age, regardless of whether they remained with the employer until that time. Employees' own contributions to their pension plans are always completely vested. In most cases, the vesting of employer-funded pension benefits must take place under one of two schedules selected by the employer:

vesting rights
Guarantee that when employees become participants in a pension plan and work a specified number of years, they will receive a pension at retirement age, regardless of whether they remained with the employer.

1. The employer may vest employees after five years and may provide zero vesting until that time.
2. The employer may vest employees over a three- to seven-year period, with at least 20 percent vesting in the third year and at least an additional 20 percent in each year after the third year.

These two schedules represent minimum requirements. Employers may vest employees more quickly if they wish. Two less-common situations have different vesting requirements. One is a "top-heavy" pension plan, meaning pension benefits for *key employees* (such as highly paid top managers) exceed a government-specified share of total pension benefits. A top-heavy plan requires faster vesting for nonkey employees. Another exception from the usual schedule involves multiemployer pension plans. These plans need not provide vesting until after 10 years of employment.

The intent of vesting requirements is to protect employees by preventing employers from terminating them before they meet retirement age in order to avoid paying pension benefits. In addition, it is illegal for employers to transfer or lay off employees as a way to avoid pension obligations, even if these changes are motivated partly by business need.[20] One way employers may legally try to minimize pension costs is in choosing a vesting schedule. For example, if many employees leave after three or four years of employment, the five-year vesting schedule would minimize pension costs.

ERISA's reporting and disclosure requirements involve the Internal Revenue Service, the Department of Labor, and employees.[21] Within 90 days after employees enter a plan, they must receive a **summary plan description (SPD),** a report that describes the plan's funding, eligibility requirements, risks, and other details. If the employee requests one, the employer must also make available an individual benefit statement, which describes the employee's vested and unvested benefits. Many employers provide such information regularly, without waiting for employee requests. This type of communication helps employees understand and value their retirement benefits.

summary plan description (SPD)
Report that describes a pension plan's funding, eligibility requirements, risks, and other details.

LO6 Describe how organizations use other benefits to match employees' wants and needs.

"Family-Friendly" Benefits

As employers have recognized the significance of employees' need to manage conflicts between their work and family roles, many have added "family-friendly" benefits to their employee benefits. These benefits include family leave policies and child care. The programs discussed here apply directly to the subset of employees with family responsibilities. However, family-friendly benefits often have spillover effects in the form of loyalty because employees see the benefits as evidence that the organization cares about its people.[22] The following types of benefits are typical:

- *Family leave*—Family or parental leave grants employees time off to care for children and other dependents. As discussed earlier in the chapter, federal law requires 12 weeks of unpaid leave. Companies may choose to offer more generous leave policies. Paid family leave remains rare in the United States, however, despite some state laws. By contrast, more than 120 countries provide paid family leave by law. The norm in Western Europe is three to four months' maternity leave at 80 to 100 percent of pay, plus additional (often unpaid) parental leave for both parents.[23]

- *Child care*—Child care benefits may take several forms, requiring different levels of organizational involvement.[24] As shown in Figure 13.6, the lowest level of involvement, offered by 19 percent of companies with at least 100 workers, is for the organization to supply and help employees collect information about the cost and quality of available child care. At the next level, organizations provide vouchers or discounts for employees to use at existing child care facilities. At the highest level of involvement, the employer provides child care at or near the work site. Staffing a child care facility is costly and involves important liability concerns. At the same time, the results of this type of benefit, in terms of reducing absenteeism and enhancing productivity, have been mixed.[25] When Providian Financial Corporation, a credit card company with headquarters in San Francisco, determined that for many of its employees, the big hurdle with child care and elder care was affordability, it set up flexible spending accounts for dependent care.[26]

Figure 13.6

Percentage of Employers Offering Various Levels of Child Care Benefits

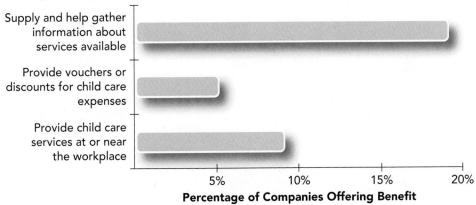

Percentage of Companies Offering Benefit

Note: Data for employers with 100 or more employees.

SOURCE: Bureau of Labor Statistics, "National Compensation Survey: Employee Benefits in Private Industry in the United States, March 2007," Summary 07-05, August 2007, http://stats.bls.gov.

- *College savings*—As workers' children grow up, their needs shift from maternity leave and child care to college tuition. Some organizations have supported this concern by sponsoring tax-favored *529 savings plans*. These plans, named after the section of the Internal Revenue Code that regulates them, let parents and other family members defer taxes on the earnings of their deposits into the 529 account. Some states also provide a (limited) tax deduction for these contributions. As an employee benefit, organizations can arrange with a broker to offer direct deposit of a portion of employees' paychecks into their accounts. Besides offering the convenience of direct deposit, employers can negotiate lower management fees. For example, Merrill Lynch charges half its usual management fee on 529 accounts set up through employers.[27]
- *Elder care*—As the population of the nation's elderly grows, so do the demands on adult children to care for elderly parents, aunts, and uncles. When these people become ill or disabled, they rely on family or professional caregivers. Responsibilities such as providing assistance, paying for professional caregivers, and locating services can be expensive, time-consuming, and exhausting, often distracting employees from their work roles. In response, many employers have added elder care benefits. These benefits typically emphasize information and support, rather than direct financial assistance. For example, organizations may provide access to counseling, flexible schedules, and printed resources. Even companies that cannot afford to offer counseling or referral services can use intranets to provide links to helpful Web sites such as the National Alliance for Caregiving (www.caregiving.org), the National Council on Aging (www. benefitscheckup.org), and the federal government's benefits information site (govbenefits.gov).[28]

Other Benefits

The scope of possible employee benefits is limited only by the imagination of the organization's decision makers. Organizations have developed a wide variety of benefits to meet the needs of employees and to attract and keep the kinds of workers who will

In order to provide a relaxed environment for their employees, one of the perks at Neversoft Entertainment is allowing employees to bring their pets to work. What other unique benefits do companies offer their employees?

be of value to the organization. Traditional extras include subsidized cafeterias, on-site health care for minor injuries or illnesses, and moving expenses for newly hired or relocating employees. Stores and manufacturers may offer employee discounts on their products.

To encourage learning and attract the kinds of employees who wish to develop their knowledge and skills, many organizations offer *tuition reimbursement* programs. A typical program covers tuition and related expenses for courses that are relevant to the employee's current job or future career at the organization. Employees are reimbursed for these expenses after they demonstrate they have completed an approved course.

Especially for demanding, high-stress jobs, organizations may look for benefits that help employees put in the necessary long hours and alleviate stress. Recreational activities such as on-site basketball courts or company-sponsored softball teams provide for social interaction as well as physical activity. Employers may reward hard-working groups or individuals with a trip for a weekend, a meal, or any activity employees are likely to enjoy. At one accounting firm, a manager made a practice of occasionally taking her team of women to a manicure salon for a break to relax and converse.[29]

L07 Explain how to choose the contents of an employee benefits package.

Selecting Employee Benefits

Although the government requires certain benefits, employers have wide latitude in creating the total benefits package they offer employees.[30] Decisions about which benefits to include should take into account the organization's goals, its budget, and the expectations of the organization's current employees and those it wishes to recruit

Table 13.2

**An Organization's
Benefits Objectives**

- To establish and maintain an employee benefit program that is based primarily on the employees' needs for leisure time and on protection against the risks of old age, loss of health, and loss of life.
- To establish and maintain an employee benefit program that complements the efforts of employees on their own behalf.
- To evaluate the employee benefit plan annually for its effect on employee morale and productivity, giving consideration to turnover, unfilled positions, attendance, employees' complaints, and employees' opinions.
- To compare the employee benefit plan annually with that of other leading companies in the same field and to maintain a benefit plan with an overall level of benefits based on cost per employee that falls within the second quintile of these companies.
- To maintain a level of benefits for nonunion employees that represents the same level of expenditures per employee as for union employees.
- To determine annually the costs of new, changed, and existing programs as percentages of salaries and wages and to maintain these percentages as much as possible.
- To self-fund benefits to the extent that a long-run cost savings can be expected for the firm and catastrophic losses can be avoided.
- To coordinate all benefits with social insurance programs to which the company makes payments.
- To provide benefits on a noncontributory basis except for dependent coverage, for which employees should pay a portion of the cost.
- To maintain continual communications with all employees concerning benefit programs.

Source: Adapted from B. T. Beam Jr. and J. J. McFadden, Employee Benefits, *3rd ed. © 1992 by Dearborn Financial Publishing, Inc. Published by Dearborn Financial Publishing, Inc., Chicago. All rights reserved.*

in the future. Employees have come to expect certain things from employers. An organization that does not offer the expected benefits will have more difficulty attracting and keeping talented workers. Also, if employees believe their employer feels no commitment to their welfare, they are less likely to feel committed to their employer.

The Organization's Objectives

A logical place to begin selecting employee benefits is to establish objectives for the benefits package. This helps an organization select the most effective benefits and monitor whether the benefits are doing what they should. Table 13.2 is an example of one organization's benefits objectives. Unfortunately, research suggests that most organizations do not have written benefits objectives.

Analytical Graphics Inc. (AGI), based in Exton, Pennsylvania, develops software that analyzes data from military equipment to help the equipment operate better. For a company that produces products that are so technical, complex, and critical, a chief objective is keeping the loyalty of talented professionals. The company's benefits policy supports these objectives by going beyond such standards as health insurance, vacations, and a 401(k) plan with employer matching contributions to such privileges as flextime, free catered meals, an exercise room, and a policy of allowing children to visit anytime and use the well-stocked playroom. Other services that make life easier for employees include oil changes in the parking lot, weekly pickup and delivery of dry cleaning, and shipping of personal packages, at cost, through the company's shipping department.[31]

Employees' Expectations and Values

Employees expect to receive benefits that are legally required and widely available, and they value benefits they are likely to use. To meet employee expectations about benefits, it can be helpful to see what other organizations offer. Employers can purchase survey information about benefits packages from private consultants. In addition, the Bureau of Labor Statistics gathers benefits data. The BLS Web site (www.bls.gov) is therefore a good place to check for free information about employee benefits in the United States. With regard to value, medical insurance is a high-value benefit because employees usually realize that surgery or a major illness can be financially devastating. Vision and dental care tend to be much less expensive, but many employees appreciate this type of coverage because so many people receive dental or vision care in the course of a year. As a result, many employers are finding that employees are even happy to pay the modest premiums for dental and vision coverage themselves because of the value they place on this benefit.[32]

Employers should also consider that the value employees place on various benefits is likely to differ from one employee to another. At a broad level, basic demographic factors such as age and sex can influence the kinds of benefits employees want. An older workforce is more likely to be concerned about (and use) medical coverage, life insurance, and pensions. A workforce with a high percentage of women of childbearing age may care more about disability or family leave. Young, unmarried men and women often place more value on pay than on benefits. However, these are only general observations; organizations should check which considerations apply to their own employees and identify more specific needs and differences. One approach is to use surveys to ask employees about the kinds of benefits they value. The survey should be carefully worded so as not to raise employees' expectations by seeming to promise all the benefits asked about at no cost to the employee.

The choice of benefits may influence current employees' satisfaction and may also affect the organization's recruiting, in terms of both the ease of recruiting and the kinds of employees attracted to the organization. For example, a benefits package that has strong medical benefits and pensions may be particularly attractive to older people or to those with many dependents. Such benefits may attract people with extensive experience and those who wish to make a long-term commitment to the organization. This strategy may be especially beneficial when turnover costs are very high. On the other hand, offering generous health care benefits may attract and retain people with high health care costs. Thus, organizations need to consider the signals sent by their benefits package as they set goals for benefits and select benefits to offer.

cafeteria-style plan
A benefits plan that offers employees a set of alternatives from which they can choose the types and amounts of benefits they want.

Organizations can address differences in employees' needs and empower their employees by offering flexible benefits plans in place of a single benefits package for all employees. These plans, often called **cafeteria-style plans,** offer employees a set of alternatives from which they can choose the types and amounts of benefits they want. The plans vary. Some impose minimum levels for certain benefits, such as health care coverage; some allow better employees to receive money in exchange for choosing a "light" package; and some let employees pay extra for the privilege of receiving more benefits. For example, some plans let employees give up vacation days for more pay or to purchase extra vacation days in exchange for a reduction in pay.

Cafeteria-style plans have a number of advantages.[33] The selection process can make employees more aware of the value of the benefits, particularly when the plan assigns each employee a sum of money to allocate to benefits. Also, the individual choice in a cafeteria plan enables each employee to match his or her needs to the company's benefits, increasing the plan's actual value to the employee. And because employees would not select benefits they don't want, the company avoids the cost of providing employees with benefits they don't value. Another way to control costs is to give employees incentives to choose lower-cost options. For example, the employee's deductible on a higher-cost health plan could be larger than on a relatively low-cost HMO.

A drawback of cafeteria-style plans is that they have a higher administrative cost, especially in the design and start-up stages. Organizations can avoid some of the higher cost, however, by using software packages and standardized plans that have been developed for employers wishing to offer cafeteria-style benefits. Another possible drawback is that employee selection of benefits will increase rather than decrease costs because employees will select the kinds of benefits they expect to need the most. For example, an employee expecting to need a lot of dental work is more likely to sign up for a dental plan. The heavy use of the dental coverage would then drive up the employer's premiums for that coverage. Costs can also be difficult to estimate when employees select their benefits.

Benefits' Costs

Employers also need to consider benefits costs. One place to start is with general information about the average costs of various benefits types. Widely used sources of cost data include the Bureau of Labor Statistics (BLS), Employee Benefit Research Institute, and U.S. Chamber of Commerce. Annual surveys by the Chamber of Commerce state the cost of benefits as a percentage of total payroll costs and in dollar terms.

Employers can use data about costs to help them select the kinds of benefits to offer. But in balancing these decisions against organizational goals and employee benefits, the organization may decide to offer certain high-cost benefits while also looking for ways to control the cost of those benefits. The highest-cost items tend to offer the most room for savings, but only if the items permit choice or negotiation. Also, as we noted earlier, organizations can control certain costs such as workers' compensation by improving their experience ratings. Cost control is especially important—and difficult—when economic growth slows or declines.

In recent years, benefits related to health care have attracted particular attention because these costs have risen very rapidly and because employers have a number of options. Concern over costs has prompted many employers to shift from traditional health insurance to HMOs and PPOs. Some employers shift more of the cost to employees. They may lower the employer's payments by increasing the amounts employees pay for deductibles and coinsurance (the employee's share of the payment for services). Or they may require employees to pay some or all of the difference in cost between traditional insurance and an HMO or PPO plan. Excluding or limiting coverage for certain types of claims also can slow the increase in health insurance costs. Employee wellness programs, especially when they are targeted to employees with risk factors and include follow-up and encouragement, can reduce risk factors for disease.[34] For more ideas on controlling the cost of health benefits, see the "HR How To" box.

HR How To

CONTROLLING THE COST OF HEALTH BENEFITS

With the cost of health care continuing to soar, employers are trying to help employees stay healthy and use their benefits efficiently. Here are some ways companies have slowed the rise in their health benefits costs:

- *Shop for bargains*—Every year, the company should research the available plans and compare quotes from different providers.

- *Know what employees care about*—Would they be willing to accept a higher deductible if it means the company can also afford prescription drug coverage?

- *Help contain health care costs*—If employees are willing to take responsibility for their own health care spending, offer a health savings account or consumer-driven health care plan. Some employees dislike these plans, but others find them financially attractive.

- *Review your claims history*—You might be able to identify correctable problems, such as heavy use of emergency rooms, perhaps because that coverage is too generous relative to benefits for office visits to the doctor.

- *Encourage healthy behavior*—Offer incentives like discounts for health club memberships, free health screenings (keep the results confidential), and lower premiums for employees who participate in a wellness program. Consider hiring or contracting with a health coach to help employees meet their wellness goals.

- *Promote a workplace culture that values healthy habits*—For example, vending machines and catered meetings should offer healthful foods.

- *Measure the results of any initiative you try*—Are premiums, health claims, or absences falling? Allow time for health benefits to have an impact; if no impact shows up, then try something different.

Sources: Steve Brooks, "Seven Steps to Lower Health Bills," *Restaurant Business*, February 2008, p. 16; Judith Nemes, "Small Firms Look for Big Savings on Health Benefits," *Chicago Tribune*, October 29, 2007, sec. 3, p. 2; and Adrienne Selko, "Employers Offering Financial Rewards for Healthy Behavior," *Industry Week*, January 1, 2008, www.industryweek.com.

Legal Requirements for Employee Benefits

LO8 Summarize the regulations affecting how employers design and administer benefits programs.

As we discussed earlier in this chapter, some benefits are required by law. This requirement adds to the cost of compensating employees. Organizations looking for ways to control staffing costs may look for ways to structure the workforce so as to minimize the expense of benefits. They may require overtime rather than adding new employees, hire part-time rather than full-time workers (because part-time employees generally receive much smaller benefits packages), and use independent contractors rather than hire employees. Some of these choices are limited by legal requirements, however. For example, the Fair Labor Standards Act requires overtime pay for nonexempt workers, as discussed in Chapter 11. Also, the Internal Revenue Service strictly limits the definition of "independent contractors," so that employees cannot avoid legal obligations by classifying workers as self-employed when the organization receives the benefits of a permanent employee. Other legal requirements involve tax treatment of benefits, antidiscrimination laws, and accounting for benefits.

Tax Treatment of Benefits

The IRS provides more favorable tax treatment of benefits classified as *qualified plans*. The details vary from one type of benefit to another. In the case of retirement plans, the advantages include the ability for employees to immediately take a tax deduction for the funds they contribute to the plans, no immediate tax on employees for the amount the employer contributes, and tax-free earnings on the money in the retirement fund.[35]

To obtain status as a qualified plan, a benefit plan must meet certain requirements.[36] In the case of pensions, these involve vesting and nondiscrimination rules. The nondiscrimination rules provide tax benefits to plans that do not discriminate in favor of the organization's "highly compensated employees." To receive the benefits, the organization cannot set up a retirement plan that provides benefits exclusively to the organization's owners and top managers. The requirements encourage employers to provide important benefits such as pensions to a broad spectrum of employees. Before offering pension plans and other benefits, organizations should have them reviewed by an expert who can advise on whether the benefits are qualified plans.

Antidiscrimination Laws

As we discussed in Chapter 3, a number of laws are intended to provide equal employment opportunity without regard to race, sex, age, disability, and several other protected categories. Some of these laws apply to the organization's benefits policies.

Legal treatment of men and women includes equal access to benefits, so the organization may not use the employee's gender as the basis for providing more limited benefits. That is the rationale for the Pregnancy Discrimination Act, which requires that employers treat pregnancy as it treats any disability. If an employee needs time off for conditions related to pregnancy or childbirth, the employee would receive whatever disability benefits the organization offers to employees who take disability leave for other reasons. Another area of concern in the treatment of male and female employees is pension benefits. On average, women live longer than men, so on average, pension benefits for female employees are more expensive (because the organization pays the pension longer), other things being equal. Some organizations have used this difference as a basis for requiring that female employees contribute more than male employees to defined benefit plans. The Supreme Court in 1978 determined that such a requirement is illegal.[37] According to the Supreme Court, the law is intended to protect individuals, and when women are considered on an individual basis (not as averages), not every woman outlives every man.

Age discrimination is also relevant to benefits policies. Two major issues have received attention under the Age Discrimination in Employment Act (ADEA) and amendments. First, employers must take care not to discriminate against workers over age 40 in providing pay or benefits. For example, employers may not set an age at which retirement benefits stop growing as a way to pressure older workers to retire.[38] Also, early-retirement incentive programs need to meet certain standards. The programs may not coerce employees to retire, they must provide accurate information about the options available, and they must give employees enough time to make a decision. In effect, employees must really have a choice about whether they retire. More recently, some employees have questioned whether it is discriminatory to require that workers over age 65 receive health benefits from Medicare, thus reducing the amount the employer spends on their medical coverage. The Equal Employment Opportunity Commission has ruled that this treatment is legal.[39]

When employers offer early retirement, they often ask employees to sign waivers saying they will not pursue claims under the ADEA. The Older Workers Benefit Protection Act of 1990 set guidelines for using these waivers.[40] The waivers must be voluntary and understandable to the employee and employer, and they must spell out the employee's rights under the ADEA. Also, in exchange for signing the waiver, the employee must receive "compensation," that is, greater benefits than he or she would otherwise receive upon retirement. The employer must inform employees that they may consult a lawyer before signing, and employees must have time to make a decision about signing—21 days before signing plus 7 days afterward in which they can revoke the agreement.

The Americans with Disabilities Act imposes requirements related to health insurance. Under the ADA, employees with disabilities must have "equal access to whatever health insurance coverage the employer provides other employees." Even so, the terms and conditions of health insurance may be based on risk factors—as long as the employer does not use this basis as a way to escape offering health insurance to someone with a disability. From the standpoint of avoiding legal challenges, an employer who has risk-based insurance and then hires an employee with a disability is in a stronger position than an employer who switches to a risk-based policy after hiring a disabled employee.[41]

Antidiscrimination laws may also apply to situations in which employers offer benefits to their retirees. In a recent case, a federal judge ruled that an employer offering health benefits to retirees could not cut back those benefits when retirees became eligible for Medicare. In other words, if some retirees are eligible for employer-provided insurance, the employer may not require that others receive Medicare coverage instead, based on their age. Some employers have addressed this requirement by eliminating health coverage for retirees.[42]

Accounting Requirements

Companies' financial statements must meet the many requirements of the Financial Accounting Standards Board (FASB). These accounting requirements are intended to ensure that financial statements are a true picture of the company's financial status and that outsiders, including potential lenders and investors, can understand and compare financial statements. Under FASB standards, employers must set aside the funds they expect to need for benefits to be paid after retirement, rather than funding those benefits on a pay-as-you-go basis. On financial statements, those funds must appear as future cost obligations.[43] For companies with substantial retirement benefits, reporting those benefits as future cost obligations greatly lowers income each year. Along with rising benefits costs, this reporting requirement has encouraged many companies to scale back benefits to retirees.

LO9 Discuss the importance of effectively communicating the nature and value of benefits to employees.

Communicating Benefits to Employees

Organizations must communicate benefits information to employees so that they will appreciate the value of their benefits. This is essential so that benefits can achieve their objective of attracting, motivating, and retaining employees. Employees are interested in their benefits, and they need a great deal of detailed information to take advantage of benefits such as health insurance and 401(k) plans. It follows that electronic technology such as the Internet and supporting databases

COMMUNICATING BENEFITS ONLINE

Putting information about benefits on the company's employee Web site makes that information readily available. Some companies focus mainly on monetary benefits, such as pay, bonuses, and stock options. Others are getting creative by showing a wider range of offerings. Some companies list training experiences and opportunities, to illustrate how the company can help employees develop their careers. Charts and graphs can show employees the value of each benefit as a proportion of their total rewards.

Boeing employees can look up their Pay and Benefits Profile online. It displays the value of medical and retirement benefits alongside the employee's salary and bonuses. The site also lists services such as wellness programs and child-care referral. Putting the benefits online enables Boeing's HR information system to tailor each display to the particular employee. It also permits interactive features, such as a "Planning for the Future" calculator, which shows the potential growth of the employee's pension and retirement savings. Users can look up an estimate of their future Social Security benefits, along with other investments they may have, to see whether they are on track to meet retirement goals. Combining this information with modeling software can let employees see how different saving strategies can affect their long-term rewards.

Sources: Drew Robb, "A Total View of Employee Rewards," *HRMagazine*, August 2007, downloaded from General Reference Center Gold, http://find.galegroup.com; and Joanne Sammer, "Tell Them about It," *HRMagazine*, November 2007, pp. 73–76.

can play a significant role in modern benefit systems. Many companies are putting benefits information on their intranets. The e-HRM box shows how online benefits communication allows employees to better understand the value of their benefits and to plan for retirement.

In actuality, employees and job applicants often have a poor idea of what benefits they have and what the market value of their benefits is. Research asking employees about their benefits has shown that employees significantly underestimate the cost and value of their benefits.[44] Probably a major reason for their lack of knowledge is a lack of communications from employers. Employees don't know what employers are spending for benefits, so many of them doubt employers' complaints about soaring costs and their impact on the company's future.[45] In one study, employees said their company neglected to tell them how to be better consumers of health care, and they would be willing to make changes in their lifestyle if they had a financial incentive to do so. Such research suggests to employers that better communication, coupled with well-designed benefits plans, will pay off in practical terms.

Employers have many options for communicating information about benefits. To increase the likelihood that employees will receive and understand the messages, employers can combine several media, such as brochures, question-and-answer meetings, intranet pages, memos, and e-mail. Some other possible media include paycheck inserts, retirement or health coaching, training programs, and benefits fairs. An investment of creativity in communications to employees can reap great returns in the form of committed, satisfied employees.

THINKING ETHICALLY

SHOULD HEALTH INSURANCE PAY FOR BIRTH CONTROL?

As we discussed in this chapter, one of the most highly valued—and expensive—employee benefits is health insurance. One way employers have dealt with the expense of this benefit is to limit the services covered. Some companies' policies, for example, have excluded coverage of contraceptives to limit costs. Organizations with religious objections to birth control have also excluded insurance coverage for such benefits.

Some employees have objected that policies excluding birth control pills but paying for other prescriptions amount to unlawful discrimination against women or unequal treatment based on pregnancy status. Federal judges in 2001 and 2003 agreed with the discrimination claims. However, in 2007, a federal appeals court ruled that an insurance plan covering the employees of Union Pacific Railroad Company did not discriminate. The court found that the Pregnancy Discrimination Act does not apply to contraceptives and that the insurance plan did not discriminate on the basis of sex because it did not cover any kind of contraceptives sold to either women or men.

The ruling may not change many benefits packages. Union Pacific began offering coverage for contraception in its health insurance before the ruling and indicated it had no plans to discontinue it. A national survey found that 89 percent of employees were enrolled in plans providing coverage for contraceptives. And a majority of states require commercial insurers to provide this coverage. Market forces may also be at work. Some observers note that paying for contraceptives is in fact cheaper than paying for pregnancies.

SOURCES: Louise Esola, "Birth Control Ruling Won't Curb Cover," *Business Insurance*, March 26, 2007; and D. Diane Hatch and James E. Hall, "Bias in Excluding Contraception Coverage?" *Workforce Management*, April 23, 2007, both downloaded from General Reference Center Gold, http://find.galegroup.com.

Questions

1. If a company decides not to offer certain benefits, such as insurance covering contraceptives, who is affected by this decision? Who is harmed? Who benefits?
2. The reasons for covering certain treatments but not others in a health care plan may be based on business criteria (cost of the coverage, attractiveness to employees) or other criteria, such as judgment about whether a treatment is ethical. Which criteria are appropriate for an employer to use?
3. Birth control is more widely available than before but is still considered unethical by some. What other kinds of medical treatment might raise ethical questions? In deciding which of these treatments a benefits package should cover, whose ethical principles should count—those of top management, the benefits manager, the company's owners, the employees, the society at large, or someone else?

SUMMARY

LO1 Discuss the importance of benefits as a part of employee compensation.

Like pay, benefits help employers attract, retain, and motivate employees. The variety of possible benefits also helps employers tailor their compensation packages to attract the right kinds of employees. Employees expect at least a minimum level of benefits, and providing more than the minimum helps an organization compete in the labor market. Benefits are also a significant expense, but employers provide benefits because employees value them and many benefits are required by law.

LO2 Summarize the types of employee benefits required by law.

Employers must contribute to the Old Age, Survivors, Disability, and Health Insurance program known as Social Security through a payroll tax shared by employers and employees. Employers must also pay federal and state taxes for unemployment insurance, based on each employer's experience rating, or percentage of employees a company has laid off in the past. State laws require that employers purchase workers' compensation insurance. Under the Family and Medical Leave Act, employees who need to care for a baby following birth or adoption or for an ill family member must be granted unpaid leave of up to 12 weeks.

LO3 Describe the most common forms of paid leave.

The major categories of paid leave are vacations, holidays, and sick leave. Paid time off may seem uneconomical, which may be the reason U.S. employers tend to offer much less vacation time than is common in Western Europe. At large U.S. companies, paid vacation is typically 10 days. The typical number of paid holidays is 10 in both Western Europe and the United States. Sick leave programs often provide full salary replacement for a limited period of time, with the amount of sick leave usually based on length of service. Policies are needed to determine how the organization will handle unused sick days at the end of each year. Some organizations let employees roll over some or all of the unused sick days into the next year, and others let unused days expire at the end of the year. Other forms of paid leave include personal days and floating holidays.

LO4   Identify the kinds of insurance benefits offered by employers.

Medical insurance is one of the most valued employee benefits. Such policies typically cover hospital expenses, surgical expenses, and visits to physicians. Some employers offer additional coverage, such as dental care, vision care, birthing centers, and prescription drug programs. Under the Consolidated Omnibus Budget Reconciliation Act of 1985, employees must be permitted to extend their health insurance coverage at group rates for up to 36 months after they leave the organization. To manage the costs of health insurance, many organizations offer coverage through a health maintenance organization or preferred provider organization, or they may offer flexible spending accounts. Some encourage healthy behaviors through an employee wellness program. Life insurance usually takes the form of group term life insurance, with the usual benefit being two times the employee's yearly pay. Employers may also offer short-term and/or long-term disability insurance, with disability payments being a percentage of the employee's salary. Some employers provide long-term care insurance to pay the costs associated with long-term care such as nursing home care.

LO5   Define the types of retirement plans offered by employers.

Retirement plans may be contributory, meaning funded by contributions from employer and employee, or noncontributory, meaning funded only by the employer. These plans may be defined benefit plans, which guarantee a specified level of retirement income, usually based on the employee's years of service, age, and earnings level. Benefits under these plans are protected by the Pension Benefit Guarantee Corporation. An alternative is to set up a defined contribution plan, such as a 401(k) plan. The employer sets up an individual account for each employee and guarantees the size of the investment into that account, rather than the amount to be

paid out on retirement. Because employees have control over investment decisions, the organization may also offer financial planning services as an employee benefit. A cash balance plan combines some advantages of defined-benefit plans and defined-contribution plans. The employer sets up individual accounts and contributes a percentage of each employee's salary. The account earns interest at a predetermined rate, so the contributions and benefits are easier to predict.

LO6   Describe how organizations use other benefits to match employees' wants and needs.

Employers have responded to work-family role conflicts by offering family-friendly benefits, including paid family leave, child care services or referrals, college savings plans, and elder care information and support. Other employee benefits have traditionally included subsidized cafeterias, on-site health clinics, and reimbursement of moving expenses. Stores and manufacturers may offer discounts on their products. Tuition reimbursement encourages employees to continue learning. Recreational services and employee outings provide social interaction as well as stress relief.

LO7   Explain how to choose the contents of an employee benefits package.

A logical place to begin is to establish organizational objectives and select benefits that support those objectives. Organizations should also consider employees' expectations and values. At a minimum, organizations offer the benefits employees have come to view as basic; some organizations go so far as to match extra benefits to individual employees' needs and interests. Cafeteria-style plans are an intermediate step that gives employees control over the benefits they receive. Employers must also weigh the costs of benefits, which are significant.

LO8   Summarize the regulations affecting how employers design and administer benefits programs.

Employers must provide the benefits that are required by law, and they may not improperly classify employees as "independent contractors" to avoid paying benefits. Tax treatment of qualified plans is favorable, so organizations need to learn the requirements for setting up benefits as qualified plans—for example, ensuring that pension plans do not discriminate in favor of the organization's highly compensated employees. Employers may not use employees' gender as the basis for discriminating against anyone, as in pension benefits on the basis that women as a group may live longer. Nor may employers discriminate against workers over age 40 in providing pay or benefits, such as pressuring older workers to retire by limiting retirement benefits. When employers offer early retirement, they must meet the requirements of the Older Workers Benefit Protection Act of 1990. Under the Americans with Disabilities Act, employers must give disabled employees equal access to health insurance. To meet the requirements of the Financial Accounting Standards Board, employers must set aside the funds they expect to need for retirement benefits ahead of time, rather than funding the benefits on a pay-as-you-go basis.

LO9 Discuss the importance of effectively communicating the nature and value of benefits to employees.

Communicating information about benefits is important so that employees will appreciate the value of their benefits. Communicating their value is the main way benefits attract, motivate, and retain employees. Employers have many options for communicating information about benefits, such as brochures, meetings, intranets, memos, and e-mail. Using a combination of such methods increases employees' understanding.

KEY TERMS

cafeteria-style plan, p. 386
cash balance plan, p. 381
Consolidated Omnibus Budget
    Reconciliation Act (COBRA),
    p. 374
contributory plan, p. 378
defined benefit plan, p. 378
defined contribution plan, p. 379
employee benefits, p. 366
Employee Retirement Income
    Security Act (ERISA), p. 379

employee wellness program (EWP),
    p. 376
experience rating, p. 369
Family and Medical Leave Act
    (FMLA), p. 370
flexible spending account, p. 376
health maintenance organization
    (HMO), p. 375
long-term disability insurance,
    p. 378
noncontributory plan, p. 378

Pension Benefit Guarantee
    Corporation (PBGC), p. 379
preferred provider organization
    (PPO), p. 376
short-term disability insurance,
    p. 377
Social Security, p. 368
summary plan description, p. 382
unemployment insurance, p. 369
vesting rights, p. 381
workers' compensation, p. 370

REVIEW AND DISCUSSION QUESTIONS

1. Why do employers provide employee benefits, rather than providing all compensation in the form of pay and letting employees buy the services they want?
2. Of the benefits discussed in this chapter, list the ones you consider essential—that is, the benefits you would require in any job offer. Why are these benefits important to you?
3. Define the types of benefits required by law. How can organizations minimize the cost of these benefits while complying with the relevant laws?
4. What are some advantages of offering a generous package of insurance benefits? What are some drawbacks of generous insurance benefits?
5. Imagine that you are the human resource manager of a small architectural firm. You learn that the monthly premiums for the company's existing health insurance policy will rise by 15 percent next year. What can you suggest to help your company manage this rising cost?
6. In principle, health insurance would be most attractive to employees with large medical expenses, and retirement benefits would be most attractive to older

employees. What else might a company include in its benefits package to appeal to young, healthy employees? How might the company structure its benefits so these employees can take advantage of the benefits they care about most?
7. What issues should an organization consider in selecting a package of employee benefits? How should an employer manage the trade-offs among these considerations?
8. How do tax laws and accounting regulations affect benefits packages?
9. What legal requirements might apply to a family leave policy? Suggest how this type of policy should be set up to meet those requirements.
10. Why is it important to communicate information about employee benefits? Suppose you work in the HR department of a company that has decided to add new benefits—dental and vision insurance plus an additional two days of paid time off for "personal days." How would you recommend communicating this change? What information should your messages include?

BUSINESSWEEK CASE

BusinessWeek   You've Got Dependents? Prove It

Many Americans are rummaging through attics and safe-deposit boxes to track down essential documents for reasons that have nothing to do with the taxman. They're preparing for an audit, but this one is being performed by their employer.

"Dependent eligibility audits," in which companies demand proof that spouses and children qualify for medical benefits, are swiftly becoming both fashionable and financially rewarding for companies frantic to curb the runaway costs of health coverage. Companies such as Boeing, General Motors, and American Airlines have been asking workers to send in marriage licenses, birth certificates, student IDs, and tax returns. The goal: to cull the benefits rolls of ineligibles, which could include ex-spouses, stepchildren who live elsewhere, or 29-year-old college grads still being claimed as dependents.

At best, the audits are a device that can save millions in an employer's health care costs, keep premiums down for legitimate beneficiaries, and catch outright fraudsters. At worst, employees who believed their family members' coverage was unassailable may discover they're out of luck. In some workplaces, morale suffers, too.

Employers are willing to risk upsetting workers because of a confluence of challenging trends. They've tried just about everything to stem the rise in health insurance expenses. Meanwhile, morphing family dynamics—high divorce rates and blended families—have helped lead to more ineligible dependents. Audits are finding up to 15 percent of those claimed as dependents aren't entitled to coverage.

Even those whose dependents are eligible may have to work hard to prove it. Take Ed Lutgen, a union shop steward coordinator in Seattle, who spent five months battling benefits bureaucrats at Boeing, where he worked for 10 years. A noncustodial parent who divorced 16 years ago, Lutgen says Boeing had never questioned the eligibility of his son, now a high school student, who had been covered since birth. A tax return showing his son as a dependent was not enough to satisfy the auditors, though a copy of his old child support order finally nailed down the coverage.

At many companies, missing the deadline for sending in paperwork risks having a dependent's coverage dropped.

Still, there are usually appeal windows of up to 60 days during which coverage can be reinstated if employees show proof. A few companies, however, are getting tough on those who procrastinate or are caught signing up an unqualified person. Some have made employees wait until the next open enrollment period if they repeatedly missed deadlines. One company even fired workers discovered to have enrolled ineligible people, because they violated its code of conduct.

Such aggressive moves are partly a response to employees who cheat the system. That has prompted a number of surprises during audits. In New Jersey, benefit plan sleuths uncovered one employee who tried to enroll 83 dependents. A California hospital found some workers had even claimed neighbors as dependents.

Audit firms say companies are often surprised by the savings. Goodyear Tire and Rubber, for instance, trimmed 13 percent of its 70,000 dependents, due to ineligibility, in its 2005 audit, saving 6 percent on costs.

Such culling is meant to help companies and workers alike lower costs, though workers may not always understand how they benefit. Auditors say many employers fail to communicate the savings. Lutgen, the Boeing veteran, has his own thoughts: "It never trickles down."

SOURCE: Keith Epstein and Jena McGregor, "You've Got Dependents? Prove It," *BusinessWeek*, November 26, 2007, downloaded from General Reference Center Gold, http://find.galegroup.com.

Questions

1. What are the advantages for an employer conducting a dependent eligibility audit? What are the disadvantages?
2. Suppose you work in human resources at a company that is planning to begin a dependent eligibility audit. Recommend how the company should measure the success of this effort.
3. Recommend how the company should communicate with employees about the audit. What should the company tell employees about the audit process and its potential advantages? What, if any, feedback will you seek?

CASE: WAL-MART EXPANDS HEALTH BENEFITS

Hordes of shoppers love Wal-Mart's low prices, but some people have criticized the ways the retail giant keeps those prices so low. One area of criticism has been the company's health care coverage. Many employees have had limited benefits, and about half have had no coverage through

Wal-Mart (many are covered through a spouse's or parent's plan, another job's benefits, or Medicaid).

Recently, that has changed. Wal-Mart announced a new, more flexible health plan. The plan eliminates extra $1,000 deductibles for hospital care and outpatient surgery. Covered employees can buy any of 2,400 generic drugs for just $4 per prescription. In contrast, brand name drugs cost $30 to $50. To emphasize preventive care, the plan offers health care credits; employees may receive a grant of $100 to $500 to be used toward health expenses such as visiting a doctor.

One challenge that remains for Wal-Mart employees is that deductibles for health care still can eat up a sizable chunk of their earnings. For a policy with low premiums of $8 a month, the annual deductible could be $2,000, more than a tenth of some employees' annual earnings. The balance between premiums and deductibles is under employees' control, however. Employees who can pay a $79 monthly premium can reduce their annual deductible to $500. Altogether, employees can customize their health plan in 50 different ways, making trade-offs among monthly premiums, annual deductibles, and the amount of the health care credit.

Another challenge is that the coverage is not available to Wal-Mart employees during their first year on the job— employees become eligible after a year. Even this policy is more generous than it had been. Until the recent changes, part-time workers became eligible for health insurance after working for Wal-Mart for two years. Still, David Nassar, executive director of the watchdog group Wal-Mart Watch, says, "Wal-Mart's waiting periods . . . are twice the national retail average" and are "a critical problem with its health care plans." More positively, Helen Darling, president of the National Business Group on Health, says, "Parts of [Wal-Mart's plan], like the $4 generics, are game-changing for the industry."

During the first month of the new insurance plan, Wal-Mart announced that the proportion of its employees with health care coverage from all sources rose from 90.4 to 92.7 percent; among these insured employees, about half received their coverage through Wal-Mart. The number of employees saying they had no health care coverage declined from 9.6 percent to just 7.3 percent. Linda Dillman, the company's executive vice president of benefits and risk management, said the increase means "the improvements we've made are being embraced by our associates and their families."

SOURCES: Michael Barbaro, "Health Plan Overhauled at Wal-Mart," *New York Times*, September 19, 2007, www.nytimes.com; "Health Insurance Plan Upgraded by Wal-Mart," *Chain Drug Review*, October 1, 2007, downloaded from General Reference Center Gold, http://find.galegroup.com; and "Wal-Mart Says More Associates Now Have Health Coverage," *Progressive Grocer*, January 23, 2008, http://find.galegroup.com.

Questions

1. How well do you think Wal-Mart's earlier, more limited health benefits supported the company's overall business strategy? How well does the new benefits plan support its strategy?
2. Why do you think Wal-Mart gave employees the option to tailor their health care coverage 50 different ways? What are the pros and cons of this approach?
3. How would you recommend that Wal-Mart communicate the plan to its employees? Consider what information the employees will need and which media will be most effective for delivering that information.

IT'S A WRAP!

www.mhhe.com/noefund3e is your source for **R**eviewing, **A**pplying, and **P**racticing the concepts you learned about in Chapter 13.

Review
- Chapter learning objectives
- Narrated lecture and iPod content

Application
- Video case and quiz: "Child Care Help"
- Self-Assessment: Will you find a job that offers the benefits you want?
- Web Exercise: Evaluate a company that helps businesses to set up intranets

Practice
- Chapter quiz

NOTES

1. S. Hamm, "A Passion for the Planet," *BusinessWeek*, August 21, 2006, www.businessweek.com; Patagonia Web site, www.patagonia.com, accessed March 11, 2008.

2. B. Gerhart and G. T. Milkovich, "Employee Compensation: Research and Practice," in *Handbook of Industrial and Organizational Psychology*, 2nd ed., ed.

M. D. Dunnette and L. M. Hough (Palo Alto, CA: Consulting Psychologists Press, 1992), vol. 3; and J. Swist, "Benefits Communications: Measuring Impact and Values," *Employee Benefit Plan Review*, September 2002, pp. 24–26.

3. S. Shellenbarger, "Companies Help Employees Cope with Caring for Parents," *Wall Street Journal*, June 21, 2007, http://online.wsj.com; and M. Freudenheim, "Some Employers Are Offering Free Drugs," *New York Times*, February 21, 2007, www.nytimes.com.

4. U.S. Department of Labor, Employment and Training Administration (ETA), "Unemployment Insurance Tax Topic," last updated July 31, 2007, http://workforcesecurity.doleta.gov; and ETA "Significant Provisions of State Unemployment Insurance Laws," January 2008, http://workforcesecurity.doleta.gov.

5. J. V. Nackley, *Primer on Workers' Compensation* (Washington, DC: Bureau of National Affairs, 1989); and T. Thomason, T. P. Schmidle, and J. F. Burton, *Workers' Compensation* (Kalamazoo, MI: Upjohn Institute, 2001).

6. B. T. Beam Jr. and J. J. McFadden, *Employee Benefits*, 6th ed. (Chicago: Dearborn Financial Publishing, 2000).

7. S. S. Muñoz, "A Good Idea, but . . . ," *Wall Street Journal*, January 24, 2005, p. R6.

8. P. Hardin, "Women Execs Should Feel at Ease about Taking Full Maternity Leave," *Personnel Journal*, September 1995, p. 19; U.S. Department of Labor Web site, www.dol.gov, 2000.

9. L. Raines, "All Work and No Play?" *Atlanta Journal-Constitution ajcjobs*, May 18, 2007, http://jobnews.ajcjobs.com; "Vacation Entitlement Survey," *HRM Guide*, June 29, 2007, www.hrmguide.com; and J. Yang, "Time Off," *Salary Negotiation*, www.salary.com, last modified November 12, 2004.

10. Employee Benefit Research Institute, "Value of Employee Benefits Constant in a Changing World," March 28, 2002, www.ebri.org.

11. J. D. Morton and P. Aleman, "Trends in Employer-Provided Mental Health and Substance Abuse Benefits," *Monthly Labor Review*, April 2005, pp. 25–35.

12. Employee Benefit Research Institute, "Typical Health Benefit Package in Private Industry," *Facts from EBRI*, April 2006, www.ebri.org.

13. R. Lieber, "New Way to Curb Medical Costs: Make Employees Feel the Sting," *Wall Street Journal*, June 23, 2004, pp. A1, A6; and R. Stolz, "Healthy Encouragement," *Human Resource Executive*, May 2, 2005, pp. 1, 22–31.

14. J. C. Erfurt, A. Foote, and M. A. Heirich, "The Cost-Effectiveness of Worksite Wellness Programs for Hypertension Control, Weight Loss, Smoking Cessation and Exercise," *Personnel Psychology* 45 (1992), pp. 5–27.

15. D. Wessel, "Enron and a Bigger Ill: Americans Don't Save," *Wall Street Journal Online*, March 7, 2002, http://online.wsj.com.

16. Pension Benefit Guaranty Corporation, "Pension Insurance Premiums Fact Sheet," Key Resources: Fact Sheets, www.pbgc.gov, accessed March 4, 2008.

17. Internal Revenue Service, "Limitation on Elective Deferrals," Plan Sponsors section of *401(k) Resource Guide*, www.irs.gov/retirement/, accessed March 4, 2008.

18. Employee Benefit Research Institute, "Retirement Trends in the United States over the Past Quarter-Century," *Facts from EBRI*, June 2007, www.ebri.org.

19. T. Lauricella, "A Lesson for Social Security: Many Mismanage Their 401(k)s," *Wall Street Journal*, December 1, 2004, http://online.wsj.com; and Eleanor Laise, "Employers Grab Reins of Workers' 401(k)s," *Wall Street Journal*, April 25, 2007, http://online.wsj.com.

20. "Supreme Court Lets Stand Third Circuit Ruling That Pension Avoidance Scheme Is ERISA Violation," *Daily Labor Report*, no. 234 (December 8, 1987), p. A-14, summarizing *Continental Can Company v. Gavalik*.

21. Beam and McFadden, *Employee Benefits*.

22. S. L. Grover and K. J. Crooker, "Who Appreciates Family Responsive Human Resource Policies: The Impact of Family-Friendly Policies on the Organizational Attachment of Parents and Non-parents," *Personnel Psychology* 48 (1995), pp. 271–88; M. A. Arthur, "Share Price Reactions to Work-Family Initiatives: An Institutional Perspective," *Academy of Management Journal* 46 (2003), p. 497; and J. E. Perry-Smith and T. Blum, "Work-Family Human Resource Bundles and Perceived Organizational Performance," *Academy of Management Journal* 43 (2000), pp. 1107–17.

23. Clearinghouse on International Developments in Child, Youth and Family Policies, "Comparative Policies and Programs," Section 1.1, Maternity, Paternity, Parental and Family Leave Policies, www.childpolicyintl.org, last updated November 2004.

24. Families and Work Institute (FWI), "The Families and Work Institute's 1998 Business Work-Life Study," FWI Web site, www.familiesandwork.org.

25. E. E. Kossek, "Diversity in Child Care Assistance Needs: Employee Problems, Preferences, and Work-Related Outcomes," *Personnel Psychology* 43 (1990), pp. 769–91.

26. B. Shutan, "Lending a Hand," *Human Resource Executive*, May 2, 2005, pp. 46–49.

27. T. Cullen, "Workplace 529 Plans May Have Lower Fees, but Also Drawbacks," *Wall Street Journal Online*, May 9, 2002, http://online.wsj.com.

28. S. Shellenbarger, "Web Sites Can Help to Ease Burden of Caring for Elders," *Wall Street Journal Online*, February 27, 2002, http://online.wsj.com.

29. S. Shellenbarger, "From Catnaps to Lunchtime Jobs: Tales about 'Undertime' at Work," *Wall Street Journal Online*, May 16, 2002, http://online.wsj.com.

30. R. Broderick and B. Gerhart, "Nonwage Compensation," in *The Human Resource Management Handbook*, eds. D. Lewin, D. J. B. Mitchell, and M. A. Zadi (San Francisco: JAI Press, 1996).

31. J. M. Von Bergen, "Pampering Employees Benefits Company," *Philadelphia Inquirer*, August 1, 2004, pp. F1–F2.

32. V. Colliver, "Balancing the Benefit Bite," *San Francisco Chronicle*, January 19, 2005, www.sfgate.com.

33. Beam and McFadden, *Employee Benefits*.

34. D. A. Harrison and L. Z. Liska, "Promoting Regular Exercise in Organizational Fitness Programs: Health-Related Differences in Motivational Building Blocks," *Personnel Psychology* 47 (1994), pp. 47–71; Erfurt et al., "The Cost-Effectiveness of Worksite Wellness Programs."

35. Beam and McFadden, *Employee Benefits*, p. 359.

36. For a description of these rules, see M. M. Sarli, "Nondiscrimination Rules for Qualified Plans: The General Test," *Compensation and Benefits Review* 23, no. 5 (September–October 1991), pp. 56–67.

37. *Los Angeles Department of Water & Power v. Manhart*, 435 U.S. S. Ct. 702 (1978), 16 E.P.D. 8250.

38. S. K. Hoffman, "Discrimination Litigation Relating to Employee Benefits," *Labor Law Journal*, June 1992, pp. 362–81.

39. "Ruling Allows Employers to Shift Retiree Health-Care Tab to Medicare," *Wall Street Journal*, December 27, 2007, http://online.wsj.com; and Barbara Rose, "Health Coverage Rule May Help Younger Retirees," *Chicago Tribune*, December 28, 2007, sec. 1, pp. 1, 2.

40. P. J. Kennedy, "Take the Money and Sue," *HRMagazine* 43, no. 5 (April 1998), pp. 105–8.

41. Hoffman, "Discrimination Litigation," p. 375.

42. A. B. Crenshaw, "Retiree Benefits Can't Be Cut at 65, Judge Says," *Washington Post*, March 31, 2005, www.washingtonpost.com.

43. A. Tergesen, "The Hidden Bite of Retiree Health," *BusinessWeek*, January 19, 2004; and D. Welch, "Has GM Outrun Its Pension Problems?" *BusinessWeek*, January 19, 2004.

44. M. Wilson, G. B. Northcraft, and M. A. Neale, "The Perceived Value of Fringe Benefits," *Personnel Psychology* 38 (1985), pp. 309–20; H. W. Hennessey, P. L. Perrewe, and W. A. Hochwarter, "Impact of Benefit Awareness on Employee and Organizational Outcomes: A Longitudinal Field Experiment," *Benefits Quarterly* 8, no. 2 (1992), pp. 90–96; and MetLife, *Employee Benefits Benchmarking Report*, www.metlife.com, accessed June 24, 2007.

45. M. C. Giallourakis and G. S. Taylor, "An Evaluation of Benefit Communication Strategy," *Employee Benefits Journal* 15, no. 4 (1991), pp. 14–18; and J. Mehring, "Health Care: Trust Issues," *BusinessWeek*, August 2, 2004, p. 28; and Employee Benefit Research Institute, "How Readable Are Summary Plan Descriptions for Health Care Plans?" *EBRI Notes*, October 2006, www.ebri.org.

Meeting Other HR Goals

PART FIVE

Collective Bargaining and Labor Relations

Introduction

The costs of health care are skyrocketing. As we discussed in the previous chapter, individuals, insurance companies, and government agencies that pick up the tab are crying out that mounting increases must be slowed. So health care providers are looking for ways to improve efficiency. At many hospitals, cost control involves asking fewer workers to do more. Nurses and other workers are expected to handle more patients, perform more tasks, and work more hours. Often, health professionals are troubled by these changes. They worry that they will burn out and that patient care will suffer. Or they worry that their employer will control costs by laying them off or refusing pay increases. These changes and pressures have led some health care workers to join labor unions. Recently, union membership among professional and technical health care workers, such as registered nurses and laboratory technologists, increased by more than 10 percent.[1]

The presence of unions at a hospital changes some aspects of human resource management by directing more attention to the interests of employees as a group. In general, employees and employers share the same interests. They both benefit when the organization is strong and growing, providing employees with jobs and employers with profits. But although the interests of employers and employees overlap, they obviously are not identical. In the case of pay, workers benefit from higher pay, but high pay cuts into the organization's profits, unless pay increases are associated with higher productivity or better customer service. Workers may negotiate differences with their employers individually, or they may form unions to negotiate on their behalf. This chapter explores human resource activities in organizations where employees belong to unions or where employees are seeking to organize unions.

We begin by formally defining unions and labor relations, and then describe the scope and impact of union activity. We next summarize government laws and regulations affecting unions and labor relations. The following three sections detail types

chapter fourteen

of activities involving unions: union organizing, contract negotiation, and contract administration. Finally, we identify ways in which unions and management are working together in arrangements that are more cooperative than the traditional labor-management relationship.

Role of Unions and Labor Relations

In the United States today, most workers act as individuals to select jobs that are acceptable to them and to negotiate pay, benefits, flexible hours, and other work conditions. Especially when there is stiff competition for labor and employees have hard-to-replace skills, this arrangement produces satisfactory results for most employees. At times, however, workers have believed their needs and interests do not receive enough consideration from management. One response by workers is to act collectively by forming and joining labor **unions,** organizations formed for the purpose of representing their members' interests and resolving conflicts with employers.

Unions have a role because some degree of conflict is inevitable between workers and management.[2] As we commented earlier, for example, managers can increase profits by lowering workers' pay, but workers benefit in the short term if lower profits result because their pay is higher. Still, this type of conflict is more complex than a simple trade-off, such as wages versus profits. Rising profits can help employees by driving up profit sharing or other benefits, and falling profits can result in layoffs and a lack of investment. Although employers can use programs like profit sharing to help align employee interests with their own, some remaining divergence of interests is inevitable. Labor unions represent worker interests and the collective bargaining process provides a way to manage the conflict. In other words, through systems for hearing complaints and negotiating labor contracts, unions and managers resolve conflicts between employers and employees.

As unionization of workers became more common, universities developed training in how to manage union-management interactions.[3] This specialty, called **labor relations,** emphasizes skills that managers and union leaders can use to foster effective labor-management cooperation, minimize costly forms of conflict (such as strikes), and seek win-win solutions to disagreements. Labor relations involves three levels of decisions:[4]

1. *Labor relations strategy*—For management, the decision involves whether the organization will work with unions or develop (or maintain) nonunion operations. This decision is influenced by outside forces such as public opinion and competition. For unions, the decision involves whether to fight changes in how unions relate to the organization or accept new kinds of labor-management relationships.
2. *Negotiating contracts*—As we will describe later in the chapter, contract negotiations in a union setting involve decisions about pay structure, job security, work rules, workplace safety, and many other issues. These decisions affect workers' and the employer's situation for the term of the contract.
3. *Administering contracts*—These decisions involve day-to-day activities in which union members and the organization's managers may have disagreements. Issues include complaints of work rules being violated or workers being treated unfairly in particular situations. A formal grievance procedure is typically used to resolve these issues.

Later sections in this chapter describe how managers and unions carry out the activities connected with these levels of decisions, as well as the goals and legal constraints affecting these activities.

LO1 Define unions and labor relations and their role in organizations.

unions
Organizations formed for the purpose of representing their members' interests in dealing with employers.

labor relations
Field that emphasizes skills managers and union leaders can use to minimize costly forms of conflict (such as strikes) and seek win-win solutions to disagreements.

Figure 14.1

10 Largest Unions in the United States

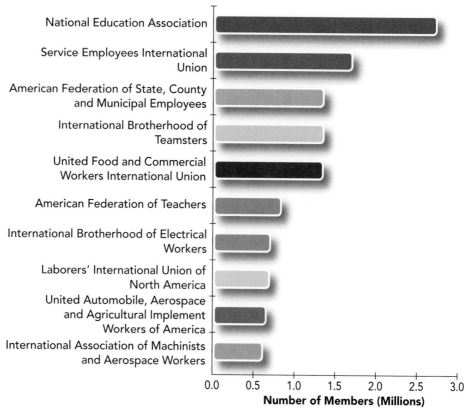

SOURCE: C. D. Gifford, *Directory of U.S. Labor Organizations* (Washington, DC: Bureau of National Affairs, 2006).

National and International Unions

Most union members belong to a national or international union. Figure 14.1 shows the membership of the 10 largest national unions in the United States. Half of these have memberships of over a million workers.

These unions may be either craft or industrial unions. The members of a **craft union** all have a particular skill or occupation. Examples include the International Brotherhood of Electrical Workers for electricians and the United Brotherhood of Carpenters and Joiners of America for carpenters. Craft unions are often responsible for training their members through apprenticeships and for supplying craft workers to employers. For example, an employer would send requests for carpenters to the union hiring hall, which would decide which carpenters to send out. In this way, craft workers may work for many employers over time but have a constant link to the union. A craft union's bargaining power depends greatly on its control over the supply of its workers.

In contrast, **industrial unions** consist of members who are linked by their work in a particular industry. Examples include the United Steelworkers of America and the Communication Workers of America. Typically, an industrial union represents many different occupations. Membership in the union is the result of working for a particular employer in the industry. Changing employers is less common than it is among craft workers, and employees who change employers remain members of the same union only if they happen to move to other employers covered by that union. Another difference is

craft union
Labor union whose members all have a particular skill or occupation.

industrial union
Labor union whose members are linked by their work in a particular industry.

that whereas a craft union may restrict the number of skilled craftsmen—say, carpenters—to maintain higher wages, industrial unions try to organize as many employees in as wide a range of skills as possible.

Most national unions are affiliated with the **American Federation of Labor and Congress of Industrial Organizations (AFL-CIO).** The AFL-CIO is not a labor union but an association that seeks to advance the shared interests of its member unions at the national level, much as the Chamber of Commerce and the National Association of Manufacturers do for their member employers. Approximately 55 national and international unions are affiliated with the AFL-CIO. An important responsibility of the AFL-CIO is to represent labor's interests in public policy issues such as labor law, economic policy, and occupational safety and health. The organization also provides information and analysis that member unions can use in their activities. In 2005, several unions broke away from the AFL-CIO to form an alliance called Change to Win. This group includes seven unions representing a membership of 5 to 6 million workers. Since the split, both groups have increased national unions' focus on strategy and organizing.[5]

Andrew Stern is president of the Service Employees International Union, the fastest-growing union in North America. He led the SEIU and six other unions in breaking away from the AFL-CIO to form Change to Win, a federation that emphasizes representation of the many workers in the high-growth service sector of the economy.

American Federation of Labor and Congress of Industrial Organizations (AFL-CIO)
An association that seeks to advance the shared interests of its member unions at the national level.

Local Unions

Most national unions consist of multiple local units. Even when a national union plays the most critical role in negotiating the terms of a collective bargaining contract, negotiation occurs at the local level for work rules and other issues that are locally determined. In addition, administration of the contract largely takes place at the local union level. As a result, most day-to-day interaction between labor and management involves the local union.

Membership in the local union depends on the type of union. For an industrial union, the local may correspond to a single large facility or to a number of small facilities. In a craft union, the local may cover a city or a region.

Typically, the local union elects officers, such as president, vice president, and treasurer. The officers may be responsible for contract negotiation, or the local may form a bargaining committee for that purpose. When the union is engaged in bargaining, the national union provides help, including background data about other settlements, technical advice, and the leadership of a representative from the national office.

Individual members participate in local unions in various ways. At meetings of the local union, they elect officials and vote on resolutions to strike. Most of workers' contact is with the **union steward,** an employee elected by union members to represent them in ensuring that the terms of the contract are enforced. The union steward helps to investigate complaints and represents employees to supervisors and other managers when employees file grievances alleging contract violations.[6] When the union deals with several employers, as in the case of a craft union, a *business representative* performs some of the same functions as a union steward. Because of union stewards' and business representatives' close involvement with employees, it is to management's advantage to cultivate positive working relationships with them.

union steward
An employee elected by union members to represent them in ensuring that the terms of the labor contract are enforced.

Figure 14.2

Union Membership Density among U.S. Wage and Salary Workers, 1973–2007

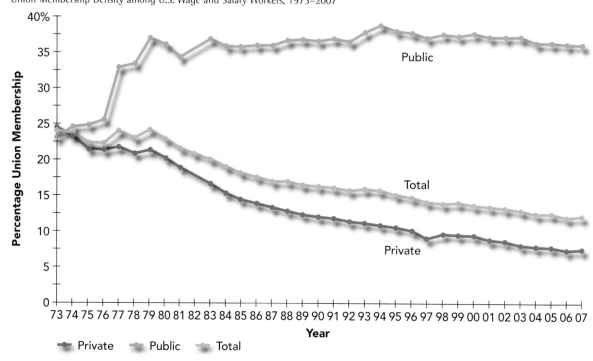

a Percentage of total, private-sector, and public-sector wage and salary workers who are union members. Beginning in 1977, workers belonging to "an employee association similar to a union" are included as members.

SOURCE: Data for 1973–2001 from B. T. Hirsch and D. A. MacPherson, *Union Membership and Earnings Data Book 2001* (Washington, DC: Bureau of National Affairs, 2002), using data from U.S. Current Population Surveys. Data for 2002 through 2007 from Bureau of Labor Statistics, "Union Affiliation Data from the Current Population Survey," http://data.bls.gov, accessed March 10, 2008.

Trends in Union Membership

Union membership in the United States peaked in the 1950s, reaching over one-third of employees. Since then, the share of employees who belong to unions has fallen. It now stands at 12.1 percent overall and 7.5 percent of private-sector employment.[7] As Figure 14.2 indicates, union membership has fallen steadily since the 1980s. Until a few years ago, the decline mostly affected the private sector, but in 2007, a slight uptick in union membership for health care, construction, and education held overall union membership steady.

The decline in union membership has been attributed to several factors:[8]

- *Change in the structure of the economy*—Much recent job growth has occurred among women and youth in the service sector of the economy, while union strength has traditionally been among urban blue-collar workers, especially middle-aged workers. Women are less likely than men to belong to unions, and services industries such as finance, insurance, and real estate have lower union representation than manufacturing. Also, much business growth has been in the South, where workers are less likely to join unions.[9]
- *Management efforts to control costs*—On average, unionized workers receive higher pay than their nonunionized counterparts, and the pressure is greater because of international competition. In the past, union membership across an industry such as

automobiles or steel resulted in similar wages and work requirements for all com-petitors. Today, U.S. producers must compete with companies that have entirely different pay scales and work rules, often placing the U.S. companies at a disadvantage.

- *Human resource practices*—Competition for scarce human resources can lead em-ployers to offer much of what employees traditionally sought through union membership.
- *Government regulation*—Stricter regulation in such areas as workplace safety and equal employment opportunity leaves fewer areas in which unions can show an ad-vantage over what employers must already offer.

As Figure 14.3 indicates, the percentage of U.S. workers who belong to unions is lower than in many other countries. More dramatic is the difference in "coverage"—the percentage of employees whose terms and conditions of employment are governed by a union contract, whether or not the employees are technically union members. In Western Europe, it is common to have coverage rates of 80 to 90 percent, so the influ-ence of labor unions far outstrips what membership levels would imply.[10] Also, em-ployees in Western Europe tend to have a larger formal role in decision making than in the United States. This role, including worker representatives on boards of direc-tors, is often mandated by the government. But as markets become more and more global, pressure to cut labor costs and increase productivity is likely to be stronger in every country. Unless unions can help companies improve productivity or organize new production facilities opened in lower-wage countries, union influence may de-cline in countries where it is now strong.

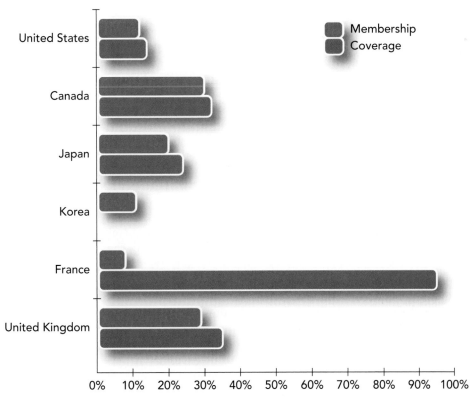

Figure 14.3

Union Membership Rates and Coverage in Selected Countries

SOURCE: J. Visser, "Union Membership Statistics in 24 Countries," *Monthly Labor Review*, January 2006, pp. 38–49.

Did You Know?

Many Union Workers Hold Government Jobs

Compared with the overall U.S. workforce, union workers are more likely to have a government job, to be 35 or older, and to work full-time. Union workers also earn more on average than nonunion workers.

Source: "Profile of Union Workers," *Business-Week,* Images, December 3, 2007, http://images. businessweek.com, citing data from Bureau of Labor Statistics.

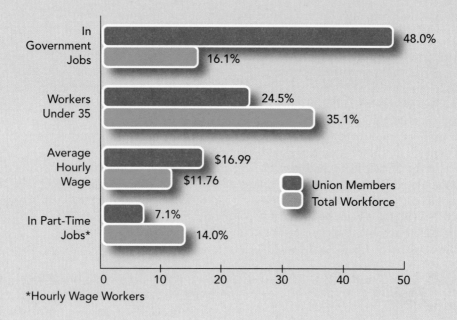

*Hourly Wage Workers

Although union members are a smaller share of the U.S. workforce, they are a significant part of many industries' labor markets. Along with strength in numbers, large unions have strength in dollars. Union retirement funds, taken together, are huge. Unions try to use their investment decisions in ways that influence businesses. The "Did You Know?" box presents some statistics on union members.

Unions in Government

Unlike union membership for workers in businesses, union membership among government workers has remained strong. Union membership in the public sector grew during the 1960s and 1970s and has remained steady ever since. Over one-third of government employees are union members, and a larger share are covered by collective bargaining agreements. One reason for this strength is that government regulations and laws support the right of government workers to organize. In 1962 Executive Order 10988 established collective bargaining rights for federal employees. By the end of the 1960s, most states had passed similar laws.

An interesting aspect of union growth among government workers is that much of it has occurred in the service industry and among white-collar employees—groups that have been viewed as difficult to organize. The American Federation of State, County and Municipal Employees (AFSCME) has about 1.4 million members. Among them are nurses, park rangers, school librarians, corrections officers, and many work-ers in clerical and other white-collar occupations.[11]

Labor relations with government workers is different in some respects, such as re-garding the right to strike. Strikes are illegal for federal workers and for state workers in most states. At the local level, all states prohibit strikes by police (Hawaii being a partial exception) and firefighters (Idaho being the exception). Teachers and state employees are somewhat more likely to have the right to strike, depending on the state. Legal or not, strikes by government workers do occur. Of the 39 strikes involv-ing 1,000 or more workers in 2000, eight involved workers in state and local government.

Impact of Unions on Company Performance

Organizations are concerned about whether union organizing and bargaining will hurt their performance, in particular, unions' impact on productivity, profits, and stock performance. Researchers have studied the general relationship between unionization and these performance measures. Through skillful labor relations, organizations can positively influence outcomes.

There has been much debate regarding the effects of unions on productivity.[12] One view is that unions decrease productivity because of work rules and limits on work-loads set by union contracts and production lost to such union actions as strikes and work slowdowns. At the same time, unions can have positive effects on productivity.[13] They can reduce turnover by giving employees a route for resolving problems.[14] Unions emphasize pay systems based on seniority, which remove incentives for em-ployees to compete rather than cooperate. The introduction of a union also may force an employer to improve its management practices and pay greater attention to em-ployee ideas.

Although there is evidence that unions have both positive and negative effects on productivity, most studies have found that union workers are more productive than nonunion workers. Still, questions remain. Are highly productive workers more likely to form unions, or does a union make workers more productive? The answer is un-clear. In theory, if unions caused greater productivity, we would expect union mem-bership to be rising, not falling as it has been.[15]

Even if unions do raise productivity, a company's profits and stock performance may still suffer if unions raise wage and benefits costs by more than the productivity gain. On average, union members receive higher wages and more generous benefits than nonunion workers, and evidence shows that unions have a large negative effect on profits. Also, union coverage tends to decline faster in companies with a lower return to shareholders.[16] In summary, companies wishing to become more competitive must continually monitor their labor relations strategy.

The studies tend to look at the average effects of unions, not at individual companies or innovative labor relations. Some organi-zations excel at labor relations, and some have worked with unions to meet business needs. For example, even though U.S. manufac-turers have outsourced or automated many jobs, a study by the National Association of Manufacturers found that 8 out of 10 had at least a moderate shortage of production workers, machinists, and craft workers. Many of these companies traditionally

Harley-Davidson and the International Association of Machinists and Aerospace Workers have cooperated to produce good results. In general, though, companies wishing to become more competitive need to continually monitor their labor relations strategies.

depended on unions to recruit and train new workers through apprenticeship programs. Some still do. At U.S. Steel, the United Steelworkers of America trains apprentices in trades including metalworking.[17]

LO2 Identify the labor relations goals of management, labor unions, and society.

Goals of Management, Labor Unions, and Society

Resolving conflicts in a positive way is usually easiest when the parties involved understand each other's goals. Although individual cases vary, we can draw some general conclusions about the goals of labor unions and management. Society, too, has goals for labor and business, given form in the laws regulating labor relations.

Management Goals

Management goals are to increase the organization's profits. Managers tend to prefer options that lower costs and raise output. When deciding whether to discourage employees from forming a union, a concern is that a union will create higher costs in wages and benefits, as well as raise the risk of work stoppages. Managers may also fear that a union will make managers and workers into adversaries or limit management's discretion in making business and employment decisions.

When an employer has recognized a union, management's goals continue to emphasize restraining costs and improving output. Managers continue to prefer to keep the organization's operations flexible, so they can adjust activities to meet competitive challenges and customer demands. Therefore, in their labor relations managers prefer to limit increases in wages and benefits and to retain as much control as they can over work rules and schedules.

Labor Union Goals

In general, labor unions have the goals of obtaining pay and working conditions that satisfy their members and of giving members a voice in decisions that affect them. Traditionally, they obtain these goals by gaining power in numbers. The more workers who belong to a union, the greater the union's power. More members translates into greater ability to halt or disrupt production. Larger unions also have greater financial resources for continuing a strike; the union can help to make up for the wages the workers lose during a strike. The threat of a long strike—stated or implied—can make an employer more willing to meet the union's demands.

As we noted earlier, union membership is indeed linked to better compensation. In 2007, private-sector unionized workers received, on average, wages 30 percent higher than nonunion workers.[18] Union membership has an even greater effect on benefits packages. Total compensation (pay plus benefits) was 43 percent higher for union members in 2007. Taking into account other influences, such as the greater ease with which unions are able to organize relatively highly paid, productive workers, researchers estimate that the total "union effect" on wages is about 10 to 15 percent.[19] In other words a union worker would earn $1.10 to $1.15 for every dollar earned by a nonunion worker.

Unions typically want to influence the *way* pay and promotions are determined. Unlike management, which tries to consider employees as individuals so that pay and promotion decisions relate to performance differences, unions try to build group solidarity and avoid possible arbitrary treatment of employees. To do so, unions focus on equal pay for equal work. They try to have any pay differences based on seniority, on the grounds that this measure is more objective than performance evaluations. As a result, where workers are represented by a union, it is common for all employees in a particular job classification to be paid at the same rate.

The survival and security of a union depend on its ability to ensure a regular flow of new members and member dues to support the services it provides. Therefore, unions typically place high priority on negotiating two types of contract provisions with an employer that are critical to a union's security and viability: checkoff provisions and provisions relating to union membership or contribution.

Under a **checkoff provision,** the employer, on behalf of the union, automatically deducts union dues from employees' paychecks. Security provisions related to union membership are *closed shop, union shop, agency shop,* and *maintenance of membership.*

The strongest union security arrangement is a **closed shop,** under which a person must be a union member before being hired. Under the National Labor Relations Act, discussed later in this chapter, closed shops are illegal. A legal membership arrangement that supports the goals of labor unions is the **union shop,** an arrangement that requires an employee to join the union within a certain time (30 days) after beginning employment. A similar alternative is the **agency shop,** which requires the payment of union dues but not union membership. **Maintenance of membership** rules do not require union membership but do require that employees who join the union remain members for a certain period of time, such as the length of the contract. As we will discuss later in the chapter, some states forbid union shops, agency shops, and maintenance of membership.

All these provisions are ways to address unions' concern about "free riders"—employees who benefit from union activities without belonging to a union. By law, all members of a bargaining unit, whether union members or not, must be represented by the union. If the union must offer services to all bargaining unit members but some of them are not dues-paying union members, the union may not have enough financial resources to operate successfully.

Societal Goals

The activities of unions and management take place within the context of society, with society's values driving the laws and regulations that affect labor relations. As long ago as the late 1800s and early 1900s, industrial relations scholars saw unions as a way to make up for individual employees' limited bargaining power.[20] At that time, clashes between workers and management could be violent, and many people hoped that unions would replace the violence with negotiation. Since then, observers have expressed concern that unions in certain industries have become too strong, achieving their goals at the expense of employers' ability to compete or meet other objectives. But even Senator Orrin Hatch, described by *BusinessWeek* as "labor's archrival on Capitol Hill," has spoken of a need for unions:

> There are always going to be people who take advantage of workers. Unions even that out, to their credit. We need them to level the field between labor and management. If you didn't have unions, it would be very difficult for even enlightened employers not to take advantage of workers on wages and working conditions, because of [competition from less-enlightened] rivals. I'm among the first to say I believe in unions.[21]

Senator Hatch's statement implies that society's goal for unions is to ensure that workers have a voice in how they are treated by their employers. As we will see in the next section, this view has produced a set of laws and regulations intended to give workers the right to join unions if they so wish.

checkoff provision
Contract provision under which the employer, on behalf of the union, automatically deducts union dues from employees' paychecks.

closed shop
Union security arrangement under which a person must be a union member before being hired; illegal for those covered by the National Labor Relations Act.

union shop
Union security arrangement that requires employees to join the union within a certain amount of time (30 days) after beginning employment.

agency shop
Union security arrangement that requires the payment of union dues but not union membership.

maintenance of membership
Union security rules not requiring union membership but requiring that employees who join the union remain members for a certain period of time.

LO3 Summarize laws and regulations that affect labor relations.

Laws and Regulations Affecting Labor Relations

The laws and regulations pertaining to labor relations affect unions' size and bargaining power, so they significantly affect the degree to which unions, management, and society achieve their varied goals. These laws and regulations set limits on union structure and administration and the ways in which unions and management interact.

National Labor Relations Act (NLRA)

National Labor Relations Act (NLRA)
Federal law that supports collective bargaining and sets out the rights of employees to form unions.

Perhaps the most dramatic example of labor laws' influence is the 1935 passage of the Wagner Act (also known as the **National Labor Relations Act,** or **NLRA**), which actively supported collective bargaining. After Congress passed the NLRA, union membership in the United States nearly tripled, from 3 million in 1933 to 8.8 million (19.2 percent of employment) in 1939.[22]

Before the 1930s, the U.S. legal system was generally hostile to unions. The courts tended to view unions as coercive organizations that hindered free trade. Unions' focus on collective voice and collective action (such as strikes and boycotts) did not fit well with the U.S. emphasis on capitalism, individualism, freedom of contract, and property rights.[23] Then the Great Depression of the 1930s shifted public attitudes toward business and the free-enterprise system. Unemployment rates as high as 25 percent and a steep fall in production between 1929 and 1933 focused attention on employee rights and the shortcomings of the economic system of the time. The nation was in crisis, and President Franklin Roosevelt responded dramatically with the New Deal. On the labor front, the 1935 NLRA ushered in an era of public policy for labor unions, enshrining collective bargaining as the preferred way to settle labor-management disputes.

Section 7 of the NLRA sets out the rights of employees, including the "right to self-organization, to form, join, or assist labor organizations, to bargain collectively through representatives of their own choosing, and to engage in other concerted activities for the purpose of collective bargaining."[24] Employees also have the right to refrain from these activities, unless union membership is a condition of employment. The following activities are among those protected under the NLRA:

- Union organizing.
- Joining a union, whether recognized by the employer or not.
- Going out on strike to secure better working conditions.
- Refraining from activity on behalf of the union.

Most employees in the private sector are covered by the NLRA. However, workers employed under the following conditions are not covered:[25]

- Employed as a supervisor.
- Employed by a parent or spouse.
- Employed as an independent contractor.
- Employed in the domestic service of any person or family in a home.
- Employed as agricultural laborers.
- Employed by an employer subject to the Railway Labor Act.
- Employed by a federal, state, or local government.
- Employed by any other person who is not an employer as defined in the NLRA.

HR How To

AVOIDING UNFAIR LABOR PRACTICES

The National Labor Relations Act prohibits employers and unions from engaging in unfair labor practices. For employers, this means they must not interfere with employees' decisions about whether to join a union and engage in union-related activities. Employers may not discriminate against employees for being involved in union activities or testifying in court about actions under the NLRA. Here are some specific examples of unfair labor practices that *employers must avoid:*

- Threatening employees with loss of their jobs or benefits if they join or vote for a union.
- Threatening to close down a plant if it is organized by a union.
- Questioning employees about their union membership or activities in a way that restrains or coerces them.
- Spying or pretending to spy on union meetings.

- Granting wage increases timed to discourage employees from forming or joining a union.
- Taking an active part in organizing a union or committee to represent employees.
- Providing preferential treatment or aid to one of several unions trying to organize employees.
- Discharging employees for urging other employees to join a union.
- Refusing to hire applicants because they are union members.
- Refusing to reinstate workers when job openings occur, on the grounds that the workers participated in a lawful strike.
- Ending operations at one facility and opening the same operations at another facility with new employees because employees at the first joined a union.

- Demoting or firing employees for filing an unfair labor practice complaint or testifying at an NLRB meeting.
- Refusing to meet with employees' representatives because the employees are on strike.
- Refusing to supply the employees' representative with cost and other data concerning a group insurance plan covering employees.
- Announcing a wage increase without consulting the employees' representative.
- Failing to bargain about the effects of a decision to close one of the employer's facilities.

Source: National Labor Relations Board, *Basic Guide to the Law and Procedures under the National Labor Relations Act* (Washington, DC: U.S. Government Printing Office, 1997); and National Labor Relations Board, "The National Labor Relations Board and You: Unfair Labor Practices," www.nlrb.gov, accessed March 17, 2008.

State or local laws may provide additional coverage. For example, California's 1975 Agricultural Labor Relations Act covers agricultural workers in that state.

In Section 8(a), the NLRA prohibits certain activities by employers as unfair labor practices. In general, employers may not interfere with, restrain, or coerce employees in exercising their rights to join or assist a labor organization or to refrain from such activities. Employers may not dominate or interfere with the formation or activities of a labor union. They may not discriminate in any aspect of employment that attempts to encourage or discourage union activity, nor may they discriminate against employees for providing testimony related to enforcement of the NLRA. Finally, employers may not refuse to bargain collectively with a labor organization that has standing under the act. For more guidance in complying with the NLRA, see the examples in the "HR How To" box.

When employers or unions violate the NLRA, remedies typically include ordering that unfair labor practices stop. Employers may be required to rehire workers, with or without back pay. The NLRA is not a criminal law, and violators may not be assigned punitive damages (fines to punish rather than merely make up for the harm done).

Laws Amending the NLRA

Originally, the NLRA did not list any unfair labor practices by unions. In later amendments to the NLRA—the Taft-Hartley Act of 1947 and the Landrum-Griffin Act of 1959—Congress established some restrictions on union practices deemed unfair to employers and union members.

Under the Taft-Hartley Act, unions may not restrain employers through actions such as the following:[26]

- Mass picketing in such numbers that nonstriking employees physically cannot enter the workplace.
- Engaging in violent acts in connection with a strike.
- Threatening employees with physical injury or job loss if they do not support union activities.
- During contract negotiations, insisting on illegal provisions, provisions that the employer may hire only workers who are union members or "satisfactory" to the union, or working conditions to be determined by a group to which the employer does not belong.
- Terminating an existing contract and striking for a new one without notifying the employer, the Federal Mediation and Conciliation Service, and the state mediation service (where one exists).

right-to-work laws
State laws that make union shops, maintenance of membership, and agency shops illegal.

The Taft-Hartley Act also allows the states to pass so-called **right-to-work laws,** which make union shops, maintenance of membership, and agency shops illegal. The idea behind such laws is that requiring union membership or the payment of union dues restricts the employees' right to freedom of association. In other words, employees should be free to choose whether they join a union or other group. Of course, unions have a different point of view. The union perspective is that unions provide services to all members of a bargaining unit (such as all of a company's workers), and all members who receive the benefits of a union should pay union dues. Figure 14.4 indicates which states currently have right-to-work laws.

The Landrum-Griffin Act regulates unions' actions with regard to their members, including financial disclosure and the conduct of elections. This law establishes and

Figure 14.4

States with Right-to-Work Laws

SOURCE: National Right to Work Legal Defense Foundation, "Right to Work States," www.nrtw.org, accessed March 17, 2008.

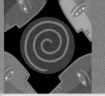

HR Oops!

Thou Shalt Not Threaten

A meatpacking company and a steel fabrication company recently ran afoul of the NLRB's requirement that employers may not interfere with union organizing by threatening or coercing employees. According to court documents, the problem at the meatpacker started when a manager saw a newspaper photo of the employee at a union rally. The manager commented to him that his presence at the rally meant he would not get a promotion. Although the manager later explained that he had intended his remark as a joke, the federal court failed to see the humor and required the company to post a notice saying it would not interfere with or coerce employees who are exercising their rights to organize.

At the steel company, the only two members of a facility's maintenance department got involved in a unionization effort. The shop foreman asked one of the maintenance workers if he thought the employees were trying to organize. When the employee said yes, the foreman said he would make the employee a manager so he couldn't be involved. He required the employee to write up disciplinary reports on two of his co-workers—a supervisory task. Later that day, the maintenance worker was fired. Again, the federal court held that these actions amounted to unlawful coercion.

Sources: Venita Jenkins, "Ruling Forbids Use of Threats," *Fayetteville (N.C.) Observer*, March 5, 2008, downloaded from General Reference Center Gold, http://find.galegroup.com; and Mary Kathryn Zachary, "Labor Law: Union Organizing Efforts Fraught with Legal Pitfalls," *Supervision*, April 2007, http://find.galegroup.com.

Questions

1. Do you agree that a comment meant as a joke can feel intimidating to an employee?

2. How can HRM professionals help supervisors avoid missteps such as the ones described here?

protects rights of union members. These include the right to nominate candidates for union office, participate in union meetings and secret-ballot elections, and examine unions' financial records.

National Labor Relations Board (NLRB)

Enforcement of the NLRA rests with the **National Labor Relations Board (NLRB).** This federal government agency consists of a five-member board, the general counsel, and 52 regional and other field offices. Because the NLRB is a federal agency, its enforcement actions are limited to companies that have an impact on interstate commerce, but as a practical matter, this extends to all but purely local businesses. For federal government workers under the Civil Service Reform Act of 1978, Title VII, the Federal Labor Relations Authority has a role similar to that of the NLRB. Many states have similar agencies to administer their laws governing state and local government workers.

The NLRB has two major functions: to conduct and certify representation elections and to prevent unfair labor practices. It does not initiate either of these actions but responds to requests for action.

The HR Oops! box shows how managers' comments and actions can considered by the NLRB as illegally interfering with union organizing.

National Labor Relations Board (NLRB)
Federal government agency that enforces the NLRA by conducting and certifying representation elections and investigating unfair labor practices.

Representation Elections

The NLRB is responsible for ensuring that the organizing process follows certain steps, described in the next section. Depending on the response to organizing efforts, the NLRB conducts elections. When a majority of workers vote in favor of a union, the

NLRB certifies it as the exclusive representative of a group of employees. The NLRB also conducts elections to decertify unions, following the same process as for representation elections.

The NLRB is also responsible for determining the appropriate bargaining unit and the employees who are eligible to participate in organizing activities. As we stated earlier, bargaining units may not include certain types of employees, such as agricultural laborers, independent contractors, supervisors, and managers. Beyond this, the NLRB attempts to group together employees who have a community of interest in their wages, hours, and working conditions. A unit may cover employees in one facility or multiple facilities within a single employer, or the unit may cover multiple employers. In general, employees on the payroll just before the ordering of an election are eligible to vote, although this rule is modified in some cases, for example, when employment in the industry is irregular. Most employees who are on strike and who have been replaced by other employees are eligible to vote in an election (such as a decertification election) that occurs within 12 months of the onset of the strike.

Prevention of Unfair Labor Practices

The handling of complaints regarding unfair labor practices begins when someone files a charge. The deadline for filing a charge is six months after the alleged unfair practice. All parties must be served with a copy of the charge. (Registered mail is recommended.) The charge is investigated by a regional office. If, after investigating, the NLRB finds the charge has merit and issues a complaint, two actions are possible. The NLRB may defer to a grievance procedure agreed on by the employer and the union; grievances are discussed later in this chapter. Or a hearing may be held before an administrative law judge. The judge makes a recommendation, which either party may appeal.

The NLRB has the authority to issue cease-and-desist orders to halt unfair labor practices. It also can order the employer to reinstate workers, with or without back pay. The NLRB can set aside the results of an election if it believes either the union or the employer has created "an atmosphere of confusion or fear of reprisals."[27] If an employer or union refuses to comply with an NLRB order, the board has the authority to petition the U.S. Court of Appeals. The court may enforce the order, recommend it to the NLRB for modification, change the order itself, or set it aside altogether.

LO4 Describe the union organizing process.

Union Organizing

Unions begin their involvement with an organization's employees by conducting an organizing campaign. To meet its objectives, a union needs to convince a majority of workers that they should receive better pay or other employment conditions and that the union will help them do so. The employer's objectives will depend on its strategy—whether it seeks to work with a union or convince employees that they are better off without union representation.

The Process of Organizing

The organizing process begins with authorization cards, such as the example shown in Figure 14.5. Union representatives make contact with employees, present their message about the union, and invite them to sign an authorization card. For the organization process to continue, at least 30 percent of the employees must sign an authorization card.

SOURCE: From J. A. Fossum, *Labor Relations: Development, Structure and Process, 2002.* Copyright © 2002 The McGraw-Hill Companies, Inc. Reprinted with permission.

If over half the employees sign an authorization card, the union may request that the employer voluntarily recognize the union. If the employer agrees, the NLRB certifies the union as the exclusive representative of employees. If the employer refuses, or if only 30 to 50 percent of employees signed cards, the NLRB conducts a secret-ballot election. The arrangements are made in one of two ways:

1. For a *consent election,* the employer and the union seeking representation arrive at an agreement stating the time and place of the election, the choices included on the ballot, and a way to determine who is eligible to vote.
2. For a *stipulation election,* the parties cannot agree on all of these terms, so the NLRB dictates the time and place, ballot choices, and method of determining eligibility.

On the ballot, workers vote for or against union representation, and they may also have a choice from among more than one union. If the union (or one of the unions on the ballot) wins a majority of votes, the NLRB certifies the union. If the ballot includes more than one union and neither gains a simple majority, the NLRB holds a runoff election.

As noted earlier, if the NLRB finds the election was not conducted fairly, it may set aside the results and call for a new election. Conduct that may lead to an election result's being set aside includes the following examples:[28]

- Threats of loss of jobs or benefits by an employer or union to influence votes or organizing activities.
- A grant of benefits or a promise of benefits as a means of influencing votes or organizing activities.
- Campaign speeches by management or union representatives to assembled groups of employees on company time less than 24 hours before an election.
- The actual use or threat of physical force or violence to influence votes or organizing activities.

After certification, there are limits on future elections. Once the NLRB has certified a union as the exclusive representative of a group of employees, it will not permit additional elections for one year. Also, after the union and employer have finished negotiating a contract, an election cannot be held for the time of the contract period or for three years, whichever comes first. The parties to the contract may agree not to hold an election for longer than three years, but an outside party (another union) cannot be barred for more than three years.

Management Strategies

Sometimes an employer will recognize a union after a majority of employees have signed authorization cards. More often, there is a hotly contested election campaign. During the campaign, unions try to persuade employees that their wages, benefits, treatment by employers, and chances to influence workplace decisions are too poor or small and that the union will be able to obtain improvements in these areas. Management typically responds with its own messages providing an opposite point of view. Management messages say the organization has provided a valuable package of wages and benefits and has treated employees well. Management also argues that the union will not be able to keep its promises but will instead create costs for employees, such as union dues and lost income during strikes.

Employers use a variety of methods to oppose unions in organizing campaigns.[29] Their efforts range from hiring consultants to distributing leaflets and letters to presenting the company's viewpoint at meetings of employees. Some management efforts go beyond what the law permits, especially in the eyes of union organizers. Why would employers break the law? One explanation is that the consequences, such as reinstating workers with back pay, are small compared to the benefits.[30] If coercing workers away from joining a union saves the company the higher wages, benefits, and other costs of a unionized workforce, management may feel an incentive to accept costs like back pay.

Supervisors have the most direct contact with employees. Thus, as Table 14.1 indicates, it is critical that they establish good relationships with employees even before there is any attempt at union organizing. Supervisors also must know what *not* to do if a union drive takes place. They should be trained in the legal principles discussed earlier in this chapter.

Union Strategies

The traditional union organizing strategy has been for organizers to call or visit employees at home, when possible, to talk about issues like pay and job security. Local unions of the Teamsters have contacted dock workers at UPS Freight terminals in 11 states and invited them to sign authorization cards. When a majority of the workers at a terminal sign cards, UPS agrees to bargain with the Teamsters at that location.[31]

Beyond encouraging workers to sign authorization cards and vote for the union, organizers use some creative alternatives to traditional organizing activities. They sometimes offer workers **associate union membership,** which is not linked to an employee's workplace and does not provide representation in collective bargaining. Rather, an associate member receives other services, such as discounts on health and life insurance or credit cards.[32] In return for these benefits, the union receives membership

associate union membership
Alternative form of union membership in which members receive discounts on insurance and credit cards rather than representation in collective bargaining.

Table 14.1

What Supervisors Should and Should Not Do to Discourage Unions

WHAT TO DO:

Report any direct or indirect signs of union activity to a core management group.

Deal with employees by carefully stating the company's response to pro-union arguments. These responses should be coordinated by the company to maintain consistency and to avoid threats or promises. Take away union issues by following effective management practices all the time:

Deliver recognition and appreciation.

Solve employee problems.

Protect employees from harassment or humiliation.

Provide business-related information.

Be consistent in treatment of different employees.

Accommodate special circumstances where appropriate.

Ensure due process in performance management.

Treat all employees with dignity and respect.

WHAT TO AVOID:

Threatening employees with harsher terms and conditions of employment or employment loss if they engage in union activity.

Interrogating employees about pro-union or anti-union sentiments that they or others may have or reviewing union authorization cards or pro-union petitions.

Promising employees that they will receive favorable terms or conditions of employment if they forgo union activity.

Spying on employees known to be, or suspected of being, engaged in pro-union activities.

Source: From J. A. Segal, "Unshackle Your Supervisors to Stay Union Free," *HR Magazine*, June 1998. Copyright © 1998 by Society for Human Resource Management. Reproduced with permission of Society for Human Resource Management via Copyright Clearance Center.

dues and a broader base of support for its activities. Associate membership may be attractive to employees who wish to join a union but cannot because their workplace is not organized by a union.

Another alternative to traditional organizing is to conduct **corporate campaigns**—bringing public, financial, or political pressure on employers during union organization and contract negotiation.[33] The Amalgamated Clothing and Textile Workers Union (ACTWU) corporate campaign against textile maker J. P. Stevens during the late 1970s was one of the first successful corporate campaigns and served as a model for those that followed. The ACTWU organized a boycott of J. P. Stevens products and threatened to withdraw its pension funds from financial institutions where J. P. Stevens officers acted as directors. The company eventually agreed to a contract with ACTWU.[34]

Another winning union organizing strategy is to negotiate employer neutrality and card-check provisions into a contract. Under a *neutrality provision*, the employer pledges not to oppose organizing attempts elsewhere in the company. A *card-check provision* is an agreement that if a certain percentage—by law, at least a majority—of employees sign an authorization card, the employer will recognize their union representation. An impartial outside agency, such as the American Arbitration Association, counts the cards. Evidence suggests that this strategy can be very effective for unions.[35]

corporate campaigns Bringing public, financial, or political pressure on employers during union organization and contract negotiation.

Decertifying a Union

The Taft-Hartley Act expanded union members' right to be represented by leaders of their own choosing to include the right to vote out an existing union. This action is called *decertifying* the union. Decertification follows the same process as a representation election. An election to decertify a union may not take place when a contract is in effect.

Research indicates that when decertification elections are held, unions typically do not fare well.[36] During the mid-1990s, unions lost about 7 out of 10 decertification elections. In another blow to unions, the number of decertification elections has increased from about 5 percent of all elections in the 1950s and 1960s to about 14 percent in recent years.

LO5 Explain how management and unions negotiate contracts.

collective bargaining Negotiation between union representatives and management representatives to arrive at a contract defining conditions of employment for the term of the contract and to administer that contract.

Collective Bargaining

When the NLRB has certified a union, that union represents employees during contract negotiations. In **collective bargaining,** a union negotiates on behalf of its members with management representatives to arrive at a contract defining conditions of employment for the term of the contract and to resolve differences in the way they interpret the contract. Typical contracts include provisions for pay, benefits, work rules, and resolution of workers' grievances. Table 14.2 shows typical provisions negotiated in collective bargaining contracts.

Collective bargaining differs from one situation to another in terms of *bargaining structure*—that is, the range of employees and employers covered by the contract. A contract may involve a narrow group of employees in a craft union or a broad group in an industrial union. Contracts may cover one or several facilities of the same employer, or the bargaining structure may involve several employers. Many more interests must be considered in collective bargaining for an industrial union with a bargaining structure that includes several employers than in collective bargaining for a craft union in a single facility.

The majority of contract negotiations take place between unions and employers that have been through the process before. In the typical situation, management has come to accept the union as an organization it must work with. The situation can be very different when a union has just been certified and is negotiating its first contract. In over one-fourth of negotiations for a first contract, the parties are unable to reach an agreement.[37]

Table 14.2

Typical Provisions in Collective Bargaining Contracts

Establishment and administration of the agreement	Bargaining unit and plant supplements
	Contract duration and reopening and renegotiation provisions
	Union security and the checkoff
	Special bargaining committees
	Grievance procedures
	Arbitration and mediation
	Strikes and lockouts
	Contract enforcement
Functions, rights, and responsibilities	Management rights clauses
	Plant removal
	Subcontracting
	Union activities on company time and premises
	Union–management cooperation
	Regulation of technological change
	Advance notice and consultation

(Continued)

Table 14.2

Concluded

Wage determination and administration	General provisions
	Rate structure and wage differentials
	Allowances
	Incentive systems and production bonus plans
	Production standards and time studies
	Job classification and job evaluation
	Individual wage adjustments
	General wage adjustments during the contract period
Job or income security	Hiring and transfer arrangements
	Employment and income guarantees
	Reporting and call-in pay
	Supplemental unemployment benefit plans
	Regulation of overtime, shift work, etc.
	Reduction of hours to forestall layoffs
	Layoff procedures; seniority; recall
	Worksharing in lieu of layoff
	Attrition arrangements
	Promotion practices
	Training and retraining
	Relocation allowances
	Severance pay and layoff benefit plans
	Special funds and study committees
Plant operations	Work and shop rules
	Rest periods and other in-plant time allowances
	Safety and health
	Plant committees
	Hours of work and premium pay practices
	Shift operations
	Hazardous work
	Discipline and discharge
Paid and unpaid leave	Vacations and holidays
	Sick leave
	Funeral and personal leave
	Military leave and jury duty
Employee benefit plans	Health and insurance plans
	Pension plans
	Profit-sharing, stock purchase, and thrift plans
	Bonus plans
Special groups	Apprentices and learners
	Workers with disabilities and older workers
	Women
	Veterans
	Union representatives
	Nondiscrimination clauses

Source: T. A. Kochan, Collective Bargaining and Industrial Relations (Homewood, IL: Richard D. Irwin, 1980), p. 29. Original data from J. W. Bloch, "Union Contracts—A New Series of Studies," Monthly Labor Review 87 (October 1964), pp. 1184–85.

Bargaining over New Contracts

Clearly, the outcome of contract negotiations can have important consequences for labor costs, productivity, and the organization's ability to compete. Therefore, unions and management need to prepare carefully for collective bargaining. Preparation includes establishing objectives for the contract, reviewing the old contract, gathering data (such as compensation paid by competitors and the company's ability to survive a strike), predicting the likely demands to be made, and establishing the cost of meeting the demands.[38] This preparation can help negotiators develop a plan for how to negotiate. Different situations and goals call for different approaches to bargaining, such as the following alternatives proposed by Richard Walton and Robert McKersie:[39]

- *Distributive bargaining* divides an economic "pie" between two sides—for example, a wage increase means giving the union a larger share of the pie.
- *Integrative bargaining* looks for win-win solutions, or outcomes in which both sides benefit. If the organization's labor costs hurt its performance, integrative bargaining might seek to avoid layoffs in exchange for work rules that improve productivity.
- *Attitudinal structuring* focuses on establishing a relationship of trust. The parties are concerned about ensuring that the other side will keep its part of any bargain.
- *Intraorganizational bargaining* addresses conflicts within union or management groups or objectives, such as between new employees and workers with high seniority or between cost control and reduction of turnover.

The collective bargaining process may involve any combination of these alternatives.

Negotiations go through various stages.[40] In the earliest stages, many more people are often present than in later stages. On the union side, this may give all the various internal interest groups a chance to participate and voice their goals. Their input helps

Patrick Dempsey and many other actors and actresses demonstrated in the Writer's Guild strike which suspended television and film production for months.

communicate to management what will satisfy union members and may help the union achieve greater solidarity. At this stage, union negotiators often present a long list of proposals, partly to satisfy members and partly to introduce enough issues that they will have flexibility later in the process. Management may or may not present proposals of its own. Sometimes management prefers to react to the union's proposals.

During the middle stages of the process, each side must make a series of decisions, even though the outcome is uncertain. How important is each issue to the other side? How likely is it that disagreement on particular issues will result in a strike? When and to what extent should one side signal its willingness to compromise?

In the final stage of negotiations, pressure for an agreement increases. Public negotiations may be only part of the process. Negotiators from each side may hold one-on-one meetings or small-group meetings where they escape some public relations pressures. A neutral third party may act as a go-between or facilitator. In some cases, bargaining breaks down as the two sides find they cannot reach a mutually acceptable agreement. The outcome depends partly on the relative bargaining power of each party. That power, in turn, depends on each party's ability to withstand a strike, which costs the workers their pay during the strike and costs the employer lost production and possibly lost customers.

When Bargaining Breaks Down

The intended outcome of collective bargaining is a contract with terms acceptable to both parties. If one or both sides determine that negotiation alone will not produce such an agreement, bargaining breaks down. To bring this impasse to an end, the union may strike, or the parties may bring in outside help to resolve their differences.

Strikes

A **strike** is a collective decision of the union members not to work until certain demands or conditions are met. The union members vote, and if the majority favors a strike, they all go on strike at that time or when union leaders believe the time is right. Strikes are typically accompanied by *picketing*—the union stations members near the worksite with signs indicating the union is on strike. During the strike, the union members do not receive pay from their employer, but the union may be able to make up for some of the lost pay. The employer loses production unless it can hire replacement workers, and even then, productivity may be reduced. Often, other unions support striking workers by refusing to cross their picket line—for example, refusing to make deliveries to a company during a strike. When the Writers Guild of America went on strike, production of television shows came to a standstill. The strike also affected the Golden Globe Awards, as actors and other union employees in the media industry refused to cross their picket lines.

The vast majority of labor-management negotiations do not result in a strike, and the number of strikes has plunged since the 1950s, as shown in Figure 14.6. The percentage of total working time lost to strikes in 2004 was a mere 0.01 percent—that is, one-hundredth of 1 percent of working time. A primary reason strikes are rare is that a strike is seldom in the best interests of either party. Not only do workers lose wages and employers lose production, but the negative experience of a strike can make future interactions more difficult. During the Writers Guild of America strike, screenwriters won some compensation for their work that is distributed over the Internet. But while television shows switched to reruns, viewers were finding new, often free content online. That could ultimately damage network TV's future.[41] When strikes do occur, the conduct of each party during the strike can do lasting harm to labor-management relations. Violence by either side or threats of job loss or actual job loss because jobs went to replacement workers can make future relations difficult. Finally, many

strike
A collective decision by union members not to work until certain demands or conditions are met.

Figure 14.6

Strikes Involving 1,000 or More Workers

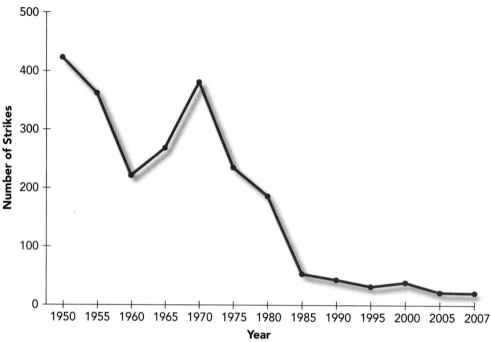

Note: Because strikes are most likely in large bargaining units, these numbers represent most lost working time in the United States.

SOURCE: Bureau of Labor Statistics, "Work Stoppage Data," http://data.bls.gov.

government employees do not have a right to strike, and their percentage among unionized employees overall has risen in recent decades, as we discussed earlier.

Alternatives to Strikes

Because strikes are so costly and risky, unions and employers generally prefer other methods for resolving conflicts. Three common alternatives rely on a neutral third party, usually provided by the Federal Mediation and Conciliation Service (FMCS):

- **Mediation** is the least formal and most widely used of these procedures. A mediator hears the views of both sides and facilitates the negotiation process. The mediator has no formal authority to dictate a resolution, so a strike remains a possibility. In a survey studying negotiations between unions and large businesses, mediation was used in almost 4 out of 10 negotiation efforts.[42]
- A **fact finder,** most often used for negotiations with governmental bodies, typically reports on the reasons for the dispute, the views and arguments of both sides, and (sometimes) a recommended settlement, which the parties may decline. The public nature of these recommendations may pressure the parties to settle. Even if they do not accept the fact finder's recommended settlement, the fact finder may identify or frame issues in a way that makes agreement easier. Sometimes merely devoting time to this process gives the parties a chance to reach an agreement. However, there is no guarantee that a strike will be avoided.
- Under **arbitration,** the most formal type of outside intervention, an arbitrator or arbitration board determines a settlement that is *binding,* meaning the parties have to

mediation
Conflict resolution procedure in which a mediator hears the views of both sides and facilitates the negotiation process but has no formal authority to dictate a resolution.

fact finder
Third party to collective bargaining who reports the reasons for a dispute, the views and arguments of both sides, and possibly a recommended settlement, which the parties may decline.

Strikes such as this one between security officers and management of several office buildings in San Francisco are costly. Both unions and employees generally prefer to resolve contract conflicts in other ways.

accept it. In conventional arbitration, the arbitrator fashions the solution. In "final-offer arbitration," the arbitrator must choose either management's or the union's final offer for each issue or for the contract as a whole. "Rights arbitration" focuses on enforcing or interpreting contract terms. Arbitration in the writing of contracts or setting of contract terms has traditionally been reserved for special circumstances such as negotiations between unions and government agencies, where strikes may be illegal or especially costly. Occasionally, arbitration has been used with businesses in situations where strikes have been extremely damaging. However, the general opinion is that union and management representatives are in the best position to resolve conflicts themselves, because they are closer to the situation than an arbitrator can be.

arbitration
Conflict resolution procedure in which an arbitrator or arbitration board determines a binding settlement.

Contract Administration

Although the process of negotiating a labor agreement (including the occasional strike) receives the most publicity, other union-management activities occur far more often. Bargaining over a new contract typically occurs only about every three years, but administering labor contracts goes on day after day, year after year. The two activities are linked, of course. Vague or inconsistent language in the contract can make administering the contract more difficult. The difficulties can create conflict that spills over into the next round of negotiations.[43] Events during negotiations—strikes, the use of replacement workers, or violence by either side—also can lead to difficulties in working successfully under a conflict.

Contract administration includes carrying out the terms of the agreement and resolving conflicts over interpretation or violation of the agreement. Under a labor contract, the process for resolving these conflicts is called a **grievance procedure.**

LO6 Summarize the practice of contract administration.

grievance procedure
The process for resolving union-management conflicts over interpretation or violation of a collective bargaining agreement.

Figure 14.7

Steps in an Employee-
Initiated Grievance
Procedure

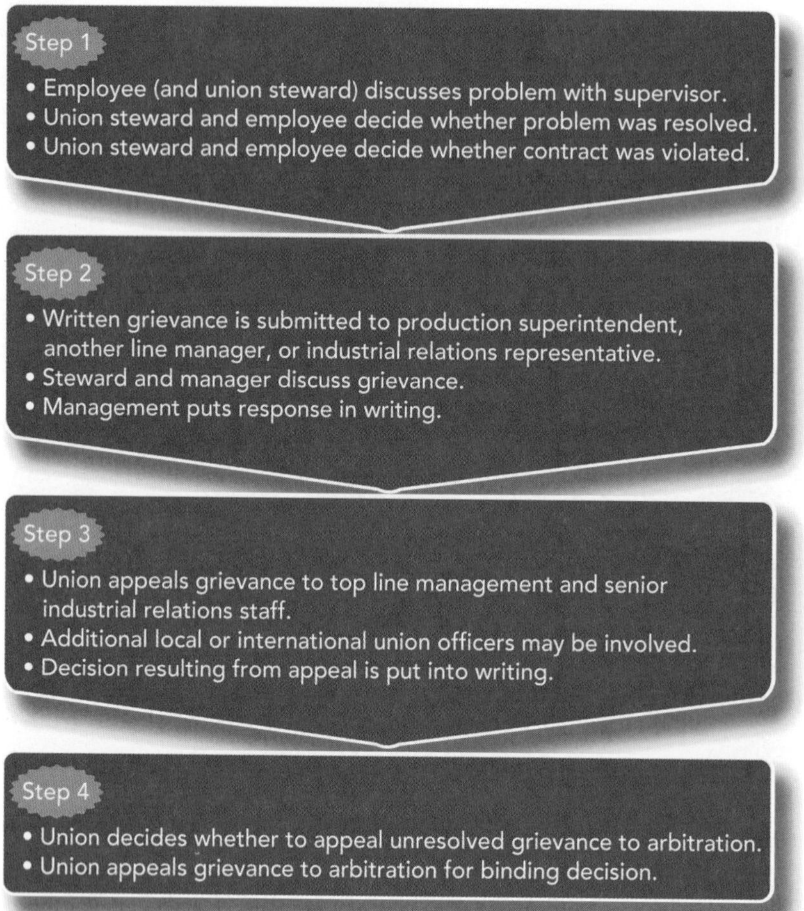

Step 1
- Employee (and union steward) discusses problem with supervisor.
- Union steward and employee decide whether problem was resolved.
- Union steward and employee decide whether contract was violated.

Step 2
- Written grievance is submitted to production superintendent, another line manager, or industrial relations representative.
- Steward and manager discuss grievance.
- Management puts response in writing.

Step 3
- Union appeals grievance to top line management and senior industrial relations staff.
- Additional local or international union officers may be involved.
- Decision resulting from appeal is put into writing.

Step 4
- Union decides whether to appeal unresolved grievance to arbitration.
- Union appeals grievance to arbitration for binding decision.

SOURCE: Adapted from T. A. Kochan, *Collective Bargaining and Industrial Relations* (Homewood, IL: Richard D. Irwin, 1980), p. 395; J. A. Fossum, *Labor Relations* (Boston: McGraw-Hill/Irwin, 2002), pp. 448–52.

This procedure has a key influence on success in contract administration. A grievance procedure may be started by an employee or discharged employee who believes the employer violated the contract or by a union representative on behalf of a group of workers or union representatives.

For grievances launched by an employee, a typical grievance procedure follows the steps shown in Figure 14.7. The grievance may be settled during any of the four steps. In the first step, the employee talks to his or her supervisor about the problem. If this conversation is unsatisfactory, the employee may involve the union steward in further discussion. The union steward and employee decide whether the problem has been resolved and, if not, whether it is a contract violation. If the problem was not resolved and does seem to be a contract violation, the union moves to step 2, putting the grievance in writing and submitting it to a line manager. The union steward meets with a management representative to try to resolve the problem. Management consults with the industrial relations staff and puts its response in writing too at this second stage. If step 2 fails to resolve the problem, the union appeals the grievance to top line management and representatives of the industrial relations staff. The union may involve more local or international officers in discussions at this stage (see step 3 in Figure 14.7). The decision resulting from the appeal is put into writing. If the grievance is still not resolved, the union may decide (step 4) to appeal the grievance to an arbitrator. If the grievance involves a discharged employee, the process may begin at step 2 or 3, however, and the time limits between steps may be shorter. Grievances filed by the union on behalf of a group may begin at step 1 or step 2.

The majority of grievances are settled during the earlier steps of the process. This reduces delays and avoids the costs of arbitration. If a grievance does reach arbitration, the arbitrator makes the final ruling in the matter. Based on a series of Supreme Court decisions, courts generally avoid reviewing arbitrators' decisions and focus only on whether the grievance involved an issue that is subject to arbitration under the contract.[44]

From the point of view of employees, the grievance procedure is an important means of getting fair treatment in the workplace. Its success depends on whether it provides for all the kinds of problems that are likely to arise (such as how to handle a business slowdown), whether employees feel they can file a grievance without being punished for it, and whether employees believe their union representatives will follow through. Under the National Labor Relations Act, the union has a *duty of fair representation*, which means the union must give equal representation to all members of the bargaining unit, whether or not they actually belong to the union. Too many grievances may indicate a problem—for example, the union members or line supervisors do not understand how to uphold the contract or have no desire to do so. At the same time, a very small number of grievances may also signal a problem. A very low grievance rate may suggest a fear of filing a grievance, a belief that the system does not work, or a belief that employees are poorly represented by their union.

What types of issues most commonly reach arbitration? According to data from the Federal Mediation and Conciliation Service, the largest share of arbitration cases involved discharge or other disciplinary actions.[45] Other issues that often reach arbitration involve wages, benefits, and the use of seniority in promotions, layoffs, work schedules, and other decisions. In reaching decisions about these and other issues, arbitrators consider a number of criteria, such as employees' understanding of the rules, the employer's consistency and fairness, and the employees' chance to present a defense and appeal a decision.[46]

Labor-Management Cooperation

The traditional understanding of union-management relations is that the two parties are adversaries, meaning each side is competing to win at the expense of the other. There have always been exceptions to this approach. And since at least the 1980s, there seems to be wider acceptance of the view that greater cooperation can increase employee commitment and motivation while making the workplace more flexible.[47] Also, evidence suggests that employees who worked under traditional labor relations systems and then under the new, more cooperative systems prefer the cooperative approach.[48]

Cooperation between labor and management may feature employee involvement in decision making, self-managing employee teams, labor-management problem-solving teams, broadly defined jobs, and sharing of financial gains and business information with employees.[49] The search for a win-win solution requires that unions and their members understand the limits on what an employer can afford in a competitive marketplace. The nearby "Best Practices" box describes how Onex Corporation has met this challenge in operating Spirit AeroSystems.

Without the union's support, efforts at employee empowerment are less likely to survive and less likely to be effective if they do survive.[50] Unions have often resisted

L07 Describe more cooperative approaches to labor-management relations.

Best Practices

Union Cooperation Helps Spirit AeroSystems Soar

A few years ago, Boeing was eager to sell off its Wichita factory, where workers made fuselages and nose cones for commercial aircraft. High wages and inflexible work rules made it difficult for the company to earn a profit, so Boeing sold to a Canadian investment firm called Onex Corporation.

The workers, represented by the International Association of Machinist & Aerospace Workers, were nervous. Often, this type of sale is followed by drastic measures to rid the workplace of the union and its higher-paid workers. In fact, Onex did lay off 800 of the plant's 4,000 employees, but it worked hard to build good relations with those who remained as it began to build a new company, called Spirit AeroSystems.

Management built up Spirit's bottom line by slashing overhead expenses and negotiating price reductions from suppliers. As managers made changes, they were open with the union and explained that they needed to make a wage cut and eliminate 15 percent of the jobs. Spirit's managers interviewed all the employees and hired the ones it thought would be most supportive of its new enterprising culture. The union worked with management to revise work rules and streamline job classifications. Still, workers were frightened and angry, as well as determined to keep their union representation.

So executives went to the union's leaders and asked what the company would need to do to win the workers' support. The union's international president, Thomas Buffenberger, replied, "If you want to share some of the pain, then give us a stake in the enterprise." And that's what Spirit did. The union members would become owners, receiving 10 percent of the ownership when the company made its initial public offering. Employee involvement teams got to work improving efficiency in every area. A year and a half later, Spirit went public, and each union member received $61,440 in cash and stock. Today, lower costs, more flexible operations, and committed employees are helping Spirit take off.

Sources: Stanley Holmes, "Soaring Where Boeing Struggled," *BusinessWeek,* February 19, 2007, downloaded from General Reference Center Gold, http://find.galegroup.com; Sidney Hill Jr., "How to Survive the 'Interesting' Times," *Manufacturing Business Technology,* April 2006, p. 56; and Molly McMillin, "Two Years after Split, Boeing Wichita Bounces Back," *Wichita (Kan.) Eagle,* September 9, 2007, http://find.galegroup.com.

employee empowerment programs, precisely because the programs try to change workplace relations and the role that unions play. Union leaders have feared that such programs will weaken unions' role as independent representatives of employee interests. Indeed, the National Labor Relations Act makes it an unfair labor practice for an employer to "dominate or interfere with the formation or administration of any labor organization or contribute financial or other support to it."

This legal requirement gave rise to concern that self-managing work teams set up by an employer could violate the NLRA. Several widely publicized rulings by the National Labor Relations Board in the mid-1990s found that worker-management committees were illegal when they were dominated by management and dealt with issues such as wages, grievances, and working conditions.[51] A team might violate national labor law when the following conditions exist:[52]

- The team addresses issues affecting nonteam employees.
- The team's issues involve matters such as wages, grievances, hours of work, and working conditions.
- The team deals with supervisors, managers, or executives on some issues.
- The company created the team or decided what it would do and how it would function.

Although employers must be careful to meet legal requirements, the NLRB has clearly supported employee involvement in decision making. For example, in a 2001 ruling, the NLRB found that employee participation committees at Crown Cork & Seal's aluminum-can factory did not violate federal labor law.[53] Those committees make and carry out decisions regarding a wide range of issues, including production, quality, training, safety, and certain types of discipline. The NLRB determined that the committees were not employer dominated. Instead of "dealing with" management, where employees make proposals for management to accept or reject, the committees exercise authority within boundaries set by management, similar to the authority of a first-line supervisor. In spite of the legal concerns, cooperative approaches to labor relations seem to contribute to an organization's success.[54]

Beyond avoiding any taint of misuse of employee empowerment, employers build cooperative relationships by the way they treat employees—with respect and fairness, in the knowledge that attracting talent and minimizing turnover are in the employer's best interests. One company that does this is General Cable's Indianapolis Compounds plant, where teams of employees, represented by the International Brotherhood of Electrical Workers, continually seek ideas to improve quality and cut inefficiency. Terry Jones, a team coordinator and union representative, says these efforts reflect "a shared attitude that's driving the push for continuous improvement."[55]

THINKING ETHICALLY

COMPANY REPUTATIONS ON THE LINE

When union-organizing efforts succeed these days, they often include a tactic known as corporate campaigns or corporate social responsibility (CSR) campaigns. In these campaigns, the organizers combine a variety of measures to raise questions about a company's reputation.

For example, when the Service Employees International Union (SEIU) set out to organize the cleaners, servers, and food preparers of Aramark, they put together a 10-city corporate campaign called the Campaign for Quality Services. One element of the strategy involved contacting the businesses that purchase food services from Aramark and promoting the union's concern that the workers were underpaid.

In Philadelphia, Aramark's headquarters city, a rally of 1,000 people gathered to voice the message that Aramark should improve the way it treats workers and customers. The union drew attention to the fact that Philadelphia's public school district had terminated its food service contract with Aramark after its cafeterias, managed by Aramark, had experienced a multimillion-dollar loss.

In Houston, city council members were invited to hear testimony from workers about how Aramark mistreated them with unfair pay practices and lacked proper concern for food safety. Also in Houston, an employee complained that she was expected to report half an hour before the start of her shift and was often not allowed to take scheduled breaks. Aramark pointed out that arriving at work early can be a wise way to avoid heavy traffic, that rest breaks are not required by law, and that employees with wage and hour complaints are encouraged to call the company's toll-free hotline.

SOURCES: L. M. Sixel, "Union Courting Aramark Workers Coast to Coast," *Houston Chronicle*, November 10, 2007; L. M. Sixel, "Union Public Relations Tactic May Not Be Helping Cause," *Houston Chronicle*, January 31, 2008; "Analysis: Unions' 'CSR' Efforts Challenge Corporations," *PR Week (US)*, June 18, 2007, all downloaded from General Reference Center Gold, http://find.galegroup.com; and SEIU, "1,000 Aramark Workers and Their Supporters March on Aramark's World Headquarters to Demand Company Do Better for Customers, Taxpayers, and Workers across the Country," news release, November 14, 2007, www.seiu.org.

Questions

1. Does a union have a *right* to make public statements about whether a company operates in a socially responsible manner? Why or why not? If a union engages in such a corporate campaign, what ethical *obligations* does it have?
2. In this example, do you think Aramark has an ethics challenge or a public relations challenge?
3. What ethical decisions can a company's management make in order to prepare itself for the possibility of this type of corporate campaign?

SUMMARY

LO1 Define unions and labor relations and their role in organizations.

A union is an organization formed for the purpose of representing its members in resolving conflicts with employers. Labor relations is the management specialty emphasizing skills that managers and union leaders can use to minimize costly forms of conflict and to seek win-win solutions to disagreements. Unions—often locals belonging to national and international organizations—engage in organizing, collective bargaining, and contract administration with businesses and government organizations. In the United States, union membership has been declining among businesses but has held steady with government employees. Unionization is associated with more generous compensation and higher productivity but lower profits. Unions may reduce a business's flexibility and economic performance.

LO2 Identify the labor relations goals of management, labor unions, and society.

Management goals are to increase the organization's profits. Managers generally expect that unions will make these goals harder to achieve. Labor unions have the goal of obtaining pay and working conditions that satisfy their members. They obtain these results by gaining power in numbers. Society's values have included the hope that the existence of unions will replace conflict or violence between workers and employers with fruitful negotiation.

LO3 Summarize laws and regulations that affect labor relations.

The National Labor Relations Act supports the use of collective bargaining and sets out the rights of employees, including the right to organize, join a union, and go on strike. The NLRA prohibits unfair labor practices by employers, including interference with efforts to form a labor union and discrimination against employees who engage in union activities. The Taft-Hartley Act and Landrum-Griffin Act establish restrictions on union practices that restrain workers, such as their preventing employees from working during a strike or determining who an employer may hire. The Taft-Hartley Act also permits state right-to-work laws.

LO4 Describe the union organizing process.

Organizing begins when union representatives contact employees and invite them to sign an authorization card. If over half the employees sign a card, the union may request that the employer voluntarily recognize the union. If the employer refuses or if 30 to 50 percent of employees signed authorization cards, the NLRB conducts a secret-ballot election. If the union wins, the NLRB certifies the union. If the union loses but the NLRB finds that the election was not conducted fairly, it may set aside the results and call a new election.

LO5 Explain how management and unions negotiate contracts.

Negotiations take place between representatives of the union and the management bargaining unit. The majority of negotiations involve parties that have been through the process before. The process begins with preparation, including research into the other side's strengths and demands. In the early stages of negotiation, many more people are present than at later stages. The union presents its demands, and management sometimes presents demands as well. Then the sides evaluate the demands and the likelihood of a strike. In the final stages, pressure for an agreement increases, and a neutral third party may be called on to help reach a resolution. If bargaining breaks down, the impasse may be broken with a strike, mediation, fact finder, or arbitration.

LO6 Summarize the practice of contract administration.

Contract administration is a daily activity under the labor agreement. It includes carrying out the terms of the agreement and resolving conflicts over interpretation or violation of the contract. Conflicts are resolved through a grievance procedure. Typically, the grievance procedure begins with an employee talking to his or her supervisor about the problem and possibly involving the union steward in the discussion. If this does not resolve the conflict, the union files a written grievance with a line manager, and union and management representatives meet to discuss the problem. If this effort fails, the union appeals the grievance to top line management and the industrial relations staff. If the appeal fails, the union may appeal the grievance to an arbitrator.

LO7 Describe more cooperative approaches to labor-management relations.

In contrast to the traditional view that labor and management are adversaries, some organizations and unions work more cooperatively. Cooperation may feature employee involvement in decision making, self-managing employee teams, labor-management problem-solving teams, broadly defined jobs, and sharing of financial gains and business information with employees. If such cooperation is tainted by attempts of the employer to dominate or interfere with labor organizations, however, such as by dealing with wages, grievances, or working conditions, it may be illegal under the NLRA. In spite of such legal concerns, cooperative labor relations seem to contribute to an organization's success.

KEY TERMS

agency shop, p. 409
American Federation of Labor and Congress of Industrial Organizations (AFL-CIO), p. 403
arbitration, p. 423
associate union membership, p. 416
checkoff provision, p. 409
closed shop, p. 409
collective bargaining, p. 418

corporate campaigns, p. 417
craft union, p. 402
fact finder, p. 422
grievance procedure, p. 423
industrial union, p. 402
labor relations, p. 401
maintenance of membership, p. 409
mediation, p. 422

National Labor Relations Act (NLRA), p. 410
National Labor Relations Board (NLRB), p. 413
right-to-work laws, p. 412
strike, p. 421
union shop, p. 409
union steward, p. 403
unions, p. 401

REVIEW AND DISCUSSION QUESTIONS

1. Why do employees join labor unions? Did you ever belong to a labor union? If you did, do you think union membership benefited you? If you did not, do you think a union would have benefited you? Why or why not?

2. Why do managers at most companies prefer that unions not represent their employees? Can unions provide benefits to an employer? Explain.

3. How has union membership in the United States changed over the past few decades? How does union membership in the United States compare with union membership in other countries? How might these patterns in union membership affect the HR decisions of an international company?

4. What legal responsibilities do employers have regarding unions? What are the legal requirements affecting unions?

5. Suppose you are the HR manager for a chain of clothing stores. You learn that union representatives have been encouraging the stores' employees to sign authorization cards. What events can follow in this process of organizing? Suggest some ways that you might respond in your role as HR manager.

6. If the parties negotiating a labor contract are unable to reach an agreement, what actions can resolve the situation?

7. Why are strikes uncommon? Under what conditions might management choose to accept a strike?

8. What are the usual steps in a grievance procedure? What are the advantages of resolving a grievance in the first step? What skills would a supervisor need so grievances can be resolved in the first step?

9. The "Best Practices" box near the end of the chapter gives an example of union-management cooperation at Spirit AeroSystems. What does the company gain from this effort? What do workers gain?

10. What are the legal restrictions on labor-management cooperation?

BUSINESSWEEK CASE

BusinessWeek   A Comeback for the UAW?

As strikes go, Chrysler's wasn't all that impressive. When Chrysler's unionized workers nationwide left their assembly line positions in early October 2007 to protest the holdup in securing a new four-year labor contract, the media reported "the second major UAW walkout in a month"—but it seemed more like a long lunch with picketing during dessert. By nightfall the parties had come to an agreement, and the next morning the newspapers chorused such headlines as "It's a New Day in Detroit" and "Detroit's 3 Finally on Track."

Really? It seems to me we've read those headlines a hundred times in the past 25 years. And each time they're wrong.

Many observers seem to believe that the Big Three's woes are all tied to union wages and the benefits its blue-collar workforce receives. But those are not their biggest problems. While the new agreements with the UAW could help, cutting labor costs won't cure what ails Detroit. In fact, just the opposite could happen.

General Motors has cried loudest about the "unfair" wage advantage the Japanese automakers enjoy. It has bemoaned what it sees as a $1,500 to $1,900 price disadvantage (owing to active and retiree health care costs) on every product it sells. Detroit spends approximately $78 an hour in blue-collar wages and benefits, while Toyota Motor spends less than $50. But a plant's productivity may be more important than actual wages paid there. Auto executives know real labor costs aren't framed just by the per-hour pay but are measured by how many vehicles the fewest workers can build in one shift. And consider Ford's last minivan attempt. No matter what Ford spent to develop or build a new minivan, it was DOA at Ford and Lincoln-Mercury dealerships. When a new vehicle comes to market and fails, the manufacturer loses hundreds of millions—if not billions—no matter what its labor costs are.

Much has been made of the fact that Detroit already spent much more than Japanese automakers in the United States for health insurance. Yet GM admitted something important after the union contracts were signed: Fully 56,000 of its remaining 74,500 blue-collar workers will be eligible for retirement by 2011. So the average age of GM's factory workers will be coming down rapidly in the near future. Theoretically this would lower costs associated with health care per employee.

At first glance, this looks to be a huge financial win for General Motors, and in the near term it is. However, it could all too easily bring the United Auto Workers roaring back to life.

Here's how it is likely to backfire. First, retired autoworkers don't get to vote on new contracts. Second, up to 56,000 of GM's 74,500 workers might be replaced either by the time of the next union negotiations or by the 2015 negotiations at the latest. Do you think the new and younger workers, paid less and getting fewer benefits, will fight to keep the retirees' benefits? A younger worker might well feel cheated and resentful.

This time around, the UAW could sign up the American workforce of foreign car companies for the same reason. The *Detroit News* reported that a secret internal Toyota report written by Seiichi Sudo, president of Toyota Engineering & Manufacturing for America, suggests that Toyota needs to get its labor costs down to whatever the prevailing wages are in the region where the factories are located. If Toyota can move more quickly to cut its labor costs because its $25 hourly wage is high compared to GM's possible $14 in some positions, then GM is putting downward pressure on Japanese wages. So the Japanese could use GM's lower wages to put downward pressure on some of their employees—and those earning Japanese wages might start to think that union representation isn't a bad idea.

SOURCE: Excerpted from Ed Wallace, "A Comeback for the UAW?" *BusinessWeek*, November 6, 2007, downloaded from General Reference Center Gold, http://find.galegroup.com.

Question

1. Why does this business writer believe union membership might become more attractive to workers at auto companies in the future? Do you agree? Why or why not?
2. Besides compensation costs, what HRM challenges do auto companies face? Which of these challenges involve labor relations?
3. Suppose GM or Toyota (choose one) hired you to advise the company about its strategy for working with or fighting the UAW. What issues would you advise the company to emphasize? What tactics would you recommend?

CASE: UNION BARISTAS AT STARBUCKS?

Starbucks, ranked near the top of *Fortune* magazine's list of the 100 Best Companies to Work for in 2008, might not seem like an obvious candidate for a union organizing campaign. But for several years, the Industrial Workers of the World (IWW) has been leading a drive to organize Starbucks workers, and the company has fought back.

Daniel Gross, a volunteer organizer for the IWW, complains that Starbucks is not as socially responsible as management would like people to think, at least not when it comes to treatment of employees. For example, only 42 percent of Starbucks employees have company-provided

health insurance. That percentage is even lower than the 47 percent at Wal-Mart, which has been widely criticized for poor compensation and benefits. Starbucks responds that over 90 percent of employees have health coverage from some source, such as a spouse or parent, and that, unlike most companies, it makes health insurance available to employees who work just 20 hours a week. In fact, Starbucks is thought to be the first major U.S. company to offer health insurance to part-timers. In New York, its typical wage for baristas—$8.75 per hour—exceeds the industry median of $7.76.

The IWW typically focuses on "direct action" to build grassroots support for unionization. Pressure on companies comes from tactics like Internet campaigns and picketing in front of stores. According to Gross, the IWW played a "substantial" role in wage increases and better working conditions at Starbucks stores. Starbucks spokesperson Tara Darrow denies that the IWW made a difference. Darrow says an employee survey found that workers want to earn more, and those results were the main reason for the pay increase that followed.

Whether or not employees need a union, Starbucks is legally required to avoid penalizing employees for the effort. In that regard, Starbucks has come under fire. The IWW claimed that in New York the company fired three employees for supporting the union, gave other union supporters negative performance appraisals, and prohibited employees from wearing union pins. The National Labor Relations Board found enough merit to the claims to schedule hearings. The company denies the charges.

Starbucks's defense grew more awkward when e-mail messages among managers became public. For example, messages indicate that when some managers learned two pro-union employees had graduated from a labor program at Cornell University, they gathered the names of other graduates and checked them against company lists to iden-tify other employees who had been in the same program. Although the research itself is not necessarily illegal, it raises questions about how managers would use what they had learned.

Company spokesperson Tara Darrow has this response: "Starbucks respects the free choice of our partners [employees] and remains committed to complying fully with all laws governing the right to organize collectively. We also are confident that our progressive, pro-partner work environment, coupled with our outstanding compensation and benefits, make unions unnecessary at Starbucks."

SOURCE: Moira Herbst, "A Storied Union Takes on Starbucks," *Business-Week*, August 2, 2007, General Reference Center Gold, http://find.galegroup.com; and Kris Maher, "Starbucks E-mails Describe Efforts to Stop Unionization," *Wall Street Journal*, January 9, 2008, http://online.wsj.com.

Questions

1. What challenges might the IWW expect to face in organizing workers at Starbucks?
2. How well do you think Starbucks is defending itself against the claims of the IWW? What other responses should it consider using?
3. If the IWW were to succeed in organizing baristas at Starbucks, what changes would you expect in the way the company manages those workers?

IT'S A WRAP!

www.mhhe.com/noefund3e is your source for Reviewing, Applying, and Practicing the concepts you learned about in Chapter 14.

Review
- Chapter learning objectives
- Narrated lecture and iPod content

Application
- Manager's Hot Seat segment: "Partnership: The Unbalancing Act"
- Video case and quiz: "Hollywood Labor Unions"
- Self-Assessment: Labor relations
- Web exercise: Understanding unions

Practice
- Chapter quiz

NOTES

1. M. Evans, "Health Workers Saying, 'Union, Yes,'" *Modern Healthcare*, February 4, 2008, downloaded from General Reference Center Gold, http://find.galegroup.com.
2. J. T. Dunlop, *Industrial Relations Systems* (New York: Holt, 1958); C. Kerr, "Industrial Conflict and Its Mediation," *American Journal of Sociology* 60 (1954), pp. 230–45.
3. See A. M. Glassman and T. G. Cummings, *Industrial Relations: A Multidimensional View* (Glenview, IL: Scott, Foresman, 1985); and W. H. Holley Jr. and K. M. Jennings, *The Labor Relations Process* (Chicago: Dryden Press, 1984).
4. T. A. Kochan, *Collective Bargaining and Industrial Relations* (Homewood, IL: Richard D. Irwin, 1980), p. 25;

and H. C. Katz and T. A. Kochan, *An Introduction to Collective Bargaining and Industrial Relations*, 3rd ed. (New York: McGraw-Hill, 2004).

5. R. J. Grossman, "Reorganized Labor," *HRMagazine*, January 2008, downloaded from General Reference Center Gold, http://find.galegroup.com.

6. Whether the time the union steward spends on union business is paid for by the employer, the union, or a combination is a matter of negotiation between the employer and the union.

7. Bureau of Labor Statistics, "Union Affiliation Data from the Current Population Survey," http://data.bls.gov, accessed March 10, 2008; and J. Smerd, "Unions Reverse Decline," *Workforce Management*, February 4, 2008, downloaded from General Reference Center Gold, http://find.galegroup.com.

8. Katz and Kochan, *An Introduction to Collective Bargaining*, building on J. Fiorito and C. L. Maranto, "The Contemporary Decline of Union Strength," *Contemporary Policy Issues* 3 (1987), pp. 12–27; G. N. Chaison and J. Rose, "The Macrodeterminants of Union Growth and Decline," in *The State of the Unions*, ed. G. Strauss et al. (Madison, WI: Industrial Relations Research Association, 1991).

9. Bureau of Labor Statistics Web site, www.bls.gov; AFL-CIO Web site, www.aflcio.org.

10. C. Brewster, "Levels of Analysis in Strategic HRM: Questions Raised by Comparative Research," Conference on Research and Theory in HRM, Cornell University, October 1997.

11. American Federation of State, County and Municipal Employees "About AFSCME," www.afscme.org, accessed March 10, 2008.

12. J. T. Addison and B. T. Hirsch, "Union Effects on Productivity, Profits, and Growth: Has the Long Run Arrived?" *Journal of Labor Economics* 7 (1989), pp. 72–105; R. B. Freeman and J. L. Medoff, "The Two Faces of Unionism," *Public Interest* 57 (Fall 1979), pp. 69–93.

13. L. Mishel and P. Voos, *Unions and Economic Competitiveness* (Armonk, NY: M. E. Sharpe, 1991); Freeman and Medoff, "Two Faces"; S. Slichter, J. Healy, and E. R. Livernash, *The Impact of Collective Bargaining on Management* (Washington, DC: Brookings Institution, 1960).

14. A. O. Hirschman, *Exit, Voice, and Loyalty* (Cambridge, MA: Harvard University Press, 1970); R. Batt, A. J. S. Colvin, and J. Keefe, "Employee Voice, Human Resource Practices, and Quit Rates: Evidence from the Telecommunications Industry," *Industrial and Labor Relations Review* 55 (1970), pp. 573–94.

15. R. B. Freeman and J. L. Medoff, *What Do Unions Do?* (New York: Basic Books, 1984); Addison and Hirsch, "Union Effects on Productivity"; M. Ash and J. A.

Seago, "The Effect of Registered Nurses' Unions on Heart-Attack Mortality," *Industrial and Labor Relations Review* 57 (2004), p. 422; and C. Doucouliagos and P. Laroche, "What Do Unions Do to Productivity? A Meta-Analysis," *Industrial Relations* 42 (2003), pp. 650–91.

16. B. E. Becker and C. A. Olson, "Unions and Firm Profits," *Industrial Relations* 31, no. 3 (1992), pp. 395–415; B. T. Hirsch and B. A. Morgan, "Shareholder Risks and Returns in Union and Nonunion Firms," *Industrial and Labor Relations Review* 47, no. 2 (1994), pp. 302–18.

17. K. Maher, "Skills Shortage Gives Training Programs New Life," *Wall Street Journal*, May 3, 2005, http://online.wsj.com.

18. Bureau of Labor Statistics, "Employer Costs for Employee Compensation Summary," news release, March 12, 2008, www.bls.gov; and Bureau of Labor Statistics, "Union Affiliation Data from the Current Population Survey," http://data.bls.gov, accessed March 12, 2008.

19. S. B. Jarrell and T. D. Stanley, "A Meta-Analysis of the Union-Nonunion Wage Gap," *Industrial and Labor Relations Review* 44 (1990), pp. 54–67; and L. Mishel and M. Walters, "How Unions Help All Workers," Economic Policy Institute Briefing Paper, August 2003, www.epinet.org.

20. S. Webb and B. Webb, *Industrial Democracy* (London: Longmans, Green, 1897); J. R. Commons, *Institutional Economics* (New York: Macmillan, 1934).

21. "Why America Needs Unions, but Not the Kind It Has Now," *BusinessWeek*, May 23, 1994, p. 70.

22. E. E. Herman, J. L. Schwartz, and A. Kuhn, *Collective Bargaining and Labor Relations* (Englewood Cliffs, NJ: Prentice Hall, 1992).

23. Kochan, *Collective Bargaining and Industrial Relations*, p. 61.

24. National Labor Relations Board, *Basic Guide to the National Labor Relations Act* (Washington, DC: U.S. Government Printing Office, 1997).

25. National Labor Relations Board, "Employees/Employers Not Covered by NLRA," Workplace Rights, www.nlrb.gov, accessed March 12, 2008.

26. National Labor Relations Board, *Basic Guide*.

27. Ibid.

28. Ibid.

29. R. B. Freeman and M. M. Kleiner, "Employer Behavior in the Face of Union Organizing Drives," *Industrial and Labor Relations Review* 43, no. 4 (April 1990), pp. 351–65.

30. J. A. Fossum, *Labor Relations*, 8th ed. (New York: McGraw-Hill, 2002), p. 149.

31. J. Gallagher, "Driving to Organize," *Traffic World*, March 3, 2008; and "UPS Freight Teamsters Gain Steam," *Traffic World*, January 28, 2008, both

downloaded from General Reference Center Gold, http://find.galegroup.com.

32. Herman et al., *Collective Bargaining*; and P. Jarley and J. Fiorito, "Associate Membership: Unionism or Consumerism?" *Industrial and Labor Relations Review* 43 (1990), pp. 209–24.

33. Katz and Kochan, *An Introduction to Collective Bargaining*; and R. L. Rose, "Unions Hit Corporate Campaign Trail," *Wall Street Journal*, March 8, 1993, p. B1.

34. Katz and Kochan, *An Introduction to Collective Bargaining*.

35. A. E. Eaton and J. Kriesky, "Union Organizing under Neutrality and Card Check Agreements," *Industrial and Labor Relations Review* 55 (2001), pp. 42–59.

36. National Labor Relations Board annual reports.

37. Chaison and Rose, "The Macrodeterminants of Union Growth and Decline."

38. Fossum, *Labor Relations*, p. 262.

39. R. E. Walton and R. B. McKersie, *A Behavioral Theory of Negotiations* (New York: McGraw-Hill, 1965).

40. C. M. Steven, *Strategy and Collective Bargaining Negotiations* (New York: McGraw-Hill, 1963); and Katz and Kochan, *An Introduction to Collective Bargaining*.

41. "The Show Will Resume," *Global Agenda*, February 12, 2008; and "Writer's Strike Ends, Viewers to Get Network Shows Again," *Information Week*, February 13, 2008, both downloaded from General Reference Center Gold, http://find.galegroup.com.

42. Kochan, *Collective Bargaining and Industrial Relations*, p. 272.

43. Katz and Kochan, *An Introduction to Collective Bargaining*.

44. *United Steelworkers v. American Manufacturing Company*, 363 U.S. 564 (1960); *United Steelworkers v. Warrior Gulf and Navigation Company*, 363 U.S. 574 (1960); *United Steelworkers v. Enterprise Wheel and Car Corporation*, 363 U.S. 593 (1960).

45. U.S. Federal Mediation and Conciliation Service, *Fifty-Ninth Annual Report, Fiscal Year 2006*, www.fmcs.gov.

46. J. R. Redecker, *Employee Discipline: Policies and Practices* (Washington, DC: Bureau of National Affairs, 1989).

47. T. A. Kochan, H. C. Katz, and R. B. McKersie, *The Transformation of American Industrial Relations* (New York: Basic Books, 1986), chap. 6; and E. Appelbaum, T. Bailey, and P. Berg, *Manufacturing Advantage: Why High-Performance Work Systems Pay Off* (Ithaca, NY: Cornell University Press, 2000).

48. L. W. Hunter, J. P. MacDuffie, and L. Doucet, "What Makes Teams Take? Employee Reactions to Work Reforms," *Industrial and Labor Relations Review* 55 (2002), pp. 448–472.

49. J. B. Arthur, "The Link between Business Strategy and Industrial Relations Systems in American Steel Minimills," *Industrial and Labor Relations Review* 45 (1992), pp. 488–506; M. Schuster, "Union Management Cooperation," in *Employee and Labor Relations*, ed. J. A. Fossum (Washington, D.C.: Bureau of National Affairs, 1990); E. Cohen-Rosenthal and C. Burton, *Mutual Gains: A Guide to Union-Management Cooperation*, 2nd ed. (Ithaca, NY: ILR Press, 1993); T. A. Kochan and P. Osterman, *The Mutual Gains Enterprise* (Boston: Harvard Business School Press, 1994); and E. Applebaum and R. Batt, *The New American Workplace* (Ithaca, NY: ILR Press, 1994).

50. A. E. Eaton, "Factors Contributing to the Survival of Employee Participation Programs in Unionized Settings," *Industrial and Labor Relations Review* 47, no. 3 (1994), pp. 371–89.

51. A. Bernstein, "Putting a Damper on That Old Team Spirit," *BusinessWeek*, May 4, 1992, p. 60; Bureau of National Affairs, "Polaroid Dissolves Employee Committee in Response to Labor Department Ruling," *Daily Labor Report*, June 23, 1992, p. A-3; and K. G. Salwen, "DuPont Is Told It Must Disband Nonunion Panels," *Wall Street Journal*, June 7, 1993, p. A2.

52. T. Kochan and P. Osterman, *The Mutual Gains Enterprise* (Boston: Harvard Business School Press, 1994), p. 202; and A. Bernstein, "Making Teamwork Work—and Appeasing Uncle Sam," *BusinessWeek*, January 25, 1993, p. 101.

53. "NLRB 4–0 Approves Crown Cork & Seal's Use of Seven Employee Participation Committees," *HR News*, September 3, 2001.

54. Kochan and Osterman, *The Mutual Gains Enterprise*; J. P. MacDuffie, "Human Resource Bundles and Manufacturing Performance: Organizational Logic and Flexible Production Systems in the World Auto Industry," *Industrial and Labor Relations Review* 48, no. 2 (1995), pp. 197–221; W. N. Cooke, "Employee Participation Programs, Group-Based Incentives, and Company Performance: A Union-Nonunion Comparison," *Industrial and Labor Relations Review* 47, no. 4 (1994), pp. 594–609; and C. Doucouliagos, "Worker Participation and Productivity in Labor-Managed and Participatory Capitalist Firms: A Meta-Analysis," *Industrial and Labor Relations Review* 49, no. 1 (1995), pp. 58–77.

55. J. Teresko, "Continuing a Winning Culture," *Industry Week*, January 2008, p. 42.

Managing Human Resources Globally

What Do I Need to Know?

After reading this chapter, you should be able to:

LO1 Summarize how the growth in international business activity affects human resource management.

LO2 Identify the factors that most strongly influence HRM in international markets.

LO3 Discuss how differences among countries affect HR planning at organizations with international operations.

LO4 Describe how companies select and train human resources in a global labor market.

LO5 Discuss challenges related to managing performance and compensating employees from other countries.

LO6 Explain how employers prepare managers for international assignments and for their return home.

Introduction

Students receiving their master's degrees from the top U.S. business schools are lining up for jobs in China, India, and Singapore as never before. The economies are booming in those parts of the world, and the graduates want to be part of the excitement while gaining valuable expertise in what are likely to be some of the world's most important markets. The employers—including investment banks, consulting firms, and multinational corporations selling consumer products, high-tech goods, and health care—are looking for people who know about business principles and also about the language and culture of the country where they will be working. Those requirements can place U.S.-born candidates at a disadvantage, but some qualify. Joseph Kauffman, for example, learned to speak Mandarin in college and worked at Coca-Cola in China between earning his undergraduate degree and enrolling in business school. His language skills and work experience helped him land a summer job with Morgan Stanley in Hong Kong.[1] At the same time that Morgan Stanley and other U.S. companies are hiring employees for assignments in other countries, foreign companies are setting up operations in the United States. Today, human resource management truly takes place on an international scale.

This chapter discusses the HR issues that organizations must address in a world of global competition. We begin by describing how the global nature of business is affecting human resource management in modern organizations. Next, we identify how global differences among countries affect the organization's decisions about human resources. In the following sections we explore HR planning, selection, training, and compensation practices in international settings. Finally, we examine guidelines for managing employees sent on international assignments.

HRM in a Global Environment

The environment in which organizations operate is rapidly becoming a global one. More and more companies are entering international markets by exporting their products, building facilities in other countries, and entering into alliances with foreign companies. At the same time, companies based in other countries are investing and setting up operations in the United States. Indeed, most organizations now function in the global economy.

LO1 Summarize how the growth in international business activity affects human resource management.

What is behind the trend toward expansion into global markets? Foreign countries can provide a business with new markets in which there are millions or billions of new customers; developing countries often provide such markets, but developed countries do so as well. In addition, companies set up operations overseas because they can operate with lower labor costs—for example, the average *monthly* wage in China is about equal to the average *daily* wage in the United States.[2] Finally, thanks to advances in telecommunications and information technology, companies can more easily spread work around the globe, wherever they find the right mix of labor costs and abilities. College graduates in India, for example, offer high intelligence and technical know-how at pay scales that are one-sixth or less the rate paid to a typical U.S. worker. A company that hires technical workers in both countries can move projects along around the clock. When one country's employees are leaving for the day, they can electronically share their work with employees in the other country, who are fresh and ready to get started.[3]

Global activities are simplified and encouraged by trade agreements among nations. For example, most countries in Western Europe belong to the European Union and share a common currency, the euro. Canada, Mexico, and the United States have encouraged trade among themselves with the North American Free Trade Agreement (NAFTA). The World Trade Organization (WTO) resolves trade disputes among more than 100 participating nations.

As these trends and arrangements encourage international trade, they increase and change the demands on human resource management. Organizations with customers or suppliers in other countries need employees who understand those customers or suppliers.

As companies in the United States and Britain cut software jobs and outsource to other countries in order to drive down costs, countries such as India continue to see employment rates rise.

Organizations that operate facilities in foreign countries need to understand the laws and customs that apply to employees in those countries. They may have to prepare managers and other personnel to take international assignments. They have to adapt their human resource plans and policies to different settings. Even if some practices are the same worldwide, the company now has to communicate them to its international workforce. A variety of international activities require managers to understand HRM principles and practices prevalent in global markets.

Employees in an International Workforce

When organizations operate globally, their employees are very likely to be citizens of more than one country. Employees may come from the employer's parent country, a

parent country
The country in which an organization's headquarters is located.

host country
A country (other than the parent country) in which an organization operates a facility.

third country
A country that is neither the parent country nor the host country of an employer.

expatriates
Employees assigned to work in another country.

host country, or a third country. The **parent country** is the country in which the organization's headquarters is located. For example, the United States is the parent country of General Motors, because GM's headquarters is in Michigan. A GM employee who was born in the United States and works at GM's headquarters or one of its U.S. factories is therefore a *parent-country national*.

A **host country** is a country (other than the parent country) in which an organization operates a facility. Great Britain is a host country of General Motors because GM has operations there. Any British workers hired to work at GM's British facility would be *host-country nationals*, that is, employees who are citizens of the host country.

A **third country** refers to a country that is neither the parent country nor the host country. (The organization may or may not have a facility in the third country.) In the example of GM's operations in Great Britain, the company could hire an Australian manager to work there. The Australian manager would be a *third-country national* because the manager is neither from the parent country (the United States) nor from the host country (Great Britain).

When organizations operate overseas, they must decide whether to hire parent-country nationals, host-country nationals, or third-country nationals for the overseas operations. Usually, they hire a combination of these. In general, employees assigned to work in another country are called **expatriates.** In the GM example, the U.S. and Australian managers working in Great Britain would be expatriates during those assignments.

The extent to which organizations use parent-country, host-country, or third-country nationals varies. In China, a challenge for companies is the limited supply of people with management expertise, so Chinese companies often recruit managers working in the United States. These managers may be U.S. citizens, Chinese citizens gaining experience in the United States, or third-country nationals, including Malaysians (many of whom are ethnic Chinese and able to communicate in their employer's language).[4] Employers can also woo candidates from China's limited talent pool by offering frequent salary reviews and tuition reimbursement to encourage learning, which is often a priority among Chinese employees.

Employers in the Global Marketplace

Just as there are different ways for employees to participate in international business—as parent-country, host-country, or third-county nationals—so there are different ways for employers to do business globally, ranging from simply shipping products to customers in other countries to transforming the organization into a truly global one, with operations, employees, and customers in many countries. Figure 15.1 shows the major levels of global participation.

Most organizations begin by serving customers and clients within a domestic marketplace. Typically, a company's founder has an idea for serving a local, regional, or national market. The business must recruit, hire, train, and compensate employees to produce the product, and these people usually come from the business owner's local labor market. Selection and training focus on employees' technical abilities and, to some extent, on interpersonal skills. Pay levels reflect local labor conditions. If the product succeeds, the company might expand operations to other domestic locations, and HRM decisions become more complex as the organization draws from a larger labor market and needs systems for training and motivating employees in several locations. As the employer's workforce grows, it is also likely to become more diverse. Even in small domestic organizations, a significant share of workers may be immigrants. In this way, even domestic companies are affected by issues related to the global economy.

Figure 15.1

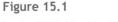

Levels of Global Participation

As organizations grow, they often begin to meet demand from customers in other countries. The usual way that a company begins to enter foreign markets is by *exporting*, or shipping domestically produced items to other countries to be sold there. Eventually, it may become economically desirable to set up operations in one or more foreign countries. An organization that does so becomes an **international organization.** The decision to participate in international activities raises a host of HR issues, including the basic question of whether a particular location provides an environment where the organization can successfully acquire and manage human resources.

While international companies build one or a few facilities in another country, **multinational companies** go overseas on a broader scale. They build facilities in a number of different countries as a way to keep production and distribution costs to a minimum. In general, when organizations become multinationals, they move production facilities from relatively high-cost locations to lower-cost locations. The lower-cost locations may have lower average wage rates, or they may reduce distribution costs by being nearer to customers. The HRM challenges faced by a multinational company are similar to but larger than those of an international organization, because more countries are involved. More than ever, the organization needs to hire managers who can function in a variety of settings, give them necessary training, and provide flexible compensation systems that take into account the different pay rates, tax systems, and costs of living from one country to another.

At the highest level of involvement in the global marketplace are **global organizations.** These flexible organizations compete by offering top products tailored to segments of the market while keeping costs as low as possible. A global organization locates each facility based on the ability to effectively, efficiently, and flexibly produce a product or service, using cultural differences as an advantage. Rather than treating differences in other countries as a challenge to overcome, a global organization treats different cultures as equals. It may have multiple headquarters spread across the globe, so decisions are more decentralized. This type of organization needs HRM practices that encourage flexibility and are based on an in-depth knowledge of differences among countries. Global organizations must be able to recruit, develop, retain, and use managers who can get results across national boundaries. The e-HRM box shows how IBM uses online tools to effectively manage its global workforce.

international organization
An organization that sets up one or a few facilities in one or a few foreign countries.

multinational company
An organization that builds facilities in a number of different countries in an effort to minimize production and distribution costs.

global organization
An organization that chooses to locate a facility based on the ability to effectively, efficiently, and flexibly produce a product or service, using cultural differences as an advantage.

ONLINE TOOLS THE LUBRICANT IN IBM'S GLOBAL MACHINE

The 20th-century IBM was a multinational corporation, with subsidiaries around the world serving local customers. Today's IBM, however, is a global organization. Its 375,000 employees on six continents are chosen as the best people in the best locations to serve clients, considering costs, available talent, access to markets, and clients' needs.

One tool that makes this machine run smoothly is a database of employee profiles, listing skill sets and availability. Employees and their managers can update the database as they complete projects and learn skills. When managers in Phoenix wanted to build a team in Brazil, they put a request on the system; within a week, they had their team.

Another tool for identifying talent is a program called Small Blue, a search engine that identifies experts in specified areas. Small Blue searches through employees' reports, e-mail, blogs, and instant messages and uses the data to rate their skills and experience. When an IBM consultant in Vancouver needed a specialist, he used Small Blue to identify knowledgeable U.S. and European employees, who recommended an expert Israeli employee.

IBM also keeps communication flowing with a social networking program called Beehive. Employees create profiles and post comments and photos related to their work and social lives. Visiting Beehive helps employees build relationships when they are too far apart for face-to-face meetings.

Sources: Steve Hamm, "International Isn't Just IBM's First Name," *BusinessWeek,* January 28, 2008, downloaded from General Reference Center Gold, http://find.galegroup.com.

---

transnational HRM system
Type of HRM system that makes decisions from a global perspective, includes managers from many countries, and is based on ideas contributed by people representing a variety of cultures.

A global organization needs a **transnational HRM system**[5] that features decision making from a global perspective, managers from many countries, and ideas contributed by people from a variety of cultures. Decisions that are the outcome of a transnational HRM system balance uniformity (for fairness) with flexibility (to account for cultural and legal differences). This balance and the variety of perspectives should work together to improve the quality of decision making. The participants from various countries and cultures contribute ideas from a position of equality, rather than the parent country's culture dominating.

Factors Affecting HRM in International Markets

LO2 Identify the factors that most strongly influence HRM in international markets.

Whatever their level of global participation, organizations that operate in more than one country must recognize that the countries are not identical and differ in terms of many factors. To simplify this discussion, we focus on four major factors:

- culture
- education
- economic systems
- political-legal systems

Culture

By far the most important influence on international HRM is the culture of the country in which a facility is located. *Culture* is a community's set of shared assumptions about how the world works and what ideals are worth striving for.[6] Cultural influences

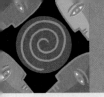

HR Oops!

Dressed for Success or a Cultural Mess?

Some days, it's hard to figure out what to wear to fit the weather. But the choice gets even harder for businesspeople who need to fit their dress to unfamiliar cultures. Learning a little about culture can prepare you, for instance, to leave a leather briefcase behind when traveling to Hindu-dominated India and to avoid white, often associated with mourning, in Asia.

Still, mistakes happen. The former medical director of an international health organization, an experienced traveler, stumbled more than once in the Middle East. Arriving at a conference in Egypt, she wore a business suit with a knee-covering skirt but quickly noticed that she "was showing more flesh than any other woman in the room." Rather than draw attention to herself, she returned to her hotel room for a pantsuit. In Iran, she tried to avoid a similar mistake by pairing a black raincoat with black trousers. The bulky outfit was uncomfortable and stood out, especially next to men in well-tailored suits. An insider might have advised a loose-fitting dress paired with flowing pants.

Of course, the culture of a particular organization matters, too. A timber company manager has learned to switch from business suits to khakis in the airport so that he fits in when he visits timber plantations.

Source: Christina Binkley, "Where Yellow's a Faux Pas and White Is Death," *Wall Street Journal*, December 6, 2007, http://online.wsj.com.

Questions

1. Why does a person's clothing affect his or her effectiveness in business settings?
2. How might an organization's HR department help its employees prepare for cultural differences when working overseas?

may be expressed through customs, languages, religions, and so on. The "HR Oops!" box shows the importance of fitting business dress to the local culture.

Culture is important to HRM for two reasons. First, it often determines the other three international influences. Culture can greatly affect a country's laws, because laws often are based on the culture's definitions of right and wrong. Culture also influences what people value, so it affects people's economic systems and efforts to invest in education.

Even more important for understanding human resource management, culture often determines the effectiveness of various HRM practices. Practices that are effective in the United States, for example, may fail or even backfire in a country with different beliefs and values.[7] Consider the five dimensions of culture that Geert Hofstede identified in his classic study of culture:[8]

1. *Individualism/collectivism* describes the strength of the relation between an individual and other individuals in the society. In cultures that are high in individualism, such as the United States, Great Britain, and the Netherlands, people tend to think and act as individuals rather than as members of a group. People in these countries are expected to stand on their own two feet, rather than be protected by the group. In cultures that are high in collectivism, such as Colombia, Pakistan, and Taiwan, people think of themselves mainly as group members. They are expected to devote themselves to the interests of the community, and the community is expected to protect them when they are in trouble.
2. *Power distance* concerns the way the culture deals with unequal distribution of power and defines the amount of

In Taiwan, a country that is high in collectivism, co-workers consider themselves more as group members instead of individuals.

439

inequality that is normal. In countries with large power distances, including India and the Philippines, the culture defines it as normal to maintain large differences in power. In countries with small power distances, such as Denmark and Israel, people try to eliminate inequalities. One way to see differences in power distance is in the way people talk to one another. In the high-power-distance countries of Mexico and Japan, people address one another with titles (Señor Smith, Smith-san). At the other extreme, in the United States, in most situations people use one another's first names—behavior that would be disrespectful in other cultures.

3. *Uncertainty avoidance* describes how cultures handle the fact that the future is unpredictable. High uncertainty avoidance refers to a strong cultural preference for structured situations. In countries such as Greece and Portugal, people tend to rely heavily on religion, law, and technology to give them a degree of security and clear rules about how to behave. In countries with low uncertainty avoidance, including Singapore and Jamaica, people seem to take each day as it comes.

4. *Masculinity/femininity* is the emphasis a culture places on practices or qualities that have traditionally been considered masculine or feminine. A "masculine" culture is a culture that values achievement, money making, assertiveness, and competition. A "feminine" culture is one that places a high value on relationships, service, care for the weak, and preserving the environment. In this model, Germany and Japan are examples of masculine cultures, and Sweden and Norway are examples of feminine cultures.

5. *Long-term/short-term orientation* suggests whether the focus of cultural values is on the future (long term) or the past and present (short term). Cultures with a long-term orientation value saving and persistence, which tend to pay off in the future. Many Asian countries, including Japan and China, have a long-term orientation. Short-term orientations, as in the cultures of the United States, Russia, and West Africa, promote respect for past tradition, and for fulfilling social obligations in the present.

Such cultural characteristics as these influence the ways members of an organization behave toward one another, as well as their attitudes toward various HRM practices. For instance, cultures differ strongly in their opinions about how managers should lead, how decisions should be handled, and what motivates employees. In Germany, managers achieve their status by demonstrating technical skills, and employees look to managers to assign tasks and resolve technical problems. In the Netherlands, managers focus on seeking agreement, exchanging views, and balancing the interests of the people affected by a decision.[9] Clearly, differences like these would affect how an organization selects and trains its managers and measures their performance.

Cultures strongly influence the appropriateness of HRM practices. For example, the extent to which a culture is individualist or collectivist will affect the success of a compensation program. Compensation tied to individual performance may be seen as fairer and more motivating by members of an individualist culture; a culture favoring individualism will be more accepting of great differences in pay between the organization's highest- and lowest-paid employees. Collectivist cultures tend to have much flatter pay structures.

Job design aimed at employee empowerment can be problematic in cultures with high "power distance." In a Mexican slipper-manufacturing plant, an effort to expand the decision-making authority of production workers stumbled when the workers balked at doing what they saw as the supervisor's proper responsibility.[10] Realizing they had moved too quickly, the plant's managers narrowed the scope of the workers' decision-making authority so they could adapt to the role. On the other hand, a factor

Best Practices

GlobalEnglish Corporation Teaches More than Vocabulary

Companies that want to help their employees do business in English may hire a training firm such as GlobalEnglish Corporation, which has 450 clients in 140 countries. Often, their people want help with a lot more than vocabulary and grammar lessons. They may already know those basics but have trouble understanding another culture's communication style.

GlobalEnglish, based in Brisbane, California, has been broadening its training to meet this need. For one client, Dubai-based Emirates Bank, the challenge is to understand accents. The bank's customers come from various countries, including Egypt, Jordan, India, and Lebanon. They are familiar with English for business matters, but each country has its own pronunciation style. So GlobalEnglish has had to move beyond exercises spoken with American and British accents.

For another client's employees, those of Computer Sciences Corporation, a struggle was how to interpret various co-workers' sense of humor. British, Danish, and Irish employees are more likely to crack jokes than employees from other parts of Europe. One French employee was offended by a British colleague calling someone "not too clever" while the three participated in a conference call. What was lighthearted to the speaker seemed rude to that listener. In another situation, a Danish team leader who poked fun at himself caused his French and German colleagues to wonder whether they should respect him. To prevent further confusion, California-based CSC has asked GlobalEnglish to develop instructions for how to recognize and interpret wisecracks.

Responding to such requests, GlobalEnglish has begun offering "Culture Notes" on its Web site. The feature offers suggestions such as the advice to "exude confidence" when communicating in the United States.

Sources: Phred Dvorak, "Plain English Gets Harder in Global Era," *Wall Street Journal,* November 5, 2007, http://online.wsj.com; and GlobalEnglish Corp., home page and "About Us," www.globalenglish.com, accessed March 31, 2008.

in favor of empowerment at that plant was the Mexican culture's high collectivism. The workers liked discussing team-related information and using the information to benefit the entire team. As in this example, a culture does not necessarily rule out a particular HRM practice, such as employee empowerment, but it should be a consideration in deciding how to carry out the practice.

Finally, cultural differences can affect how people communicate and how they coordinate their activities. In collectivist cultures, people tend to value group decision making, as in the previous example. When a person raised in an individualistic culture must work closely with people from a collectivist culture, communication problems and conflicts often occur. People from the collectivist culture tend to collaborate heavily and may evaluate the individualistic person as unwilling to cooperate and share information with them. Cultural differences in communication affected the way a North American agricultural company embarked on employee empowerment at its facilities in the United States and Brazil.[11] Empowerment requires information sharing, but in Brazil, high power distance leads employees to expect managers to make decisions, so they do not desire information that is appropriately held by managers. Empowering the Brazilian employees required involving managers directly in giving and sharing information to show that this practice was in keeping with the traditional chain of command. Also, because uncertainty avoidance is another aspect of Brazilian culture, managers explained that greater information sharing would reduce uncertainty about their work. At the same time, greater collectivism in Brazil made employees comfortable with the day-to-day communication of teamwork. The individualistic U.S. employees needed to be sold more on this aspect of empowerment. To learn how one company is helping employers cope with these challenges, see the "Best Practices" box.

Because of these challenges, organizations must prepare managers to recognize and handle cultural differences. They may recruit managers with knowledge of other cultures or provide training, as described later in the chapter. For expatriate assignments, organizations may need to conduct an extensive selection process to identify individuals who can adapt to new environments. At the same time, it is important to be wary of stereotypes and avoid exaggerating the importance of cultural differences. Recent research that examined Hofstede's model of cultural differences found that differences among organizations within a particular culture were sometimes larger than differences from country to country.[12] This finding suggests that it is important for an organization to match its HR practices to its values; individuals who share those values are likely to be interested in working for the organization.

Education and Skill Levels

Countries also differ in the degree to which their labor markets include people with education and skills of value to employers. As discussed in Chapter 1, the United States suffers from a shortage of skilled workers in many occupations, and the problem is expected to increase. For example, the need for knowledge workers (engineers, teachers, scientists, health care workers) is expected to grow almost twice as fast as the overall rate of job growth in the United States.[13] On the other hand, the labor markets in many countries are very attractive because they offer high skills and low wages.

Educational opportunities also vary from one country to another. In general, spending on education is greater per pupil in high-income countries than in poorer countries.[14] Poverty, diseases such as AIDS, and political turmoil keep children away from school in some areas. A concerted international effort to provide universal access to primary education has dramatically reduced the number and proportion of children without access to schooling. However, the problem persists in sub-Saharan Africa and is significant but declining in South Asia.[15]

Companies with foreign operations locate in countries where they can find suitable employees. The education and skill levels of a country's labor force affect how and the extent to which companies want to operate there. In countries with a poorly educated population, companies will limit their activities to low-skill, low-wage jobs. In contrast, India's large pool of well-trained technical workers is one reason that the country has become a popular location for outsourcing computer programming jobs.

Economic System

A country's economic system, whether capitalist or socialist, as well as the government's involvement in the economy through taxes or compensation, price controls, and other activities, influences human resource management practices in a number of ways.

As with all aspects of a region's or country's life, the economic system and culture are likely to be closely tied, providing many of the incentives or disincentives for developing the value of the labor force. Socialist economic systems provide ample opportunities for educational development because the education system is free to students. At the same time, socialism may not provide economic rewards (higher pay) for increasing one's education. In capitalist systems, students bear more of the cost of their education, but employers reward those who invest in education.

The health of an economic system affects human resource management. In developed countries with great wealth, labor costs are relatively high. Such differences show up in compensation systems and in recruiting and selection decisions.

In general, socialist systems take a higher percentage of each worker's income as the worker's income increases. Capitalist systems tend to let workers keep more of their earnings. In this way, socialism redistributes wealth from high earners to the poor, while capitalism apparently rewards individual accomplishments. In any case, since the amount of take-home pay a worker receives after taxes may thus differ from country to country, in an organization that pays two managers in two countries $100,000 each, the manager in one country might take home more than the manager in the other country. Such differences make pay structures more complicated when they cross national boundaries, and they can affect recruiting of candidates from more than one country.

Political-Legal System

A country's political-legal system—its government, laws, and regulations—strongly impinges on human resource management. The country's laws often dictate the requirements for certain HRM practices, such as training, compensation, hiring, firing, and layoffs. As we noted in the discussion of culture, the political-legal system arises to a large degree from the culture in which it exists, so laws and regulations reflect cultural values.

Students at the University of Warsaw in Poland are provided with a government-supported education. In general, former Soviet bloc countries tend to be generous in funding education, so they tend to have highly educated and skilled labor forces. Capitalist countries such as the United States generally leave higher education up to individual students to pay for, but the labor market rewards students who earn a college degree.

For example, the United States has led the world in eliminating discrimination in the workplace. Because this value is important in U.S. culture, the nation has legal safeguards such as the equal employment opportunity laws discussed in Chapter 3, which affect hiring and other HRM decisions. As a society, the United States also has strong beliefs regarding the fairness of pay systems. Thus, the Fair Labor Standards Act (discussed in Chapter 11), among other laws and regulations, sets a minimum wage for a variety of jobs. Other laws and regulations dictate much of the process of negotiation between unions and management. All these are examples of laws and regulations that affect the practice of HRM in the United States.

Similarly, laws and regulations in other countries reflect the norms of their cultures. In Western Europe, where many countries have had strong socialist parties, some laws have been aimed at protecting the rights and benefits of workers. Until recently, workers in Germany and France had 35-hour workweeks, but under growing pressure to adopt the "Anglo-Saxon model" emphasizing productivity, many have made concessions. The European Union's standard permits workweeks of up to 48 hours.[16]

An organization that expands internationally must gain expertise in the host country's legal requirements and ways of dealing with its legal system, often leading organizations to hire one or more host-country nationals to help in the process. Some countries have laws requiring that a certain percentage of the employees of any foreign-owned subsidiary be host-country nationals, and in the context of our discussion here, this legal challenge to an organization's HRM may hold an advantage if handled creatively.

LO3 Discuss how differences among countries affect HR planning at organizations with international operations.

Human Resource Planning in a Global Economy

As economic and technological change creates a global environment for organizations, human resource planning is involved in decisions about participating as an exporter or as an international, multinational, or global company. Even purely domestic companies may draw talent from the international labor market. As organizations consider decisions about their level of international activity, HR professionals should provide information about the relevant human resource issues, such as local market pay rates and labor laws. When organizations decide to operate internationally or globally, human resource planning involves decisions about where and how many employees are needed for each international facility.

Decisions about where to locate include HR considerations such as the cost and availability of qualified workers. In addition, HR specialists must work with other members of the organization to weigh these considerations against financial and operational requirements. For example, one reason that Toyota built manufacturing facilities in the United States was to address U.S. customers' concerns over U.S. jobs being lost to foreign auto companies. However, the company has tended to locate its factories in lower-wage areas of the United States (away from union strongholds) and also has facilities in Mexico, where it can serve North America as economically as possible.[17]

Other location decisions involve outsourcing, described in Chapter 2. Many companies have boosted efficiency by arranging to have specific functions performed by outside contractors. Many—but not all—of these arrangements involve workers outside the United States in lower-wage countries.[18]

In Chapter 5, we saw that human resource planning includes decisions to hire and lay off workers to prepare for the organization's expected needs. Compared with other countries, the United States allows employers wide latitude in reducing their workforce, giving U.S. employers the option of hiring for peak needs, then laying off employees if needs decline. Other governments place more emphasis on protecting workers' jobs. European countries, and France in particular, tend to be very strict in this regard.

LO4 Describe how companies select and train human resources in a global labor market.

Selecting Employees in a Global Labor Market

Many companies such as Microsoft have headquarters in the United States plus facilities in locations around the world. To be effective, employees in the Microsoft Mexico operations in Mexico City must understand that region's business and social culture. Organizations often meet this need by hiring host-country nationals to fill most of their foreign positions. A key reason is that a host-country national can more easily understand the values and customs of the local workforce than someone from another part of the world can. Also, training for and transporting families to foreign assignments is more expensive than hiring people in the foreign country. Employees may be reluctant to take a foreign assignment because of the difficulty of moving overseas. Sometimes the move requires the employee's spouse to quit a job, and some countries will not allow the employee's spouse to seek work, even if jobs might be available.

Even so, organizations fill many key foreign positions with parent-country or third-country nationals. Sometimes a person's technical and human relations skills outweigh the advantages of hiring locally. In other situations, such as the shortage of U.S. knowledge workers, the local labor market simply does not offer enough qualified people. At organizations located where needed skills are in short supply, hiring immigrant employees may be part of an effective recruitment and selection strategy.[19] Of the two largest categories of foreign workers employed in the United States, one group consists of professionals with the particular qualifications needed to fill a job.[20] The other group comprises employees of multinational companies who are transferred to the United States from their employer's facilities in another country. The terrorist attacks of September 11, 2001, have not changed the basics of selecting these employees, but they have raised some security issues. One is that the government may move more deliberately (and thus more slowly) in approving visas for immigrants. Employers may be required to provide more paperwork, such as annual reports to show they can pay the immigrant's salary and, for some kinds of positions, job descriptions clarifying that the worker will not be in a situation where he or she could harm the United States. Another issue is that foreign travelers to and from the United States, including the organization's immigrant workers, may have to contend with more delays and red tape. The primary impact on employers is that they must be more patient in completing the hiring process.[21]

Qualities associated with success in foreign assignments are the ability to communicate in the foreign country, flexibility, enjoying a challenging situation, and support from family members. What would persuade you to take a foreign assignment?

Whether the organization is hiring immigrants or selecting parent-country or third-country nationals for foreign assignments, some basic principles of selection apply. Selection of employees for foreign assignments should reflect criteria that have been associated with success in working overseas:

- Competency in the employee's area of expertise.
- Ability to communicate verbally and nonverbally in the foreign country.
- Flexibility, tolerance of ambiguity, and sensitivity to cultural differences.
- Motivation to succeed and enjoyment of challenges.
- Willingness to learn about the foreign country's culture, language, and customs.
- Support from family members.[22]

In research conducted a number of years ago, the factor most strongly influencing whether an employee completed a foreign assignment was the comfort of the employee's spouse and family.[23] Personality may also be important. Research has found successful completion of overseas assignments to be most likely among employees who are extroverted (outgoing), agreeable (cooperative and tolerant), and conscientious (dependable and achievement oriented).[24]

Qualities of flexibility, motivation, agreeableness, and conscientiousness are so important because of the challenges involved in entering another culture. The emotions that accompany an overseas assignment tend to follow a cycle like that in Figure 15.2.[25] For a month or so after arriving, the foreign worker enjoys a "honeymoon"

Honeymoon → Culture shock → Learning → Adjustment

Figure 15.2

Emotional Cycle Associated with a Foreign Assignment

SOURCE: Adapted from C. Lachnit, "Low-Cost Tips for Successful Inpatriation," *Work-force*, August 2001, p. 44.

of fascination and euphoria as the employee enjoys the novelty of the new culture and compares its interesting similarities to or differences from the employee's own culture. Before long, the employee's mood declines as he or she notices more unpleasant differences and experiences feelings of isolation, criticism, stereotyping, and even hostility. As the mood reaches bottom, the employee is experiencing **culture shock,** the disillusionment and discomfort that occur during the process of adjusting to a new culture and its norms, values, and perspectives. Eventually, if employees persist and continue learning about their host country's culture, they develop a greater understanding and a support network. As the employee's language skills and comfort increase, the employee's mood should improve as well. Eventually, the employee reaches a stage of adjustment in which he or she accepts and enjoys the host country's culture.

culture shock
Disillusionment and discomfort that occur during the process of adjusting to a new culture.

Even if the organization determines that the best candidate for a position is someone from another country, employers often have difficulty persuading candidates to accept foreign assignments. Not only do the employee and employee's family have to contend with culture shock, but the employee's spouse commonly loses a job when an employee makes a foreign move. Some organizations solve this problem with a compromise: the use of **virtual expatriates,** or employees who manage an operation abroad without locating permanently in that country.[26] They take frequent trips to the foreign country, and when they are home, they use modern technology such as videoconferencing and e-mail to stay in touch. An assignment as a virtual expatriate may be less inconvenient to family members and less costly to the employer. The arrangement does have disadvantages. Most notably, by limiting personal contact to sporadic trips, the virtual expatriate will likely have a harder time building relationships.

virtual expatriates
Employees who manage an operation abroad without permanently locating in the country.

Training and Developing a Global Workforce

In an organization whose employees come from more than one country, some special challenges arise with regard to training and development: (1) Training and development programs should be effective for all participating employees, regardless of their country of origin; and (2) When organizations hire employees to work in a foreign country or transfer them to another country, the employer needs to provide the employees with training in how to handle the challenges associated with working in the foreign country.

Training Programs for an International Workforce

Developers of effective training programs for an international workforce must ask certain questions.[27] The first is to establish the objectives for the training and its content. Decisions about the training should support those objectives. The developers should next ask what training techniques, strategies, and media to use. Some will be more effective than others, depending on the learners' language and culture, as well as the content of the training. For example, in preparation U.S. employees might expect to discuss and ask questions about the training content, whereas employees from other cultures might consider this level of participation to be disrespectful, so for them some additional support might be called for. Language differences will require translations and perhaps a translator at training activities. Next, the developers should identify any other interventions and conditions that must be in place for the training to meet its objectives. For example, training is

CULTURAL DIMENSION	IMPACT ON TRAINING
Individualism	Culture high in individualism expects participation in exercises and questioning to be determined by status in the company or culture.
Uncertainty avoidance	Culture high in uncertainty avoidance expects formal instructional environments. Less tolerance for impromptu style.
Masculinity	Culture low in masculinity values relationships with fellow trainees. Female trainers are less likely to be resisted in low-masculinity cultures.
Power distance	Culture high in power distance expects trainer to be expert. Trainers are expected to be authoritarian and controlling of session.
Time orientation	Culture with a long-term orientation will have trainees who are likely to accept development plans and assignments.

TABLE 15.1

Effects of Culture on Training Design

Source: Based on B. Filipczak, "Think Locally, Act Globally," Training, January 1997, pp. 41–48.

more likely to meet its objectives if it is linked to performance management and has the full support of management. Finally, the developers of a training program should identify who in the organization should be involved in reviewing and approving the training program.

The plan for the training program must consider international differences among trainees. For example, economic and educational differences might influence employees' access to and ability to use Web-based training. Cultural differences may influence whether they will consider it appropriate to ask questions and whether they expect the trainer to spend time becoming acquainted with employees or to get down to business immediately. Table 15.1 provides examples of how cultural characteristics can affect training design. For additional suggestions on providing effective training programs to an international workforce, see the "HR How To" box.

Cross-Cultural Preparation

When an organization selects an employee for a position in a foreign country, it must prepare the employee for the foreign assignment. This kind of training is called **cross-cultural preparation,** preparing employees to work across national and cultural boundaries, and it often includes family members who will accompany the employee on the assignment. The training is necessary for all three phases of an international assignment:

1. Preparation for *departure*—language instruction and an orientation to the foreign country's culture.
2. The *assignment* itself—some combination of a formal program and mentoring relationship to provide ongoing further information about the foreign country's culture.
3. Preparation for the *return* home—providing information about the employee's community and home-country workplace (from company newsletters, local newspapers, and so on).

cross-cultural preparation
Training to prepare employees and their family members for an assignment in a foreign country.

HR How To

DELIVERING TRAINING IN OTHER COUNTRIES

Training professionals offer the following ideas for preparing and delivering training programs overseas:

- *Know your goals*—Clarify what the overseas training is supposed to achieve. Don't assume that if overseas operations save money, the training will be cheaper, too. You'll need to find qualified trainers, stay in contact with them across time zones, and perhaps translate materials into another language. Trainers may have high travel expenses. If efficiency is your goal, computer-based training may cost far less than classroom training. If your goal is to convey the organization's culture, you probably will want someone to travel to the training site.

- *Keep an eye on quality*—You need a plan to train your overseas trainers to meet the same quality standards you have at headquarters. Trainers need to know the course material as well as trainees' language and culture. Specific, quantifiable quality measures are especially important for training done far away.

- *Be clear about standards for confidentiality and intellectual property*—Especially if training is to be conducted in a country with lax laws regarding ownership of training materials, you will need a plan for protecting authors' and publishers' rights.

- *Know the local laws that affect training programs*—When Liverpool, Mexico's largest department store chain, wanted to set up a formal training program, called Liverpool Virtual University, it needed to obtain approval from that country's education authorities, who were reluctant to recognize a new educational institution. Also, Liverpool's training was to be conducted mostly online, and the Mexican regulators were unfamiliar with evaluating this type of education process. The effort succeeded, but the government hurdles were some of the most difficult the company faced.

Sources: Holly Dolezalek, "It's a Small World," *Training,* January 2008, pp. 22–26; and Desda Moss, "A Lesson in Learning," *HRMagazine,* November 2007, downloaded from General Reference Center Gold, http://find.galegroup.com.

Methods for providing this training may range from lectures for employees and their families to visits to culturally diverse communities.[28] Employees and their families may also spend time visiting a local family from the country where they will be working. In the later section on managing expatriates, we provide more detail about cross-cultural preparation.

U.S.-based companies sometimes need to be reminded that foreign employees who come to the United States ("inpatriates") need cross-cultural preparation as much as U.S. employees sent on foreign assignments.[29] In spite of the many benefits of living in the United States, relocation can be challenging for inpatriates. In fact, in the Global Relocation Trends 2000 Survey Report, the United States was listed as among the most challenging foreign assignments.[30] For example, inpatriates exposed to the United States through Hollywood and TV shows often worry about safety in their new homes. In many parts of the world, a middle manager or professional's lifestyle may include servants, and the cost of rental housing is far less. As with expatriates, organizations can prepare inpatriate employees by providing information about getting the resources they need to live safely and comfortably in their new surroundings. HR personnel may be able to identify local immigrant communities where their inpatriate employees can go to shop for familiar foods and hear their native language.

Global Employee Development

At global organizations, international assignments are a part of many career paths. The organization benefits most if it applies the principles of employee development in deciding which employees should be offered jobs in other countries. Career development helps expatriate and inpatriate employees make the transitions to and from their assignments and helps the organization apply the knowledge the employees obtain from these assignments.

Performance Management across National Boundaries

LO5 Discuss challenges related to managing performance and compensating employees from other countries.

The general principles of performance management may apply in most countries, but the specific methods that work in one country may fail in another. Therefore, organizations have to consider legal requirements, local business practices, and national cultures when they establish performance management methods in other countries. Differences may include which behaviors are rated, how and the extent to which performance is measured, who performs the rating, and how feedback is provided.[31]

For example, National Rental Car uses a behaviorally based rating scale for customer service representatives. To measure the extent to which customer service representatives' behaviors contribute to the company's goal of improving customer service, the scale measures behaviors such as smiling, making eye contact, greeting customers, and solving customer problems. Depending on the country, different behaviors may be appropriate. In Japan, culturally defined standards for polite behavior include the angle of bowing as well as proper back alignment and eye contact. In Ghana and many other African nations, appropriate measures would include behaviors that reflect loyalty and repaying of obligations as well as behaviors related to following regulations and procedures.

The extent to which managers measure performance may also vary from one country to another. In rapidly changing regions, such as Southeast Asia, the organization may have to update its performance plans more often than once a year.

Feedback is another area in which differences can occur. Employees around the world appreciate positive feedback, but U.S. employees are much more used to direct feedback than are employees in other countries. In Mexico managers are expected to provide positive feedback before focusing the discussion on behaviors the employee needs to improve.[32] At the Thai office of Singapore Airlines, managers resisted giving negative feedback to employees because they feared this would cause them to have bad karma, contributing to their reincarnation at a lower level in their next life.[33] The airlines therefore allowed the managers to adapt their feedback process to fit local cultures.

Compensating an International Workforce

The chapters in Part 4 explained that compensation includes decisions about pay structure, incentive pay, and employee benefits. All these decisions become more complex when an organization has an international workforce. In a recent survey of employers with international operations, 85 percent said they have a global compensation strategy to guide compensation decisions for employees at all levels and in all countries where they operate.[34] Still, HR specialists may need to make extra efforts to

Figure 15.3

Earnings in Selected Occupations in Seven Cities

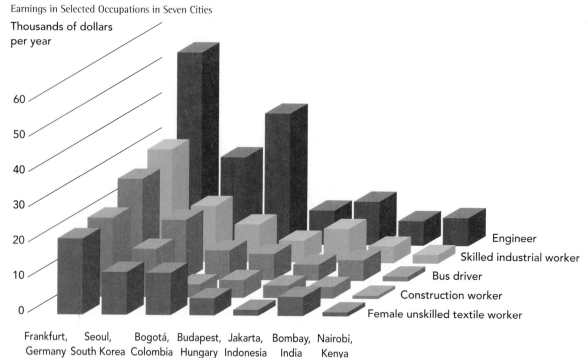

Note: Earnings are adjusted to reflect purchasing power.

SOURCE: From *World Development Report 1995*. Workers in an Integrating World by World Bank. Copyright 1995 by World Bank. Reprinted with permission of World Bank via Copyright Clearance Center.

administer these systems effectively. In half of the companies surveyed, the person in charge of HRM in one country reports to the head of that company's operations, rather than to the leader of HRM at headquarters.

Pay Structure

As Figure 15.3 shows, market pay structures can differ substantially across countries in terms of both pay level and the relative worth of jobs. For example, compared with the labor market in Frankfurt, Germany, the markets in Budapest, Hungary, and in Bombay, India, provide much lower pay levels overall. The latter two labor markets also exhibit less of a pay difference for jobs requiring greater skill and education.

Differences such as these create a dilemma for global companies: Should pay levels and differences reflect what workers are used to in their own countries? Or should they reflect the earnings of colleagues in the country of the facility, or earnings at the company headquarters? For example, should a German engineer posted to Bombay be paid according to the standard in Frankfurt or the standard in Bombay? If the standard is Frankfurt, the engineers in Bombay will likely see the German engineer's pay as unfair. If the standard is Bombay, the company will likely find it impossible to persuade a German engineer to take an assignment in Bombay. Dilemmas such as these make a global compensation strategy important as a way to show employees that the pay structure is designed to be fair and related to the value that employees bring to the organization.

These decisions affect a company's costs and ability to compete. The average hourly labor costs in industrialized countries such as the United States, Germany, and Japan are far higher than these costs in newly industrialized countries such as Mexico, Hong Kong, and Korea.[35] As a result, we often hear that U.S. labor costs are too high to allow U.S. companies to compete effectively unless the companies shift operations to low-cost foreign subsidiaries. That conclusion oversimplifies the situation for many companies. Merely comparing wages ignores differences in education, skills, and productivity.[36] If an organization gets more or higher-quality output from a higher-wage workforce, the higher wages may be worth the cost. Besides this, if the organization has many positions requiring highly skilled workers, it may need to operate in (or hire immigrants from) a country with a strong educational system, regardless of labor costs. Finally, labor costs may be outweighed by other factors, such as transportation costs or access to resources or customers. When a production process is highly automated, differences in labor costs may not be significant.

At the same time, the challenge of competing with organizations in low-wage countries can be very difficult. China, for example, has invested in vocational schools, which provide training for skilled factory jobs. Chinese universities graduate a much larger share of engineers than U.S. universities. These schools are flooding the Chinese labor market with talent, so that even as high-tech manufacturing spreads to many Chinese cities, the need for workers is easy to fill. For Chinese workers, even experienced engineers, the result is that pay is growing but remains low compared to rates in other countries.[37]

Incentive Pay

Besides setting a pay structure, the organization must make decisions with regard to incentive pay, such as bonuses and stock options. Although stock options became a common form of incentive pay in the United States during the 1990s, European businesses did not begin to embrace this type of compensation until the end of that decade.

However, the United States and Europe differ in the way they award stock options. European companies usually link the options to specific performance goals, such as the increase in a company's share price compared with that of its competitors.

Employee Benefits

As in the United States, compensation packages in other countries include benefits. Decisions about benefits must take into account the laws of each country involved, as well as employees' expectations and values in those countries. Some countries require paid maternity leave, and some countries have nationalized health care systems, which would affect the value of private health insurance in a compensation package. Pension plans are more widespread in parts of Western Europe than in the United States and Japan. Over 90 percent of workers in Switzerland have pension plans, as do all workers in France. Among workers with pension plans, U.S. workers are significantly less likely to have defined benefit plans than workers in Japan or Germany.

Paid vacation, discussed in Chapter 13, tends to be more generous in Western Europe than in the United States. Figure 15.4 compares the number of hours the average employee works in various countries. Of these countries, only in South Korea and Poland do workers put in more hours than U.S. workers. In the other countries, the norm is to work fewer hours than a U.S. worker over the course of a year.

Figure 15.4

Average Hours Worked in
Selected Countries

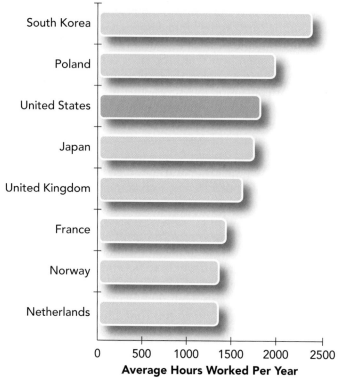

SOURCE: PriceWaterhouseCoopers, *Key Trends in Human Capital: A Global
Perspective, 2006*, Publications, www.pwc.co.uk, accessed March 19, 2008.

International Labor Relations

Companies that operate across national boundaries often need to work with unions in
more than one country. Organizations establish policies and goals for labor relations,
for overseeing labor agreements, and for monitoring labor performance (for example,
output and productivity).[38] The day-to-day decisions about labor relations are usually
handled by each foreign subsidiary. The reason is that labor relations on an international scale involve differences in laws, attitudes, and economic systems, as well as
differences in negotiation styles.

At least in comparison with European organizations, U.S. organizations exert more
centralized control over labor relations in the various countries where they operate.[39]
U.S. management therefore must recognize differences in how various countries understand and regulate labor relations. For example, in the United States, collective
bargaining usually involves negotiations between a union local and an organization's
management, but in Sweden and Germany, collective bargaining generally involves
negotiations between an employers' organization and a union representing an entire
industry's employees.[40] Legal differences range from who may form a union to how
much latitude an organization is allowed in laying off workers. In China, for example,
the government recently passed a law requiring employers to give new employees
shorter probationary periods, consider workers' dependents in making layoff decisions,
pay severance to fired workers, and give the Communist Party–run union more power
in negotiating contracts and work rules.[41] In Germany, because labor representatives
participate on companies' boards of directors, the way management handles labor
relations can affect a broad range of decisions.[42] Management therefore has an incentive to build cooperative relationships.

International labor relations must also take into account that negotiations between labor and management take place in a different social context, not just different economic and legal contexts. Cultural differences that affect other interactions come into play in labor negotiations as well. Negotiators will approach the process differently depending on whether the culture views the process as primarily cooperative or competitive and whether it is local practice to negotiate a deal by starting with the specifics or agreeing on overall principles.[43] Working with host-country nationals can help organizations navigate such differences in negotiation style.

Due to the Multi Fibre Agreement which governs trade in the textile and clothing industry, the once prosperous clothing industry in Cambodia is falling to competitors in countries such as China. Many fear employees being laid off will be pushed to prostitution or become victims of human trafficking.

Managing Expatriates

At some point, most international and global organizations assign managers to foreign posts. These assignments give rise to significant human resource challenges, from selecting managers for these assignments to preparing them, compensating them, and helping them adjust to a return home. The same kinds of HRM principles that apply to domestic positions can help organizations avoid mistakes in managing expatriates: planning and goal setting, selection aimed at achieving the HR goals, and performance management that includes evaluation of whether the overseas assignment delivered value relative to the costs involved.[44]

Selecting Expatriate Managers

The challenge of managing expatriate managers begins with determining which individuals in the organization are most capable of handling an assignment in another country. Expatriate managers need technical competence in the area of operations, in part to help them earn the respect of subordinates. Of course, many other skills are also necessary for success in any management job, especially one that involves working overseas. Depending on the nature of the assignment and the culture where it is located, the organization should consider each candidate's skills, learning style, and approach to problem solving. Each of these should be related to achievement of the organization's goals, such as solving a particular problem, transferring knowledge to host-country employees, or developing future leaders for the organization.[45]

A successful expatriate manager must be sensitive to the host country's cultural norms, flexible enough to adapt to those norms, and strong enough to survive the culture shock of living in another culture. In addition, if the manager has a family, the family members must be able to adapt to a new culture. Adaptation requires three kinds of skills:[46]

1. Ability to maintain a positive self-image and feeling of well-being.
2. Ability to foster relationships with the host-country nationals.
3. Ability to perceive and evaluate the host country's environment accurately.

In a study that drew on the experience of people holding international assignments, expatriates told researchers that the most important qualities for an expatriate manager are, in order of importance, family situation, flexibility and adaptability, job knowledge and motivation, relational skills, and openness to other cultures.[47] To assess candidates' ability to adapt to a new environment, interviews should address topics such as the ones listed in Table 15.2. The interviewer should be certain to give

Table 15.2

Topics for Assessing Candidates for Overseas Assignments

Motivation
- Investigate reasons and degree of interest in wanting to be considered.
- Determine desire to work abroad, verified by previous concerns such as personal travel, language training, reading, and association with foreign employees or students.
- Determine whether the candidate has a realistic understanding of what working and living abroad require.
- Determine the basic attitudes of the spouse toward an overseas assignment.

Health
- Determine whether any medical problems of the candidate or his or her family might be critical to the success of the assignment.
- Determine whether he or she is in good physical and mental health, without any foreseeable change.

Language ability
- Determine potential for learning a new language.
- Determine any previous language(s) studied or oral ability (judge against language needed on the overseas assignment).
- Determine the ability of the spouse to meet the language requirements.

Family considerations
- How many moves has the family made in the past among different cities or parts of the United States?
- What problems were encountered?
- How recent was the last move?
- What is the spouse's goal in this move?
- What are the number of children and the ages of each?
- Has divorce or its potential, or death of a family member, weakened family solidarity?
- Will all the children move? Why or why not?
- What are the location, health, and living arrangements of grandparents and the number of trips normally made to their home each year?
- Are there any special adjustment problems that you would expect?
- How is each member of the family reacting to this possible move?
- Do special educational problems exist within the family?

Resourcefulness and initiative
- Is the candidate independent; can he make and stand by his decisions and judgments?
- Does she have the intellectual capacity to deal with several dimensions simultaneously?
- Is he able to reach objectives and produce results with whatever personnel and facilities are available, regardless of the limitations and barriers that might arise?
- Can the candidate operate without a clear definition of responsibility and authority on a foreign assignment?
- Will the candidate be able to explain the aims and company philosophy to the local managers and workers?
- Does she possess sufficient self-discipline and self-confidence to overcome difficulties or handle complex problems?
- Can the candidate work without supervision?
- Can the candidate operate effectively in a foreign environment without normal communications and supporting services?

Adaptability
- Is the candidate sensitive to others, open to the opinions of others, cooperative, and able to compromise?
- What are his reactions to new situations, and efforts to understand and appreciate differences?
- Is she culturally sensitive, aware, and able to relate across the culture?
- Does the candidate understand his own culturally derived values?
- How does the candidate react to criticism?

(Continued)

Table 15.2 **Concluded**

- What is her understanding of the U.S. government system?
- Will he be able to make and develop contacts with peers in the foreign country?
- Does she have patience when dealing with problems?
- Is he resilient; can he bounce back after setbacks?

Career planning
- Does the candidate consider the assignment anything other than a temporary overseas trip?
- Is the move consistent with her progression and that planned by the company?
- Is his career planning realistic?
- What is the candidate's basic attitude toward the company?
- Is there any history or indication of interpersonal problems with this employee?

Financial
- Are there any current financial and/or legal considerations that might affect the assignment, such as house purchase, children and college expenses, car purchases?
- Are financial considerations negative factors? Will undue pressures be brought to bear on the employee or her family as a result of the assignment?

Source: Excerpted with permission, pages 55–57 from "Multinational People Management: A Guide for Organizations and Employees," by David M. Noer. Copyright © 1975 by the Bureau of National Affairs, Inc. Washington, DC 20037. Published by the Bureau of National Affairs, Inc., Washington, DC 20037. For copies of BNA Books publications call toll free 1-800-960-1220.

candidates a clear and complete preview of the assignment and the host-country culture. This helps the candidate evaluate the assignment and consider it in terms of his or her family situation, so the employer does not violate the employee's privacy.[48]

Preparing Expatriates

Once the organization has selected a manager for an overseas assignment, it is necessary to prepare that person through training and development. Because expatriate success depends so much on the entire family's adjustment, the employee's spouse should be included in the preparation activities. Employees selected for expatriate assignments already have job-related skills, so preparation for expatriate assignments often focuses on cross-cultural training—that is, training in what to expect from the host country's culture. The general purpose of cross-cultural training is to create an appreciation of the host country's culture so expatriates can behave appropriately.[49] Paradoxically, this requires developing a greater awareness of one's own culture, so that the expatriate manager can recognize differences and similarities between the cultures and, perhaps, home-culture biases. Consider, for example, the statements in Figure 15.5, which are comments made by visitors to the United States. Do you think these observations accurately describe U.S. culture?

On a more specific level, cross-cultural training for foreign assignments includes the details of how to behave in business settings in another country—the ways people behave in meetings, how employees expect managers to treat them, and so on. As an example, Germans value promptness for meetings to a much greater extent than do Latin Americans—and so on. How should one behave when first meeting one's business counterparts in another culture? The "outgoing" personality style so valued in the United States may seem quite rude in other parts of the world.[50]

Employees preparing for a foreign assignment also need information about such practical matters as housing, schools, recreation, shopping, and health care facilities in the country where they will be living. This is a crucial part of the preparation.

LO6 Explain how employers prepare managers for international assignments and for their return home.

Figure 15.5

Impressions of Americans: Comments by Visitors to the United States

"Americans seem to be in a perpetual hurry. Just watch the way they walk down the street. They never allow themselves the leisure to enjoy life; there are too many things to do."

—A visitor from India

"The American is very explicit; he wants a 'yes' or 'no.' If someone tries to speak figuratively, the American is confused."

—A visitor from Ethiopia

"The tendency in the United States to think that life is only work hits you in the face. Work seems to be the one type of motivation."

—A visitor from Colombia

"The first time . . . my [American] professor told me, 'I don't know the answer, I will have to look it up,' I was shocked. I asked myself, 'Why is he teaching me?' In my country, a professor would give the wrong answer rather than admit ignorance."

—A visitor from Iran

SOURCE: J. Feig and G. Blair, *There Is a Difference*, 2nd ed. (Washington, DC: Meridian House International, 1980), cited in N. Adler, *International Dimensions of Organizational Behavior*, 2nd ed. (Boston: PWS-Kent, 1991).

Communication in another country often requires a determined attempt to learn a new language. Some employers try to select managers who speak the language of the host country, and a few provide language training. Most companies assume that employees in the host country will be able to speak the host country's language. Even if this is true, host country nationals are not likely to be fluent in the home country's language, so language barriers remain.

Along with cross-cultural training, preparation of the expatriate should include career development activities. Before leaving for a foreign assignment, expatriates should discuss with their managers how the foreign assignment fits into their career plans and what types of positions they can expect upon their return. This prepares the expatriate to develop valuable skills during the overseas assignment and eases the return home when the assignment is complete.

When the employee leaves for the assignment, the preparation process should continue.[51] Employees need a chance to discuss their experiences with other expatriates, so they can learn from their failures and successes. The organization may provide a host-country mentor or "assimilator" to help expatriates understand their experiences. Successful expatriates tend to develop a bicultural or multicultural point of view, so as they spend more time in the host country, the value of their connections to other expatriates may actually increase.

Managing Expatriates' Performance

Performance management of expatriates requires clear goals for the overseas assignment and frequent evaluation of whether the expatriate employee is on track to meet those goals. Steven Miranda, vice president of human resources at Lucent Technologies, recommends using phone calls, e-mail, and face-to-face meetings to assess the expatriate's performance frequently during the first five or six months of the assignment. The information can help management decide whether to give the expatriate employee additional authority. When the goal of the overseas assignment is to prepare host-country nationals to manage the operation, the evaluations should consider those employees' performance as well.[52]

Compensating Expatriates

One of the greatest challenges of managing expatriates is determining the compensation package. Most organizations use a *balance sheet approach* to determine the total amount of the package. This approach adjusts the manager's compensation so that it gives the manager the same standard of living as in the home country plus extra pay for the inconvenience of locating overseas. As shown in Figure 15.6, the balance sheet

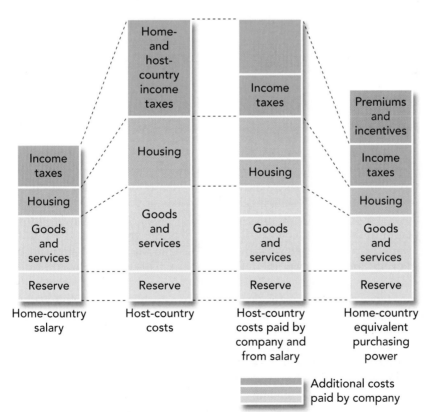

Figure 15.6

The Balance Sheet for Determining Expatriate Compensation

SOURCE: C. Reynolds, "Compensation of Overseas Personnel," in *Handbook of Human Resource Administration*, 2nd ed., ed. J. J. Famularo (New York: McGraw-Hill, 1986), p. 51. Reprinted with permission. Copyright © 1986 by The McGraw-Hill Companies, Inc.

Did You Know?

Moscow and London Top Priciest Cities

Expatriates spend more for housing, transportation, food, clothing, and other living expenses in Moscow than in any other major city, according to a survey by Mercer Human Resources Consulting.

Mercer's list of the 50 most expensive cities includes only two in North America: New York (15th place) and Los Angeles (42nd). The top five are shown in the figure below.

Source: Mercer Human Resources Consulting, "Moscow Tops Mercer's Cost of Living List; London Is Close Behind," www.mercer.com, last updated June 18, 2007.

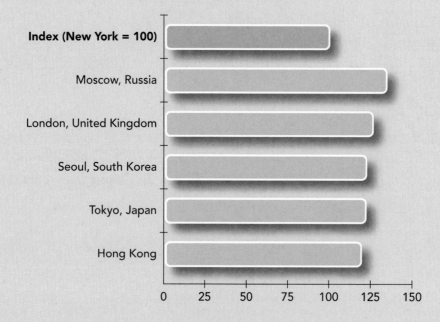

approach begins by determining the purchasing power of compensation for the same type of job in the manager's own country—that is, how much a person can buy, after taxes, in terms of housing, goods and services, and a reserve for savings. Next, this amount is compared with the cost (in dollars, for a U.S. company) of these same expenses in the foreign country. In Figure 15.6, the greater size of the second column means the costs for a similar standard of living in the foreign country are much higher in every category except the reserve amount. This situation would be likely in one of the cities identified in the "Did You Know?" box. For the expatriate in this situation, the employer would pay the additional costs, as shown by the third column. Finally, the expatriate receives additional purchasing power from premiums and incentives. Because of these added incentives, the expatriate's purchasing power is more than what the manager could buy at home with the salary for an equivalent job. (Compare the fourth column with the first.) In practice, the total cost of an international assignment is three to five times the employee's salary in the host country.[53] To restrain spending, some organizations are sending expatriates on shorter assignments. For instance, on an assignment of less than a year, an expatriate generally would not move his or her family, substantially reducing the cost of relocation and eliminating the need to cover children's education expenses.

After setting the total pay, the organization divides this amount into the four components of a total pay package:

1. *Base salary*—Determining the base salary is complex because different countries use different currencies (dollars, yen, euros, and so on). The exchange rate—the rate at which one currency may be exchanged for another—constantly shifts in response to a host of economic forces, so the real value of a salary in terms of dollars is constantly changing. Also, as discussed earlier, the base salary may be comparable to the pay of other managers at headquarters or comparable to other managers at the foreign subsidiary. Because many organizations pay a salary premium as an incentive to accept an overseas assignment, expatriates' salaries are often higher than pay for staying at headquarters.

2. *Tax equalization allowance*—Companies have different systems for taxing income, and in many countries, tax rates are much higher than in the United States. Usually, the employer of an expatriate withholds the amount of tax to be paid in the parent country, then pays all of the taxes due in the country where the expatriate is working.

3. *Benefits*—Most benefits issues have to do with whether an employee can use the same benefits in the foreign country. For example, if an expatriate has been contributing to a pension plan in the United States, does this person have a new pension in the foreign country? Or can the expatriate continue to contribute to the U.S. pension plan? Similarly, health benefits may involve receiving care at certain health facilities. While the person is abroad, does the same health plan cover services received in the foreign country? In one case, flying a manager back to the United States for certain procedures actually would have cost less than having the procedures done in the country where the person was working. But the company's health plans did not permit this alternative. An employer may offer expatriates additional benefits to address the problem of uprooting the spouse when assigning an employee overseas.

4. *Allowances to make a foreign assignment more attractive*—Cost-of-living allowances make up the differences in expenses for day-to-day needs. Housing allowances ensure that the expatriate can maintain the same standard of living as in the United States. Education allowances reimburse expatriates who pay tuition for their children to attend private English-speaking schools. Relocation allowances cover the expenses of making the move to the foreign country, including transportation, shipping or storage of possessions, and expenses for temporary housing until the employee can rent or purchase a home.

Figure 15.7 is an example of a summary sheet for an expatriate manager's compensation package, showing a variety of allowances.

Helping Expatriates Return Home

As the expatriate's assignment nears its end, the human resource department faces a final challenge: helping the expatriate make the transition back to his or her home country. The process of preparing expatriates to return home from a foreign assignment is called **repatriation.** Reentry is not as simple as it might sound. Culture shock takes place in reverse. The experience has changed the expatriate, and the company's and expatriate's home cultures have changed as well. Also, because of differences in economies and compensation levels, a returning expatriate may experience a decline in living standards. The standard of living for an expatriate in many countries includes maid service, a limousine, private schools, and clubs.

Companies are increasingly making efforts to help expatriates through this transition. Two activities help the process along: communication and validation.[54]

repatriation
The process of preparing expatriates to return home from a foreign assignment.

Figure 15.7

International Assignment
Allowance Form

John H. Doe	1 October 2004
Name	**Effective date**
Singapore	Manager, SLS./Serv. AP/ME
Location of assignment	**Title**

Houston, Texas	1234	202	202
Home base	**Emp. no.**	**LCA code**	**Tax code**

Reason for Change:　　　　International Assignment

	Old	New
Monthly base salary	_____	$5,000.00
Living cost allowance	_____	$1,291.00
Foreign service premium	_____	$ 750.00
Area allowance	_____	-0-
Gross monthly salary	_____	$7,041.00
Housing deduction	_____	$ 500.00
Hypothetical tax	_____	$ 570.00
Other	_____	_____
Net monthly salary	_____	$5,971.00

_____　　　_____
Prepared by　　　　　　　**Date**

_____　　　_____
Vice President, Human Resources　　**Date**

Communication refers to the expatriate receiving information and recognizing changes while abroad. The more the organization keeps in contact with the expatriate, the more effective and satisfied the person will be upon return. The expatriate plays a role in this process as well. Expatriates should work at maintaining important contacts in the company and industry. Communication related to career development before and during the overseas assignment also should help the employee return to a position that is challenging and interesting. Validation means giving the expatriate recognition for the overseas service when this person returns home. Expatriates who receive praise and recognition from colleagues and top managers for their overseas service and future contribution have fewer troubles with reentry than those whose contributions are disregarded. Validation should also include planning for how the returning employee will contribute to the organization. What skills will this person bring back? What position will he or she fill? The new skills may be much more than knowledge of a particular culture. For example, the person may have learned how to lead or negotiate with a diverse group of people.[55]

THINKING ETHICALLY

CARRYING ETHICS STANDARDS ABROAD

Deloitte Touche Tohmatsu applies a uniform set of ethical standards to its employees, who work in almost 150 different countries. Wherever they work, DTT's employees are expected to abide by the standards of honesty and integrity, professional behavior, competence, objectivity, confidentiality, fair business practices, responsibility to society, respect and fair treatment, and accountability and decision making (leading by example). The firm has one advantage, at least: Its professional employees share the values of their profession, even if they come from a variety of cultural backgrounds. For other companies, the political, cultural, and economic realities of a host country may be extremely different from those of the parent country, causing ethical dilemmas.

Consider companies that market clothing in the United States that is manufactured in low-wage countries where living standards are far from those in the United States. Critics have objected to the practice of selling goods made in "sweatshops," factories where working conditions are unhealthy and unsafe. Typically, the U.S. marketer doesn't hire its own manufacturing employees but instead contracts with manufacturing firms in low-wage countries, so the U.S. company has limited direct control over working conditions.

To exert some control over working conditions, Gap Inc. requires that all its suppliers guarantee they will adhere to local labor laws, not use child labor or forced labor, and meet other standards of its Vendor Code of Conduct. It sends more than 90 full-time inspectors to

its contractors, checking more than 2,000 factories each year. In one recent year, the company canceled contracts with almost two dozen factories that had violated the code of conduct.

But in a recent case, London's *Observer* newspaper reported that it had found workers as young as 10 making Gap clothes at a filthy sweatshop in New Delhi, India. Some reportedly worked 16 hours a day sewing clothing by hand but were not paid because they were still "trainees." One child told the *Observer* that if children cried or did not work hard enough, they could be beaten. Gap responded by saying it would convene a meeting of all its Indian suppliers to "forcefully reiterate" its policy against child labor.

SOURCES: Deloitte Touche Tohmatsu, "About Deloitte" and "Ethics & Compliance," www.deloitte.com/dtt/, accessed March 31, 2008; "Gap Vows Action after Child Labor Report," *Yahoo News*, October 29, 2007, http://news.yahoo.com; and Gap Inc., "Social Responsibility: Improving Factory Conditions," www.gapinc.com, accessed March 31, 2008.

Questions

1. Does a company bear responsibility for the ethical practices of its suppliers? Why or why not?
2. Suppose you work in Gap's HR department. How does the publicity about working conditions in overseas factories affect HRM at your company?
3. How can HRM support ethical conduct at Deloitte Touche Tohmatsu? At Gap? Is its role at these two companies different?

SUMMARY

LO1 Summarize how the growth in international business activity affects human resource management.

More and more companies are entering international markets by exporting and operating foreign facilities. Organizations therefore need employees who understand customers and suppliers in other countries. They need to understand local laws and customs and be able to adapt their plans to local situations. To do this organizations may hire a combination of parent-country, host-country, and third-country nationals. They may operate on the scale of an exporter or an international, global, or multinational organization. A global organization needs a transnational HRM system, which makes decisions from a global perspective, includes managers from many countries, and is based on ideas contributed by people representing a variety of cultures.

LO2 Identify the factors that most strongly influence HRM in international markets.

By far the most important influence is the culture of each market—its set of shared assumptions about how the world works and what ideals are worth striving for. A culture has the dimensions of individualism/collectivism, high or low power distance, high or low uncertainty avoidance, masculinity/femininity, and long-term or short-term orientation. Countries also differ in the degree to which their labor markets include people with education and skills of value to employers. Another influence on international HRM is the foreign country's political-legal system—its government, laws, and regulations. Finally, a country's economic system, capitalist or socialist, as well as the government's involvement in the country's economy, such as through taxes and price controls, is a strong factor determining HRM practices.

LO3 Discuss how differences among countries affect HR planning at organizations with international operations.

As organizations consider decisions about their level of international activity, HR professionals should provide information about the relevant human resource issues. When organizations decide to operate internationally or globally, HR planning involves decisions about where and how many employees are needed for each international facility. Some countries limit employers' ability to lay off workers, so organizations would be less likely to staff for peak periods. Other countries allow employers more flexibility in meeting human resource needs. HRM professionals need to be conversant with such differences.

LO4 Describe how companies select and train human resources in a global labor market.

Many organizations with foreign operations fill most positions with host-country nationals. These employees can more easily understand the values and customs of the local workforce, and hiring locally tends to be less expensive than moving employees to new locations. Organizations also fill foreign positions with parent-country and third-country nationals who have human relations skills associated with success in foreign assignments. They also may use "virtual expatriates," who do not go abroad for an extended period. When sending employees on foreign assignments, organizations prepare the employees (and often their families) through cross-cultural training. Before the assignment, the training provides instruction in the foreign country's language and culture. During the assignment, there is communication with the home country and mentoring. For the return home the employer provides further training.

LO5 Discuss challenges related to compensating employees from other countries.

Pay structures can differ substantially among countries in terms of pay level and the relative worth of jobs. Organizations must decide whether to set pay levels and differences in terms of what workers are used to in their own countries or in terms of what employees' colleagues earn at headquarters. Typically, companies have resolved this dilemma by linking pay and benefits more closely to those of the employee's country, but this practice may be weakening so that it depends more on the nature and length of the foreign assignment. These decisions affect the organization's costs and ability to compete, so organizations consider local labor costs in their location decisions. Along with the basic pay structure, organizations must make decisions regarding incentive pay, such as bonuses and stock options. Laws may dictate differences in benefit packages, and the value of benefits will differ if a country requires them or makes them a government service.

LO6 Explain how employers prepare managers for international assignments and for their return home.

When an organization has selected a manager for an overseas assignment, it must prepare the person for the experience. In cross-cultural training the soon-to-be expatriate learns about the foreign culture he or she is heading to, and studies her or his own home-country culture as well for insight. The trainee is given a detailed briefing on how to behave in business settings in the new country. Along with cross-cultural training, preparation of the expatriate should include career development activities to help the individual acquire valuable career skills during the foreign assignment and at the end of the assignment to handle repatriation successfully. Communication of changes at home and validation of a job well done abroad help the expatriate through the repatriation process.

KEY TERMS

cross-cultural preparation, p. 447
culture shock, p. 446
expatriates, p. 436
global organization, p. 437

host country, p. 436
international organization, p. 437
multinational company, p. 437
parent country, p. 436

repatriation, p. 459
third country, p. 436
transnational HRM system, p. 438
virtual expatriates, p. 446

REVIEW AND DISCUSSION QUESTIONS

1. Identify the parent country, host country(ies), and third country(ies) in the following example: A global soft-drink company called Cold Cola has headquarters in Atlanta, Georgia. It operates production facilities in Athens, Greece, and in Jakarta, Indonesia. The company has assigned a manager from Boston to head the Athens facility and a manager from Hong Kong to manage the Jarkarta facility.

2. What are some HRM challenges that arise when a U.S. company expands from domestic markets by exporting? When it changes from simply exporting to operating as an international company? When an international company becomes a global company?

3. In recent years, many U.S. companies have invested in Russia and sent U.S. managers there in an attempt to transplant U.S.-style management. According to Hofstede, U.S. culture has low power distance, uncertainty avoidance, and long-term orientation and high individuality and masculinity. Russia's culture has high power distance and uncertainty avoidance, low masculinity and long-term orientation, and moderate individuality. In light of what you know about cultural differences, how well do you think U.S. managers can succeed in each of the following U.S.-style HRM practices? (Explain your reasons.)
   a. Selection decisions based on extensive assessment of individual abilities.
   b. Appraisals based on individual performance.
   c. Systems for gathering suggestions from workers.
   d. Self-managing work teams.

4. Besides cultural differences, what other factors affect human resource management in an organization with international operations?

5. Suppose you work in the HR department of a company that is expanding into a country where the law and culture make it difficult to lay off employees. How should your knowledge of that difficulty affect human resource planning for the overseas operations?

6. Why do multinational organizations hire host-country nationals to fill most of their foreign positions, rather than sending expatriates for most jobs?

7. Suppose an organization decides to improve collaboration and knowledge sharing by developing an intranet to link its global workforce. It needs to train employees in several different countries to use this system. List the possible cultural issues you can think of that the training program should take into account.

8. For an organization with operations in three different countries, what are some advantages and disadvantages of setting compensation according to the labor markets in the countries where the employees live and work? What are some advantages and disadvantages of setting compensation according to the labor market in the company's headquarters? Would the best arrangement be different for the company's top executives and its production workers? Explain.

9. What abilities make a candidate more likely to succeed in an assignment as an expatriate? Which of these abilities do you have? How might a person acquire these abilities?

10. In the past, a large share of expatriate managers from the United States have returned home before successfully completing their foreign assignments. Suggest some possible reasons for the high failure rate. What can HR departments do to increase the success of expatriates?

BUSINESSWEEK CASE

BusinessWeek From Georgia to Tanzania

Gary Stowe has done business globally in the cotton and cattle industries for a quarter century. But now the entrepreneur is embarking on his biggest challenge, establishing a beef production company in the East African republic of Tanzania. Stowe, who has 15 full-time employees in his Chihuahua Cattle & Cotton, based in Albany, Georgia, is aiming not only for commercial success but also to modernize the agricultural sector in Tanzania. Stowe spoke recently to columnist Karen E. Klein. Edited excerpts follow.

What does your company do?
We buy U.S. cotton gins that are 10 to 15 years old and obsolete due to new technology, refurbish them, and sell them abroad through agents in 22 countries. There's a large market for refurbished cotton gins, particularly in the Third World.

What are the plans for the new business?
We've founded a joint venture called Triple S Beef in Shinyanga, Tanzania. That's in the northern part of the country. We'll begin by selling local beef on the national market, and once we get the packing house [to fully meet] European and American standards, we'll begin to export into the Middle East. Of course, everyone's goal is to export to the European and U.S. markets eventually.

How did you come up with the idea of starting a business in Tanzania?
I've traveled extensively in Africa for more than 10 years, doing sales and service for our cotton gins. I noticed that there are cattle on every corner, and I found out the price of beef was very inexpensive. Then I discovered a meatpacking plant that someone started to build in 1978. They got about 85 percent of the construction work done on it, ran out of money, and quit. This facility has a rail line on one side and electrical power lines on the other. It seemed like an ideal opportunity.

And I like Tanzania. It's a young democracy with a good, sound government and no internal political struggles. The government has been very supportive of us, from regional economic commissioners all the way up to the president's cabinet.

What are the unique challenges of working in East Africa?

There is zero irrigation in the region, so we intend to drill our own wells. English is pretty widespread, but Swahili is the native language. There is no refrigeration, so we'll have to power our own refrigeration in the packing plant and in our trucks. All our machinery and supplies will have to be imported. The good news is that communications are much better than they used to be, which will allow me to continue my business here in the United States and go back and forth to Tanzania frequently. Cell phone service is good all over Africa. We'll probably put in a satellite system and our own servers for Internet access.

Of course, there's a huge labor force that's much less expensive than in the West, and the raw product will be much less expensive, so overall we hope we have a lot more margin than we would for a similar operation in the United States, but things are not really as cheap as they look from the outside.

Why is that?

You have to provide a lot of benefits for your workforce, in terms of health care, education, and training. These people expect to become your family, not just your employees, and you grow to feel a great responsibility toward them. We plan to develop a labor pool management program and human resource training initiatives to help them adapt to modern farming, ranching, and meatpacking techniques. We also want to present genetic improvement programs to the local cattle farmers and train them in energy- and water-saving techniques.

SOURCE: Excerpted from Karen E. Klein, "Going Global: From Georgia to Tanzania," *BusinessWeek*, October 11, 2007, downloaded from General Reference Center Gold, http://find.galegroup.com.

Questions

1. Of the major factors affecting international HRM and described in this chapter—cultural, educational, economic, and political-legal—which has Stowe considered? Overall, does each factor seem favorable for his enterprise in Tanzania?
2. Of the business challenges and plans that Stowe describes, which are related to HRM?
3. Would you recommend that Stowe turn to a U.S. HR expert (parent-country national) or a Tanzanian HR expert (host-country national) to develop his compensation package for his Tanzanian employees? From what country would you recommend he obtain trainers for his workers? Why?

CASE: CULTURE CLASHES MAKE CHANGE DIFFICULT AT SAP

Software giant SAP is based in Germany and is seeking to develop more efficient global operations. At the beginning of this decade, about two-thirds of its managers were German, and most key projects were led from its headquarters in Walldorf, Germany. The company's leaders hoped SAP could become more agile and creative by bringing in a more diverse group of employees and sharing responsibility.

Unlike the more typical route to globalization by setting up sales offices and manufacturing facilities, SAP introduced change from the top down. The company made English its official language, even for meetings at headquarters. It hired foreign managers, making them half of the company's top management. It placed product development under the leadership of Shai Agassi, based in Palo Alto, California. Agassi was charged with overseeing development groups in eight centers around the world.

One objective for the globalized SAP was to develop and implement software much faster. The process of creating a new program at SAP had been taking at least a year, as programmers in Walldorf carefully worked out each problem. The resulting programs were complex and difficult to install and didn't work well with other companies' products.

At the same time, the Internet was making customers' software more interconnected and increasing the pace of change. To keep up, SAP would have to change as well.

SAP hired programmers in India and China, as well as in Germany and the United States. German programmers focused on the coding associated with the software's main tasks, American employees more often addressed programming that affects the user's experience, and Indian programmers worked on updating and fixing the code in older programs. Some human resource functions were outsourced to Prague, in Eastern Europe.

The changes frightened many of the German employees, who worried they would lose their jobs and the company would lose its reputation for quality. Agassi assigned a group of 10 software developers to create 100 programs for analyzing data such as defects in parts. Their deadline: just 12 weeks. The developers first insisted the task was impossible, but when Agassi wouldn't back down, they found a way to meet the deadline by writing a program that would write other programs. Still, they worried that working so fast would ultimately lead to problems with quality.

Employees in Germany complained about the move away from "good, old German engineering" and the requirement that they speak English in meetings. They criticized the "Americanization of SAP." Eventually, they rallied enough support to form a workers' council, similar to a union, to help workers find other jobs at SAP when positions were moved to other countries. So far, though, the company has avoided layoffs at headquarters—in fact, it has hired programmers.

Personnel director Klaus Heinrich guided American executives in working with engineers in each country. For example, he urged them to manage German workers by making a good impression with hard work and quality. Managers learned to give German employees plenty of leeway and give Indian employees plenty of attention. Still, Agassi, the U.S.-based head of product development, resigned out of frustration with the level of conflict.

SOURCE: Based on Phred Dvorak and Leila Abboud, "SAP's Plan to Globalize Hits Cultural Barriers," *Wall Street Journal*, May 11, 2007, http://online.wsj.com.

Questions

1. In your opinion, what aspects of the changes at SAP would be most difficult for the German employees? Which would be most difficult for the SAP employees in other countries?
2. What HRM activities or functions were affected by the changes described in this case?
3. Imagine you are an HR consultant called in to advise the leadership at SAP. Suggest a few ways the company can overcome cultural barriers that are affecting its efforts to become more creative and agile.

IT'S A WRAP!

www.mhhe.com/noefund3e is your source for Reviewing, Applying, and Practicing the concepts you learned about in Chapter 15.

Review
- Chapter learning objectives
- Narrated lecture and iPod content

Application
- Manager's Hot Seat segment: "Cultural Differences: Let's Break a Deal"
- Video case and quiz: "Outsourcing"
- Self-Assessment: How much do you know about global HRM?
- Web Exercise: Compare labor statistics for different countries

Practice
- Chapter quiz

NOTES

1. E. White, "For M.B.A. Students, a Good Career Move Means a Job in Asia," *Wall Street Journal*, May 10, 2005, http://online.wsj.com.
2. V. Masch, "A Radical Plan to Manage Globalization," *BusinessWeek Online*, February 14, 2007, downloaded from Business & Company Resource Center, http://galenet.galegroup.com.
3. D. Kirkpatrick, "The Net Makes It All Easier—Including Exporting U.S. Jobs," *Fortune*, May 2003, www.fortune.com.
4. A. Browne, "Chinese Recruit Top Executives Trained Abroad," *Wall Street Journal*, November 30, 2004, pp. B1, B8; and J. P. Izquierdo, "Five Practical Strategies for Building a Chinese Workforce," *Industry Week*, November 1, 2007, www.industryweek.com.
5. N. Adler and S. Bartholomew, "Managing Globally Competent People," *The Executive* 6 (1992), pp. 52–65.
6. V. Sathe, *Culture and Related Corporate Realities* (Homewood, IL: Richard D. Irwin, 1985); and M. Rokeach, *Beliefs, Attitudes, and Values* (San Francisco: Jossey-Bass, 1968).
7. N. Adler, *International Dimensions of Organizational Behavior*, 2nd ed. (Boston: PWS-Kent, 1991).
8. G. Hofstede, "Dimensions of National Cultures in Fifty Countries and Three Regions," in *Expectations in Cross-Cultural Psychology*, eds. J. Deregowski, S. Dziurawiec, and R. C. Annis (Lisse, Netherlands: Swets and Zeitlinger, 1983); and G. Hofstede, "Cultural Constraints in Management Theories," *Academy of Management Executive* 7 (1993), pp. 81–90.

9. Hofstede, "Cultural Constraints in Management Theories."

10. W. A. Randolph and M. Sashkin, "Can Organizational Empowerment Work in Multinational Settings?" *Academy of Management Executive* 16, no. 1 (2002), pp. 102–15.

11. Ibid.

12. B. Gerhart and M. Fang, "National Culture and Human Resource Management: Assumptions and Evidence," *International Journal of Human Resource Management* (forthcoming).

13. L. A. West Jr. and W. A. Bogumil Jr., "Foreign Knowledge Workers as a Strategic Staffing Option," *Academy of Management Executive* 14, no. 4 (2000), pp. 71–83.

14. Organization for Economic Cooperation and Development, *Education at a Glance 2007: Highlights,* http://www.oecd.org/dataoecd/36/5/39290975.pdf, accessed March 20, 2008.

15. World Bank, "The State of Education," *EdStats,* www.worldbank.org, accessed March 20, 2008.

16. European Union, "Organisation of Working Time," Employment Rights and Work Organisation: Health, Hygiene and Safety at Work, http://europa.eu, last updated July 24, 2007; and PriceWaterhouseCoopers, *Key Trends in Human Capital: A Global Perspective, 2006,* Publications, www.pwc.co.uk, accessed March 19, 2008.

17. N. Shirouzu, "Toyota's New U.S. Plan: Stop Building Factories," *Wall Street Journal,* June 20, 2007, http://online.wsj.com.

18. A. Rutkoff, "Firms Expect to Increase IT Outsourcing, Survey Shows," *Wall Street Journal,* June 7, 2005, http://online.wsj.com.

19. West and Bogumil, "Foreign Knowledge Workers as a Strategic Staffing Option."

20. G. Flynn, "Hiring Foreign Workers in a Post-9/11 World," *Workforce,* July 2002, pp. 78–79.

21. Ibid; and S. Ladika, "Unwelcome Changes," *HRMagazine,* February 2005, downloaded from Infotrac at http://web5.infotrac.galegroup.com.

22. W. A. Arthur Jr. and W. Bennett Jr., "The International Assignee: The Relative Importance of Factors Perceived to Contribute to Success," *Personnel Psychology* 48 (1995), pp. 99–114; and G. M. Spreitzer, M. W. McCall Jr., and J. D. Mahoney, "Early Identification of International Executive Potential," *Journal of Applied Psychology* 82 (1997), pp. 6–29.

23. J. S. Black and J. K. Stephens, "The Influence of the Spouse on American Expatriate Adjustment and Intent to Stay in Pacific Rim Overseas Assignments," *Journal of Management* 15 (1989), pp. 529–44.

24. P. Caligiuri, "The Big Five Personality Characteristics as Predictors of Expatriates' Desire to Terminate the Assignment and Supervisor-Rated Performance," *Personnel Psychology* 53 (2000), pp. 67–88.

25. C. Lachnit, "Low-Cost Tips for Successful Inpatriation," *Workforce,* August 2001, pp. 42–44, 46–47.

26. J. Flynn, "E-mail, Cell Phones, and Frequent-Flier Miles Let 'Virtual' Expats Work Abroad but Live at Home," *Wall Street Journal,* October 25, 1999, p. A26.

27. D. M. Gayeski, C. Sanchirico, and J. Anderson, "Designing Training for Global Environments: Knowing What Questions to Ask," *Performance Improvement Quarterly* 15, no. 2 (2002), pp. 15–31.

28. J. S. Black and M. Mendenhall, "A Practical but Theory-Based Framework for Selecting Cross-Cultural Training Methods," in *Readings and Cases in International Human Resource Management,* eds. M. Mendenhall and G. Oddou (Boston: PWS-Kent, 1991), pp. 177–204.

29. Lachnit, "Low-Cost Tips for Successful Inpatriation."

30. Ibid., citing research jointly sponsored by GMAC Global Relocation Services/Windham International, the National Foreign Trade Council, and SHRM Global Forum.

31. D. D. Davis, "International Performance Measurement and Management," in *Performance Appraisal: State of the Art in Practice,* ed. J. W. Smither (San Francisco: Jossey-Bass, 1998), pp. 95–131.

32. M. Gowan, S. Ibarreche, and C. Lackey, "Doing the Right Things in Mexico," *Academy of Management Executive* 10 (1996), pp. 74–81.

33. L. S. Chee, "Singapore Airlines: Strategic Human Resource Initiatives," in *International Human Resource Management: Think Globally, Act Locally,* ed. D. Torrington (Upper Saddle River, NJ: Prentice Hall, 1994), pp. 143–59.

34. "Global Compensation Strategies and HR," *HRMagazine,* May 2005, downloaded from Infotrac at http://web5.infotrac.galegroup.com.

35. Sparks, Bikoi, and Moglia, "A Perspective on U.S. and Foreign Compensation Costs in Manufacturing."

36. See, for example, A. E. Cobet and G. A. Wilson, "Comparing 50 Years of Labor Productivity in U.S. and Foreign Manufacturing," *Monthly Labor Review,* June 2002, pp. 51–63; and M. Hayes, "Precious Connection," *Information Week Online,* October 20, 2003, www.informationweek.com.

37. P. Wonacott, "China's Secret Weapon: Smart, Cheap Labor for High-Tech Goods," *Wall Street Journal,* March 14, 2002, pp. A1, A6.

38. P. J. Dowling, D. E. Welch, and R. S. Schuler, *International Human Resource Management,* 3rd ed. (Cincinnati: South-Western, 1999), pp. 235–36.

39. Ibid.; J. La Palombara and S. Blank, *Multinational Corporations and National Elites: A Study of Tensions*

(New York: Conference Board, 1976); A. B. Sim, "Decentralized Management of Subsidiaries and Their Performance: A Comparative Study of American, British and Japanese Subsidiaries in Malaysia," *Management International Review* 17, no. 2 (1977), pp. 45–51; Y. K. Shetty, "Managing the Multinational Corporation: European and American Styles," *Management International Review* 19, no. 3 (1979), pp. 39–48; and J. Hamill, "Labor Relations Decision-Making within Multinational Corporations," *Industrial Relations Journal* 15, no. 2 (1984), pp. 30–34.

40. Dowling, Welch, and Schuler, *International Human Resource Management*, p. 231.

41. D. Roberts, "Rumbles over Labor Reform," *BusinessWeek*, March 12, 2007, p 57; Sarah Schafer, "Now They Speak Out," *Newsweek*, May 28, 2007, downloaded from General Reference Center Gold, http://find.galegroup.com; and "China Passes Workers' Rights Law," *UPI NewsTrack*, June 30, 2007, http://find.galegroup.com.

42. J. K. Sebenius, "The Hidden Challenge of Cross-Border Negotiations," *Harvard Business Review*, March 2002, pp. 76–85.

43. Ibid.

44. E. Krell, "Evaluating Returns on Expatriates," *HRMagazine*, March 2005, downloaded from Infotrac at http://web5.infotrac.galegroup.com.

45. Ibid.; and M. Harvey and M. M. Novicevic, "Selecting Expatriates for Increasingly Complex Global Assignments," *Career Development International* 6, no. 2 (2001), pp. 69–86.

46. M. Mendenhall and G. Oddou, "The Dimensions of Expatriate Acculturation," *Academy of Management Review* 10 (1985), pp. 39–47.

47. Arthur and Bennett, "The International Assignee."

48. J. I. Sanchez, P. E. Spector, and C. L. Cooper, "Adapting to a Boundaryless World: A Developmental Expatriate Model," *Academy of Management Executive* 14, no. 2 (2000), pp. 96–106.

49. P. Dowling and R. Schuler, *International Dimensions of Human Resource Management* (Boston: PWS-Kent, 1990).

50. Sanchez, Spector, and Cooper, "Adapting to a Boundaryless World."

51. Ibid.; and Lachnit, "Low-Cost Tips for Successful Inpatriation."

52. F. Jossi, "Successful Handoff," *HRMagazine*, October 2002, pp. 49–52.

53. Krell, "Evaluating Returns on Expatriates"; and L. G. Klass, "Fed Up with High Costs, Companies Thin the Ranks of 'Career Expats,'" *Workforce Management*, October 2004, downloaded from Infotrac at http://web5.infotrac.galegroup.com.

54. Adler, *International Dimensions of Organizational Behavior*.

55. L. G. Klaff, "The Right Way to Bring Expats Home," *Workforce*, July 2002, pp. 40–44.

Creating and Maintaining High-Performance Organizations

What Do I Need to Know?

After reading this chapter, you should be able to:

LO1 Define high-performance work systems, and identify the elements of such a system.

LO2 Summarize the outcomes of a high-performance work system.

LO3 Describe the conditions that create a high-performance work system.

LO4 Explain how human resource management can contribute to high performance.

LO5 Discuss the role of HRM technology in high-performance work systems.

LO6 Summarize ways to measure the effectiveness of human resource management.

Introduction

Does human resource management really help an organization meet its business goals? Joseph Nour would surely say yes. A few years ago, the chief executive officer of Protus IP Solutions was dealing with a terrible 60 percent employee turnover. Even worse, no one really knew why people were quitting. If the departing employees had an exit interview, the notes were simply filed away unread. For help in solving the problem, Nour hired Janice Vanderburg as director of human resources. Vanderburg discovered that HR practices had failed to keep pace with the start-up company's quick growth. She conducted surveys and learned that many employees had trouble communicating with managers, didn't know what was expected of them, and saw no clear career path at the company. Vanderburg began developing Protus's managers, helping them communicate with and develop their staff. She introduced performance management software that would help managers give employees better feedback and track their progress. She established a logical pay structure and made sure employees knew about all the benefits for which they are eligible. Now turnover at the 140-employee company is just 15 percent a year—far from ideal but a vast improvement for the technology company.[1]

The experience of Protus IP Solutions shows that high-tech products and rapid growth do not guarantee business success. Someone in the organization has to recognize how business activities, management style, and strategy changes will affect the organization's people. The organization must design work and performance management systems so that they bring out the best in the employees. These challenges are some of the most crucial responsibilities of human resource management.

This chapter summarizes the role of human resource management in creating an organization that achieves a high level of performance, measured in such terms as long-term profits, quality, and customer satisfaction. We begin with a definition of

chapter sixteen

high-performance work systems and a description of these systems' elements and outcomes. Next, we identify the conditions that contribute to high performance. We explain how the various HRM functions can contribute to high performance. Finally, we introduce ways to measure the effectiveness of human resource management.

High-performance Work Systems

The challenge facing managers today is how to make their organizations into **high-performance work systems,** with the right combination of people, technology, and organizational structure to make full use of resources and opportunities in achieving their organizations' goals. To function as a high-performance work system, each of these elements must fit well with the others in a smoothly functioning whole. Many manufacturers use the latest in processes including flexible manufacturing technology, total quality management, and just-in-time inventory control (meaning parts and supplies are automatically restocked as needed), but of course these processes do not work on their own; they must be run by qualified people. Organizations need to determine what kinds of people fit their needs, and then locate, train, and motivate those special people.[2] According to research, organizations that introduce integrated high-performance work practices usually experience increases in productivity and long-term financial performance.[3]

Creating a high-performance work system contrasts with traditional management practices. In the past, decisions about technology, organizational structure, and human resources were treated as if they were unrelated. An organization might acquire a new information system, restructure jobs, or add an office in another country without considering the impact on its people.[4] More recently, managers have realized that success depends on how well all the elements work together. For instance, after visiting hundreds of manufacturing facilities to prepare his company's annual Harbour Report on the state of the automotive industry, Ron Harbour has found that manufacturing is first of all a "people system" that depends on clear processes and worker involvement, not just sophisticated machinery. Harbour has also concluded that the most productive operations apply ideas from line workers and use strategies that work well with their own people, rather than simply copying other companies.

Elements of a High-Performance Work System

As shown in Figure 16.1, in a high-performance work system, the elements that must work together include organizational structure, task design, people (the selection, training, and development of employees), reward systems, and information systems, and human resource management plays an important role in establishing all these.

Organizational structure is the way the organization groups its people into useful divisions, departments, and reporting relationships. The organization's top management makes most decisions about structure, for instance, how many employees report to each supervisor and whether employees are grouped according to the functions they carry out or the customers they serve. Such decisions affect how well employees coordinate their activities and respond to change. In a high-performance work system, organizational structure promotes cooperation, learning, and continuous improvement.

Task design determines how the details of the organization's necessary activities will be grouped, whether into jobs or team responsibilities. In a high-performance work system, task design makes jobs efficient while encouraging high quality. In Chapter 4, we discussed how to carry out this HRM function through job analysis and job design.

LO1 Define high-performance work systems, and identify the elements of such a system.

high-performance work system
The right combination of people, technology, and organizational structure that makes full use of the organization's resources and opportunities in achieving its goals.

Figure 16.1

Elements of a
High-Performance
Work System

The right *people* are a key element of high-performance work systems. HRM has a significant role in providing people who are well suited and well prepared for their jobs. Human resource personnel help the organization recruit and select people with the needed qualifications. Training, development, and career management ensure that these people are able to perform their current and future jobs with the organization.

Reward systems contribute to high performance by encouraging people to strive for objectives that support the organization's overall goals. Reward systems include the performance measures by which employees are judged, the methods of measuring performance, and the incentive pay and other rewards linked to success. Human resource management plays an important role in developing and administering reward systems, as we saw in Chapters 8 through 12.

The final element of high-performance work systems is the organization's *information systems*. Managers make decisions about the types of information to gather and the sources of information. They also must decide who in the organization should have access to the information and how they will make the information available. Modern information systems, including the Internet, have enabled organizations to share information widely. HR departments take advantage of this technology to give employees access to information about benefits, training opportunities, job openings, and more, as we will describe later in this chapter.

In a high-performance work system, all the elements—people, technology, and organizational structure—work together for success.

L02 Summarize the outcomes of a high-performance work system.

Outcomes of a High-Performance Work System

Consider the practices of steel minimills in the United States. Some of these mills have strategies based on keeping their costs below competitors' costs; low costs let them operate at a profit while winning customers with low prices. Other steel minimills focus on "differentiation," meaning they set themselves apart in some way other

Figure 16.2

Outcomes of a High-Performance Work System

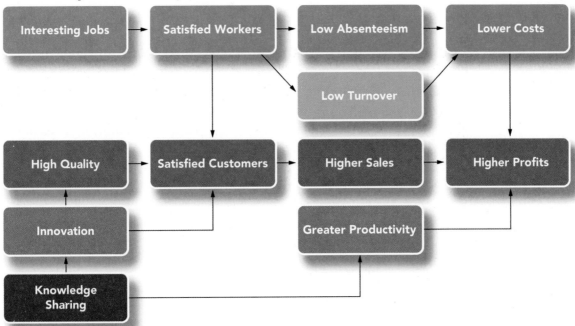

than low price—for example, by offering higher quality or unusual product lines. Research has found that the minimills with cost-related goals tend to have highly centralized structures, so managers can focus on controlling through a tight line of command. These organizations have low employee participation in decisions, relatively low wages and benefits, and pay highly contingent on performance.[5] At minimills that focus on differentiation, structures are more complex and decentralized, so authority is more spread out. These minimills encourage employee participation and have higher wages and more generous benefits. They are high-performance work systems. In general, these differentiator mills enjoy higher productivity, lower scrap rates, and lower employee turnover than the mills that focus on low costs.

Outcomes of a high-performance work system thus include higher productivity and efficiency. These outcomes contribute to higher profits. A high-performance work system may have other outcomes, including high product quality, great customer satisfaction, and low employee turnover. Some of these outcomes meet intermediate goals that lead to higher profits (see Figure 16.2). For example, high quality contributes to customer satisfaction, and customer satisfaction contributes to growth of the business. Likewise, improving productivity lets the organization do more with less, which satisfies price-conscious customers and may help the organization win over customers from its competitors. Other ways to lower cost and improve quality are to reduce absenteeism and turnover, providing the organization with a steady supply of experienced workers. In the previous example of minimills, some employers keep turnover and scrap rates low. Meeting those goals helps the minimills improve productivity, which helps them earn more profits.

In a high-performance work system, the outcomes of each employee and work group contribute to the system's overall high performance. The organization's individuals and groups work efficiently, provide high-quality goods and services, and so on, and in this way, they contribute to meeting the organization's goals. When the organization adds or changes goals, people are flexible and make changes as needed to meet the new goals.

LO3 Describe the conditions that create a high-performance work system.

Conditions That Contribute to High Performance

Certain conditions underlie the formation of a high-performance work system:[6]

- Teams perform work.
- Employees participate in selection.
- Employees receive formal performance feedback and are actively involved in the performance improvement process.
- Ongoing training is emphasized and rewarded.
- Employees' rewards and compensation relate to the company's financial performance.
- Equipment and work processes are structured, and technology is used to encourage maximum flexibility and interaction among employees.
- Employees participate in planning changes in equipment, layout, and work methods.
- Work design allows employees to use a variety of skills.
- Employees understand how their jobs contribute to the finished product or service.
- Ethical behavior is encouraged.

Practices involving rewards, employee empowerment, and jobs with variety contribute to high performance by giving employees skills, incentives, knowledge, autonomy—and satisfaction, another condition associated with high performance. Ethical behavior is a necessary condition of high performance because it contributes to good long-term relationships with employees, customers, and the public.

Teamwork and Empowerment

As we discussed in Chapter 2, today's organizations empower employees. They expect employees to make more decisions about how they perform their jobs. One of the most popular ways to empower employees is to design work so that it is performed by teams. On a work team, employees bring together various skills and experiences to produce goods or provide services. The organization may charge the team with making decisions traditionally made by managers, such as hiring team members and planning work schedules. Teamwork and empowerment contribute to high performance when they improve job satisfaction and give the organization fuller use of employees' ideas and expertise.

For empowerment to succeed, managers must serve in linking and coordinating roles[7] and provide the team with the resources it needs to carry out its work. The manager should help the team and its members interact with employees from other departments or teams and should make sure communication flows in both directions—the manager keeps the team updated on important issues and ensures that the team shares information and resources with others who need them. At the Global Engineering Manufacturing Alliance (GEMA) plant in Dundee, Michigan, teamwork is designed to achieve the primary goal—to be the world's most productive engine plant. All employees, including the engineers, are either members or leaders of six-person teams. Groups of three employees work rotating shifts so that they know and work with one another around the

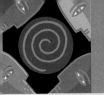

HR Oops!

Losing Retirees' Knowledge

Young employees hired fresh out of college may bring an organization knowledge of the latest tools, techniques, and technology. But employees nearing retirement have had the chance to develop deep wisdom from experience. With so much to gain from both types of workers, you might think that employers would work to ensure that knowledge is shared between the generations.

If so, you would often be wrong. In practice, according to a recent survey, employers have been careless about ensuring that their experienced employees' knowledge is transferred before they retire. Only 4 percent have a formal process for capturing and transferring retiring employees' knowledge; another 23 percent have an informal process for doing so. By far the greatest share, 44 percent, say they have no knowledge transfer process and no plans to create one. In addition, experienced employees complain that employers are reluctant to continue investing in their development, because they expect them to leave soon.

Source: Michael Laff, "Knowledge Walks out the Door," *T&D,* January 2008, p. 20.

Questions

1. What do organizations lose when experienced workers retire? Why do you think many employers are unwilling to spend money on knowledge transfer?

2. Suggest two or three ways an organization might capture experienced employees' knowledge. Generally speaking, what costs would your ideas involve?

---

clock. Team members are carefully selected to ensure they can handle the problem-solving responsibilities that GEMA has delegated to its teams. Technology such as large electronic display screens lets team members monitor productivity and delays, so they can identify when they are succeeding and when problems need to be resolved. All employees, not just managers or engineers, are empowered to solve problems. Employees who develop innovative solutions receive bonuses.[8]

Knowledge Sharing

For more than a decade, managers have been interested in creating a **learning organization,** that is, an organization in which the culture values and supports lifelong learning by enabling all employees to continually acquire and share knowledge. The people in a learning organization have resources for training, and they are encouraged to share their knowledge with colleagues. Managers take an active role in identifying training needs and encouraging the sharing of ideas.[9] An organization's information systems, discussed later in this chapter, have an important role in making this learning activity possible. Information systems capture knowledge and make it available even after individual employees who provided the knowledge have left the organization. Ultimately, people are the essential ingredients in a learning organization. They must be committed to learning and willing to share what they have learned. The "HR Oops!" box emphasizes the need to capture and share the knowledge of perhaps the most valuable people in a company, employees nearing retirement age.

A learning organization has several key features:[10]

- It engages in **continuous learning,** each employee's and each group's ongoing efforts to gather information and apply the information to their decisions. In many organizations, the process of continuous learning is aimed at improving quality. To engage in continuous learning, employees must understand the entire work system they participate in, the relationships among jobs, their work units, and the

learning organization
An organization that supports lifelong learning by enabling all employees to acquire and share knowledge.

continuous learning
Each employee's and each group's ongoing efforts to gather information and apply the information to their decisions in a learning organization.

organization as a whole. Employees who continuously learn about their work system are adding to their ability to improve performance.

- Knowledge is *shared.* Therefore, to create a learning organization, one challenge is to shift the focus of training away from merely teaching skills and toward a broader focus on generating and sharing knowledge.[11] In this view, training is an investment in the organization's human resources; it increases employees' value to the organization. Also, training content should be related to the organization's goals. Human resource departments can support the creation of a learning organization by planning training programs that meet these criteria, and they can help to create systems for creating, capturing, and sharing knowledge.
- *Critical, systematic thinking* is widespread. This occurs when organizations encourage employees to see relationships among ideas and to test assumptions and observe the results of their actions. Reward systems can be set up to encourage employees and teams to think in new ways.
- The organization has a *learning culture*—a culture in which learning is rewarded, promoted, and supported by managers and organizational objectives. This culture may be reflected in performance management systems and pay structures that reward employees for gathering and sharing more knowledge. A learning culture creates the conditions in which managers encourage *flexibility* and *experimentation.* The organization should encourage employees to take risks and innovate, which means it cannot be quick to punish ideas that do not work out as intended.
- *Employees are valued.* The organization recognizes that employees are the source of its knowledge. It therefore focuses on ensuring the development and well-being of each employee.

The experience of Lopez Foods shows that the qualities of a learning organization aren't limited just to high-tech industries. Lopez Foods, which makes beef and sausage patties, involved employees in making production more efficient. Working with consultants, Lopez managers and engineers diagrammed production processes on huge sheets of brown paper hung on the walls. They made sticky notes available so that any worker passing by could post notes correcting the information or making suggestions based on their day-to-day experience on the front lines. Not only did the practice improve the quality of information, but it also engaged workers in the improvement process so that they remain committed to making suggestions and helping their company become more efficient. The company also improved the communication of performance feedback, now posting hourly performance indicators, and it pays production workers modest but regular bonuses for exceeding productivity targets.[12]

Job Satisfaction

A condition underpinning any high-performance organization is that employees experience job satisfaction—they experience their jobs as fulfilling or allowing them to fulfill important values. Research supports the idea that employees' job satisfaction and job performance are related.[13] Higher performance at the individual level should contribute to higher performance for the organization as a whole. A study by Watson Wyatt Worldwide found that companies with high employee commitment (which includes employees' satisfaction with their jobs and the company) enjoyed higher total returns to shareholders, a basic measure of a company's financial performance.[14] The relationship between satisfaction and performance also relates to nonprofit and government organizations. In a survey by the Partnership for Public Service and American University, the Nuclear Regulatory Commission and Government Accountability Office showed the

Did You Know?

Employees Equally Satisfied at Best Government Agencies, Average Business

Federal government employees who rated their satisfaction with their job and work environment were most satisfied at the Nuclear Regulatory Commission. While the top five agencies had much higher satisfaction rates than other government agencies, their scores weren't much higher than the overall average for large businesses. Here are the top five and their averages:

Sources: Partnership for Public Service, "Welcome to the 2007 Best Places to Work Rankings," http://bestplacestowork.org, accessed March 27, 2008; and Stephen Barr, "Nuclear Regulatory Commission Ranks as Top Workplace," *Washington Post,* April 20, 2007, www.washingtonpost.com.

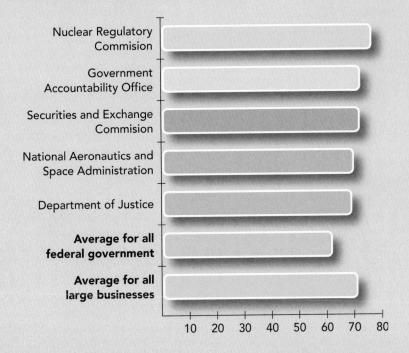

highest degrees of employee satisfaction, as the "Did You Know?" box shows. They far outranked the bottom agencies, the Department of Homeland Security (index of 49.8) and Small Business Administration (43.4).[15] How would you expect these differences to play out in terms of the agencies' effectiveness?

Chapter 10 described a number of ways organizations can promote job satisfaction. They include making jobs more interesting, setting clear and challenging goals, and providing valued rewards that are linked to performance in a performance management system that employees consider fair. For example, the Nuclear Regulatory Commission's top agency score for employee satisfaction is based partly on its relatively high ratings for fair and timely rewards, effective training and development, and satisfactory compensation, as well as solid

Research has found that teachers' job satisfaction is associated with high performance of the schools where they teach. What are other ways in which organizations can promote and foster job satisfaction?

475

teamwork—being part of a work group with good communication, a friendly work atmosphere, and high-quality output.[16]

Some organizations are moving beyond concern with mere job satisfaction and are trying to foster employees' *passion* for their work. Passionate people are fully engaged with something so that it becomes part of their sense of who they are. Feeling this way about one's work has been called *occupational intimacy*.[17] People experience occupational intimacy when they love their work, when they and their co-workers care about one another, and when they find their work meaningful. Human resource managers have a significant role in creating these conditions. For example, they can select people who care about their work and customers, provide methods for sharing knowledge, design work to make jobs interesting, and establish policies and programs that show concern for employees' needs. Such efforts may become increasingly important as the business world increasingly uses employee empowerment, teamwork, and knowledge sharing to build flexible organizations.[18]

Ethics

In the long run, a high-performance organization meets high ethical standards. Ethics, defined in Chapter 1, establishes fundamental principles for behavior, such as honesty and fairness. Organizations and their employees must meet these standards if they are to maintain positive long-term relationships with their customers and their community.

Ethical behavior is most likely to result from values held by the organization's leaders combined with systems that promote ethical behavior. Charles O. Holliday Jr., the chairman and chief executive officer of Du Pont Company, is an example of an executive who cares about ethics. For Holliday, ethics is a matter of behaving in ways that promote trust: "Just saying you're ethical isn't very useful. You have to earn trust by what you do every day."[19] Holliday experienced this kind of leadership himself when he first joined Du Pont. The CEO at that time, Dick Heckert, told him, "This company lives by the letter of its contracts and the intent of those contracts," speaking with such conviction that he imprinted the lesson on Holliday's mind.

A number of organizational systems can promote ethical behavior.[20] These include a written code of ethics that the organization distributes to employees and expects them to use in decision making. Publishing a list of ethical standards is not enough, however. The organization should reinforce ethical behavior. For example, performance measures should include ethical standards, and misdeeds should receive swift discipline, as described in Chapter 10. The organization should provide channels employees can use to ask questions about ethical behavior or to seek help if they are expected to do something they believe is wrong. Organizations also can provide training in ethical decision making.

As these examples suggest, ethical behavior is a human resource management concern. The systems that promote ethical behavior include such HRM functions as training, performance management, and discipline policies. A reputation for high ethical standards can also help a company attract workers—and customers—who share those high standards. UPS is committed to living up to the words of its founder, Jim Casey: "We have become known to all who deal with us as a people of integrity, and that priceless asset is more valuable than anything we possess." UPS has a written code of conduct, published in a detailed booklet that offers regularly updated examples. All employees must read and give their written acceptance of that code when they join the company. Employees who have questions about particular situations or who see ethical problems within the company may call a hotline, staffed by a vendor. The vendor compiles information from the calls and forwards it to the UPS compliance department, which distributes the issues to the appropriate departments. The majority of situations are handled by the human resource department; other departments, including legal and security, handle the other concerns. Unit managers receive summary reports, and their responses to concerns play a role in their performance evaluations. Even if their unit has relatively few complaints, managers are expected to take action.[21]

HRM's Contribution to High Performance

LO4 Explain how human resource management can contribute to high performance.

Management of human resources plays a critical role in determining companies' success in meeting the challenges of a rapidly changing, highly competitive environment.[22] Compensation, staffing, training and development, performance management, and other HRM practices are investments that directly affect employees' motivation and ability to provide products and services that are valued by customers. A study by Watson Wyatt Worldwide found that significant improvements in major HR practices, including reward systems, recruitment, and employee retention, led to significant increases in the value of a company's stock.[23] Table 16.1 lists examples of HRM practices that contribute to high performance.

Research suggests that it is more effective to improve HRM practices as a whole than to focus on one or two isolated practices, such as the organization's pay structure or selection system.[24] Also, to have the intended influence on performance, the HRM practices must fit well with one another and the organization as a whole.[25] An example of an organization that has achieved this fit is ConAgra Foods, described in the "Best Practices" box.

Job Design

For the organization to benefit from teamwork and employee empowerment, jobs must be designed appropriately. Often, a high-performance work system places employees in work teams where employees collaborate to make decisions and solve problems. Individual employees also may be empowered to serve on teams that design jobs and work processes. For example, the members of the staff of a ThedaCare health clinic in Wisconsin evaluated the process of office visits, looking for a way to shrink the average length of a visit from an hour to 30 minutes. They drew a chart showing the typical steps involved in serving a patient with pneumonia and discovered that of the 68 steps identified, only 17 were considered valuable. They determined that instead of requiring patients to walk down the hall to a laboratory to have blood drawn, they could have a

Table 16.1

HRM Practices That Can Help Organizations Achieve High Performance

- HRM practices match organization's goals.
- Individuals and groups share knowledge.
- Work is performed by teams.
- Organization encourages continuous learning.
- Work design permits flexibility in where and when tasks are performed.
- Selection system is job related and legal.
- Performance management system measures customer satisfaction and quality.
- Organization monitors employees' satisfaction.
- Discipline system is progressive.
- Pay systems reward skills and accomplishments.
- Skills and values of a diverse workforce are valued and used.
- Technology reduces time and costs of tasks while preserving quality.

Best Practices

ConAgra Foods' High Performance in a Tough Industry

ConAgra Foods operates in the meat-processing business, known best for tough jobs, stiff price competition, and low-wage work. In an industry like that, you might be surprised to discover that ConAgra is committed to employee engagement in a high-performance work system. In fact, ConAgra adopted its ConAgra Performance System (CPS) precisely because it was determined to operate efficiently by empowering employees to identify and seek solutions to problems.

At the heart of the CPS is communication. The company provides workers with monthly reports on industry and company performance. It asks them to speak up when they see poor job design. Employees are committed to the effort because they understand that well-designed work and efficient operations make their jobs safer, more orderly, and more secure. In addition, gainsharing pay at many facilities is tied to improvements in output and costs. In a recent year, the CPS saved the company $30 million. Employee engagement (measured with surveys) rose so much that the company's consultants "asked us to double-check the numbers," according to Peter Perez, executive vice president of human resources.

Salaried workers at ConAgra are also empowered to make process improvements through an initiative called Roadmap, in which they evaluate each step of their work flow. To make their work more motivating and to lower turnover, the company is focusing on employee development. Hiring decisions focus on identifying employees with the potential to move up in the company hierarchy. The company has been increasing the percentage of its internal promotions, with a long-term goal of 85 to 90 percent internal promotions.

ConAgra's industry challenges show no sign of easing, but Perez is encouraged by recent survey results showing that 79 percent of its employees are proud to work for the company, 14 percentage points above the previous year.

Source: Fay Hansen, "The Toughest HR Job in America: Managing in a Maelstrom," *Workforce Management*, February 18, 2008, downloaded from General Reference Center Gold, http://find.galegroup.com; "About Us," company Web site, www.conagrafoodscompany.com, accessed April 8, 2008.

technician visit the examination room to draw blood. Changes such as these cut patients' waiting time from 30 minutes to just 9. The nature of certain jobs also changed. Six assistants had been assigned to work with individual doctors; in the redesigned process, these assistants were pooled to work wherever they were needed most.[26]

Recruitment and Selection

At a high-performance organization, recruitment and selection aim at obtaining the kinds of employees who can thrive in this type of setting. These employees are enthusiastic about and able to contribute to teamwork, empowerment, and knowledge sharing. Qualities such as creativity and ability to cooperate as part of a team may play a large role in selection decisions. High-performance organizations need selection methods that identify more than technical skills like ability to perform accounting and engineering tasks. Employers may use group interviews, open-ended questions, and psychological tests to find employees who innovate, share ideas, and take initiative.

Training and Development

When organizations base hiring decisions on qualities like decision-making and teamwork skills, training may be required to teach employees the specific skills they need to perform the duties of their job. Extensive training and development also are part of a learning organization, described earlier in this chapter. And when organizations delegate many decisions to work teams, the members of those teams likely will benefit from participating in team development activities that prepare them for their roles as team members.

Employee development is an important factor in IBM's top ranking in a study of the "Top 20 Companies for Leaders," jointly conducted by Hewitt Associates and *Chief Executive* magazine. According to Randall MacDonald, IBM's senior vice president of human resources, IBM had determined that leadership was one of four areas it had to focus on to achieve high performance. So the company charged all its existing leaders with developing future leaders. Once a year, IBM calls together its top managers to select candidates for leadership development, and they work with the candidates to create a development plan that meets their personal goals. By making leadership development a part of the company's routine processes, IBM removes the fear that coaching one's replacement threatens one's own career.[27]

Performance Management

In a high-performance organization, employees know the organization's goals and what they must do to help achieve those goals. HR departments can contribute to this ideal through the design of the organization's performance management system. As we discussed in Chapter 8, performance management should be related to the organization's goals. For example, at Extreme Logic, high performance comes from clear communication about what kinds of behavior are needed. On its intranet, the Atlanta-based software company publishes attributes and behaviors associated with success in each job, as well as the performance standard for each attribute and behavior. Employees can go online at any time to gauge whether they are meeting those standards.[28]

To develop future leaders, new IBM managers participate in IBM's Basic Blue program for an intensive nine-month training program. IBM is considered one of the best companies in the development of future leaders.

Figure 16.3

Employee Performance as a Process

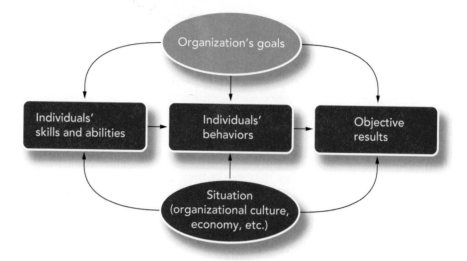

To set up a performance management system that supports the organization's goals, managers need to understand the process of employee performance. As shown in Figure 16.3, individual employees bring a set of skills and abilities to the job, and by applying a set of behaviors, they use those skills to achieve certain results. But success is more than the product of individual efforts. The organization's goals should influence each step of the process. The organization's culture and other factors influence the employees' abilities, behaviors, and results. Sometimes uncontrollable forces such as the current economic conditions enter the picture, it mustn't be forgotten—for example, a salesperson can probably sell more during an economic expansion than during an economic slowdown.

This model suggests some guidelines for performance management. First, each aspect of performance management should be related to the organization's goals. Business goals should influence the kinds of employees selected and their training, the requirements of each job, and the measures used for evaluating results. Generally, this means the organization identifies what each department must do to achieve the desired results, then defines how individual employees should contribute to their department's goals. More specifically, the following guidelines describe how to make the performance management system support organizational goals:[29]

- *Define and measure performance in precise terms*—Focus on outcomes that can be defined in terms of how frequently certain behaviors occur. Include criteria that describe ways employees can add value to a product or service (such as through quantity, quality, or timeliness). Include behaviors that go beyond the minimum required to perform a job (such as helping co-workers).
- *Link performance measures to meeting customer needs*—"Customers" may be the organization's external customers, or they may be internal customers (employees receiving services from a co-worker). Service goals for internal customers should be related to satisfying external customers.
- *Measure and correct for the effect of situational constraints*—Monitor economic conditions, the organization's culture, and other influences on performance. Measures of employees' performance should take these influences into account.

This approach, along with the guidelines in the "HR How To" box, gives employees the information they need to behave in ways that contribute to high performance.

HR How To

CREATING USEFUL PERFORMANCE MEASURES AND STANDARDS

Managers are used to seeing performance data about costs, revenues, and employee turnover. But to get a real handle on the day-to-day activities that affect the bottom line, they need to figure out which factors really matter and how to measure them. Several companies' experiences offer some examples:

- Wells Fargo arranges for the Gallup Organization to conduct regular surveys of employee attitudes and compute a "happy-to-grumpy ratio." The bank has found that a high ratio translates into more productive workers and more satisfied customers.

- Lowell Bryan, a McKinsey consultant, advocates measuring profit per employee. One advantage of this measurement is that it is easy to compute and hard to fudge.

- Pitney Bowes used data about employees' health claims and absenteeism to learn how to make its health insurance more cost effective. It also established voluntary targets employees can use to improve their health at minimal expense.

- *Analytics* take the performance measures and find links among them, for example, between employee satisfaction and productivity. Thinking

about analytics—the practical application of measurements—ensures that performance measurement is actually useful. Best Buy measured employee engagement for several years and then compared it with sales. For every 0.1 percent increase in employee engagement, a Best Buy store's sales role by $100,000. This information helps Best Buy evaluate whether more dollars spent on employee engagement are a good investment.

Source: Scott Leibs, "Measuring Up," *CFO*, June 2007, downloaded from General Reference Center Gold, http://find.galegroup.com.

In addition, organizations should help employees identify and obtain the abilities they need to meet their performance goals.

Compensation

Organizations can reinforce the impact of this kind of performance management by linking compensation in part to performance measures. Chapter 12 described a number of methods for doing this, including merit pay, gainsharing, and profit sharing. Lincoln Electric has for decades paid its production workers a piecework rate. Not only does this motivate individual employees to look for the most efficient ways to do their jobs, but because the company is known for this compensation method, it attracts workers who value working hard in order to earn more. In addition, Lincoln has been paying all of its employees a profit-sharing bonus "every year since 1934," in the words of Lincoln's CEO John M. Stropki Jr.[30] Compensation systems also can help to create the conditions that contribute to high performance, including teamwork, empowerment, and job satisfaction. For example, as discussed in Chapter 12, compensation can be linked to achievement of team objectives.

Organizations can increase empowerment and job satisfaction by including employees in decisions about compensation and by communicating the basis for decisions about pay. When the organization designs a pay structure, it can set up a task force that includes employees with direct experience in various types of jobs. Some organizations share financial information with their employees and invite them to recommend pay increases for themselves, based on their contributions. Employees also may participate in setting individual or group goals for which they can receive bonuses. Research has found that employee participation in decisions about pay policies is linked to greater satisfaction with the pay and the job.[31] And as we discussed in Chapter 11, when organizations explain their pay structures to employees, the communication can enhance employees' satisfaction and belief that the system is fair.

HRM Technology

LO5 Discuss the role of HRM technology in high-performance work systems.

Human resource departments can improve their own and their organization's performance by appropriately using new technology. New technology usually involves *automation*—that is, using equipment and information processing to perform activities that had been performed by people. Over the last few decades, automation has improved HRM efficiency by reducing the number of people needed to perform routine tasks. Using automation can free HRM experts to concentrate on ways to determine how human resource management can help the organization meet its goals, so technology also can make this function more valuable.[32] For example, information technology provides ways to build and improve systems for knowledge generation and sharing, as part of a learning organization. Among the applications are databases or networking sites where employees can store and share their knowledge, online directories of employee skills and experiences, and online libraries of learning resources, such as technical manuals and employees' reports from seminars and training programs.

HRM Applications

As computers become ever more powerful, new technologies continue to be introduced. In fact, so many HRM applications are developed for use on personal computers that publications serving the profession (such as *HR Magazine* and *Workforce Management*) devote annual issues to reviewing this software. Some of the technologies that have been widely adopted are transaction processing, decision support systems, and expert systems.[33]

transaction processing Computations and calculations involved in reviewing and documenting HRM decisions and practices.

Transaction processing refers to computations and calculations involved in reviewing and documenting HRM decisions and practices. It includes documenting decisions and actions associated with employee relocation, training expenses, and enrollments in courses and benefit plans. Transaction processing also includes the activities required to meet government reporting requirements, such as filling out EEO-1 reports, on which employers report information about employees' race and gender by job category. Computers enable companies to perform these tasks more efficiently. Employers can fill out computerized forms and store HRM information in databases (data stored electronically in user-specified categories), so that it is easier to find, sort, and report.

decision support systems Computer software systems designed to help managers solve problems by showing how results vary when the manager alters assumptions or data.

Decision support systems are computer software systems designed to help managers solve problems. They usually include a "what if?" feature that managers can use to enter different assumptions or data and see how the likely outcomes will change. This type of system can help managers make decisions for human resource planning. The manager can, for example, try out different assumptions about turnover rates to see how those assumptions affect the number of new employees needed. Or the manager can test a range of assumptions about the availability of a certain skill in the labor market, looking at the impact of the assumptions on the success of different recruiting plans. Possible applications for a decision support system include forecasting (discussed in Chapter 5) and succession planning (discussed in Chapter 9).

expert systems Computer systems that support decision making by incorporating the decision rules used by people who are considered to have expertise in a certain area.

Expert systems are computer systems that incorporate the decision rules used by people who are considered to have expertise in a certain area. The systems help users make decisions by recommending actions based on the decision rules and the information provided by the users. An expert system is designed to recommend the same actions that a human expert would in a similar situation. For example, an expert system could guide an interviewer during the selection process. Some organizations use expert systems to help employees decide how to allocate their money for benefits (as in a cafeteria plan) and help managers schedule the labor needed to complete projects. Expert systems can deliver both high quality and lower costs. By using the decision processes of experts, an expert system helps many people to arrive at decisions that reflect the expert's knowledge. An expert system helps avoid the errors that can result from fatigue and decision-making biases, such as biases in appraising employee performance, described in Chapter 8. An expert system can increase efficiency by enabling fewer or less-skilled employees to do work that otherwise would require many highly skilled employees.

In modern HR departments, transaction processing, decision support systems, and expert systems often are part of a human resource information system. Also, these technologies may be linked to employees through a network such as an intranet. Information systems and networks have been evolving rapidly; the following descriptions provide a basic introduction.

Human Resource Information Systems

A standard feature of a modern HRIS is the use of *relational databases*, which store data in separate files that can be linked by common elements. These common elements are fields identifying the type of data. Commonly used fields for an HR database include name, Social Security number, job status (full- or part-time), hiring date, position, title, rate of pay, citizenship status, job history, job location, mailing address, birth date, and emergency contacts. A relational database lets a user sort the data by any of the fields. For example, depending on how the database is set up, the user might be able to look up tables listing employees by location, rates of pay for various jobs, or employees who have completed certain training courses. This system is far more sophisticated than the old-fashioned method of filing employee data by name, with one file per employee.

The ability to locate and combine many categories of data has a multitude of uses in human resource management. Databases have been developed to track employee benefit costs, training courses, and compensation. The system can meet the needs of line managers as well as the HR department. On an oil rig, for example, management might look up data listing employee names along with safety equipment issued and appropriate skill certification. HR managers at headquarters might look up data on the same employees to gather information about wage rates or training programs needed. Another popular use of an HRIS is applicant tracking, or maintaining and retrieving records of job applicants. This is much faster and easier than trying to sort through stacks of résumés. With relational databases, HR staff can retrieve information about specific applicants or obtain lists of applicants with specific skills, career goals, work history, and employment background. Such information is useful for HR planning, recruitment, succession planning, and career development. Taking the process a step further, the system could store information related to hiring and terminations. By analyzing such data, the HR department could measure the long-term success of its recruiting and selection processes.

One of the most creative developments in HRIS technology is the **HR dashboard,** a display of a series of HR-related indicators, or measures, showing human resource

HR dashboard
A display of a series of HR measures, showing human resource goals and objectives and progress toward meeting them.

eHRM

HUMAN CAPITAL MANAGEMENT SYSTEMS

As HRIS software becomes more advanced, it increasingly takes the form of powerful suites with names such as *human capital management*. As the name implies, a human capital management suite brings together various applications associated with managing an organization's human resources.

For example, Oracle Corporation offers the E-Business Human Resources Management System (HRMS), which managers can use to enter requests for new employees, post job openings online,

receive and process applications, enter changes to an employee's work status (such as a promotion or unpaid leave), apply for benefits, and more. Scheduling and compensation management are other HR-related activities handled by such programs.

The systems can also provide decision support. When managers at Sony Computer Entertainment need someone to work on a project, they use a program from WorkforceLogic that leads them through a series of questions and

then recommends whether the position should be filled by an employee or by an independent contractor. Tyco International uses a program called CareerTracker, which not only collects data on performance standards and appraisals but also plots performance data for individuals so that managers can readily identify top performers and areas for intervention.

Source: Sue Hildreth, "HR Gets a Dose of Science," *Computerworld,* February 5, 2007, downloaded from General Reference Center Gold, http://find.galegroup.com.

goals and objectives and the progress toward meeting them. Managers with access to the HRIS can look at the HR dashboard for an easy-to-scan review of HR performance. For example, at Cisco Systems, employee development is a priority, so its HR dashboard includes a measure that tracks how many employees move and why.[34] By looking for divisions in which many employees make many lateral and upward moves, Cisco can identify divisions that are actively developing new talent. The "eHRM" box shows how companies are using sophisticated software applications to track and analyze human resource data.

Human Resource Management Online: E-HRM

During the last decade or so, organizations have seen the advantages of sharing information in computer networks. At the same time, the widespread adoption of the Internet has linked people around the globe. As we discussed in Chapter 2, more and more organizations are engaging in e-HRM, providing HR-related information over the Internet. Because much human resource information is confidential, organizations may do this with an intranet, which uses Internet technology but allows access only to authorized users (such as the organization's employees). For HR professionals, Internet access also offers a way to research new developments, post job openings, trade ideas with colleagues in other organizations, and obtain government documents. In this way, e-HRM combines company-specific information on a secure intranet with links to the resources on the broader Internet.

A benefit of e-HRM is that employees can help themselves to the information they need when they need it, instead of contacting an HR staff person. For example, employees can go online to enroll in or select benefits, submit insurance claims, or fill out employee satisfaction surveys. This can be more convenient for the employees, as well as more economical for the HR department.

Most administrative and information-gathering activities in human resource management can be part of e-HRM. For example, online recruiting has become a significant part of the total recruiting effort, as candidates submit résumés online. Employers go online to retrieve suitable résumés from job search sites or retrieve information from forms they post at their own Web sites. For selection decisions, the organization may have candidates use one of the online testing services available; these services conduct the tests, process the results, and submit reports to employers. Aspects of job design can be automated; at United Parcel Service, for example, a software system maps out each day's route for drivers to minimize wasted time and gasoline.[35] Online appraisal systems can help managers make pay decisions consistent with company policies and employee performance. Many types of training can be conducted online, as we discussed in Chapter 7. Employees at Capital One can download podcasts of training modules in the financial service company's audio learning program.[36] Online surveys of employee satisfaction can be quick and easy to fill out. Besides providing a way to administer the survey, an intranet is an effective vehicle for communicating the results of the survey and management's planned response.

Online recruiting offers many benefits to the company and the potential employee. Companies are able to easily post job openings and retrieve résumés, and most importantly, it allows them to voice the message of their company. Potential employees also benefit by having the ability to research the company, search for job openings, and submit their résumés. The Internet is fast becoming an excellent source for recruiting.

Not only does e-HRM provide efficient ways to carry out human resource functions, it also poses new challenges to employees and new issues for HR managers to address. The Internet's ability to link people anytime, anywhere has accelerated such trends as globalization, the importance of knowledge sharing within organizations, and the need for flexibility. These trends, in turn, change the work environment for employees. For example, employees in the Internet age are expected to be highly committed but flexible, able to move from job to job. Employees also may be connected to the organization 24/7. In the car, on vacation, in airports, and even in the bathroom, employees with handheld computers can be interrupted by work demands. Organizations depend on their human resource departments to help prepare employees for this changing work world through such activities as training, career development, performance management, and benefits packages that meet the need for flexibility and help employees manage stress.

Effectiveness of Human Resource Management

LO6 Summarize ways to measure the effectiveness of human resource management.

In recent years, human resource management at some organizations has responded to the quest for total quality management by taking a customer-oriented approach. For an organization's human resource division, "customers" are the organization as a whole and its other divisions. They are customers of HRM because they depend on HRM to provide a variety of services that result in a supply of talented, motivated employees. Taking this customer-oriented approach, human resource management defines its customer groups, customer needs, and the activities required to meet those needs, as shown in Table 16.2. These definitions give an organization a basis for defining goals and measures of success.

Depending on the situation, a number of techniques are available for measuring HRM's effectiveness in meeting its customers' needs. These techniques include

Table 16.2

Customer-Oriented
Perspective of Human
Resource Management

WHO ARE OUR CUSTOMERS?	WHAT DO OUR CUSTOMERS NEED?	HOW DO WE MEET CUSTOMER NEEDS?
Line managers	Committed employees	Qualified staffing
Strategic planners	Competent employees	Performance management
Employees		Rewards
		Training and development

reviewing a set of key indicators, measuring the outcomes of specific HRM activity, and measuring the economic value of HRM programs.

Human Resource Management Audits

HRM audit
A formal review of the outcomes of HRM functions, based on identifying key HRM functions and measures of business performance.

An **HRM audit** is a formal review of the outcomes of HRM functions. To conduct the audit, the HR department identifies key functions and the key measures of business performance and customer satisfaction that would indicate each function is succeeding. Table 16.3 lists examples of these measures for a variety of HRM functions: staffing, compensation, benefits, training, appraisal and development, and overall effectiveness. The audit may also look at any other measure associated with successful management of human resources—for instance, compliance with equal employment opportunity laws, succession planning, maintaining a safe workplace, and positive labor relations. An HRM audit using customer satisfaction measures supports the customer-oriented approach to human resource management.

After identifying performance measures for the HRM audit, the staff carries out the audit by gathering information. The information for the key business indicators is usually available in the organization's documents. Sometimes the HR department has to create new documents for gathering specific types of data. The usual way to measure customer satisfaction is to conduct surveys. Employee attitude surveys, discussed in Chapter 10, provide information about the satisfaction of these internal customers. Many organizations conduct surveys of top line executives to get a better view of how HRM practices affect the organization's business success. To benefit from the HR profession's best practices, companies also may invite external auditing teams to audit specific HR functions. For example, the European Foundation of Management Development has audited management training at Novartis, which markets health care products.[37] In the United States, the American Society for Training and Development conducts similar assessments.

Analyzing the Effect of HRM Programs

Another way to measure HRM effectiveness is to analyze specific programs or activities. The analysis can measure a program's success in terms of whether it achieved its objectives and whether it delivered value in an economic sense. For example, if the organization sets up a training program, it should set up goals for that program, such as the training's effects on learning, behavior, and performance improvement (results). The analysis would then measure whether the training program achieved the preset goals. Novartis analyzes the quality of its training programs by assessing whether they meet particular goals, such as preparing managers to meet leadership standards. As soon as a training program ends, participants are asked to rate the experience. Several months later, the training department measures whether participants' performance improved or behavior changed. Overall employee evaluations of company leadership also are measured against the use of management training.[38]

Table 16.3

Key Measures of Success for an HRM Audit

BUSINESS INDICATORS	CUSTOMER SATISFACTION MEASURES
Staffing	
Average days taken to fill open requisitions	Anticipation of personnel needs
Ratio of acceptances to offers made	Timeliness of referring qualified workers to line supervisors
Ratio of minority/women applicants to representation in local labor market	Treatment of applicants
Per capita requirement costs	Skill in handling terminations
Average years of experience/education of hires per job family	Adaptability to changing labor market conditions
Compensation	
Per capita (average) merit increases	Fairness of existing job evaluation system in assigning grades and salaries
Ratio of recommendations for reclassification to number of employees	Competitiveness in local labor market
Percentage of overtime hours to straight time	Relationship between pay and performance
Ratio of average salary offers to average salary in community	Employee satisfaction with pay
Benefits	
Average unemployment compensation payment (UCP)	Promptness in handling claims
Average workers' compensation payment (WCP)	Fairness and consistency in the application of benefit policies
Benefit cost per payroll dollar	Communication of benefits to employees
Percentage of sick leave to total pay	Assistance provided to line managers in reducing potential for unnecessary claims
Training	
Percentage of employees participating in training programs per job family	Extent to which training programs meet the needs of employees and the company
Percentage of employees receiving tuition refunds	Communication to employees about available training opportunities
Training dollars per employee	Quality of introduction/orientation programs
Employee appraisal and development	
Distribution of performance appraisal ratings	Assistance in identifying management potential
Appropriate psychometric properties of appraisal forms	Organizational development activities provided by HRM department
Overall effectiveness	
Ratio of personnel staff to employee population	Accuracy and clarity of information provided to managers and employees
Turnover rate	Competence and expertise of staff
Absenteeism rate	Working relationship between organizations and HRM department
Ratio of per capita revenues to per capita cost	
Net income per employee	

Source: Excerpted with permission, Chapter 1.5, "Evaluating Human Resource Effectiveness" (pp. 187–227) by Anne S. Tsui and Luis R. Gomez-Mejia from Human Resource Management: Evolving Roles & Responsibilities, *edited by Lee Dyer. Copyright © 1988 by The Bureau of National Affairs, Inc., Washington, DC. For copies of BNA Books publications call toll free 1-800-960-1200.*

The analysis can take an economic approach that measures the dollar value of the program's costs and benefits. Successful programs should deliver value that is greater than the programs' costs. Costs include employees' compensation as well as the costs to administer HRM programs such as training, employee development, or satisfaction surveys. Benefits could include a reduction in the costs associated with employee absenteeism and turnover, as well as improved productivity associated with better selection and training programs.

In general, HR departments should be able to improve their performance through some combination of greater efficiency and greater effectiveness. Greater efficiency means the HR department uses fewer and less-costly resources to perform its functions. Greater effectiveness means that what the HR department does—for example, selecting employees or setting up a performance management system—has a more beneficial effect on employees' and the organization's performance. For example, Home Depot tracks a variety of measures to see whether it is effective at meeting goals for attracting, motivating, and keeping skilled employees. The company uses a database that includes data on job applications, career paths, performance ratings, employee satisfaction, and attrition (employees leaving the company). Managers can analyze the data by region, district, and store, as well as compare numbers over time.[39]

HRM's potential to affect employees' well-being and the organization's performance makes human resource management an exciting field. As we have shown throughout the book, every HRM function calls for decisions that have the potential to help individuals and organizations achieve their goals. For HR managers to fulfill that potential, they must ensure that their decisions are well grounded. The field of human resource management provides tremendous opportunity to future researchers and managers who want to make a difference in many people's lives.

THINKING ETHICALLY

CAN HRM BUILD AN ETHICAL CULTURE?

A recent survey commissioned by Deloitte & Touche USA and Junior Achievement asked high school students if they would do something unethical to "get ahead" if they were certain not to be caught. In other words, given a choice between integrity and personal gain, what would they choose? Most of the students said they would not act unethically, but 22 percent said they would. How does that attitude affect employers? If these students continue to have the same outlook, in the next generation of American workers, one out of five will be willing to put personal gain ahead of integrity.

In this book, we have tried to make the case that effective human resource management contributes to ethical behavior, in part because organizations that embrace high ethical standards perform well over the long term. Customers want to buy from companies they can trust, and employees want to work for companies where they feel good about themselves and what they do.

According to the Ethics Resource Center, employees' commitment, performance, and satisfaction are higher in an organization with an ethical culture and climate, and their rates of misconduct are lower. An ethical culture is one that teaches employees that "doing the right thing matters," expects them to be ethical, and reinforces ethical behavior. An ethical climate is one in which people's attitudes, perceptions, and decisions reflect moral principles. The Ethics Resource Center says this combination of culture and climate is most likely in an organization where ethical conduct is measured and where leaders model and reward ethical behavior.

SOURCES: Barry Salzbert, "Shaping the Workforce of the Future," *BusinessWeek,* October 29, 2007, www.businessweek.com; and Ethics Resource Center, "Ethical Culture Building: A Modern Business Imperative," Executive Summary, www.ethics.org, accessed March 10, 2008.

Questions

1. Do you agree with the idea that ethical behavior is linked to high performance? Why or why not? If you were an HR manager, would you want to measure whether this relationship between ethics and performance exists in your organization? Why or why not?

2. Based on what you have learned about HRM in this course, how can HR managers contribute to building and maintaining an ethical culture? (For ideas, you might want to look up the Code of Ethical and Professional Standards at the Web site of the Society for Human Resource Management, www.shrm.org.)

3. How can HR managers contribute to building and maintaining an ethical climate?

SUMMARY

LO1 Define high-performance work systems, and identify the elements of such a system.

A high-performance work system is the right combination of people, technology, and organizational structure that makes full use of the organization's resources and opportunities in achieving its goals. The elements of a high-performance work system are organizational structure, task design, people, reward systems, and information systems. These elements must work together in a smoothly functioning whole.

LO2 Summarize the outcomes of a high-performance work system.

A high-performance work system achieves the organization's goals, typically including growth, productivity, and high profits. On the way to achieving these overall goals, the high-performance work system meets such intermediate goals as high quality, innovation, customer satisfaction, job satisfaction, and reduced absenteeism and turnover.

LO3 Describe the conditions that create a high-performance work system.

Many conditions contribute to high-performance work systems by giving employees skills, incentives, knowledge, autonomy, and employee satisfaction. Teamwork and empowerment can make work more satisfying and provide a means for employees to improve quality and productivity. Organizations can improve performance by creating a learning organization, in which people constantly learn and share knowledge so that they continually expand their capacity to achieve the results they desire. In a high-performance organization, employees experience job satisfaction or even "occupational intimacy." For long-run high performance, organizations and employees must be ethical as well.

LO4 Explain how human resource management can contribute to high performance.

Jobs should be designed to foster teamwork and employee empowerment. Recruitment and selection should focus on obtaining employees who have the qualities necessary for teamwork, empowerment,

and knowledge sharing. When the organization selects for teamwork and decision-making skills, it may have to provide training in specific job tasks. Training also is important because of its role in creating a learning organization. The performance management system should be related to the organization's goals, with a focus on meeting internal and external customers' needs. Compensation should include links to performance, and employees should be included in decisions about compensation. Research suggests that it is more effective to improve HRM practices as a whole than to focus on one or two isolated practices.

LO5 Discuss the role of HRM technology in high-performance work systems.

Technology can improve the efficiency of the human resource management functions and support knowledge sharing. HRM applications involve transaction processing, decision support systems, and expert systems, often as part of a human resource information system using relational databases, which can improve the efficiency of routine tasks and the quality of decisions. With Internet technology, organizations can use e-HRM to let all the organization's employees help themselves to the HR information they need whenever they need it.

LO6 Summarize ways to measure the effectiveness of human resource management.

Taking a customer-oriented approach, HRM can improve quality by defining the internal customers who use its services and determining whether it is meeting those customers' needs. One way to do this is with an HRM audit, a formal review of the outcomes of HRM functions. The audit may look at any measure associated with successful management of human resources. Audit information may come from the organization's documents and surveys of customer satisfaction. Another way to measure HRM effectiveness is to analyze specific programs or activities. The analysis can measure success in terms of whether a program met its objectives and whether it delivered value in an economic sense, such as by leading to productivity improvements.

KEY TERMS

continuous learning p. 473
decision support systems p. 482
expert systems p. 482

high-performance work systems
  p. 469
HR dashboard p. 483

HRM audit p. 486
learning organization p. 473
transaction processing p. 482

REVIEW AND DISCUSSION QUESTIONS

1. What is a high-performance work system? What are its elements? Which of these elements involve human resource management?

2. As it has become clear that HRM can help create and maintain high-performance work systems, it appears that organizations will need two kinds of human resource professionals: One kind focuses on identifying how HRM can contribute to high performance. The other kind develops expertise in particular HRM functions, such as how to administer a benefits program that complies with legal requirements. Which aspect of HRM is more interesting to you? Why?

3. How can teamwork, empowerment, knowledge sharing, and job satisfaction contribute to high performance?

4. If an organization can win customers, employees, or investors through deception, why would ethical behavior contribute to high performance?

5. How can an organization promote ethical behavior among its employees?

6. Summarize how each of the following HR functions can contribute to high performance.
   a. Job design
   b. Recruitment and selection
   c. Training and development
   d. Performance management
   e. Compensation

7. How can HRM technology make a human resource department more productive? How can technology improve the quality of HRM decisions?

8. Why should human resource departments measure their effectiveness? What are some ways they can go about measuring effectiveness?

BUSINESSWEEK CASE

BusinessWeek Customer Service Champs

Bob Emig was flying home from St. Louis on Southwest Airlines this past December when an all-too-familiar travel nightmare began to unfold. After his airplane backed away from the gate, he and his fellow passengers were told the plane would need to be de-iced. When the aircraft was ready to fly two and a half hours later, the pilot had reached the hour limit set by the Federal Aviation Administration, and a new pilot was required. By that time, the plane had to be de-iced again. Five hours after the scheduled departure time, Emig's flight was finally ready for takeoff.

A customer service disaster, right? Not to hear Emig tell it. The pilot walked the aisles, answering questions and offering constant updates. Flight attendants, who Emig says "really seemed like they cared," kept up with the news on connecting flights. And within a couple of days of arriving home, Emig, who travels frequently, received a letter from Southwest that included two free round-trip ticket vouchers. "I could not believe they acknowledged the situation and apologized," says Emig. "Then they gave me a gift, for all intents and purposes, to make up for the time spent sitting on the runway."

Emig's "gift" from the airline was not the result of an unusually kind customer service agent who took pity on his plight. Nor was it a scramble to make amends after a disastrous operational fiasco. Rather, it was standard procedure for Southwest Airlines, which almost six years ago created a new high-level job that oversees all proactive customer communications. Fred Taylor, who was plucked from the field by President Colleen C. Barrett to fill the role, coordinates information that's sent to all frontline reps in the event of major flight disruptions. But he's also charged with sending out letters, and in many cases flight vouchers, to customers caught in major storms, air traffic snarls, or other travel messes—even those beyond Southwest's control—that would fry the nerves of a seasoned traveler. "It's not something we had to do," says Taylor. "It's just something we feel our customers deserve."

As Southwest recognizes, providing great customer service is much more than just a job for the front lines or the call centers. It takes coordination from the top, bringing together people, management, technology, and processes to put customers' needs first. Refining time-tested concepts and coming up with cutting-edge ideas is critical for managing rank-and-file workers and measuring what customers think.

In BusinessWeek's first-ever ranking of the best providers of customer service, we set out to find the service champions, but also to dig into the techniques, strategies, and tools they use to make the customer king. Most of the names on our list share a few important traits. They emphasize employee loyalty as much as customer loyalty, keeping their people happy with generous benefits and perks. Most of the companies on our list also know how to respond when service goes wrong, as Southwest did in Emig's case.

The connection between satisfied employees and contented customers is hardly a new concept: Any business school student can recite by heart the concept of the "service–profit chain," which draws the inextricable link between the front line and satisfied customers. But new research from Katzenbach Partners offers an updated metaphor. The firm stresses the importance of the "empathy engine," which looks at the role of the entire organization, including middle and senior management, in providing great service. If that engine is thought of as a heart, "the whole company has to pump the customer through it," says Traci Entel, a principal at Katzenbach Partners who recently studied 13 leading service companies' best practices. "It starts much further back, with how they organize themselves, and how they place value on thinking about the customer."

SOURCE: Excerpted from Jena McGregor, "Customer Service Champs," *BusinessWeek*, March 5, 2007, www.businessweek.com.

Questions

1. Which characteristics of high-performance organizations does Southwest Airlines demonstrate?
2. How can an organization recruit and select people who have the level of commitment to customer service described here?
3. What other HRM practices can reinforce and maintain an organizationwide commitment to superior customer service?

CASE: CAN REELL PRECISION MANUFACTURING BE A HIGH PERFORMER AGAIN?

Reell Precision Manufacturing, a small manufacturing company based in Minnesota, was founded by three partners who envisioned a company that simultaneously values business success and ethical principles. They named their company *Reell* (pronounced "ray-EL"), using a German word for "honest, trustworthy and good" to represent the company's commitment to those values in its products and its treatment of employees and customers.

The three founders decided their company would be run differently from a traditional organization. First, they decided, all three of them would have to agree on major decisions. In effect, they would be co-CEOs. In practice, this required the company's leaders to cooperate and think through ideas carefully; employees came to see their leaders as thoughtful and as good listeners. Second, all Reell's products would be the best quality. In addition, all employees would be expected to put their families ahead of work. Finally, according to the company's Declaration of Belief, all employees must "do what is 'right' even if it does not seem to be profitable, expedient, or conventional."

Reell makes specialty parts that apply torque—twisting force. An early test of the founders' beliefs came in 1975, a few years after the company's launch, when their only customer at the time (3M) canceled the remainder of its order. The partners managed to land a new client, Xerox, but sales were down drastically. The co-CEOs addressed the problem by cutting their own pay 50 percent and asking their employees to take a 10 percent pay cut. That way, they survived the downturn without layoffs.

Business took off years later, when Hewlett Packard asked Reell to develop a hinge for what was then a new concept: a laptop computer. The hinge would have to hold the screen's position—common today but innovative then. As the company met the demand for this new product, it grew from 10 employees to 200-plus. These employees took on responsibility for living up to Reell's values. They checked quality and made decisions based on their ethical principles. When they could not find a solution alone, they worked with their colleagues, going to the top only when they couldn't solve a problem together. When times were good, workers earned generous bonuses. The founders paid themselves no more than seven times an entry-level employee's earnings. The company also set up an employee stock ownership plan.

When laptops and their parts were still considered novel and innovative, Reell thrived. But problems began when heavier competition drove manufacturing overseas. The owners had to make a significant decision: would they sell hinges to Asian computer makers, knowing the price competition could become stiff? They decided that the company's future survival depended on taking that risk. In the meantime, two of the founders retired. The board brought in a new leader, former Kodak executive Eric Donaldson, so that the remaining founder could continue the tradition of co-CEOs. At first the decision to sell in Asia meant rapid growth in volume, but eventually the shift to greater volume also brought demands for further price breaks and volatile sales as customers moved from one supplier to another. The board decided that shared leadership was no longer effective, and the third founder left.

Under Donaldson's leadership, the focus has shifted to efficiency improvement. Wages have stagnated, and workers are unhappy. Many see the loss of a culture they valued and have left the company; employee turnover has doubled. Donaldson insists that the changes are the only way to preserve Reell in challenging times.

SOURCES: Bo Burlingham, "Paradise Lost," *Inc.*, February 2008, www.inc.com; and Reell Precision Manufacturing, "About Reell," www.reell.com, accessed April 7, 2008.

Questions

1. In this description of Reell under its original founders, what qualities of a high-performance organization did the company exhibit?

2. What qualities of a high-performance organization were lacking?

3. Imagine you are an HR manager or consultant at Reell. What actions would you recommend the company take to weather the increased competition while restoring employee engagement? Do your recommendations focus on financial goals, employee satisfaction, or both?

IT'S A WRAP!

www.mhhe.com/noefund3e is your source for Reviewing, Applying, and Practicing the concepts you learned about in Chapter 16.

Review
- Chapter learning objectives
- Narrated lecture and iPod content
- Test Your Knowledge: Levels of Strategy

Application
- Manager's Hot Seat segment: "Change: More Pain than Gain?"
- Video case and quiz: "HR in Alignment"
- Self-Assessments: Your Career in HR
- Web exercise: High Performance Work Systems

Practice
- Chapter quiz

NOTES

1. S. Covel, "Tech Company Stems Departures by Listening to Employees' Needs," *Wall Street Journal*, January 24, 2008, http://online.wsj.com.

2. S. Snell and J. Dean, "Integrated Manufacturing and Human Resource Management: A Human Capital Perspective," *Academy of Management Journal* 35 (1992), pp. 467–504.

3. M. A. Huselid, "The Impact of Human Resource Management Practices on Turnover, Productivity, and Corporate Financial Performance," *Academy of Management Journal* 38 (1995), pp. 635–72; U.S. Department of Labor, *High-Performance Work Practices and Firm Performance* (Washington, DC: U.S. Government Printing Office, 1993); and J. Combs, Y. Liu, A. Hall, and D. Ketchen, "How Much Do High-Performance Work Practices Matter? A Meta-Analysis of Their Effects on Organizational Performance," *Personnel Psychology* 59 (2006), pp. 501–28.

4. R. N. Ashkenas, "Beyond the Fads: How Leaders Drive Change with Results," *Human Resource Planning* 17 (1994), pp. 25–44; and C. Slater, "The Truth Shall Set You Free," *Fast Company*, May 2004, pp. 78–79, 82–83.

5. J. Arthur, "The Link between Business Strategy and Industrial Relations Systems in American Steel Minimills," *Industrial and Labor Relations Review* 45 (1992), pp. 488–506.

6. J. A. Neal and C. L. Tromley, "From Incremental Change to Retrofit: Creating High-Performance Work Systems," *Academy of Management Executive* 9 (1995), pp 42–54; and M. A. Huselid, "The Impact of Human Resource Management Practices on Turnover, Productivity, and Corporate Financial Performance," *Academy of Management Journal* 38 (1995), pp. 635–72.

7. D. McCann and C. Margerison, "Managing High-Performance Teams," *Training and Development Journal*, November 1989, pp. 52–60.

8. J. Marquez, "Engine of Change," *Workforce Management*, July 17, 2006, pp. 20–30.

9. D. Senge, "The Learning Organization Made Plain and Simple," *Training and Development Journal*, October 1991, pp. 37–44.

10. M. A. Gephart, V. J. Marsick, M. E. Van Buren, and M. S. Spiro, "Learning Organizations Come Alive," *Training and Development* 50 (1996), pp. 34–45.

11. T. T. Baldwin, C. Danielson, and W. Wiggenhorn, "The Evolution of Learning Strategies in Organizations: From Employee Development to Business Redefinition," *Academy of Management Executive* 11 (1997), pp. 47–58; and J. J. Martocchio and T. T. Baldwin, "The Evolution of Strategic Organizational Training," in *Research in Personnel and Human Resource Management* 15, ed. G. R. Ferris (Greenwich, CT: JAI Press, 1997), pp. 1–46.

12. A. Hanacek, "Star Power," *National Provisioner*, February 2008, downloaded from General Reference Center Gold, http://find.galegroup.com.

13. T. A. Judge, C. J. Thoresen, J. E. Bono, and G. K. Patton, "The Job Satisfaction-Job Performance Relationship: A Qualitative and Quantitative Review," *Psychological Bulletin* 127 (2001), pp. 376–407; and R. A. Katzell, D. E. Thompson, and R. A. Guzzo, "How Job Satisfaction and Job Performance Are and Are Not Linked," *Job Satisfaction*, eds. C. J. Cranny, P. C. Smith, and E. F. Stone (New York: Lexington Books, 1992), pp. 195–217.

14. Watson Wyatt Worldwide, *WorkUSA 2002: Weathering the Storm* (Watson Wyatt, October 2002, www.humancapitalonline.com).

15. Partnership for Public Service, "Welcome to the 2007 Best Places to Work Rankings," http://bestplacestowork.org, accessed March 27, 2008; and Stephen Barr, "Nuclear Regulatory Commission Ranks as Top Workplace," *Washington Post*, April 20, 2007, www.washingtonpost.com.

16. Partnership for Public Service, "Welcome to the 2007 Best Places to Work Rankings."

17. P. E. Boverie and M. Kroth, *Transforming Work: The Five Keys to Achieving Trust, Commitment, and Passion in the Workplace* (Cambridge, MA: Perseus, 2001), pp. 71–72, 79.

18. R. P. Gephart Jr., "Introduction to the Brave New Workplace: Organizational Behavior in the Electronic Age," *Journal of Organizational Behavior* 23 (2002), pp. 327–44.

19. C. Hymowitz, "CEOs Must Work Hard to Maintain Faith in the Corner Office," *Wall Street Journal*, July 9, 2002, p. B1.

20. K. Maher, "Wanted: Ethical Employer," *Wall Street Journal*, July 9, 2002, pp. B1, B8.

21. R. F. Stolz, "What HR Will Stand For," *Human Resource Executive*, January 2003, pp. 1, 20–28.

22. W. F. Cascio, *Costing Human Resources: The Financial Impact of Behavior in Organizations*, 3rd ed. (Boston: PWS-Kent, 1991); and Watson Wyatt Worldwide, *Watson Wyatt's Human Capital Index: Human Capital as a Lead Indicator of Shareholder Value*, 2001/2002 Survey Report (Watson Wyatt, October 2002, www.humancapitalonline.com).

23. Watson Wyatt, *Watson Wyatt's Human Capital Index*.

24. B. Becker and M. A. Huselid, "High-Performance Work Systems and Firm Performance: A Synthesis of Research and Managerial Implications," in *Research in Personnel and Human Resource Management* 16, ed. G. R. Ferris (Stamford, CT: JAI Press, 1998), pp. 53–101.

25. B. Becker and B. Gerhart, "The Impact of Human Resource Management on Organizational Performance: Progress and Prospects," *Academy of Management Journal* 39 (1996), pp. 779–801.

26. B. Wysocki Jr., "To Fix Health Care, Hospitals Take Tips from Factory Floor," *Wall Street Journal*, April 9, 2004, pp. A1, A6.

27. "Leadership: Ripe for Change," *Human Resource Executive*, 2002, pp. 60, 62+ (interview with Randall MacDonald).

28. C. M. Solomon, "HR's Push for Productivity," *Workforce*, August 2002, pp. 28–33.

29. H. J. Bernardin, C. M. Hagan, J. S. Kane, and P. Villanova, "Effective Performance Management: A Focus on Precision, Customers, and Situational Constraints," in *Performance Appraisal: State of the Art in Practice*, ed. J. W. Smither (San Francisco: Jossey-Bass, 1998), p. 56.

30. M. Lewis Jr., "The Heat Is On," *Inside Business*, October 2007, downloaded from General Reference Center Gold, http://find.galegroup.com.

31. L. R. Gomez-Mejia and D. B. Balkin, *Compensation, Organizational Strategy, and Firm Performance* (Cincinnati: South-Western, 1992); and G. D. Jenkins and E. E. Lawler III, "Impact of Employee Participation in Pay Plan Development," *Organizational Behavior and Human Performance* 28 (1981), pp. 111–28.

32. S. Shrivastava and J. Shaw, "Liberating HR through Technology," *Human Resource Management* 42, no. 3 (2003), pp. 201–17.

33. R. Broderick and J. W. Boudreau, "Human Resource Management, Information Technology, and the Competitive Edge," *Academy of Management Executive* 6 (1992), pp. 7–17.

34. N. Lockwood, *Maximizing Human Capital: Demonstrating HR Value with Key Performance Indicators* (Alexandria, VA: SHRM Research Quarterly, 2006).

35. D. Foust, "How Technology Delivers for UPS," *BusinessWeek*, March 5, 2007, p. 60.

36. "Outstanding Training Initiatives: Capital One, Audio Learning in Stereo," *Training*, March 2006, p. 64.

37. K. Whitney, "Novartis: Using Analytics to Enhance Leadership Training," *Chief Learning Officer*, March 2007, www.clomedia.com.

38. Ibid.

39. R. F. Stolz, "CEOs Who 'Get It,'" *Human Resource Executive*, March 16, 2005, pp. 1, 18–25.

Glossary

achievement tests   Tests that measure a person's existing knowledge and skills.

action learning   Training in which teams get an actual problem, work on solving it and commit to an action plan, and are accountable for carrying it out.

adventure learning   A teamwork and leadership training program based on the use of challenging, structured outdoor activities.

affirmative action   An organization's active effort to find opportunities to hire or promote people in a particular group.

agency shop   Union security arrangement that requires the payment of union dues but not union membership.

alternative dispute resolution (ADR)   Methods of solving a problem by bringing in an impartial outsider but not using the court system.

alternative work arrangements   Methods of staffing other than the traditional hiring of full-time employees (for example, use of independent contractors, on-call workers, temporary workers, and contract company workers).

American Federation of Labor and Congress of Industrial Organizations (AFL-CIO)   An association that seeks to advance the shared interests of its member unions at the national level.

apprenticeship   A work-study training method that teaches job skills through a combination of on-the-job training and classroom training.

aptitude tests   Tests that assess how well a person can learn or acquire skills and abilities.

arbitration   Conflict resolution procedure in which an arbitrator or arbitration board determines a binding settlement.

assessment center   A wide variety of specific selection programs that use multiple selection methods to rate applicants or job incumbents on their management potential.

assessment   Collecting information and providing feedback to employees about their behavior, communication style, or skills.

associate union membership   Alternative form of union membership in which members receive discounts on insurance and credit cards rather than representation in collective bargaining.

avatars   Computer depictions of trainees, which the trainees manipulate in an online role-play.

balanced scorecard   A combination of performance measures directed toward the company's long- and short-term goals and used as the basis for awarding incentive pay.

behavior description interview (BDI)   A structured interview in which the interviewer asks the candidate to describe how he or she handled a type of situation in the past.

behavioral observation scale (BOS)   A variation of a BARS which uses all behaviors necessary for effective performance to rate performance at a task.

behaviorally anchored rating scale (BARS)   Method of performance measurement that rates behavior in terms of a scale showing specific statements of behavior that describe different levels of performance.

benchmarking   A procedure in which an organization compares its own practices against those of successful competitors.

benchmarks   A measurement tool that gathers ratings of a manager's use of skills associated with success in managing.

bona fide occupational qualification (BFOQ)   A necessary (not merely preferred) qualification for performing a job.

cafeteria-style plan   A benefits plan that offers employees a set of alternatives from which they can choose the types and amounts of benefits they want.

cash balance plan   Retirement plan in which the employer sets up an individual account for each employee and contributes a percentage of the employee's salary; the account earns interest at a predefined rate.

checkoff provision   Contract provision under which the employer, on behalf of the union, automatically deducts union dues from employees' paycheecks.

closed shop   Union security arrangement under which a person must be a union member before being hired; illegal for those covered by the National Labor Relations Act.

coach   A peer or manager who works with an employee to motivate the employee, help him or her develop skills, and provide reinforcement and feedback.

cognitive ability tests   Tests designed to measure such mental abilities as verbal skills, quantitative skills, and reasoning ability.

collective bargaining   Negotiation between union representatives and management representatives to arrive at a contract defining conditions of employment for the term of the contract and to administer that contract.

commissions   Incentive pay calculated as a percentage of sales.

compensatory model   Process of arriving at a selection decision in which a very high score on one type of assessment can make up for a low score on another.

concurrent validation   Research that consists of administering a test to people who currently hold a job, then comparing their scores to existing measures of job performance.

Consolidated Omnibus Budget Reconciliation Act (COBRA)   Federal law that requires employers to permit employees or their dependents to extend their health insurance coverage at group rates for up to 36 months following a qualifying event, such as a layoff, reduction in hours, or the employee's death.

construct validity   Consistency between a high score on a test and high level of a construct such as intelligence or leadership ability, as well as between mastery of this construct and successful performance of the job.

content validity   Consistency between the test items or problems and the kinds of situations or problems that occur on the job.

continuous learning   Each employee's and each group's ongoing efforts to gather information and apply the information to their decisions in a learning organization.

contributory plan   Retirement plan funded by contributions from the employer and employee.

coordination training   Team training that teaches the team how to share information and make decisions to obtain the best team performance.

core competency   A set of knowledges and skills that make the organization superior to competitors and create value for customers.

corporate campaigns   Bringing public, financial, or political pressure on employers during union organization and contract negotiation.

craft union   Labor union whose members all have a particular skill or occupation.

criterion-related validity   A measure of validity based on showing a substantial correlation between test scores and job performance scores.

critical-incident method   Method of performance measurement based on managers' records of specific examples of the employee acting in ways that are either effective or ineffective.

cross-cultural preparation   Training to prepare employees and their family members for an assignment in a foreign country.

cross-training   Team training in which team members understand and practice each other's skills so that they are prepared to step in and take another member's place.

culture shock   Disillusionment and discomfort that occur during the process of adjusting to a new culture.

decision support systems   Computer software systems designed to help managers solve problems by showing how results vary when the manager alters assumptions or data.

defined benefit plan   Pension plan that guarantees a specified level of retirement income.

defined contribution plan   Retirement plan in which the employer sets up an individual account for each employee and specifies the size of the investment into that account.

delayering   Reducing the number of levels in the organization's job structure.

development   The acquisition of knowledge, skills, and behaviors that improve an employee's ability to meet changes in job requirements and in customer demands.

differential piece rates   Incentive pay in which the piece rate is higher when a greater amount is produced.

direct applicants   People who apply for a vacancy without prompting from the organization.

disability   Under the Americans with Disabilities Act, a physical or mental impairment that substantially limits one or more major life activities, a record of having such an impairment, or being regarded as having such an impairment.

disparate impact   A condition in which employment practices are seemingly neutral yet disproportionately exclude a protected group from employment opportunities.

disparate treatment   Differing treatment of individuals, where the differences are based on the individuals' race, color, religion, sex, national origin, age, or disability status.

diversity training   Training designed to change employee attitudes about diversity and/or develop skills needed to work with a diverse workforce.

downsizing   The planned elimination of large numbers of personnel with the goal of enhancing the organization's competitiveness.

downward move   Assignment of an employee to a position with less responsibility and authority.

due-process policies   Policies that formally lay out the steps an employee may take to appeal the employer's decision to terminate that employee.

EEO-1 report   The EEOC's Employer Information Report, which details the number of women and minorities employed in nine different job categories.

e-learning   Receiving training via the Internet or the organization's intranet.

electronic human resource management (e-HRM)   The processing and transmission of digitized HR information, especially using computer networking and the Internet.

employee assistance program (EAP)   A referral service that employees can use to seek professional treatment for emotional problems or substance abuse.

employee benefits   Compensation in forms other than cash.

employee development   The combination of formal education, job experiences, relationships, and assessment of personality and abilities to help employees prepare for the future of their careers.

employee empowerment   Giving employees responsibility and authority to make decisions regarding all aspects of product development or customer service.

Employee Retirement Income Security Act (ERISA) Federal law that increased the responsibility of pension plan trustees to protect retirees, established certain rights related to vesting and portability, and created the Pension Benefit Guarantee Corporation.

employee stock ownership plan (ESOP)   An arrangement in which the organization distributes shares of stock to all its employees by placing it in a trust.

employee wellness program (EWP)   A set of communications, activities, and facilities designed to change health-related behaviors in ways that reduce health risks.

employment at will   Employment principle that if there is no specific employment contract saying otherwise, the employer or employee may end an employment relationship at any time, regardless of cause.

equal employment opportunity (EEO)   The condition in which all individuals have an equal chance for employment, regardless of their race, color, religion, sex, age, disability, or national origin.

Equal Employment Opportunity Commission (EEOC)   Agency of the Department of Justice charged with enforcing Title VII of the Civil Rights Act of 1964 and other antidiscrimination laws.

ergonomics   The study of the interface between individuals' physiology and the characteristics of the physical work environment.

ethics   The fundamental principles of right and wrong.

exempt employees   Managers, outside salespeople, and any other employees not covered by the FLSA requirement for overtime pay.

exit interview   A meeting of a departing employee with the employee's supervisor and/or a human resource specialist to discuss the employee's reasons for leaving.

expatriates   Employees assigned to work in another country.

experience rating   The number of employees a company has laid off in the past and the cost of providing them with unemployment benefits.

experiential programs   Training programs in which participants learn concepts and apply them by simulating behaviors involved and analyzing the activity, connecting it with real-life situations.

expert systems   Computer systems that support decision making by incorporating the decision rules used by people who are considered to have expertise in a certain area.

external labor market   Individuals who are actively seeking employment.

externship   Employee development through a full-time temporary position at another organization.

fact finder   Third party to collective bargaining who reports the reasons for a dispute, the views and arguments of both sides, and possibly a recommended settlement, which the parties may decline.

Fair Labor Standards Act (FLSA)   Federal law that establishes a minimum wage and requirements for overtime pay and child labor.

Family and Medical Leave Act (FMLA)   Federal law requiring organizations with 50 or more employees to provide up to 12 weeks of unpaid leave after childbirth or adoption; to care for a seriously ill family member; or for an employee's own serious illness.

Fleishman Job Analysis System   Job analysis technique that asks subject-matter experts to evaluate a job in terms of the abilities required to perform the job.

flexible spending account   Employee-controlled pretax earnings set aside to pay for certain eligible expenses such as health care expenses during the same year.

flextime   A scheduling policy in which full-time employees may choose starting and ending times within guidelines specified by the organization.

forced-distribution method   Method of performance measurement that assigns a certain percentage of employees to each category in a set of categories.

forecasting   The attempts to determine the supply of and demand for various types of human resources to predict areas within the organization where there will be labor shortages or surpluses.

four-fifths rule   Rule of thumb that finds evidence of discrimination if an organization's hiring rate for a minority group is less than four-fifths the hiring rate for the majority group.

gainsharing   Group incentive program that measures improvements in productivity and effectiveness objectives and distributes a portion of each gain to employees.

generalizable   Valid in other contexts beyond the context in which the selection method was developed.

glass ceiling   Circumstances resembling an invisible barrier that keep most women and minorities from attaining the top jobs in organizations.

global organization   An organization that chooses to locate a facility based on the ability to effectively, efficiently, and flexibly produce a product or service, using cultural differences as an advantage.

graphic rating scale   Method of performance measurement that lists traits and provides a rating scale for each trait; the employer uses the scale to indicate the extent to which an employee displays each trait.

green-circle rate   Pay at a rate that falls below the pay range for the job.

grievance procedure   The process for resolving union-management conflicts over interpretation or violation of a collective bargaining agreement.

health maintenance organization (HMO)   A health care plan that requires patients to receive their medical care from the HMO's health care professionals, who are often paid a flat salary, and provides all services on a prepaid basis.

high-performance work system   An organization in which technology, organizational structure, people, and processes all work together to give an organization an advantage in the competitive environment.

host country   A country (other than the parent country) in which an organization operates a facility.

hot-stove rule   Principle of discipline that says discipline should be like a hot stove, giving clear warning and following up with consistent, objective, immediate consequences.

hourly wage   Rate of pay for each hour worked.

HR dashboard   A display of a series of HR measures, showing the measure and progress toward meeting it.

HRM audit   A formal review of the outcomes of HRM functions, based on identifying key HRM functions and measures of business performance.

human capital   An organization's employees, described in terms of their training, experience, judgment, intelligence, relationships, and insight.

human resource information system (HRIS)   A computer system used to acquire, store, manipulate, analyze, retrieve, and distribute information related to an organization's human resources.

human resource management (HRM)   The policies, practices, and systems that influence employees' behavior, attitudes, and performance.

human resource planning   Identifying the numbers and types of employees the organization will require in order to meet its objectives.

Immigration Reform and Control Act of 1986   Federal law requiring employers to verify and maintain records on applicants' legal rights to work in the United States.

Improshare   A gainsharing program in which the gain is the decrease in the labor hours needed to produce one unit of product, with the gains split equally between the organization and its employees.

incentive pay   Forms of pay linked to an employee's performance as an individual, group member, or organization member.

industrial engineering   The study of jobs to find the simplest way to structure work in order to maximize efficiency.

industrial union Labor union whose members are linked by their work in a particular industry.

instructional design A process of systematically developing training to meet specified needs.

interactional justice A judgment that the organization carried out its actions in a way that took the employee's feelings into account.

internal labor force An organization's workers (its employees and the people who have contracts to work at the organization).

international organization An organization that sets up one or a few facilities in one or a few foreign countries.

internship On-the-job learning sponsored by an educational institution as a component of an academic program.

involuntary turnover Turnover initiated by an employer (often with employees who would prefer to stay).

job A set of related duties.

job analysis The process of getting detailed information about jobs.

job description A list of the tasks, duties, and responsibilities (TDRs) that a particular job entails.

job design The process of defining how work will be performed and what tasks will be required in a given job.

job enlargement Broadening the types of tasks performed in a job.

job enrichment Empowering workers by adding more decision-making authority to jobs.

job evaluation An administrative procedure for measuring the relative internal worth of the organization's jobs.

job experiences The combination of relationships, problems, demands, tasks, and other features of an employee's job.

job extension Enlarging jobs by combining several relatively simple jobs to form a job with a wider range of tasks.

job hazard analysis technique Safety promotion technique that involves breaking down a job into basic elements, then rating each element for its potential for harm or injury.

job involvement The degree to which people identify themselves with their jobs.

job posting The process of communicating information about a job vacancy on company bulletin boards, in employee publications, on corporate intranets, and anywhere else the organization communicates with employees.

job rotation Enlarging jobs by moving employees among several different jobs.

job satisfaction A pleasant feeling resulting from the perception that one's job fulfills or allows for the fulfillment of one's important job values.

job sharing A work option in which two part-time employees carry out the tasks associated with a single job.

job specification A list of the knowledge, skills, abilities, and other characteristics (KSAOs) that an individual must have to perform a particular job.

job structure The relative pay for different jobs within the organization.

job withdrawal A set of behaviors with which employees try to avoid the work situation physically, mentally, or emotionally.

knowledge workers Employees whose main contribution to the organization is specialized knowledge, such as knowledge of customers, a process, or a profession.

labor relations Field that emphasizes skills managers and union leaders can use to minimize costly forms of conflict (such as strikes) and seek win-win solutions to disagreements.

leaderless group discussion An assessment center exercise in which a team of five to seven employees is assigned a problem and must work together to solve it within a certain time period.

leading indicators Objective measures that accurately predict future labor demand.

learning management system (LMS) A computer application that automates the administration, development, and delivery of training programs.

learning organization An organization that supports lifelong learning by enabling all employees to acquire and share knowledge.

long-term disability insurance Insurance that pays a percentage of a disabled employee's salary after an initial period and potentially for the rest of the employee's life.

maintenance of membership Union security rules not requiring union membership but requiring that employees who join the union remain members for a certain period of time.

management by objectives (MBO) A system in which people at each level of the organization set goals in a process that flows from top to bottom, so employees at all levels are contributing to the organization's overall goals;

these goals become the standards for evaluating each employee's performance.

material safety data sheets (MSDSs)   Forms on which chemical manufacturers and importers identify the hazards of their chemicals.

mediation   Conflict resolution procedure in which a mediator hears the views of both sides and facilitates the negotiation process but has no formal authority to dictate a resolution.

mentor   An experienced, productive senior employee who helps develop a less experienced employee (a protégé).

merit pay   A system of linking pay increases to ratings on performance appraisals.

minimum wage   The lowest amount that employers may pay under federal or state law, stated as an amount of pay per hour.

mixed-standard scales   Method of performance measurement that uses several statements describing each trait to produce a final score for that trait.

multinational company   An organization that builds facilities in a number of different countries in an effort to minimize production and distribution costs.

multiple-hurdle model   Process of arriving at a selection decision by eliminating some candidates at each stage of the selection process.

Myers-Briggs Type Indicator (MBTI)®   Psychological inventory that identifies individuals' preferences for source of energy, means of information gathering, way of decision making, and lifestyle, providing information for team building and leadership development.

National Labor Relations Act (NLRA)   Federal law that supports collective bargaining and sets out the rights of employees to form unions.

National Labor Relations Board (NLRB)   Federal government agency that enforces the NLRA by conducting and certifying representation elections and investigating unfair labor practices.

needs assessment   The process of evaluating the organization, individual employees, and employees' tasks to determine what kinds of training, if any, are necessary.

nepotism   The practice of hiring relatives.

noncontributory plan   Retirement plan funded entirely by contributions from the employer.

nondirective interview   A selection interview in which the interviewer has great discretion in choosing questions to ask each candidate.

nonexempt employees   Employees covered by the FLSA requirements for overtime pay.

Occupational Safety and Health Act (OSH Act)   U.S. law authorizing the federal government to establish and enforce occupational safety and health standards for all places of employment engaging in interstate commerce.

Occupational Safety and Health Administration (OSHA)   Labor Department agency responsible for inspecting employers, applying safety and health standards, and levying fines for violation.

Office of Federal Contract Compliance Procedures (OFCCP)   The agency responsible for enforcing the executive orders that cover companies doing business with the federal government.

offshoring   Moving operations from the country where a company is headquartered to a country where pay rates are lower but the necessary skills are available.

on-the-job training (OJT)   Training methods in which a person with job experience and skill guides trainees in practicing job skills at the workplace.

open-door policy   An organization's policy of making managers available to hear complaints.

organization analysis   A process for determining the appropriateness of training by evaluating the characteristics of the organization.

organizational behavior modification (OBM)   A plan for managing the behavior of employees through a formal system of feedback and reinforcement.

organizational commitment   The degree to which an employee identifies with the organization and is willing to put forth effort on its behalf.

orientation   Training designed to prepare employees to perform their jobs effectively, learn about their organization, and establish work relationships.

outcome fairness   A judgment that the consequences given to employees are just.

outplacement counseling   A service in which professionals try to help dismissed employees manage the transition from one job to another.

outsourcing   Contracting with another organization (vendor, third party provider or consultant) to provide services.

paired-comparison method   Method of performance measurement that compares each employee with each other employee to establish rankings.

panel interview   Selection interview in which several members of the organization meet to interview each candidate.

parent country   The country in which an organization's headquarters is located.

pay differential   Adjustment to a pay rate to reflect differences in working conditions or labor markets.

pay grades   Sets of jobs having similar worth or content, grouped together to establish rates of pay.

pay level   The average amount (including wages, salaries, and bonuses) the organization pays for a particular job.

pay policy line   A graphed line showing the mathematical relationship between job evaluation points and pay rate.

pay ranges   A set of possible pay rates defined by a minimum, maximum, and midpoint of pay for employees holding a particular job or a job within a particular pay grade.

pay structure   The pay policy resulting from job structure and pay level decisions.

peer review   Process for resolving disputes by taking them to a panel composed of representatives from the organization at the same levels as the people in the dispute.

Pension Benefit Guarantee Corporation (PBGC)   Federal agency that insures retirement benefits and guarantees retirees a basic benefit if the employer experiences financial difficulties.

performance management   The process through which managers ensure that employees' activities and outputs contribute to the organization's goals.

person analysis   A process for determining individuals' needs and readiness for training.

personnel selection   The process through which organizations make decisions about who will or will not be allowed to join the organization.

piecework rate   Rate of pay for each unit produced.

Position Analysis Questionnaire (PAQ)   A standardized job analysis questionnaire containing 194 questions about work behaviors, work conditions, and job characteristics that apply to a wide variety of jobs.

position   The set of duties (job) performed by a particular person.

predictive validation   Research that uses the test scores of all applicants and looks for a relationship between the scores and future performance of the applicants who were hired.

preferred provider organization (PPO)   A health care plan that contracts with health care professionals to provide services at a reduced fee and gives patients financial incentives to use network providers.

procedural justice   A judgment that fair methods were used to determine the consequences an employee receives.

profit sharing   Incentive pay in which payments are a percentage of the organization's profits and do not become part of the employees' base salary.

progressive discipline   A formal discipline process in which the consequences become more serious if the employee repeats the offense.

promotion   Assignment of an employee to a position with greater challenges, more responsibility, and more authority than in the previous job, usually accompanied by a pay increase.

protean career   A career that frequently changes based on changes in the person's interests, abilities, and values and in the work environment.

psychological contract   A description of what an employee expects to contribute in an employment relationship and what the employer will provide the employee in exchange for those contributions.

readability   The difficulty level of written materials.

readiness for training   A combination of employee characteristics and positive work environment that permit training.

realistic job preview   Background information about a job's positive and negative qualities.

reality check   Information employers give employees about their skills and knowledge and where these assets fit into the organization's plans.

reasonable accommodation   An employer's obligation to do something to enable an otherwise qualified person to perform a job.

recruiting   Any activity carried on by the organization with the primary purpose of identifying and attracting potential employees.

recruitment   The process through which the organization seeks applicants for potential employment.

red-circle rate   Pay at a rate that falls above the pay range for the job.

reengineering   A complete review of the organization's critical work processes to make them more efficient and able to deliver higher quality.

referrals   People who apply for a vacancy because someone in the organization prompted them to do so.

reliability The extent to which a measurement is from random error.

repatriation The process of preparing expatriates to return home from a foreign assignment.

right-to-know laws State laws that require employers to provide employees with information about the health risks associated with exposure to substances considered hazardous.

right-to-work laws State laws that make union shops, maintenance of membership, and agency shops illegal.

role ambiguity Uncertainty about what the organization expects from the employee in terms of what to do or how to do it.

role analysis technique A process of formally identifying expectations associated with a role.

role conflict An employee's recognition that demands of the job are incompatible or contradictory.

role overload A state in which too many expectations or demands are placed on a person.

role The set of behaviors that people expect of a person in a particular job.

Rucker plan A gainsharing program in which the ratio measuring the gain compares labor costs to the value added in production (output minus the cost of materials, supplies, and services).

sabbatical A leave of absence from an organization to renew or develop skills.

salary Rate of pay for each week, month, or year worked.

Scanlon plan A gainsharing program in which employees receive a bonus if the ratio of labor costs to the sales value of production is below a set standard.

selection The process by which the organization attempts to identify applicants with the necessary knowledge, skills, abilities, and other characteristics that will help the organization achieve its goals.

self-assessment The use of information by employees to determine their career interests, values, aptitudes, and behavioral tendencies.

self-service System in which employees have online access to information about HR issues and go online to enroll themselves in programs and provide feedback through surveys.

sexual harassment Unwelcome sexual advances as defined by the EEOC.

short-term disability insurance Insurance that pays a percentage of a disabled employee's salary as benefits to the employee for six months or less.

simple ranking Method of performance measurement that requires managers to rank employees in their group from the highest performer to the poorest performer.

simulation A training method that represents a real-life situation, with trainees making decisions resulting in outcomes that mirror what would happen on the job.

situational interviews A structured interview in which the interviewer describes a situation likely to arise on the job, then asks the candidate what he or she would do in that situation.

skill-based pay systems Pay structures that set pay according to the employees' levels of skill or knowledge and what they are capable of doing.

Social Security The federal Old Age, Survivors, Disability, and Health Insurance (OASDHI) program, which combines old age (retirement) insurance, survivor's insurance, disability insurance, hospital insurance (Medicare Part A), and supplementary medical insurance (Medicare Part B) for the elderly.

standard hour plan An incentive plan that pays workers extra for work done in less than a preset "standard time."

stock options Rights to buy a certain number of shares of stock at a specified price.

straight piecework plan Incentive pay in which the employer pays the same rate per piece, no matter how much the worker produces.

strike A collective decision by union members not to work until certain demands or conditions are met.

structured interview A selection interview that consists of a predetermined set of questions for the interviewer to ask.

succession planning The process of identifying and tracking high-potential employees who will be able to fill top management positions when they become vacant.

summary plan description Report that describes a pension plan's funding, eligibility requirements, risks, and other details.

task analysis The process of identifying and analyzing tasks to be trained for.

team leader training Training in the skills necessary for effectively leading the organization's teams.

teamwork   The assignment of work to groups of employees with various skills who interact to assemble a product or provide a service.

technic of operations review (TOR)   Method of promoting safety by determining which specific element of a job led to a past accident.

third country   A country that is neither the parent country nor the host country of an employer.

360-degree performance appraisal   Performance measurement that combines information from the employee's managers, peers, subordinates, self, and customers.

total quality management (TQM)   A companywide effort to continuously improve the ways people, machines, and systems accomplish work.

training   An organization's planned efforts to help employees acquire job-related knowledge, skills, abilities, and behaviors, with the goal of applying these on the job.

transaction processing   Computations and calculations involved in reviewing and documenting HRM decisions and practices.

transfer of training   On-the-job use of knowledge, skills, and behaviors learned in training.

transfer   Assignment of an employee to a position in a different area of the company, usually in a lateral move.

transitional matrix   A chart that lists job categories held in one period and shows the proportion of employees in each of those job categories in a future period.

transnational HRM system   Type of HRM system that makes decisions from a global perspective, includes managers from many countries, and is based on ideas contributed by people representing a variety of cultures.

trend analysis   Constructing and applying statistical models that predict labor demand for the next year, given relatively objective statistics from the previous year.

unemployment insurance   A federally mandated program to minimize the hardships of unemployment through payments to unemployed workers, help in finding new jobs, and incentives to stabilize employment.

Uniform Guidelines on Employee Selection Procedures   Guidelines issued by the EEOC and other agencies to identify how an organization should develop and administer its system for selecting employees so as not to violate antidiscrimination laws.

union shop   Union security arrangement that requires employees to join the union within a certain amount of time (30 days) after beginning employment.

union steward   An employee elected by union members to represent them in ensuring that the terms of the labor contract are enforced.

unions   Organizations formed for the purpose of representing their members' interests in dealing with employers.

utility   The extent to which something provides economic value greater than its cost.

validity   The extent to which performance on a measure (such as a test score) is related to what the measure is designed to assess (such as job performance).

vesting rights   Guarantee that when employees become participants in a pension plan and work a specified number of years, they will receive a pension at retirement age, regardless of whether they remained with the employer.

virtual expatriates   Employees who manage an operation abroad without permanently locating in the country.

virtual reality   A computer-based technology that provides an interactive, three-dimensional learning experience.

voluntary turnover   Turnover initiated by employees (often when the organization would prefer to keep them).

work flow design   The process of analyzing the tasks necessary for the production of a product or service.

workers' compensation   State programs that provide benefits to workers who suffer work-related injuries or illnesses, or to their survivors.

workforce utilization review   A comparison of the proportion of employees in protected groups with the proportion that each group represents in the relevant labor market.

yield ratio   A ratio that expresses the percentage of applicants who successfully move from one stage of the recruitment and selection process to the next.

Photo Credits

Name and Company Index

505

Subject Index